KT-440-598

GUINNESS WORLD RECORDS 2015

Largest yo-yo

On 15 Sep 2012, Beth Johnson (USA) got her "Whoa-Yo" yo-yo to go-go to cheers from onlookers in LaRue, Ohio, USA. Measuring a record 3.63 m (11 ft 9 in) in diameter and weighing 2.09 tonnes (4,620 lb), the disc plunged 36.5 m (120 ft) on a rope attached to a 68-tonne (150,000-lb) crane before rebounding.

Diamonds

All the diamonds ever polished in history would fill just **one double-decker bus**

FACT

This scintillating Snoopy also features 783 black diamonds and a collar made from 415 red ruby gemstones!

Most valuable Snoopy

On 13 Nov 2009, to celebrate the 60th anniversary of Charles Schulz's cartoon-strip canine Snoopy, Tse Sui Luen Jewellery of Hong Kong, China, created a 14-cm-tall (5.5-in) "Diamond Snoopy" encrusted with 9,917 diamonds. Also known as "The Ever-Shining Star", the 207-carat creation went on sale with a price tag of HK$2,888,880 (£224,960; $372,750).

Largest diamond in the universe

BPM 37093 is a white dwarf star 50 light years from Earth in the constellation of Centaurus. In 2004, astronomers from the Harvard-Smithsonian Center for Astrophysics in Massachusetts, USA, deduced that the carbon white dwarf had crystallized into a diamond some 4,000 km (2,500 mi) across. The star has been nicknamed "Lucy" after The Beatles' song "Lucy in the Sky with Diamonds". Assuming the cost of £1,000 per carat, Lucy would set you back £10,000,000,000,000,000, 000,000,000,000,000,000, 000 (£10 undecillion).

Largest brilliant-cut diamond

A 545.67-carat "brilliant" diamond known as the "Golden Jubilee Diamond" was purchased from the diamond specialist group De Beers by a syndicate of Thai businessmen and in 1995 was presented to the King of Thailand to commemorate his golden jubilee. It is now mounted in the Thai royal sceptre.

Largest cut fancy black diamond

An unnamed fancy black diamond containing small red diamond crystals was polished into 55 facets over several years and finished in Jun 2004. It weighs 555.55 carats – the repetitive use of the number five is culturally significant in the Islamic world – and was inspired by Ran Gorenstein (BEL), who also commissioned it.

Most diamonds in one ring

The "Tsarevna Swan" ring, which was created by the Lobortas Classic Jewelry House (UKR), is white gold set with 2,525 diamonds. Fully wearable, it was presented and measured in Kiev, Ukraine, on 21 Jul 2011.

Most valuable casino chip

A casino chip designed by Gerald N Lewy (CAN) was valued at CAN$450,000 (£287,000) on 30 May 2013. The 22-carat pink gold chip is set with 173 round brilliant-cut diamonds – 17 of them around the rim – and 64 natural pink diamonds.

Most expensive diamond per carat

The diamond-price record per carat is £854,700 ($1,375,938) for a 7.03-carat fancy vivid-blue modified rectangular brilliant-cut diamond sold by Sotheby's on 12 May 2009. It was cut from an original stone that weighed 26.58 carats.

Most valuable boots

A pair of size-6 ankle boots made with 4,738 g (167 oz) of gold and covered in 39,083 natural

Most valuable materials in a work of art

For the Love of God by Damien Hirst (UK) is a human skull encrusted with 8,601 flawless diamonds, including a 52.4-carat pink diamond in the forehead. The total 1,106.18 carats of diamonds were reported to cost a dazzling £12 m ($23.7 m).

ANATOMY OF A DIAMOND: THE "BRILLIANT" CUT

A diamond is "cut" – that is, shaped and polished – to enhance its beauty and brilliance.

Top view

Enlarged girdle

Side view

Bottom view

Upper girdle facet

Star facet

Upper main facet

Girdle

Lower girdle facet

Pavilion main facet

Table

Culet: flattened apex of the lower facets (optional) *Enlarged culet*

Pavilion: lower part of the cut diamond, usually with 25 facets

Crown: upper part of the cut diamond, usually with 33 facets

"Baby" Williams

The latest fashion accessory for any self-respecting rapper is "grillz" – i.e., diamond dentures. The king of bling is undoubtedly Bryan "Baby" Williams (USA), who reportedly spent a record $500,000 (£312,500) on having his teeth permanently fitted with 18-carat white gold and platinum crowns set with asher-cut diamonds.

fancy coloured diamonds weighing 1,550 carats was unveiled by Diarough/UNI-Design and A F Vandevorst (BEL) in Dec 2013. The boots were valued at $3.1 m (£1.93 m).

Most expensive diamond sold at auction

On 12 Nov 2013, the "Pink Star" – a flawless pink diamond – was sold to an anonymous bidder for 76,325,000 Swiss francs (£52.07 m; $83.01 m) at Christie's in Geneva, Switzerland. The oval-shaped 59.60-carat diamond is mounted on a ring and measures 2.69 x 2.06 cm (1.06 x 0.81 in). It took two years to cut.

Most faceted diamond

Diamonds are cut with varying numbers of facets to enhance their sparkle (see below), the most common being the 57 or 58 facets of the brilliant cut found in most engagement rings. The "Brilliant Lady 21" cut, which was created by Louis Verelst (BEL), has 221 facets, producing a large number of reflections and resulting in increased brilliance.

Actual Size

Largest diamond pendant

The largest non-religious pendant is "Crunk Ain't Dead", owned by hip-hop artist Lil' Jon (USA). With 3,576 white diamonds, it weighs 977.6 g (2 lb 2.4 oz) without its chain.

Largest uncut diamond

The largest ever single rough uncut diamond was the "Cullinan", which weighed 3,106.75 carats when found in 1905 in South Africa. It was cut into nine smaller diamonds, the largest of which, the "Great Star of Africa", weighs 530.2 carats and tops the royal sceptre (left) wielded by the UK's Queen Elizabeth II. The next largest fragment – the "Second Star of Africa" – sits in the Queen's Imperial State Crown.

Most valuable necklace

"The Incomparable" contains a 407.48-carat flawless diamond and 102 "satellite" diamonds. Manufactured by the jewellers Mouawad, based in Switzerland, it was valued on 13 Feb 2013 at £35 m ($55 m). The flawless diamond was discovered in the Congo some 30 years ago in a pile of kimberlite, a by-product of diamond mining.

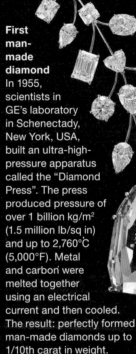

First man-made diamond

In 1955, scientists in GE's laboratory in Schenectady, New York, USA, built an ultra-high-pressure apparatus called the "Diamond Press". The press produced pressure of over 1 billion kg/m^2 (1.5 million lb/sq in) and up to 2,760°C (5,000°F). Metal and carbon were melted together using an electrical current and then cooled. The result: perfectly formed man-made diamonds up to 1/10th carat in weight.

The **largest man-made cut diamond** is a 2.16-carat synthetic marquis-cut diamond created by the Scio Diamond Technology Corporation (USA). The 13.42-mm (0.5-in) diamond was tested in Apr 2013 by the Gemological Institute of America.

FACT

The Incomparable appeared on eBay in 2002 with a starting price of £15 m but failed to sell.

Actual Size

First 100% diamond ring

On 8 Mar 2012, Shawish Jewellery (CHE) unveiled the first ring to be made entirely from a diamond. The 150-carat creation is reportedly worth £43.5 m ($70 m).

i Rock stars: diamonds defined

Diamond – the world's **hardest natural substance** – is a mineral formed 140–200 km down in the Earth's mantle. It is a form (allotrope) of the chemical element carbon (C) in which the atoms are arranged in a tetrahedral crystalline formation. Diamonds are measured in carats, with one carat equal to 200 mg. For each carat of diamond mined, 250 tonnes of earth is excavated.

Largest heist: the 90-second break-in

At lunchtime on 28 Jul 2013, an armed man entered the Carlton International hotel (right) in Cannes, France. His target: jewellery worth 103 m euros (£89 m). He single-handedly pulled off the biggest diamond heist ever, in just one-and-a-half minutes. The diamond-encrusted watches, rings and earrings he stole (left) belonged to Lev Leviev – a Soviet-born Israeli diamond and property mogul – and had been on display in an exhibition at the hotel.

British Library
Cataloguing-in-publication data: a catalogue record for this book is available from the British Library

ISBN: 978-1-908843-62-3

This book is dedicated to Chris Bernstein

For a complete list of credits and acknowledgements, turn to p.252.

Records are made to be broken – indeed, it is one of the key criteria for a record category – so if you find a record that you think you can beat, tell us about it by making a record claim. Find out how on p.5. Always contact us before making a record attempt.

Check the official website – www.guinnessworldrecords.com – regularly for record-breaking news, plus video footage of record attempts. You can also join and interact with the Guinness World Records online community.

Sustainability
The paper used for this edition is manufactured by UPM Plattling, Germany. The production site has forest certification and its operations have both ISO14001 environmental management system and EMAS certification to ensure sustainable production.

UPM Papers are true Biofore products, produced from renewable and recyclable materials.

OFFICIALLY AMAZING

© 2014 GUINNESS WORLD RECORDS LIMITED
No part of this book may be reproduced or transmitted in any form or by any means, electronic, chemical, mechanical, including photography, or used in any information storage or retrieval system without a licence or other permission in writing from the copyright owners.

Editor-in-Chief
Craig Glenday

Senior Managing Editor
Stephen Fall

Layout Editors
Ian Cranna,
Rob Dimery,
Lucian Randall

Assistant Editor
Roxanne Mackey

Editorial Team
Theresa Bebbington (Americanization),
Marie Lorimer (indexing),
Matthew White (proofreading)

Picture Editor
Michael Whitty

Deputy Picture Editor
Fran Morales

Talent/Picture Researcher
Jenny Langridge

Picture Researcher
Laura Nieberg

VP Publishing
Jenny Heller

Director of Procurement
Patricia Magill

Publishing Manager
Jane Boatfield

Publishing Executives
Ebyan Egal,
Charlie Peacock

Production Consultants
Roger Hawkins,
Dennis Thon

Printing & Binding
MOHN Media Mohndruck GmbH, Gütersloh, Germany

Cover Production
Hololens Technology Co, Ltd;
Simon Thompson (API Laminates Ltd);
Bernd Salewski (GT Produktion)

Augmented Reality
Mustard Design Limited;
Anders Ehrenborg (Robert Wadlow modelling and texturing)

Design
Paul Wylie-Deacon, Richard Page, Matt Bell at 55design.co.uk

Original Photography
Richard Bradbury, Anne Caroline, Kimberly Cook, Matt Crossick, Daniel Deme, James Ellerker, Jarek Jõepera, Paul Michael Hughes, Shinsuke Kamioka, Ranald Mackechnie, Kevin Scott Ramos, Chris Skone-Roberts, Philip Robertson, Ryan Schude

Editorial Consultants
Mark Aston, Jan Bondeson, Iain Borden, Martyn Chapman, Nicholas Chu, Sammpa von Cyborg, Steven Dale, Joshua Dowling, Dick Fiddy, David Fischer, Mike Flynn, Justin Garvanovic, Ben Hagger, Ralph Hannah, David Hawksett, Eberhard Jurgalski, David Lardi, Glen O'Hara, Ocean Rowing Society, Paul Parsons, Clara Piccirillo, Dr Karl Shuker, Matthew White, World Sailing Speed Record Council, Stephen Wrigley, Robert Young

President: Alistair Richards
SVP Americas: Peter Harper
President (Greater China): Rowan Simons
VP Japan: Erika Ogawa
Country Manager, UAE: Talal Omar

PROFESSIONAL SERVICES
EVP Finance, Legal, HR & IT:
Alison Ozanne
Financial Controller: Scott Paterson
Management Accountants: Daniel Ralph, Shabana Zaffar
Assistant Accountant: Kimberley Dennis
Accounts Payable Assistant:
Victoria Aweh
Accounts Receivable Manager: Lisa Gibbs
Head of Legal & Business Affairs:
Raymond Marshall
Legal & Business Affairs Manager:
Michael Goulbourn
Legal & Business Affairs Executive:
Xiangyun Rablen
Director of IT: Rob Howe
Senior Developer: Philip Raeburn
Developer: Lewis Ayers
Desktop Support: Ainul Ahmed
Head of HR: Jane Atkins
Office Manager (UK): Jacqueline Angus
HR & Office Manager (Americas):
Morgan Wilber
Office Manager (Japan): Fumiko Kitagawa
Office Manager (Greater China): Tina Shi
Office Assistant (Greater China):
Sabrine Wang

TELEVISION
Director of TV Content & Sales:
Rob Molloy
TV Distribution Manager:
Denise Carter Steel

GLOBAL MARKETING
SVP Global Marketing: Samantha Fay
Marketing Director (Americas):
Stuart Claxton
Marketing Director (Greater China):
Sharon Yang
Senior PR Manager (Americas):
Jamie Antoniou

PR & Marketing Executive (Americas):
Sara Wilcox
Marketing Managers: Justine Tommey (UK), Tanya Batra (UK & EMEA)
Marketing Executives: Aurora Bellingham (UK), Christelle BeTrong (UK), Asumi Funatsu (Japan), Mayo Ma (Greater China)
PR Director (UK): Amarilis Whitty
PR & Sales Promotion Manager (Japan):
Kazami Kamioka
PR Managers (UK): Tandice Abedian, Damian Field
PR Executive (UK): Jamie Clarke
PR Assistant (Greater China): Leila Wang
Director of Digital Content & Marketing:
Katie Forde
Digital Manager: Kirsty Brown
Digital Video Producer: Adam Moore
Community Manager: Dan Thorne
Online Editor: Kevin Lynch
Designer: Neil Fitter
Design Executive: Jon Addison
Designer (Japan): Momoko Cunneen
Content Manager (Americas): Mike Janela
Digital & Publishing Content Manager (Japan): Takafumi Suzuki
Digital Manager (Greater China):
Jacky Yuan

GWR CREATIVE
VP Creative: Paul O'Neill
Programme Manager, Attractions:
Louise Toms

COMMERCIAL SALES
SVP Sales UK & EMEA: Nadine Causey
VP Commercial: Andrew Brown
Publishing, Sales & Product Director (Americas): Jennifer Gilmour
Content Director (Greater China):
Angela Wu
Head of Publishing Sales (EL):
John Pilley
Sales & Distribution Manager (UK & international): Richard Stenning
Head of Commercial Accounts & Licensing (UK): Samantha Prosser
Licensing Manager, Publishing:
Emma Davies

Commercial Director (Greater China):
Blythe Fitzwiliam
Business Development Manager (Americas): Amanda Mochan
Head of Commercial Sales & Marketing (Japan): Kaoru Ishikawa
Senior Account Manager:
Vihag Kulshrestha
Account Managers:
Dong Cheng (China), Ralph Hannah (UK/Paraguay), Annabel Lawday (UK), Takuro Maruyama (Japan), Nicole Pando (USA), Lucie Pessereau (UK), Terje Purga (UK), Nikhil Shukla (India), Seyda Subasi-Gemici (Turkey), Charlie Weisman (USA)
Commercial Assistant (Greater China):
Catherine Gao

RECORDS MANAGEMENT
SVP Records: Marco Frigatti
Director of RMT: Turath Alsaraf
Head of Records Management:
Carlos Martinez (Japan), Kimberly Partrick (Americas), Charles Wharton (Greater China)
Database Manager: Carim Valerio
Adjudications Manager: Benjamin Backhouse
Team Leader, RMT (UK): Jacqueline Fitt
Specialist Records Managers (UK):
Anatole Baboukhian, Louise McLaren, Elizabeth Smith
Records Managers (Americas):
Alex Angert, Evelyn Carrera, Michael Empric, Johanna Hessling, Annie Nguyen, Philip Robertson
Records Managers (Greater China):
John Garland, Lisa Hoffman
Records Managers (Japan):
Mariko Koike, Aya McMillan, Mai McMillan, Justin Patterson, Gulnaz Ukassova
Records Managers (UK):
Jack Brockbank, Fortuna Burke, Tom Ibison, Sam Mason, Mark McKinley, Eva Norroy, Anna Orford, Pravin Patel, Glenn Pollard, Chris Sheedy, Lucia Sinigagliesi, Victoria Tweedy, Lorenzo Veltri, Aleksandr Vypirailenko
Senior Project Manager (UK): Alan Pixsley
Project Managers: Samer Khallouf (UAE), Paulina Sapinska (UK)
Project Co-ordinator (UK): Shantha Chinniah

Guinness World Records Limited has a very thorough accreditation system for records verification. However, while every effort is made to ensure accuracy, Guinness World Records Limited cannot be held responsible for any errors contained in this work. Feedback from our readers on any point of accuracy is always welcomed.

Guinness World Records Limited uses both metric and imperial measurements. The sole exceptions are for some scientific data where metric measurements only are universally accepted, and for some sports data. Where a specific date is given, the exchange rate is calculated according to the currency values that were in operation at the time. Where only a year date is given, the exchange rate is calculated from 31 Dec of that year. "One billion" is taken to mean one thousand million.

Appropriate advice should always be taken when attempting to break or set records. Participants undertake records entirely at their own risk. Guinness World Records Limited has complete discretion over whether or not to include any particular record attempts in any of its publications. Being a Guinness World Records record holder does not guarantee you a place in any Guinness World Records publication.

Be a record-breaker

Have you got a **record-breaking talent** to share?

Anyone can set a record and there are more ways of doing it now than ever before. It's free of charge and you can apply right away at **www.guinnessworldrecords.com**. When we started in 1955, record holders could only appear in the book – now you can get on TV, appear at live events or get your attempt on our website.

FACT

You can attempt a world record right now by visiting **www. guinnessworldrecords. com/challengers** and, once you get the green light, you can upload a video of your attempt. You'll soon hear – GWR adjudicate every week.

Start

Do you know which record you want to attempt?

If you think you've got what it takes to tackle an existing record, we want to hear from you. Want to try something new? We are equally excited by new ideas, so let us know right away.

YES → **NO** →

Register online

Head on over to **www.guinnessworld records.com** and click on "Register" at the top of the screen. It's a matter of minutes to set up your account and you're almost set. Have you got the guidelines yet?

NO

YES

Read, watch, browse

Keep reading the book! You'll find ideas there and in our TV shows and you can check out the latest action on the website at **www. guinnessworldrecords. com**. This will give you a sense of the records that we usually accept.

Record rules

If your chosen record already exists (or we like your idea), we'll send you the guidelines that anyone must follow when making an attempt. If you've submitted an idea and we don't accept it, we will tell you why.

Collect evidence

Make sure you give yourself plenty of time to practise your record attempt. When you're ready to go, you'll have to be careful to collect all the evidence we need to ensure your best chance of a successful attempt.

Just the facts

Gather your evidence and send it to us. Depending on the record, we'll need independent eyewitness statements, photos, video and other proof outlined in the guidelines. Now just wait to hear... Did you break your record?

Finish

You're a record-breaker!

If you've followed the rules and beaten an existing record or even set a new one, you'll receive a letter of confirmation. You will also be sent your official Guinness World Records certificate welcoming you into the family of record holders. Congratulations! If you're very lucky, you may even make it into next year's book.

NO **YES**

Better luck next time

You may not be successful, but don't give up! Come back and try again or choose a different record for another chance to receive that world-famous certificate.

Inside 2015

What's new in the world's **best-selling annual book**?

All-new Augmented Reality!

Download our FREE "See It 3D" app now and see some of your favourite record holders come to life. Simply point your mobile phone or tablet device at the pages where you see the "SEE IT 3D" icon and you'll be able to meet a giant, explore the depths of the ocean and even battle with cheesy maggots in a fun new videogame.

Augmented Reality (AR) software works by harnessing the camera of your tablet device or smartphone and using it to detect elements on the printed page. This triggers the device to display 3D images on the screen. Today, the technology behind it allows for virtual-reality environments, interactive 3D animations and even games, such as the one below…

PLAY THE AR GAME: Maggot Splat!

Try the **SEE IT 3D** experience now by downloading the app and playing this new game, inspired by the record for the **most dangerous cheese**!

Casu marzu is a Sardinian cheese that is deliberately left to rot, allowing flies to lay eggs and hatch thousands of maggots inside the cheese. This apparently improves the taste, although it can leave you with stomach pains. Your challenge is to splat the maggots as they ping themselves out of the cheese – just like they do in Sardinia. Register your high score and you could even win yourself an official Guinness World Records certificate! Good luck!

1 DOWNLOAD THE FREE "SEE IT 3D" APP

Download on the App Store

ANDROID APP ON Google play

GUINNESSWORLDRECORDS.COM/SEEIT3D

2 LOOK FOR THE "SEE IT 3D" SYMBOL ON THE COVER OR INSIDE THE BOOK

3 USING THE APP, VIEW THE BOOK AND WATCH THE RECORD HOLDERS APPEAR IN 3D!

#seeit3d

Share your AR experience with us:

Facebook.com/ GuinnessWorldRecords

Twitter.com/ GWR

Youtube.com/ guinnessworldrecords

Plus.Google.com/ +guinnessworldrecords

Instagram.com/ guinnessworldrecords

CONTENTS

QUOTE

"When one thinks of Guinness World Records, automatically 'extraordinary' and 'remarkable' comes to mind. So for me to win, I am truly honoured and delighted."
Usain Bolt

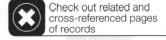 Check out related and cross-referenced pages of records

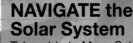

NAVIGATE the Solar System p.20
Take a trip to Mars, Saturn and the rest of the Solar System from the comfort of your armchair

EXPLORE the ocean depths p.42
Turn your device into a deep-sea explorer and encounter the creatures of the deep

ENCOUNTER the most venomous spider p.60
Get dangerously close to the Brazilian wandering spider... without actually putting your life at risk!

MEET the performing Pomeranian p.66
Go walkies with Jiff the dog and watch as the cool canine pulls off some of his trademark tricks

SIZE-UP with the tallest man p.80
Get the exclusive chance to meet the most iconic record holder of all time. Robert Pershing Wadlow stood 2.72 m (8 ft 11.1 in) tall – how do you measure up?

#seeit3d
The SEE IT 3D app comes with a built-in camera feature, so snap yourself and your friends alongside the AR record holders and share your images with us.

Editor's letter

Globally, **only 7.6% of claims** became official world records this year

Welcome to this special diamond anniversary edition of the world's **biggest-selling annual book**. We may be entering our 60th year, but we're not looking to retire and collect our pensions just yet! While this year's book revisits six ever-changing decades of record-breaking, we've still squeezed in every major new and updated record from the last year, so expect the usual mix of unrivalled sporting achievements, talented pets, cutting-edge scientific discoveries and the most remarkable human beings on the planet...

Most "drunken sailor" dance steps in 30 seconds

In *Strictly Come Dancing*'s annual "It Takes Two" challenge, the show's professionals compete to set a dance record. On 22 Nov 2013, newcomer Kevin Clifton achieved an unbeaten 77 "drunken sailor" steps in 30 sec. This is a three-step sequence, so Kevin, pictured here with GWR adjudicator Elizabeth Smith, actually completed 231 separate moves, or nearly four per sec!

439 made it into our database as official Guinness World Records titles, so thanks and congratulations to everyone who received their official GWR certificate.

As ever, the scope of record-breaking in the UK is impressive, ranging from the very British **most cups of tea made in one hour** (1,608 by a team of 12 from Burco Water Boilers in London) and the **oldest newspaper delivery woman** (88-year-old Beryl Walker of Gloucester; see p.77) to the fearless, such

First radio station to reach a million YouTube subscribers

Back in 2006, Radio 1 launched a YouTube channel, and on 19 Jan 2014 it became the first station to sign up its millionth subscriber. Radio 1's pioneering visuals include parody videos, such as a take on Miley Cyrus' "Wrecking Ball" featuring a naked Greg James (above, clothed, with fellow presenter Fearne Cotton).

How to have a record-breaking Christmas!

Serial record-breaker Gino D'Acampo (below left) added two more certificates to his collection. He and Keith Lemon (below right) pulled the **most Christmas crackers in one minute** – 45 – on the *Through the Keyhole Christmas Special* on 15 Dec 2013. And with Melanie Sykes, he donned the **most jumpers worn in one minute** – 11 – on *Let's Do Christmas with Gino & Mel* (inset) on 24 Dec.

as the **most axe juggling catches** (369 by Chris Marley in Sheffield) and the **fastest water speed record blindfolded** (150.6 km/h or 93.58 mph by Mike Newman in Devon).

We've had schools getting involved (**largest gathering of people**

There's been no let-up in the demand for record-breaking, with around 50,000 new claims, enquiries and updates filling our inboxes and mail trays over the past 12 months. We've had correspondence and claims from around the world, from Afghanistan (**longest chain of paper dolls**: a successful attempt, at 6.5 km or 40.3 mi) to Zimbabwe (**longest live DJ set**: TBC, but the current record of 168 hr will be hard to beat!) alongside enquiries from as far afield as East Timor, Tongo and Tajikistan.

The UK remains a key country for record-breaking,

with 6,672 claims registered, putting it in second place behind the USA, with a whopping 13,352 applications. Of the UK's claims, a healthy

Most rugby passes in one minute (pair)

The highest number of passes – 59 – was achieved by former England rugby internationals Ben Kay (right) and Austin Healey (hidden) on the set of BT Sport's *Rugby Tonight* TV show in London on 22 Jan 2014.

Fastest 100 x 100-m swimming relay

A 100-strong team from Swim4Leukaemia UK set a new relay record of 1 hr 29 min 3 sec at Ponds Forge in Sheffield on 1 Feb 2014. The event was organized by Great Britain swimmer Lewis Coleman (pictured with brother Oliver and adjudicator Kirsty Bennett) after his mother was diagnosed with acute lymphoblastic leukaemia.

wearing onesies: 1,184 by Ringwood School in Hampshire), the armed forces (most people dipping egg soldiers: 178 members of the Allied Rapid Reaction Corps at Imjin Barracks in Gloucestershire) and, of course, the celebrities that you'll find dotted throughout the book.

WHAT'S NEW?

As well as all these new records, because it's our 60th birthday, we've decided to trace the evolution of some of your favourite record categories. You'll find "Flashback" features at the beginning of each chapter.

Most stairs descended by a slinky

On 18 Feb 2014, Marty Jopson (left) – the resident scientist on the BBC's *The One Show* – and Cambridge University's Senior Lecturer in Engineering, Dr Hugh Hunt (right), succeeded in encouraging a slinky to "walk" down 30 stairs. The boffins are pictured here alongside GWR adjudicator Mark McKinley.

Each one explores a record-breaking topic – such as 60 years in space (p.16), new animal discoveries (p.44) and communications technology (p.180) – and traces how the records have evolved since our first book in 1955. We've also dipped into our earlier editions to bring you the occasional bite-sized Flashbacks on the regular pages, comparing records from the past to those of today.

One of the reasons for the success of Guinness World Records over the past 60 years is that we've always tried to embrace any new habits, fashions or technologies. We're not a dusty reference book – we reflect what's happening around us. This year is no exception, which is why you'll find new categories for topics such as 3D printing (p.206), Instagram and Twitter (p.138), alternative transport (p.190) and digital piracy (p.174). Look out, too, for some 2013 "neologies" (newly coined words), such as "bitcoin" (p.135) "twerking" (p.117) and "selfies" (p.207).

NEW DESIGN

We've also refreshed the design this year – riffing on the concept of "diamonds" and "tablet typography" – courtesy of the creatives at 55 Design. To that end,

Fastest 400-m freestyle (female, S6)

We were delighted this year to finally present swimmer Eleanor ("Ellie") Simmonds with her Guinness World Records certificate for the **fastest women's 400 m freestyle (S6)**. Ellie won gold at the 2012 Paralympic Games on 1 Sep 2012, finishing in a world-beating time of 5 min 19.17 sec.

we've introduced a new element we're calling the Control Strip. You'll find this design feature along the bottom of most of the regular spreads. This space is dedicated to fact boxes, glossaries, the aforementioned Flashback panels and infographics, giving you extra record data at a glance.

Yet another new feature for this book is the Gallery. These spreads showcase some of the amazing photography that Guinness World Records has shot over the years. Picture Editor Michael Whitty and his team have once again been travelling the world to bring you the best new images,

Most entries in a two-person pantomime animal race

Fifty-three teams (106 participants) competed in a 100-m panto-horse race organized by ITV's *This Morning* for their Christmas appeal at Kempton Park racecourse on 5 Dec 2013. Seen with their GWR certificate are presenter Jeff Brazier and guest commentator Jon Culshaw.

Most people riding a kitesurf board

Sir Richard Branson has been breaking records again. He's pictured here kitesurfing with Alice Galliers (UK), Susi Mai (DEU) and Alison Di Spaltro (USA) in the British Virgin Islands on 2 Feb 2014. He also took part in the **largest kitesurf armada**, leading 318 kitesurfers off Hayling Island in Hampshire on 15 Sep 2013.

Editor's letter

Collections corner

Obsessive collectors usually make for great photographic subjects, as these two British record holders attest. Ian O'Brien of Manchester is obsessed with *Doctor Who* and keeps his collection in his living room. Meanwhile, James Bond fanatic Nick Bennett of Warrington needs an entire warehouse – at a secret location (naturally) – for his collection. Find out how many items the pair own, and discover some of the other weird and wonderful collections in our archives, on pp.90–1.

so look out for the likes of Jiff the dog from the USA (**fastest 5 metres on front paws**, p.67), the QTvan from the UK (**smallest caravan**, p.192) and the Fisarmonica Gigante from Italy (**largest accordion**, see p.97).

FREE APP

Back by popular demand is our SEE IT 3D Augmented Reality (AR) feature. Check out how to access a wealth of 3D and interactive animations – and how to download the free app – on pp.6–7. Among the amazing visuals on offer this year is an actual-size render of Robert Pershing Wadlow, the world's

tallest man ever (p.81), giving you the unique chance to have your photograph taken alongside this classic record holder. Many thanks to Mustard Design (UK) for their cutting-edge work on these added extras.

Staying with digital matters, we were excited to welcome our 4-millionth Facebook fan in April, and we've signed up to Instagram and Flickr to share some of the hundreds of incredible photographs and videos that come into our offices every week. We're also closing in on our 500,000th follower on the GWR YouTube channel, and our Twitter following has reached 87.2K. Okay, we're a long way off Katy Perry (**most followers on Twitter**) and Shakira (**most "liked" person on Facebook**) – see p.166 – but our job is to monitor and disseminate records, not to break them!

While we're in the digital realm, be sure to check out

Longest knitted bunting line

On 14 Oct 2011, *Woman's Weekly* magazine put the finishing touches to a knitted bunting line measuring 3,212.41 m (10,539 ft 4.5 in). It wasn't until 8 Jul 2013, however, that the bunting was finally hung, in London, and the GWR certificate issued. In all, 926 people knitted a total of 13,428 triangles. With 25 m (82 ft) of wool in each triangle, 335.7 km (208.5 mi) of wool was used in all.

Largest videogame tournament

We were delighted this year to present Ralph Straus, Head of Brand Management at FIFA, with yet another certificate for the largest gaming contest. The most recent FIFA Interactive World Cup – held from 1 Oct 2012 to 8 May 2013 – nearly doubled its 2011/12 participation record of 1,306,821, with an incredible 2,541,519 gamers.

the Challengers section of our website. This gives wannabe record holders fast access to an official Guinness World Records adjudicator for a series of do-try-this-at-home record categories such as Food & Drink, Sports & Fitness and Videogames. You'll find out how it works at *www. guinnessworldrecords.com/ challengers*.

The most exciting aspect of working at Guinness World Records is getting to meet the record holders face to face, and this year we've had some memorable encounters. We've had

Highest-grossing opening weekend for a 2D movie

In May 2014, Tom Hardy (UK) accepted a certificate for *The Dark Knight Rises*' opening weekend of 20–22 Jul 2012, when it grossed a record-breaking £103.9 m globally. Tom, who played Bane, the villain of the movie, accepted the certificate at London's iconic Tower Bridge.

Most seats sat on in one minute

As part of a head-to-head challenge in aid of Sport Relief on 13 Mar 2014, Robbie Savage (above right, with GWR's Mark McKinley) managed to sit on 86 seats in 60 sec at Wembley Stadium. Savage beat fellow football pundit Alan Shearer (above left, with GWR's Tom Ibison) by a single seat! Over the following five days, the duo went on to sit in every seat in the stadium!

the honour of presenting certificates to some of the sporting world's greatest legends, including Pelé (see p.239) and Haile Gebrselassie (far right and p.212), as well as welcoming adventurers and pioneers to our offices (see below and pp.142–57).

We're indebted, as always, to our countless record claimants and fans. Of course, we try to answer every email and letter, although we can't find room for every single new record approved – our annual book features only about 10% of all the superlatives we have on file, and includes

those classic records that have stood the test of time. So if you've achieved a record and you haven't been selected, better luck next time...

One of the most touching letters we received this past year was from a young man named Stephen Sutton, who had been diagnosed at the age of 15 with terminal cancer. Stephen created a "bucket list" of things he wanted to achieve before his death, one of which was to get his name in the *Guinness World Records* book.

Stephen's campaign made global news, and his efforts to raise money for the Teenage Cancer Trust resulted in £3 m (and

counting) of donations. Sadly, in May, just as the book went to press, Stephen passed away, but not, as you'll find out on p.255, before fulfilling his wish of becoming an official record-breaker.

If you've also made it your life's ambition to get your name in the *Guinness World Records* book, then apply now! Record-breaking is free and open to absolutely everyone – you'll discover

Fastest-run 20,000 m (male)

When runner Haile Gebrselassie (ETH) visited London to act as a pace-setter in the 2014 Marathon, we took the chance to recognize his record 20,000-m run – 56 min 26 sec – in Ostrava, Czech Republic, on 27 Jun 2007. For more sports records, see pp.208–47.

Most heads shaved simultaneously

A headcount of 179 scalps and 179 shavers was achieved by *The Ray D'Arcy Show* (IRL) in Dublin, Ireland, on 21 Feb 2014 as part of Today FM's Shave or Dye 2014 campaign. The event, staged in the Mansion House, was in aid of the Irish Cancer Society. Adjudicator Anna Orford (front, centre) holds the official GWR confirmation.

how on p.5. We need you to keep on breaking those records. Sixty years ago, it wasn't possible to make a transatlantic phone call (p.180) and no human had set foot on the Moon (p.16). Imagine where we might be in 60 years' time...

Craig Glenday,
Editor-in-Chief

For more outdoor feats, turn to pp.142–57.

Adventurers at GWR HQ

Record-breaking visitors to GWR this year included mountain pioneer Christian Stangl (AUT, right), teenage polar explorer Lewis Clarke (UK, above right), and ocean rowers Jamie Sparks and Luke Birch (both UK, above left). To celebrate and acknowledge some recent adventurers, we commissioned a series of portraits, which you'll find in the Great Journeys chapter starting on p.142.

Officially Amazing!

Celebrating the 60-year story of the **biggest-selling annual**

In the 1950s, Sir Hugh Beaver (left) – Managing Director of the Guinness Brewery – had the idea for a book of world records that might help settle arguments in pubs. Sixty years on, the idea of superlatives continues to fascinate and excite... and inspires millions of people to strive for immortality by becoming record holders themselves.

"Turn the heat of argument into the light of knowledge." This was the remit of the first ever edition of *The Guinness Book of Records*, which itself had its origins in an argument. On 10 Nov 1951, during a shooting party at North Slob, by the River Slaney in County Wexford, Ireland, Sir Hugh Beaver (1890–1967) – MD of the Guinness Brewery – and his fellow fowl-hunters failed to bag some golden plovers flying overhead. Could the plover be the fastest game bird in Europe? A debate ensued, but no answer could be found, not even in the well-stocked library of Sir Hugh's host later that evening.

It occurred to Sir Hugh that people across the UK and Ireland would be arguing over all sorts of topics, and that perhaps a book should be published to settle those debates. If he could create such a book, he could even give it away to some of the 80,000 or so pubs in the UK as part of a promotion to sell more Guinness stout. To help him with his plan, he needed to locate a fact-finding agency, and luckily an underbrewer at the Guinness Brewery in Park Royal, London, had the answer: the McWhirter twins.

That underbrewer was Chris Chataway (1931–2014), an amateur athlete who acted as pacemaker for Roger Bannister, who on 6 May 1954 had broken the four-minute mile – a feat once thought to be impossible. The timekeeper for the race was Norris McWhirter (1925–2004), who, along with his identical twin Ross (1925–75), had recently set up a fact-finding agency in London.

1973 Broadcaster David Frost (second on left) acquires TV rights for GWR specials. The *Hall of Fame* special seen above appeared in 1986.

1972 In the UK, the BBC produce a spin-off of TV show *Blue Peter* called *Record Breakers*, hosted by Roy Castle (right) and the McWhirter twins; it runs for nearly 30 years.

1998 *Guinness World Records Primetime* debuts on Fox TV on 27 Jul 1998, hosted by Mark Thompson, and runs for 53 episodes.

1954 Sir Hugh Beaver invites the McWhirter twins to start work on a book of superlatives

1955 Twins Ross (left) and Norris McWhirter publish the first edition of *The Guinness Book of Records* for the Guinness Brewery.

1956 The first US edition is published

1962 First French edition

1963 First German edition

1967 First Japanese, Danish and Norwegian editions

1968 First Swedish, Finnish and Italian editions

1971 First Dutch edition

1975 First GWR museum opens in the Empire State Building, New York, USA

1976 First Czech edition

1977 First Hebrew, Serbo-Croat and Icelandic editions

1978 First Slovenian edition

THE GUINNESS BOOK OF RECORDS 1986
OUT OF THIS WORLD

THE GUINNESS BOOK OF RECORDS 1998
THE GUINNESS BOOK OF RECORDS 1997
GUINNESS BOOK OF RECORDS 1996
RECORDS 1994
THE GUINNESS BOOK OF RECORDS 1989
GUINNESS BOOK OF RECORDS 1992

1999 GWR launches its first UK TV show, named simply *Guinness World Records*, hosted by football star Ian Wright.

Sir Hugh commissioned the McWhirters to create his book of superlatives, and in 1954 the twins set up an office in a disused gym at 107 Fleet Street in London. Under the name Guinness Superlatives, they spent an intense few months researching and collating the first edition of *The Guinness Book of Records*, which was bound on 27 Aug 1955.

While it was initially intended as a promotional item, the book had a life beyond the bars, and when *The Guinness Book of Records* was offered up for the public to buy (minus the beer-proof coating!)

in October of that year, it became an instant best-seller, and has remained at the top of the charts ever since. Within a year, it had launched in the USA – as *The Guinness Book of World Records* – and today is available in more than 100 countries in up to 20 languages.

In the years since its debut, the book has had a change of owner – it was sold by the Guinness Brewery in 1999 – and

a change of name to its current title *Guinness World Records*, reflecting the fact that it's more than just a book: it also has TV shows, museums, websites, digital apps, ebooks and, most recently, live events.

RECORD ADJUDICATION

As the accepted global arbiter of record-breaking achievement, Guinness

Experience GWR live

Look out for the exciting new Guinness World Records Attractions, the first of which is scheduled to open in 2015. See records come to life using cutting-edge digital technology, and attempt your own records in front of official GWR adjudicators.

World Records now processes around 50,000 claims a year, and has sent adjudicators as far afield as the bottom of the ocean and the top of the Burj Khalifa, the world's **tallest building**. We've expanded into larger premises in London, and opened new offices in New York (USA), Tokyo (JPN), Beijing (CHN) and Dubai (UAE), with more record representatives and

editorial consultants dotted all around the world.

As you'll see in this year's edition, we continue to evolve and adapt, reflecting the ever-shifting modern landscape and providing a snapshot of the universe in which we live. As long as humans continue to push the limits of what's possible, we'll be there with our stopwatches and counters, documenting and ratifying the achievements. And the next 60 years will undoubtedly be as fascinating and record-breaking as the last.

2006 Editor-in-Chief Craig Glenday welcomes the King of Pop, Michael Jackson, to the London offices on the eve of the 2006 World Music Awards, where Jackson's *Thriller* album is acknowledged as the **biggest-selling album of all time**.

2005 Her Majesty, Queen Elizabeth II, receives a copy of our 50th anniversary edition from GWR President Alistair Richards.

1996 GWR opens an office in New York, USA

2000 guinnessworldrecords.com launches

2003 The 100-millionth copy of the book is sold

2005 First annual Guinness World Records Day

2013 Hong Kong actor Jackie Chan accepts his two GWR certificates, for **most stunts by a living actor** (more than 100 films) and **most credits in one movie** (15).

2010 GWR app launches; Office opened in Tokyo, Japan

2012 Office opened in Beijing, China

2013 Office opened in Dubai, UAE

2015 GWR celebrates its 60th anniversary

GUINNESS WORLD RECORDS 2005

SPECIAL 50TH ANNIVERSARY EDITION

GUINNESS WORLD RECORDS 2006
GUINNESS WORLD RECORDS 2004
GUINNESS WORLD RECORDS 2003

GUINNESS WORLD RECORDS 2009

GUINNESS WORLD RECORDS 2015

INSIDE: ALL-NEW AUGMENTED REALITY!

GUINNESS WORLD RECORDS 2013
RECORDS 2011
RECORDS 2010
RECORDS 2008

Space

This **gallery of galaxies** illustrates the beauty of our Universe... *not* shown to scale!

1. Youngest galaxy
In Feb 2014, astronomers discovered galaxy Abell 2744-Y1, the light from which takes just over 13 billion years to reach Earth. Around 30 times smaller than the Milky Way, it is producing 10 times more stars.

2. Most common type of galaxy
Spiral galaxies such as Messier 101, pictured here by the *Hubble* space telescope, account for 77% of all galaxies. Our Milky Way is also a spiral galaxy, characterized by spiral arms wound around a brighter core.

3. First discovered spiral galaxy
William Parsons, 3rd Earl of Rosse (IRL), identified M51 (the "Whirlpool Galaxy") as a spiral in 1845. He used the *Leviathan*, then the world's **largest telescope**, at Birr Castle, County Offaly, Ireland.

4. Closest galaxy to the Milky Way
The Canis Major dwarf galaxy lies an average of 42,000 light years from the centre of our galaxy. It was only found in 2003 as it was difficult to detect behind the plane of our own spiral galaxy as seen from Earth.

5. Most remote object visible to the naked eye
The Andromeda galaxy, known as Messier 31, is about 2.5 million light years from Earth. Runner-up in this category is Messier 33, a spiral galaxy that can be glimpsed at a distance of 2.53 million light years.

6

7

8

10

9

6. Densest galaxies
Ultra Compact Dwarf (UCD) galaxies, such as M60-UCD1 (pictured), contain around a hundred million stars squashed into a space measuring 200 light years across.

7. Largest satellite galaxy
Of the 15 minor satellite galaxies orbiting the Milky Way, the largest and brightest is the Large Magellanic Cloud, some 160,000 light years from the centre of the Milky Way.

8. Fastest approaching galaxy
The Universe might be expanding but M86, a lenticular galaxy around 52 million light years away in the Virgo Cluster, is moving towards us at a rate of 419 km/s (260 mi/s).

9. Largest galaxy
IC 1101, in the Abell 2029 cluster, has a major diameter of 5.6 million light years – 80 times the diameter of the Milky Way – and a light output equivalent to 2 trillion times that of the Sun. It may be the result of many smaller galaxies merging.

10. Most massive galaxy cluster
"El Gordo" is the nickname of a galaxy cluster 7 billion light years away. Discovered via a disturbance in the cosmic microwave background, El Gordo is actually two clusters colliding at a rate of several million km/h.

Milestones in space

NASA's five Space Shuttles spent some **1,320 days** in space

No human had crossed the edge of space when GWR started in 1955. It wasn't until 1961 that the milestone was reached, but the pioneers of space exploration went on to rack up achievements at a blistering pace – visiting the Moon, building space stations and sending rovers to Mars and a probe beyond our Solar System.

It is testament to the power of human imagination that space flight quickly became an accepted part of everyday thought and discussion. Our concept of an expanding future for space exploration occupies much of our science-fiction film and television, and even cash-strapped nations compete to send probes to our sister planets.

The conquest of space was kickstarted as part of the increasingly bitter Cold War in the 1950s between the USA and the USSR. In 1955, both powers announced their intention to launch satellites, and the Soviets were the first to achieve the **first artificial satellite** with *Sputnik 1* in 1957. They were again the first to launch a man into space in 1961. Keen to catch up, US President Kennedy promised that the USA would be the first to get humans on the Moon. "We choose to go to the Moon in this decade," he said in 1962, "…because that challenge is one that we are willing to accept, one we are unwilling to postpone."

With that bold declaration, the space race became hotter than ever and the brightest and bravest ensured it changed humanity and the way we saw our planet and our place in the Solar System.

First flight between space stations: Mir EO-1 is the first expedition to the Soviet *Mir* space station. Its crew, Leonid Kizim and Vladimir Solovyov, launch from Earth on 13 Mar 1986, reach *Mir* two days later and remain docked for six weeks. *Mir* deorbits some 15 years later on 23 Mar 2001. More than 100 people visit over its life span.

1986

First untethered space walk: US astronaut Bruce McCandless II tests the Manned Maneuvering Unit (MMU) from the Space Shuttle *Challenger* on 7 Feb 1984.

1984

First manned maiden space flight: John Young and Robert Crippen (both USA) launch the inaugural orbital mission of the Space Shuttle *Columbia* on 12 Apr 1981. It is the first time a new spacecraft system is piloted in space without a prior unmanned flight.

1981

Farthest distance travelled on another world: The unmanned Soviet *Lunokhod 2* rover travels 42 km on the Moon between 16 Jan and 23 Jun 1973.

1973

Farthest distance from Earth reached by humans: The crew of *Apollo 13* reach 400,171 km above the Earth's surface on the "dark" (far) side of the Moon at 1:21 a.m. BST on 15 Apr 1970. They are 254 km above the lunar surface.

1970

First men on the Moon: Neil Armstrong (USA), commander of the *Apollo 11* mission, takes his first small step at 2:56 a.m. GMT on 21 Jul 1969, followed on to the surface of the Moon by Edwin "Buzz" Aldrin Jr (USA).

1969

First manned space flight: Russian cosmonaut, Flight Major Yuri Gagarin, achieves an altitude of 327 km in *Vostok 1* on 12 Apr 1961. Gagarin completes a single orbit of the Earth (still the **shortest orbital flight**) and ejects 108 min into the flight as planned.

1961

SPACE PIONEERS

1961

Yuri Gagarin: first man in space
Gagarin's flight of 12 Apr (see above) hit a speed of 40,868.6 km/h and made him a Soviet hero. Tragically, he was killed in a jet flight in 1968, aged just 34.

1963

Valentina Tereshkova: first woman in space
Launched in *Vostok 6* from Kazakhstan on 16 Jun, Tereshkova (USSR) flew for 2 days 22 hr 50 min. She went on to be politically prominent in the USSR.

1965

Alexey Leonov: first spacewalk
Leonov (USSR) conducted the first ever extra-vehicular activity (EVA) – aka spacewalk – when he exited the *Voskhod 2* craft for 12 min on 18 Mar 1965.

1969

Neil Armstrong: first men on the Moon
The commander of the *Apollo 11* mission was the first to walk on the surface of the Moon. He had learned to fly aged 15, even before he got his driving licence.

1969

"Buzz" Aldrin: first men on the Moon
In 2013, Aldrin (USA) looked back: "Neil had an optimistic way of using the word 'beautiful'. But when I looked out, it wasn't beautiful. It was desolate."

1972

Eugene Cernan: longest manned lunar mission
The US mission commander spent 74 hr 59 min 40 sec with Schmitt (see right) on the Moon on 7–19 Dec. *Apollo 17* was the last manned Moon mission.

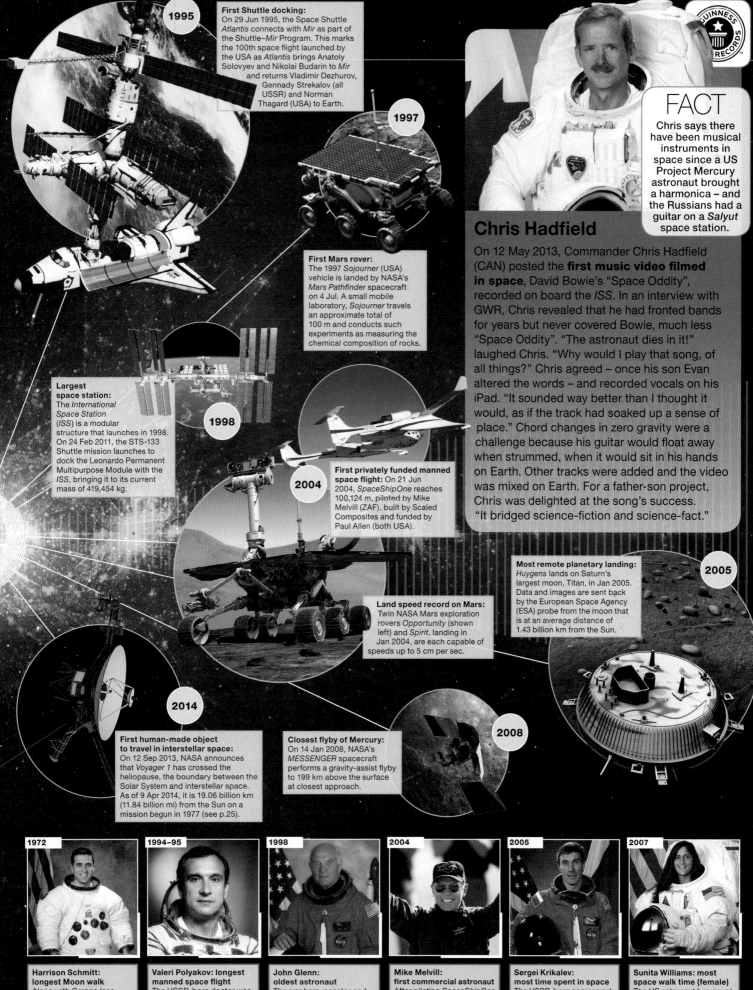

1995

First Shuttle docking: On 29 Jun 1995, the Space Shuttle *Atlantis* connects with *Mir* as part of the Shuttle–*Mir* Program. This marks the 100th space flight launched by the USA as *Atlantis* brings Anatoly Solovyev and Nikolai Budarin to *Mir* and returns Vladimir Dezhurov, Gennady Strekalov (all USSR) and Norman Thagard (USA) to Earth.

1997

First Mars rover: The 1997 *Sojourner* (USA) vehicle is landed by NASA's *Mars Pathfinder* spacecraft on 4 Jul. A small mobile laboratory, *Sojourner* travels an approximate total of 100 m and conducts such experiments as measuring the chemical composition of rocks.

GUINNESS RECORDS

FACT
Chris says there have been musical instruments in space since a US Project Mercury astronaut brought a harmonica – and the Russians had a guitar on a *Salyut* space station.

Chris Hadfield

On 12 May 2013, Commander Chris Hadfield (CAN) posted the **first music video filmed in space**, David Bowie's "Space Oddity", recorded on board the *ISS*. In an interview with GWR, Chris revealed that he had fronted bands for years but never covered Bowie, much less "Space Oddity". "The astronaut dies in it!" laughed Chris. "Why would I play that song, of all things?" Chris agreed – once his son Evan altered the words – and recorded vocals on his iPad. "It sounded way better than I thought it would, as if the track had soaked up a sense of place." Chord changes in zero gravity were a challenge because his guitar would float away when strummed, when it would sit in his hands on Earth. Other tracks were added and the video was mixed on Earth. For a father-son project, Chris was delighted at the song's success. "It bridged science-fiction and science-fact."

Largest space station: The *International Space Station* (*ISS*) is a modular structure that launches in 1998. On 24 Feb 2011, the STS-133 Shuttle mission launches to dock the Leonardo Permanent Multipurpose Module with the *ISS*, bringing it to its current mass of 419,454 kg.

1998

2004

First privately funded manned space flight: On 21 Jun 2004, *SpaceShipOne* reaches 100,124 m, piloted by Mike Melvill (ZAF), built by Scaled Composites and funded by Paul Allen (both USA).

Most remote planetary landing: *Huygens* lands on Saturn's largest moon, Titan, in Jan 2005. Data and images are sent back by the European Space Agency (ESA) probe from the moon that is at an average distance of 1.43 billion km from the Sun.

2005

Land speed record on Mars: Twin NASA Mars exploration rovers *Opportunity* (shown left) and *Spirit*, landing in Jan 2004, are each capable of speeds up to 5 cm per sec.

2014

First human-made object to travel in interstellar space: On 12 Sep 2013, NASA announces that *Voyager 1* has crossed the heliopause, the boundary between the Solar System and interstellar space. As of 9 Apr 2014, it is 19.06 billion km (11.84 billion mi) from the Sun on a mission begun in 1977 (see p.25).

Closest flyby of Mercury: On 14 Jan 2008, NASA's *MESSENGER* spacecraft performs a gravity-assist flyby to 199 km above the surface at closest approach.

2008

1972

Harrison Schmitt: longest Moon walk Along with Cernan (see left), the US geologist spent 7 hr 37 min on the Moon on 12 Dec, the pair covering 20.4 km and taking extensive samples.

1994–95

Valeri Polyakov: longest manned space flight The USSR-born doctor was sent to the *Mir* space station on 8 Jan 1994 and, after a space flight lasting 437 days 17 hr 58 min, landed – in full health – on 22 Mar 1995.

1998

John Glenn: oldest astronaut The war hero, senator and first American to orbit Earth (USA, b. 18 Jul 1921) made a 1998 comeback on 29 Oct on the Space Shuttle, aged 77 years 103 days.

2004

Mike Melvill: first commercial astronaut After piloting *SpaceShipOne* in 2004 (see above), the pioneer was awarded the first commercial astronaut wings by the US Federal Aviation Administration.

2005

Sergei Krikalev: most time spent in space The USSR-born cosmonaut notched up 803 days 9 hr in space, including stints on *Mir*, Space Shuttles and the *ISS*. He retired from active space flight in 2007.

2007

Sunita Williams: most space walk time (female) The US astronaut has spent a total of 50 hr 40 min on space walks. In Sep 2012 she carried out external repairs to the power supply unit of the *ISS*.

Universe

Twin sunsets: the planet **Kepler-47b** is lit by two stars

FACT
Gamma-ray bursts are the Universe's most powerful events and thought to be the birth cries of black holes, as supermassive stars exhaust their fuel and collapse to a singularity.

GRB 130427A

Most massive black hole

On 5 Dec 2011, astronomers using the *Gemini North*, *Keck II* and *Hubble* observatories reported a supermassive black hole in the centre of elliptical galaxy NGC 4889, some 336 million light years away. The black hole's mass is estimated at 20 billion times that of the Sun.

Largest cloud of primordial hydrogen
First discovered in 2000, LAB-1 is an astronomical object known as a Lyman-alpha blob. Measuring c. 300,000 light years across and some 11.5 billion light years from Earth, LAB-1 is a cloud of hydrogen gas that has yet to coalesce into galaxies. The blob is glowing – possibly due to the light from galaxies within that have already formed. Owing to its distance we see LAB-1 as it was when the Universe was only around 15% of its current age.

Largest void
The Giant Void is a very large region of space with an abnormally low density of galaxies and other matter within the constellation Canes Venatici. Also known as the "Giant Void in NGH (Northern Galactic Hemisphere)", the "Canes Venatici Supervoid", or its more scientific designation AR-Lp 36, is the largest confirmed void to date in the visible Universe. With an estimated diameter of 300–400 Mpc (1–1.3 billion light years), its geometric centre is approximately 1.5 billion light years away.

Densest known galaxy
M60-UCD1, announced in Sep 2013, is a type of galaxy called an Ultra Compact Dwarf (UCD). This class was discovered in 1999 by astrophysicists led by Dr Michael Drinkwater (UK). These galaxies are potentially left-over building blocks that once formed much larger galaxies. Half of the

First sighting of an extragalactic planet

In 2009, astronomers announced that they had seen a planet in the Andromeda galaxy, 2.2 million light years away. It became visible when it passed in front of a star, an event known as "microlensing", when the light of a star is magnified by an object passing in front. The Andromeda event was first seen in 2004, when it was believed to be owing to a binary star.

Highest-energy gamma rays from a gamma-ray burst

In May 2013, NASA announced that its *Fermi* gamma-ray space telescope had detected a burst measuring at least 94 billion electron volts (35 billion times the energy of normal, visible light). This explosion, known as GRB 130427A, came from a galaxy 3.6 billion light years away.

mass of M60-UCD1 is found within a radius of only 80 light years, making the density of stars 15,000 times greater than our area of the Milky Way.

Most distant dwarf galaxy
In 2012, astronomers led by Dr Simona Vegetti of the Massachusetts Institute of Technology announced the discovery of a dwarf galaxy orbiting a large elliptical galaxy some 10 billion light years away. Undetectable by telescope, its gravity causes light distortion that gives it away. It's possible the galaxy is composed exclusively of dark matter, or it may contain stars that are too dim to be visible at this distance.

See Earth from space on pp.34–35

Our very first record
We opened our first edition in 1955 with "remotest known bodies". The record went to an "extra-galactic nebulae at a distance of some 1,000 million light-years". In Mar 2014, the most distant confirmed galaxy is z8-GND-5296: its light takes some 13.3 billion years to reach us on Earth.

COSMOLOGICAL COMPOSITION

Astronomers once thought that the Universe was composed largely of "stuff" – i.e., stars and planets made of atoms and heavy elements. However, observations of how galaxies move suggest that most of the total mass of the Universe is invisible. It is currently understood that the majority of the Universe is "dark" energy and matter; the stars and planets, plus the interstellar hydrogen and other gases and dust, account for just c. 5%.

KEY:
- Dark energy
- Dark matter
- Free hydrogen and helium, other gases, dust, stars, planets

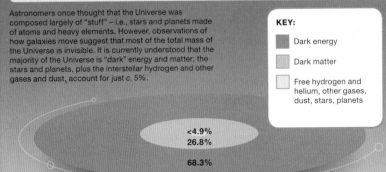

<4.9%
26.8%
68.3%

We are all stardust

You're older than you might think – most of the elements in your body include atoms that arose during the Big Bang, 13.82 billion years ago.
The astronomer and influential science communicator Carl Sagan (USA, 1934–96), host of the original *Cosmos* TV show in 1980, famously wrote: "The nitrogen in our DNA, the calcium in our teeth, the iron in our blood, the carbon in our apple pies were made in the interiors of collapsing stars. We are made of star-stuff."

Most distant black hole

A supermassive black hole resides in the centre of quasar ULAS J112001.48+064124.3. In terms of redshift (a light measurement – higher than 1.4 means the source is receding at more than the speed of light), it measures 7.085. This black hole was announced in Jun 2011 and emits radiation from superheated matter that surrounded it less than 770 million years after the Big Bang.

Longest galactic jet

An energetic jet of matter emitted from a supermassive black hole in the centre of galaxy CGCG 049-033 measures 1.5 million light years long. Life on any planets in the path of the jet stream would be extinguished.

Highest electrical current
Scientists at the University of Toronto, Canada, have made the "shocking" discovery of the highest known electrical current in the Universe. Generated by a cosmic jet more

than 2 billion light years away in a galaxy known as 3C303, the electrical current is measured at 1E18 amps (1 followed by 18 zeros). The scientists used the effect of the current on radio waves coming from the galaxy to measure this tremendous amount of electrical energy, which is most likely generated by magnetic fields from a black hole at the centre of the galaxy. The resulting jet of matter extends into space to around 150,000 light years – possibly the largest bolt of lightning ever seen.

Most distant supernova
A Type IIn supernova some 11 billion light years away was located using data from the Canada-France-Hawaii Telescope. In 2009, astronomers announced they had seen a galaxy that brightened momentarily with a spectrum characterized by a very narrow colour band of emitted light from hydrogen as it burns.

Oldest light
The Cosmic Microwave Background (CMB) is radiation that formed 380,000 years after the Big Bang. When the Universe was born, a tremendous amount of light was generated that remains all pervasive. The CMB can be seen as photons coming from all directions. The 2013 *Planck* map of CMB showed, among other things, that the Universe is older than thought, at 13.82 billion years.

Smallest extrasolar planet
Kepler-37b is a planet only slightly larger than the Moon. It orbits the star Kepler-37, around 210 light years from Earth in the constellation of Lyra. Its discovery by NASA's *Kepler* space observatory – the mission launched to carry

out research into habitable planets – was announced on 20 Feb 2013. Kepler-37b is only 1,930 km (1,199 mi) across, making it smaller than the planet Mercury.

Most magnetic object

If a magnetar flew within 161,000 km (100,000 mi) of Earth, it could strip the data off every credit card. Fortunately, there have been fewer than a dozen identified examples of these neutron stars (which come from the dead core of collapsed stars densely packed to the size of a city). Magnetars, thought to originate from the supernovae of massive stars, have magnetic fields that are up to a trillion times the size of, for example, a hospital MRI machine.

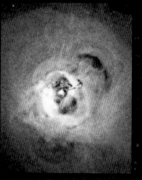

Deepest note

The Universe's lowest note is caused by acoustic waves generated by a supermassive black hole. It is in the centre of the Perseus cluster of galaxies (above), 250 million light years away. The sound – a B-flat note, 57 octaves below middle C – propagates through thin gas surrounding the black hole.

Largest structure

The Hercules-Corona Borealis Great Wall consists of a staggeringly huge cluster of galaxies and other normal matter measuring 10 billion light years across and about 10 billion light years from Earth. Superclusters are bound by gravity; this one was announced in Nov 2013 by astronomers who mapped it by charting gamma-ray bursts (pictured) in the region.

FACT
Light travels at 300,000 km/s and a light year measures how far light travels in a year.

Nothing to see here: dark matter

Astronomers in the 1970s, particularly Vera Rubin (right), measured the velocities of stars in other galaxies and noticed that the stars at the galaxies' edges moved faster than predicted. To reconcile the observations with the law of gravity, scientists proposed that there is matter we can't see and called it "dark matter". This, the most common form of matter, neither emits nor absorbs light and radiation as stars and planets do. Measuring the effect of dark matter in gravitational terms, scientists have proposed that together with dark energy it makes up 95% of the Universe.

The hole truth

Nearest distance between two black holes: two orbiting black holes in quasar SDSS J153636.22+044127.0, separated by just one-third of a light year

Closest black hole to Earth: V4641 Sgr, discovered 1,600 light years away

Closest supermassive black hole to Earth: Sagittarius A*, centre of the Milky Way, 27,000 light years away

○ ○ ○

Solar System

The word "planet" derives from the ancient Greek for **"wandering star"**

Most tails for an asteroid

On 10 Sep 2013, the *Hubble* telescope spotted a bizarre asteroid with six distinct tails like a comet. The 480-m-wide (1,570-ft) asteroid P/2013 P5 is likely to have the tails owing to the pressure of solar radiation, which has increased the asteroid's spin so much that mass is lost from its own rotation.

MERCURY

Largest impact basin on Mercury
The Caloris Basin has a diameter of *c.* 1,550 km (950 mi) and is surrounded by 2-km-high (1.2-mi) mountains. It was formed 3.8–3.9 billion years ago when a 100-km-wide (60-mi) object struck.

Fastest planet
Mercury takes 87.96 days to orbit the Sun at an average distance of 57.9 million km (35.9 million mi), giving an average speed of 172,248 km/h (107,030 mph) – almost twice as fast as Earth.

VENUS

Brightest planet
With a maximum magnitude of -4.4, Venus is the brightest planet visible from Earth with the naked eye.

First thunder heard on another planet
On 25 Dec 1978, the USSR's *Venera 11* lander touched down on Venus. Among its instruments was an acoustic detector, which heard an 82-dB sound of unknown origin. A Venusian thunder clap is the most likely explanation.

EARTH

Densest planet
Earth is the densest planet, with an average density of 5.517 times that of water.

Deepest crater
The Earth's Moon is home to the largest and deepest known crater in the Solar System. The South Pole-Aitken impact basin on the far side of the Moon is 2,250 km (1,400 mi) in diameter and has an average depth of 12,000 m (39,000 ft).

Fastest trip to the *ISS*
The fastest time to reach the *International Space Station* (*ISS*) from launch to dock is 5 hr 39 min, achieved on 29 May 2013 UTC by the crew of Expedition 36 on board the *Soyuz TMA-09M* (inset). They launched from Baikonur in Kazakhstan at 8:31 p.m. UTC and docked with the *ISS*'s "Rassvet" module at 2:10 a.m. UTC on 30 May.

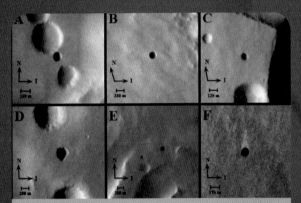

First caves on another planet

In Mar 2007, images from NASA's *Mars Odyssey* showed the discovery of what appeared to be seven circular pits on Mars' surface with entrances to underground caverns. In only one of the seven pits does a floor appear to be visible, at least 130 m (426 ft) below the surface.

MARS

Highest clouds
In Aug 2006, European scientists reported their discovery of clouds some 90–100 km (55–62 mi) above the surface of Mars. Detected by an instrument on board the European Space Agency's *Mars Express* orbiter, the clouds are made of carbon dioxide ice crystals. If the density of this upper atmosphere is greater than thought, it will mean more aerobraking for landing ships.

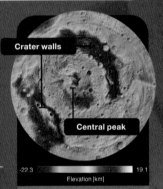

Crater walls

Central peak

-22.3   Elevation [km]   19.1

Tallest central peak for an impact crater
Rheasilvia is a 505-km-wide (313-mi) impact crater on asteroid 4Vesta between Mars and Jupiter. At its centre is a peak rising a record 20 km (12 mi) above the crater floor (the central red feature seen on the satellite image above).

MAGNIFICENT MOUNTAINS: OLYMPUS, KEA AND EVEREST

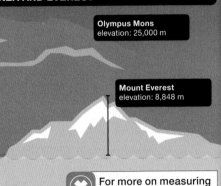

Olympus Mons on Mars is the **highest mountain in the Solar System**, with an elevation (peak height) of 25 km – nearly three times that of Everest. However, Everest isn't Earth's highest mountain when Mauna Kea on Hawaii is measured from base to peak.

Olympus Mons
elevation: 25,000 m

Mount Everest
elevation: 8,848 m

Mauna Kea
elevation: 4,205 m
(base to peak: 10,205 m)

Sea level

 For more on measuring mountains, see p.36

Size matters
In our 1955 edition, the most remote planet was assumed to be Pluto, with a mean distance from the Sun of 5.9×10^9 km. Pluto was discovered on 18 Feb 1930 by Clyde Tombaugh, an astronomer working at the Lowell Observatory in the USA. Today, Pluto no longer holds the record, as over the years astronomers raised doubts over its planetary status, citing its diminutive size and erratic orbit. In 2006, the International Astronomical Union offered a new definition of a planet; Pluto didn't qualify, and its status was revised to "dwarf planet".

FACT
You could fit one million Earths inside the Sun.

Beyond the Solar System
Voyager I, the **most remote man-made object**, is, as of 15:26 GMT on 6 Feb 2014, a distance of 19,034,504,880 km from Earth. Having left the Solar System in Aug 2012, it is now travelling through interstellar space.

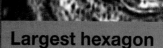

Largest area of surface ice

Almost all of the ice on Mars' surface is in the poles. The southern cap is the largest at around 420 km (260 mi) across, and contains enough water to cover the entire planet in a layer 11 m (36 ft) deep.

JUPITER

Most moons to a planet

As of 2013, 67 natural satellites of Jupiter have been discovered. Most are small, irregularly shaped bodies of ice and rock, and many are almost certainly captured asteroids.

One of the Jovian moons, Ganymede, has the **greatest mass of a moon in the Solar System**. It is twice as heavy as Earth's Moon and has a width of 5,267 km (3,273 mi).

SATURN

Least dense planet

Saturn is mainly composed of hydrogen and helium, the two lightest elements in the Universe. It would float on water if there was a bathtub large enough to hold it.

Tallest clouds

A massive vortex of clouds – roughly five times higher than Earth's hurricanes – was discovered to be at Saturn's south pole in 2006.

NEPTUNE

Farthest planet in the Solar System

Since Pluto's demotion from "planet" status in 2006 (see below left), Neptune is the farthest planet from the Sun. At a distance of 4.5 billion km (2.8 billion mi) away, it orbits at 5.45 km/s (3.38 mi/s) and takes 164.79 years to complete each orbit.

Fastest winds

There are no faster winds in our Solar System than those on Neptune. NASA's *Voyager 2* probe measured winds of around 2,400 km/h (1,500 mph) in 1989.

Largest hexagon

The largest hexagon in our Solar System is on Saturn's North Pole, where a massive pattern of hexagonal clouds, with sides measuring around 13,800 km (8,500 mi) in length, is located. It was first seen by the *Voyager* in the early 1980s and has since been studied in more detail, proving that it has lasted for at least 30 years.

SEE IN 3D WITH THE FREE APP

Augmented Reality alert! 3D ON THIS PAGE

Saturn

Uranus

Neptune

Jupiter

FACT

Saturn has the largest ring system: billions of tiny, orbiting particles of dust and ice, equivalent in mass to 30 million Mount Everests.

Largest planet

Our Solar System's mightiest body is Jupiter, with an equatorial diameter of 143,884 km (89,405 mi) and a polar diameter of 133,708 km (83,082 mi). Its mass and volume are around 317 and 1,323 times that of Earth respectively. Jupiter also has the **shortest day of any planet in the Solar System**, at just 9 hr 55 min 29.69 sec.

Earth

Mars

Mercury

Venus

Scaled-up: the Sweden Solar System

When the Stockholm (now Ericsson) Globe Arena opened in Sweden in Feb 1989 as the world's **largest hemispherical building**, it gave two Swedish academics an idea: if the 110-m-wide building was considered a scaled-down Sun, how far away would the planets lie, and what size would they be? Nils Brenning and Gösta Gahm went on to champion the **largest representation of the Solar System** – a 1:20-million-scale "model" that stretches 950 km across the country, with planets, minor planets and comets represented by scaled globes or artworks at their relative distances apart.

Mercury (25 cm wide), 2.9 km away

Earth (65 cm wide), 7.6 km away

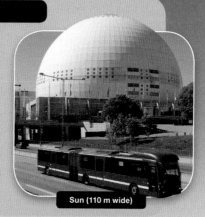
Sun (110 m wide)

Glossary

Dwarf planet: a body with enough mass to form a spherical shape, but not enough gravitational attraction to clear its orbit of debris as it circles the Sun.

Light year: the distance that light travels in one year in a vacuum: some 9.46 trillion km (9.46×10^{12} km).

Mass: a measure of the quantity of matter in a body as well as its inertia.

Weight: the force of an object due to gravity.

Comets

Halley's Comet should make its next appearance in **2061**

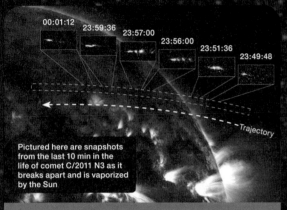

00:01:12 23:59:36 23:57:00 23:56:00 23:51:36 23:49:48

Trajectory

Pictured here are snapshots from the last 10 min in the life of comet C/2011 N3 as it breaks apart and is vaporized by the Sun

Comet up close

Nucleus: dust, rocky debris and frozen gas
Coma: cloud of evaporated gases and dust around nucleus
Hydrogen envelope: gets larger as comet nears the Sun
Dust tail: follows comet's orbit; may be 150 million km long
Ion tail: made up of ionized gases flowing along the magnetic field lines of the plasma of the solar wind

Dust tail

Ion tail

Nucleus

Coma

Hydrogen envelope

First comet observed being destroyed by the Sun

On 6 Jul 2011, NASA's Solar Dynamics Observatory captured images of comet C/2011 N3's demise. The comet had a nucleus 9–45 m (29–147 ft) wide and got within 100,000 km (62,100 mi) of the Sun's surface, moving at about 2.1 million km/h (1.3 million mph), before breaking up and being vaporized.

Largest source of comets
Beyond Neptune's orbit lie the Kuiper Belt, the Scattered Disc and the Oort Cloud, collectively known as Trans-Neptunian Objects. The Oort Cloud contains trillions of cometary nuclei. It surrounds the Sun at a distance of c. 50,000 Astronomical Units (1 AU = distance from the Earth to the Sun), around 1,000 times the distance from the Sun to Pluto. Scientists believe the cloud to be the source of most of the comets that visit the inner Solar System.

Longest comet tail
The tail of comet Hyakutake measured 570 million km (350 million mi) long – more than 3 AU. The tail was discovered by Geraint Jones of Imperial College, London, UK, on 13 Sep 1999, using data gathered by the ESA/NASA spacecraft *Ulysses* on a chance encounter with the comet on 1 May 1996.

Closest approach to Earth by a comet
On 1 Jul 1770, travelling at 138,600 km/h (86,100 mph), Lexell's Comet came within 2,200,000 km (1,360,000 mi) – or just 0.015 AU – of Earth.

Most recent Great Comet

Great Comets are those that become extremely bright in the night sky. The most recent Great Comet was Comet McNaught, first discovered by Robert McNaught (AUS) in 2006. At its peak brightness, on 12 Jan 2007, its tail measured a maximum of 35° long in the sky.

First cometary soft lander

Launched on 2 Mar 2004, the European Space Agency's (ESA) Rosetta mission will rendezvous with comet 67P/Churyumov-Gerasimenko in 2014. The spacecraft will study and map the comet then release the *Philae* lander, which will anchor itself to the surface of the 4-km-wide (2.4-mi) comet with harpoons and will survive for at least a week.

Smallest comet visited by a spacecraft
NASA's *Deep Impact* spacecraft, launched on 12 Jan 2005, was re-tasked as the EPOXI mission on 3 Jul 2007 with the goal of studying extrasolar planets and performing a flyby of comet 103P/Hartley. The flyby occurred

COSMIC PATH: A COMET'S JOURNEY THROUGH SPACE

A comet's coma and tails form during its journey around the Sun. One tail is composed of dust; the other is an ion (gas) tail. Solar wind and radiation angle the tails away from the comet

Dust tail is pushed out by sunlight

Earth's orbit

Ion tail is swept back by solar wind

solar wind

solar radiation

Tail points away from Sun

Coma forms when comet is about five times farther from the Sun than Earth is

Nucleus warms. Ice starts turning to gas

Coma and tail disappear as comet gets farther from Sun's warmth

Larger than we thought...

In 1955, *The Guinness Book of Records* said that it was estimated that no comet head contains "mass in excess of 20 miles [30 km] in diameter" and that the longest tail "may trail out to 200 million miles [300 million km]". The **largest comet** now known is Chiron, which has a diameter of 182 km and a tail that has measured up to 1,273 million km in length.

Glossary

Asteroid: inactive body of rock and metal orbiting the Sun.

Comet: cluster of ice, dust, rock and frozen gas left over from the birth of the Solar System. When it passes near the Sun, a coma and tail can often be seen (pictured above).

Meteor: rock that enters the Earth's atmosphere and burns up into a "shooting star". See p.32.

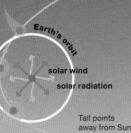

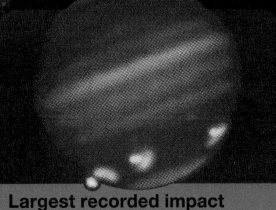

Largest recorded impact in the Solar System

From 16 to 22 Jul 1994, more than 20 fragments of comet Shoemaker-Levy 9 collided with Jupiter. The greatest impact was of the "G" fragment, which exploded with the energy of roughly 600 times the nuclear arsenal of the world, equivalent to 6 million megatons of TNT.

on 4 Nov 2010 as *Deep Impact* passed within 700 km (430 mi) of the nucleus. The comet is around 2.25 km (1.4 mi) long and has a mass of around 300 million tonnes (590 billion lb).

Most distant observations of a comet
On 3 Sep 2003, the European Southern Observatory in Paranal, Chile, released an image of Halley's Comet at 4,200 million km (2,600 million mi) from the

First comet discovered to be periodic

Halley's Comet, aka 1P/Halley, orbits the Sun every 75.32 years. Sightings of this comet go back to at least 240 BC, but it was English astronomer Edmond Halley who, in 1705, first realized that observations of this comet were of the same object and predicted its return for the year 1758. The main picture (below left) shows a Babylonian clay tablet from *c.* 164 BC that mentions the comet. The inset, from the Bayeux Tapestry (made *c.* 1100), depicts the comet along with Latin text stating: "These [people] are looking in wonder at the star."

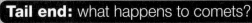

First comet sample returned

Encountering the comet Wild 2 (below) in early 2004, the *Stardust* spacecraft swept up tiny samples of cometary dust in an aerogel collector (above) and returned the material to Earth on 15 Jan 2006. Its ongoing analysis is providing insights into the chemical make-up of this icy, primordial body.

Sun. It shows Halley as a fuzzy dot with a brightness of magnitude of 28.2, nearly a billion times fainter than the faintest objects visible with the naked eye.

Largest observed coma
The coma of the Great Comet of 1811 – discovered on 25 Mar 1811 by French astronomer Honoré Flaugergues – had a diameter of about 2 million km (1.2 million mi).

First anti-comet medication

Halley's Comet visited the inner Solar System in 1910. Earth passed through its tail, which included the toxic gas cyanogen. Needless panic-buying of gas masks, "anti-comet umbrellas" and "anti-comet pills" followed.

First impact on a comet

On 4 Jul 2005, a 350-kg (770-lb) copper "bullet" from NASA's *Deep Impact* craft hit comet Tempel 1 at 10.3 km/s (6.4 mi/s). The impact – equivalent to that of 4.7 tonnes (10,360 lb) of TNT – created a crater 100 m (330 ft) wide and 30 m (100 ft) deep.

Tail end: what happens to comets?

The "death" of a comet can come about in a variety of different ways. Not all comets are tied to an orbit around the Sun, and some of them simply fly out of the Solar System. Each time a comet passes the Sun, it loses samples of dust and ice; if all of the ice is lost, the comet can become an inactive, asteroid-like structure. Alternatively, complete loss of ice can result in the comet breaking up into dust clouds. Finally, comets can meet a violent end when their orbit results in them crashing into a moon or planet. Our own Moon (right) is pockmarked with impact craters caused by comets and asteroids crashing into its surface.

Comet watch

Closest comet flyby by a spacecraft: *Giotto* flew within 200 km of Grigg-Skjellerup on 10 Jul 1992.

Most comet tails met by a spacecraft: *Ulysses* flew through the tails of Hyakutake (1996), McNaught-Hartley (2004) and McNaught (2007).

Most comets discovered by a spacecraft: The *SOHO* (*Solar and Heliospheric Observatory*) had discovered 2,574 comets by Dec 2013.

SETI

SETI stands for the **Search for Extraterrestrial Intelligence**

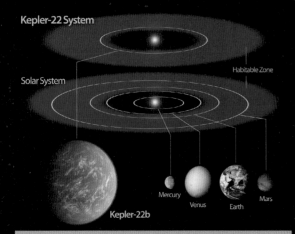

Kepler-22 System

Solar System

Habitable Zone

Mercury
Venus
Earth
Mars

Kepler-22b

First Earth-like planet

On 5 Dec 2011, Kepler-22b was announced as the first of more than 700 planets thought to reside within the habitable zone of its star, some 600 light years away. At 2.4 times the size of Earth, the planet orbits its Sun-like star in around 290 days. If the planet has an Earth-like greenhouse effect, then its surface temperature could be 22°C (72°F).

First known pulsar
On 28 Nov 1967, British astronomers Jocelyn Bell Burnell and Antony Hewish spotted a radio signal from another star. All stars emit radio signals, but this turned on and off with perfect regularity: one pulse lasting 0.04 sec every 1.3373 sec. The pair playfully named the phenomenon "LGM-1" ("Little Green Men 1"). In fact, they had found what would be called a pulsar – a portmanteau of "pulsating star". Pulsars are the rapidly rotating remnants left over by a supernova – and their behaviour is entirely natural, if very precise. The first was later named CP 1919.

Largest planet-hunter space telescope
NASA's Kepler space telescope was launched on 7 Mar 2009 on a Delta II rocket from Cape Canaveral, USA. The spacecraft measures 2.7 x 4.7 m (8 ft 10 in x 15 ft 5 in) and follows an Earth-trailing heliocentric orbit. It can capture images of planets outside the Solar System, called exoplanets or extrasolar planets, using a mirror 1.4 m (4 ft 7 in) in diameter and a 95-megapixel camera. As of Feb 2014, it has identified 961 exoplanets – over half of the total discoveries of the past 20 years – and 2,903 unconfirmed candidates.

Most Earth-like exoplanet
The Earth Similarity Index (ESI) is a system devised to categorize and rate the increasing number of exoplanetary candidates. It rates how similar each is to Earth, based on size, density, escape velocity and surface temperature. The ranking ranges from zero to 1, with Earth's value at 1. The exoplanet ranking highest on the ESI is KOI-3284.01, detected by the Kepler telescope in 2012 and given an ESI rating of 0.9. The planet may or may not be rocky, but it does have the potential for liquid water.

First physical message sent into deep space

Pioneer 10 is a NASA probe launched on 3 Mar 1972. A gold-strengthened aluminium plaque was fixed to the outside showing a man and woman, to scale with the probe, along with a map of the Solar System and the location of the Sun relative to pulsars in our galaxy. The probe's mission was to make the **first Jupiter flyby**, achieved on 3 Dec 1973.

First digital time capsule chosen by public vote

A radio telescope at Yevpatoria in Ukraine sent a radio message on 9 Oct 2008 to the planet Gliese 581c, orbiting a star some 20.3 light years from Earth. Images of landmarks and celebrities (such as singer Cheryl Cole, pictured) were sent, as well as 501 text messages from Bebo users. The message is due to reach Gliese 581c in 2029.

Oldest unexplained extrasolar signal
On 15 Aug 1977, astronomer Jerry Ehman (USA) detected a radio signal using the *Big Ear* radio telescope at the Ohio State University, USA. The signal was monitored for 72 sec and closely matched the expected profile of an extraterrestrial signal. Ehman circled the readout and wrote "Wow!". It has never been detected again.

VOYAGER GOLDEN RECORD

Explanation of the *Voyager* Golden Record cover by NASA

Plan of record: binary code defining speed around the edge

Elevation of record: showing position of record cartridge

Sun location: defined by 14 pulsars of known direction from the Sun

Wave form of video signals on recording: binary code gives time of scan

Video image frame information: decoded properly, first image is a circle

Two lowest states of hydrogen with spin moments of proton and electron: clock reference for diagrams and decoded pictures

Lisa Vanderperre-Hirsch

Grey aliens are alleged beings of wildly varying description, although they are often shown with oversized heads and black eyes. Lisa Vanderperre-Hirsch (USA) has the **largest collection of grey alien memorabilia**, with 547 individual items as of 20 Nov 2011 in Florida, USA. Lisa's collection includes posters, calendars and even alien-themed toilet paper.

i Listening time

The amount of radio telescope capacity used for SETI is much less than is popularly assumed. Project Phoenix was given the **largest allocation for a single SETI project** at Arecibo to analyse patterns in radio signals. It used about 5% of the total observatory time (2,400 hr) from Sep 1998 to Mar 2004. Worldwide, just 30 or so scientists and engineers work full-time in SETI.

Most powerful radio signal aimed into space

On 16 Nov 1974, scientists at the Arecibo radio telescope in Puerto Rico sent a message containing basic data on humanity (right). The binary radio signal was broadcast to the M13 globular cluster in the constellation of Hercules and lasted 169 sec. It will arrive in 25,000 years at a strength 10 million times that of radio signals from our Sun. Any reply will take another 25,000 years to return to Earth.

Most remote man-made object

Voyager 1, launched on 5 Sep 1977, is a space probe whose primary mission was to perform flybys of Jupiter and Saturn. As of 9 Apr 2014, it is 19.06 billion km (11.84 billion mi) from the Sun. *Voyager 1* and *Voyager 2* each contain a tougher version of a vinyl record: a gold-plated copper disc with stylus and instructions to alien life on how to play it (see *Voyager Golden Record*). The disc carries 116 images encoded in audio form and natural sounds of Earth, greetings in 59 languages and music.

First report of a "flying saucer"

UFOs have been recorded for hundreds of years

in various forms, but it was the sighting by pilot Kenneth Arnold on 24 Jun 1947 that saw newspapers coin the term "flying saucer". Arnold didn't use the exact phrase to describe the nine objects he saw in the sky near Mount Rainier in Washington, USA, though he did say they were like saucers, discs or pie-plates.

First UFO landing pad

St Paul in Alberta, Canada, is a prairie town with an official UFO landing pad, opened on 3 Jun 1967 by Canada's Minister of National Defence. The saucer-shaped concrete platform sits above a pile

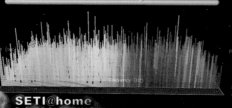

Longest-running SETI project

SETI@home, developed by the University of California, USA, is a crowdsourcing project that harnesses the power of PCs to process vast amounts of data. Signals from the Arecibo radio telescope were first made available for download on 17 May 1999 in a screensaver. The most intriguing discovery to date was a signal called SHGb02+14a, found in Mar 2003, that does not correspond to any known galactic phenomena.

of welcoming stones from each province of Canada. A sign declares the pad to be "a symbol of our faith that mankind will maintain the outer universe free from national wars and strife". Inside the pad is a time capsule to be opened on its centenary in 2067.

Largest civilian UFO investigative group

The Mutual UFO Network (MUFON) is an American-based organization that investigates UFO sightings. There are branches all over the world and more than 3,000 members. MUFON was started in May 1969.

Largest UFO convention

The 23rd International UFO Congress was held in Scottsdale in Arizona, USA, on 12–16 Feb 2014. An average of 1,500 people attended events throughout the week on topics such as official cover-ups, exopolitics, black projects, crop circles and visitations.

First equation estimating intelligent life in our galaxy

In 1961, US astronomer Frank Drake devised an equation to give estimates of the number of planets inhabited by intelligent life:

$$N = R_* F_p N_e F_l F_i F_c L$$

While some of these variables (see glossary below) are extremely speculative, Drake himself estimated the number of advanced civilizations in our galaxy to be as high as 10,000.

$10,000,000.00
UFO ABDUCTION
INSURANCE

First insurance against alien abduction

The UFO Abduction Insurance Co (USA) offers an insurance policy costing $19.95 (£12) that pays out $10 m (£6.06 m) to abductees. Proof of abduction is all that is required – an extraterrestrial signature will suffice.

The Drake equation

N number of civilizations for possible radio communication

R. average star formation rate in our galaxy

F$_p$ fraction of those stars with planets

N$_e$ average of planets that might support life

F$_l$ fraction of those planets that develop life

F$_i$ fraction of those planets that develop civilizations

F$_c$ fraction of civilizations that develop detectable technology

L length of broadcast time of such civilizations

Life on Mars: examining the evidence

Astronomer Giovanni Schiaparelli (ITA) was the **first person to gather scientific evidence concerning life on Mars**. In 1877, he described telescopic observations of the planet that included *canali*, or channels – a network of lines across the surface. *Canali* was mistranslated as "canals" and later observers mapped them in detail, believing them to be structures built by a civilization rather than natural channels. As telescopes became more powerful, and space probes sent information from the surface, the "canals" were shown to be geological features.

Observatories

An **11,000-year-old site** in Turkey is thought to have been an early form of observatory

Largest array of radio telescopes

The VLA (Very Large Array) of the US National Science Foundation has 27 mobile antennae on rails in a Y-shaped arrangement. Each arm of the Y is 21 km (13 mi) long and each antenna has a dish that measures 25 m (82 ft) in diameter. The VLA, completed in 1980, is located 80 km (50 mi) west of Socorro in New Mexico, USA.

LARGEST...

Primary mirror (non-segmented)

The largest observatory mirrors are those in the dual-tube Large Binocular Telescope (see right), but the largest *single* primary mirror forms part of Japan's Subaru Telescope on Mauna Kea, Hawaii, USA. The 8.2-m-wide (26-ft 10-in) mirror is made from 20-cm-thick (8-in) glass weighing 22.8 tonnes (50,265 lb). With the help of 261 actuators to constantly keep the mirror focused, warping is limited to less than 0.1 microns (0.00001 millimetres).

Cosmic ray telescope

The Pierre Auger Observatory is a vast array of 1,600 particle detectors looking for very high-energy cosmic ray particles, which it is thought may be produced by supermassive black holes. Only one high-energy particle falls per 1 km² (0.39 sq mi) in a century, so the observatory is arranged over a 3,000-km² (1,158-sq-mi) area of Argentina – in an area larger than Luxembourg.

Highest astronomical observatory

The University of Tokyo Atacama Observatory (TAO) was established in Chile at an altitude of 5,640 m (18,500 ft) – double the height at which altitude sickness typically occurs. TAO perches on the summit of Cerro Chajnantor in the Atacama Desert. The observatory has an infrared telescope that was completed in Mar 2009.

Dish radio telescope

The Arecibo Observatory (see also p.25) was considered impressive enough to star in the finale to the 1995 James Bond movie *GoldenEye*. The

Deepest observatory

The Sudbury Neutrino Observatory (SNOLAB) is 2,075 m (6,800 ft) down a mine in Ontario, Canada. There, shielded from cosmic rays that affect experiments into low-energy solar neutrinos, it searches for cosmic dark matter and supernova neutrino.

Largest robotic telescope

The Liverpool Telescope receives requests for data online and autonomously "decides" which observations to make. Located on La Palma in the Canary Islands with a 2-m (6.5-ft) mirror, the Liverpool reserves 5% of its observing time for use by schools.

HIGHEST OBSERVATORIES

5,640 m	University of Tokyo Atacama Observatory (TAO), Chile
5,230 m	Chacaltaya Astrophysical Observatory, Bolivia
5,200 m	James Ax Observatory, Chile
5,190 m	Atacama Cosmology Telescope, Chile
5,105 m	Llano de Chajnantor Observatory (APEX), Chile
5,100 m	Shiquanhe Observatory (NAOC Ali Observatory), Tibet
5,080 m	Llano de Chajnantor Observatory (QUIET), Chile
5,000 m	Llano de Chajnantor Observatory (ALMA), Chile
4,860 m	Atacama Submillimeter Telescope Experiment, Chile
4,600 m	Large Millimeter Telescope, Mexico

Sea level

Scope for improvement

The **largest reflector telescope** in our 1955 edition was the Hale Telescope of the California Institute of Technology on Palomar Mountain, USA, with its 5.1-m-wide unsegmented mirror. The record today – now categorized as the **largest unsegmented primary mirror** – is held by the 8.2-m-wide Subaru Telescope on Mauna Kea (see above). The **largest land-based telescope** in *absolute* terms, though, is the segmented Gran Telescopio Canarias (right) at 10.4 m wide.

Glossary

Actuator: motor that moves the mirror or changes its shape in large reflecting telescopes

Aperture: the opening in a telescope (or camera) that determines how much light enters and gets focused

First light: inaugural use of a telescope to record an astronomical image

Primary mirror: the main light-gathering surface of a reflecting telescope

Largest binocular telescope

The Large Binocular Telescope in Arizona, USA, comprises two identical telescopes, each with an 8.4-m-wide (27-ft 6-in) primary mirror. Working in tandem, they have an equivalent light-gathering power of a single mirror 11.8 m (38 ft 8 in) in diameter and are able to achieve the image sharpness of a 22.8-m-wide (74-ft 9-in) aperture.

c. 3,200 km (2,000 mi) apart. The arms of these facilities are each 4 km (2.4 mi) long, providing LIGO with a high level of sensitivity. The detectors are currently being upgraded to continue the search for gravitational waves predicted in Einstein's general theory of relativity.

Liquid mirror
The Large Zenith Telescope (LZT), east of Vancouver in Canada, uses a mirror made from liquid mercury. By spinning the 3-tonne (6,613-lb), 6-m-diameter

Largest movable motor-driven structure on land

The Robert C Byrd Green Bank Telescope is a radio telescope at the National Radio Astronomy Observatory in West Virginia, USA. The dish measures 100 x 110 m (328 x 360 ft), and its highest point stands 146 m (480 ft) above the ground. The structure is fully steerable, and can observe the whole sky from five degrees above the horizon.

distinctive design consists of a dish with a diameter of 305 m (1,000 ft), covering 7.48 ha (18.5 acres) – about the same as 14 American football fields. The dish is covered by 38,778 aluminium panels. A steerable arm measuring 100 m (328 ft) is above the dish, allowing more of the sky to be seen.

Gravitational wave detector
The Laser Interferometry Gravitational Wave Observatory (LIGO) consists of two similar L-shaped structures based in Louisiana and Washington (USA),

Largest concentration of high-altitude telescopes

Kitt Peak in Arizona, USA, is a 2,096-m (6,876-ft) mountain whose atmospheric clarity has attracted 24 major telescopes on its summit since 1958. Two are radio telescopes and the others are optical telescopes. The largest structure is the Nicholas U Mayall Telescope, a 4-m (13-ft) mirror housed in a 57-m-tall (187-ft) building that can be seen from a distance of 80 km (50 mi).

(19-ft 8-in) mercury mirror, the liquid forms a concave mirror shape. As a zenith telescope it is limited by looking straight up, but it is more economical as mercury is less expensive than glass mirrors.

Refracting telescope
Refracting telescopes use lenses to gather and focus light, as opposed to reflecting telescopes that use mirrors. The 1897 Yerkes Observatory in Wisconsin, USA, has a primary lens with a diameter of 1.02 m (3 ft 4 in).

Largest Cherenkov telescope

The H.E.S.S. II telescope – the newest part of the High Energy Stereoscopic System – has a diameter of 28 m (91 ft 10 in) and a total collecting surface area of 614 m^2 (6,609 sq ft). It detects faint Cherenkov radiation, which is produced by particles travelling faster than the speed of light. H.E.S.S. II saw its first light in Khomas Highland, Namibia, on 26 Jul 2012.

FACT
The H.E.S.S. II is larger than many telescopes but, as a Cherenkov detector, it is in a different category to true imaging telescopes.

Mirror call: largest telescope

The Gran Telescopio Canarias (GTC) is the **largest land-based optical telescope**, boasting a mirror with an effective aperture of 10.4 m. This is also the world's **largest segmented primary mirror**, consisting of 36 hexagonal pieces, each of which can be moved separately to help counter the blurring effect of Earth's atmosphere on stellar light. The GTC, located at an altitude of 2,267 m on La Palma in the Canary Islands, has produced images of the Milky Way at a resolution 60 million times greater than human vision.

FACT
Three big competitors in the next generation of observatories are the Giant Magellan Telescope (La Serena, Chile), the Thirty Meter Telescope (Mauna Kea, Hawaii) and the European Extremely Large Telescope (Cerro Armazones, Chile). Due for completion in the next decade or so, their budgets will average around £700 m.

Earth

If all the oceans were combined into a single drop of water, it would be **1,371 km** wide

Tallest illuminated icefalls

The waterfalls of Eidfjord in Norway plunge noisily some 500 m (1,640 ft) in summer. In the winter, when temperatures can drop to -26°C (-15°F), the water is frozen in its tracks. In Jan 2013, climbers Stephan Siegrist and Dani Arnold (pictured climbing, with Martin Echsner belaying), photographer Thomas Senf and sports-equipment manufacturer Mammut captured images of these "icefalls" at night. Illuminations were provided by lamps, torches and flares, and involved 700 m (2,300 ft) of cables.

FACT
The dramatic light show was inspired by stories of the Norse frost giants – a race formed from the drip of an icicle as the fires of creation met the lifeless snows that had come before.

The history of humanity is defined by our insatiable quest to explore and learn more about our planet. Ever since early explorers crossed the oceans in search of new lands, we have used the latest technology to watch the weather and monitored seas to predict storms. Today, technology is used by scientists to measure the health of the planet.

Our knowledge of the systems governing the Earth has increased exponentially over the last 60 years, with ever more accurate sensors and comprehensive coverage in telecommunications to monitor the movement of the land and the action of the seas. We are constantly seeking to understand the most intimate secrets of the powerful forces that sweep across our world.

Scientists are now able to make measurements of the magnetic properties of the planet, the strength of its gravity field has been mapped at all points to aid in construction projects, and we send robotic vehicles to test environments in which we could not survive.

More recently, advanced systems for data collection have helped us to chart the rate of climate change. Every year we are accumulating a more accurate picture of human processes, such as agricultural irrigation and deforestation. As we do so, we are discovering not only how our planet works but how better to respect and protect it.

The **first successful weather satellite** was the USA's *TIROS-1*, which was launched on 1 Apr 1960. "TIROS" – the "Television Infra Red Observation Satellite" – remained operational for 78 days, during which time it employed its high- and low-resolution cameras to record images of cloud formations (inset) that were used by meteorologists worldwide to understand weather systems.

The **longest-operating Earth-observation satellite** was *Landsat 5*, developed by NASA and launched on 1 Mar 1984 from Vandenberg Air Force Base, California, USA. Managed by the National Oceanic and Atmospheric Administration (1984–2000) and later the US Geological Survey (2001–13), it was decommissioned in 2013 after capturing more than 2.5 million images of Earth's surface during its 150,000 orbits.

2004

1984

1975

1960

1958

1955

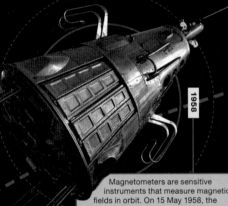

Magnetometers are sensitive instruments that measure magnetic fields in orbit. On 15 May 1958, the **first satellite magnetometer** was launched on board the Soviet Union's *Sputnik 3* – a conical satellite 3.57 m (11 ft 8 in) long and 1.73 m (5 ft 8 in) wide at its base. It weighed 1,327 kg (2,925 lb) and possessed 12 scientific instruments (below). The satellite remained in orbit until 6 Apr 1960.

The **first geostationary weather satellite** – *GOES-1* (Geostationary Operational Environmental Satellite) – was launched from Cape Canaveral, Florida, USA, on 16 Oct 1975. The principal instrument on board was the Visible Infrared Spin Scan Radiometer (VISSR), which provided day and night imagery of cloud conditions over the full-disk (inset). The satellite had the capability to relay meteorological data from more than 10,000 locations into a central processing centre in order to build weather-prediction models.

The Argo programme uses the **largest fleet of ocean sensors** to monitor global ocean current patterns. The 3,600 free-floating, robotic Argo sensors (mapped below) drift to depths of 2,000 m (6,560 ft) and rise to transmit data via satellites. By Nov 2012, Argo had collected its millionth profile of temperature and salinity – twice the number obtained by all research vessels during the 20th century.

60 YEARS OF WEATHER EXTREMES

1959

Greatest snowfall
From 13 to 19 Feb, snow fell to a depth of 4,800 mm on Mount Shasta Ski Bowl in northern California, USA.

1964

Driest place
From 1964 to 2001, the average annual rainfall for the Quillagua meteorological station in the Atacama Desert, Chile, was just 0.5 mm.

1966

Highest annual mean temperature
Dallol in Ethiopia recorded a record annual mean temperature of 34°C for the six years between 1960 and 1966.

1970

Most intense rainfall
Basse-Terre, Guadeloupe, in the Caribbean, recorded 38.1 mm of rain in one minute on 26 Nov. This is the accepted highest figure, although scientists agree that it is difficult to assess exact rainfall readings over very short periods.

1983

Lowest temperature recorded on Earth
On 21 Jul, temperatures at the Soviet Union's Vostok research station in Antarctica plunged to -89.2°C. The site was chosen for research with the aim of drilling into ancient ice.

On 7 Jul 2005, scientists were able to perform the **first accurate sea-level monitoring by satellite** using a number of different instruments (such as the *Gravity Recovery and Climate Experiment* – or *GRACE* – satellite, above). Satellite data was collected on changes in Earth's gravitational field, the mass of polar ice caps, and ocean topography and circulation (inset). Using this data, it was determined that, in the last 50 years, the rate at which the sea level is rising is 1.8 mm per year – although in the last 12 years, this rate has increased to 3 mm per year.

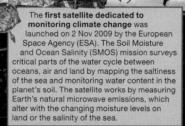

FACT
The radiometric temperature was measured by the amount of radiation (or lack of it) from the Antarctic Ridge.

The **lowest radiometric Earth temperature recorded by satellite** is -93.2°C, on a high ridge in Antarctica, as preliminarily announced by NASA in Dec 2013. Data was collected by satellites including NASA's *Terra* (right) over 32 years and it was found that the dry and clear air of the Antarctic allows heat to be efficiently radiated into space.

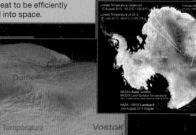

The **first satellite dedicated to monitoring climate change** was launched on 2 Nov 2009 by the European Space Agency (ESA). The Soil Moisture and Ocean Salinity (SMOS) mission surveys critical parts of the water cycle between oceans, air and land by mapping the saltiness of the sea and monitoring water content in the planet's soil. The satellite works by measuring Earth's natural microwave emissions, which alter with the changing moisture levels on land or the salinity of the sea.

2005 · 2006 · 2009 · 2013 · 2015

The **fastest-melting Antarctic glacier** is Pine Island Glacier, which is dropping in height by up to 16 m (52 ft) a year, scientists discovered. Key data came from *Autosub* (below), an autonomous submarine which was sent under the vast glacier to reveal it has become detached from an undersea ridge, allowing warm water to flow under it and increase the rate of melt.

The **largest-ever unmanned Earth-observation satellite** was *Envisat*, a European Space Agency satellite. It weighed 8,100 kg and measured 26 x 10 x 5 m, orbiting at an altitude which ranged from 785 to 791 km. *Envisat* monitored Earth's land and oceans, ice caps (inset) and atmosphere with an array of instruments, before abruptly going silent on 8 Apr 2012 after 10 years in orbit.

From its launch in 2009 until its burn-up in 2013, ESA's *Gravity Field and Steady-State Ocean Circulation Explorer* (*GOCE*, above) was the **most accurate gravity-mapping satellite**, working to 1 milliGal (a unit used to measure the gravitational field).

The **highest-resolution maps of Earth's gravity field**, however, were created in 2013 by an Australian-German team using data obtained from the US Space Shuttle. The maps (right) improved the resolution of previous global gravity field maps by a factor of 40, and revealed that the pull of gravity is at its strongest at the North Pole; the lowest is at the top of the Huascarán mountain in the Andes.

1994

Longest-lasting cyclone
Hurricane/typhoon John formed on 11 Aug in the eastern Pacific Ocean. It lasted for 31 days and travelled the **farthest distance for a tropical cyclone**: 13,280 km.

1998

Largest coral reef die-off
In 1998, around 16% of all coral reefs were destroyed or damaged in a once-in-a-millennium event. The 1998 El Niño phenomenon may have triggered the disaster.

2008

Highest ocean temperature
In Aug 2008, scientists announced that they had recorded water at 464°C spewing from a hydro-thermal vent ("black smoker") on the ocean floor 3,000 m deep at the Mid-Atlantic Ridge.

2013

Largest measured tornado
A tornado with a diameter of 4.18 km was measured using Doppler radar by the US National Weather Service on 31 May in El Reno, Oklahoma, USA.

Greatest temperature range
Verkhoyansk, in the Siberian "Pole of Cold" in the east of Russia. Temperatures have ranged 105°C: from a record low of -68°C to a record high of 37°C.

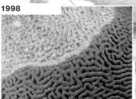

It came from outer space

Almost 100 tonnes of meteoroid material enters Earth's atmosphere every day

Farthest sample-and-return mission

On 13 Jun 2010, the contents of Japanese space probe *Hayabusa* were retrieved in Australia after a sampling mission to the 25143 Itokawa asteroid some 300 million km (65.6 million mi) away. The probe had landed on 25 Nov 2005, and the samples it collected – 1,500 tiny grains of dust – are the **first material returned from an asteroid**. The inset picture above shows Masaharu Nakagawa (left), science and technology minister for Japan, and *Hayabusa* project leader Junichiro Kawaguchi.

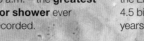

Fastest meteor shower
The Leonids are a shower of meteors entering Earth's atmosphere at around 71 km/s (44 mi/s) and begin to glow at an altitude of some 155 km (96 mi). The motion of the parent meteoroid stream, from comet 55P/Tempel–Tuttle, accounts for the speed. It is directly opposite to the orbital motion of Earth around the Sun, resulting in an almost head-on collision between the tiny particles and the Earth annually on 15–20 Nov.

Every 33 years, the Leonids look even more impressive as their parent comet swoops near the Sun. On 16–17 Nov 1966, the Leonid meteors were visible to lucky sky-watchers between western North America and eastern Russia (then USSR), passing over Arizona, USA, at a rate of 2,300 per min for 20 min from 5 a.m. – the **greatest meteor shower** ever recorded.

First accurately predicted asteroid impact
Analysis of the orbit of asteroid 2008 TC3 indicated that it would hit Earth 21 hr after being discovered on 6 Oct 2008. At 2:46 a.m. on 7 Oct 2008, the asteroid – measuring a few metres across – exploded 37 km (23 mi) above Sudan with the force of 1 kiloton. Passengers travelling in a plane saw the flash from a distance of 750 nautical mi (1,389 km; 863 mi).

Heaviest man-made object to re-enter the atmosphere

The Russian space station *Mir* came out of orbit during a successful controlled re-entry of Earth's atmosphere on 23 Mar 2001. After 15 years in space, the 130-tonne (286,600-lb) laboratory broke into pieces that splashed down in the ocean east of New Zealand. **The largest space station** is now the *International Space Station*.

Greatest impact on Earth
The most widely accepted theory of how the Moon came into being is that it was part of the Earth until 4.5 billion years ago. A planet the size of Mars is thought to have collided with the young Earth, shearing off much of the mantle and sending huge chunks of it into orbit. Over time, this debris collected under its own gravity to form the Moon.

Greatest recorded impact on Earth (unmeasured)
On 30 Jun 1908, the disintegration of an asteroid 10 km (6 mi) above the basin of the Podkamennaya Tunguska River in Russia resulted in a huge explosion. An area of 3,900 km² (1,500 sq mi) was devastated by the break-up of the meteoroid, which released as much energy as up to

First identified impact crater

The Barringer Meteorite Crater, aka Meteor Crater, in Arizona, USA, measures around 1.2 km (0.74 mi) in diameter and 173 m (570 ft) deep. It was proposed in 1891 to be the result of a meteorite impact, and later determined to be the crater of an iron meteorite. Scientists believe that it landed some 49,000 years ago, with a force 150 times greater than that of the atomic bomb dropped on Hiroshima in 1945.

> ## GLOBAL IMPACT SITES

Meteorite impacts confirmed with shock waves or chemical evidence

Diameter (km):
- <10
- 11–50
- 51–100
- 101–300
- Highly probable based on geological evidence

Source: www.impacts.rajmon.cz

Glossary

Meteoroid: metallic or rocky fragments, usually from a comet or asteroid and typically less than 1 m wide; smaller fragments are known as micrometeoroids.

Meteor: a meteoroid that streaks through the atmosphere emitting heat and light; a "shooting star".

Meteorite: meteoroid that survives Earth's atmosphere and lands on the ground.

Most people injured in a meteoroid explosion

There have been no confirmed human fatalities found in modern research into meteorite impacts. The worst effects recorded were on 15 Feb 2013 when a meteoroid exploded over Chelyabinsk Oblast in the Urals in Russia. Around 1,200 people were injured, mostly from flying glass caused by the shock wave following the fireball. Astronomer Alan Harris has calculated that the odds of being killed by an asteroid are 1 in 700,000. Scientists have suggested an asteroid bigger than 10 km (6.2 mi) across would kill most of humanity; fortunately, these only arrive once every 100 million years.

Largest meteorites
• **Overall:** Hoba meteorite – 59 tonnes (130,000 lb), found in 1920 at Hoba West in Namibia.
• **Exhibited in a museum:** Cape York meteorite – 30,883 kg (68,085 lb), found in 1897 near Cape York in the west of Greenland; now at the Hayden Planetarium in New York City, USA.
• **From Mars:** Zagami meteorite – 18 kg (40 lb), found on 3 Oct 1962 near Zagami, Nigeria.

Largest tektite
Tektites are glassy pieces of rock formed by the melting and cooling of terrestrial rocks after meteor impacts. A tektite weighing 10.8 kg (23 lb 13 oz) was discovered in 1971 in Thailand.

A fragment from the Chelyabinsk Oblast meteorite (see left) recovered from Chebarkul Lake was placed in a local museum in 2013. Early analysis by scientists suggests that the meteor is of a common type known as ordinary chondrite.

Big Muley, aka sample 61016, came back with *Apollo 16* on 27 Apr 1972. At 11.7 kg, it is the **heaviest rock returned from space**. All rock returned so far is lunar, from the Apollo and Luna programmes (see below).

Of the roughly 50 known meteorites on Earth that have originated from the Moon, the **largest lunar meteorite** is Kalahari 009, with a mass of 13.5 kg (29 lb 12 oz). It was discovered in the Kalahari Desert in Botswana in Sep 1999.

First person hit by space junk

The first and only person to be hit by a man-made object from orbit is Lottie Williams (USA). On 22 Jan 1997, in Tulsa, Oklahoma, USA, she was hit in the shoulder by a piece of blackened metal about 15 cm (6 in) long that NASA tests showed was probably from a *Delta II* rocket. Williams was unhurt.

five times that of all explosives used in World War II. While there are no exact figures on record from 1908, there are accurate measurements of the recent **greatest measured impact on Earth**. This was the Chelyabinsk impact of 15 Feb 2013 (see above).

Largest impact crater on Earth

The Vredefort crater, near Johannesburg in South Africa, may have lost the title of **oldest impact crater** to Greenland's Maniitsoq crater (see right), but it remains the largest crater, with an estimated diameter of around 300 km (186 mi). The crater was formed by an impact that occurred about 2 billion years ago.

Oldest impact crater on Earth

On 29 Jun 2012, scientists at the Geological Survey of Denmark and Greenland announced that they had discovered an impact crater in Greenland that could be 3 billion years old. Known as the Maniitsoq crater, the structure is around 100 km (62 mi) across. Much of it has eroded and it may once have been much bigger. If such a crater was formed in an impact with Earth today, most life would be wiped out.

North-west Africa 7325 (NWA 7325) was discovered in Morocco in 2012 and is thought to be the **first meteorite from Mercury**. Fragments, weighing 345 g, are chemically consistent with data sent back from a Mercury-orbiting mission.

Crash trash: NASA litter fine

On 11 Jul 1979, the defunct US space station *Skylab* (left) re-entered Earth's atmosphere and disintegrated. Large chunks of the station survived to crash in Western Australia, and the Australian Shire of Esperance imposed a AUS$400 (now £800) fine on NASA for littering, which NASA didn't pay. The bill was finally settled on their behalf in 2009 by US radio host Scott Barley, who raised the money from his audience for the 30th anniversary of *Skylab*'s demise. Pieces of *Skylab* are on display in Esperance's museum, as is a poster declaring the fine paid.

In 1979, a spaceship **crashed** over Esperance. We fined them $400 for **littering**. **PAID IN FULL**
Esperance

ℹ Sample-and-return

Numerous space missions have sought to return sample material to Earth:
• Apollo (1969–72): 2,415 samples of Moon rock weighing a total of 382 kg
• Luna (1959–76): Soviet robotic probe missions that collected 326 g of lunar samples
• Orbital Debris Collector on *Mir* (1996–97) brought back interplanetary dust
• *Genesis* (2001–04): NASA project to collect solar wind molecules (**first material collected beyond the Moon**)

⟲ Earth from space

Approximately **2,500 man-made satellites** – both working and defunct – orbit Earth

First image of Earth from lunar orbit

NASA's Apollo precursor *Lunar Orbiter 1* snapped Earth on 23 Aug 1966 while orbiting the Moon (original shot, above right). Modern technology has allowed for the rendering of higher resolution images from the original sources and the result was unveiled in 2008 (below right).

First full-view colour photograph of Earth

On 10 Nov 1967, NASA satellite *ATS-3* took a photograph of Earth while in geostationary orbit 37,000 km (23,000 mi) above Brazil.

First "Earthrise" viewed by humans

Apollo 8 was a manned spacecraft that orbited the Moon on 23–24 Dec 1968. On Christmas Eve, crew members Frank Borman, Bill Anders and Jim Lovell (all USA) captured an iconic image of fragile beauty that became known as "Earthrise" and is credited with inspiring increased environmental awareness.

First image of Earth and the Moon in a single frame from space

On 18 Sep 1977, NASA's *Voyager 1* probe was on the way to Jupiter when it captured the Earth and Moon from a distance of 11.66 million km (7.25 million mi). The image of the Moon was far dimmer than the Earth and had to be artificially enhanced by a factor of three to be visible.

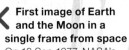

Most distant image of Earth

The image called "the pale blue dot" was taken by *Voyager 1* on 14 Feb 1990, from almost 6.5 billion km (4 billion mi) away, on the request of astronomer Carl Sagan. "Every 'superstar', every 'supreme leader', every saint and sinner in the history of our species lived there," said Sagan, "on a mote of dust suspended in a sunbeam."

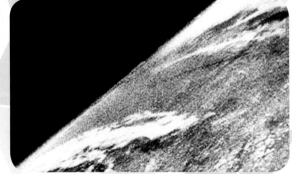

First image of Earth from space

A former Nazi V-2 rocket was launched by the USA on 24 Oct 1946 in New Mexico, USA, with a camera taking a frame every 1.5 sec. The rocket soared 104 km (65 mi) before crashing, with the film preserved in a steel enclosure.

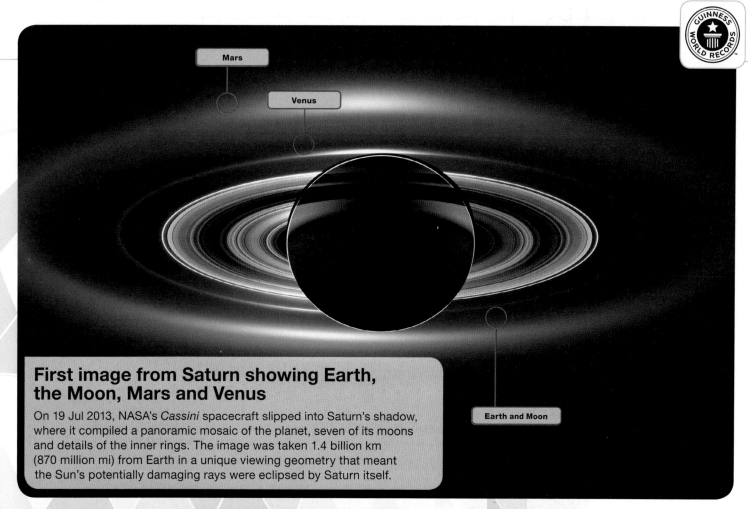

Mars

Venus

Earth and Moon

First image from Saturn showing Earth, the Moon, Mars and Venus

On 19 Jul 2013, NASA's *Cassini* spacecraft slipped into Saturn's shadow, where it compiled a panoramic mosaic of the planet, seven of its moons and details of the inner rings. The image was taken 1.4 billion km (870 million mi) from Earth in a unique viewing geometry that meant the Sun's potentially damaging rays were eclipsed by Saturn itself.

Largest geological structure discovered from space

The "bullseye" of the Richat Structure in the Sahara desert of Mauritania was discovered from orbit by US astronauts Jim McDivitt and Ed White during the *Gemini IV* mission in Jun 1965. It has a diameter of 50 km (30 mi).

First Earth image from Martian orbit

On 8 May 2003, NASA's *Mars Global Surveyor* spacecraft turned its Mars Orbiter Camera back to Earth and captured it from 139 million km (86 million mi) away. The inset above shows Earth, with North and South America visible, and the Moon. At the bottom of the main picture (left) is Jupiter.

First high-resolution image of a total solar eclipse from lunar orbit
The Earth looks like a diamond ring in this full solar eclipse series taken by Japan's unmanned *Kaguya*, aka the SELENE mission, on 10 Feb 2009.

Mountains

Every rise of 305 m in altitude lowers the **boiling point of water** by 1°C

Highest Arctic mountain

The summit of Gunnbjørn Fjeld in Greenland's Watkins Range reaches 3,694 m (12,119 ft) above sea level. It is a type of mountain known as a "nunatak", a rocky peak poking through a glacier or ice field. On the other side of the world, the **highest mountain in Antarctica** is Vinson Massif, one of the Seven Summits, whose peak reaches 4,892 m (16,050 ft) above sea level.

Highest mountain

The summit of Mount Everest, a Himalayan peak on the border between Tibet and Nepal, is at an altitude of 8,848 m (29,029 ft), higher than any other mountain. For more about the conquests of Everest, see p.148.

Tallest mountain face

The Rupal face of Nanga Parbat, located in the western Himalayas, Pakistan, is a single rise of approximately 5,000 m (16,000 ft) from the valley floor to the summit. The mountain itself, which reaches an altitude of 8,125 m (26,656 ft), is the highest mountain in Pakistan and the eighth highest in the world.

Largest vertical extent

Both the highest and the lowest points on Earth's exposed surface are in the continent of Asia. Mount Everest, with its peak at 8,848 m above sea level, and the Dead Sea, with its surface at 422 m (1,384 ft) below sea level, make Asia the continent with the largest difference in vertical extent of 9,270 m (30,413 ft).

Highest mountain tabletop

Monte Roraima, on the border of Brazil, Guyana and Venezuela, is a sandstone plateau measuring 2,810 m (9,220 ft) in height. Its harsh environment has deterred human presence and predators; as a result, around one-third of its plant species are unique to the mountain.

Highest polar ice cap

Dome Argus is a vast ice plateau near the centre of East Antarctica. Its highest point is some 4,093 m (13,428 ft) above sea level. It is Antarctica's highest ice feature and overlies the 1,200-km-long (745-mi) Gamburtsev Mountain Range. For more on the formation of this record-breaking range, see p.37.

FACT
The Tibetan Plateau covers an area larger than Western Europe.

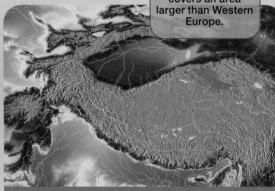

Largest plateau

The most extensive high plateau is the Tibetan Plateau, which covers 1.85 million km² (715,000 sq mi) of Central Asia. Its average altitude is 4,900 m (16,000 ft). The Himalayan mountain range, to the south of the plateau, is home to 30 of the world's tallest mountains.

Tallest mountain

Measured from its submarine base in the Hawaiian Trough to its peak, Mauna Kea (White Mountain) on the island of Hawaii, USA, has a combined height of 10,205 m (33,480 ft), of which 4,205 m (13,796 ft) is above sea level.

MOUNTAIN RANGES

Largest

A mountain range is a series of mountains, or hills, that are connected in some way. The Himalayas, in Asia, is the largest mountain range, incorporating 96 of the 109 peaks measuring more than 7,300 m (24,000 ft).

Longest continental

The Andes in South America is 7,600 km (4,700 mi) long. It spans seven countries – from Venezuela to Argentina – and includes some of the highest mountains on Earth. More than 50 of the Andes

FACT
Monte Roraima is thought to have inspired Arthur Conan Doyle's novel *The Lost World*.

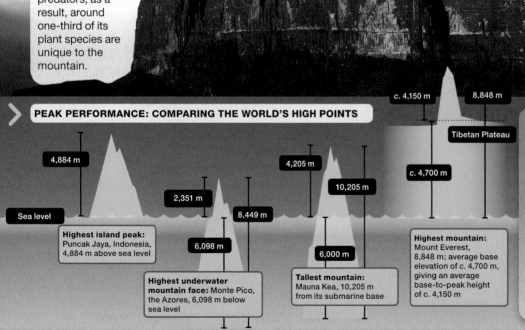

PEAK PERFORMANCE: COMPARING THE WORLD'S HIGH POINTS

- 4,884 m
- Sea level
- Highest island peak: Puncak Jaya, Indonesia, 4,884 m above sea level
- 2,351 m
- 6,098 m
- Highest underwater mountain face: Monte Pico, the Azores, 6,098 m below sea level
- 8,449 m
- 6,000 m
- 4,205 m
- 10,205 m
- Tallest mountain: Mauna Kea, 10,205 m from its submarine base
- c. 4,150 m
- 8,848 m
- Tibetan Plateau
- c. 4,700 m
- Highest mountain: Mount Everest, 8,848 m; average base elevation of c. 4,700 m, giving an average base-to-peak height of c. 4,150 m

Moving mountains

Sixty years ago, the height of Mount Everest changed overnight! The Great Trigonometrical Survey of India, a broad study that took place during the 19th century, calculated the height of the summit to be 8,840 m in 1856. In 1955, however, this figure was adjusted to the present altitude of 8,848 m. The mountain was given its present name in 1865, in honour of Sir George Everest (above). As British Surveyor General in India from 1830 to 1843, he had a major role in mapping the Indian subcontinent.

of the Cordillera Blanca. The mountain range contains 33 peaks of more than 5,500 m (18,000 ft) in addition to 80 glaciers and 120 glacial lakes.

Longest submarine

The Mid-Ocean Ridge runs 65,000 km (40,000 mi) from the Arctic Ocean to the Atlantic Ocean, around Africa, Asia and Australia, and under the Pacific Ocean to the west coast of North America. Its peaks reach 4,200 m (13,800 ft) above the base ocean depth.

Fastest-rising mountain

Nanga Parbat in Pakistan is growing taller at a rate of 7 mm (0.27 in) per year. The mountain is part of the Himalayan Plateau, which was formed when India began colliding with the Eurasian continental plate between 50 million and 30 million years ago.

Greatest vertical drop

Mount Thor on Baffin Island in Nunavut, Canada, is a granite peak whose west face consists of a vertical drop of 1,250 m (4,101 ft). It is technically an overhang, with the average angle of repose of the cliff being at 105° – or 15° beyond the vertical.

peaks reach at least 6,000 m (20,000 ft) high and for most of its extent the range is some 300 km (200 mi) wide.

Highest coastal

The Sierra Nevada de Santa Marta is an isolated range of mountains located in Colombia, separated from the Andes. The range rises to an elevation of 5,775 m (18,946 ft) above sea level. Its considerable biodiversity

led UNESCO to designate the mountains as a biosphere reserve in 1979.

Highest tropical

Huascarán National Park in Peru's Cordillera Blanca ("White Range") mountain range has its highest point at 6,768 m (22,204 ft) above sea level. The protected area covers approximately 340,000 ha (840,100 acres) and covers almost the whole

Highest free-standing mountain

Mount Kilimanjaro in Tanzania, Africa, is 5,895 m (19,341 ft) above sea level. It is the fourth highest of the world's Seven Summits and the highest mountain in Africa. Standing independent of any range, Kilimanjaro is a dormant or extinct stratovolcano that last erupted around 200,000–150,000 years ago.

Oldest

The Barberton Greenstone Belt in South Africa, also known as the Makhonjwa Mountains, is formed of rocks dating back 3.6 billion years. It was here, in 1875, that the first gold in South Africa was discovered. The mountains rise some 1,800 m (5,900 ft) above sea level.

Smallest

The Sutter Buttes of California, USA, are the eroded remains of a volcano that was active around 1.6–1.4 million years ago. They are isolated within the flat-floored Sacramento Valley and reach a maximum height of 628 m (2,060 ft), with a base diameter of around 16 km (10 mi).

Cold mountain: peaks under the ice

The Gamburtsev Mountain Range in eastern Antarctica extends for some 1,200 km across the continent. It reaches 2,700 m high but is permanently buried under more than 600 m of ice, making it the world's **largest subglacial mountain range**.

Studies suggest that the Gamburtsev may date back 1 billion years, the result of mini-continents converging to form a supercontinent and forcing the land between them into a mountain range. In time, this range collapsed under its own weight and was eroded down to a residual root. Tectonic movement tore the land into separate continents and created a rift from present-day eastern Antarctica to India; the root, warmed by the rifting, forced up the land to form eastern Antarctica. As Earth cooled, this land became covered in an ice sheet the size of Canada.

Ice sheet

Gamburtsev Mountain Range

Root

FACT

Chimborazo, an inactive stratovolcano located in the Andes, is 6,268 m tall – more than 2,000 m shorter than Mount Everest. Because it is located on the equator, however – which bulges outwards more than the rest of the globe – scientists believe that its summit is the **most distant point on Earth from the planet's core.**

Blue planet

Oceans provide **190 times as much living space** as soil, air and fresh water combined

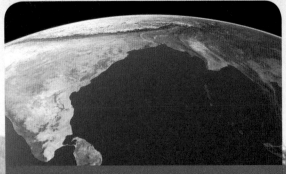

FACT
Superior is one of the Great Lakes of North America, along with Michigan, Huron, Erie and Ontario. Spanning over 1,200 km, they contain about a fifth of the world's surface fresh water – only the polar ice caps have more.

Largest freshwater lake

Lake Superior is shared by Canada and the USA, bordered by Ontario and Minnesota to the north and west, and Wisconsin and Michigan to the south. The lake covers 82,100 km² (31,700 sq mi). Lake Baikal in Siberia, Russia, has the **greatest volume for a freshwater lake**, estimated at 23,000 km³ (5,500 cu mi).

Largest bay

The Bay of Bengal in the Indian Ocean covers an area of 2.17 million km² (839,000 sq mi). One quarter of the world's population of 7.2 billion live in the countries bordering it: Sri Lanka, India, Bangladesh, Myanmar and Malaysia.

Chesapeake Bay is the **largest bay by shore length**, stretching 18,804 km (11,684 mi) along the Atlantic coast of Maryland and Virginia, USA.

Biggest rise in sea level since the last ice age
Meltwater Pulse 1A was an event occurring around 14,500 years ago, when sea levels rose by c. 20 m (65 ft) in less than 500 years. Approximately 3,000 years earlier, as the ice sheets of the last ice age began to retreat, they added fresh water to the oceans. Global sea levels rose at an average of some 1 cm (0.4 in) per year until Meltwater Pulse 1A speeded things up, probably due to a partial collapse of the Antarctic ice sheets.

Lowest river

The Jordan River begins in Israel at an elevation of 2,814 m (9,232 ft) and flows 251 km (155 mi) south to the Dead Sea. Its lowest elevation here is 416 m (1,361 ft) below sea level.

This elevation makes the Dead Sea itself the **lowest exposed body of water**. Bordering Israel and Jordan, it is 80 km (50 mi) long and measures 18 km (11 mi) at its widest point.

Highest river

The Yarlung Zangbo has an average elevation of 4,000 m (13,100 ft). It rises in Tibet, runs for 2,000 km (6,550 mi) through China, and becomes the Brahmaputra River in India. It enters the ocean in the Bay of Bengal, where it meets the Ganges to form the **largest delta**, covering 75,000 km² (30,000 sq mi).

Largest pink lake

A combination of micro-organisms and minerals gives Lake Retba, or Lac Rose, in Senegal, its distinctive hue. At 7.5 km² (2.7 sq mi), it may be the biggest, but it's far from unique. Examples can be found in Canada (Dusty Rose Lake in British Columbia), Spain (two saltwater lakes near Torrevieja) and Australia (Lake Hillier). Lakes become pink through algae, or from organisms that produce carotenoids (as occur in carrots), such as the sea salt field *Dunaliella salina*.

Oldest body of seawater
The US Geological Survey studied a body of groundwater more than 1,000 m (3,280 ft) below Chesapeake Bay in the USA. They reported that it dated from the early Cretaceous North Atlantic period, between 145 and 100 million years ago.

Largest desert lake
Lake Turkana, in the Great Rift Valley, Kenya, has a surface area of 6,405 km² (2,472 sq mi) – the equivalent of around 90 soccer pitches.

Oldest lake
Lake Baikal in Russia is up to 25 million years old. It formed following a tectonic rift in the Earth's crust.

WATER BODIES: LONGEST RIVERS, LARGEST OCEANS

Top 10 longest rivers
1. Nile, Egypt, 6,650 km
2. Amazon, Brazil, 6,400 km
3. Yangtze, China, 6,300 km
4. Mississippi, USA, 6,275 km
5. Yenisei, Russia, 5,539 km
6. Huang He, China, 5,464 km
7. Ob–Irtysh, Russia, 5,410 km
8. Paraná, Brazil, 4,880 km
9. Congo, Congo, 4,700 km
10. Amur–Argun, Russia, 4,444 km

Land area 34.2%
Arctic Ocean 2.8%
Southern Ocean 4.0%
Indian Ocean 13.4%
Atlantic Ocean 15.1%
Pacific Ocean 30.5%

Largest tidal bores

A tidal bore arises when the Sun, Moon and Earth align to form dramatic tidal conditions. A solitary wave travels with great speed up a narrow river, forcing the flow upstream.

In 1955, the **largest tidal bore** was the Tsien Tang Kiang, attaining "a height of up to 25 feet [7.62 m] and a speed of 13 knots". We later reported the 1993 incident in which one of these waves reached Hangzhou Bay, China. It rose to 9 m, was 300 km long and pushed 9 million litres of water per sec to the shore, resulting in multiple fatalities.

Glossary

Acoustic doppler current profiler (ADCP, or ADP): a meter that measures the velocities of water currents across a range of depths, by referencing the acoustic properties of sound waves.

Biome: a substantial community of flora and fauna that occurs naturally in a specific environment such as desert, grassland, tundra, forest or ocean.

Delta: an area of land, created from sediment, that forms at the mouth of a large river.

Deepest river

In Jul 2008, scientists from the US Geological Survey and the American Museum of Natural History discovered that the Congo River, which spans 10 countries in Africa, has a maximum depth of at least 220 m (722 ft). The measurements were performed in the Lower Congo River using echo sounders, advanced GPS and acoustic doppler current profilers.

OCEANS

Deepest point
Challenger Deep, located in the Mariana Trench in the Pacific Ocean, is 10,911 m (35,797 ft) at its deepest point. Mount Everest would entirely fit in it, with its peak 2,000 m (6,560 ft) below the surface.

Largest biome
The area in open ocean – away from both seabed and shore – is called the pelagic zone. Globally, its volume is 1.3 billion km³ (319 million cu mi) and it supports life, making it by far the largest biome. It has many of the planet's larger animals, including whales.

Largest continuous ocean current system
The system of ocean circulation that transports cold and salty deep water is called the thermohaline conveyor belt ("thermo" from heat and "haline" from salinity). The water is slowly transported from the north Atlantic down to the

Southern Ocean, where it travels east and north to the Indian and Pacific oceans. Here, it rises and becomes warm, travelling back west, where it sinks once again in the north Atlantic. The complete cycle can last for a thousand years.

WATERFALLS

Largest waterfall ever
Dry Falls, near Missoula in Montana, USA, is all that remains of a waterfall that stretched over 5.6 km (3.5 mi) and was 115 m (380 ft) high. It burst into life when the water from a massive glacial lake – formed 18,000 years ago – broke through the ice, causing a catastrophic flood.

Highest underwater waterfall
The Denmark Strait Cataract is underwater in the Denmark Strait, which separates Greenland and Iceland. The 3.5-km (2.17-mi) waterfall carries around 5 million m³ (176.5 million cu ft) of water per sec. The Cataract, the **largest waterfall** of any

Largest area of bioluminescence

Legends of a "milky sea" date far back in naval history. In 2005, scientists at the US Naval Research Laboratory used satellite imagery to confirm detailed log reports made by the British ship SS *Lima* in 1995. They described an area in the Indian Ocean, near Somalia, measuring around 14,000 km² (5,400 sq mi). Vast amounts of bioluminescent bacteria, possibly *Vibrio harveyi*, are believed to be responsible.

kind, is formed as cold, denser seawater drops from the Greenland Sea into the slightly warmer Irminger Sea.

Largest plunge pool
Plunge pools form at the base of waterfalls as a result of water erosion. Perth Canyon is a plunge pool off the coast of Australia that measures *c.* 300 m (1,000 ft) deep and 12 km² (4.62 sq mi) in area. The prehistoric pool was created when the region was above sea level.

Greatest waterfall flow
Boyoma Falls in the Democratic Republic of the Congo flows at a rate of 17,000 m³ (600,000 cu ft) per sec. It has seven drops along 100 km (60 mi) of the Lualaba River.

Largest lake within a lake

Manitou Lake occupies an area of 106 km² (41 sq mi). It is located on the **largest island in a lake**, Manitoulin Island (see above), which covers 2,766 km² (1,068 sq mi) of the Canadian section of Lake Huron. Another geographical nesting doll is Vulcan Point, the **largest island in a lake on an island in a lake on an island**. The 40-m (130-ft) island sits in Crater Lake, the central crater of the Taal volcano in Lake Taal on the island of Luzon in the Philippines.

Tide of filth: a drop in the ocean

The **largest ocean rubbish site** is in the North Pacific Gyre (right), a vortex of slowly revolving ocean water that naturally concentrates ever increasing amounts of floating litter in its centre. Much of it is made up of plastic, which never degrades but breaks down into tiny fragments that pollute down to 10 m below the surface. These tiny, toxic chunks enter the food chain and studies now suggest that waste outweighs nutritious plankton by a factor of six to one. Plastic bags account for over 50% of all marine litter, the **greatest ocean pollutant** (left).

In deep water

Deepest lake: Lake Baikal, Russia, 1,637 m deep

Deepest hypersaline lake: The Dead Sea, Israel/Jordan, 378 m deep and more than eight times saltier than seawater

Deepest brine pool: Orca Basin, Gulf of Mexico, 2,200 m below sea level, filled with water around eight times saltier than the Gulf

Caves

It typically takes **100,000 years** for a cave to grow large enough to accommodate humans

Longest cave system

It has taken some 25 million years for Mammoth Cave to form through the weathering action of the Green River and its tributaries. Situated in Mammoth Cave National Park in Kentucky, USA, the system is a network of limestone caves, of which 644 km (400 mi) have been explored so far.

Longest gypsum cave

Gypsum, a soft mineral, is used to make a type of plaster called plaster of Paris. A cave system called Optymistychna ("Optimistic"), near Korolivka, Ukraine, occurs in a layer of gypsum around 20 m (65 ft 7 in) thick. It has

Longest underground river

In Mar 2007, cave divers Stephen Bogaerts (UK) and Robbie Schmittner (DEU) announced that they had discovered a 153-km-long (95-mi) river beneath the Yucatán Peninsula in Mexico. The river, which has many twists and turns, spans around 10 km (6 mi) of land.

Longest sea cave

Matainaka Cave on New Zealand's South Island is 1,540 m (5,052 ft) long and is still forming through wave action from the sea. This length is more than three times that of its nearest rival, Mercer Bay Cave in New Zealand, which extends to 470 m (1,542 ft). The **largest sea cave** is in the Sea Lion Caves in Oregon, USA. One chamber is 95 m (310 ft) long, 50 m (165 ft) wide and 15 m (50 ft) high, in a 400-m-long (1,315-ft) passage.

been mapped so far at 236 km (146 mi) in length, under an area covering 2 km² (0.7 sq mi).

Deepest blue hole

Blue holes are found at or just below sea level, and were once dry caves or shafts. They filled with seawater as the ice caps melted and the water levels rose during the last ice age. Dean's Blue Hole is 76 m (250 ft) wide, a vertical shaft that sinks for 202 m (662 ft) at Turtle Cove on the Atlantic edge of The Bahamas. It contains 1.1 million m³ (11.8 million cu ft) of water.

Deepest ice cave descent

Janot Lamberton (FRA) descended to 202 m (662 ft) in a glacial cave

in Greenland. The cave, reached by Lamberton in 1998, was formed by a river of melt water during the Arctic summer.

Deepest lava cave

Lava tubes are formed by streaming lava under the hard surface of a lava flow. While a volcano is erupting, the tubes drain lava away, before the rock cools and the process results in a long, cave-like channel. The deepest and longest example is Kazumura Cave in Hawaii, USA. It is 65.5 km (40.7 mi) long, and descends to a depth of 1,101 m (3,614 ft).

Largest cave chamber

A chamber is the largest order of space in a cave. It is often formed at a junction of passages, where erosion and collapse have exposed more rock, and its maximum size is dictated by the strength of the ceiling. The Sarawak Chamber in the Lubang Nasib Bagus cave of Sarawak, Borneo, is 700 m (2,300 ft) long. Its average width is 300 m (980 ft) and it is at least 70 m (230 ft) high. By way of comparison, that's nearly as long as seven soccer pitches, and taller than Nelson's Column in Trafalgar Square, London.

Oldest caves

The Sudwala Caves in Mpumalanga, South Africa, are c. 240 million years old. The series of caves is believed to have formed from Precambrian dolomite rock dating back 3.8 billion years. As well as providing shelter for prehistoric humans, it has been used in modern times for ammunition storage and as a concert venue. The bat guano (droppings) found there are used as fertilizer.

Longest explored cave system underwater

Sistema Ox Bel Ha ("Three Paths of Water" in Mayan), in the state of Quintana

LONGEST CAVES

1. **Mammoth Cave**, USA, 644 km
2. **Sistema Sac Actun**, Mexico, 310.72 km
3. **Jewel Cave National Monument**, USA, 267.57 km
4. **Sistema Ox Bel Ha**, Mexico, 243.03 km
5. **Optymistychna Cave**, Ukraine, 236 km
6. **Wind Cave**, USA, 228.24 km
7. **Lechuguilla Cave**, USA, 222.57 km
8. **Hölloch**, Switzerland, 200.42 km
9. **Fisher Ridge Cave System**, USA, 197.18 km
10. **Gua Air Jernih (Clearwater Cave)**, Malaysia, 197.08 km

Source: www.caverbob.com

⚡ Deepest cave

The same year that we published our first edition, we said that six French speleologists discovered the Berger cave near Grenoble in France in Jul 1955. We called it the **deepest cave**, at 2,959 ft (902 m).

Today, Gouffre Berger is no longer quite the awesome challenge it once was, and is regularly explored by groups of up to 200. We also now know it is 1,122 m deep and that Krubera Cave in Georgia is nearly twice as deep (see right).

ᴀᴢ Glossary

Cave: natural chamber or series of chambers in the ground, hillsides or cliffs.

Caving (or **potholing** or **spelunking**): recreational exploration of caves.

Speleology: scientific study of caves, including their structure, properties, history, occupants and the process by which they form (speleogenesis).

○ ○ ○

Largest cave

Vietnamese farmer Ho Khanh found a cave in central Vietnam in 1991 – and then forgot where it was. It wasn't until 2009 that he guided a UK team to Hang Son Doong ("Mountain River Cave"), which is 200 m (655 ft) high, 150 m (490 ft) wide and at least 6.5 km (4 mi) long. Tourists with £1,800 ($3,000) to spare can now visit it – although first they must trek for over a day through jungle and abseil 79 m (260 ft) to the entrance.

Longest stalactite
Stalactites form to hang from a cave ceiling. The longest free-hanging example is 28 m (92 ft) and hangs in the Gruta do Janelão in Minas Gerais, Brazil.

Tallest stalagmite
A stalagmite is the opposite of a stalactite. It is built up from the floor and the tallest is reported to measure some 70 m (230 ft). It is located in Zhijin Cave in Guizhou Province, China.

Tallest natural cave column
A column measuring 61.5 m (201 ft 8 in) in a cave at Tham Sao Hin, Thailand, was created by the merging of a stalactite and stalagmite. Where the two formations met they became one column.

Deepest unbroken vertical shaft in a cave

Straight, natural shafts are challenges for cavers – essentially, they are sheer drops without ledges. The Miao Keng Cave, near Tian Xing in China, has a continuous shaft 501 m (1,643 ft) deep that takes around two hours to abseil. The shaft is around two-thirds of the height of the tallest building – the 828-m (2,716-ft) Burj Khalifa in Dubai, UAE.

Roo, Mexico, is a series of underwater passages accessed by surface lakes. As of Mar 2014, according to cave researcher Bob Gulden at caverbob. com, 243 km (151 mi) of the system has been mapped.

Greatest vertical extent for a flowstone cascade
Flowstone cascades form in sheets when limestone-saturated water runs down cave walls and floors, leaving behind calcite deposits that solidify over time. The largest vertical extent is 150 m (492 ft), in the Lechuguilla Cave in Carlsbad Caverns National Park, New Mexico, USA.

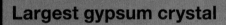

Largest gypsum crystal

The Cave of Crystals, below Naica mountain in the Chihuahuan Desert, Mexico, contains translucent single crystals of gypsum measuring up to 11 m (36 ft) long and weighing up to 55 tonnes (121,200 lb). They began to form hundreds of thousands of years ago, when the cave was filled with warm, mineral-rich water.

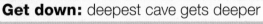

Get down: deepest cave gets deeper

It's not often that a geological feature breaks its own record, but that's exactly what happened with the **deepest cave**, Krubera Cave (left). Or rather, Gennady Samokhin (pictured right), a Ukrainian caver, extended the known depth of the cave on 10 Aug 2012 by 6 m. The cave in the Arabika Massif, Georgia, now has an explored depth of 2,197 m. The new area is in a sump (submerged section) called Dva Kapitana ("Two Captains") that Samokhin suspects may extend by as much as 10 km, all the way to the Black Sea. Samokhin was also a member of the previous record attempt team in 2007.

Underground music

Deepest live radio broadcast: two-hour CBC Radio Points North (CAN) show, 2,340 m down in Creighton Mine in Ontario, Canada, 24 May 2005

Largest natural underground musical instrument: the Great Stalacpipe Organ – stalactites covering 1.4 ha that produce tones when struck with mallets linked to a keyboard in Luray Caverns, Virginia, USA

Deepest concert underground: Agonizer (FIN), 1,271 m below sea level at Pyhäsalmi Mine in Pyhäjärvi, Finland, 4 Aug 2007

There are an estimated **7.77 million animal species** on Earth; to date, only 12% have been described

SEE IT
3D
WITH THE
FREE APP

Largest fish

The largest living fish is the rare plankton-feeding whale shark (*Rhincodon typus*), which is found in the warmer areas of the Atlantic, Pacific and Indian oceans. The largest scientifically recorded example was 12.65 m (41 ft 6 in) long – about the same length as three-and-a-half Mini Cooper cars – and measured 7 m (23 ft) around the thickest part of the body. It was captured off Baba Island near Karachi, Pakistan, on 11 Nov 1949 and weighed an estimated 21 tonnes (46,000 lb).

Augmented Reality alert!
3D
ON
THIS
PAGE

FACT

A whale shark egg – the **largest of all fish eggs** – is typically the same size as an American football!

⚡ New discoveries

It is a tragic but inescapable fact that animal species are becoming extinct all the time – in many cases, as a direct result of human activity. Happily, it is also true that even today a surprising number of previously unknown, entirely new animal species are coming to light: 15,000 each year, on average.

Many of the new species being discovered are small, inconspicuous creatures: mostly insects, worms and other diminutive invertebrates. But quite a few much more sizeable and very spectacular animals are also being uncovered, and on a global scale, not just in a few specific locations.

To demonstrate this heartening and ongoing revelation of previously unknown life forms, our expert Dr Karl Shuker highlights some of the most notable new animal species

that have come to light over the past six decades. All of these creatures have been found, formally described and classified by scientists since the first edition of the *Guinness Book of Records* was published in 1955, and every one is a GWR record holder.

At the bottom of these pages we present 10 of the most recent, and most remarkable, animal finds. Encouragingly, the evidence on these pages suggests that there are still plenty of new species waiting to be discovered!

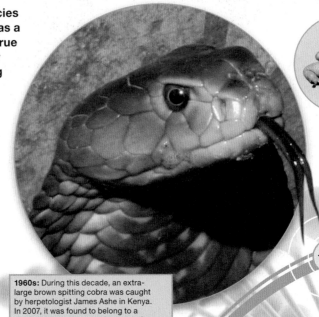

Largest species of poison-dart frog: South America's poison-dart frogs have toxic skin secretions used by native Indian tribes to tip their blowgun darts. The largest species, the 30-g (1-oz) Colombian golden poison-dart frog (*Phyllobates terribilis*), remained undiscovered by science until 1974.

1970s

1960s: During this decade, an extra-large brown spitting cobra was caught by herpetologist James Ashe in Kenya. In 2007, it was found to belong to a previously unknown species – at *c.* 3 m (9 ft) long, the **largest species of spitting cobra** – which was formally named *Naja ashei*, or Ashe's giant spitting cobra.

1970s: In 1977, scientists on board US research submarine *Alvin* discovered an astonishing new ecosystem thriving around hydrothermal vents on the seafloor off the Galápagos Islands, Ecuador. Among the fauna were new species such as the giant tube worm (*Riftia pachyptila*), with huge, red, plume-like tentacles. It was the **first known ecosystem not to derive its primary energy from sunlight**, which can't penetrate down to it, but from chemical energy instead, released by bacteria.

1960s

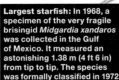

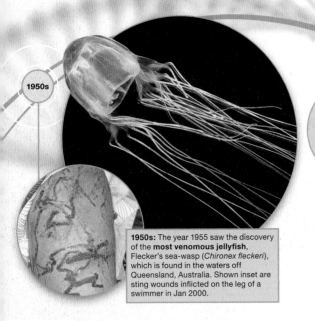

1950s

Largest species of gerbil: Discovered in the 1960s, the great gerbil (*Rhombomys opimus*) can exceed 40 cm (1 ft 3 in) in length. It is native to Turkmenistan, Kazakhstan, Mongolia and several other central and east-central Asian countries.

1950s: The year 1955 saw the discovery of the **most venomous jellyfish**, Flecker's sea-wasp (*Chironex fleckeri*), which is found in the waters off Queensland, Australia. Shown inset are sting wounds inflicted on the leg of a swimmer in Jan 2000.

Largest starfish: In 1968, a specimen of the very fragile brisingid *Midgardia xandaros* was collected in the Gulf of Mexico. It measured an astonishing 1.38 m (4 ft 6 in) from tip to tip. The species was formally classified in 1972.

TEN OF THE MOST RECENT ARRIVALS. NEWEST...

Amphibian	Ape	Bird of prey	Cat	Freshwater cetacean

2013 Botsford's leaf-litter frog (*Leptolalax botsfordi*) was formally described and classified in late 2013. It was discovered in the high elevations of Vietnam's Mount Fansipan, the tallest mountain in Indochina.	**2010** The northern buff-cheeked gibbon (*Nomascus annamensis*) is native to the tropical rainforests between Vietnam, Laos and Cambodia. It is distinguished from similar-looking species by its characteristic vocalizations.	**2010** Formally described and named in 2010, the Socotra buzzard (*Buteo socotraensis*) is native exclusively to the Socotra archipelago, a group of tiny islands forming part of Yemen in the Arabian peninsula.	**2013** The selkirk rex is also known as the poodle cat because of its thick, curly fur, composed of three separate layers. The breed was developed from a spontaneous genetic mutation originating in Montana, USA, in 1987.	**2014** *Inia araguaiaensis*, the Araguaian boto, was officially described and named in Jan 2014. It is a species of freshwater dolphin native to the Araguaia River basin of Brazil, and is the first such discovery for almost a century.

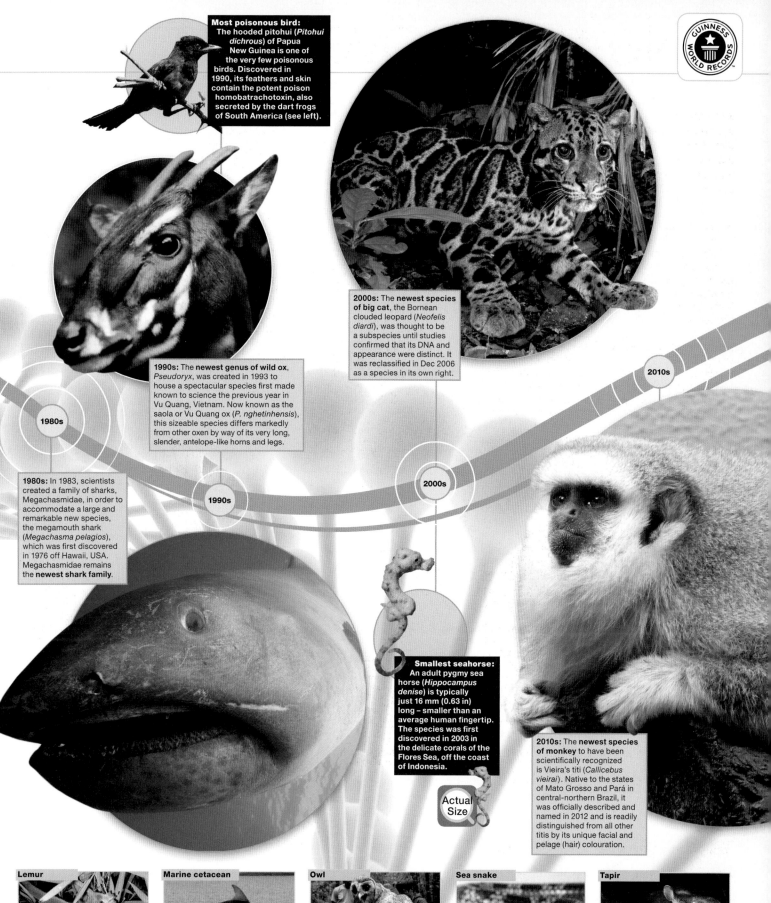

Most poisonous bird: The hooded pitohui (*Pitohui dichrous*) of Papua New Guinea is one of the very few poisonous birds. Discovered in 1990, its feathers and skin contain the potent poison homobatrachotoxin, also secreted by the dart frogs of South America (see left).

2000s: The **newest species of big cat**, the Bornean clouded leopard (*Neofelis diardi*), was thought to be a subspecies until studies confirmed that its DNA and appearance were distinct. It was reclassified in Dec 2006 as a species in its own right.

1990s: The **newest genus of wild ox**, *Pseudoryx*, was created in 1993 to house a spectacular species first made known to science the previous year in Vu Quang, Vietnam. Now known as the saola or Vu Quang ox (*P. nghetinhensis*), this sizeable species differs markedly from other oxen by way of its very long, slender, antelope-like horns and legs.

2010s

1980s

1980s: In 1983, scientists created a family of sharks, Megachasmidae, in order to accommodate a large and remarkable new species, the megamouth shark (*Megachasma pelagios*), which was first discovered in 1976 off Hawaii, USA. Megachasmidae remains the **newest shark family**.

1990s

2000s

Smallest seahorse: An adult pygmy sea horse (*Hippocampus denise*) is typically just 16 mm (0.63 in) long – smaller than an average human fingertip. The species was first discovered in 2003 in the delicate corals of the Flores Sea, off the coast of Indonesia.

Actual Size

2010s: The **newest species of monkey** to have been scientifically recognized is Vieira's titi (*Callicebus vieirai*). Native to the states of Mato Grosso and Pará in central-northern Brazil, it was officially described and named in 2012 and is readily distinguished from all other titis by its unique facial and pelage (hair) colouration.

Lemur

2013
The Marohita mouse lemur (*Microcebus marohita*) and Anosy mouse lemur (*M. tanosi*) are native to Madagascar, as are all lemurs. Each was distinguished from similar species of mouse lemur by sequencing its genes.

Marine cetacean

2012
The latest marine cetacean to have been scientifically recognized is the Burrunan dolphin (*Tursiops australis*), which was officially described and named in 2012. It is endemic to the coastal waters of south-eastern Australia.

Owl

2013
The Seram masked owl (*Tyto almae*) was described and named in 2013, but was first known to science in 1987 when a specimen was photographed (but not collected) in the wild. It is native to the Indonesian island of Seram.

Sea snake

2012
The mosaic sea snake (*Aipysurus mosaicus*) is known from a single specimen in Copenhagen's Natural History Museum. Caught in the 19th century, in the seas between New Guinea and Australia, it was only made a new species in 2012.

Tapir

2013
Brazil's kabomani tapir (*Tapirus kabomani*) is one of the largest new mammals to have been discovered for a century, but is the **smallest living species of tapir**, weighing on average a very modest 110 kg (242 lb).

Mammals

The rare **bowhead whale** (*Balaena mysticetus*) can live for longer than a century

Largest feline carnivore

The male Siberian tiger (*Panthera tigris altaica*) averages 3.15 m (10 ft 4 in) from nose to tail, stands 99–107 cm (3 ft 3 in–3 ft 6 in) to its shoulder and weighs around 265 kg (580 lb). There are about 360 of the tigers in existence – a recovery from a low of 20–30 in the 1930s.

CARNIVORES

Largest bear ever
The tyrant polar bear (*Ursus maritimus tyrannus*) evolved from an isolated population of Arctic brown bears during the mid-Pleistocene epoch (250,000–100,000 years ago). With a body length of 3.7 m (12 ft 2 in), and a height to the shoulder of 1.83 m (6 ft), it could weigh more than a tonne (2,200 lb). The tyrant was the first form of polar bear.

Oldest brown bear in captivity
On 24 May 2013, a 50-year-old European brown bear (*Ursus arctos*) named Andreas died in a sanctuary built by the World Society for the Protection of Animals in northern Greece. The average life span in the wild is 25 years.

Largest euplerid
Euplerids were once classed in the civet family and are also known as Madagascan civets. The largest of the 10 species is the fossa (*Cryptoprocta ferox*), which has the size and look of a small puma. It is 70–80 cm (2 ft 3 in–2 ft 7 in) long with a tail of 65–70 cm (2 ft 1 in–2 ft 3 in), and weighs 5.5–8.6 kg (12 lb 2 oz–18 lb 15 oz).

Oldest big-cat fossil
In 2010, fossils from a previously unknown species similar to a snow leopard were unearthed in the Himalayas. The fossils of this species – named *Panthera blytheae* – have been dated to between 4.1 and 5.95 million years old, which supports the theory that big cats evolved in central Asia – not Africa – and spread outwards.

Newest species of wild cat
Formally named in 2013, the southern Brazilian oncilla (*Leopardus guttulus*) inhabits the Atlantic Forest to the south of the country. They do not interbreed with oncillas elsewhere in Brazil.

Rarest fox
The island fox (*Urocyon littoralis*) is native to six of the eight Channel Islands in California, USA, each of which has its own separate subspecies of this species. In 2002, a total of 1,500 specimens was estimated (some of the subspecies numbered fewer than 100). Since then the species has continued to decline, due in part to predation by golden eagles, disease parasites and habitat destruction. The International Union for Conservation of Nature (IUCN) categorize it as "Critically Endangered".

Rarest raccoon
The Cozumel or pygmy raccoon (*Procyon pygmaeus*) is found on the tiny Cozumel Island, off Mexico's Yucatán Peninsula, which is 478 km² (184.5 sq mi) in area. The raccoon is listed as "Critically Endangered" by the IUCN: only 250–300 specimens are now believed to exist.

Most expensive species in captivity

The giant panda (*Ailuropoda melanoleuca*) indigenous population is owned by China. Four US zoos each pay an annual fee of $1 m (£0.5 m) to China to lease a pair. Cub births, bamboo production and security all add to the cost. But it can be worth it: Edinburgh Zoo in the UK reported a 51% increase in visitors during the year after giant pandas Sunshine and Sweetie took up residence.

Fastest marine mammal

On 12 Oct 1958, a bull killer whale (*Orcinus orca*) an estimated 6.1–7.6 m (20–25 ft) in length was timed at 55.5 km/h (34.5 mph) in the north-eastern Pacific. Similar speeds have also been reported for Dall's porpoise (*Phocoenoides dalli*) in short bursts.

 Bear necessities

Largest home range for a land-based mammal: polar bears (*Ursus maritimus*) cover Arctic areas of 30,000 km² – the size of Italy – in a year.

Most sensitive nose for a land mammal: typically, polar bears can detect prey such as seals from more than 30 km away and even when the prey is under ice.

Richest bear's milk: polar-bear milk contains up to 48.4% fat, which is as rich as cream and vital in order to build up the fat reserves in cubs so that they can withstand the extreme conditions.

Fattiest diet: in the spring and summer months, polar bears dine on ringed seal pups, which have up to 50% body fat.

Blue whale: the biggest heart on Earth

Weighing up to 160 tonnes, the blue whale (*Balaenoptera musculus*) is the **largest mammal**, and the **largest animal** known to have existed. Pictured is a model of a blue whale's heart, made for Museum of New Zealand Te Papa Tongarewa by Human Dynamo Workshop. A blue whale's car-sized heart weighs *c.* 680 kg and is the **largest heart** of any animal. It beats 4–8 times a minute (**slowest heartbeat**).

Smallest family of land carnivores

Two families of land carnivores contain just one single species each. They are Nandiniidae, containing the nandinia (*Nandinia binotata*) of Africa, and Ailuridae, containing as its own living species the lesser or red panda (*Ailurus fulgens*) of Asia.

CETACEANS

Largest cetacean

A female blue whale (*Balaenoptera musculus*) killed at Twofold Bay in New

Largest cetacean family

The term "cetacean" describes whales, dolphins and porpoises. Dolphins (*Delphinidae*) have 37 living species, not all of which are called dolphins. This diverse family also includes pilot whales and killer, false killer and pygmy killer whales. They all breathe through a blow hole situated on top of their heads.

Largest terrestrial carnivore

The polar bear (*Ursus maritimus*) weighs 400–600 kg (880–1,320 lb) and is 2.4–2.6 m (7 ft 10 in–8 ft 6 in) long. It feeds on the **largest prey**, killing walruses up to 500 kg (1,100 lb) and beluga whales of 600 kg (1,322 lb) to fill a stomach capacity of *c.* 68 kg (150 lb), or 4 kg (9 lb) heavier than an adult human male.

South Wales, Australia, in 1910 measured 29.57 m (97 ft) long.

The **smallest cetaceans** are the Hector's dolphin (*Cephalorhynchus hectori*) and the vaquita (*Phocoena sinus*), both of which grow to a length of just 1.2 m (3 ft 11 in).

The **smallest species of baleen whale** (toothless but possessing baleen plates for filtering food from water) is the pygmy right whale (*Caperea marginata*) – native to the Southern Ocean – at 6–6.5 m (19 ft 8 in–21 ft 3 in) long and weighing 3–3.5 tonnes (6,600–7,700 lb).

Deepest mammal dive

Scientists recorded a 2,000-m (6,500-ft) dive, lasting 1 hr 13 min, by a bull sperm whale (*Physeter macrocephalus*) off the coast of Dominica in 1991.

In 1989, a male northern elephant seal (*Mirounga angustirostris*) was recorded diving to 1,529 m (5,017 ft) off the coast of California, USA, the **deepest dive by a pinniped**.

Largest carnivore

Male (bull) southern elephant seals (*Mirounga leonina*) weigh up to 3,500 kg (7,720 lb), with an average length of 5 m (16 ft 4 in). Also the **largest pinnipeds**, they dwarf even the polar bear (*U. maritimus*, left) and are found in the sub-Antarctic islands.

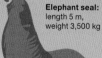 For animals closer to home, try p.64

CARNIVORE AND CETACEAN SIZES

Male Siberian tiger: length 3.15 m, weight 265 kg

Polar bear: length 2.6 m, weight 600 kg

Adult human male: height 1.75 m, weight 64 kg

Elephant seal: length 5 m, weight 3,500 kg

Killer whale: length 9 m, weight 10 tonnes

Common dolphin: length 2.6 m, weight 80 kg

Hector's dolphin: length 3 ft 11 in weight 40–60 kg

Blue whale: length 24 m, weight 160 tonnes

Glossary

Carnivore: meat-eating animal (order Carnivora)

Cetacean: aquatic mammal (order Cetacea). Divided into two main groups: toothed whales (dolphins, porpoises, smaller whales) and baleen whales (large filter-feeders).

Pinniped: carnivorous, semi-aquatic marine mammal (order Pinnipedia). Comprises seals, sea lions and the walrus.

Mammals

The cries of male howler monkeys can be heard from **5 km away**

Largest monkey

The male mandrill (*Mandrillus sphinx*) of equatorial West Africa has a head and body length of 61–76 cm (2 ft–2 ft 6 in) and a tail measuring 5.2–7.6 cm (2–3 in). Males average 25 kg (55 lb) but can weigh 54 kg (119 lb). The mandrill's distinctive blue rump, red-striped face and yellow beard make it one of the most vividly coloured mammals.

CHIROPTERANS

Largest bat colony
Up to 20 million female Mexican free-tailed bats (*Tadarida brasiliensis*) and offspring live in Bracken Cave in San Antonio, Texas, USA. Up to 500 baby bats occupy 0.09 m² (1 sq ft) of space. The colony's nightly flight out for food forms a column that can be picked up on the local airport radar.

Largest bat family
As of Nov 2013, there were 300 species of vesper bat (Vespertilionidae), with new ones described every year. Among the members are the common pipistrelles, the European serotine, the noctules, the tube-nosed, the mouse-eared, and the rare barbastelle.

Longest gestation period for a bat
The common vampire bat (*Desmodus rotundus*) has a gestation period of seven to eight months, and when the baby bat is born it suckles its mother for an additional nine months and sometimes even longer. Native to Mexico, Central America and South America, vampire bats feed solely on blood.

INSECTIVORES

Largest mammalian brain-to-body mass
Shrews have brains that constitute 10% of their total body weight.

Most dangerous insectivore
The solenodon is a small, innocuous-looking rat-like Caribbean mammal. The Haitian solenodon (*Solenodon paradoxus*) and the rare Cuban solenodon (*Solenodon cubanus*) have toxic saliva that is potentially dangerous to humans.

Largest bat
Bats are the only mammals capable of true flight (i.e., by flapping wings), rather than gliding. The largest are the flying foxes or fruit bats (Pteropodidae), which can have a wing-span of 1.7 m (5 ft 7 in).

Smallest primate

The pygmy mouse lemur (*Microcebus myoxinus*) from Madagascar is about 62 mm (2.4 in) long with a tail of 136 mm (5.3 in) and an average weight of 30.6 g (1.1 oz). A white stripe runs from nose to forehead, and a black stripe runs down its back.

Heaviest tree shrew
Tree shrews resemble squirrels with pointed snouts and no whiskers. Fully grown male specimens of the Mindanao tree shrew (*Urogale everetti*), native to the Philippines, have been recorded weighing 350 g (12 oz).

Most sensitive animal organ
The star-nosed mole (*Condylura cristata*) takes its name from its 22-probed nose covered with 25,000 sensory receptors – five times the amount of touch-sensitive nerve fibres in a human hand.

FACT
Shrews have a big appetite: in just one day, they can eat their own body weight in bugs and worms!

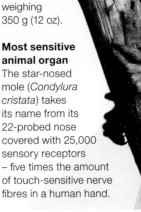

Smallest monkey

Pygmy marmosets (*Callithrix pygmaea*) weigh 15 g (0.53 oz) at birth and grow to an average of 119 g (4.19 oz). They are 136 mm (5.3 in) long, excluding tail. Despite their size, pygmy marmosets can leap 5 m (16 ft 5 in) in the air.

CHIROPTERAN, INSECTIVORE AND PRIMATE SIZES

Male eastern lowland gorilla: height 1.75 m, weight 163 kg

Mandrill: height 61–76 cm, weight 25 kg

Large and gigantic flying fox (fruit bat): wing-span 1.7 m, weight 1.6 kg

Giant otter shrew: head-to-tail length 64 cm, weight 950 g

Moonrat: head-to-tail length 43–71 cm, weight 1–2 kg

Koala bears

Sleepiest marsupial: because of its low-quality diet of eucalyptus leaves, koalas (*Phascolarctos cinereus*) spend up to 18 hr out of every 24 asleep.

Largest koala litter: two – a pair of identical twins called Euca and Lyptus born on 10–11 Apr 1999 in Queensland, Australia.

Oldest koala: Sarah, who died in 2001 aged 23 years, was born in 1978 and lived at the Lone Pine Koala Sanctuary in Queensland, Australia; koalas typically live for 16 years in captivity.

Oldest koala sanctuary: the Lone Pine Koala Sanctuary, where Sarah lived; it was established in 1927 by Claude Reid (AUS) and still operates today.

Largest insectivore

The moonrat (*Echinosorex gymnurus*) is neither a rat nor from the Moon! Found in south-east Asia, it is actually a giant relative of the hedgehog, but with thick fur instead of spikes. It is 26–46 cm (10 in–1 ft 6 in) long with a tail of 17–25 cm (6–9 in), and weighs 1–2 kg (2 lb 3 oz–4 lb 6 oz).

MARSUPIALS

Longest proportionate animal caecum
A caecum is a kind of pouch in the large intestine, which in herbivores contains bacteria that help to break down the cellulose present in plant material. The largest in the animal kingdom relative to body size belongs to the koala (*Phascolarctos cinereus*). It is 2 m (6 ft 7 in) long and 10 cm (4 in) in diameter, while the koala's own body length is just 60–85 cm (2–2 ft 9 in).

Most nipples
The female shrewish short-tailed opossum (*Monodelphis sorex*) has up to 27 nipples (or "mammae"), despite being tiny: 11–13 cm (4–5 in) with a tail of 6.5–8.5 cm (2.5–3.3 in).

Most northerly marsupial
The Virginia opossum (*Didelphis virginiana*) is the only species of marsupial that lives north of Mexico. It has been recorded as far north as south-western Ontario in Canada.

PRIMATES

Largest primate
The male eastern lowland gorilla (*Gorilla beringei graueri*), found in the eastern Congo, weighs up to 163 kg

(360 lb) and has a typical bipedal height of up to 1.75 m (5 ft 9 in). The tallest recorded in the wild, however, was a 1.95-m (6-ft 5-in) mountain bull shot in the eastern Congo on 16 May 1938.

Largest nocturnal primate
The aye-aye (*Daubentonia madagascariensis*) from Madagascar is rodent-like but closely related to lemurs. Under threat for being seen as an omen of death, the aye-aye weighs 2.7 kg (5 lb 15 oz) and averages 65 cm (2 ft) in length for the male, more than half of which is accounted for by its long tail.

Smallest loris
Lorises are small, nocturnal primates related to lemurs

Actual Size

Smallest mammal
Kitti's hog-nosed bat (*Craseonycteris thonglongyai*), aka the bumblebee bat, is 29–33 mm (1.14–1.29 in) long. Found in caves in Thailand and Myanmar, it was rated as "vulnerable" on the International Union for Conservation of Nature (IUCN) red list of threatened species.

and bushbabies. The smallest is the pygmy slow loris (*Nycticebus pygmaeus*), which measures 19.5–23 cm (7.6–9 in) in length, with a tail averaging 1.8 cm (0.7 in). It weighs 36–58 g (1–2 oz).

Smallest mammal on land
Savi's pygmy shrew (*Suncus etruscus*) is no bigger than a human thumb. Its body measures 36–53 mm (1.4–2 in) and its tail 24–29 mm (0.9–1.1 in). It weighs just 1.5–2.6 g (0.05–0.09 oz).

Largest mammal to build a nest

Male African gorillas (*Gorilla gorilla*) measure 1.7–1.8 m (5 ft 6 in–6 ft) and weigh 136–227 kg (300–500 lb). They create a new ground nest from the surrounding vegetation every day. The nests are circular and typically measure 1 m (3 ft 3 in) in diameter. Some lighter members of the troop build in trees and many make a separate nest during the day for a nap. These constructions are also the **largest nests built by a mammal**.

FACT
The **largest primate of all time** was *Gigantopithecus blacki* – a veritable King Kong, now extinct for 100,000 years – standing 3 m tall and weighing 1.58 tonnes.

Largest marsupial: red kangaroo

There are nearly 60 species of kangaroo, the biggest being the red (*Macropus rufus*) from the dry centre of Australia. The male red measures 1.8 m tall and 2.85 m long, and can weigh 90 kg. Reds arrive as the **largest newborn marsupial**, but because all marsupials are born very early, the reds weigh just 0.75 g; it would take 36,000 newborns to equal their mother's weight. The **longest jump by a kangaroo** was in New South Wales, Australia, in 1951, when a female bounded 12.8 m.

Glossary

Chiropteran: has forelimbs modified as wings; uses echolocation to navigate

Insectivore: insect-eating mammal

Marsupial: characterized by pouch in which mother carries her young

Primate: has large brain and flexible hands and feet, includes humans

○ ○ ○

Mammals

Giraffes give birth standing up, so newborn calves typically fall 1.5 m to the ground

RODENTS

First domesticated rodent
The guinea pig or South American cavy (*Cavia porcellus*) was first bred as a food animal in the Andes in around 5000 BC. It is thought to be a domesticated version of the montane guinea pig (*C. tschudii*) native to the mountains of Peru.

Longest-lived rodent
Africa's naked mole rat (*Heterocephalus glaber*) spends its life in underground burrow systems located beneath East Africa's drier tropical grasslands, and can live for 28 years.

Smallest gliding rodent
The pygmy scalytail (*Idiurus zenkeri*) is also known as a flying mouse. Native to Central and East Africa, it has a maximum length of 18 cm (7 in), of which its long, feather-like tail accounts for more than half. It has a gliding membrane between the forelimb and hind limb on each side of its body, which it expands when leaping from a tree, enabling it to glide through the air.

Largest rodent ever
Josephoartigasia monesi was a 2-million-year-old fossil species that lived in what is today coastal Uruguay. It is currently known only from a single skull measuring 53 cm (1 ft 9 in) long, from which scientists estimate that the complete animal probably weighed 1 tonne (2,200 lb).

Largest jerboa
Jerboas are desert-dwelling rodents that jump and leap on their hind legs like miniature kangaroos. The suitably named great jerboa (*Allactaga major*) has an uppermost head-and-body length of 18 cm (7 in), with a tail that can grow to 26 cm (10.2 in). It primarily inhabits deserts in Russia, Kazakhstan, Turkmenistan and Uzbekistan.

Smallest ungulate
The lesser Malay mouse deer (*Tragulus javanicus*) has a body length of 42–55 cm (1 ft 5 in–1 ft 9 in), a shoulder height of 20–25 cm (8–10 in) and weighs 1.5–2.5 kg (3 lb 4 oz–5 lb 8 oz). Primarily nocturnal, this small ungulate is rarely seen.

Tallest mammal
Giraffes (*Giraffa camelopardalis*) are found in the dry savannah and open woodland areas of sub-Saharan Africa. An adult male giraffe typically measures between 4.6 m and 5.5 m (15–18 ft) in height.

Largest squirrel
The Indian or Malabar giant squirrel (*Ratufa indica*) is endemic to deciduous and moist evergreen forests in peninsular India. It can grow to 1 m (3 ft 3 in) long, of which its long bushy tail constitutes two-thirds.

Fewest teeth for a rodent
Also known as the small-toothed moss-mouse, and native to Indonesia and Papua New Guinea, Shaw Mayer's shrew mouse (*Pseudohydromys ellermani*) has eight teeth – four incisors and four molars, with no canines or premolars.

The **most teeth for a rodent** is the silvery mole rat (*Heliophobius argenteocinereus*). Native to Central and East Africa, including Tanzania, Kenya and the Democratic Republic of the Congo, it has no fewer than 24 grinding teeth (premolars and molars) plus four incisors: 28 teeth in all.

Largest rhinoceros
Restricted to southern Africa, the southern white rhinoceros (*Ceratotherium simum simum*) can grow to a length of 4.2 m (13 ft 9 in), with an uppermost shoulder height of 1.85 m (6 ft) and weight of 3.6 tonnes (7,930 lb).

Jumbo size: African elephant

The adult male African elephant (*Loxodonta africana*) is not only the **largest ungulate** but also the **largest land mammal**. It typically stands 3–3.7 m at the shoulder and, at 4–7 tonnes, can weigh more than 100 average-sized men. The tallest in Africa are members of the endangered desert race from Damaraland in Namibia. A bull elephant shot near Sesfontein in Damaraland on 4 Apr 1978 was the tallest recorded example. It measured 4.42 m in a line from the shoulder to the base of the forefoot – as tall as a London double-decker bus!

AZ Glossary

Rodent: largest order of mammals, found on every continent except Antarctica; characterized by their paired upper and lower incisor teeth ("rodent" means "gnawing").

Ungulate: broadly defined as a mammal with hooves (enlarged, modified toenails that, unlike claws and nails, support its weight).

UNGULATES

Smallest rhinoceros

Once widespread across south-eastern Asia but now confined to Sumatra, the Malay Peninsula and Borneo, the Sumatran rhinoceros (*Dicerorhinus sumatrensis*) has a maximum head-and-body length of 3.18 m (10 ft 5 in), tail length of 70 cm (2 ft 3 in) and shoulder height of 1.45 m (4 ft 9 in).

Largest herd of white deer

Within the former Seneca Army Depot in Seneca County, New York, USA, is a herd of some 300 white

Least classifiable mammal

The African aardvark (*Orycteropus afer*) has cylindrical teeth unlike those of any other mammal and claws rather than the hooves of other ungulates. It has its own order – Tubulidentata ("tube teeth").

Largest deer

A male Alaskan moose (*Alces alces gigas*) standing 2.34 m (7 ft 8 in) tall and weighing an estimated 816 kg (1,800 lb) was shot in the Yukon territory of Canada in Sep 1897. The **smallest deer** is the northern pudu (*Pudu mephistophiles*), which grows to 35 cm (1 ft 1 in) tall at the shoulder and weighs up to 6 kg (13 lb 3 oz). It is found in Colombia, Ecuador and Peru.

deer. Their species is the North American white-tailed deer (*Odocoileus virginianus*), and their white coat results from a recessive non-albino mutant gene allele.

The **rarest deer** is the Bawean (*Hyelaphus kuhlii*), limited to the tiny Indonesian island of Bawean. Fewer than 250 mature individuals are believed to exist. It is categorized as "Critically Endangered" by the International Union for Conservation of Nature (IUCN).

Largest camel

The dromedary or one-humped camel (*Camelus dromedarius*) has a top head-and-body length of 3.5 m (11 ft 5 in), with a maximum shoulder height of 2.4 m (7 ft 10 in), and can weigh 690 kg (1,520 lb). Native to the Middle East, it survives today as a feral animal only in Australia and Spain.

Largest wild pig

Central Africa's giant forest hog (*Hylochoerus meinertzhageni*) has a head–body length of 2.1 m (6 ft 10 in), a shoulder height of 1.05 m (3 ft 5 in) and can weigh 275 kg (600 lb).

Actual Size

Smallest rodent

Both the northern pygmy mouse (*Baiomys taylori*, above) of Mexico and the USA and the Baluchistan pygmy jerboa (*Salpingotulus michaelis*) of Pakistan have a 3.6-cm (1.4-in) head-to-body length and 7.2-cm (2.8-in) tail.

Longest hair for a domestic cattle breed

The domestic cattle (*Bos taurus*) with the longest hair is the Highland cattle. Originating in Scotland but subsequently exported worldwide, this famously hirsute breed has an average hair length of 35 cm (1 ft 1 in). This is measured from the length of the "dossan" (fringe) and also the length of hair in the ears.

RODENT AND UNGULATE SIZES

Never forget...
The **largest land mammal** (African elephant) is nearly 3 million times heavier than the **smallest** (pygmy shrew)!

Giraffe: height 4.6–5.5 m, weight 1.6 tonnes

Adult male African elephant: height 3–3.7 m, weight 4–7 tonnes

Southern white rhinoceros: length 4.2 m, weight 3.6 tonnes

Capybara: length 1.3 m, weight 79 kg

Lesser Malay mouse deer: length 42–55 cm, weight 1.5–2.5 kg

Pygmy mouse: height 3.6 cm, tail length 7.2 cm

FACT

The World Wildlife Fund (WWF) has five ungulates on its critically endangered list: saola (*Pseudoryx nghetinhensis*), Sumatran elephant (*Elephas maximus sumatranus*), Sumatran rhinoceros (*Dicerorhinus sumatrensis*), black rhinoceros (*Diceros bicornis*) and Javan rhinoceros (*Rhinoceros sondaicus*).

Birds

Owls can rotate their heads a full **270°** in either direction

Largest owl
The European race of the eagle owl (*Bubo bubo*) has an average length of 66–71 cm (2 ft 2 in–2 ft 4 in), an average weight of 1.6–4 kg (3 lb 8 oz–8 lb 13 oz) and a wing-span of more than 1.5 m (5 ft).

Largest woodpecker
The imperial woodpecker (*Campephilus imperialis*) measures up to 60 cm (1 ft 11 in) long. It was formerly widespread across Mexico, but owing to extensive habitat destruction its numbers rapidly plummeted. The last confirmed sighting was in 1956, but observations by locals continued into the mid-1990s. It is categorized as "Critically Endangered", possibly extinct, by the International Union for Conservation of Nature (IUCN).

Longest-toed bird (relative to body)
The chicken-sized northern jacana (*Jacana spinosa*) has four toes, each about 7 cm (2.8 in) long. When fully extended, they span 168 cm² (26 sq in), enabling the bird to walk on lily pads and other floating vegetation.

Loudest parrot
Research conducted at San Diego Zoo in California, USA, recorded shrieks reaching 135 decibels by the Moluccan (salmon-crested) cockatoo (*Cacatua moluccensis*), native to the Moluccas in Indonesia.

Fastest wingbeat
During its diving courtship displays, the ruby-throated hummingbird (*Archilochus colubris*) has a wingbeat rate of 200 beats per sec, as opposed to the 90 beats per sec produced by other hummingbirds.

Smallest swan
The smallest swan – but largest species of South American waterfowl – is the black-necked swan

Smallest bird
Male bee hummingbirds (*Mellisuga helenae*) of Cuba measure 57 mm (2.24 in) long, half of which is the bill and tail. They weigh just 1.6 g (0.056 oz), generally regarded as the lowest limit for warm-blooded animals. Females are slightly larger.

Actual Size

(*Cygnus melancoryphus*). It grows up to 1.24 m (4 ft) long, with a wing-span of 1.77 m (5 ft 9 in). The coscoroba swan (*Coscoroba coscoroba*) is slightly smaller, but is no longer thought to be closely related to true swans and may well be a swan in name only.

Rarest heron
The global population of the imperial (white-bellied) heron (*Ardea insignis*) is estimated at no more than 400 birds and is thought to be decreasing. It is categorized as "Critically Endangered" by the IUCN. The species is native to the eastern Himalayan foothills of India, Myanmar, Bhutan and possibly Bangladesh but is now extinct in Nepal.

Rarest kingfisher
The Tuamotu kingfisher (*Todiramphus gambieri*) is confined entirely to a very small area on the single island of Niau in the Tuamotu Archipelago of French Polynesia. Only 125–135 birds still exist as of 2013. It is threatened by non-native rats and cats, as well as by cyclone-induced habitat destruction.

FACT
Birds are closely related to dinosaurs. In the USA, there are plans to retro-engineer a dinosaur using chicken DNA.

Largest toucan
The largest species of toucan is the toco toucan (*Ramphastos toco*), which weighs up to 876 g (1 lb 14 oz) and grows up to 65 cm (2 ft 1 in) long – a third of which is its huge bill. Males are larger than females. It is native to much of eastern and central South America, but particularly Brazil.

⚡ Brink of extinction
The North American ivory-billed woodpecker (*Campephilus principalis*) remains the **rarest bird**. Sixty years ago, we said that it "may even be extinct. It is believed that less than a dozen still exist in the Florida area." Today, our consultant Karl Shuker says, "I consider there to be good evidence that it survives, albeit very precariously."

Ostr-etch: tall story
The North African ostrich (*Struthio camelus camelus*) is the **largest living bird**. Males have been recorded at 2.75 m tall and weighing 156.5 kg. It cannot fly, but makes up for it by being the **fastest flightless bird on land**, reaching 72 km/h. Its powerful strides can exceed 7 m and are comparable to those of the **fastest land mammal**, the cheetah. It can also attack with a powerful kick. Because of its size, the ostrich is also the bird that lays the **smallest eggs relative to body weight**: only 1.4–1.5% of its total mass.

Fastest bird diving

The peregrine falcon (*Falco peregrinus*) – found on almost all continents – is thought to reach a terminal velocity of around 300 km/h (186 mph) in a diving stoop. At this point it is the fastest animal on the planet. Bad news for any prey below...

Fastest bird in level flight

In a report published by French and British researchers working in the sub-Antarctic, the average estimated ground speed for a satellite-tagged grey-headed albatross (*Thalassarche chrysostoma*) is 127 km/h (78.9 mph), sustained for more than 8 hr while returning to its nest at Bird Island, South Georgia, in the middle of a storm.

Actual Size

Largest family of birds

The Tyrannidae family of tyrant flycatchers has more than 400 species, including the brown-crested flycatcher (*Myiarchus tyrannulus*, above left), lesser kiskadee (*Philohydor lictor*, below left) and vermilion flycatcher (*Pyrocephalus rubinus*, below). Highly diverse in form, these insectivorous birds live in North, Central and South America.

Most airborne bird

After leaving its nesting grounds as a youngster, the sooty tern (*Sterna fuscata*) remains aloft for 3–10 years while maturing, settling on water from time to time before returning to land to breed as an adult.

The **longest bird migration** is that of the Arctic tern (*Sterna paradisaea*). It breeds north of the Arctic Circle, then flies south to the Antarctic for the northern winter and back again – a round trip of approximately 80,467 km (50,000 mi).

Smallest flightless bird

Found only on a small area of land in the South Atlantic, the Inaccessible Island rail (*Atlantisia rogersi*) weighs a mere 40 g (1.4 oz). First discovered in 1870, the birds are around the size of a three-day-old chicken.

The **longest time for a bird to learn to fly** is exhibited by the wandering albatross (*Diomedea exulans*), whose chicks take 278–280 days on average to make their first flight after hatching. Because it takes so long for the young albatross to get to this stage, the adults breed only once every two years.

Most expensive pigeon

On 18 May 2013, pigeon breeder Leo Heremans (BEL) sold his racing pigeon for 310,000 euros (£260,000; $400,000) on www.pipa.be. The pigeon, Bolt, was named after world-record-holding Jamaican sprinter Usain Bolt and will be used for breeding.

Shortest bills

The shortest avian bills in relation to body length belong to the smaller swifts (Apodidae family), and in particular to the glossy swiftlet (*Collocalia esculenta*), whose bill is almost non-existent.

Longest bills

The Australian pelican (*Pelecanus conspicillatus*) is the bill to beat, at 34–47 cm (1 ft 1 in–1 ft 6.5 in). But the **longest beak in relation to body length** is that of the sword-billed hummingbird (*Ensifera ensifera*) of the Andes from Venezuela to Bolivia. The beak measures 10.2 cm (4 in), making it longer than its body without the tail.

> TOP OF THE BILL: BIRDS SEEDED

Black-legged falconet: head-to-tail length 14–15 cm, weight 35 g

Bee hummingbirds: length 57 mm, weight 1.6 g

Andean condor: wing-span 3.2 m, weight 15 kg

Male wandering albatross: wing-span 3.63 m, weight 5.9–12.7 kg

North African ostrich: height 2.75 m, weight 156.5 kg

Best of the nests

- **Highest nest:** marbled murrelets (*Brachyramphus marmoratus*) nest as high up as 45 m.
- **Largest ground nest:** malleefowl (*Leipoa ocellata*) nests contain up to 229 m³ of matter and weigh as much as 300 tonnes.
- **Longest nest burrow:** rhinoceros auklet (*Cerorhinca monocerata*) nest burrows typically measure 2–3 m long.

Reptiles & amphibians

More than **6,000 species of lizard** are known to exist

Heaviest venomous snake

The eastern diamondback rattlesnake (*Crotalus adamanteus*) weighs 5.5–6.8 kg (12–15 lb), with the biggest on record at 15 kg (34 lb). Other contenders are the king cobra (*Ophiophagus hannah*), up to 9 kg (20 lb), and the gaboon viper (*Bitis gabonica*), weighing 8.5 kg (18 lb 12 oz).

Fastest lizard
The Costa Rican spiny-tailed iguana (*Ctenosaura similis*) can attain a land speed of 34.9 km/h (21.7 mph).

Highest frequency frog croak
The concave-eared torrent frog (*Odorrana tormota*) of eastern China croaks at a frequency of 128 kHz

– an ultrasonic emission well beyond the range of human hearing (which cannot detect sound frequencies above 20 kHz). The reason that

this frog produces such a high-frequency croak is to overcome the very loud low-frequency sound of the waterfalls near which it lives in order to communicate with others of its species.

Largest caiman
Caimans are alligator-related crocodilians and, of their six species, the largest is the black caiman (*Melanosuchus niger*). Old males can sometimes exceed 5 m (16 ft 5 in) in length and 400 kg (880 lb) in weight. The black caiman is native to rivers and swamps in the Amazon basin.

Largest frog

The goliath frog (*Conraua goliath*) is 30 cm (1 ft) long on average, the same size as a rabbit. The largest individual specimen was captured in Apr 1889 in Cameroon with an overall length of 87.63 cm (2 ft 10.5 in). Classified as "endangered" by the International Union for Conservation of Nature (IUCN), the frog is found mainly in Central Africa.

Largest plant-eating lizard
Jim Morrison, singer with The Doors, called himself "The Lizard King". In his honour, an extinct species of iguana was named *Barbaturex morrisoni*. It was almost 2 m (6 ft 6 in) in length and inhabited what is now Burma during the Eocene epoch, some 40–36 million years ago. High temperatures may have helped the lizard evolve to its unusual size.

Most poisonous newt
The California newt (*Taricha torosa*) is poisonous all

Rarest tree frog
Rabbs' fringe-limbed tree frog (*Ecnomiohyla rabborum*) was only discovered by science in 2005, and just one living specimen is currently known to exist. The male lives at the Atlanta Botanical Garden in Georgia, USA.

Longest iguana species

The green, or common, iguana (*Iguana iguana*) can exceed 2 m (6 ft 6 in) in length. Found in an extensive range from Brazil and Paraguay to as far north as Mexico and the Caribbean, they are among the largest lizards in the Americas. Iguanas live near water and are excellent swimmers, feeding largely on leaves, flowers and fruit.

⚡ Longest frog jump

A frog-jumping contest recorded in our 1955 edition produced the **longest frog jump** by an amphibian athlete named Can't Take It. On 17 May 1953, before a crowd of 30,000 in California, USA, it soared 4.73 m. The record was leapfrogged with a stunning performance by a South African sharp-nosed frog (*Ptychadena oxyrhynchus*) named Santjie, who was competing in a triple jump. On 21 May 1977, Santjie flew 10.3 m – about half the length of a basketball court.

REPTILE SCALES

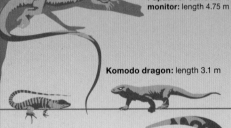

Papuan or Salvadori's monitor: length 4.75 m

Komodo dragon: length 3.1 m

Galápagos giant tortoise: length 1.35 m

Estuarine or saltwater crocodile length 7 m

Black-and-white tegu: length 1.4 m

Reticulated python: length 10 m (longest specimen discovered)

Largest tegu

The black-and-white or Argentine giant tegu (*Tupinambis merianae*) is native to east and central South America and can grow to 1.4 m (4 ft 7 in) in length and weigh 7 kg (15 lb 7 oz). Tegus are predatory, and popularly kept as pets by reptile fanciers.

Smallest lizard family
The Lanthanotidae family of lizards has just one member – the earless monitor (*Lanthanotus borneensis*). This is an evolutionary oddity known only in Sarawak, Borneo. It lacks external ears, and the nearest relatives of this small family are the true monitors and the venomous Gila monster and beaded lizards.

Smelliest species of frog
The skunk frog (*Aromobates nocturnus*) of Venezuela is well named. Measuring 6.2 cm (2.44 in) long, it is a member of the poison-arrow frog family (Dendrobatidae), yet its defensive skin secretion contains not toxin but the same stink-producing compound present in the anal emissions of mammalian skunks.

over: its skin, muscles and blood contain tetrodotoxin, a toxic and powerful nerve poison that is a hundred times more deadly than cyanide. It's the same stuff that makes the pufferfish (Tetraodontidae) the **most poisonous edible fish**. The newt itself is immune to the effects of venom.

Smallest crocodilian

Females of the dwarf caiman (*Paleosuchus palpebrosus*) of northern South America rarely exceed a length of 1.2 m (4 ft) and males often don't grow over 1.5 m (4 ft 11 in). They are generally nocturnal and usually solitary.

Most legs for a worm lizard

As their name suggests, worm lizards resemble earthworms and are generally limbless. But four of the 180-plus species – known as ajolotes (*Bipes* spp.) and confined to Mexico – possess a pair of small forelimbs with large clawed feet positioned behind the head. These limbs are sometimes mistaken for ears!

Actual Size

Most geographically restricted python
Liasis mackloti savuensis is confined to the tiny Indonesian island of Savu, south of Java, from which it gets its common name: the Savu Island python. Savu is the largest of the three Savu Islands, whose total area is only 460.84 km² (178 sq mi).

Most powerful species of vertebrate
In terms of watts of power generated per kilogram of muscle, the giant palm salamander (*Bolitoglossa dofleini*) of Central America is the strongest vertebrate species. Its tongue explodes outwards at 18,000 watts per kg (818 watts per lb) of muscle. It is believed that elastic collagen tissue in the salamander's tongue stores up energy prior to its explosive release, much like a stretched rubber band or a bowstring drawn back.

FACT

A typical Salvadori's monitor might have a body of 1.2 m but a tail of more than double that: up to 2.7 m. By comparison, the average Komodo dragon is 2.25 m long.

Longest lizard

While the **largest lizard** overall may be the bulky Komodo dragon (*Varanus komodoensis*), Salvadori's monitor (*Varanus salvadorii*) has an impressive tail to tell. Its lengthy appendage brings the total length of the Papua New Guinean lizard up to a maximum of 4.75 m (15 ft 7 in).

Scaled up: long snakes

The reticulated python (*Python reticulatus*) of Indonesia, south-east Asia and the Philippines is the world's **longest snake**. A specimen measured in Indonesia in 1912 was 10 m long – equivalent in length to the outstretched arms of eight adult men.

Pictured is Si Belang, a 6.05-m-long python adopted by the Toe family in Borneo. The 60-kg snake lives, sleeps, eats and even bathes with the family – including three-year-old Karim. Si Belang is not a threat to the Toes as he recognizes them as his own family and their home as his territory.

 I toad you so

Largest toad: cane toad (*Bufo marinus*), 2.65 kg; 53.9 cm long.

Most paternal amphibian: male midwife toad (*Alytes obstetricans*), carries eggs around its thighs until they hatch.

Smallest toad: *Bufo taitanus beiranus* from Africa, 2.4 cm in length.

Fishes

The whale shark is **not a shark**; a starfish is **not a fish**; an electric eel is **not an eel**

Largest carp species

The Siamese giant carp (*Catlocarpio siamensis*), aka giant barb, is the largest of the cyprinid (carp) family. The longest specimens currently reported – such as the 102-kg (225-lb) barb above – are around 1.8 m (5 ft 10 in) in length, while the longest known specimen was 3 m (9 ft 10 in).

long, almost twice the length of the whale shark, the **largest fish** alive today (see p.42).

Largest freshwater fish

The largest fish that spends its whole life in fresh or brackish water is the Mekong giant catfish (*Pangasianodon gigas*), principally of the Mekong River basin, and *Pangasius sanitwongsei*, mainly of the Chao Phraya River basin, both native to south-east Asia. Both species are reputed to grow to 3 m (9 ft 10 in) and weigh 300 kg (660 lb). The *Arapaima gigas* of South America is reported to reach 4.5 m (14 ft 9 in) long, but it weighs only 200 kg (440 lb).

Smallest fish

The smallest adult fish – and indeed the **smallest vertebrate** – is a sexually mature male *Photocorynus spiniceps*, which measures just 6.2 mm (0.24 in) long and is found in the Philippine Sea. This species of anglerfish reproduces through sexual parasitism. The male permanently attaches itself to the larger female by biting her back, belly or sides and effectively turning her into a hermaphrodite.

The **smallest freshwater fish** is the dwarf pygmy goby (*Pandaka pygmaea*), a colourless and nearly transparent species found in the streams and lakes of Luzon in the

Actual Size

Slowest fish

The slowest-moving marine fish are the sea horses (family Syngnathidae), of which there are just over 30 species. Some of the smaller species such as the dwarf sea horse (*Hippocampus zosterae*, above), which reaches a maximum length of only 4.2 cm (1.6 in), probably never attain speeds of more than 0.016 km/h (0.001 mph).

Largest fish ever

In 2008, two palaeontology students discovered a specimen of the marine fossil species *Leedsichthys problematicus* in clay pits near Peterborough in Cambridgeshire, UK. Dating back 155 million years, this particular specimen measured 22 m (72 ft)

Longest bony fish

The lengthiest of the bony or "true" fishes (class Pisces, aka Osteichthyes – see Glossary, below) is the oarfish (*Regalecus glesne*), or the "King of the Herrings", which has worldwide distribution. In *c.* 1885, a 7.6-m-long (25-ft) example weighing 272 kg (600 lb) was caught by fishermen off Pemaquid Point in Maine, USA. The specimen pictured here was found dead in the water off Toyon Bay, California, USA, on 13 Oct 2013 by staff of the Catalina Island Marine Institute; it measured 5.5 m (18 ft) long.

FACT

An oarfish seen swimming by a team of scientists off New Jersey, USA, in 1963 was estimated to be 15.2 m long!

Longing for the sea? Turn to p.38

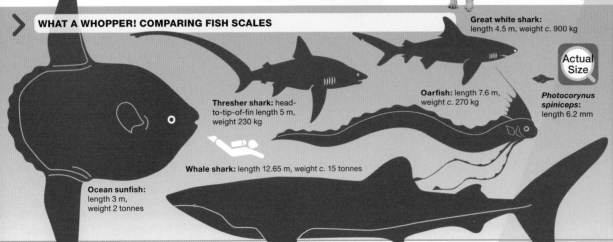

> ## WHAT A WHOPPER! COMPARING FISH SCALES

Great white shark: length 4.5 m, weight *c.* 900 kg

Thresher shark: head-to-tip-of-fin length 5 m, weight 230 kg

Oarfish: length 7.6 m, weight *c.* 270 kg

Actual Size

Photocorynus spiniceps: length 6.2 mm

Whale shark: length 12.65 m, weight *c.* 15 tonnes

Ocean sunfish: length 3 m, weight 2 tonnes

Glossary

Chondrichthyes: cartilaginous fish; have skeletons made of cartilage – a flexible but firm tissue less stiff than bone.
Osteichthyes: bony fish; have skeletons made from bone. There are *c.* 28,000 species of Osteichthyes, accounting for 96% of all fish species. They also form the **largest class of vertebrates** (animals with backbones).

FACT
Thresher sharks are believed to use their tails to herd and then stun schools of milling fish ready for eating.

Longest fin

All three species of thresher shark (family Alopiidae) have a huge, scythe-shaped caudal (tail) fin that is roughly as long as the body itself. The largest and most common species, *Alopias vulpinus*, found worldwide in temperate and tropical seas, grows to 6 m (19 ft 8 in) in length, of which almost 3 m (9 ft 10 in) consists of this greatly elongated upper tail fin.

Philippines. Males are only 7.5–9.9 mm (0.29–0.38 in) long and weigh just 4–5 mg.

Highest living fish
The Tibetan loach (family Cobitidae) is found at an altitude of 5,200 m (17,060 ft) in the Himalayas.

Longest fish migration
Many fish species undertake long annual migrations between their feeding grounds. The longest straight-line distance known to have been covered by a fish is 9,335 km (5,800 mi) for a bluefin tuna (*Thunnus thynnus*) that was dart-tagged off Baja California, Mexico, in 1958, and caught 483 km (300 mi) south of Tokyo, Japan, in Apr 1963.
The **longest journey by a freshwater fish** is some 4,800–6,400 km (3,000–4,000 mi), taking about six months, by the European eel (*Anguilla anguilla*). This species spends between seven and 15 years in fresh

water in Europe, before abruptly evolving into breeding condition, changing colour to become silver, and growing a longer snout and larger eyes. The much-altered animal then begins a marathon trek to the species' spawning grounds in the Sargasso Sea, east of North America.

Most venomous fish
Poisonous creatures contain poison within their bodies, which they pass on to any creatures that consume, or even touch them, while venomous creatures inject

venom into their victims. The stonefish (family Synanceiidae) of the tropical waters of the Indo-Pacific are highly venomous. *Synanceia horrida* has the largest venom glands of any known fish. Direct contact with the spines of its fins, which contain a strong neurotoxic poison, can prove fatal.
The **most poisonous fish** is the puffer fish (*Tetraodon*) of the Red Sea and Indo-Pacific region, which produces a fatally poisonous toxin called tetrodotoxin. Its ovaries, eggs, blood, liver, intestines

FACT
Technically, there is no such thing as a "fish" – the creatures on these pages are from many different animal families.

Heaviest bony fish

The ocean sunfish (*Mola mola*) has been recorded weighing 1,995 kg (4,400 lb) and measuring 3 m (10 ft) from fin tip to fin tip. *Mola mola* – named from the Latin for "millstone" in reference to its shape – is found in all oceans in tropical or temperate climates and feeds on zooplankton, small fishes and algae. Sharks and rays, by contrast, are cartilaginous, not bony as in the case of the ocean sunfish.

FACT
There are more fish in the Amazon River than there are in all of Europe.

Fastest fish
The cosmopolitan sailfish (*Istiophorus platypterus*) is considered to be the fastest species of fish over short distances, although practical difficulties make measurements extremely hard to secure. Trials at the Long Key Fishing Camp in Florida, USA, suggested a top speed of 109 km/h (68 mph).

and, to a lesser extent, its skin, contain tetrodotoxin. Less than 0.1 g (0.004 oz) of this is enough to kill a human adult in as little as 20 min.

Most ferocious freshwater fish
Piranhas are renowned for their ferocity, particularly those of the genera *Serrasalmus* and *Pygocentrus*, found in the large rivers of South America. Attracted to blood and frantic splashing, a school of piranhas can within minutes strip an animal as large as a horse of its flesh, leaving only its skeleton.

Shark attack: great white shark

The **largest predatory fish** is the great white shark (*Carcharodon carcharias*, from the Greek for "sharp-toothed"). Adults average 4.3–4.6 m in length – as long as a typical family saloon car – and generally weigh 900 kg. There is plenty of circumstantial evidence to suggest that some great whites grow to more than 6 m in length, and there have even been claims of huge specimens up to 10 m long. Pictured here is a lucky seal escaping the jaws of a great white, snapped in Jul 2013 off the coast of Seal Island, South Africa, by photographer David Jenkins.

 Freshwater giant

According to our 1955 edition, the **largest freshwater fish** was the 6.7-m-long giant Russian sturgeon (*Acipenser*), found in the Volga River. "However, we now know that this is not an exclusively freshwater species," says our animal consultant Dr Karl Shuker. "At 3 m, the largest fish that spends its whole life in fresh water is Asia's Mekong giant catfish." (see p.56)

Crustaceans

A female skeleton shrimp **consumes the male** shortly after mating

Most abundant animal

Copepods, found almost everywhere with water, comprise 12,000 species and form groups that can reach a trillion individuals. Most are less than 1 mm (0.04 in) long.

Deepest-living crustacean

In Nov 1980, live amphipods were found at a depth of 10,500 m (34,450 ft) in Challenger Deep, the **deepest point on Earth**, in the Mariana Trench of the western Pacific Ocean.

Longest journey by a crab

In Dec 2006, it was reported that an American Columbus crab (*Planes minutus*) had been discovered washed up but still alive on a beach in Bournemouth, UK – 8,000 km (5,000 mi) from its home in the Sargasso Sea, east of Florida, USA. The 15-cm (6-in) crab is believed to have made its journey by clinging to barnacles on a buoy for three months, surviving storms, predators and sharp changes in sea temperature.

Fastest-swimming crustacean

Henslow's swimming crab (*Polybius henslowii*), native to the eastern Atlantic Ocean, has been timed at 1.3 m/s (4 ft 3 in/s) in captivity. It is likely that it would be able to swim even faster under natural conditions in the wild.

First venomous crustacean

Xibalbanus (previously *Speleonectes*) *tulumensis* feeds upon other crustaceans. Its claws inject a cocktail of chemicals including a paralysing neurotoxin similar to rattlesnake venom. The toxin breaks down the victim's body tissues, turning it into liquid to be sucked up from its prey's exoskeleton. The blind crustacean inhabits underwater caves of the Caribbean, Canary Islands and Western Australia. *Xibalbanus tulumensis* is a member of the remipede class and is the only crustacean that possesses venom.

Largest freshwater crustacean

The Tasmanian giant freshwater crayfish (*Astacopsis gouldi*) is also the **largest freshwater invertebrate** of any kind. Native to small streams in Tasmania, Australia, it can measure 80 cm (2 ft 7 in) and weigh 5 kg (11 lb). Overfishing and habitat loss have seen the species decline and it is listed as endangered.

Largest extent of colour vision

Stomatopods such as mantis shrimps have eight different types of colour photoreceptor in their eyes (humans have three). These reef-dweller crustaceans can distinguish numerous shades within the electromagnetic spectrum's ultraviolet waveband – entirely invisible to humans. Their clear-eyed vision is used to identify prey (which is often semi-transparent) and dodge predators.

FACT

Pictured inset is a 1-m-long American lobster found off the coast of Maine, USA, on 17 Feb 2012. The 18-kg beast was dubbed Rocky before being released back into the wild.

Heaviest marine crustacean

The American or North Atlantic lobster (*Homarus americanus*) is the heaviest marine crustacean. On 11 Feb 1977, a specimen weighing 20.14 kg (44 lb 6 oz) and measuring 1.06 m (3 ft 6 in) from tail fan to the tip of its largest claw was caught off Nova Scotia, Canada. It was sold to a New York restaurant owner.

CRUSTACEAN LENGTHS

Tasmanian giant freshwater crayfish: 80 cm

Robber or coconut crab: 1 m

Giant spider crab: leg-span 3.69 m

Giant acorn barnacle: 7 cm

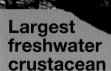

Actual Size

Parasitic pea crab: 6.3 mm

Common sea slater: 3 cm

Water fleas (branchiopods): 0.25 mm

Glossary

Arthropod: animal from the phylum Arthropoda (meaning "jointed leg") that includes insects, arachnids and crustaceans; arthropods account for 80% of all animal species.

Crustacean: a group (or sub-phylum) of arthropod comprising 67,000 described species, from the minuscule 0.094-mm-long *Stygotantulus stocki* up to the giant spider crab (*Macrocheira kaempferi*) with its 3.69-m span from claw to claw (see above right). They are distinguished from other groups of arthropods by their two-parted limbs and the form taken by their larvae.

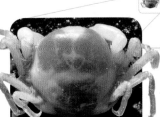

Actual Size

Smallest crab

Parasitic pea crabs (*Pinnotheres pisum*) can measure 6.3 mm (0.25 in) across. They live in the organ cavity of bivalve molluscs – such as oysters ·and mussels – where they tuck into food collected by their molluscan host's gills.

Sharpest night vision for an animal

Gigantocypris is a marine crustacean living at depths of more than 1,000 m (3,300 ft) with almost no sunlight. But this genus of ostracod has eyes with an f-number (a measure of light sensitivity) of 0.25. In comparison, humans measure around f-2.55. Each eye possesses a pair of high-powered parabolic reflectors that direct the dim light on to the retina.

Largest barnacle

The giant acorn barnacle (*Balanus nubilus*) stands up to 12.7 cm (5 in) high and measures 7 cm (2.76 in) across. It lives as far down as 91 m (300 ft) and its side plates withstand strong currents. The barnacle is food for whelk snails, which can drill into the shell.

Largest copepod

Pennella balaenopterae is a parasite living on the backs of fin whales (*Balaenoptera physalus*). It can attain a length of 32 cm (1 ft 0.5 in).

Largest woodlouse

The common sea slater (*Ligia oceanica*) can grow up to 3 cm (1.2 in) long and is twice as long as it is broad. Its speed when startled has earned it the nickname "sea cockroach". It is an aquatic species that breathes air and lives on rocky coasts of temperate waters.

Largest marine crustacean

The giant spider crab (*Macrocheira kaempferi*), found off the south-eastern coast of Japan, has a leg-span of up to 3.69 m (12 ft 1.5 in). Pictured here is "Big Daddy", whose leg-span of 3.11 m (10 ft 2.5 in) makes him the **widest crustacean in captivity**. The leggy crab – named after a famous British wrestler – was measured at Sea Life in Blackpool, UK, on 8 Aug 2013.

Rarest crayfish

The endangered Shasta crayfish (*Pacifastacus fortis*) is native to Shasta County in California, USA, where it is found along portions of the Pit River. It occurs in only 13 km² (5 sq mi) of the river and its fragmented population probably numbers no more than 300 in total.

Smallest crustacean

Stygotantulus stocki measures 0.094 mm (0.003 in), also making it the **smallest arthropod** of any kind. It is an ectoparasite – a parasite on the surface – of crustaceans called harpacticoid copepods. The **smallest non-parasitic crustaceans** are water fleas (branchiopods) of the genus *Alonella*. These freshwater fleas measure less than 0.25 mm (0.009 in).

Fastest land crustacean

Tropical ghost crabs of the genus *Ocypode* can scuttle up to 2 m/s (6 ft/s) – not bad for sideways sprinters. This is equivalent to a human running at 324 km/h (201 mph).

Coconut crab: island monster

The **largest** (and **heaviest**) land-living **crustacean** is the robber or coconut crab (*Birgus latro*), which lives on tropical islands and atolls in the Indo-Pacific. It can weigh as much as 4.1 kg and has a leg-span of up to 1 m. This type of hermit crab feeds on rotting coconuts, although it will eat a variety of other food. It has been hunted almost to extinction on many islands in the Indian and Pacific Oceans, owing to both its size and its use as a culinary delicacy. The young are hatched in the sea but return to land and lose the ability to survive in the water.

i Hermit crabs

Hermit crabs (Paguroidea) aren't true crabs (they have three rather than four pairs of walking legs), but they are crustaceans. They don't have shells; instead, they reuse those that have been abandoned by other creatures. The hermit crab is the **animal with the most chromosomes** (the body's hereditary information), with 127 pairs, compared with just 23 pairs in humans.

Insects & arachnids

For every human, there are an estimated **1.4 billion insects** alive right now

SEE IT 3D WITH THE FREE APP

The **fastest insect wing-beat** under natural conditions is 62,760 beats per min by a tiny midge of the genus *Forcipomyia*.

Most venomous spider

The Brazilian wandering spiders of the genus *Phoneutria* are highly venomous, particularly the Brazilian huntsman (*P. fera*), which has the most active neurotoxic venom of any living spider. Just 0.006 mg of its venom is sufficient to kill a mouse.

Largest appetite relative to weight

The caterpillar of the North American silk moth (*Antheraea polyphemus*) eats more food relative to its own body weight than any other animal. Living on the leaves of oak, birch, willow and maple trees, it eats up to 86,000 times its own weight during the first 56 days of its life.

Fastest insect
A speed of 5.4 km/h (3.36 mph), or 50 body lengths per sec, was registered by *Periplaneta americana* – the familiar American cockroach of the order Dictyoptera – in 1991.

The **fastest caterpillar** is the larva of the mother-of-pearl moth (*Pleuroptya ruralis*), which can travel at 1.37 km/h (0.8 mph).

The **fastest flying insect** is the Australian dragonfly (*Austrophlebia costalis*), at 58 km/h (36 mph) in short bursts. In 1917, a ground velocity of 98.6 km/h (61.3 mph) was recorded over 73–82 m (240–270 ft).

Least classifiable insect

A newly discovered nymph (juvenile) form of planthopper resembles nymphs from at least four taxonomic families but has defied classification. It was found in the rainforest of south-eastern Suriname.

Actual Size

Most toxic insect venom

Pogonomyrmex maricopa is a stinging species of harvester ant native to Arizona, USA. The LD_{50} value of its venom (the dosage required to kill 50% of mice subjected to it) is 0.12 mg/kg when injected intravenously into mice.

Actual Size

Loudest insect
The African cicada (*Brevisana brevis*), discovered in 1850, produces a calling song with a mean sound pressure level of 106.7 decibels at a distance of 50 cm (1 ft 7 in). Songs play a vital role in cicada communication and reproduction.

Most aggressive butterfly
The powerful flier *Charaxes candiope* of Uganda actively dive-bombs people who invade its territory.

Longest insect tongue

Most times for an insect to moult
All insects moult several times during the course of their lifetime. Up to 60 moults have been recorded for the fire brat (*Thermobia domestica*), a primitive, wingless insect that is widely distributed in North America and other temperate regions

Largest ant

The wingless queen of the fulvous driver ant *Dorylus fulvus* is native to South Africa. It grows to a maximum length of 5 cm (1.9 in), some 2 cm (0.7 in) longer than the male of the species. The term "fulvous" describes the ant's characteristic tawny-brown colouration.

Actual Size

> **OUTSIZED INSECTS, CENTIPEDES AND ARACHNIDS**

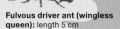

Fulvous driver ant (wingless queen): length 5 cm

Titan beetle: body length 15 cm

Giant centipede: length 26 cm

Hercules beetle: length including horns 17 cm

Giant water bug: length 11.5 cm

Chan's megastick: length 35.5 cm

Goliath bird-eating spider: leg-span 28 cm

worldwide. The fire brat moults throughout its life, whereas most insects only do so during their juvenile (nymph, or larval) stage.

Most dangerous bee
The Africanized honey bee (*Apis mellifera scutellata*) will generally only attack when provoked but is persistent in pursuit. It is very aggressive and fiercely protective of territories up to a 0.8-km (0.5-mi) radius. Its venom is no more potent than that of other bees, but it attacks in swarms so the number of stings inflicted can be fatal.

Most bee stings removed
The greatest number of bee stings sustained by any surviving human subject

Hardiest beetle

The most indestructible beetle is a small species known as *Niptus hololeucus*. Researcher Malcolm Burr has revealed that no fewer than 1,547 specimens were discovered alive inside a bottle of casein protein that had been stoppered for 12 years.

Actual Size

is 2,443, by Johannes Relleke at the Kamativi tin mine, Gwaii River, in Wankie District, Zimbabwe (then Rhodesia), on 28 Jan 1962. All the stings were removed and counted.

Most painful insect sting
In 1983, entomologist Justin O Schmidt (USA) published a detailed pain index of insect stings, based on a four-point scale. The most painful sting, registering 4.0+ on his index, was that of the bullet ant (*Paraponera clavata*), native to Central

Fastest spider

Actual Size

The giant house spider (*Tegenaria gigantea*) is native to North America. An adult female studied during tests in the UK in 1970 attained a running speed of 1.90 km/h (1.18 mph) over short distances. This is equivalent to covering 33 times her own body length in 10 sec.

and South America. Schmidt described its sting as "like walking over flaming charcoal with a 3-in [8-cm] rusty nail in your heel".

LARGEST...

Wasp
A female giant tarantula-hawk wasp (*Pepsis heros*) found in Peru had a wing-span of 12.15 cm (4.75 in) and body length of *c.* 6.2 cm (2.25 in).

Actual Size

Heaviest moth

Native to Australia, the heaviest species of moth is the giant wood moth (*Endoxyla cinereus*). The weightiest specimen on record is an adult female that measured 31.2 g (1.1 oz). Females have a wing-span of approximately 25 cm (9.8 in), while males are only about half that size.

Actual Size

Lowest temperature endured by insects

The woolly bear caterpillar of the Greenland tiger moth (*Gynaephora groenlandica*) lives in the high Arctic. It can survive being frozen at -50°C (-58°F) for 10 months of the year.

Bee
Females of the king bee (*Chalicodoma pluto*) from the Moluccas Islands of Indonesia measure

3.9 cm (1.5 in) long. The **smallest species of bee** is *Perdita minima* of south-western USA – measuring just under 2 mm (0.07 in) long and weighing only 0.333 mg (that's 3,030 bees to the gram, or 85,133 to the ounce).

Scorpion
A specimen of *Heterometrus swannerdami* found during World War II in the village of Krishnarajapuram, India, measured 29.2 cm (11.5 in) in length from the tips of the pedipalps (pincers) to the end of the sting.

Cockroach
A preserved female *Megaloblatta longipennis* in the collection of Akira Yokokura (JPN) measures 9.7 cm (3.8 in) long and 4.5 cm (1.75 in) across.

Augmented Reality alert!
3D ON THIS PAGE

Heaviest praying mantis

Actual Size

Native to India, Myanmar, Nepal and Sri Lanka, the weightiest species of praying mantis is the giant Asian mantis *Hierodula membranacea*. The heaviest specimen on record was a well-fed female that was reliably weighed and found to tip the scales at 9 g (0.3 oz) – approximately the same as nine paper clips.

Longest insect tongue

The tongue, or proboscis, of Morgan's sphinx (hawk) moth (*Xanthopan morganii praedicta*) measures up to 35 cm (1 ft 1 in) – more than twice the entire length of the moth itself. This enables the moth to reach the nectar deep inside the star-shaped flowers of the comet, or Darwin's orchid. The insect is native to Madagascar.

Actual Size

 Apian alert: bees at risk

Since around 2006, many bee populations have collapsed – a phenomenon known as colony collapse disorder. Possible causes include poisoning from pesticides, destruction of the bees' natural environments and parasites that feed on bees' blood. The welfare of the bee impacts directly on our own food chain: with no bees to pollinate them, up to half of our fruit and vegetable plants would disappear, along with animal-feed crops.

Bee-suited: attracting a mantle

A "mantle" is an enormous cluster of bees that forms a protective layer around the queen bee. By wearing the queen in a locket around the neck, an individual can encourage a mantle of bees to form around their body. This rippling mass of bees can weigh many kilograms, with the **heaviest mantle of bees** record currently standing at 61.2 kg – about the same weight as an adult man – by Ruan Lianming (CHN) on 6 May 2012. Ruan used 56 queens to attract an estimated 621,000 bees in Fengxin County, Jiangxi Province, China.

What's the buzzzzz?

First use of apitherapy: The Greek physician Galen (AD 129–200) is said to have used honey and bee venom to treat baldness.

Largest bee house: A bee house measuring 13 x 1.27 x 0.36 m was built in Barking, London, UK, on 18 Jun 2011.

Largest wasp nest: A nest measuring 3.7 x 1.75 m and *c.* 5.5 m in circumference was found at Waimauku, New Zealand, in Apr 1963.

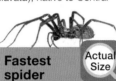

Mostly molluscs

Octopuses don't have eight legs – they have **two legs and six arms**

Deepest octopus
The dumbo octopus (*Grimpoteuthis*) lives as far down as 1,500 m (5,000 ft). Its body, 20 cm (7.8 in) long, is soft and semi-gelatinous, enabling the octopus to resist the great pressure found at this depth. It travels by moving its fins, pulsing its webbed arms (octopus limbs are called arms rather than tentacles) or pushing water through a funnel as a form of jet propulsion.

Most bioluminescent octopus
Squids include many bioluminescent species but only *Stauroteuthis syrtensis* lights up the octopus world in a significant way. It uses a row of sucker-like structures that glow blue-green and emit light at 470 nanometres (a wavelength that travels well under water). Researchers believe the flashing entices prey within reach.

Smallest octopus
With an average arm span of less than 5.1 cm (2 in), *Octopus arborescens* is the smallest species. It is found in Sri Lanka.

First complete nervous system
In 2013, scientists announced a nervous system had been found in a 3-cm-long (1.18-in) fossil belonging to a previously unknown species of segmented marine arthropod. This creature is an ancestor of chelicerates (spiders, scorpions and horseshoe crabs). Belonging to the extinct genus *Alalcomenaeus*, it lived more than 520 million years ago in the Cambrian period in the seas of south-west China.

Heaviest colossal squid
Colossal squid are shorter than giant squid but they make up for it in weight. One specimen of adult male colossal squid (*Mesonychoteuthis hamiltoni*) weighed c. 450 kg (990 lb) when caught by fishermen in the Ross Sea of Antarctica in 2007.

Rarest jellyfish
The Cookii Monster (*Crambione cookii*) of Australia is pink, 50 cm (1 ft 8 in) long and very venomous. Recorded in 1910 in Cooktown, Queensland, the species disappeared until a specimen was caught in 2013 off Queensland's Sunshine Coast by Puk Scivyer of nearby UnderWater World, where it now resides.

Largest invertebrate
An Atlantic giant squid (*Architeuthis dux*) that washed up in Thimble Tickle Bay, Newfoundland, Canada, on 2 Nov 1878 had a body measured at 6.1 m (20 ft) long and one tentacle reaching 10.7 m (35 ft), giving a total of 16.8 m (55 ft). Pictured is a giant squid snapped in Feb 1996 in New Zealand.

Largest clam
The marine giant clam (*Tridacna gigas*) lives on the Indo-Pacific coral reefs. A specimen measuring 1.15 m (3 ft 9 in) and weighing 333 kg (734 lb) was collected off Ishigaki Island, Okinawa, Japan, in 1956. It was examined in 1984 when experts estimated that it weighed over 340 kg (750 lb) when alive.

Most venomous gastropod
Predatory marine shells called cone shells (genus *Conus*) deliver a fast-acting neurotoxic venom. While several species are capable of delivering enough toxin to kill humans, the geographer cone (*C. geographus*) of the Indo-Pacific is particularly dangerous and should never be handled.

Longest bivalve mollusc
Bivalves, such as clams and oysters, have a hinged shell. The longest bivalve is the giant shipworm (*Kuphus polythalamia*), a marine species that lives in a tubular shell. The longest specimen measured 1.53 m (5 ft).

⊗ For news of life off Earth, turn to p.24

Big suckers: giant octopus

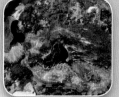

The **largest octopus** is the Pacific giant octopus (*Enteroctopus dofleini*, right), the biggest specimen of which sported an arm-span of 9.6 m – the same arm-span of eight adult men! Despite their size, they are not exempt from predators but, like most cephalopods, they have a good defence mechanism: above left is a Pacific giant squirting a plume of ink in its wake as it evades attack. They are also masters of camouflage and can change colour – and even texture – to match their surroundings (bottom left).

FACT
Centipedes don't have 100 legs but do have an uneven number of leg pairs.

ⓘ Full of venom
All octopuses, cuttlefish and some squid are venomous. Fortunately, only the venom of one – the blue-ringed octopus – is powerful enough to kill humans.

Largest snail

An individual African giant snail (*Achatina achatina*) was recorded at 39.3 cm (1 ft 3.5 in) when fully extended, with a shell length of 27.3 cm (10.75 in). Weighing 900 g (2 lb), this specimen was named Gee Geronimo and was kept in Hove in the UK after being collected in Sierra Leone in Jun 1976.

FACT

Gee Geronimo's owner, Chris Hudson (UK), got divorced after his wife complained that the house was too full of snails – and that he even had a bucket of them under their bed.

Actual Size

LARGEST...

Centipede

The giant centipede (*Scolopendra gigantea*) of Central and South America is 26 cm (10 in) long. It preys on mice, lizards and frogs – and one group was found in Venezuela hanging upside down from cave roofs to feed on bats. The centipede uses modified jaws to catch its food, delivering venom that feels like an insect sting in humans and can cause swelling and fever.

Millipede

A fully grown African giant black millipede (*Archispirostreptus gigas*) owned by Jim Klinger of Coppell, Texas, USA, measures 38.7 cm (1 ft 3.2 in)

Oldest mollusc

In Oct 2007 at Bangor University in Wales, UK, scientists announced that the annual growth rings in the shell of a quahog clam (*Arctica islandica*) showed it to be 405–410 years old. This was later revised to 507. Alas, the clam was killed in dating.

in length and 6.7 cm (2.6 in) in circumference, and has 256 legs. The average length for this type of millipede is 16–28 cm (6–11 in).

Horseshoe crab

The Atlantic horseshoe crab (*Limulus polyphemus*) measures up to 60 cm (1 ft 11.5 in) in length, yet despite its name it is not a crab. An aquatic relative of arachnids, its appearance has been relatively unchanged for millions of years.

Marine snail

The largest marine gastropod is the trumpet or baler conch (*Syrinx aruanus*)

of Australia. A specimen collected in 1979 had a shell 77.2 cm (2 ft 6.4 in) long, with a maximum girth of 1.01 m (3 ft 3.75 in). It weighed nearly 18 kg (40 lb) when alive.

Eye-to-body ratio

Vampyroteuthis infernalis – the "vampire squid from hell" – has a body measuring 28 cm (11 in) in length and eyes with a diameter of 2.5 cm (0.9 in). The ratio is almost 1:11 – the human equivalent of eyes the size of table tennis bats! Squid also have the largest eyes in absolute terms (see below).

Newest slug

Science was already aware of the giant pink slug (*Triboniophorus aff. graeffei*) of New South Wales, Australia, but it was thought to be an unusual colour variety of the red triangle slug (*Triboniophorus graeffei*). In Jun 2013, genetic results revealed it to be a species in its own right.

SIZING CEPHALOPODS, MYRIAPODS AND MOLLUSCS

Ash-black slug: length 30 cm

Atlantic horseshoe crab: length 60 cm

Giant centipede: length 26 cm

African giant black millipede: length 38.7 cm

African giant snail: snout-to-tail length 39.3 cm

Atlantic giant squid: length up to 16.8 m, has the **largest eye of any animal** (above), at 40 cm in diameter

 Superlative squid

Smallest: 1.27-cm-long *Parateuthis tunicata*.

Most bioluminescent: firefly squid (*Watasenia scintillans*) emit flashes of light.

First video of giant squid in natural habitat: Jul 2012, filmed south of Tokyo in the Pacific Ocean.

First giant squid captured: seven juveniles caught off the coast of New Zealand in Mar 2002.

Pets

There are **70 million** pet dogs and **74.1 million** pet cats in the USA

Oldest bearded dragon

Guinness (b. 26 Jul 1997), a bearded dragon owned by Nik Vernon (UK), was 16 years 129 days old when he died on 2 Dec 2013. Bearded dragons generally live to about eight years in the wild in Australia and typically a maximum of 14 years in captivity.

Largest breed of spaniel

Named after Clumber Park in Nottingham, UK, the Clumber spaniel has been a favourite of aristocracy and royalty. The breed standard specifies a weight of 39 kg (86 lb) and a height of 51 cm (20 in). The Clumber is loyal but a little demanding: its white coat sheds throughout the year, and the breed tends to slobber and snore.

Smallest breed of poodle

Poodles can be found in standard, miniature and – the smallest – toy categories. To qualify, a toy poodle must have a maximum height to the withers of either 28 cm (11 in) or 25.4 cm (10 in), depending on the guidelines of different international bodies.

Oldest pig ever

Pig Floyd (b. 17 Feb 1992) – a pot-bellied pig owned by Kris and Tricia Fernandez of Baton Rouge, Louisiana, USA – was 21 years 166 days old when assessed on 2 Aug 2013.

More amazing animals: pp.66–67

First pet hedgehog

A relative of the Algerian hedgehog (*Atelerix algirus*) was domesticated during the 4th century BC by the Romans. They were primarily raised for their meat and quills, but were also kept as pets, as several different species are today. Modern popular breeds are the Egyptian long-eared hedgehog (*Hemiechinus auritus auritus*), the Indian long-eared hedgehog (*H. collaris*) and the African pygmy hedgehog (*A. albiventris*), which is a hybrid of the Algerian and the four-toed hedgehog.

Most intelligent breed of dog

The Border collie is the smartest pooch of all, followed by the poodle and German shepherd, according to Professor Stanley Coren (USA) of the University of British Columbia, Canada, and

200 professional dog obedience judges. Top dogs understand a vocabulary of 250 words – as many as a two-year-old human child. Bottom of the class are the bulldog, the Basenji and, last of all, the Afghan hound.

Most expensive sheepdog

Shepherd Eddie Thornalley (UK) bought Marchup Midge (both above) from UK breeder and trainer Shaun Richards at an auction in Skipton in North Yorkshire, UK, on 26 Oct 2012. His winning bid was £10,080 ($16,216).

COLOSSAL COMPANIONS

Tallest horse: 2.10 m, Big Jake, Belgian gelding

Tallest donkey: 1.72 m, Romulus, American Mammoth Jackstock

Largest pet canary: 22 cm, Parisian frill

Largest pony breed: 1.52 m, Connemara

Tallest male dog: 111.8 cm, Zeus, Great Dane

Tallest female dog: 98.15 cm, Morgan, Great Dane

Tallest domestic cat: 48.3 cm, Trouble, Savannah Islands

Largest domestic rabbit: 91 cm, Flemish giant rabbit

Top cats

Most popular in politics: Socks was adopted by future President Bill and Hillary Clinton (USA) in 1991. During his eight-year stint at the White House, Socks was said to have received 75,000 letters and parcels a week.

Most travelled: In Feb 1984, Hamlet escaped from his cage on a flight from Toronto in Canada and became caught behind aeroplane panelling for over seven weeks, accidentally travelling nearly 965,000 km.

Wealthiest: In 1988, Ben Rea (UK) bequeathed his £7-million ($12.5-million) fortune to Blackie, the last of the 15 cats he shared his mansion with.

i Nero the friendly lion

George Wombwell (UK, 1777–1850) had a successful travelling menagerie. It included Nero, a lion so docile that he refused to fight dogs when his owner arranged a bout. Wombwell's tomb is still viewable today: he was buried in London's gothic Highgate Cemetery, under a statue of sleepy Nero, lying with his head on his paws.

Shortest cat

Lilieput, a nine-year-old female Munchkin cat, measured 13.34 cm (5.25 in) from the floor to the shoulders on 19 Jul 2013. She is owned by Christel Young of Napa, California, USA.

Gone but not fur-gotten is Colonel Meow (inset), the characterful **cat with the longest fur**, who passed away on 30 Jan 2014. His fur measured 22.87 cm (9 in) and his owner was Anne Marie Avey (USA).

Smallest breed of horse

Originally developed in Argentina in 1868, the smallest recognized breed of horse is the Falabella miniature horse, which has an average height at the withers of 8 hands (81.2 cm; 32 in). While miniature horses are shorter, they are also smaller – their limbs and body grow in proportion. The use of a "hand" (10.1 cm; 4 in) as a unit of measurement goes back to ancient Egypt.

Largest breed of horse

The English Shire horse is a type of draught horse. Stallions stand 17 hands (173 cm; 5 ft 8 in) or even taller at maturity. It was one of these working animals that was the **tallest** and **heaviest** horse ever to be documented. Sampson (later renamed Mammoth) was a Shire gelding born in 1846. By 1850, he measured 21.2½ hands (2.19 m; 7 ft 2.5 in) and later weighed 1,524 kg (3,359 lb). Mammoth was bred by Thomas Cleaver of Toddington Mills in Bedfordshire, UK.

Largest breed of pony

The Connemara pony of North America ranges in height from 13 to 15 hands (132–152.4 cm; 4 ft 4 in–5 ft).

The **smallest breed of pony** is the Shetland pony. Often used by children learning to ride, its maximum accepted height is 107 cm (3 ft 6 in) at the withers, with a minimum of 71 cm (2 ft 4 in). Dwarf ponies have a genetic mutation that may make them smaller, but the Shetland pony is the smallest of the pure breeds.

Tallest donkey

Romulus is an American Mammoth Jackstock who measured 17 hands (1.72 m; 5 ft 8 in) tall on 8 Feb 2013. He is owned by Cara and Phil Yellott of Red Oak in Texas, USA. His brother, Remus, was measured at over 16 hands (1.62 m; 5 ft 4 in). The minimum height for the big breed is 14.2 hands (1.47 m; 4 ft 10 in).

Tallest dogs

Zeus (USA, left), a Great Dane, measured 111.8 cm (3 ft 8 in) tall on 4 Oct 2011. Owned by Denise Doorlag and family of Otsego in Michigan, USA, Zeus is both the **tallest male dog** and the **tallest dog ever**. The **tallest female dog** is also a Great Dane: Morgan, owned by Dave and Cathy Payne of Melbourne in Ontario, Canada, measured 98.15 cm (3 ft 2.6 in) to the shoulder on 9 Jan 2013. The two dogs met for the first time in Oct 2013.

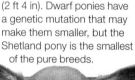

Smallest dog

Vanesa Semler of Dorado, Puerto Rico, owns a female Chihuahua called Milly, who measured 9.65 cm (3.8 in) tall on 21 Feb 2013. As a puppy, she was fed using an eyedropper and was small enough to fit on a teaspoon.

First pets: domestic bliss

As our ancestors formed settlements, animals became domesticated for practical uses. They were used for food and clothing or would help us work. Dogs became the **first domestic animals**, around 13,000 BC in the Middle East. The bones of the **oldest known domestic cat** date back 9,500 years, and were discovered in a neolithic village on Cyprus next to its presumed owner. Records of the **first domestic elephants** tell of their use as beasts of burden at least 4,000 years ago in the present-day area covering Pakistan and India.

And finally...

- **Longest tail on a dog:** Finnegan, from Calgary, Canada, is an Irish wolfhound with a 72.29-cm tail, as of 15 Aug 2013.
- **Largest donation of pet food in one week:** Full Stride Media (Pty) Ltd (ZAF) collected 10,009 kg of pet food for animal charities between 6 and 13 Oct 2013 in Johannesburg, South Africa.

Animals in action

GWR's human talent always faces fierce **furry or feathered competition**...

Most treats balanced on a dog's nose
Despite his name, Monkey is a dog, and on 2 Jul 2013 he balanced 26 treats on his nose, appearing with handler Meghan Fraser (USA) on the set of *Guinness World Records Unleashed* in California, USA.

Most drink cans opened by a parrot
Zac the macaw opened 35 cans using just his beak in San Jose, California, USA, on 12 Jan 2012. The talented bird also set the record for the **most slam dunks by a parrot in one minute**, with 22 dunks into a specially designed net on 30 Dec 2011.

Longest jump by a cat
Flying feline Alley cat-apulted himself to a record with a 1.82-m (6-ft) leap on 27 Oct 2013. Alley, a rescue cat owned by Samantha Martin (USA), is part of the Amazing Acro-Cats touring show.

Fastest 30 m on a scooter by a dog
Owner Karen Cobb (USA) didn't need to do much to encourage her enthusiastic four-year-old Briard, Norman, to scoot 30 m (98 ft) in 20.77 sec, at All-Tournament Players Park in Georgia, USA, on 12 Jul 2013.

FACT
Nifty Norman also rides bicycles (with stabilizers, of course), skateboards and surfboards.

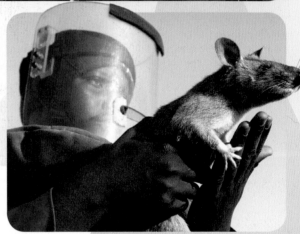

Largest working rodent
The Gambian giant pouched rat (*Cricetomys gambianus*) measures 90 cm (3 ft) long and is used to sniff out landmines in Mozambique.

The rats are trained to associate the scent of explosives with a food reward and identify the presence of explosives by grooming and scratching at the earth.

Highest-ranking penguin

Colonel-in-Chief Sir Nils Olav is the male king penguin mascot of Norway's Hans Majestet Kongens Garde (King's Guard) unit. He lives in the UK's Edinburgh Zoo, which received its first king penguin, from Norway, in 1913. In 1972, when the Norwegian King's Guard visited the zoo, a penguin was adopted and was named Nils Olav in honour of King Olav V. The current incumbent became Colonel-in-Chief on 18 Aug 2005.

Fastest dog to retrieve a person from water

Search-and-rescue dog Jack, a black vom Mühlrad, is handled by Hans-Joachim Brückmann (DEU). On 11 Jun 2013, Jack retrieved one of his handler's assistants from a distance of 25 m (82 ft) in 1 min 36.81 sec on the Kaarster See lake in Kaarst, Germany.

First dog to detect diabetic episodes

Armstrong the Labrador was trained in 2003 by Mark Ruefenacht (USA) to detect, via scent, the chemical changes leading to hypoglycaemia (low blood sugar) – a condition that can cause a diabetic to slip into a coma. The Dogs for Diabetics charity was founded in 2004, following Armstrong's success.

SEE IT 3D WITH THE FREE APP

FACT

Jiff appeared in a Katy Perry video ("Dark Horse", 2013) and in the film *Adventures of Bailey: A Night in Cowtown* (USA, 2013).

Augmented Reality alert! 3D ON THIS PAGE

Fastest 10 m on hind legs by a dog

Jiff the Pomeranian covered 10 m (32 ft) in 6.56 sec at TOPS Kennels in Grayslake, Illinois, USA, on 9 Sep 2013. The plucky Pom, who performs various tricks, can also walk on his front paws (inset), covering 5 m (16 ft) in a record 7.76 sec – the **fastest 5 m on front legs by a dog**.

Plants

A notch or limb on a tree stays the **same distance** from the ground

First use of spices in cooking

Garlic mustard plant seeds were used between 6,150 and 5,800 years ago (around 4000 BC). In 2013, archaeologists announced that the spice had been found in European pottery shards.

Largest cashew nut tree

Natal's cashew tree (*Anacardium occidentale*) in Rio Grande do Norte, Brazil, covers approximately 7,500 m² (80,700 sq ft) with a perimeter of around 500 m (1,640 ft). That's a lot of nuts – indeed, the yield is up to 80,000 fruit per year. Some estimate the tree to be up to 1,000 years old, though it is also said that it was planted in 1888 by local fisherman Luiz Inácio de Oliveira.

to survive adverse surface conditions throughout the seasons. The largest is produced by the titan arum (*Amorphophallus titanum*) and commonly weighs around 50 kg (110 lb). The heaviest specimen weighed 117 kg (257 lb 15 oz) and was recorded in 2006 in the Botanical Garden of Bonn University in Germany.

The titan arum is also the **smelliest plant** when it blooms – which is fortunately relatively rarely. It releases an odour, comparable to that of rotten flesh, that can be smelled at a great distance to attract the carrion beetles and flesh flies that pollinate it. Like the **largest living flower** (right), its stench gives it the nickname "corpse flower".

Shiniest living objects

Marble berry (*Pollia condensata*) is a 1-m-tall (3-ft 3-in) herb native to Ghana. Resembling Christmas baubles, its vivid fruit is approximately 30% as reflective as a silver mirror. This is the highest reported light reflectivity of any biological material.

Largest corm

A corm is an underground plant stem that is used for storage by some plants

Largest horsetail

One of the oldest plant genera to survive, horsetail is a living fossil. It is the only surviving member of the

Largest branched inflorescence

A branched inflorescence is a cluster of flowers on a multi-branched stem as opposed to a single stem. The largest is that of the talipot palm (*Corypha umbraculifera*), which consists of up to several million creamy-white flowers. The palm is native to parts of India and Sri Lanka. Its inflorescence grows at the apex of the tree's trunk and is 6–8 m (19–26 ft) long.

Largest water lily

Native to freshwater lakes and bayous in the Amazon basin, the giant water lily (*Victoria amazonica*) has floating leaves measuring up to 3 m (10 ft) across and is held in place on an underwater stalk 7–8 m (23–26 ft) long. The leaves are supported by rib-like crossridges that are said to have inspired the metal girders of Crystal Palace in London, UK, built in 1851.

FACT

If evenly distributed, a mature giant water lily leaf can support up to 45 kg of weight.

Equisetopsida class, which once featured strongly in late Mesozoic period forests for up to 100 million years. Today, the Mexican giant horsetail (*Equisetum myriochaetum*) is the largest species, a primeval-looking plant reaching 7.3 m (24 ft) in height.

Largest poppy flowers
Coulter's Matilija poppy (*Romneya coulteri*) has silky white flowers around an eye-catching ball of golden stamens and grows to 13 cm (5.12 in) across. It can be found in southern California, USA, and northern Mexico and its bold display of flowers makes it a popular ornamental plant.

LARGEST PLANT SIZES

Redwood: height 115.24 m

Puya raimondii: height 10.7 m

Raffia palm: leaf length 20 m, stalk length 4 m

Talipot palm: length 6–8 m

Rafflesia arnoldii: width 91 cm, weight 11 kg

Giant water lily: width up to 3 m

⚡ Palmed off

Before the leaf of the raffia palm took the record, it was the giant water lily that was considered the **largest leaf**, in 1955 reported as 6.4 m. Back then, it was called *Victoria regina* before the name *Victoria amazonica* became widely used. Its common name is the royal water lily.

ℹ Trees of the Amazon

The Amazon basin and Guiana Shield area of South America has an estimated 16,000 tree species, of which just 227 species (1.4%) account for half of all Amazon trees. The rarest 11,000 species account for just 0.12% of the total number of trees in the region. The study from which this data is extracted, published in *Nature* in 2013, suggests that there is a total of 400 billion trees alive today in the Amazon rainforest.

Most massive plant by area

A network of quaking aspen trees (*Populus tremuloides*) grows in the Wasatch mountains, Utah, USA, covering 43 ha (106 acres) and weighing an estimated 6,000 tonnes (13,227,700 lb), making it also the **heaviest organism**. The clonal system is genetically uniform and acts as a single organism, with all the component trees changing colour or shedding leaves in unison. The network looks like a forest, but it is made up of plants that have grown from the root system of a single tree dating back at least 80,000 years.

Smallest bromeliad

While the best-known member of the bromeliad clan is the pineapple, its unlikely relation is Spanish moss (*Tillandsia usneoides*). Neither a moss nor Spanish, the beard-like growth is made up of the smallest bromeliads, with slender stems bearing tiny flowers and a series of leaves that cling together. It produces hanging thread-like chains that stretch up to 6 m (19 ft 8 in) long.

Tallest banksia

Banksias are Australian wildflowers of the genus Banksia, some of which are so large that they grow as tall as trees. The tallest species are the coast banksia (*Banksia integrifolia*) and the river banksia (*B. seminuda*), both of which can grow to 30 m (100 ft).

Tallest cycad

Cycads can look like palm trees and are sometimes grouped with them, but they are coning plants (like pine trees). Hope's cycad (*Lepidozamia hopei*) from Queensland, Australia, is the largest, growing to heights of 15 m (49 ft).

Tallest moss

Dawson's giant moss (*Dawsonia superba*), native to New Zealand, can grow to 60 cm (23.6 in) tall, even though its spores are no more than 0.01 mm in size.

Largest living flower

Rafflesia arnoldii gets its nickname "corpse flower" owing to its smell of rotting flesh (see also **smelliest plant**, left). And there is a lot of flower to sniff – it measures up to 91 cm (3 ft) across and weighs up to 11 kg (24 lb), with petals that are 1.9 cm (0.75 in) thick. The rare flower is native to south-east Asia and grows as a parasite inside and upon jungle vines.

i Assassin bugs

A trick employed by some carnivorous plants is to use "assassin bugs", which live unthreatened on the plant itself. The bugs feed off the trapped prey and the plant then absorbs what it needs from the bugs' excrement.

Actual Size

Largest prey of carnivorous plants

Of all the carnivorous plants, the ones that digest the largest prey belong to the Nepenthaceae family (genus *Nepenthes*). Both *N. rajah* and *N. rafflesiana* have been known to eat large frogs, birds and even rats. These species are commonly found in the rainforests of Asia, in particular Borneo, Indonesia and Malaysia. By using their colour, smell and nectar to attract prey, the plants then trap, kill and digest enzymes, before absorbing what is needed for nutrition.

Vaulting ambition: seed storage

The Svalbard Global Seed Vault is an underground facility located on the Norwegian island of Spitsbergen designed to store samples of the world's seeds as insurance against threats to biodiversity. Opened on 26 Feb 2006, it is the **largest seed vault**. The goal of the project is to store a total of 4.5 million samples (about 2 billion seeds) from 100 countries and – as of 2013 – more than 770,000 samples had been deposited. The vault cost £5 m and the location – 130 m into the permafrost of a mountain – was chosen for being the best suited to keeping the temperature of samples at a stable 18°C.

👁 Marine plants

Deepest: algae at 269 m, found by Mark and Diane Littler (both USA), The Bahamas, Oct 1984

Fastest growing: giant kelp (*Macrocystis pyrifera*), growing 34 cm per day

Largest clonal colony: DNA-sharing colony of Neptune grass, aka Mediterranean tapeweed (*Posidonia oceanica*), 8 km across, Mediterranean Sea, discovered 2006

:Humans

The surface area of a human lung is equivalent to the **size of a tennis court**

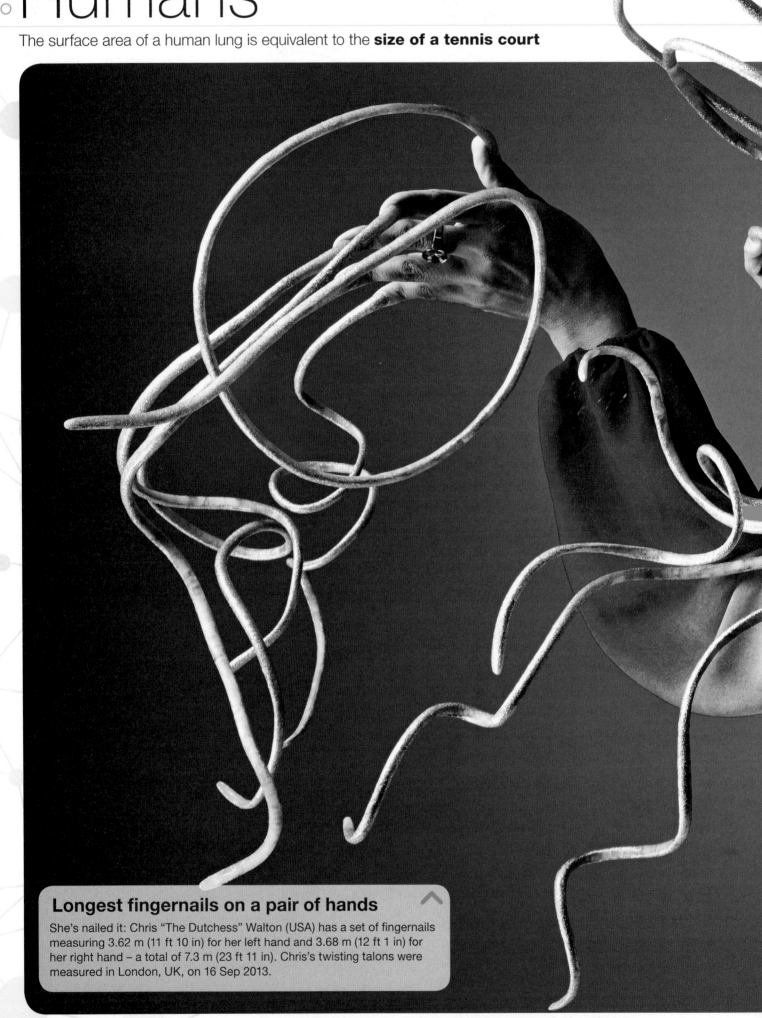

Longest fingernails on a pair of hands

She's nailed it: Chris "The Dutchess" Walton (USA) has a set of fingernails measuring 3.62 m (11 ft 10 in) for her left hand and 3.68 m (12 ft 1 in) for her right hand – a total of 7.3 m (23 ft 11 in). Chris's twisting talons were measured in London, UK, on 16 Sep 2013.

Contents

FACT
Fingernails grow at around 3.5 mm per month. And men's nails usually grow faster than women's.

Changing shapes

One constant in Guinness World Records' 60-year history has been the popularity of the Human Body chapter. It's the part of the book that most people flick to first, and many of the colourful characters who've filled the pages over the years have attained iconic status. Here, we look back at how some of these records have changed since our first edition in 1955.

Ask anyone to name a favourite record holder from the *Guinness World Records* book and the chances are they'll recall someone from the Human Body chapter. With visually striking record holders such as Robert Wadlow (**tallest man ever**), Lee Redmond (**longest fingernails**) and Robert Earl Hughes (**largest chest measurement** and former **heaviest man**), it comes as no surprise. It helps that their stories are so memorable. Who could forget that Wadlow died as a result of a blister from ill-fitting footwear? Or that Hughes was buried in a coffin the size of a piano case?

In this Flashback, we examine a selection of iconic Human Body superlatives that appeared in our first edition and identify who now holds the record. In some cases, such as the **tallest man ever**, the record hasn't changed in 60 years; in others, such as the **longest hair**, the current claimant has surpassed the original holder by a long way…

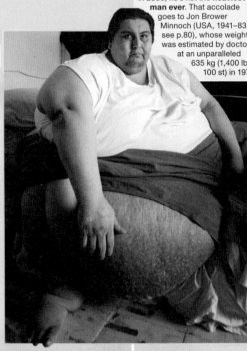

Longest moustache
Measured at 4.29 m (14 ft) on 4 Mar 2010, the face furniture of Ram Singh Chauhan (IND) earned him a place in the record books for the longest 'tache of all time. Ram started growing his facial hair in 1970 and, with his wife's help, grooms his whiskers daily with coconut and mustard oils.

Heaviest living male
Although his peak weight of 560 kg (1,235 lb; 88 st 3 lb) secured Manuel Uribe (MEX, pictured) the extant world record in 2006, he's not the **heaviest man ever**. That accolade goes to Jon Brower Minnoch (USA, 1941–83, see p.80), whose weight was estimated by doctors at an unparalleled 635 kg (1,400 lb; 100 st) in 1978.

Most children delivered at a single birth to survive
Nadya Suleman (USA) claimed headlines across the world on 26 Jan 2009 when she gave birth to six boys and two girls in Bellflower, California, USA. Dubbed "Octomom" by the US press, Suleman conceived with the aid of *in vitro* fertilization (IVF), swelling her family from six children to 14.

Oldest living woman
As we go to press, 115-year-old Misao Okawa of Japan is the oldest woman – and **oldest person** – alive on Earth (see p.76). She's not the **oldest woman ever**, of course: the all-time holder, also a woman, is Jeanne Louise Calment (FRA), who died on 4 Aug 1997 at the remarkable age of 122 years 164 days.

2015
1955

Most children	Oldest woman	Longest moustache	Heaviest man

"Multiple births"
Our first edition mentions fanciful accounts of women having as many as 36 children in a single birth (illustrated right is "Dorothea", who reportedly had 11 babies in 1755). Turning to "medically more acceptable cases", however, we go on to discuss the five Dionne babies – then, one of only three examples of quintuplets to survive – born on 28 May 1934.

YVONNE   EMILIE   MARIE   CECILE   ANNETTE

"Oldest centenarians"
Longevity is a subject that has clearly always been controversial. "Few subjects have been so obscured by deceit and falsehood", we wrote in 1955. The oldest woman then on record "for whom there exists acceptable evidence" was vicar's daughter Katherine Plunkett of County Louth, Ireland, who lived for 111 years 328 days from 1820 to 1932.

"Longest moustache"
Our earliest edition makes reference to Mr John Roy of Glasgow, UK, whose 41.91-cm-long (16.5-in) moustache is the "longest moustache owned by a member of Britain's 'Handlebar Club'." Roy, a smoker, once tried to have his moustache insured because of the fire risk, but couldn't afford the premiums.

"Heaviest heavyweight"
Now known as the man with the **widest chest measurement** (315 cm; 10 ft 4 in), Robert Earl Hughes' (USA) first appearance in GWR was as the **heaviest living man**, at 429 kg (946 lb; 67 st 8 lb). We also named the "heaviest man recorded in medical history" as Miles Darden (USA, 1799–1857), who peaked "slightly in excess of 1,000 lb (71 st 6 lb)" – or just over 453 kg.

Tallest living man
Towering 81.2 cm (2 ft 8 in) over GWR Editor-in-Chief Craig Glenday is Sultan Kösen of Turkey, who took the title of tallest living man – and human – in Feb 2009. Currently standing at 251 cm (8 ft 3 in), Sultan is one of just eight people over 8 ft (243 cm) to be ratified in the past 60 years.

FACT
As a teenager, Sultan was signed to play basketball for Galatasaray in Turkey but proved too tall to compete!

FACT
In 1955, we reported on a man claiming to be the world's tallest human at 289 cm (9 ft 6 in), but who actually turned out to be 222 cm (7 ft 3.5 in) when assessed medically!

Shortest living man and **woman**
Pictured here is GWR's Head of Records, Marco Frigatti, with the current shortest living humans. Jyoti Amge (IND, right) measured 62.8 cm (24.7 in) in Nagpur, India, on 16 Dec 2011 while, two months later, at a clinic in Kathmandu, Nepal, on 26 Feb 2012, Chandra Bahadur Dangi (NPL, left) reached just 54.6 cm (21.5 in). Mr Dangi is also officially ratified as the **shortest man ever measured** using modern medical equipment.

Longest hair (female)
The world's lengthiest locks (female) belong to Xie Qiuping of China at 5.62 m (18 ft 5.5 in). She has been growing her hair since 1973, from the age of 13. "It's no trouble at all. I'm used to it," she said. "But you need patience and you need to hold yourself straight when you have hair like this."

Greatest vocal range
Brazil's Georgia Brown has a vocal range that spans an incredible eight octaves (from G2 to G10), as verified at Aqui Jazz Atelier Music School in São Paulo on 18 Aug 2004 – a record that has remained unchallenged for more than a decade!

FACT
Xie travels with an assistant to hold her hair and help her manage her plentiful tresses.

| Longest hair | Greatest vocal range | Tallest man | Shortest man and woman |

"Longest tresses"
The "longest recorded feminine tresses", we said in 1955, "appear to be those of the 19th-century exhibitionist named Miss Owens, which were measured at 8 ft 3 in [251.4 cm]". Millie Owens was the "Queen of Long Hair" and enjoyed a career showing off her tresses and selling picture postcards.

"Greatest range"
The singer with the greatest range in 1955 was named as Miss Yma Sumac (born Zoila Augusta Emperatriz Chávarri del Castillo, 1922–2008), an acclaimed soprano from Peru: "She is reputed to have a range of five octaves from A# to B."

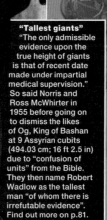

"Tallest giants"
"The only admissible evidence upon the true height of giants is that of recent date made under impartial medical supervision." So said Norris and Ross McWhirter in 1955 before going on to dismiss the likes of Og, King of Bashan at 9 Assyrian cubits (494.03 cm; 16 ft 2.5 in) due to "confusion of units" from the Bible. They then name Robert Wadlow as the tallest man "of whom there is irrefutable evidence". Find out more on p.81.

"Shortest dwarfs"
Sixty years ago, we named Miss Edith Barlow (below right) as the UK's "shortest living dwarf", at 55.8 cm (22 in), making her the world's **shortest living woman** by default. Only Walter Boehning, aka Böning (DEU, d. 1955, below) was shorter in absolute terms, claiming to be the "smallest dwarf in the world" at an unconfirmed height of just 52 cm (20.5 in). By 1964, Boehning was removed from the book owing to a lack of supporting evidence for his claimed stature.

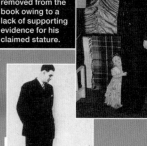

Senses & perception

The eyes can process around **36,000 pieces of information** every hour

FACT
Quieter V6 engines were introduced in the 2014 season – to the disappointment of many F1 fans!

Noisiest workplace

The loudest place on Earth that any human works for a sustained period is the cockpit of a Formula One racing car. For a driver sitting directly in front of the engine, the noise level has been measured at 140 dB. All drivers wear tailor-made earplugs.

HEARING

Highest detectable pitch

The upper limit of human hearing is accepted to be 20,000 Hz (hertz, or cycles per second), although this figure decreases with age. By way of comparison, bats emit pulses at up to 90,000 Hz.

The average accepted **lowest detectable pitch** by the human ear is 20 Hz, although in ideal conditions a young person can hear frequencies down to 12 Hz. Inaudible infrasound waves in the range of 4–16 Hz can be felt by the human body as physical vibrations.

Smallest bone

The stapes or stirrup bone measures 2.6–3.4 mm (0.1–0.13 in) in length and weighs 2–4.3 mg. One of the three auditory ossicles in the middle ear, the stapes plays a vital role in hearing.

SIGHT

Farthest object visible to the naked eye

Gamma-ray bursts are the birth cries of black holes. At 2:12 EDT on 19 Mar 2008, NASA's *Swift* satellite detected a gamma-ray burst from a galaxy some 7.5 billion light years away. Some 30–40 sec later, the optical counterpart of the burst was seen on Earth and captured by a robotic telescope. The explosion, known as GRB 080319B, was visible to the naked eye for around 30 sec.

Most active muscle

Scientists have estimated that human eye muscles move more than 100,000 times a day. Many of these rapid eye movements take place during the dreaming phase of sleep.

Most sensitive colour vision

The average human eye can perceive approximately a million colours. Our powers of colour vision derive from three types of cone cells in the eye, each responsive to different wavelengths of light. Our brains combine the signals to produce the perception of colour. Work completed by neuroscientist Gabriele Jordan at the University of Newcastle, UK, proved that some people have four cones,

Most valuable tongue

On 9 Mar 2009, Lloyd's reported that the tongue of Gennaro Pelliccia (UK) was insured for £10 m ($14 m). Pelliccia tastes every single batch of coffee beans made for Costa Coffee (UK) stores and has now learned to distinguish between thousands of different flavours.

enabling them to see more colours – about 99 million more, in fact. Jordan and her team created a test in which three subtle colour circles flashed on a screen. Only one person was able to distinguish them every time – an English female doctor known as "cDa29" – who has the most sensitive colour vision measured.

SMELL

Smelliest substance

The man-made foul-smelling substances "Who-Me?" and "US Government Standard Bathroom Malodor" have five and eight chemical

Quietest place

Tests performed on 18 Oct 2012 in the Anechoic Test Chamber at Orfield Laboratories in Minneapolis, Minnesota, USA, gave a background noise reading of just -13 dBA (decibels A-weighted). The term "dBA" denotes sound levels audible to the human ear – i.e., excluding extreme highs and lows.

HOW MANY SENSES DO WE HAVE?

Conventionally, we think of ourselves as having five senses: sight, hearing, taste, touch and smell. But if to "sense" something simply means to be aware of it, then we have many more than just these five "primary" senses. Here are a few others to consider:

Temperature: we can tell hot from cold and adjust accordingly

Pain: a mechanism for the body to sense damage

Balance: we are sensitive to body movement, direction and acceleration

Kinesthetics: the brain's parietal cortex enables us to tell where every part of our body is in relation to its other parts. (Test this by trying to touch your nose with your eyes closed!)

Interoception: our internal senses alert us when we are feeling hungry or tired

Time: we sense time passing

i Listen up: the decibel scale

The loudness, or intensity, of a sound is usually measured in decibels (dB). Decibels are calculated according to a logarithmic scale, which increases by a set ratio.

Total silence would measure 0 dB; a sound 10 times greater would be 10 dB, but a sound 100 times louder than 0 dB would measure only 20 dB, and sounds 1,000 times louder than 0 dB would register just 30 dB.

Listed here are typical decibel readings, recorded from a distance of 10 m away from the source.

DECIBEL (dB) READINGS

All readings from 10-m distance

dB	Sound
150	Jet engine
114	Train whistle
110	Subway train
107	Pneumatic riveter
89	Power saw
64	City traffic from inside car
46	Normal piano practice

Mapping the senses

This oddly shaped figure is a "sensory homunculus". This is what you'd look like if your body parts were in proportion to the areas of the brain concerned with sensory perception. Based on a model at the UK's Natural History Museum, it shows which areas of our bodies are the most sensitive to touch.

TOUCH

Most touch-sensitive part of the body
Our fingers have the highest density of touch receptors in the body. So sensitive are our fingers that we can distinguish two points of contact just 2 mm (0.07 in) apart. They can also detect a movement of just 0.02 microns – that's 200-thousandths of a millimetre (or 31-millionths of an inch).

TASTE

Bitterest substance
The bitterest-tasting substances are based on the denatonium cation and have been produced commercially as benzoate and saccharide. Taste detection levels are as low as just one part in 500 million, while a dilution of just one part in 100 million will leave a lingering taste.

Actual Size

FACT
The term "homunculus" was coined by alchemists in the 17th century and means simply "little person".

Most valuable nose
On 19 Mar 2008, Lloyd's reported that Ilja Gort (NLD) had his nose insured for 5 m euro (£3.9 m; $7.8 m). Gort, the owner of the vineyard Château la Tulipe de la Garde in Bordeaux, France, insured his nose in an attempt to protect his livelihood.

ingredients respectively. Bathroom Malodor smells primarily of human faeces and becomes incredibly repellant to people at a ratio of just two parts per million. It was originally developed to test the power of deodorizing products.

Smelliest molecule
The chemicals ethyl mercaptan (C_2H_5SH) and butyl seleno-mercaptan (C_4H_9SeH) have a distinctive smell reminiscent of a combination of rotting cabbage, garlic, onions, burnt toast and sewer gas.

Sweetest substance
Thaumatin, aka talin, from arils (appendages found on certain seeds) of the katemfe plant (*Thaumatococcus daniellii*) found in West Africa, is 3,250 times sweeter than sugar when compared with a 7.5% sucrose solution.

Lips have many sense receptors – which is one of the reasons why babies put objects into their mouths to learn about them.

When it comes to detecting our world, the tongue is highly sensitive, with a very dense concentration of neural connections.

Our fingers feel the world in sensory high definition by containing the highest density of touch receptors in the body. Sense receptors are more concentrated in smaller fingers. As a result, women tend to have a more developed tactile sensitivity than men.

The calves are among the least sensitive body parts – the brain can only distinguish two points of contact around 45 mm apart, compared with 2 mm for the fingers.

The 100,000–200,000 sense receptors on the sole of each foot help stabilize the whole body. They are at their most effective when we walk barefoot.

Talking scents: our sense of smell

Smell accounts for around 80% of our sense of taste. The first sense to develop, it is functional before we are born and is generally most sensitive in childhood. We can detect some 10,000 odours, but prolonged exposure to a smell causes our awareness of it to reduce quickly. We are more sensitive to smells in spring and summer, as the air is more moist then; exercise also increases the moisture in our nostrils, improving our sense of smell. Women have a stronger sense of smell than men – it is particularly acute during pregnancy.

Smells enter the nasal vestibule (nostril), where small hairs filter out dust and other fine particles. At the top of the nasal cavity are *c.* 40 million olfactory receptor cells, which detect the odourant molecules and send a message to the brain. When you eat, you "taste" the food using these same cells, which detect food odours in the mouth.

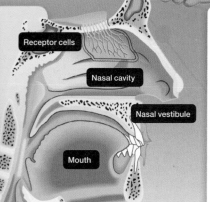

Receptor cells

Nasal cavity

Nasal vestibule

Mouth

And finally...
• **Longest echo:** 1 min 15 sec by Trevor Cox and Allan Kilpatrick (both UK) inside a disused oil tank at Inchindown in Highland, UK, on 3 Jun 2012.
• **Fastest time to boil water by passing electricity through body:** 1 min 22.503 sec, to heat 150 ml of water from 25°C to 97°C by Slavisa "Biba" Pajkic (SRB) in Istanbul, Turkey, on 13 Jul 2013.

Oldest people

The number of people over 65 is expected to **double to 800 million** by 2025

Largest gathering of centenarians

On 19 May 2013, the Regency Jewish Heritage Nursing & Rehabilitation Center in Somerset, New Jersey, USA, hosted a gathering of 31 people aged 100 years or over – only two of whom were men. Their combined ages stretched back to about 1100 BC, when the ancient Phoenicians were inventing the alphabet.

television, the modern motor car and aeroplanes. When asked on her 120th birthday what she expected of the future, she replied: "A very short one."

Parent-child (aggregate)
The highest combined age for a parent and child alive at the same time is 215 years in the case of 119-year-old Sarah Knauss (USA, 1880–1999) and her 96-year-old daughter Kathryn Knauss Sullivan (USA, 1903–2005). Knauss was the second-oldest human ever, reaching 119 years 97 days.

Adoptive parent
Frances Ensor Benedict (USA, 1918–2012) was 83 years 324 days old when she adopted her foster daughter Jo Anne

Oldest solo parachute jump (female)

Dilys Margaret Price (UK, b. 3 Jun 1932) made a parachute jump at Langar Airfield in Nottingham, UK, on 13 Apr 2013 at the age of 80 years 315 days. The **oldest solo parachute jump (male)** was made by Milburn Hart (USA, 1908–2010) in Washington, USA, on 18 Feb 2005. He was 96 years 63 days old.

Oldest competitive sprinter

Hidekichi Miyazaki (JPN, b. 22 Sep 1910) was 103 years 15 days old when he competed at the International Gold Masters in Kyoto, Japan, on 6 Oct 2013. He took part in the 100 m race, which he finished in 34.10 sec, shaving 2.67 sec off his previous best.

Longest separated twins
Twins Ann and Elizabeth were born to unmarried mother Alice Lamb in Aldershot, Hampshire, UK, on 28 Feb 1936. A decision was made to separate the twins for adoption, and Ann grew up unaware of her sister Lizzie, who now lives in Portland, Oregon, USA. The pair were finally reunited on 1 May 2014 after a record 77 years 289 days.

OLDEST...

Person (ever)
The greatest fully authenticated age to which any human has ever lived is 122 years 164 days by Jeanne Louise Calment (FRA, 21 Feb 1875–4 Aug 1997). She lived through two World Wars and the development of

Oldest BASE jumper

Donald Cripps (USA, b. 12 Sep 1929) was 84 years 37 days old when he parachuted off the 267-m-high (876-ft) New River Gorge Bridge near Fayetteville in West Virginia, USA, on 19 Oct 2013. BASE jumping – from **B**uildings, **A**ntennas, **S**pans (bridges) and **E**arth (cliffs) – is the most dangerous form of parachuting, owing to the short falls involved.

Benedict Walker (USA) on 5 Apr 2002 in Putnam County, Tennessee, USA. At 65 years 224 days, Jo Anne (b. 24 Aug 1936) is also the **oldest adoptee**.

Fashion model
Aged 85 years 295 days as of 22 Apr 2014, Daphne Selfe (UK, b. 1 Jul 1928) is the oldest professional fashion model. Her 60-year career includes appearances for Dolce & Gabbana and Gap, modelling in *Vogue* and *Marie Claire*, and posing for photographers David Bailey and Mario Testino.

Actor to win an Oscar
Christopher Plummer (UK, b. 13 Dec 1929) was 82 years 65 days old when he won the 2012 Best Supporting Actor Oscar for *Beginners* (2010).

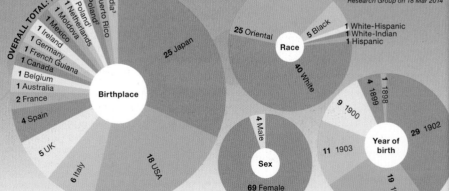

SUPERCENTENARIANS OF 111+ BY COUNTRY, AGE, SEX AND RACE

Last audit taken by the Gerontology Research Group on 18 Mar 2014

OVERALL TOTAL: 73
1 India[3]
1 Puerto Rico
1 Poland[2]
1 Netherlands
1 Moldova
1 Mexico
1 Ireland
1 Germany
1 French Guiana
1 Canada
1 Belgium
1 Australia
2 France
4 Spain
5 UK
6 Italy
18 USA
25 Japan

Birthplace

Race
25 Oriental
5 Black
40 White
1 White-Hispanic
1 White-Indian
1 Hispanic

Sex
4 Male
69 Female

Year of birth
1 1898
4 1899
9 1900
11 1903
19 1901
29 1902

¹ then Austrian Empire, ² then Russian Empire, ³ then British Empire

Lying about age is nothing new

In our first edition, we cautioned against "deceit and falsehood" encountered in claimed ages. Using information investigated by the Canadian government, we listed the greatest age reached by a male as 113, by Pierre Joubert, a French Canadian bootmaker (b. 15 Jul 1701, buried 18 Nov 1814). An investigation in 1990, however, established that Joubert was actually 82 at the time of his death, and that the person buried in 1814 was Joubert's homonymous ("same name") son, born in 1732.

FACT

Life expectancy has risen worldwide on average by four months each year since 1970.

My life will go on

The greatest age reached by a survivor of the *Titanic* was 104 years 72 days. Mary Wilburn, née Davis (UK, 1883–1987), was 28 when the ship sank in 1912.

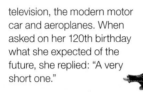

Oldest living person

Misao Okawa (JPN, b. 5 Mar 1898) turned 116 in 2014. Misao, who lives in a nursing home in Osaka, Japan, became the **oldest living woman** on 12 Jan 2013 and **oldest living person** on 12 Jun 2013. She is also the ninth oldest verified person ever.

OLDEST SUPERCENTENARIANS

As of 14 Apr 2014, there were 74 people whose age had been verified as passing the 111-year mark. The estimated worldwide total of living supercentenarians is 300–450 persons.

Who	Born	How old?
Misao Okawa (JPN)	5 Mar 1898	116 years 40 days
Jeralean Talley (USA)	23 May 1899	114 years 326 days
Susannah Mushatt Jones (USA)	6 Jul 1899	114 years 282 days
Bernice Madigan (USA)	24 Jul 1899	114 years 264 days
Emma Morano-Martinuzzi (ITA)	29 Nov 1899	114 years 136 days
Anna Henderson (USA)	5 Mar 1900	114 years 40 days
Antonia Gerena Rivera (USA)	19 May 1900	113 years 330 days
Ethel Lang (UK)	27 May 1900	113 years 322 days
Nabi Tajima (JPN)	4 Aug 1900	113 years 253 days
Blanche Cobb (USA)	8 Sep 1900	113 years 218 days

Source: Gerontology Research Group

Oldest living man

Shortly before going to press, we heard of the passing of Arturo Licata (ITA, 2 May 1902–24 Apr 2014), who had briefly been the oldest living man, aged 111 years 357 days at his death. His successor, Dr Alexander Imich (POL/RUS, now USA, b. 4 Feb 1903), took the title at the age of 111 years 79 days. He is pictured here in his Upper West Side home in New York.

Oldest newspaper delivery person (female)

Aged 88 years 346 days as of 27 Mar 2014, Beryl Walker (UK, b. 15 Apr 1925) was still delivering newspapers six mornings a week in Gloucester, Gloucestershire, UK. She has now given up her evening round.

The **oldest actress to win an Oscar** is Jessica Tandy (UK, 1909–1994), who won the 1990 Best Actress award at 80 years 295 days for the title role in *Driving Miss Daisy* (1989).

Newspaper delivery person
Ted Ingram (UK, b. 14 Feb 1920) delivered the *Dorset Echo* from the 1940s until 9 Nov 2013, when he was 93 years 268 days old.

Soccer referee
As of 14 Apr 2013, Peter Pak-Ngo Pang (USA, b. IDN, 4 Nov 1932) was still refereeing in the adult men's league in San Jose, California, USA, aged 80 years 161 days.

Convicted bank robber
On 23 Jan 2004, 92-year-old J L Hunter Rountree (USA, b. 1911) received 12 years 7 months for robbing a bank (unarmed) in Texas, USA.

Oldest dance troupe

The Hip Op-eration Crew (NZ) are hip-hop dancers whose ages range from 67 to 95, giving an average of 79 years 197 days (as of 10 May 2014). The 23 core members, from the small island of Waiheke, New Zealand, include 12 in their eighties and nineties. Their performances include a guest slot at 2013's World Hip Hop Dance Championship final in Las Vegas, Nevada, USA. Respect.

Theatre actor
On 29 Nov 2013, Radu Beligan (ROM, b. 14 Dec 1918) was still performing at the National Theatre in Bucharest, Romania, at 94 years 350 days old.

Painter
Alphaeus Philemon Cole (USA, 1876–1988), whose work is in the permanent collections of the National Portrait Gallery (UK) and the Brooklyn Museum (USA), painted and exhibited his work up to the age of 103. A portraitist, Cole began his art career in the 1890s with Seurat and Signac as contemporaries.

Chess master
Zoltan Sarosy (HUN, b. 23 Aug 1906) was the Canadian Correspondence Chess Champion three times (1967, 1972, 1981) and, according to ChessGames.com, continues to play at 107 years of age.

Elder statesmen: current national leaders

Combining political power with staying power, Shimon Peres (right), the ninth President of Israel, is the **oldest living head of state**. Born Szymon Perski in Wiszniew, Poland (now Vishnyeva, Belarus), on 2 Aug 1923, he celebrated his 90th birthday in 2013.

Only six months younger is the President of Zimbabwe, Robert Mugabe (left, top), born on 21 Feb 1924. Almost exactly a year younger than Peres is Saudi Arabia's King Abdullah bin Abdulaziz al-Saud (left). Born on 1 Aug 1924, he has already outlived two of his crown prince heirs.

Longest careers

Professional hairdresser: Dorothy McKnight (USA, b. 27 Feb 1922) of Lake Worth, Florida, USA, since 13 Jun 1939.

Church pianist/organist: Martha Godwin (USA, b. 17 Jan 1927) in Southmont, North Carolina, USA, since Apr 1940.

Stuntman: Rocky Taylor (UK, b. 28 Feb 1945), since Mar 1961. He appeared in *World War Z* (released Jun 2013).

○ ○ ○

Body parts

Adults are made up of around **7,000,000,000,000,000,000,000,000,000** atoms

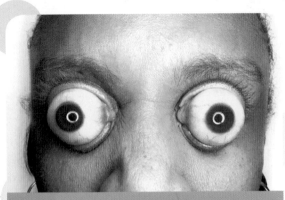

Farthest eyeball pop

Kim Goodman (USA) popped her eyeballs to a protrusion of 12 mm (0.47 in) beyond her eye sockets in Istanbul, Turkey, on 2 Nov 2007, beating her previous record of 11 mm (0.43 in) from 1998. Kim discovered her talent when she was hit on the head by a hockey mask, but can now pop her eyes out on cue.

Stretchiest skin

Garry Turner (UK) is able to stretch the skin of his abdomen to a distended length of 15.8 cm (6.25 in) due to a rare medical condition called Ehlers-Danlos Syndrome. With this condition, the collagen that strengthens the skin and determines its elasticity becomes defective, resulting in, among other things, a loosening of the skin and "hypermobility" of the joints.

Largest hairy family

Victor "Larry" Gomez, Gabriel "Danny" Ramos Gomez, Luisa Lilia De Lira Aceves and Jesus Manuel Fajardo Aceves (all MEX) are four of a family of 19 that span five generations with a rare condition called congenital generalized hypertrichosis, characterized by excessive facial and torso hair. The women are covered with a light-to-medium coat of hair while the men have thick hair on approximately 98% of their body apart from their hands and feet.

Hairiest teenager

In 2010, trichologists (medical experts specializing in hair) used the Ferriman-Gallwey method to evaluate the hirsutism (hairiness) of Supatra "Nat" Sasuphan (THA, b. 5 Aug 2000). Ten areas of her body were scored from 1 to 4 according to the density of the hair. Nat received a score of 4 on four areas: face, neck, chest and upper back.

LARGEST…

Human skull

The largest documented skull was that of an adult male with a 1,980-cm³ (120-cu-in) cranial capacity. The average skull has a capacity of 950–1,800 cm³ (57.9–109 cu in), depending on age and size.

Longest fingernails on one hand

The aggregate measurement of the five nails on Shridhar Chillal's (IND) left hand was 7.05 m (23 ft 1.5 in) on 4 Feb 2004. His thumbnail was the longest, at 1.58 m (5 ft 2.2 in), and his index finger was the shortest, at 1.31 m (4 ft 3.5 in). Chillal stopped cutting his fingernails in 1952.

Hands

Robert Wadlow's (USA) hands measured 32.3 cm (1 ft 0.75 in) from wrist to tip of middle finger, which isn't surprising given his status as **tallest man ever** (see p.80–81). The current **tallest man**, Sultan Kösen (TUR, see p.80), has the **largest hands on a living person**, at 28.5 cm (11.22 in) long.

Feet

If cases of elephantiasis are excluded, the largest feet ever measured belonged

Longest tongue

Nick "The Lick" Stoeberl's (USA) lengthy licker measured 10.10 cm (3.97 in) from tip to closed lip when examined in Salinas, California, USA, on 27 Nov 2012. The bank teller and stand-up comedian has been known to use his tongue – wrapped in cling film – to paint works of art!

Fellow American Chanel Tapper has the record for the **longest tongue (female)**, measuring 9.75 cm (3.80 in) when examined in California, USA, on 29 Sep 2010.

TALLEST AND SHORTEST

250 cm	
200 cm	
150 cm	
100 cm	
50 cm	

Robert Wadlow 272.0 cm
John William Rogan 264.0 cm
John F Carroll 263.5 cm
Väinö Myllyrinne 251.4 cm
Sultan Kösen 251.0 cm
Don Koehler 248.9 cm
Bernard Coyne 248.9 cm
Zeng Jinlian 248.0 cm
Patrick Cotter (O'Brien) 246.4 cm
Brahim Takioullah 246.3 cm

Chandra Bahadur Dangi 54.6 cm
Gul Mohammed 57.0 cm
Junrey Balawing 59.9 cm
Pauline Musters 61.0 cm
Jyoti Amge 62.8 cm
Madge Bester 65.0 cm
Younis Edwan 65.0 cm
Calvin Phillips 67.0 cm
Khagendra Thapa Magar 67.08 cm
Lin Yih-Chih 67.5 cm

 The skinny on weight loss

In 1955, we reported on a 79-cm-tall dwarf as the "thinnest human": "The lowest recorded human bodyweight was the 12 lb [5.44 kg] of the Welshman, Hopkin Hopkins, at his death in Glamorganshire in March 1754. At no time in his 17 years of life did he attain a weight of more than the 17 lb [7.7 kg] he was at 14 years."

The record, since retitled **lightest person** and now open only to adults aged 18 or older, is held by 67-cm-tall Lucia Xarate (aka Lucia Zarate, MEX, 1863–89), whose adult weight peaked (aged 20) at 5.9 kg.

i **Simmonds' disease**

The lightest recorded adults of average height are those suffering from Simmonds' disease (hypophyseal cachexia) – a failure of the pituitary gland. Losses of up to 65% of the original bodyweight have been recorded in females, with a low of 20 kg (3 st 3 lb) documented in the case of Emma Schaller (USA, 1868–90), who stood 1.57 m tall.

Widest tongue

At its widest point, Byron Schlenker's (USA) tongue measures 8.3 cm (3.26 in). Three separate measurements were made in New Hartford, New York, USA, on 30 Oct 2013 – 8.2 cm (3.22 in), 8.4 cm (3.30 in) and 8.3 cm (3.26 in) – with the average taken as the final record value.

to Robert Wadlow, who wore US size 37AA shoes (UK 36) – the equivalent of 47 cm (1 ft 6.5 in).

The **largest feet on a living person** are those of Brahim Takioullah (MAR) – at 246.3 cm (8 ft 1 in), the world's second-tallest living human – whose left foot measured 38.1 cm (1 ft 3 in) and his right 37.5 cm (1 ft 2.76 in) on 24 May 2011.

Breasts
Annie Hawkins-Turner (USA) has an under-breast measurement of 109.22 cm (43 in) and an around-chest-over-nipple measurement of 177.8 cm (70 in). She currently wears a US size 52I bra, but needs a 48V, which is not manufactured.

Tonsils
The palantine tonsils (the lymphatic tissue at the back of the mouth) of Justin Werner (USA) measured 5.1 x 2.8 x

had a 100% covering of black inked over his existing tattoos and is now adding white designs on top of the black, and coloured designs on top of the white.

Maria Jose Cristerna (MEX) is the **most tattooed woman**: she had a total body coverage of 96% on 8 Feb 2011.

Piercings (lifetime)
Elaine Davidson (BRA/UK) had been pierced 4,225 times as of 8 Jun 2006. She also received the **most piercings in a single count** when

Largest gape

A mouth gape stretches from the incisal edge of the maxillary central incisors to the incisal edge of the mandibular central incisors. J J Bittner (USA, right) is able to open his mouth to a gape of 8.4 cm (3.30 in). Meanwhile, Francisco Domingo Joaquim "Chiquinho" (AGO, inset) has the **widest mouth**, measuring 17 cm (6.69 in) on 18 Mar 2010 in Rome, Italy.

2 cm (2.1 x 1.1 x 0.7 in) and 4.7 x 2.6 x 2 cm (1.9 x 1 x 0.7 in). They were removed at the ExcellENT Surgery Center in Topeka, Kansas, USA, on 18 Jan 2011.

MOST...

Tattoos
The ultimate in multi-layered tattooing is represented by Lucky Diamond Rich (AUS, b. NZ), who has spent more than 1,000 hr having his body modified. Lucky

462 were documented in one sitting on 4 May 2000.

Rolf Buchholz (DEU) had the **most piercings in a single count (male)**, with 453 on 5 Aug 2010. As of 16 Dec 2012, Rolf had 516 modifications, including subdermal horn implants and magnetic fingertips, making him the **most modified person**.

Hair-raising: incredible coiffures

Joining the GWR family in 2013 was Alan Edward Labbe (right) of Waltham, Massachusetts, USA, whose hairdo – measured at 1.54 m in circumference on 26 Jul – earned him a certificate for the **largest male afro**. Alan joins the likes of Eric Hahn (USA, left), whose 68.58-cm barnet was verified as the **tallest Mohican** on 14 Nov 2008, and Xie Qiuping (CHN, bottom left), who has grown the **longest hair (female)** – her terrific tresses, last measured on 8 May 2004, stretch for 5.62 m.

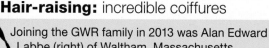

Hole again

Most piercings...
• **On a senior citizen (single count):** "Prince Albert", aka John Lynch (UK), 241, as of 17 Oct 2008
• **In the tongue:** Francesco Vacca (USA), 16, as of 17 Feb 2012
• **On the face:** Axel Rosales (ARG), 280, as of 17 Feb 2012

○ ○ ○

◎ Extreme bodies

Kuwaiti citizens have the **highest body mass index**: 27.5 for men, 31.4 for women

Tallest living person

At 251 cm (8 ft 3 in), Sultan Kösen (TUR) had feared that he might be too tall to find true love. But on 26 Oct 2013, his dream of finding a soulmate came true when he married 175-cm-tall (5-ft 9-in) Merve Dibo in Mardin, Turkey.

FACT

Sultan is 76 cm (2 ft 6 in) taller than Merve, but the **greatest height difference in a married couple** is 94.5 cm (3 ft 1 in) for France's Fabien and Natalie Pretou.

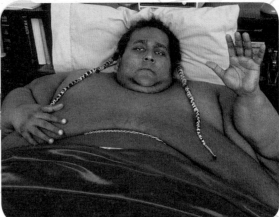

Heaviest twins

Billy Leon (1946–79) and Benny Loyd (1946–2001) McCrary, alias McGuire (both USA), were average in size until the age of six. But by Nov 1978, Billy and Benny weighed 337 kg (743 lb; 53 st) and 328 kg (723 lb; 51 st 9 lb) respectively. Each brother had a waist measuring 2.13 m (6 ft 11.8 in) in circumference.

Largest waist

At his peak weight of approximately 1,200 lb (544 kg; 85 st), Walter Hudson (USA, 1944–91) had a waist measurement of 302 cm (9 ft 11 in).

Heaviest woman ever

Rosalie Bradford (USA) was claimed to have registered a peak weight of around 1,200 lb (544 kg; 85 st) in Jan 1987. Although she had some success in controlling her size, it continued to be a problem throughout her life and she died from weight-related complications in Nov 2006.

Heaviest living man

In 2006, Manuel Uribe (MEX) peaked in weight at 560 kg (1,235 lb; 88 st 3 lb), but by Mar 2012 he had slimmed down to 444.6 kg (980 lb; 70 st). He remains the heaviest living man weighed by GWR.

FACT

GWR discovered Manuel after he asked for help to lose weight on Mexican television.

FACT

The **heaviest man ever** was Jon Brower Minnoch (USA, 1941–83), whose weight peaked at an estimated 1,400 lb (635 kg; 100 st).

Largest chest measurement
Robert Earl Hughes (USA, 1926–58) had a chest circumference of 315 cm (10 ft 4 in). In our first edition of 1955, he was listed as the **heaviest human**, with a weight of 429.6 kg (946 lb; 67 st 8 lb), although when he was weighed shortly before his death he had reached 484 kg (1,067 lb; 76 st 3 lb).

Shortest woman ever
Pauline Musters (NLD) was born in Ossendrecht, Netherlands, on 26 Feb 1876, measuring 30.5 cm (12 in). By the time she died of pneumonia with meningitis on 1 Mar 1895 in New York City, USA, at the age of 19, she had grown to only 61 cm (2 ft).

Shortest living woman
Jyoti Amge (IND) was measured at 62.8 cm (2 ft 0.7 in) on 16 Dec 2011 – her 18th birthday. She towers over the **shortest living man** (and **shortest man ever**), Chandra Bahadur Dangi (NPL), who was measured at 54.6 cm (1 ft 9.5 in) tall on 26 Feb 2012.

SEE IN 3D WITH THE FREE APP

GUINNESS WORLD RECORDS

Augmented Reality alert! 3D ON THIS PAGE

Tallest man ever

Robert Pershing Wadlow of Alton, Illinois, USA, was listed as the tallest man in our first edition and his record has never been beaten. When last measured, on 27 Jun 1940, he was 2.72 m (8 ft 11.1 in). He died less than a month later, on 15 Jul.

Family matters

In Senegal, the average household has **8.9 family members**; in Germany, it's just 2.0

FACT
In Tudor and medieval England, the term "family" also included servants.

Highest combined age for nine living siblings
As of 24 Jun 2013, the nine Melis siblings born to Francesco Melis and his wife Eleonora Mameli of Perdasdefogu, Italy, had an aggregate age of 828 years 45 days.

Largest family reunion
On 12 Aug 2012, at Saint-Paul-Mont-Penit in Vendée, France, 4,514 members of the Porteau-Boileve family came together for a truly great reunion.

Largest proportion of children
Niger has the highest proportion of children, with 50% of the total population aged 0–14 years old in 2012.
The **smallest proportion of children** is that of the two Special Administrative Regions of China: Hong Kong and Macau. Just 12% of their respective populations were aged 0–14 in 2012.

Lowest birth rate
In 2011, Germany had the lowest crude birth rate – the number of babies born per 1,000 people – with 8.1 births. In the same year, Germany had the 16th-largest population in the world, at 82.2 million.
As of 2011, Niger remained the country with the **highest birth rate** with 48.2 births.

Greatest number of descendants
In polygamous countries, the number of descendants can become incalculable. In terms of documented cases, at the time of his death in 1992, Samuel S

Most twins in one academic year at a school

A total of 24 pairs of twins were enrolled in fifth grade at Highcrest Middle School in Wilmette, Illinois, USA, for the academic year 2012–13. That's eight more pairs than the previous record holders!

Mast, aged 96, of Fryburg in Pennsylvania, USA, was known to have 824 living descendants. The roll call comprised 11 children, 97 grandchildren, 634 great-grandchildren and 82 great-great-grandchildren.
Although it is impossible to verify the figures, the last Sharifian Emperor of Morocco, Moulay Ismail (1672–1727), was reputed to have fathered 525 sons and 342 daughters by 1703. His 700th son was reported to have been born in 1721.

Most prolific mother
A total of 69 children were born to the wife of Feodor Vassilyev (1707–c. 1782), a peasant from Shuya, Russia. In 27 confinements, she gave birth to 16 pairs of twins, seven sets of triplets and four sets of quadruplets.

Most children delivered in a single birth
Nine children were born to Geraldine Brodrick (AUS) at the Royal Hospital for Women in Sydney, Australia, on 13 Jun 1971. All the children (five boys and four girls) died within six days.

Running in the family

The **most family members from multiple generations to complete a marathon** is eight, by the Shoji family (JPN, above) at the 40th Honolulu Marathon in Hawaii, USA, on 9 Dec 2012. The **most siblings to complete a marathon** is 16, by the Kapral family (USA, inset) in Appleton, Wisconsin, USA, on 20 Sep 2009.

MOST EXPENSIVE WEDDINGS

- Diana Spencer to Prince Charles, 1981, $110 m
- Vanisha Mittal to Amit Bhatia, 2004, $66 m
- Kate Middleton to Prince William, 2011, $34 m (estimated)
- Coleen McLoughlin to Wayne Rooney, 2008, $8 m
- Chelsea Clinton to Marc Mezvinsky, 2010, $5 m
- Liza Minnelli to David Gest, 2002, $4.2 m
- Elizabeth Taylor to Larry Fortensky, 1991, $4 m
- Heather Mills to Paul McCartney, 2002, $3.6 m
- Elizabeth Hurley to Arun Nayar, 2007, $2.6 m
- Christina Aguilera to Jordan Bratman, 2005, $2.2 m

Source: Business Insider. Figures adjusted for inflation.

⚡ **Consecutive births of twins**

On 5 Feb 1955, Gail Taylor (USA), a twin (of sibling Dale), gave birth to twins of her own, Janet and Joyce. As an adult, Janet gave birth to twins too – Debra and Daniel – and, incredibly, Debra followed suit, giving birth to twins Nathan and Alexander: a record four generations of twins.

The Taylors (above) share their record with the Rollings family (UK). Twins Elizabeth and Olga were born on 3 Dec 1916. On 20 Jul 1950, their nieces Margaret and Maureen Hammond arrived, and their own nieces – Fay and Fiona O'Connor – followed on 26 Feb 1977. Finally, Fay and Fiona's nieces Kacie and Jessica Fawcett were born on 12 Jan 2002.

Oldest first-time grandmother

Marianne Wallenberg (DEU, b. 7 Feb 1913) was 95 years 81 days old when her first grandson, Joshua Fritz Wallenberg (CAN), was born at Sinai Hospital in Toronto, Ontario, Canada, on 29 Apr 2008. Joshua's twin, Karina Diana, was delivered at the same birth.

On 26 Jan 2009, Nadya Suleman (USA) gave birth to six boys and two girls at the Kaiser Permanente Medical Center in Bellflower, California, USA – the **most children delivered in a single birth to survive**. The babies were conceived with the aid of *in vitro* fertilization (IVF) treatment and were nine weeks premature when they were delivered by Caesarean section.

Heaviest birth
Giantess Anna Bates (née Swan, CAN), who measured 241.3 cm (7 ft 11 in), gave birth to a boy weighing 9.98 kg (22 lb) and measuring 71.12 cm (2 ft 4 in) at her home in Seville, Ohio, USA, on 19 Jan 1879. The baby died 11 hr later.

Donna Simpson (USA) weighed 241 kg (532 lb) when she delivered daughter Jacqueline in Feb 2007, making her the **heaviest woman to give birth**.

Lightest birth
The lightest birth for a surviving infant of which there is evidence is 260 g (9.17 oz) for Rumaisa Rahman (USA), born at Loyola University Medical Center in Maywood, Illinois, USA, on 19 Sep 2004 after a gestation period of just 25 weeks 6 days.

Rumaisa was born with her twin sister Hiba, who weighed 580 g (1 lb 4.4 oz). Together, they hold the record for the **lightest birth for twins**, with a total weight of 840 g (1 lb 13.57 oz).

Longest interval between birth of triplets
The greatest gap between the birth of a first and third triplet was 66 hr 50 min for the arrival of Christine, Catherine and Calvin, children of Louise and Robert Jamison (all USA) in 1956. Christine was born at 3.05 a.m. on 2 Jan, Catherine was born at 10 a.m. on 3 Jan, and Calvin was born at 9.55 p.m. on 4 Jan.

Peggy Lynn (USA) gave birth to a girl, Hanna, on

11 Nov 1995. Hanna's twin, Eric, was not delivered until 2 Feb 1996 – 84 days later – at the Geisinger Medical Center in Pennsylvania, USA – a delay that represents the **longest interval between the birth of twins**.

Largest gathering of...
• **Multiple births:** 4,002 sets (3,961 pairs of twins, 37 sets of triplets, four sets of quads) amassed outside Taipei City Hall in Chinese Taipei on 12 Nov 1999.

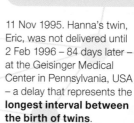

Longest marriage

Herbert Fisher (USA, 1905–2011) and Zelmyra Fisher (USA, 1907–2013) were married on 13 May 1924 in North Carolina, USA. They had been married 86 years 290 days at the time of Herbert's death.

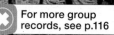

• **People born via IVF:** 1,232, by The Infertility Fund R.O.C. in Taichung, Chinese Taipei, on 16 Oct 2011.

• **People born prematurely:** 386, by UNICEF in Buenos Aires, Argentina, on 30 Sep 2012.

• **People with the same birthday:** 228 people, all born on 4 Jul, by Stichting Apenheul (NLD) in Apeldoorn, Netherlands, on 4 Jul 2012.

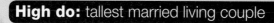

Most bridesmaids to a bride

Nisansala Kumari Ariyasiri (LKA) was attended to by a record retinue of 126 bridesmaids at her wedding to Nalin Pathirana at the Avenra Garden Hotel in Negombo, Colombo, Sri Lanka, on 8 Nov 2013. Around 700 guests were also present.

⊗ For more group records, see p.116

High do: tallest married living couple

On 4 Aug 2013, Sun Mingming – the world's **tallest active basketball player** – and handball player Xu Yan (both CHN) were married in Beijing, China, generating speculation that they had become the world's **tallest married couple**.

On 14 Nov 2013, Guinness World Records was able to confirm this as a record when the towering twosome were measured by doctors at the Oasis Healthcare Centre in Beijing in the presence of official adjudicators. Mingming and Yan reached 236.17 cm and 187.3 cm respectively, giving a record combined height of 423.47 cm and beating the previous record by 4.37 cm.

FACT

The **tallest married couple ever recorded** in history was Anna Haining Swan (CAN) and Martin van Buren Bates (USA), whose combined height was 477.52 cm when they married in St Martin-in-the-Fields church in Trafalgar Square, London, UK, on 17 Jun 1871. Anna later gave birth to the **heaviest baby** (see main text above).

Medical bag

The 14th-century outbreak of the Black Death killed up to **200 million** people

Largest waiting mortuary

German physician Christoph Wilhelm Hufeland (1762–1836) designed "waiting hospitals" to avoid burying the living. The largest of these was in Munich around 1880, and had room for 120 corpses. "Patients" were tied to an alarm system triggered by movement.

First three-headed baby

In 1834, Dr Raina and Dr Galvagni (both ITA) described a stillborn, three-headed infant. This was the

to 26 Dec 1898. He was an assistant to the coffin's inventor, Count Michel de Karnice-Karnicki (RUS). It had a periscope-like tube reaching above ground to allow in air for the prematurely buried. Lorenzo said of his Christmas break that it had been "damned smelly down there".

Lightest person

Lucia Zarate (aka Xarate, MEX) weighed 1.1 kg (2 lb 6 oz) at birth and 2.1 kg (4 lb 11 oz) at the age of 17. By 1884, when she was 20, she weighed 5.9 kg (13 lb). Born with a variant of dwarfism, she reached a height of 67 cm (2 ft 2 in).

Longest human horn

There are many historical instances of humans growing large horns, usually from the head. Madame Dimanche (FRA), who lived in Paris, France, in the early 19th century, had a horn measuring 25 cm (10 in) in length and 5 cm (2 in) in diameter at the base.

First recorded case of congenital hypertrichosis

The hirsute covering of Petrus Gonzales (ESP, b. 1537) was caused by congenital hypertrichosis lanuginosa. Educated at the court of the French king Henri II, he married a wife who did not share his condition.

First recorded lithopedion

The 1582 autopsy on 68-year-old Madame Colombe Chatri (FRA) revealed an ossified child (lithopedion or "stone-child"). The foetus had died in pregnancy and was calcified by her body to prevent infection from the tissue.

First proven case of superfetation

Superfetation is the conception of twins from two different menstrual cycles – and potentially different fathers. A 1980 case of disputed paternity of twins in Germany used genetic testing to establish the putative father of Twin Two with 99.995% probability, while excluding him as the father of Twin One.

Smallest waist

Ethel Granger (UK, 1905–82) reduced her natural waist from 56 cm (1 ft 10 in) to 33 cm (1 ft 1 in) from 1929 to 1939 by wearing ever tighter corsets. The same measurement was matched by actress Mlle Polaire, aka Émilie Marie Bouchaud (FRA, 1874–1939).

First safety coffin

Duke Ferdinand of Brunswick-Wolfenbüttel (DEU) suffered from taphophobia (see below). Ahead of his death in 1792, he ordered a coffin with a window, an air hole, and a lid that was unlockable instead of nailed down.

Faroppo Lorenzo (ITA) underwent the **longest voluntary burial** in a safety coffin, from 17 Dec

First documented account of a pig-faced lady

Papers published by G J Boekenoogen (NLD) trace the legend of girls born with the face of a pig back to the 1630s. A Dutch print goes farther back, recounting the story of a girl from 1621 who grew up to eat from a trough and talk in grunts. Such fanciful accounts were spread in pamphlets and ballads that were in general circulation during the 17th and 18th centuries.

TOP 10 CAUSES OF DEATH WORLDWIDE IN 2011

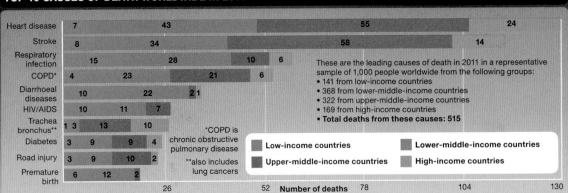

These are the leading causes of death in 2011 in a representative sample of 1,000 people worldwide from the following groups:
- 141 from low-income countries
- 368 from lower-middle-income countries
- 322 from upper-middle-income countries
- 169 from high-income countries
- Total deaths from these causes: 515

Cause	Low-income	Lower-middle-income	Upper-middle-income	High-income
Heart disease	7	43	55	24
Stroke	8	34	58	14
Respiratory infection	15	28	10	6
COPD*	4	23	21	6
Diarrhoeal diseases	10	22	2	1
HIV/AIDS	10	11	7	
Trachea bronchus**	1 3	13	10	
Diabetes	3	9	9	4
Road injury	3	9	10	2
Premature birth	6	12	2	

*COPD is chronic obstructive pulmonary disease

**also includes lung cancers

Number of deaths: 26   52   78   104   130

Legend:
- Low-income countries
- Lower-middle-income countries
- Upper-middle-income countries
- High-income countries

Source: World Health Organization, 2013

Glossary

Hypertrichosis: abnormal growth of hair; the condition can be congenital (from birth). Hairiness can be assessed using the Ferriman-Gallwey method (see p.78).

Taphophobia: the fear of being buried alive. This was a pressing concern before doctors were able to reliably detect signs of life in people who might appear to be deceased.

First recorded asymmetrical conjoined twins

Lazarus Colloredo (ITA, b. 1617) had a parasitic twin complete with head and three deformed extremities growing from his chest. The twin was apparently considered to be a separate individual as he was given the name Joannes Baptista. Lazarus toured to exhibit his twin, who displayed some reaction to stimulus, implying limited autonomous functionality.

first recorded instance of extreme conjoined twinning, as one of the necks had two heads.

Longest human tail
Indian plantation worker Chandre Oram showed a tail measuring 33 cm (1 ft 1 in) in length to the world's media in 2008. Other notable cases include a 12-year-old boy in French Indochina who was said to have sported a 22.8-cm (9-in) tail. In 1901, anatomist Dr Ross Granville Harrison described a baby boy with a 7.6-cm-long (3-in) tail that was examined by Harrison after amputation.

Most ascarides expelled
Ascarides are roundworm parasites that live in the small intestine. They sometimes appear by the hundreds, but in 1880, Dr Fauconneau-Dufresne reported on the case of a Frenchman who had managed to expel around 5,000 ascarides in less than three years, largely through vomiting.

Most tapeworms expelled
It is possible for more than one tapeworm to exist in the body. In 1883, Dr Aguiel described an unnamed patient who expelled a 1-kg (2-lb 3-oz) lump containing 34.5 m (113 ft 2 in) of tapeworm. Three years later, Dr Garfinkel saw a peasant with 72.5 m (238 ft) of tapeworm with 12 heads.

Most children born to unseparated conjoined twins

Chang and Eng Bunker (1811–74) were born in Thailand, then called Siam – the origin of the now-defunct term "Siamese twins". The two men fathered 21 children, the descendents of whom held their 24th annual reunion in Mount Airy, North Carolina, USA, in 2013.

Longest nose ever
Thomas Wedders (UK) was a travelling circus sideshow act in the 1770s, with a nose that was reputed to measure 19 cm (7.5 in) long.

Most deadly outbreak of listeriosis
Sources differ, but somewhere between 47 and 84 people were killed in California, USA, in the 1985 outbreak of listeriosis. It was caused by the bacteria listeria in cheese and, even at the lowest figure, it remains the instance with the highest number of fatalities. It is also the deadliest outbreak of bacterial food-borne disease in the USA.

Oldest dwarf
Hungarian-born Susanna Bokoyni of New Jersey, USA, was 105 when she died on 24 Aug 1984. Born in Apr 1879, she was 101.5 cm (3 ft 4 in) tall and is one of two centenarian dwarfs on record, the other being Anne Clowes (UK). Anne died on 5 Aug 1784 aged 103 and was 114 cm (3 ft 9 in) tall.

Oldest ever male conjoined twins
Giacomo and Giovanni Battista Tocci (ITA) were born on 4 Oct 1877 and lived to be 63. They were separate above the waist, but shared an abdomen, pelvis and two legs. Having made money from touring Europe and the USA, they retired from public life.

Together: conjoined twins

Masha and Dasha Krivoshlyapova (both USSR, left) suffered from *dicephalus tetrabrachius dipus* (two heads, four arms, and two legs), a very rare form of conjoined twinning. They were born on 3 Jan 1950 and, until their death on 17 Apr 2003, were the **oldest living conjoined female twins**. The title then went to the craniopagus (joined at the head) twins born on 18 Sep 1961 as Lori and Dori Schappell (both USA, right). As of 8 May 2014 they were 52 years 232 days old. In 2007, Dori announced that he was transgender, identifying himself as a male called George.

FACT
The decision to separate conjoined twins is not taken lightly, and many twins – such as Lori and George (left) and Chang and Eng Bunker (above) – opt to stay together. Complications arise when twins share vital organs. In the case of the Bunkers, their livers were fused but the procedure to separate them would, today, be relatively simple; not so back in the 1800s, hence their decision to stay together.

:Recordmania

Mania: noun, from the Greek, *be mad*; an excessive enthusiasm or passion

Largest collection of soft-drink cans

Davide Andreani's (ITA) mania for Coca-Cola cans began at the age of five, when he started collecting unfamiliar tins brought home by his father from European business trips. At the last count, confirmed on 14 Aug 2013, Coke addict Davide owned a record 10,558 unique single-brand cans from 87 countries.

Contents

FACT
Most of Davide's cans are unopened. He empties them by piercing a hole in the bottom to stop the cans exploding!

⚡ Mr Versatility

No sooner had work started on the first edition of *The Guinness Book of Records* in London than a boy was born in New York City, USA, who would go on to become the undisputed king of record-breaking. His name was Keith Furman, but today he's better known by his spiritual name: Ashrita.

That the man who holds the Guinness World Records title for **most Guinness World Records titles held** was born within a month of the company is a coincidence, but it's a joyous one. Keith Furman was born on 16 Sep 1954. It would be 25 years before he set the first of many Guinness World Records,

but he has achieved more in 36 years than most people could do in 10 lifetimes.

The manager of a health food store, Furman was given the name Ashrita – Sanskrit for "Protected by God" – by his spiritual teacher Sri Chinmoy (IND, 1931–2007), who taught him self-transcendence and meditation. Using these lessons, Ashrita set his first record in 1979 – achieving 27,000 star jumps (jumping jacks) – and he hasn't looked back. As of 1 May 2014, he had set 521 records, of which 182 are still current.

Come with us on a journey through just some of the records set by Mr Versatility…

> ## ⓘ For the record
> Ashrita set his 100th record on 24 Sep 2005, **spinning the largest hula hoop** – 4.8 m (16 ft) in diameter – three times around his waist on the set of *Richard & Judy* in London, UK.

Ashrita… in his own words

"My teacher's philosophy of self-transcendence – of overcoming your limits and making progress spiritually, creatively and physically using the power of meditation – really thrills me. If you can connect with your inner source and be receptive to a higher Grace, you can accomplish anything.

"Attempting records has become an inherent part of my spiritual journey. I scour the *Guinness World Records* book looking for categories I think will be challenging and fun. Many of the records involve child-like activities such as juggling, hopscotch, unicycling, pogo-sticking and balancing objects on my head and chin. I get joy not only in practising the activity itself, but also in seeing my progress towards achieving a goal. The particular event is unimportant as long as it gives you the opportunity to dance on the edge of your capacity."

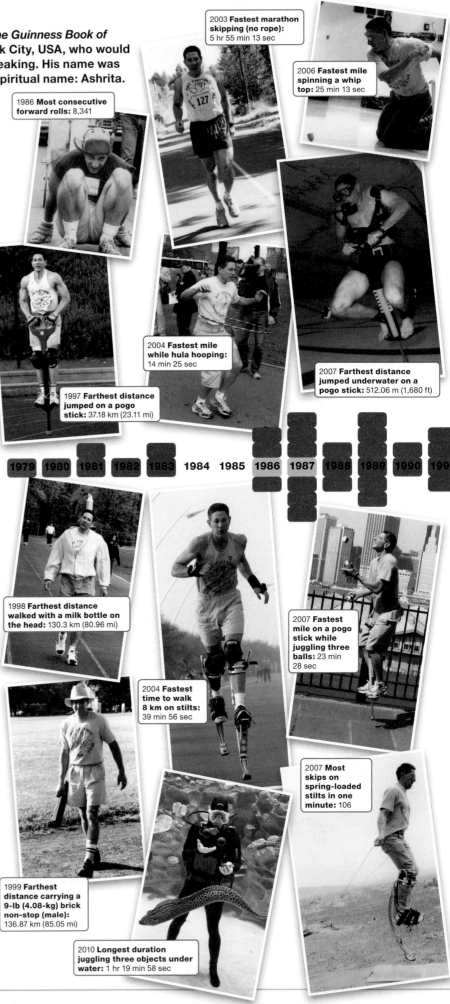

2003 **Fastest marathon skipping (no rope):** 5 hr 55 min 13 sec

2006 **Fastest mile spinning a whip top:** 25 min 13 sec

1986 **Most consecutive forward rolls:** 8,341

2004 **Fastest mile while hula hooping:** 14 min 25 sec

2007 **Farthest distance jumped underwater on a pogo stick:** 512.06 m (1,680 ft)

1997 **Farthest distance jumped on a pogo stick:** 37.18 km (23.11 mi)

1979 1980 1981 1982 1983 **1984 1985** 1986 1987 1988 1989 1990 1991

1998 **Farthest distance walked with a milk bottle on the head:** 130.3 km (80.96 mi)

2004 **Fastest time to walk 8 km on stilts:** 39 min 56 sec

2007 **Fastest mile on a pogo stick while juggling three balls:** 23 min 28 sec

2007 **Most skips on spring-loaded stilts in one minute:** 106

1999 **Farthest distance carrying a 9-lb (4.08-kg) brick non-stop (male):** 136.87 km (85.05 mi)

2010 **Longest duration juggling three objects under water:** 1 hr 19 min 58 sec

FURMAN'S FAVOURITES

Ashrita has broken records on all seven continents, including the **fastest mile on a pogo stick** in Antarctica and the **fastest mile on a kangaroo ball (spacehopper)** along the Great Wall of China. Here, he picks his most memorable records.

Most consecutive forward rolls	8,341
Farthest distance with milk bottle on head	130.3 km
Pogo-stick jumping (in Mount Fuji foothills)	18.60 km
Underwater pogo-stick jumping (in the Amazon River)	3,647 jumps 3 hr 40 min
Fastest sack race mile (against a yak)	16 min 41 sec
Most star jumps – Ashrita's first record!	27,000
Pool cue balancing (at the pyramids, Egypt)	11.3 km
Fastest mile pushing an orange with nose	22 min 41 sec
Fastest 8 km on stilts	39 min 56 sec
Fastest 5 km skipped without a rope	30 min

Key

Record set then later lost

Still holds record

Current as of 1 May 2014

2011 **Most apples snapped in one minute:** 40

2011 **Most baseballs held in a glove:** 24

2009 **Fastest 10 m balancing a pool cue on the chin:** 3.02 sec

2008 **Fastest mile on stilts:** 12 min 23 sec

1993 1994 1995 1996 1997 1998 1999 2000 2001 2002 2003 2004 2005 2006 2007 2008 2009 2010 2011 2012 2013 2014

2009 **Fastest mile balancing a book on the head:** 8 min 27 sec

2010 **Fastest one-mile piggy-back race:** 12 min 47 sec

2010 **Longest control of a golf ball with one club:** 1 hr 20 min 42 sec

2012 **Longest duration balancing a chainsaw on the chin:** 1 min 25.01 sec

2010 **Fastest 100 m frog jumping:** 7 min 18 sec

2012 **Fastest mile bounce-juggling three objects:** 7 min 27 sec

2012 **Fastest 5 km joggling in swim fins:** 32 min 3 sec

Collections

There are an estimated **five million stamp collectors** in the USA

Pizza boxes

When Scott Wiener (USA) orders a pizza, he's usually more interested in the box than the food. As of 23 Oct 2013, the pizza buff – who has even written a book about his passion, *Viva La Pizza!: The Art of the Pizza Box* – had amassed a collection of 595 boxes from 42 different countries.

These are the latest collections to be added to the GWR database:

Airline boarding passes

Having flown with 90 airlines in 28 years, João Gilberto Vaz of Brasilia, Brazil, had saved 2,558 boarding passes as of 23 Jan 2014. He flies an average of 91.35 flights per year.

Bagpipes
Daniel Fleming of Cleethorpes in Lincolnshire, UK, owned 105 sets of playable bagpipes as of 24 Oct 2013.

Coins from the same year
Rahul G Keshwani (IND) has 11,111 coins from the year 1989. The collection, made up of the defunct 25-paise coin, was verified on 28 Jul 2013 in Mumbai, India.

Cookery books
Sue Jimenez (USA/CAN) had 2,970 cookbooks as of 14 Jul 2013 in Albuquerque, New Mexico, USA.

Electronic calculators
Gerhard Wenzel (DEU) has no fear of wrongly counting his collection of calculators

Fake food

Plastic food replicas are a common sight in Japanese restaurants… and in the home of Akiko Obata in Sanbu-gun, Chiba, Japan. Obata's collection of 8,083 fake dishes – plus food-related keyrings, toys and magnets – was verified on 24 Jan 2014.

– not with 4,113 examples to help tot them up, as of 7 Sep 2013, in Solingen, Germany.

Ganesha-related items
Ram and Lalita Kogata (IND) own 10,631 items relating to Ganesha, the Hindu god with the head of an elephant. Their collection was counted on 14 Sep 2013 in Udaipur, Rajasthan, India. The couple also have the **largest collection of Ganesha statues**, with 2,930.

Gift cards (gift tokens)
In 2007, teenage brothers Aaron and David Miller (USA/CAN) wanted to make shopping with their mother more interesting, so they started to collect gift tokens. As of 30 Aug 2013, they had amassed 3,215 different cards.

Horse-related items
Equine enthusiast Edgar Rugeles (COL) had collected 2,762 models of

Doctor Who memorabilia

Ian O'Brien (UK) had acquired 1,573 unique items relating to everyone's favourite Timelord, as of 6 Sep 2013, in his home in Manchester, UK. He started his collection in 1974 with a yellow Dalek (a Louis Marx toy) and received *The Dr Who Annual* every Christmas. His personal favourites are a TARDIS console released by Dapol and a very rare nursery toy Dalek by Selcol.

TOP 10 LARGEST CATEGORIES OF COLLECTIONS

1: Tobacco
4.65 million items

2: Human body
2.17 million items

3: Publishing
1.65 million items

4: Food and drink
1.45 million items

5: Clothing and accessories
806,698 items

Total:
12,558,180
as of 22 Apr 2014

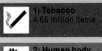
6: Leisure, games and hobbies
551,046 items

7: Travel
459,249 items

8: Stationery
381,101 items

9: Household
237,006 items

10: Animal
184,946 items

Stamps featuring…

Paintings: J M van der Leeuw (NLD), 19,284 stamps as of 25 May 2013 in Wageningen, Netherlands

Sea life: Samhar Moafaq Noori Ahmed (IRQ), 2,775 stamps as of 16 Nov 2013 in Leeds, Yorkshire, UK

First-day covers: George Vavvas (GRC), 7,215 stamps as of 6 Apr 2013 in Ioannina, Greece

Popes: Magnus Andersson (SWE), 1,580 stamps as of 16 Nov 2010 in Falun, Sweden

Glossary

Bibliophilism: enthused book collecting

Cagophily: key collecting

Cartophily: cigarette- or chewing-gum-card collecting

Labeorphily: beer-bottle-label collecting

Philately: postage-stamp collecting

Timbromania: mania for collecting postage stamps

○ ○ ○

CHARACTER COLLECTIONS

Collection	Amount	Record holder	Date counted
X-Men	15,400	Eric Jaskolka (USA)	28 Jun 2012
James Bond (see below)	12,463	Nick Bennett (UK)	21 Nov 2013
Winnie the Pooh	10,002	Deb Hoffmann (USA)	14 Sep 2013
Mickey Mouse	6,726	Janet Esteves (USA)	11 Nov 2013
Conan the Barbarian	4,670	Robert and Patricia Leffler (both USA)	2 Apr 2003
Hello Kitty	4,519	Asako Kanda (JPN)	14 Aug 2011
Trolls	2,990	Sherry Groom (USA)	26 Oct 2012
Donald Duck	2,775	Steffen Gerdes (DNK)	27 Jun 2012
1 The Simpsons	2,580	Cameron Gibbs (AUS)	20 Mar 2008
2 Batman	2,501	Kevin Silva (USA)	25 Oct 2013
Doctor Who (see opposite page)	1,573	Ian O'Brien (UK)	6 Sep 2013
3 Charlie's Angels	1,460	Jack Condon (USA)	6 Feb 2007
Superman	1,253	Herbert Chavez (PHL)	22 Feb 2012
Daleks	1,202	Rob Hull (UK)	14 May 2013
Harry Potter	807	Jayne Gradel (USA)	13 Jun 2013

horses, among other items of horse memorabilia, as of 26 Aug 2013, in Bogotá, Colombia.

Keys
Lisa J Large of Kansas City, Missouri, USA, owned 3,604 different keys as of 20 Nov 2013.

Ozzy Osbourne memorabilia
As of 18 Oct 2013, Claus Solvig of Rødovre, Denmark, had acquired 1,811 items relating to heavy-metal legend Ozzy Osbourne.

James Bond memorabilia

Nick Bennett (UK) began his bond with Bond in 1995 and his collection of 12,463 items, as verified on 21 Nov 2013, is now housed in a warehouse in Warrington, UK. The collection includes Roger Moore's shoes from *The Man with the Golden Gun* (UK, 1974), a unique 007 doll worth in the region of £10,000 ($16,000) and a speedboat from *Live and Let Die* (UK, 1973).

Collect call: anything goes

Guinness World Records has at least 169 collection categories for which a record has yet to be awarded. Now's the time to check behind the sofa – perhaps you have the **largest collection of...** *Alice in Wonderland* memorabilia; Aloha (Hawaiian) shirts; autographed golf balls; autographed soccer memorabilia; baby bibs; baseball jerseys; basketball memorabilia; beauty pageant sashes; bedpans; boxed PC games; branded tins; Buddhist statues; camel-related items; candy canes; cleaning brushes; collie-related items; crotcheted items... Find out how to register your claim on p.5.

And finally...

• *The Nightmare Before Christmas* memorabilia: William Wong (HKG) owns 2,020 items (18 Feb 2014).

• *Star Wars* memorabilia: Steve Sansweet (USA) has 300,000 unique *Star Wars* items in California, USA. Of these, 92,240 had been catalogued by 4 May 2014.

• Clothing labels: Paul Brockmann (USA) has amassed 4,120 labels (11 Mar 2014).

Model-making

Airfix originally sold **inflatable rubber toys**; it didn't sell model-making kits until 1952

Largest toothpick sculpture

Michael Smith (USA) used more than 3 million toothpicks to create "Alley", a 4.5-m-long (15-ft) alligator that weighed 132.4 kg (292 lb) when measured in Prairieville, Louisiana, USA, on 22 Mar 2005.

Largest display of toothpick sculptures

A full miniature orchestra – comprising 62 musicians with their instruments, plus a conductor – was modelled by Go Sato (CAN) using

Largest model aircraft kit

In the TV series *Toy Stories* (BBC, 2009), presenter James May (UK) took part in the construction of a model aircraft from a fully scaled-up Airfix kit, resulting in a 1:1 replica of a Supermarine Spitfire Mk1 with a wing-span of 11.2 m (36 ft 9 in) and a length of 9.12 m (29 ft 11 in). It was built at the Royal Air Force Museum Cosford in Shropshire, UK.

12,500 toothpicks and displayed in Ottawa, Ontario, Canada, on 18 Jun 2013.

Largest Plasticine model

Martin and Nigel Langdon (UK) have spent thousands of hours since the early 1960s painstakingly modelling their ideal city with more than 226 kg (500 lb) of Plasticine. The model, complete with Roman-style colosseum and American-inspired

skyscrapers, now covers an area 4.5 m (15 ft) long by 1.2 m (4 ft) wide. The only things not made of Plasticine are the tree trunks, which are made of dyed matchsticks.

Largest matchstick model

"Cathedrals of the Sea" is a North Sea oil production platform modelled from 4,075,000 matchsticks. It was made by David Reynolds (UK) and completed in Jul 2009.

Tallest toothpick sculpture

Stan Munro (USA) created a model of the Burj Khalifa tower in Dubai, UAE, the world's **tallest building**. The 5.09-m-tall (16-ft 8-in) sculpture was measured at the Phelps Art Center in Phelps, New York, USA, on 22 Jun 2013. It took Munro around six months to make and includes approximately 250,000 toothpicks.

Largest collection of military models

Francisco Sánchez Abril (ESP) started collecting miniature military vehicles in 1958 and, as of Feb 2012, had amassed 2,815 unique items representing the military might of 25 countries.

Largest model airport

Knuffingen Airport, located at Miniatur Wunderland in Hamburg, Germany, is built to a scale of 1:87. The 45.9-m² (494-sq-ft) model is based on the

Tallest matchstick model

A scale replica of the Eiffel Tower, built from matchsticks by Toufic Daher (LBN), stands at 6.53 m (21 ft 5 in) tall. It was unveiled at City Mall, Beirut, Lebanon, on 11 Nov 2009 in celebration of GWR Day.

> **HOW TO MAKE A SHIP-IN-A-BOTTLE**

01 Choose a bottle with a fairly large neck and paint a sea effect inside the bottle.

02 Using wood, build the hull of the ship. Build everything except for the mast, sails, and the sails' support beams (spars). Make sure it can fit through the neck of the bottle. Paint.

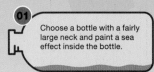

03 Make the masts. Create a hinge using wire, which is used to bend the sails, in the base of each mast. Make the sails and spars.

04 Make holes in each mast and run a line of thread through them. Attach the masts and rigging to the hull of the ship; lay them flat along its length.

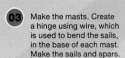

05 Push the ship through the bottle's neck. Colour putty to represent the sea. When the putty sets, the ship should be stable.

06 Gently pull the thread running through the masts, so that they rise vertically on their wire hinges.

07 Fasten the masts by applying glue to their bases. Insert a cork to seal the bottle.

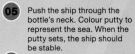

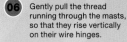

Pietro D'Angelo

Since 2008, Italian artist Pietro D'Angelo has been creating a series of sculptures made from paperclips – all hand-made in his own home. Created in 2008, Pietro's *Pole Dance* is the **tallest paperclip sculpture** in the world, stretching 2.28 m. Each sculpture takes Pietro two to three months to produce and includes 10–20,000 paperclips. The dextrous D'Angelo used iron paperclips at first, but now has stainless steel versions specially made for him by a paperclip factory.

Largest collection of dioramas

A diorama is a 3D model of a landscape or scene containing numerous elements, and the largest collection on record is owned by Nabil Karam (LBN). Among his 333 dioramas – which were counted in Zouk, Lebanon, on 17 Nov 2011 – are famous battles, a train station, an airport and scenes from classic movies.

Smallest ship-in-a-bottle

In 1956, Arthur V Pedlar (UK) constructed a ship inside a 1-cc glass phial measuring 2.38 cm (0.9 in) long and 0.9 cm (0.3 in) wide, with a neck of just 0.2 cm (0.07 in). The galleon had three masts, five sails and three flags.

Largest display of ships-in-a-bottle

Kjell Birkeland (NOR) owned a fleet of 655 model ships, as of 15 Feb 2013. The bottled boats are displayed at the Arendal Bymuseum in Arendal, Norway.

Largest ship-in-a-bottle

"Nelson's Ship in a Bottle" is a scale replica of HMS *Victory* contained within a giant bottle. The artwork was made by Yinka Shonibare MBE (UK) and measures 4.7 m (15 ft 5 in) in length and 2.8 m (9 ft 2 in) in diameter. It was originally displayed on the Fourth Plinth in Trafalgar Square, London, UK, in 2010.

international airport serving Hamburg, and took seven years to complete.

Fastest rocket-powered model car

The Heathland School Rocket Car Club in Hounslow, UK, built "Möbius" – a jet-propelled model car that reached a speed of 329.84 km/h (204.95 mph) on 14 Jun 2013.

Longest model train

A model train measuring 282.11 m (925 ft 6 in) and comprising 31 locomotives and 1,563 carriages was constructed by the Wilmington Railroad Museum Model Railroad Committee. It was presented in Wilmington, North Carolina, USA, on 23 Apr 2011.

The **longest model train track** is the Great American Railway, which boasts a total of more than 15.2 km (9.5 mi) of HO (1:87 scale) track. Built by Bruce Williams Zaccagnino (USA), it is the star exhibit at the Northlandz attraction in Flemington, New Jersey, USA.

Most model rocket kits launched simultaneously

Boy Scout Jacob Smith (USA) launched 3,130 model rockets at once to commemorate the 100th anniversary of the Boy Scouts of America. The launch took place in College Station, Texas, USA, on 9 Oct 2010.

Largest Dalek sculpture

Snugburys Ice Cream (UK) has been making straw sculptures for over 10 years and, in 2013, constructed a 10.6-m-tall (35-ft) Dalek. The sculpture, made in celebration of *Doctor Who*'s 50th anniversary, took 700 hr to complete and used 6 tonnes (13,440 lb) of straw and 5 tonnes (11,200 lb) of steel.

Mini-marvel: Queen Mary's Dolls' House

Built in 1921–24 by architect Sir Edwin Landseer Lutyens (UK) at a scale of 1:12, Queen Mary's Dolls' House includes plumbing, electricity and a cellar stocked with drinkable wine. It is the **most visited dolls' house**, having been on display for many years at Windsor Castle in Windsor, UK, which attracted more than 9 million visitors between 2004 and 2013 alone. Its miniature library contains the **most works of literature made for a dolls' house**: the 206 unique literary works include a handwritten book of poetry by Rudyard Kipling and *How Watson Learned the Trick*, a story specially written by Arthur Conan Doyle.

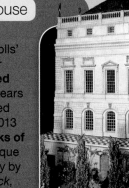

i Diminutive domiciles

Also known as "baby houses", these dolls' houses' date back at least to the 16th century. The early versions were usually replicas of grand houses of rich families rather than toys. By the 18th century, "doll cabinets" – miniature houses set in fine cabinets – were common. The Victorian era saw the birth of the dolls' house as we know it today: a beautifully crafted child's plaything.

:Big stuff

The **Great Wall of China** is big – but it's a myth that it is visible from the Moon

Largest poster

The boss of all posters is a poster to promote *Boss*, a 2013 Bollywood film. It took 30 hr to print and had an area of 3,234 m² (34,814 sq ft) – longer than 12 tennis courts. It was made by Team Akshay (IND) and Macro Art Ltd (UK) and unveiled on 3 Oct 2013.

Hot dog cart
Marcus Daily (USA) built a 3.72-m-tall (12-ft 3-in) cart that, despite its size, is mobile, although at 7.06 m (23 ft 2 in) in length, it moves with difficulty. Marcus plans to turn the cart – which set the record on 28 Oct 2013 in Union, Missouri, USA – into a permanent restaurant.

Knitting needles
Despite being 3.98 m (13 ft 0.75 in) long, needles made by Jim Bolin were used by Jeanette Huisinga (both USA) to knit a square of 10 x 10 stitches at Monroe Elementary School in Casey, Illinois, USA, on 20 May 2013.

Megaphone
Members of the public were encouraged to make their thoughts heard loud and clear with a massive megaphone measuring 2.43 m (8 ft) long. It was built by Bezoya (ESP) in Madrid, Spain, on 10 Oct 2013.

FACT
The lamp was switched on using a timer, and its base was used as seating.

Largest floor lamp
Fredrik and Martin Raddum (NOR) were the bright sparks behind a lamp measuring 9.16 m (30 ft) high in Oslo, Norway, in Feb 2013. The lamp shade is made of polyester and fibreglass and is 3.98 m (13 ft) in diameter. The supporting pole is made of steel.

LARGEST...

Envelope
Ajmal Khan Tibbiya College (IND) made an envelope measuring 17.86 m (58 ft 7 in) in length and 13.10 m (42 ft 11.7 in) in width in Aligarh, Uttar Pradesh, India, on 3 Apr 2013.

Model tooth
A massive molar measuring 8.23 m (27 ft) tall was made by Sensodyne (MEX) and displayed in Mexico City's Parque México on 25 Nov 2013 to raise awareness of tooth decay.

Oil lamp
An oil lamp with a volume of 652.8 litres (143 gal) was commissioned by the municipality of Almócita in Almeria, Spain, as part of their celebrations for The Night of the Oil Lamps festival held on 11 May 2013.

Paintbrush
Indian artist Sujit Das made a paintbrush measuring 8.5 m (28 ft) long and weighing 22 kg (48 lb 8 oz). It was used at Nagaon Government Boys' High School in Nagaon, India, on 19 Jun 2012 to paint portraits of Mahatma Gandhi, Bhagat Singh and Bishnu Prasad Rabha.

Longest golf club
Karsten Maas (DNK) made a 4.37-m-long (14-ft 5-in) long golf club and drove a ball 165.46 m (542 ft 10 in) at the Golf in Wall course in Wall, Germany, on 30 Apr 2013. Karsten, who performs in his own trick golf shows, last set the record in 2009. Normal golf drivers are usually around 1.14–1.22 m (3 ft 9 in–4 ft).

Longest board cut from one tree
Daniel Czapiewski (POL) cut a board measuring 46.53 m (152 ft 7 in) in Szymbark, Poland, on 9 Jun 2012. For more from Daniel Czapiewski, see Big Orchestra on pp.96–97.

XL XMAS

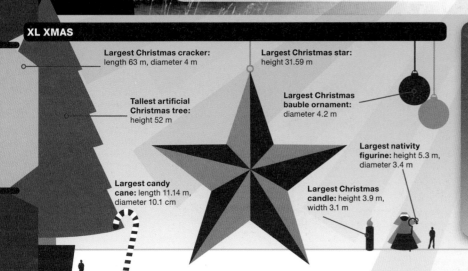

Largest Christmas cracker: length 63 m, diameter 4 m

Largest Christmas star: height 31.59 m

Tallest artificial Christmas tree: height 52 m

Largest Christmas bauble ornament: diameter 4.2 m

Largest candy cane: length 11.14 m, diameter 10.1 cm

Largest nativity figurine: height 5.3 m, diameter 3.4 m

Largest Christmas candle: height 3.9 m, width 3.1 m

Big news

In 1955, we reported on the "most massive single issue of a newspaper yet published": a 490-page edition of the *New York Times* from 12 Sep 1954. This has since been beaten by the 14 Sep 1987 Sunday edition of *The New York Times* – a single issue that contained 1,612 pages. At a back-breaking 5.4 kg, it's also the **heaviest newspaper ever**.

Making it supersized

"Big stuff" records typically require claimants to recreate a scaled-up version of a regular-sized object, maintaining proportions where possible and using the same construction materials. Although guidelines may vary, we expect the supersized version to be functional – a giant pencil should still be able to write, for example, no matter how big!

Largest clothes peg

Karl Josef Biller (DEU, pictured right) devised a fully functioning wooden clothes peg – just don't get your finger caught in it! It measured 3.5 m (11 ft 5 in) long and 65 cm (2 ft) high and was unveiled on 9 Sep 2012 in Regensburg, Germany.

Postbox

A 68.484-m³ (2,418.49-cu-ft) postbox was erected by Yamaguchi University's Choshu Enjoying Science Innovation Project in Ube, Yamaguchi, Japan, on 27 Dec 2012. A first-class effort all round!

Silver ring

A 91.32-kg (201-lb 5-oz) ring made from 99.99% pure silver was created by Valentine Diamond (TUR). The ring, which has an inner diameter of 92 cm (3 ft), was measured in Istanbul, Turkey, on 27 Sep 2013.

Sandcastle

Ed Jarrett (USA) became king of the (sand) castle with his 11.63-m-tall (38-ft 2-in) effort at Point Pleasant Beach in New Jersey, USA, on 29 Oct 2013.

Playing cards

A pack of playing cards measuring 1.295 m x 0.939 m (4 ft 3 in x 3 ft 1 in) was unveiled by Viejas Casino & Resort in Alpine, California, USA, on 12 Sep 2013. The cards were played in a hand of blackjack on the world's **largest blackjack table** – a fully functioning gaming table covering an area of 206.85 m² (2,226.51 sq ft) – made to celebrate the venue's 21st anniversary.

Paper aircraft

It's one thing to make a paper plane with a wing-span of 18.21 m (59 ft 9 in); it's another to make it fly. Yet Braunschweig Institute of Technology (DEU) did just that in Braunschweig, Germany, on 28 Sep 2013. Launched from a 2.47-m-high (8-ft) platform, the aircraft flew 18 m (59 ft).

Wooden spoon

A traditional folk art spoon made by Centrul Cultural Mioveni of Romania measured 17.79 m (58 ft 4 in) long in Mioveni, Romania, on 7 Jun 2013.

Largest Santa Claus

Shopping Center Norte unveiled a Santa towering 20 m (65 ft 7 in) tall, 7 m (23 ft) wide and 4 m (13 ft) deep in São Paulo, Brazil, on 7 Nov 2013. It was estimated that up to 5 million shoppers would pass through the mall over Christmas to admire the styrofoam and fibreglass giant. Next to Santa was a wrapped present that itself stood 4 m (13 ft) high.

Largest soccer shirt

The Nigerian national squad – the Super Eagles – had a shirt made by Guinness Nigeria plc. It measured 73.55 m (241 ft) wide and 89.67 m (294 ft) long in Lagos, Nigeria, on 25 Jan 2013.

FACT

In Brazil, Santa Claus is known as Papai Noel. He comes through the window and hides presents in shoes left out for him.

Knitty gritty: longest scarf

Helge Johansen (NOR) is no knit-wit: he's the proud creator of the world's **longest knitted scarf**. It's taken the nimble-fingered Norwegian 30 years to knit his neck-warmer to an incredible 4,565.46 m – as long as 550 London double-decker buses or sufficient to stretch the entire length of Central Park in Manhattan, New York, USA. In order to measure his knitwear for Guinness World Records Day 2013, Helge unravelled his scarf – which he usually keeps in a ball (right) – in a sports centre in Oslo, Norway, snaking the scarf in dozens of tight loops (left).

And finally...

- **Largest marquee:** 40,473.85 m², erected by Barrett-Jackson Auction Company in Scottsdale, Arizona, USA, in Jan 2014.
- **Largest spade:** 4.5 m tall with a 95.6-cm-wide blade, by Rollins Bulldog Tools in Harlow, UK, on 27 Sep 2013.
- **Largest flag (draped):** 101,978 m², by Moquim Al Hajiri in Doha, Qatar, on 16 Dec 2013.

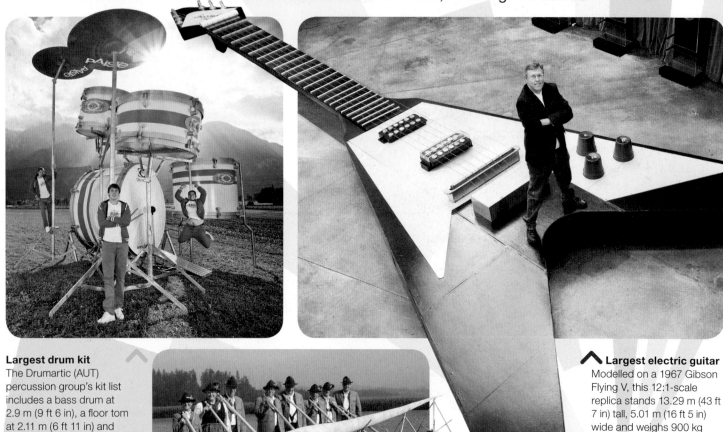Big orchestra

The word "orchestra" comes from the ancient Greek *orcheisthai*, meaning **"to dance"**

Largest drum kit
The Drumartic (AUT) percussion group's kit list includes a bass drum at 2.9 m (9 ft 6 in), a floor tom at 2.11 m (6 ft 11 in) and a rack tom at 1.57 m (5 ft 2 in). The hi-hat cymbals are 1.73 m (5 ft 8 in) wide. Their huge creation is called Big Boom.

Largest electric guitar
Modelled on a 1967 Gibson Flying V, this 12:1-scale replica stands 13.29 m (43 ft 7 in) tall, 5.01 m (16 ft 5 in) wide and weighs 900 kg (2,000 lb). It was made by Scott Rippetoe (USA, above) and students from Conroe Independent School District Academy of Science & Technology in Texas, USA. It was first played on 6 Jun 2000, some seven months after work began.

Longest alphorn
Seven months in the making, "Corno vivo Oli" is 26.46 m (86 ft 9 in) long and weighs 92.5 kg (203 lb 14 oz). It was made by the Rottumtaler Alphornbläser (DEU) out of a single Douglas fir and was presented and measured in Bellamont, Germany, on 16 Sep 2012.

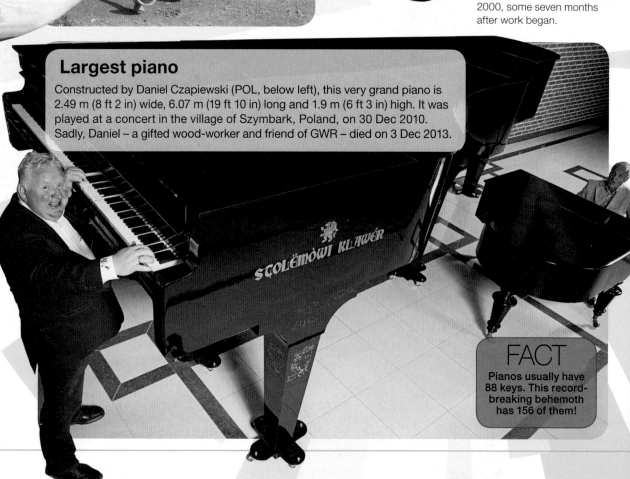

Largest piano

Constructed by Daniel Czapiewski (POL, below left), this very grand piano is 2.49 m (8 ft 2 in) wide, 6.07 m (19 ft 10 in) long and 1.9 m (6 ft 3 in) high. It was played at a concert in the village of Szymbark, Poland, on 30 Dec 2010. Sadly, Daniel – a gifted wood-worker and friend of GWR – died on 3 Dec 2013.

STOLĖMÒWI KLAWÈR

> **FACT**
> Pianos usually have 88 keys. This record-breaking behemoth has 156 of them!

Largest accordion
This 2.53-m-tall (8-ft 3-in), 1.9-m-wide (6-ft 2-in) and 85-cm-deep (2-ft 9-in) squeeze box weighs about 200 kg (440 lb). Built by Giancarlo Francenella (ITA, above, with his daughter Laura), the instrument is named "Fisarmonica Gigante" and was completed in 2001.

Most pieces in a drum kit
In terms of individual elements, the largest drum set belongs to Dr Mark Temperato (USA, above) and comprises 813 pieces. They were counted in Lakeville, New York, USA, on 21 Mar 2013. It takes a team of four people more than 20 hr to set up this colossal kit, and around 45 minutes to hit every piece of percussion in it. Beat that!

Largest violin

Created by the Vogtland masters of violin- and bow-making (DEU), this giant violin is 4.27 m (14 ft) long, has a maximum width of 1.4 m (4 ft 7 in) and is played with a 5.2-m-long (17-ft) bow.

Largest saxophone
With a tube length of 6.74 m (22 ft 1 in) and a bell diameter of 39.1 cm (1 ft 3 in), this super-sized sax was created by J'Élle Stainer (BRA) for the company Below65-4hz.com (ITA) to mark the 200th anniversary of Adolphe Sax. It stands 2.74 m (8 ft 11 in) tall, weighs 28.6 kg (63 lb 0.8 oz) and was measured in Cerveteri, Italy, on 3 Aug 2013. Above, project co-ordinator Gilberto Lopes tries it out.

Fun with food

Americans eat **75 litres of popcorn** a year – enough to fill a bath tub!

Most pancakes made in one hour

Ross McCurdy (USA) singlehandedly made 1,092 pancakes in Kingston, Washington, USA, on 13 Aug 2013.

The **most pancakes made in eight hours by a team** is 76,382, by Batter Blaster (USA) on 9 May 2009.

Fastest field-to-oven-cooked loaf

Australian farmer Neil Unger had long wanted to take the "paddock to plate" challenge. The record had stood unbroken since 1999, but with a team of assistants he took wheat from a field to produce 13 loaves of bread (a "baker's dozen") in 16 min 30.83 sec. The feat took place in Cawdor, New South Wales, Australia, on 11 Jan 2013.

Fastest time to eat a bowl of pasta

Furious Pete, aka Peter Czerwinski (CAN, pictured on p.99), ate a bowl of pasta in 41 sec on the set of *Abenteuer Leben* (Kabel eins) in Sankt Peter-Ording, Germany, on 13 Jul 2013.

Fastest time to eat a jam doughnut with no hands

Oli White (UK) used no hands and didn't lick his lips as he hoovered up a jam doughnut in 28.75 sec at Alexandra Palace in London, UK, on 17 Aug 2013. It was the third time in the space of a year that the GWR YouTube presenter managed to break the record.

Most bites in one minute while juggling apples

Entertainer and juggler Michael Goudeau (USA) took 151 bites from three apples while juggling for 1 min on the set of *Guinness World Records Unleashed* in Los Angeles, California, USA, on 20 Jun 2013.

Most Bhut Jolokia chilli peppers eaten in two minutes

The Bhut Jolokia, or ghost chilli, rates at approximately 1,000,000 on the Scoville scale (see below). On 19 Jun 2013, Jason McNabb (USA) ate 66 g (2.33 oz) of these chillis – more than 13 whole peppers – in Los Angeles, California, USA.

FACT
Ghost peppers can burn bare skin, so always wear latex gloves if handling.

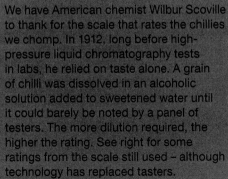

MOST...

Bananas sliced with a sword on a slackline in one minute
A slackline is similar in look to a tightrope, but is slung much closer to the ground. Veteran record-breaker Ashrita Furman (USA) balanced on a slackline as he was thrown 36 bananas, each of which he cut in two in New York, USA, on 3 Aug 2013.

Spice up your life: the Scoville scale

We have American chemist Wilbur Scoville to thank for the scale that rates the chillies we chomp. In 1912, long before high-pressure liquid chromatography tests in labs, he relied on taste alone. A grain of chilli was dissolved in an alcoholic solution added to sweetened water until it could barely be noted by a panel of testers. The more dilution required, the higher the rating. See right for some ratings from the scale still used – although technology has replaced tasters.

Chilli	Scoville rating
Peperoncini	100–500
Jalapeño	2,500–5,000
Cayenne	30,000–50,000
Tabasco	
Scotch bonnet	80,000–300,000
Bhut Jolokia	800,000–1.04 million
Naga viper	1.38 million
Carolina reaper (pictured left)	1.56 million (the **hottest chilli**)

 Egg-streme efforts

Fastest time to crush 10 eggs: 12.64 sec, Mauro Vagnini (ITA), Milan, Italy, 28 Apr 2011

Most standing jumps on to raw eggs without breaking them: nine, Lan Guangping (CHN), Beijing, China, 9 Sep 2013

Most eggs held in one hand: 27, Silvio Sabba (ITA), Milan, Italy, 19 May 2013

FACT

Sabering a bottle of champagne was popular during the Napoleonic Wars. The bottle is held at about 20° and the sabre used to crack the collar; the pressure in the bottle then sends the top flying off.

Champagne bottles sabered in one minute

"Sabrage" is a technique used to open champagne by holding the bottle at an angle and sliding a sabre (sword) up the neck deftly enough to slice off the collar and cork. On 8 Sep 2013, Mitchell Ancona (USA) sabered open 34 bottles in a minute in Ridgefield, Connecticut, USA.

The **most champagne bottles sabered at once** is 277, by Centro Empresarial e Cultural de Garibaldi in Rio Grande do Sul, Brazil, on 5 Oct 2013.

Using the conventional method of opening, UK TV chef Gino D'Acampo (ITA) recorded the **most champagne corks popped in one minute**, with seven on 29 Jul 2013.

Cream-filled sponge cakes eaten in one minute

Competitive eater Patrick Bertoletti (USA) tucked away 16 creamy sponge delights in Los Angeles, USA, on 26 Jun 2013.

Eggs held unbroken on a roller-coaster

Özgür Tuna held 110 eggs in a basket while Udo Baron (both DEU) gave him advance warning of the roller-coaster turns. The pair were at Europa-Park in Rust, Germany, on 21 Jun 2013.

Hamburgers eaten in three minutes

Takeru Kobayashi (JPN) ate 11 hamburgers in Istanbul, Turkey, on 5 Jun 2013.

Ice-cream scoops balanced on one cone

Dimitri Panciera (ITA) balanced 85 scoops at a festival of ice-cream in Zoppè di Cadore, Italy, on 21 Jul 2013.

Most nuts crushed by sitting down in 30 seconds

Cherry Yoshitake (JPN) crushed 48 walnuts using his buttocks at the Wakamiya Hachimangu shrine in Kawasaki, Kanagawa, Japan, on 15 Jan 2013.

Fastest time to eat three éclairs

Furious Pete demolished three chocolate éclairs in 18.02 sec at MEATMarket in Covent Garden, London, UK, on 10 Jul 2013. That day he also set a gastronomic record for the **most hamburgers eaten in one minute**, with four. Fans follow his antics on YouTube, with his videos having notched up more than 115 million views by 1 Feb 2014.

Mustard drunk in 30 seconds

Denis Klefenz (DEU) consumed 294 g (10.37 oz) from a tube of Kühne Senf Mittelscharf German mustard on 20 Jun 2013.

Walnuts crushed by hand in one minute

Not content with crushing 131 walnuts in his hand in 60 sec on 10 Dec 2012, Ashrita Furman went on to set another nutty record, for the **most walnuts cracked against the head in one minute**: 44, on 8 Jan 2013. Both were set in New York, USA.

Fastest time to drink one litre of lemon juice

Michael Jenkins (USA) won a three-way head-to-head challenge by drinking a litre of lemon juice through a straw in a record time of 54.1 sec in Los Angeles, California, USA, on 20 Jun 2013, beating the next fastest time by 10 sec.

100% Pure

Lemon Juice
Not From Concentrate

Trenchermen: eating to excess

A "trencher" was a medieval bowl carved out of a loaf of stale bread and, as the first edition of *The Guinness Book of Records* explained in 1955, "trencherman" was the name given to a glutton who enjoys food to excess, often setting records in the process. However, we went on to say that trenchermen records did not match "those suffering from the rare disease of bulimia (morbid desire to eat) and polydipsia (pathological thirst). Some bulimia patients have to spend 15 hr a day eating, with an extreme consumption of 174 kg of food in six days by Matthew Daking, aged 12, in 1743... Some polydipsomaniacs are unsatisfied by less than 54.5 litres of liquid a day."

FAST FOOD: FROM SWIFT SWALLOWERS TO NIMBLE NIBBLERS

- 61.46 sec, **eat 500 g of cranberry sauce**, Erkan Mustafa (UK)
- 54 sec, **eat three mince pies**, Robert Edward Lee (AUS)
- 50.08 sec, **wrap five portions of chips**, Stephanie Celik (UK)
- 41 sec, **eat a bowl of pasta**, "Furious" Peter Czerwinski (CAN)
- 36.10 sec, **eat three pickled eggs**, Kyle Thomas Moyer (USA)
- 18.02 sec, **eat three chocolate éclairs**, Peter Czerwinski (CAN)
- sec, **eat a slice of toast**, Anthony Falzon (MLT)

seconds

And finally...

- **Most cappuccinos made in one hour:** 289 by Suzanne Stagg (AUS) in Hobart, Tasmania, Australia, on 29 Nov 2013

- **Largest cream tea party:** 510 people in Buxton, Derbyshire, UK, on 24 Nov 2013

- **Most people dunking cookies:** 1,796 by Oreo India at I.I.T., Mumbai, India, on 22 Dec 2013

Big food

There are **more Indian restaurants** in London than in Mumbai and New Delhi combined

Largest samosa

On 22 Jun 2012, chefs and students at Bradford College in West Yorkshire, UK, cooked up a super-sized Indian pastry weighing 110.8 kg (244 lb 4 oz) and measuring 1.35 m (4 ft 5 in) long, 85 cm (2 ft 9 in) wide and 29 cm (11 in) high. The team dubbed their world-beater "Big Bertha".

LARGEST...

Bowl of apple sauce
Musselman's Apple Sauce (USA) produced a bowl of apple sauce weighing 324.8 kg (716 lb) at the Baltimore Running Festival in Maryland, USA, on 12 Oct 2013.

Cheesecake
Philadelphia Cream Cheese (USA) created a cheesecake weighing in at 3,129 kg (6,900 lb) in Lowville,

New York, USA, on 21 Sep 2013. It measured 2.29 m (7 ft 6.2 in) in diameter and 78.7 cm (2 ft 7 in) tall.

Chewing gum stick
Japanese firm Lotte produced the biggest stick of chewing gum, in Sapporo, Hokkaido, Japan, on 5 Oct 2013. It measured

1.085 m (3 ft 6.7 in) long, 29.4 cm (11.57 in) wide and 2.9 cm (1.14 in) deep.

Chocolate mousse
A mousse weighing 225.3 kg (496 lb 12 oz) – as heavy as three average men – was whipped up for charity at the Aventura Mall in Florida, USA, on 6 Oct 2012.

FACT
This titanic turkey tea is free for anyone who can eat it – solo – within 45 min!

Largest Christmas dinner

This 9.6-kg (21-lb 2-oz) festive feast for one comprises a turkey, carrots, parsnips, broccoli, cauliflower, roast potatoes, "pigs in blankets" and 25 Brussels sprouts. It was on the menu of The Duck Inn in Oakenshaw, UK, on 24 Dec 2013.

Cinnamon roll
Weighing the equivalent of five adult women, the largest cinnamon roll tipped the scales at 276 kg (609 lb) and was baked by the Second Floor Bakery in Holland, Michigan, USA, on 4 May 2013. The roll measured 1.83 m (6 ft) in diameter and was 17.8 cm (7 in) deep.

Largest macaron tower

Sebastien Laurent (FRA) created a 12-tier, 6.7-m (21-ft 11-in) display that comprised 8,540 macarons at Château de Montjoux in Thonon-les-Bains, France, on 8 Jun 2013.

Crab cake
Made from fresh Maryland blue crab meat, the largest crab cake weighed 136 kg (300 lb). It was made by Handy International Incorporated (USA) in Timonium, Maryland, USA, on 1 Sep 2012.

Rocky road
On 25 Jan 2013, Australian confectionery company Darrell Lea created a "rocky road" – a candy bar of chocolate, nut, marshmallow and biscuit – that weighed 261.2 kg (575 lb 13.5 oz).

Largest pizza commercially available

Big Mama's & Papa's Pizzeria's Giant Sicilian pizza measures 1.37 x 1.37 m (4 ft 6 in x 4 ft 6 in). Sold at six locations in Los Angeles, USA, it's large enough to feed between 50 and 100 people. The outsize snack will set you back $199.99 (£124.18) plus tax.

FACT
First made in Naples, Italy, pizzas originally used dough and tomatoes but no cheese.

★ Big burger recipe ★

The Black Bear Casino Resort (USA) share their recipe for the **largest hamburger.** You will need:

913.54 kg beef (about 3.5 cows)
23.8 kg tomatoes
22.7 kg lettuce
27.2 kg onions
8.6 kg pickles
18.1 kg American cheese
7.5 kg bacon

Cook the beef for 4 hr on a 4.5-m skillet, using a crane to flip the patty. Once it's done, add toppings and serve in a giant bun!

CAN I HAVE SOME MORE, PLEASE?

A standard bath tub holds 80 litres. So how long do you think it would take you to drink all these record-breakers?   = 25 bath tubs

Largest cocktail 39,746.82 litres

Largest bowl of soup 26,658 litres

Largest cup of coffee 13,200 litres

Largest cup of hot chocolate 3,331.16 litres

ℹ Waste not, want not

GWR insists that the products of all "big food" record attempts must be consumed to avoid wastage. At most record attempts, food is eaten by participants or spectators, distributed to food banks or sold off to raise money for charity. If food is not eaten, or becomes inedible in the process of being prepared, it will not qualify as a record.

HUMONGOUS HELPINGS

Most of the records on these pages are for one huge item of food. But in the table below, you'll find records for the largest overall servings – ordinary food served in extraordinary amounts.

What	Quantity	Who	Date
Baked potatoes	1,716.6 kg (3,784 lb 7 oz)	Comité Organizador de Fegasur (PER)	9 Jun 2012
1 Chilli con carne	1,097.7 kg (2,420 lb)	Chris' Dream Chili Team (USA)	15 Jun 2013
Chips (fries)	448 kg (987 lb 10 oz)	Adventure Island (UK)	29 Jun 2011
Dumplings	685 kg (1,510 lb 2 oz)	A Chang Meat Dumpling Restaurant (TPE)	18 Nov 2012
2 Fish and chips	47.75 kg (105 lb 4 oz)	Fish and Chips@ LTD (UK)	30 Jul 2012
Fruit salad	6,935.88 kg (15,291 lb)	University of Massachusetts Dining Services (USA)	2 Sep 2013
3 Lobster	510.99 kg (1,126 lb 8 oz)	International Lobster Festivals, Inc. and San Pedro Fish Markets (USA)	14 Sep 2013
Mussels	4,898 kg (10,798 lb 3 oz)	Havfruen Fiskerestaurant (NOR)	3 Aug 2012
Papas rellenas	846.9 kg (1,867 lb 1 oz)	Municipality of Ventanilla, Sociedad Peruana Cebiche Más Grande del Mundo, and APRIEG (all PER)	29 Sep 2013
Pastries	39,550 pastries	2023 Metre Barış ve Kardeşlik Böregi (TUR)	3 Jun 2012

Smoothie
More than 3,200 bananas were liquidized by the Cabot Creamery Cooperative in New York City, USA, on 3 May 2013 to make a 1,514-litre (333-gal) smoothie – enough to fill at least 16 average-sized bath tubs!

LONGEST...

Black pudding
Created in Burgos, Spain, during the city's year as the Spanish Capital of Gastronomy 2013, a black pudding was measured at 175.7 m (576 ft 5 in). Weighing in at 211 kg (465 lb), the *morcilla* was made by more than 450 volunteers, following the local recipe: pork, pork fat, horcal onion, bahia rice, lard, pork blood, spices and salt, in a casing of tripe.

Cake roll
Starting on 16 Apr 2013, it took 66 pastry chefs from Japan's Kai Corporation two days to create a strawberry-topped cream sponge roll measuring 130.68 m (428 ft 8 in) in Tokyo, Japan.

Fruit cake
A fruit cake measuring 503.34 m (1,651 ft 4 in) – as long as nine jumbo jets parked wing to wing – was made by Panaderia Schick at the Centro Comercial Managua in Nicaragua on 17 Nov 2013.

Garlic bread
Etienne Thériault (CAN) created a stick of garlic bread 16.71 m (54 ft 10 in) long at École Ola-Léger in Bertrand, New Brunswick, Canada, on 6 Jul 2013.

Hot dog
A hot dog measuring 203.8 m (668 ft 7 in) was created by Novex SA in the city of Mariano Roque Alonso, Paraguay, on 15 Jul 2011 – long enough to fill 1,132 regular hot dog buns!

Ice-cream dessert
On 18 Aug 2013, a 380.97-m (1,249-ft 11-in) line of ice-cream scoops decorated with chocolate syrup, nuts and sprinkles was served up – in an array of (clean!) gutter pipes – by PGA National Resort & Spa and Luke's Ice Cream in Palm Beach Gardens, Florida, USA.

Largest serving of doughnuts

MEGA Alma-Ata shopping and entertainment mall in Almaty, Kazakhstan, fried up 667 kg (1,470 lb) of *baursaks* (sweetened fluffy dough) on 2 Nov 2013. A specially constructed wooden barrel was needed to hold the doughnuts.

Ham-made: grow your own burger

Professor Mark Post (left), a Dutch vascular biologist at Maastricht University in the Netherlands, demonstrated the **first laboratory-grown beef burger** during a launch event in London, UK, on 5 Aug 2013. The *in vitro* meat – the first example of what its creator says could provide an answer to global food shortages and help combat climate change – was fried in a pan and tasted by two volunteers.

The result of years of research by Post, the meat in the burger was made by knitting together around 20,000 strands of protein cultured from cattle stem cells in his lab. Post and his team are working to show that meat grown in petri dishes might one day be a true alternative to meat from livestock.

✋ And finally...

- **Largest gingerbread house:** 1,110.1 m³ (internal volume), built by Traditions Club (USA) on 30 Nov 2013.
- **Largest bag of crisps:** 1,141 kg, by Corkers Crisps (UK) on 13 Sep 2013.
- **Longest line of sandwiches:** 3,865.7 m of sandwiches with chocolate and hazelnut spread, by Nocilla (ESP) on 1 Jun 2013.

⊙ Curious claimants

You don't need to be **Usain Bolt or Edmund Hillary** to be a record-breaker… luckily for this heroic lot!

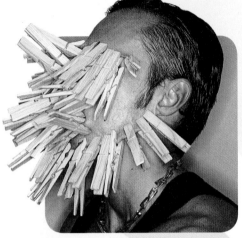

Silvio Sabba

With 48 current Guinness World Records to his name – all achieved in less than three years – Italy's Silvio Sabba is one of our most prolific claimants and king of the one-minute records. He's pictured here attempting the **most matchsticks stacked into a tower** (74), **most dice stacked using chopsticks** (44) and **most clothes pegs clipped to the face** (51).

28
Number of dice that Silvio stacked into a tower – using just his mouth – in a minute on 3 Jul 2013.

Simon Elmore
Here's a record that really sucks! Britain's Simon Elmore managed to stuff 400 regular drinking straws into his gob at once on 6 Aug 2009. And, as per Guinness World Records guidelines, he held them in place for a full 10 seconds. Unfortunately for Simon, he was two straws short of his personal goal, but he still did enough to earn himself the world record.

Gary Duschl
The latest surveyor's report on Gary Duschl's (USA) epic **longest chewing gum wrapper chain** gives a total length of 23.9 km (14.8 mi) – that's almost 230 soccer pitches long! Gary has been linking gum wrappers since 11 Mar 1965, and as of Mar 2014 has made 3,743,076 links to 1,871,538 wrappers.

Nathan Dickens

There was plenty of bizarre behaviour on American TV when *Guinness World Records Unleashed* aired in 2013. Among the records established was the **most targets hit by blindfolded tennis serves in two minutes** (15), by the USA's Nathan Dickens.

Stephen Kish
A regular in the first series of the BBC's *Officially Amazing* TV show, "Sizzlin'" Stephen Kish (UK) pinged his way to a record for the **most ping pong balls bounced into a pint glass in one minute** (six).

Michael Pericoloso

Putting the "breaking" into record-breaking is Michael Pericoloso (USA), who earned his certificate for the **most yard sticks broken over the head in one minute** (37) on *Guinness World Records Unleashed* in Jun 2013. Ouch!

John Cassidy ∧
When it comes to balloon-shaping, John Cassidy (USA) leaves the competition feeling deflated. John's records include the **fastest time to create a balloon dog sculpture** (6.5 sec), the **most balloon sculptures made in one minute** (13) and the **most made in one hour** (747).

Crying over spilt milk
Skimmed milk is best for this attempt – if you use full-fat milk, the fat tends to clog up the tear ducts!

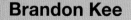

Brandon Kee

Ever heard the phrase "Don't shoot 'til you see the whites of his eyes"? It could've been coined for Brandon "Youngblood" Kee (USA), holder of the record for the **fastest time to hit five targets by squirting milk from the eye** (34.9 sec). How does he get it there? He snorts it up his nose then forces it out of his tear ducts! Eye caramba!

Take the challenge
Got a unique talent or record-worthy party piece? If so, visit our Challengers website – **guinnessworldrecords. com/challengers** – where you can attempt a record of your own and upload a video to one of our adjudicators.

Show of strength

Danish strongman John Holtum could **catch cannonballs** fired straight at him

title 15 times between 1999 and 2013. The nine events include standing chop, hot saw, springboard chop and 18-m (60-ft) speed climb. The World Championships are held annually in Hayward, Wisconsin, USA.

The **most Lumberjack World Championships won by a woman** is nine, by Nancy Zalewski (USA). She won the title of Lady Jill (men are lumberjacks, women are lumberjills) in 2003–04 and 2007–13. The All-Around Lady Jill title is given to the woman who scores highest over the entire competition.

Heaviest weight lifted by pierced ears

Johnny Strange (UK) lifted a 14.9-kg (32-lb 13.5-oz) keg that was attached to a hook through his pierced ears in Doncaster, South Yorkshire, UK, on 12 Oct 2013. Along with Daniella D'Ville (opposite), Johnny performs as part of the Institution of Human Marvels.

Most frying pans rolled in one minute

Steve Weiner (USA) rolled 12 frying pans in Los Angeles, California, USA, on 25 Jun 2013. The **most frying pans rolled by a female** is five, by Polish powerlifter Aneta Florczyk in Beijing, China, on 14 Nov 2008.

Fastest time to pull a train over 20 metres using rice-bowl suction
By pressing a bowl on his abdominal muscles, Zhang Xingquan (CHN) created enough suction to pull a train weighing 132 tonnes (291,000 lb), with two drivers weighing 150 kg (330 lb). It took him 1 min 18.92 sec to cover 20 m (65 ft 6 in) in Erlianhaote, Inner Mongolia, China, on 24 Jul 2013.

Greatest weight lifted in one hour by kettlebell snatch
On 23 Dec 2013, Sergey Trifanov (BLR) lifted 30,012 kg (66,165 lb) by

snatching kettlebells at the State Technological University in Vitebsk, Belarus.

Most baseball bats broken with the back in one minute
Matt Dopson (USA) was on the set of *Guinness World Records Unleashed* to snap 19 baseball bats over his back in Los Angeles, California, USA, on 24 Jun 2013.

Most wins of the Lumberjack World Championships
Jason Wynyard (NZ) won the Tony Wise All-Around Champion

Most apples crushed with the bicep in one minute

Mama Lou, aka Linsey Lindberg (USA), used muscle power to squash eight apples in Los Angeles, California, USA, on 26 Jun 2013. Once an accountant, she quit to be a performer and now blows up and pops hot water bottles and rips telephone directories in half.

> HEAVIEST WEIGHT LIFTED BY...

Nose (floss): Christopher Snipp (UK), 11 May 2013 — **15.8 kg**

Tongue: Thomas Blackthorne (UK), 1 Aug 2008 — **12.5 kg**

4.12 kg — Forehead (hooks): Burnaby Q Orbax (CAN), 21 Jun 2013

14.9 kg — Ears: Johnny Strange (UK), 12 Oct 2013

63.8 kg — Beard: Antanas Kontrimas (LTU), 26 Jun 2013

32.6 kg — Nipples: "The Baron" (FIN), 19 Jul 2013

4.12 kg — Cheeks (hooks): Sweet Pepper Klopek (CAN), 21 Jun 2013

67.5 kg — Little fingers: Kristian Holm (NOR), 13 Nov 2008

8.67 kg — Fingernail: Chikka Bhanu Prakash (IND), 20 Nov 2011

23 kg — Toes: Guy Phillips (UK), 28 May 2011

👁 Pulling vehicles

Heaviest road vehicle pulled by teeth: Igor Zaripov (RUS), double-decker bus weighing 12,360 kg in London, UK, on 15 Oct 2012

Heaviest train pulled by teeth: Velu Rathakrishnan (MYS), two trains weighing 260.8 tonnes in Kuala Lumpur, Malaysia, on 18 Oct 2003

Heaviest vehicle pulled by nipples: "The Great Nippulini", aka Sage Werbock (USA), a wagon loaded with people weighing a total of 988.5 kg in Milan, Italy, on 25 Mar 2011

ℹ Greatest weight lifted

"The greatest weight ever raised by a human being", according to our 1955 book, "is 4,333 lb (1.84 tons) [1,965 kg] by the 25-stone [158.7-kg] French-Canadian Louis Cyr (1863–1912) in Chicago in 1896 in a back-lift (weight raised off trestles). Cyr had a 60½-in [153.6-cm] chest and 22-in [55.8-cm] biceps." Today, the fully notarized record stands at 2,422 kg for two cars (plus drivers) on a platform backlifted by Gregg Ernst (CAN) in Jul 1993.

○ ○ ○

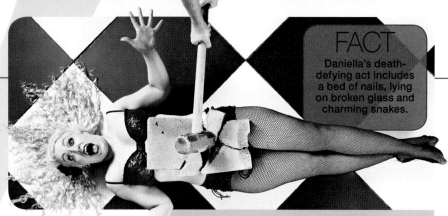

FACT

Daniella's death-defying act includes a bed of nails, lying on broken glass and charming snakes.

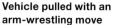

HEAVIEST...

Boat pulled by a team of swimmers

A team of 73 people organized by lifeguard association SLRG Luzern (CHE) pulled a boat weighing 323.2 tonnes (712,534 lb) on 14 Sep 2013 in Lucerne, Switzerland. They took 4 min 34.72 sec to pull the boat 100 m (328 ft).

George Olesen (DNK) recorded the **heaviest boat pulled by an individual**. The boat was a ferry weighing 10,300 tonnes (22.7 million lb) and he heaved it 5.1 m (16 ft 8.8 in) in Gothenburg, Sweden, in Jun 2000.

Tyre spun around the body

As well as breaking records with ordinary hula hoops, Paul Blair (USA) has shaken his stuff with a tyre weighing 52.9 kg (116 lb 10 oz). Paul, who performs as Dizzy Hips, set his latest record on 8 Sep 2013.

For more physical feats, turn to p.118

Fastest time to break 16 concrete blocks on the body (female)

Daniella D'Ville, aka Danielle Martin (UK), had 16 concrete blocks smashed on her body – one at a time – in 30.40 sec with a sledgehammer wielded by fellow performer Johnny Strange (UK) at the Tattoo Jam in Doncaster, South Yorkshire, UK, on 12 Oct 2013. Each of the slabs had a minimum density of 650 kg/m³ (41 lb/cu ft).

Heaviest weight lifted by beard

Antanas Kontrimas (LTU) used his beard to lift 63.8 kg (141 lb) – in the shape of *Rekorlar Dünyası* presenter Gupse Özay'ın – in Istanbul, Turkey, on 26 Jun 2013. It was his 10th consecutive successful attempt at a record he first set in 2000, when he lifted 55.7 kg (122 lb 11 oz).

Vehicle pulled with an arm-wrestling move

Kevin Fast (CAN) challenged a truck to an arm-wrestling contest – and won! With his elbow on a table in an arm-wrestling position, the multiple record holder pulled a truck weighing 11,060 kg (24,380 lb) in Cobourg, Ontario, Canada, on 26 Apr 2013. Kevin also holds records for the **heaviest aircraft pulled by a man** (a Boeing C-17 Globemaster III weighing 188.83 tonnes; 416,299 lb), and the **heaviest house pulled by a man** (35.9 tonnes; 79,145 lb). You can also see him setting a new caber-tossing record on p.112.

Yoke walk over 10 metres

The yoke is a metal bar carried over the shoulders with weights either side. Patrik Baboumian (DEU, b. IRN) carried a weight of 555 kg (1,224 lb) in Toronto, Ontario, Canada, on 8 Sep 2013.

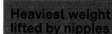

Heaviest weight lifted by nipples

"The Baron" (FIN) is no stranger to tricks involving extremely close encounters with drills, hooks and nails, not to mention fire. He topped the lot by lifting 32.6 kg (71 lb 14 oz) with his nipples at Bush Hall in London, UK, on 19 Jul 2013.

Weight lifted with one ear using a clamp

Rakesh Kumar (IND) used an ear clamp to lift 82.6 kg (182 lb 1 oz) in Istanbul, Turkey, on 25 Jul 2013.

Vehicle pulled with ears (female)

On 20 Jun 2013, Asha Rani (IND) used both ears to pull a 1,700-kg (3,745-lb) van in Leicestershire, UK. Back in Aug 2012, she pulled a double-decker bus – at 12,101 kg (26,678 lb), the **heaviest vehicle pulled by a woman using her hair** – a distance of 17.2 m (56 ft 5 in).

Gym king: endurance weightlifter

Eamonn Keane (IRL) holds 22 records, as of Mar 2014, for endurance weightlifting. The champion lifter's most recent feat was the **most weight lifted by incline dumbbell flies in one minute** (in which dumbbells are held in each hand on an incline bench before bringing them together over the chest), with 2,160 kg in Louisburgh, Ireland, on 16 Oct 2013. His oldest record still standing dates back to 2003: the **heaviest weight lifted in one hour by bench press**, an astonishing 138,480 kg. He did 1,280 repetitions with 90.7 kg and 493 reps with 45.3 kg.

And finally...

- **Heaviest vehicle pulled over 100 ft (female):** Lia Grimanis (CAN) pulled a truck cab weighing 8,083 kg in Toronto, Ontario, Canada, on 12 Dec 2013.
- **Most kettlebell weight lifted in one minute with alternating floor presses:** Anatoly Ezhov (BLR) lifted 4,080 kg – 170 reps of a 24-kg kettlebell lift – in Zurich, Switzerland, on 27 Feb 2014.

Flexible friends

Overall, **women are more flexible** than men of the same age

Fastest time to cram into a box (male)

Mr Yogi Laser, aka Kenneth Greenaway (USA), took 5.35 sec to squeeze into a box measuring 50.8 x 50.8 x 44.4 cm (20 x 20 x 17.5 in) in California, USA, on 27 Jun 2013. The **fastest time to cram into a box (female)** – a space of just 52 x 45 x 45 cm (20.4 x 17.7 x 17.7 in) – is 4.78 sec, by Skye Broberg (NZ) on 15 Sep 2011.

Fastest escape from a straitjacket

Sofia Romero (UK) freed herself from a regulated Posey straitjacket in 4.69 sec at the Aylestone Leisure Centre in Leicester, UK, on 9 Jun 2011.

The **fastest escape from a straitjacket and chains while suspended** is 10.6 sec and was achieved by Lucas Wilson (CAN) at Holy Trinity Catholic High School in Simcoe, Ontario, Canada, on 8 Jun 2012.

Wilson also recorded the **fastest escape from a straitjacket underwater** – 23.16 sec – at École St Patrick high school in Yellowknife, Northwest Territories, Canada, on 5 Oct 2013.

Most people belly dancing simultaneously

Danone Canarias (ESP) organized a mass belly dance involving 842 performers at Playa de Las Canteras in Las Palmas, Gran Canaria, Spain, on 29 May 2011.

YOGA

Longest yoga chain

A chain of 696 students from the CK School of Practical Knowledge (IND) formed a yoga chain in Cuddalore, India, on 30 Jan 2013. They performed five different yoga poses, including: Cow's Face (Gomukhasana), Child's (Balasana), Half Lotus (Padmasana) and Easy Seated (Sukhasana).

Longest yoga marathon (female)

During a 32-hr marathon, Yasmin Fudakowska-Gow (CAN) completed 1,008 yoga positions at Om West Centre Holistique in Quebec, Canada, on 2–3 Aug 2010.

The **longest yoga marathon (male)** lasted 29 hr 4 min and was achieved by Michael Schwab (AUT) in Vienna, Austria, on 26–27 Sep 2009.

ACROBATICS

Longest backflip

Lukas Steiner (AUT) carried out a 4.26-m (13-ft 11.7-in) backflip in Milan, Italy, on 28 Apr 2011.

Most jackhammer hops in one minute

Bryan Nguyen (USA) performed 49 jackhammer hops – a staple breakdancing move – in a minute on the set of *Guinness World Records Unleashed* in Los Angeles, California, USA, on 19 Jun 2013. The guidelines require that the hand leaves the ground on each hop.

Steiner also recorded the **longest jump from feet to handstand (male)**. From a standing start, he leapt 2.55 m (8 ft 4.39 in), landed on his hands and pressed himself into a handstand, held for 5 sec. The attempt was undertaken in Mittweida, Germany, on 10 Nov 2011.

Longest time to hold the Marinelli bend position

This extraordinarily demanding position requires the performer to sustain his or her entire body weight via a mouth grip on a short pole. Tsatsral Erdenebileg (MNG) maintained a Marinelli bend for 4 min 17 sec on the set of *Rekorlar Dünyası* in Istanbul, Turkey, on 17 Jul 2013.

LARGEST ACTIVITY EVENTS

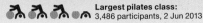

Largest aerobics display: 50,420 participants, 15 Aug 2011

Largest yoga class: 29,973 students, 19 Nov 2005

Largest dance class: 9,223 participants, 30 Apr 2010

 = 1,000 participants

Largest Zumba class: 6,671 participants, 15 Sep 2012

Largest pilates class: 3,486 participants, 2 Jun 2013

 Largest limbo dance: 1,208 children, 1 Oct 2011

Glossary

Parkour: the discipline of moving rapidly through a typically urban environment, by means of performing acrobatic feats such as jumping, climbing and flipping to negotiate obstacles. It began in France and was popularized by David Belle and Sébastien Foucan. Parkour practitioners are known as "traceurs", as they "trace" their way through their environment.

FACT

US gymnast George Eyser won six medals at the 1904 Olympics – despite his wooden leg.

Supple difference

Babies have a greater amount of soft cartilage than bone. In time, much of this hardens into bone – which is why adults are so much less flexible than babies.

On 24 May 2010, Chase Armitage (UK) performed the **longest backflip off a wall**, measuring 3.48 m (11 ft 5 in), for *Zheng Da Zong Yi – Guinness World Records Special* in Beijing, China.

The **most backflips against a wall in one minute** is 29, by Miguel Marquez (ESP) for the same TV series in Beijing, China, on 19 Jun 2009.

Most circular jumps on a wall in one minute
To make a circular jump, performers use only their hands to spin the body 360° against a wall. On 24 Mar 2010, Aung Zaw Oo (USA) carried out 11 circular jumps on a wall in Rome, Italy.

Longest forward-jump flip/somersault
Hasit Savani (UK) achieved a 6-m (19-ft 7-in) forward-jump flip at Talacre Community Sports Centre in London, UK, on 15 Feb 2012.

Most forward-roll frontflips in one minute
Mathew Kaye (UK) managed 17 forward-roll frontflips in a minute at Parkour Park in Chineham, Hampshire, UK, on 8 Sep 2010. On the same day, he also recorded the **most pistol squats on a scaffold pole in one minute**, with 29. A pistol squat is a bodyweight squat done on one leg to full depth. Mathew can be seen performing parkour in Coldplay's video for "Charlie Brown" (2011).

Farthest arrow shot using feet

Nancy Siefker (USA) shot an arrow into a target 6.09 m (20 ft) away using only her feet on the set of *Guinness World Records Unleashed* in Los Angeles, California, USA, on 20 Jun 2013. The guidelines require that the target should be no more than 30 cm (12 in) in diameter. However, Nancy, a circus performer, hit a target measuring just 13.9 cm (5.5 in).

Most hula hoops spun simultaneously around the waist (team)

Marawa the Amazing (AUS) and her Majorettes whirled into the record books by spinning 264 hula hoops at once at the Shaftesbury Theatre in London, UK, on 14 Nov 2013, in celebration of Guinness World Records Day. For more Marawa, spin over to p.112.

Oldest person to perform a backflip
Walter Liesner (DEU, b. 14 Jan 1913) was 94 years 268 days old when he backflipped into a swimming pool in Wetzlar, Germany, on 9 Oct 2007. Walter, a part-time gymnastics teacher for most of his life, shot to local fame aged 17 when he performed a handstand on the handrail at the top of the Wetzlar church tower, 42 m (137 ft) above the ground.

Joint session: pros and cons of hypermobility

People with extreme flexibility are often said to be double-jointed or even triple-jointed. There is disagreement about the accuracy of these terms, however, and some scientists prefer the term "hypermobility" to describe unusually unrestricted joint movements. For dancers or gymnasts, such flexibility can improve performance, but can also give rise to problems including dislocation of the joints, back pain and damage to soft tissue. Super-flexibility, however, can be helpful to contortionists such as Zlata, aka Julia Gunthel (DEU, left, **fastest time to burst three balloons with the back**: 12 sec), and Daniel Browning Smith (USA, right), who achieved the **fastest time to enter a locked straitjacket** (2 min 8 sec) on 16 Aug 1999.

Handcuff escapology

Fastest escape from handcuffs underwater: 3.425 sec, Thomas Blacke (USA), 25 Oct 2011

Fastest escape from double-locked handcuffs: 1.59 sec, Chad Netherland (USA), 8 Jan 2011

Most handcuff escapes in one hour: 627, Zdeněk Bradáč (CZE), 12 Feb 2010

○ ○ ○

Performers

"Circus" is from the Latin for "**ring**" – rounded arena for entertainment

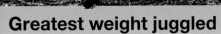

Most soap bubbles blown inside one large bubble

Andy Lin, aka Kuo-Sheng Lin (TWN), blew 152 soap bubbles inside a larger bubble at the World Trade Center in Taipei City, Chinese Taipei, on 23 Dec 2011. On 17 Apr 2012, Kuo-Sheng also set a record for the **most bounces of a soap bubble**, with 195 consecutive bounces.

Eichholz went 15.66 m (51 ft 4 in) in Beijing, China, on 9 Sep 2013.

Greatest height by a human cannonball
The Bullet, aka David Smith, Jr (USA), was fired 26 m (85 ft) vertically on 8 Jul 2013 in California City, California, USA. He also holds the record for the **farthest distance for a human cannonball**, with 59.05 m (193 ft 8.8 in) in Milan, Italy, on 10 Mar 2011. Cannonballing began on 2 Apr 1877, when 14-year-old Zazel, aka Rosa Richter

Greatest weight juggled

Ukrainian strongman Hercules, aka Denys Ilchenko, juggled three tyres weighing a total of 26.98 kg (59 lb 7 oz) in Nairn in the Scottish Highlands, UK, on 17 Jul 2013. The tyres stayed aloft for 32.43 sec on Denys's third attempt.

Farthest distance walked balancing a lawnmower on the chin
Multiple record holder The Space Cowboy, aka Chayne Hultgren (AUS), walked 28.4 m (93 ft 2 in) with an unpowered lawnmower on his chin in Sydney, Australia, on 14 Nov 2013. His other records include the **most**

hat flicks from foot to head on a unicycle in one minute, with 10 in London, UK, on 28 Sep 2012.

Greatest distance travelled on a slackline by unicycle
Slacklines are less rigid to cross than tightropes and German "extreme unicyclist" Lutz

⊗ More performance feats on p.104

(UK), became the **first human cannonball**. She was shot a distance of 6 m (20 ft) at Westminster Aquarium in London, UK.

Largest free-floating soap bubble
SamSam BubbleMan, aka Sam Heath (UK), made a bubble indoors with a volume of 3.3 m³ (117 cu ft) on 11 Jan 2013 in London, UK, for *Officially Amazing* (Lion TV).

Most apples held in own mouth and chainsawed in one minute

Johnny Strange (UK) chainsawed eight apples in his mouth in a minute at Doncaster's Tattoo Jam in South Yorkshire, UK, on 12 Oct 2013. Teaming up with Daniella D'Ville (see opposite), Johnny also set a record for the **most apples held in the mouth and cut in half by chainsaw in one minute**, with 12.

Most poi weaves in one minute
Poi is the art of swinging weights on lengths of material in different rhythmic patterns. Joe Dickinson (UK)

LARGEST ANIMAL CIRCUS ACTS

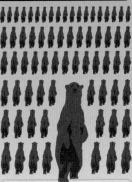

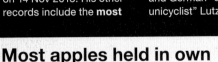

Lions: 40, Alfred Schneider (UK), Bertram Mills Circus, London, UK, 1925

Mixed lions and tigers: 43, Clyde Beatty (USA), 1938

Polar bears: 60–70, Willy Hagenbeck (DEU), Circus Paul Busch, Berlin, Germany, 1904

⚡ **Circus animals**

As the graphic to the left suggests, Guinness World Records has had a long and varied history of documenting records involving circus animals. Today, circuses are much more sensitive to the welfare of animals, and many have banned animal acts outright. Similarly, we no longer monitor records involving circus animals where we cannot be 100% sure of the animals' treatment and welfare.

 ○○○

Jeff Dunham

American ventriloquist and stand-up comedian Jeff Dunham holds the record for the **most tickets sold for a stand-up comedy tour** – his "Spark of Insanity" tour, which was performed in 386 venues worldwide from 13 Sep 2007 to 21 Aug 2010, sold an incredible 1,981,720 tickets, presumably leaving Dunham laughing all the way to the bank.

 ○○○

Most swords swallowed underwater

The Space Cowboy, aka Chayne Hultgren (AUS), swallowed three swords underwater at the Olympic Park Aquatic Centre in Sydney, Australia, on 14 Nov 2013.

achieved 74 three-beat poi weaves in one minute at the Secret Garden Party in Cambridgeshire, UK, on 22 Jul 2012.

Youngest person to do a quadruple somersault
Michael Martini (ITA, b. 17 Nov 1999) performed a quadruple somersault aged 13 years 196 days at Circo Orfei in Massafra, Italy, on 1 Jun 2013. Michael is a professional performer; GWR does not otherwise monitor this category for under-16s.

JUGGLING

Fastest time for a pair to exchange costumes while juggling
Matt Baker and Joe Ricci (both USA) swapped outfits in 2 min 52 sec in Jiangsu, China, on 8 Jan 2014. The two men also recorded

Most rotations of a sword balanced on a dagger

Specialist circus sideshow performer Daniella D'Ville, aka Danielle Martin (UK), set a new record when she rotated a sword balanced on a dagger nine times in a minute at Doncaster's Tattoo Jam on 12 Oct 2013.

13 changeovers – passing while leaping over each other – the **most complete changeovers juggling three objects in one minute**, on 1 Jan 2012.

Greatest distance on a slackline while juggling three objects
Carson Firth (USA) combined slacklining with juggling to walk a record 8.65 m (28 ft 4 in) in Florida, USA, on 9 Aug 2013.

Most melons chopped on the stomach on a nail bed

Daniella D'Ville had 10 watermelons sliced on her stomach while lying on a bed of nails at Doncaster's Tattoo Jam on 12 Oct 2013.
The **most watermelons chopped on the stomach in one minute** (no bed of nails) is 48, sliced by Bipin Larkin on Ashrita Furman (both USA) in Jamaica, New York, USA, on 30 Nov 2012.

Most consecutive axe juggling catches
Having demonstrated the potency of his axes by chopping wood, Max Winfrey (USA) juggled three of them, making 163 catches, in Winter Garden, Florida, USA, on 7 Jun 2013.

Most objects juggled while sword swallowing
The Space Cowboy juggled five balls after swallowing a sword in London, UK, on 14 Sep 2012. Luther Bangert (USA) matched this feat in Iowa City, USA, on 7 Jul 2013. Luther kept

Longest career as a ringmaster

Norman Barrett (UK) had been a ringmaster for 56 years, as of 20 Mar 2014. But he didn't need to run away to join the circus – his father owned one and he was born into the life on 20 Dec 1935. Norman was 12 when he first performed.

the balls aloft for 11.72 sec; The Space Cowboy kept them airborne for 6.5 sec.

Most juggling catches on a circus pole in one minute
Isabelle Noël (DEU), a performer and circus teacher, perched

on a 49-m (160-ft) pole to make 179 catches at Europa-Park in Rust, Germany, on 21 Jun 2013.

Cirque du Soleil: circus maximus

Montreal-based Cirque du Soleil, co-founded and run by Guy Laliberté (CAN), is the **largest circus organization**, with 19 touring and resident global productions. The record-breaking company (see right) turns over more than US$1 bn (£600 m) annually and has 5,000 employees. Cirque du Soleil faces increased competition and tougher markets, but Laliberté still found the time and money to enjoy a $35-m (£22-m) break on the *International Space Station* in 2009 – one of seven visitors since 2001 to experience the **most expensive tourist trip**.

Cirque du Soleil presents...
Most people simultaneously stilt-walking in multiple venues: 1,908 on 16 Jun 2009.
Largest underwater stage hydraulic lift system: Handling Specialty Manufacturing (CAN) built a 339-m² stage in a pool of 5.6 million litres of water in 1999 for Cirque du Soleil!
Fastest 50 m hand-walking on stilts: Carlos Rodriguez Diaz (CUB), 1 min 30 sec in Florida, USA, on 16 Jun 2009

Indoor pursuits

A 3 x 3 Rubik's Cube has **43,252,003,274,489,856,000** permutations

Most people playing pinball simultaneously

On 16 May 2013, 100 paddle flippers amassed at First Canadian Place in Toronto, Canada, to play pinball. The free-to-play event was organized by the Stratford Festival to promote the Avon Theatre's production of *Tommy*, the musical that features the song "Pinball Wizard".

Largest plastic-cup pyramid in 30 minutes

Uri, Jonathan, Daniel and Oded Ish-Shalom (all USA) built a pyramid comprising 652 plastic cups in 30 min in Jerusalem, Israel, on 22 Feb 2012.

Fastest sport stacking (individual cycle stack)

William Polly (USA) set an individual cycle stack time of 5.59 sec at the WSSA US National Sport Stacking Championships in Maryland, USA, on 24 Mar 2013.

Most people playing a board game simultaneously

The Dokter Toy company (IDN) assembled 1,239 people to play the Crazy Birds

board game in Tribeca Central Park, Jakarta, Indonesia, on 16 Jun 2013.

Longest board game marathon

Brett Carow and Sam Hennemann (both USA) played 116 back-to-back games of Strat-O-Matic Baseball for 61 hr 2 min in New York City, USA, on 7–9 Jun 2012.

CHESS

Fastest time to arrange a chess set

Ray Butler (USA) set up a chess board in 41.87 sec in Las Vegas, Nevada, USA, on 18 Sep 2013. The **fastest time to arrange a set by a team of two** is 41.24 sec, by Tyler Eichman and John Walker (both USA) in Oconto, Wisconsin, USA, on 27 Nov 2013.

Longest chess marathon

On 17–19 Dec 2010, Daniel Häußler and Philipp Bergner (both DEU) played chess for 40 hr 20 min in Ostfildern,

Germany. Häußler won 191 to Bergner's 114 games, with 50 draws.

Most chess games played in one location

The Sports Authority of Gujarat (IND) ran 20,480 games simultaneously at the University of Gujarat Sports Grounds in Ahmedabad, India, on 24 Dec 2010.

Largest chess set

On 27 May 2009, the Medicine Hat Chess Club

Most Scrabble opponents played at once

Chris May (AUS) won 25 of the 28 games of Scrabble he played simultaneously at Oxford University Press in Oxford, UK, on 11 Jun 2013. Then ranked No.9 in the world at Scrabble, May took more than four hours to finish all the games.

of Alberta, Canada, unveiled a set measuring 5.89 m (19 ft 4 in) on each side. The king was 1.19 m (3 ft 10 in) tall and 37.4 cm (1 ft 2 in) wide at its base.

DOMINOES

Most dominoes toppled by an individual

Liu Yang (CHN) single-handedly arranged then toppled 321,197 dominoes at CITIC Guoan Grand Epoch City in Beijing, China, on 31 Dec 2011.

Largest ball bath

On 30 Oct 2013, the swimming pool at the Kerry Hotel in Pudong, Shanghai, China, was drained and filled with one million green and pink balls as part of Breast Cancer Awareness Month. The balls, which covered a surface area of 315.6 m² (3,397 sq ft), were later sold to raise funds for charity.

HOW THE MIGHTY HAVE FALLEN: MOST DOMINOES TOPPLED BY A GROUP

■ = 15,000 dominoes

Value	Country	Year
1,605,757	Netherlands	1998
2,472,480	Netherlands	1999
2,751,518	China	1999
3,407,535	China	2000
3,847,295	Netherlands	2002
3,992,397	Netherlands	2004
4,002,136	Netherlands	2005
4,079,381	Netherlands	2006
4,345,027	Netherlands	2008
4,491,863	Netherlands	2009

FACT

The current record for the **most dominoes toppled by a group** was set on Domino Day 2009, aka "The World in Domino – The Show with the Flow", on 13 Nov. The dominoes were set up by 89 builders in the WTC Expo centre in Leeuwarden, Netherlands.

Tallest domino structure

A domino tower 6.02 m (19 ft 9.2 in) high and consisting of 11,465 dominoes was erected and toppled by Yspertal Domino Team (AUT) in Yspertal, Austria, on 3 Nov 2013. Pictured is Marcel Pürrer, one of the team of four who built the tower.

FACT

The tower formed the final part of a 100,101-domino array built by 44 people over four days.

Most solves in Rubik's Cube competitions in a single year

In 2012, Sébastien Auroux (DEU) solved 2,033 Rubik's Cubes in official World Cube Association competitions. This equates to 5.5 competitive solves every day and doesn't include any cubes solved outside of formal events.

MOST SOLVES OF RUBIK'S CUBES IN ONE YEAR

Name	Solves	Attempts	Year
Sébastien Auroux (DEU)	2,033	2,122	2012
François Courtès (FRA)	1,651	1,780	2013
Zoé de Moffarts (BEL)	1,518	1,575	2012
Arnaud van Galen (NLD)	1,481	1,568	2012
Erik Akkersdijk (NLD)	1,477	1,609	2010
Jan Bentlage (DEU)	1,452	1,517	2012
Bence Barát (HUN)	1,349	1,392	2010
Clément Gallet (FRA)	1,213	1,249	2011
Tim Reynolds (USA)	1,205	1,281	2012
Laura Ohrndorf (DEU)	1,193	1,295	2013

Source: World Cube Association, as of 31 Dec 2013

Longest domino wall

Germany's Sinners Domino Entertainment holds multiple records for setting up and toppling dominoes. On 6 Jul 2012, at the Wolfgang Ernst Gymnasium School in Büdingen, Germany, Sinners erected – then toppled – a 30-m-long (98-ft 5-in) wall built from 31,405 dominoes. On the same day, Sinners also set a record for the **most dominoes toppled in a pyramid**, with 13,486.

Not content with this, they were back in action on 23 Oct 2012, this time in Kefenrod, Germany, with the **most dominoes toppled in 30 seconds**, setting up and toppling 60 pieces.

Six months later, Sinners set another record for the **most toppled in a spiral**, with 55,555 on 12 Jul 2013.

Most toppled in one minute

Gemma Hansen (UK) set up and toppled 75 dominoes at Butlin's in Minehead, UK, on 7 Aug 2010. At the 2011 event, also on 7 Aug, Andy James (UK) stacked 39 dominoes in a single pile: the **most dominoes stacked in one minute**. Paul Lusher (UK) equalled his record on 4 Sep 2011.

World Cube Association fastest single solves

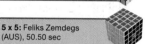
2 x 2: Christian Kaserer (ITA), 0.69 sec

3 x 3: Mats Valk (NLD), 5.55 sec

4 x 4: Feliks Zemdegs (AUS), 24.66 sec

5 x 5: Feliks Zemdegs (AUS), 50.50 sec

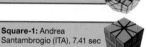
6 x 6: Kevin Hays (USA), 1 min 40.86 sec

7 x 7: Bence Barát (HUN), 2 min 40.11 sec

Megaminx: Simon Westlund (SWE), 42.28 sec

Square-1: Andrea Santambrogio (ITA), 7.41 sec

Pyraminx: Oscar Roth Andersen (DEN), 1.36 sec

Skewb: Brandon Harnish (USA), 2.19 sec

Rubik's Clock: Sam Zhixiao Wang (CHN), 5.27 sec

Correct as of 26 Feb 2014

Captains of cup: sport stacking

The eighth annual STACK UP! was organized by the World Sport Stacking Association (USA) on 14 Nov 2013. They assembled more than half a million people to record the **most people sport stacking in multiple venues**. Speed stackers use special cups that they arrange in specific sequences as fast as possible and then take them down again, often too quickly for a casual observer to follow. The 555,932 stackers represented 2,631 schools and organizations from 29 countries. Stacking fans claim that it improves hand and eye coordination with its emphasis on dexterity.

Pricey pastimes

Most expensive...
Toy model car: 1930s W E Boyce delivery van, £19,975 ($35,728).
Mickey Mouse toy: clockwork Mickey Mouse motorcycle, £51,000 ($83,466).
Toy soldier: 1963 prototype G I Joe, $200,000 (£124,309).
Doll: 1914 French doll by Albert Marque, $263,000 (£162,181).

Skateboarding was **banned in Norway** from 1978 to 1989 because of the high accident rate

Most waterskiers towed by one boat

On 27 Jan 2012, a total of 145 skiers were towed behind a boat at the Horsehead Water Ski Club in Strahan, Tasmania, Australia.

BUNGEE

Highest dunk of a doughnut

Ron Jones (USA) dunked a doughnut by bungee from 60.55 m (198 ft 8 in) into a coffee cup measuring 8.89 cm (3.5 in) in diameter in California City, California, USA, on 7 Jul 2013.

Highest bungee jump dive into water

Raymond Woodcock (UK) was aged 72 when he bungee-jumped 115.9 m (380 ft) from a crane into water in Chepstow, UK, on 18 Aug 2013.

Fastest 100 m in high-heeled roller-skates

Marawa Ibrahim (AUS) glided 100 m in 26.10 sec in Regent's Park, London, UK, on 21 Aug 2013 while wearing her custom-made 13-cm-high (5.1-in) high-heeled roller-skates. "Marawa the Amazing", as she is known, manages a troupe of majorettes who perform in the UK.

Most jumps in one hour

Mike Heard (NZ) jumped 80 times under Auckland Harbour Bridge on 16 Sep 2011, using a cord measuring 9.5 m (31 ft 2 in).

The **most bungee jumps in 24 hours** stands at 105, by Kevin Scott Huntly (ZAF) at Bloukrans Bridge, Garden Route, South Africa, on 8 May 2011. His time was 7 hr 42 min – an average of one jump every 4.5 min, with a cord measuring 40 m (131 ft 3 in).

FLYING DISC (FRISBEE)

Fastest relay over 20 m

On 6 May 2012, a team of five threw a disc in 8.74 sec. Tim, Daniel, Lindsey and Elyse Habenicht and Cliff West (all USA) were in College Station, Texas, USA.

Longest throw caught by a dog

Robert McLeod (CAN) threw a disc 122.5 m (402 ft) to Davy Whippet in Thorhild, Alberta, Canada, on 14 Oct 2012.

Another canine disc master is Beibei the border collie. His owner Liu Haiwang (CHN) helped him set the **most catches by a dog over 10 m in three minutes**, with 18 in Beijing, China, on 7 Sep 2013.

Longest throw to hit a target

Brodie Smith (USA) dunked a disc into a basketball hoop from 45.7 m (150 ft) in Patterson Park in Austin, Texas, USA, on 3 Dec 2013. Brodie was not allowed to hit the backboard in the attempt.

Most drink cans hit in one minute

Robert McLeod (CAN) hit 28 cans at Edgemont World Health club in Calgary, Canada, on 28 Jan 2012. His other achievements include setting the **longest throw, run and catch on ice skates**, with 73.2 m (240 ft) on 24 Feb 2013, and the **longest time for a disc to stay aloft thrown from ice skates**, with 12.03 sec in Edmonton, Canada, on 23 Feb 2013.

FACT

Marawa's flair and coordination with the hula hoop took her to the semi-finals of *Britain's Got Talent* in 2011.

POGO STICK

Fastest mile dribbling a basketball

On 9 Aug 2013, Ashrita Furman (USA) pogo-sticked a mile – while controlling a bouncing basketball – in 23 min 2.91 sec in New York City, USA. Ashrita's eight pogo records include the **fastest mile**, set on 24 Jul 2001 at 12 min 16 sec.

Most caber tosses in three minutes

Kevin Fast (CAN) tossed 14 cabers in Quinte West, Ontario, Canada, on 7 Sep 2013. Kevin has been setting records for many years and currently holds eight records for feats of strength.

POGO POWER: BOUNCING INTO THE RECORD BOOKS

Fastest one mile: 12 min 16 sec, Ashrita Furman (USA), 24 Jul 2001

Most balloons popped in one minute: 57, Mark Aldridge (UK), 1 Apr 2010

Most consecutive front flips: 5, Jake Gartland (USA), 28 Jul 2011

Most consecutive backflips: 17, Fred Grzybowski (USA), 19 Dec 2013

Farthest distance underwater: 512.06 m, Ashrita Furman (USA), 1 Aug 2007

 Get your skates on

Fastest time to roller-skate across the USA: Russell "Rusty" Moncrief (USA), 69 days 8 hr 45 min, 15 Mar 2002.

Fastest time to roller-skate the length of the UK: Damian Magee (UK), 9 days 5 hr 23 min, 19–28 Jun 1992.

Tallest moving human pyramid on roller-skates: NSA Roller Gymnastics Team (USA), four storeys high, Pennsylvania, USA, 1985.

Longest journey by water jet pack

On 8 Nov 2013, TV presenter Pollyanna Woodward (UK) jetted off from Gozo Marina in Malta using a jet pack that draws in water and forces it out under pressure, providing lift. She covered a record 36.45 km (22.64 mi) in 4 hr 45 min.

Most consecutive jumps
James Roumeliotis (USA) recorded 70,271 consecutive pogo jumps – i.e., without a break and without falling off – at Pogopalooza 10 in New York, USA, on 26 Jul 2013.

James had previously set the record for the **most bounces in a pogo marathon**, with an ankle-crushing 206,864 jumps. His attempt took 20 hr 13 min at Pogopalooza 8 in California, USA, on 29 Jul 2011. James commented afterwards, "My calves are killing me. My ankles are swollen. I can't actually feel my hands, my right thumb especially."

ROLLER-SKATING

Longest forward jump
Jeff Dupont (USA) jumped 6.18 m (20 ft 3 in) without using a ramp at the Willamalane Center for Sports and Recreation in Springfield, Oregon, USA, on 12 Feb 2012.

Highest forward flip jump on a pogo stick
Biff Hutchison (USA) jumped 2.49 m (8 ft 2 in) in Tompkins Square Park, New York, USA, on 27 Jul 2013. The next day he set the **highest jump on a pogo stick** at 2.93 m (9 ft 7.5 in).

Longest cumulative abseil in one hour – team of 10

In a stunt organized by ECCO Shoes (DEU), 10 abseilers – all wearing high heels – descended the 103.4-m-tall (339-ft 2-in) Park Inn hotel in Berlin, Germany, in one hour on 6 Jul 2013. A total of 32 descents were logged: a cumulative distance of 3.3 km (2.05 mi).

Most spins while carrying two people
On 10 Dec 2012, Liu Jiangshan made 17 consecutive 360° spins on roller-skates while hanging on to Wang Chenyu and Yang Liangliang (all CHN) in Beijing, China.

SLINGSHOT

Longest slingshot
The greatest distance achieved launching an object from a sling is 477.10 m (1,565 ft 4 in), using a 1.27-m-long (4-ft 2-in) sling and a 62-g (2.25-oz) dart, by David Engvall (USA) at Baldwin Lake, California, USA, on 13 Sep 1992.

Most cans hit in one minute
Michael McClure (USA) used metal balls to strike 13 drinks cans with a slingshot – from 10 m (33 ft) – at the East Coast Slingshot Tournament in Alverton, Pennsylvania, USA, on 8 Jun 2013.

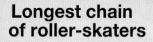

Longest chain of roller-skaters

The Clyde 1 radio station and ScotRail (both UK) set in motion 254 participants in a roller-skating line in Glasgow, UK, on 8 Sep 2013. They were led by Clyde 1 DJ Diane Knox-Campbell.

Pie's the limit: flying disc history

As long ago as ancient Greece, the discus was in use (right), and a clay disc found in Utah, USA, suggests that Native Americans used something similar. In the 1870s in Connecticut, USA, a baker called Russell Frisbie started stamping "Frisbie's pies" on the base of his light, circular tins. Students at nearby Yale played throw and catch with the tins, shouting "Frisbie!" as an alert. In California, Wham-O adopted the name for its plastic disc, changed the spelling and patented the Frisbee. More than 100 million Frisbees have now been produced, but the bakery itself closed in 1958.

FACT
Mountain biking was adopted as an Olympic sport in 1996. BMX followed in 2008.

Did you know?
In the late 1990s, the US Marine Corps experimented with skateboards in urban-military exercises, using them to detect tripwires in buildings and draw out sniper fire.

Wheelie good

The **skateboard ollie** is named after its inventor, Alan "Ollie" Gelfand

Longest vehicle drift

In a drift, a driver controls a vehicle through a sustained rear-wheel skid. Johan Schwartz (USA) maintained an 84.13-km (51.27-mi) drift at the BMW Performance Center in Spartanburg, South Carolina, USA, on 11 May 2013.

First double loop by a car
Gary Hoptrough (UK) conquered the "Deadly 720" by completing two 8-m-diameter (26-ft) 360° loops in a Rage R180 buggy on *Top Gear Live* at Moses Mabhida Stadium in Durban, South Africa, on 16 Jun 2012.

Longest individual ATV side wheelie
On 30 Oct 2012, Daniel Adams (USA) executed a 27.17-km (16.89-mi) wheelie on the side wheels of an all-terrain vehicle (ATV) near Grantsville in Utah, USA.

Longest UTV ramp jump
Tanner Godfrey (USA) made a 32.08-m (105-ft 3-in) ramp jump in a utility terrain vehicle (UTV) at Eureka Casino Resort in Mesquite, Nevada, USA, on 22 Feb 2013.

BICYCLE

Most 180° jumps in one minute
The greatest number of 180° jumps on a bicycle in a minute is 43, by Daniel Rall (DEU) at Comtech Arena in Aspach, Germany, on 13 Jul 2013.

Highest vertical drop
Wayne Mahomet (UK) made a vertical drop of 4.1 m (13 ft 5 in) on his bicycle at the Dounby Show in Dounby, Orkney Islands, UK, on 8 Aug 2013.

Fastest 10-obstacle slalom (blindfolded)
On 23 Jul 2013, Juan Ruiz (MEX) negotiated his bicycle around 10 obstacles set randomly on a 20-m (66-ft) slalom course in 25.43 sec on the set of *Guinness World Records – Rekorlar Dünyası* in Istanbul, Turkey. Juan has been blind since birth and used echolocation to achieve the feat.

Fastest 100 miles
Ian Cammish (UK) took 3 hr 11 min 11 sec to cycle 100 mi (161 km) on 10 Aug 1993.

The **fastest 100 miles by a woman** is 3 hr 49 min 42 sec, by Pauline Strong (UK) on 18 Oct 1991.

Farthest wheelie on front wheel with feet off the pedals
Andreas Lindqvist (SWE) carried out a 316-m (1,036-ft

Longest wheelie by a skid loader

On 28 Jul 2012, Jake R Hatch (USA) carried out a 21.88-m-long (71-ft 9-in) wheelie in a Bobcat skid steer at Taylor Rodeo Grounds in Taylor, Arizona, USA.

8-in) front-wheel wheelie without his feet touching the pedals of his bike on the set of *Guinness Rekord TV* at Liljeholmshallen, Stockholm, Sweden, on 6 Oct 2001.

On the same show, Lindqvist also performed the **longest duration bicycle wheelie on the front wheel with feet off the pedals**, staying aloft for 2 min 20 sec.

Most BMX megaspins in 30 seconds
A BMX megaspin involves standing on a rear peg, holding on to the handlebars and, with the front wheel raised, kicking the rear tyre so that the bike spins. On 19 Jul 2013, pro rider Takahiro Ikeda (JPN) performed 45 spins in 30 sec in Kōtō, Tokyo, Japan.

MOTORCYCLE

Longest jump with backflip on a minimoto
On 9 Oct 2012, Ricardo Piedras (ESP) carried out a 14.74-m-long (48-ft 4-in) jump with backflip on a minimoto (minibike) in Barcelona, Spain.

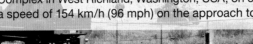

Longest dirt-to-dirt motorcycle ramp jump

The greatest distance covered in a dirt-to-dirt motorcycle ramp jump is 90.69 m (297 ft 6 in), by Alex Harvill (USA) at the Horn Rapids Motorsports Complex in West Richland, Washington, USA, on 6 Jul 2013. He reached a speed of 154 km/h (96 mph) on the approach to the take-off ramp.

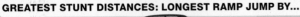

> ## GREATEST STUNT DISTANCES: LONGEST RAMP JUMP BY...

Car in reverse: 18.62 m, *Top Gear* stuntman (UK)

Skateboard: 24 m, Danny Way (USA)

Rollerblades: 30 m, Chris Haffey (USA)

Bicycle (assisted): 35.63 m, Colin Winkelmann (USA)

Monster truck: 65.43 m, Dan Runte (USA)

Car: 81.9 m, Travis Pastrana (USA)

Motorcycle: 106.98 m, Robbie Maddison (USA)

FACT
The 2011 film *Drive* (USA), starring Ryan Gosling, was directed by Nicolas Winding Refn, who has never owned a driving licence.

0 m

Shortest braking distance by a vehicle on ice

On 8 Jan 2013, Fulda Reifen – a tyre brand of Goodyear Dunlop Tires Germany – set a braking distance of 48.132 m (157 ft 11 in) for a car driven at 48.5 km/h (30.1 mph) on the frozen Schwatka Lake near Whitehorse, Yukon, Canada.

Longest stoppie

The greatest distance for a stoppie (aka endo or front-wheel wheelie) on a motorcycle is 402.42 m (1,320 ft 4 in). It was achieved by Jesse Toler (USA) at the Charlotte Diesel Super Show staged at the ZMAX Dragway in North Carolina, USA, on 5 Oct 2012.

Most switchback zero rotations in one minute

For this record, a rider must be seated back-to-front on a motorcycle ("switchback zero"), without touching it with his or her hands, and rotate the machine through 360°. On 22 Aug 2013, British rider Mark Van Driel completed a total of 13 motorcycle switchback zero rotations in one minute on the set of *Officially Amazing* in Mildenhall, Suffolk, UK.

Most steps climbed by bicycle

Krystian Herba (POL) climbed all 2,754 steps of the World Financial Center in Shanghai, China, by bike on 17 Mar 2013. He did so, without touching the walls or putting his feet on the floor, in a time of 1 hr 21 min 53 sec.

SKATEBOARD

Fastest 110-m hurdles by hippy jumps

A hippy jump involves jumping off a moving board and over an obstacle while the skateboard passes beneath. Steffen Köster (DEU) hippy-jumped along a 110-m (360-ft) hurdle course in 29.98 sec in Rust, Germany, on 19 Jun 2013.

Fastest time to slalom 100 cones

On 16 Aug 2013, Jānis Kuzmins (LVA) slalomed his board through 100 cones in 19.41 sec on the set of *CCTV Guinness World Records Special* at the Asia-Pacific Experimental School of Beijing Normal University in Beijing, China.

Farthest distance in 24 hours

Andrew Andras (USA) travelled 431.33 km (261.8 mi) on his skateboard in 24 hr at the Homestead-Miami Speedway in Homestead, Florida, USA, on 7–8 Jan 2013. On the same date and at the same venue, Colleen Pelech (USA) achieved the **farthest distance travelled on a skateboard in 24 hours (female)**: 269.08 km (167.2 mi).

Fastest 400-m hurdles on a bicycle

On 26 Aug 2013, Austrian cyclist Thomas Öhler negotiated a 400-m hurdles course by bicycle in 44.62 sec in Linz, Austria.

Most ollie 180s in a minute

Eric Carlin (USA) performed 25 skateboard ollie 180s in 60 sec in Mount Laurel, New Jersey, USA, on 2 Jul 2013.

Longest stationary manual

Brendon Davis (USA) remained stationary on one set of wheels for 19 min 39.56 sec at the Society skate shop in San Carlos, California, USA, on 11 May 2013.

Most shove-its

On 5 Sep 2013, Gabriel Pena (USA) executed 33 shove-its (a 180°-or-more board spin) in 30 sec in Houston, Texas, USA.

Fastest motorcycle wheelie on ice

On 27 Jan 2013, Ryan Suchanek (USA) carried out a wheelie at a speed of 174.6 km/h (108.5 mph) across the frozen Lake Koshkonong in Wisconsin, USA. In doing so, he broke his own existing world record by 21.7 km/h (13.5 mph). The speed was measured over a distance of 100 m (328 ft).

> **FACT**
> Ryan Suchanek (left) rode a 2005 Kawasaki ZX10R. Its tyres were studded to provide better traction on ice.

Monster feats: *Bigfoot*

It may have recorded the **longest monster truck ramp jump** with a leap of 65.43 m, but *Bigfoot 18* isn't the biggest in the *Bigfoot* family. *Bigfoot 5*, built in 1986, has the accolade of being the **largest monster truck**, standing 4.7 m tall with 3-m-high tyres and weighing in at 17 tonnes. The man behind the monsters is Bob Chandler (USA), who began building them in 1975 as a way of publicizing his four-wheel-drive centre in Missouri, USA.

Glossary

Caballerial: a 360° turn with the skater's back facing the ramp. Named after Steve Caballero.

McTwist: a 540° turn on a ramp.

Ollie: a jump in which the tail of the board is smacked ("popped") on the ground. In a "nollie", the nose of the board hits the ground.

Railslide: sliding the underside of the board along an object. ○ ○ ○

Mass participation

A gathering of 9,768 firefighters in Oct 2011 is almost **four times the population** of the Falkland Islands

Loudest stadium crowd roar

Fans of the Seattle Seahawks (USA) achieved a 137.6-dB(A) roar at CenturyLink Stadium in Seattle, Washington, USA, on 2 Dec 2013, in a match against the New Orleans Saints. The term "dB(A)" denotes decibel levels audible to the human ear – i.e., excluding extreme highs and lows.

LARGEST...

AED training session
Automated External Defibrillators (AED) diagnose and treat heart conditions. A training session for 2,109 participants on the machines was held by AED4all.com, Anne-Marie Willems and René Verlaak (all NLD) in Nijmegen, Netherlands, on 29 May 2013.

Baking lesson
Much dough was kneaded by 426 students of Green Grin Club Limited, Grin Kitchen Limited and Ma On Shan Tsung Tsin secondary school (all HKG) in Hong Kong, China, on 7 Sep 2013.

Barbecue
Try to guess how much food you need for a barbecue for 45,252 people. Ingredients used by Estado de Nuevo León (MEX) included 15.5 tonnes (34,000 lb) of angus beef with 18 tonnes (39,500 lb) of onions and 15 tonnes (33,000 lb) of corn tortillas, topped with 16 tonnes (35,000 lb) of salsa. It took place in Parque Fundidora in Monterrey, Mexico, on 18 Aug 2013.

Barefoot walk
The National Service Scheme Cell of Acharya Nagarjuna University (IND) took 7,050 people for a shoe-free stroll in Guntur, Andhra Pradesh, India, on 12 Dec 2012.

Gathering of professional clown doctors
Clown doctors can ease difficult and frightening procedures in hospital for sick young people. On 30 Jan 2013, a group of 153 clowns marked the 20th anniversary of the clown doctoring work done by the Theodora Foundation, headquartered in Bern, Switzerland.

Largest horse race

The Federation of Mongolian Horse Racing Sport and Trainers registered 4,249 runners in an 18-km (11.18-mi) race in Khui Doloon Khudag, Ulan Bator, Mongolia, on 10 Aug 2013. The youngest rider was seven and the oldest was 79.

Largest gathering of people dressed as penguins

Children's hospice Richard House got 325 oversized penguins to waddle together in Wood Wharf, London, UK, on Guinness World Records Day on 13 Nov 2013.

GREATEST GATHERINGS

Largest religious crowd: 30 million, India, 2013

Largest funeral: 15 million, India, 1969

Largest papal crowd: 4 million, Philippines, 1995

Largest gathering of Sikhs: 3.5 million, India, 1999

Largest anti-war rally: 3 million, Italy, 2003

Big banquets

In our 1962 edition, one of the earliest examples of a mass participation record was reported. "Lyons catered for the world's largest banquet at Olympia, London, on 8th August, 1925. A total of 6,600 guests were seated at 5 miles of tables served by 1,360 waitresses supported by 700 cooks and porters. The occasion was a War Memorial fund raising effort by Freemasons."

LARGEST GATHERING OF PEOPLE DRESSED...

	Category	People	Organizer/Event	Location	Date
1	as Mohandas Gandhi	2,955	Sowdambikaa Group of Schools	Tiruchirappalli, India	11 Oct 2013
	with false moustaches	2,268	City of Fairfield & Fairfield RAGBRAI Committee	Fairfield, Iowa, USA	26 Jul 2013
2	as witches	1,607	La Bruixa d'Or	Sort, Lleida, Spain	16 Nov 2013
3	as *Star Trek* characters	1,063	Media 10 Ltd	ExCeL, London, UK	20 Oct 2012
4	as Saint Patrick	882	Saint Brigid's National School	Castleknock, Dublin, Ireland	14 Mar 2013
	as fairies	871	St Giles Hospice	Lichfield, Staffordshire, UK	22 Jun 2013
	as Superman	867	Escapade, Kendal Calling	Lowther Deer Park, Cumbria, UK	27 Jul 2013
	in one-piece pyjamas (onesies)	752	Henry Allen Onesie Angels	StadiumMK, Milton Keynes, UK	2 Nov 2013
	as nurses	691	Dubai Health Authority	Dubai, UAE	24 Jan 2014
	as trees	516	Ośrodek Kultury Leśnej w Gołuchówie	Gołuchów, Poland	30 Sep 2013
	as cows	470	Chick-fil-A	George Mason University, Virginia, USA	2 Jul 2013
	as monks	463	Ardfert Central National School	Ardfert, County Kerry, Ireland	11 May 2013
	in Disney costumes	361	Walsgrave Church of England Primary School	Coventry, UK	12 Jul 2013

Carolling
The Waukesha Downtown Business Association (USA) cajoled 1,822 carol singers in Waukesha, Wisconsin, USA, on 22 Nov 2013.

On a single bed
Leaving no room to roll over, 54 people were crammed on a single bed by Xilinmen Furniture in Beijing, China, on 7 Sep 2013.

Blowing bubble gum bubbles
Lester B Pearson Public School in Aurora, Canada, organized 544 people to simultaneously blow gum bubbles on 6 Jun 2013.

Blowing up balloons
A different kind of blowing saw Bayer Yakuhin (JPN) organize 2,639 simultaneous balloon inflations on 14 Jan 2014, in Osaka, Japan.

Painting buildings at once
On 18 May 2013, Slovenian paint manufacturer Helios put 1,272 painters to work across nine venues.

Most people twerking
On 25 Sep 2013, GWR adjudicator Charlie Weisman witnessed 358 people twerking simultaneously in New York City, USA. The event was organized by hip-hop artist Big Freedia (USA).

MOST PEOPLE...

On the same drum
Queen's "We Will Rock You" was an anthemic choice for 263 people playing a drum measuring 10 m (32 ft 9 in) in diameter and 1.6 m (5 ft 2 in) high. Organized by PLAY (POL), the event took place at Przystanek Woodstock in Kostrzyn nad Odra, Poland, on 2 Aug 2013.

Singing a national anthem simultaneously
A total of 121,653 employees from the Sahara India Pariwar company sang India's national anthem in Lucknow, India, on 6 May 2013.

Largest gathering of zombies
A brain-munching 9,592 members of the walking dead did the New Jersey Zombie Walk in Asbury Park, New Jersey, USA, on 5 Oct 2013. They shuffled their way to regaining the record from the Zombie Pub Crawl of Minneapolis, USA.

Hindu pilgrimage: Kumbh Mela festival
Between 80 and 100 million people attended the 55-day Kumbh Mela festival, which began in Allahabad, India, in Jan 2013. A Hindu pilgrimage to bathe in a sacred river is usually held every three years in one of four cities, but 2013 was a special version, the Maha Kumbh Mela, which occurs every 144 years. The city prepared for the onslaught – more than the entire population of the UK – with 14 temporary hospitals, 243 doctors on call, around 30,000 police and security staff on duty and 40,000 toilets. The cost was approximately 11.5 bn rupees (£129 m), but it was hoped that the festival would earn as much as 120 bn rupees (£1.3 bn).

And finally...
• **Most people shaking cocktails simultaneously:** 1,710, Diageo (UK), 18 Sep 2013
• **Most people popping party poppers:** 743, Grey Court School (UK), 17 Jul 2013
• **Longest high-five chain:** 695 people, St Francis of Assisi Primary School and Calwell High School (both AUS), 27 Sep 2013

○ ○ ○

No pain, no gain

Owing to a genetic anomaly, **redheads** are more susceptible to pain

Longest time spent in full-body contact with ice

Wim Hof (NLD) spent 1 hr 53 min 2 sec immersed in ice in Naarden, Netherlands, on 18 Oct 2013. When it comes to withstanding sub-zero temperatures, Wim has consistently proved himself to be one cool customer: he has held this record 16 times in the past.

Longest time in full-body contact with snow

Oleksiy Gutsulyak (UKR) endured 60 min 8 sec of close contact with snow in the Kyrylo Tryliovski City Park in Kolomyia, Ukraine, on 25 Jan 2013.

Longest time to hold the breath voluntarily (male)

Stig Severinsen (DNK) held his breath underwater for exactly 22 min at the London School of Diving in London, UK, on 3 May 2012. The female record is held by Karoline Mariechen Meyer (BRA), who held her breath for 18 min 32.59 sec in the Racer Academy swimming pool in Florianópolis, Brazil, on 10 Jul 2009.

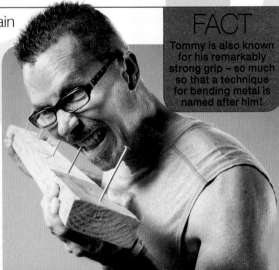

FACT
Tommy is also known for his remarkably strong grip – so much so that a technique for bending metal is named after him!

Most nails removed from wood with teeth in one minute

Tommy Heslep (USA) yanked 16 nails from a length of wood using just his teeth in a nail-biting 60 sec on the set of *Guinness World Records Unleashed* in Los Angeles, California, USA, on 19 Jun 2013. Around 135 kg (300 lb) of pressure was needed to remove each nail.

Longest full-body burn (without oxygen)

The greatest duration for a full-body burn without oxygen is 5 min 25 sec. The fiery feat was accomplished by Jayson Dumenigo (USA) in Santa Clarita, California, USA, on 27 Mar 2011.

The **most people to perform simultaneous full-body burns** is 21, achieved during an event organized by Ted Batchelor and Hotcards.com (both USA) at the Hotcards Burn in Cleveland, Ohio, USA, on 19 Oct 2013.

The **fastest time to run through 10 locked and burning doors** is 12.84 sec, performed by Chris Roseboro (USA) on

Most animal traps released on the body in one minute

On 12 Oct 2013, Johnny Strange (UK) set off six vintage animal traps on his body in a minute at Doncaster's Tattoo Jam, held at Doncaster Racecourse in South Yorkshire, UK. All of the traps were once used to catch rabbits. It's one of six GWR records that this sideshow entertainer extraordinaire currently holds.

GREATEST DISTANCES RUN ON A TREADMILL IN...

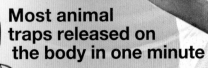

- **1 week (female):** 833.05 km, Sharon Gayter (UK), 14–21 Dec 2011
- **1 week (male):** 822.31 km, Pierre-Michael Micaletti (FRA), 13–19 May 2012
- **48 hr (male):** 405.22 km, Tony Mangan (IRL), 22–24 Aug 2008
- **48 hr (female):** 309.8 km, Martina Schmit (AUT), 10–12 Mar 2006
- **24 hr (male):** 257.88 km, Suresh Joachim (AUS), 28–29 Nov 2004
- **24 hr (female):** 247.2 km, Edit Bérces (HUN), 8–9 Mar 2004
- **12 hr (male):** 123.4 km, Eusébio Bochons (CHE/ESP), 7 Dec 2013
- **12 hr (female):** 96.8 km, Theresa Dugwell (CAN), 2 Mar 2013

⚡ Lasting achievements

You might think that the human capacity for athletic endurance was fairly well set by now, but committed individuals have a way of confounding expectations. Back in 1998, Rory Coleman (UK) held the record for the **fastest time to run 100 miles on a treadmill (male)**, with a time of 23 hr 43 min. By 2003, Andrew Rivett (UK) was more than 7 hr faster (16 hr 23 min 16 sec). The current record, held by Suresh Joachim (AUS), is 13 hr 42 min 33 sec – around 10 hr faster than the 1998 record holder!

FACT
William Staub created the home treadmill in the 1960s. It was initially sold under the name PaceMaster.

ℹ️ Dreading the tread

Treadmills were once a common feature in UK prisons. Engineer William Cubitt (UK) introduced them *c.* 1818, variously to supply power, grind corn and punish prisoners. They were abolished in 1898.

the set of *Guinness World Records Unleashed* in California City, California, USA, on 7 Jul 2013.

Most nails inserted into the nose in 30 seconds
Burnaby Q Orbax (CAN) inserted 12 nails into – then out of – his nose, one at a time, in 30 sec in London, UK, on 22 Jun 2013. Each nail was 10 cm (4 in) long.

Heaviest vehicle pulled using a hook through the nasal cavity and mouth
On 5 Jun 2013, Ryan Stock (CAN) pulled a 983-kg (2,167-lb) Volkswagen Beetle – with two women inside it – using a hook fed through his nasal cavity and out of his mouth for *Rekorlar Dünyası* in Istanbul, Turkey.

MOST...

Arrows broken by the neck in one minute
Fitness enthusiast Michael Gillette (USA) snapped 12 arrows by placing the sharp end of each one against his throat – in the

jugular notch – and forcing the other end against a wall in Los Angeles, California, USA, on 27 Jun 2013.

Ceramic slabs broken by the head by forward flips in one minute
In just 60 sec, Michael Gonzalez (USA) smashed 43 ceramic slabs with his head, following a forward flip, on the set of *Guinness World Records Unleashed* in Los Angeles, California, USA, on 2 Jul 2013.

Concrete blocks broken in one minute (male)
Ali Bahçetepe (TUR) smashed 1,175 concrete blocks by hand in Datça Cumhuriyet Meydanı, Turkey, on 17 Nov 2012.

Ali is something of a past master when it comes to concrete deconstruction. Over the years, he has also recorded the **most concrete blocks broken in 30 seconds** (683) and the **most concrete blocks broken in one stack** (36).

Ice blocks broken by a human battering ram
Uğur Öztürk (TUR) rammed through 14 ice blocks for *Rekorlar Dünyası* in Istanbul, Turkey, on 26 Jun 2013.

GUINNESS WORLD RECORDS

FACT
There were 3,000 nails in the board on Jon's chest and the board weighed 56 kg.

Most rope skips on a bed of nails over a person
As if lying on a bed of nails isn't testing enough, Amy Bruney skipped 117 times on top of a bed of nails balanced over her husband Jon Bruney (both USA) on the set of *Guinness World Records Unleashed* in Los Angeles, California, USA, on 25 Jun 2013.

Most coconuts smashed with the elbows in one minute
On 24 Jun 2013, actor and martial arts expert Jeffrey James Lippold (USA) used his elbows to smash through 21 coconuts in one minute on the set of *Guinness World Records Unleashed* in Los Angeles, California, USA.

Pine boards broken with the elbow in one minute
Mohammad Rashid (PAK) broke 68 pine boards with his elbow in one minute at the Punjab Youth Festival in Lahore, Pakistan, on 13 Mar 2013. At the same event on the same day, 1,450 attendees also set the record for the **most people arm wrestling**.

The following year, perhaps looking for less painful records to attempt, the festival organizers formed the **largest human flag**, involving 28,957 participants at the National Hockey Stadium in Lahore on 15 Feb.

Hard to beat: Paddy Doyle
If one man knows all about pushing the body to the limits of its physical capacity, it's Paddy Doyle (UK). This tough and tenacious character has been setting and breaking GWR endurance records for years – his oldest current record goes all the way back to 1989 (**most push-ups in 12 hours:** 19,325)! Along the way, he's also survived the **most competitive full-contact rounds** (6,324) and performed the **most push-ups using the back of the hands in one hour carrying a 40-lb pack** (663). See right for more examples of Doyle's derring-do.

 Paddy Doyle takes the strain

Most star jumps in one minute carrying a 100-lb pack: 33, on 10 Nov 2013

Most step-ups in one minute carrying a 100-lb pack: 31, on 17 Aug 2013

Fastest cross-country half marathon carrying a 100-lb pack: 4 hr 18 min, on 22 Jun 2013

Most squat thrusts in one minute with a 40-lb pack: 21, on 28 Mar 2011

o o o

Modern world

Largest collection of US presidential memorabilia >

Ronald Wade (USA) owned 6,960 items of memorabilia with a US presidential theme as of 14 Oct 2013. Ronald started his collection with a badge at the age of 10, and after graduation became a White House page during Richard Nixon's presidency (1969–74). He has also donated many items to the Bush Library outside Dallas and has had a replica of the Oval Office built in his house in Longview, Texas.

Contents

FACT

The site for the White House was chosen by the first US president, George Washington, in 1791. John Adams, the second president, was the first one to actually live there, in 1800.

Richest people

Even if he spent $1 m a day, it would still take the **richest man** nearly 200 years to spend all of his cash!

Meet the oil barons, retail magnates and tech tycoons who are all members of the exclusive Guinness World Records Super-Rich Club – the 16 men (and yes, they're all men, and all but four of them American) who've held the record for the wealthiest living person over the past 60 years.

"The meek shall inherit the Earth, but not its mineral rights." So said Jean Paul Getty (USA), the oil baron who was the world's **richest person** for seven of the last 60 years. He was not alone in oil – one in four of our featured billionaires owed their megabucks to a vice-like grip on our natural resources.

Oil is no longer such a king. More recent entrants to the Billionaires' Club found their fortunes by trading in less tangible goods such as software and media rights, or have a near magical ability to read the stock markets.

In real terms, the richest man to emerge since we started publishing in 1955 is Bill Gates (USA). Adjusted for inflation, his software-based fortune via Microsoft reached an almost inconceivable $120 bn (£75 bn) in 2000. It was built on the back of the dot-com boom, which, in the USA, saw the value of shares on the NASDAQ stock exchange more than double in the year up to 10 Mar 2000. Alas, all good things come to an end, and the wheel of fortune crushed many of those same companies: just 12 months later, most NASDAQ dot-coms had ceased trading.

Bill Gates survived, although, by the end of 2001, even he was down to his last $77.8 bn (£48.5 bn).

Al Capone

Our 1960 edition records the belief that Chicago gangster Al Capone (USA, 1899–1947) held the record for the **highest gross income ever achieved in a single year by a private citizen**. Adjusted for inflation, in 1927 he earned $1.41 bn (£0.83 bn) from a trade we said included "illegal liquor trading and alky-cookers (illicit stills)" as well as "dog tracks, dance halls... and vice".

FACT
The business card of gangster Alphonse Gabriel "Al" Capone read: "Second-hand furniture dealer."

King Bhumibol Adulyadej

One surefire way to riches is to be born to them. Thailand's King Bhumibol Adulyadej, with assets of $30 bn (£21 bn), is the **richest monarch**. Here, he is with Brunei's Sultan Haji Hassanal Bolkiah (left), the second richest monarch with a mere $20 bn (£14 bn) – but what's a few billion between royal friends?

FACT
Guinness World Records has been published every year since 1955, with the exception of 1957, 1959 and 1963. We have included the record for the **richest person** in every edition.

FACT
J T Williamson's wealth was never stated explicitly in the first *Guinness Book of Records*; his entry merely stated that his wealth "transcends all other personal fortunes".

Chart axis labels: $100 bn, $90 bn, $80 bn, $70 bn, $60 bn, $50 bn, $40 bn, $30 bn, $20 bn, $10 bn; 1955, 1960, 1965, 1970, 1975

THE GWR RICH LIST: HIGHEST ROLLERS, 1955–2015

John Thoburn Williamson
(CAN, 1907–58)
Record: 1955–56
Industry: Minerals, founded Williamson diamond mine
Peak: $60 m
Adjusted: $514 m

Jean Paul Getty
(USA, 1892–1976)
Record: 1958, 1960–61, 1964–67
Industry: Oil, building on empire of father George Franklin Getty
Peak: $3 bn
Adjusted: $22.2 bn

Haroldson Lafayette Hunt
(USA, 1889–1974)
Record: 1962
Industry: Oil empire based in Texas, after running cotton plantation
Peak: $2 bn
Adjusted: $15.2 bn

Howard Hughes
(USA, 1905–76)
Record: 1968–71
Industry: Inherited father's tool business, moved into aviation, also film production
Peak: $1.37 bn
Adjusted: $9 bn

Daniel K Ludwig
(USA, 1897–1992)
Record: 1972–77, 1979–81
Industry: Shipping, oil, banking, cattle, insurance, property, hotels
Peak: $3 bn
Adjusted: $16.5 bn

John D MacArthur
(USA, 1897–1978)
Record: 1978
Industry: Insurance (with wife Catherine), property, mainly in Florida, USA
Peak: $1.72 bn
Adjusted: $6 bn

Forrest Mars, Sr
(USA, 1904–99)
Record: 1982–83
Industry: Food, building on father's Mars candy business, leaving company in 1969
Peak: $1 bn
Adjusted: $12.3 bn

David Packard
(USA, 1912–96)
Record: 1984–85
Industry: IT and computing, co-founding Hewlett-Packard with Bill Hewlett in 1939
Peak: $1.8 bn
Adjusted: $3.98 bn

Adjusted wealth estimated in 2014 using the consumer price list

TOP 10 RICHEST PEOPLE IN 2014

Of the **richest person** record holders over the last 60 years, only three feature in the current top 10.

Name	Amount	Industry	Age
● Bill Gates (USA)	$75.9 bn	Software	58
● Carlos Slim Helú (MEX)	$71 bn	Telecoms	73
Amancio Ortega (ESP)	$62.7 bn	Textiles	77
● Warren Buffett (USA)	$58.6 bn	Investment	83
Ingvar Kamprad (SWE)	$51.9 bn	Retail	87
Charles Koch (USA)	$46.9 bn	Engineering	78
David Koch (USA)			73
Larry Ellison (USA)	$43 bn	Software	69
Christy Walton (USA)	$36.9 bn	Retail	59
Sheldon Adelson (USA)	$35.4 bn	Casinos	80

Wealth average taken from: bloomberg.com, celebritynetworth.com, citywire.co.uk, forbes.com, londonlovesbusiness.com and nationaljournal.com

FACT
If Bill Gates were still worth $120 bn today, his wealth would be greater than the GDP of 134 of the world's 192 countries.

i Who wants to be a quadrillionaire?

In Jun 2013, it was reported that Christopher Reynolds (USA) became the **first trillionaire** and **first quadrillionaire** when a (brief) bank error in his favour resulted in a balance of $92,233,720,368,547,800 in his PayPal account. Reportedly, when asked what he would have spent the money on, Reynolds said, "I probably would have paid down the national debt." He would have been able to do that and then some, given that his balance was 1,200 times greater than the GDP of every country in the world combined!

Key

Each bar represents the dollar value of each person in a given year; bars are shown to scale based on their *actual* known wealth at the time, plus this figure *adjusted* for inflation to the value at today's figures.

inflation adjusted ——

actual ——

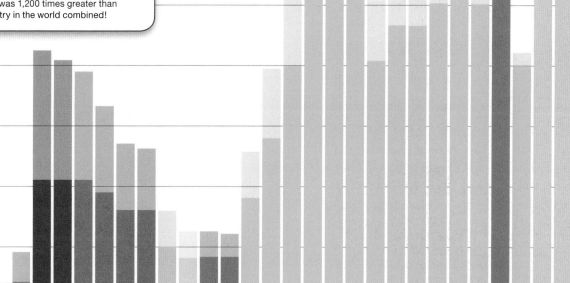

1980   1985   1990   1995   2000   2005   2010

Gordon Getty (USA, b. 1933)
Record: 1986
Industry: Father's oil empire, selling to Texaco in contentious deal for $10 bn in 1984
Peak: $4.1 bn
Adjusted: $9.06 bn

Sam Walton (USA, 1918–92)
Record: 1987–88
Industry: Retailing empire based around Walmart chain stores, founded 1962
Peak: $21 bn
Adjusted: $42.4 bn

Yoshiaki Tsutsumi (JPN, b. 1934)
Record: 1989–1992
Industry: Developing and expanding father's property-based business empire
Peak: $21 bn
Adjusted: $38.9 bn

S Robson Walton (USA, b. 1944)
Record: 1993
Industry: Oldest son of Sam Walton, chairman of Walmart (biggest retailer in 2013)
Peak: $10 bn
Adjusted: $15.9 bn

John Werner Kluge (DEU, 1914–2010)
Record: 1994
Industry: Mainly media, including TV, radio and advertising
Peak: $8.1 bn
Adjusted: $12.5 bn

Warren Buffett (USA, b. 1930)
Record: 1995–96, 2009
Industry: Investing in a diverse range of companies all over the world
Peak: $62 bn
Adjusted: $66.1 bn

Bill Gates (USA, b. 1955)
Record: 1997–2008, 2010, 2014
Industry: Software engineering, founder of Microsoft
Peak: $90 bn
Adjusted: $120 bn

Carlos Slim Helú (MEX, b. 1940)
Record: 2011–13
Industry: Telecoms, after stockbroking, investment and general business
Peak: $74 bn
Adjusted: $74 bn

World at war

There has not been a 25-year period without war since **1495**

Least peaceful country

Created by the Institute for Economics and Peace, the Global Peace Index ranks countries by the safety of their citizens, the extent of conflict and the degree of militarization. The index runs from 1 to 5, where 1 represents peace. As of 2013, Afghanistan was rated least at peace (3.440), with Somalia second-least peaceful and Syria third.

Least secure nation in relation to nuclear weapons
In 2012, the Economist Intelligence Unit and the Nuclear Threat Initiative (a non-governmental organization) reported that of the 32 nations with more than 1 kg (2.2 lb) of weapons-grade nuclear material, North Korea is the least secure. The state's leader, Kim Jong-un – aged 31, according to official reports – is the **youngest state leader to control nuclear weapons**.
As of 2012, these sources rank Australia as the **most secure nation in relation to nuclear weapons**.

Largest refugee camp

According to the humanitarian aid charity Cooperative for Assistance and Relief Everywhere (CARE), the Dadaab refugee camp in Kenya, Africa, is the largest in the world. On 29 Apr 2013, its registered refugee population stood at 423,496 – nearly five times the size the camp was originally built to accommodate. Most of the refugees are from neighbouring Somalia.

Most peaceful country
As of 2013, Iceland was No.1 on the Global Peace Index (see above) with a score of 1.162. Denmark was second and New Zealand was ranked third.

Highest defence budget
The USA had a defence budget totalling $645.7 bn (£399.3 bn) in 2012.

Longest civil war of modern times

The civil war in Myanmar started shortly after the country – formerly known as Burma – achieved independence from the UK on 4 Jan 1948, and it continues to the present day. Small armed groups are active in the west and, according to Amnesty International, clashes in Rakhine State started in Jun 2012 and have continued since.

Most civilian deaths in an undeclared civil war
Accurately recording deaths in any conflict is difficult and subject to variation of numbers. However, the United Nations estimated on 24 Jul 2013 that 100,000 people had died in Syria since the start of hostilities in Mar 2011. On 24 Sep 2013, France is reported to have told the UN General Assembly that 120,000 people had been killed in Syria. In Oct 2013, the Syrian Observatory for Human Rights, based in the UK, also reported 120,000 fatalities.

Deadliest conflict for children (current)
In the Nov 2013 report "Stolen Futures" (spanning Mar 2011 to Aug 2013) by the Oxford Research Group, 11,420 victims aged 17 and under are believed to have been killed in the Syrian civil war. Of these, more than 112 were tortured, 389 were killed by sniper fire and some 764 were summarily executed.

HIGHEST DEATH TOLLS IN CONFLICTS SINCE 1955

††††††††††††††††††††††††††††††††††††††
Second Congo War 2.5–5.4 million, 1998–2003

†††††††††
Vietnam War 800,000–3.8 million, 1955–75

††††††††††† **Nigerian Civil War** 1–3 million, 1967–70

†††††††††† **Soviet War in Afghanistan** c. 960,000–1.6 million, 1979–89

††††††††† **Iran-Iraq War** c. 1 million, 1980–88

††††††††† **Second Sudanese Civil War** c. 1 million, 1983–2005

††††††††† **Mozambican Civil War** 900,000–1 million, 1975–94

†††††††† **Rwandan Civil War** 800,000–1 million, 1990–93

†††††††† **First Congo War** 800,000, 1996–97

†††††† **Eritrean War of Independence** 570,000, 1961–91

KEY:
† x1 = 100,000 deaths
†††††††††††
= lowest estimate
†††††††††††
= highest estimate

FACT
During World War I, the average life expectancy of soldiers in the trenches was around six weeks.

Nothing civil about war
Civil wars have brought about the death of around 25 million people since the conclusion of the last global conflict in 1945.

Casualties of war
The first *Guinness Book of Records* was published only 10 years after the end of World War II. That conflict featured in our debut edition as the **bloodiest war**, with overall casualties of around 56.4 million. Poland suffered most in proportion to its population, with 6,028,000 (or 17.2%) of its 35,100,000 citizens killed. It is a measure of the magnitude of this loss of life that it still represents history's **highest wartime death toll**.

Most terrorist attacks per country

The survey "Country Reports on Terrorism 2012", published in May 2013 by the US National Consortium for the Study of Terrorism and Responses to Terrorism, identified Pakistan as the country with the most terrorist attacks during 2012. It saw 1,404 attacks during that 12-month period, in which 1,848 people were killed and 3,643 injured. Iraq was placed second in the survey and Afghanistan third.

The number of Syrian child refugees is now 1 million (the **most refugee children**), most of whom are under the age of 11.

Most refugees by country of origin
According to UNHCR, the UN refugee agency, a combined total of

2,585,605 refugees had escaped from Afghanistan as of Jan 2013, the greatest number from any country.

The **country with the largest population of refugees** is Pakistan. In Jan 2013, it housed 1,638,456 refugees, nearly all of whom have fled from Afghanistan.

Largest peacekeeping force (one operation)
A United Nations Protection Force (UNPROFOR) peacekeeping mission was deployed in the former Yugoslavia from Feb 1992 to Mar 1995. In Sep 1994, the mission reached a strength of 39,922 military personnel, including a "Rapid Reaction Force".

At present, the UN is undertaking 15 peacekeeping operations worldwide, with one special political mission in Afghanistan. The **largest peacekeeping force deployed on one operation (present day)** is the stabilization mission in the Democratic Republic of the Congo. Of the 26,024 UN personnel deployed there, 19,557 are military troops.

Lowest score on the Press Freedom Index
Based on data for deaths, violence, censorship, media independence and other factors, the African

dictatorship of Eritrea is rated as the country with the least press freedom, according to the 2013 Press Freedom Index.

According to the Committee to Protect Journalists, as of 19 Dec 2013 the **most dangerous country for the media (current year)** was Syria: 21 journalists were killed there in 2013. In all, 52 journalists were killed in 2013 worldwide with a "confirmed" motive – i.e., where a murder is

Largest special forces

Special forces are trained military units with non-conventional tasks. North Korea has the largest such force, with around 60,000 operatives and some 130,000 personnel with special forces-like characteristics, according to US military officials.

in direct reprisal for their work, or in crossfire, combat or during dangerous assignments, such as coverage of a street protest.

First post-World War II head of state convicted by an international war crimes court
The international Special Court for Sierra Leone based in the Hague, Netherlands, found Charles Taylor, the ex-President of Liberia, Africa, guilty of 11 crimes. These included rape, murder and the use of child soldiers during the civil war in Sierra Leone between 1991 and 2002, in which around 50,000 people died. He was sentenced to 50 years' imprisonment in May 2012 for aiding the rebels who committed atrocities.

Largest emergency aid appeal

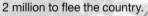

On 7 Jun 2013, the United Nations launched an appeal for $5 bn (£3 bn) in humanitarian aid for Syria to help more than 10 million people by the end of that year. The UN estimates that 4 million children are in need of humanitarian assistance as a result of the three-year conflict. The war has forced more than 6 million people out of their homes and caused 2 million to flee the country.

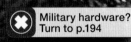

Military hardware?
Turn to p.194

Remote-controlled death: striking drones

Drones are remotely controlled, armed and unmanned aerial vehicles. According to non-governmental organizations and Pakistan government sources cited by Amnesty International in its "Will I Be Next?" report on US drone strikes in Pakistan, the USA launched some 330–374 drone strikes in that country between 2004 and Sep 2013. Another estimate, from the New America Foundation public policy institute, puts the figure at 364 US drone strikes in Pakistan as of Jul 2013. Either estimate represents the **most drone strikes**.

Waging warfare

Shortest war: between Britain and Zanzibar (now part of Tanzania); lasted from 9:00 a.m. to 9:45 a.m. on 27 Aug 1896

Longest continuous international war: Thirty Years War (1618–48), between various European countries; ended with Peace of Westphalia

Highest death toll from a civil war: Russian Civil War (1917–22), with the death of c. 1.5 million soldiers and more than 8 million civilians

ooo

Hot spots

The **average life expectancy in 1955** was 48 years; today, it is 67.2

Most murders per country

There were 47,106 murders in Brazil during 2012, corresponding to 24.5 homicides per 100,000 of the population. In Nov 2012, protesters concerned by these figures amassed outside the Brasilia National Congress, where more than 900 blood-red bricks were laid out: one for each victim in a typical week.

Most dangerous place to fly
The 2012 Annual Review of the International Air Transport Association (IATA) reported that the most dangerous place to fly is Africa – nine times more dangerous than the global average. In 2011, Africa suffered 3.27 aircraft destroyed or written off for every million flights taken. Reasons included an ageing fleet of turbo-prop aircraft, and inadequate air-traffic control.

Country with the highest percentage of the poor
Despite India's growing economy, its borders contain 41.01% of the world's poor. China comes second with 22.12%. The UN Department of Economic and Social Affairs defines poverty as "equating to those who earn $1.25 [80p] a day or less".

Deadliest place to travel by road

In 2013, the World Health Organization reported that the Dominican Republic recorded 41.7 road deaths per 100,000 population during the year 2010, the highest rate of nations with a population of over 1 million. Globally, 1.24 million people died on the road in 2010.

Lowest GDP per head
Gross Domestic Product (GDP) reflects all the goods and services produced by a nation in a year, stated as a value per head of population. The citizens of Malawi, an East African country with an undeveloped economy, have a GDP per head of $223 (£132). Luxembourg has the **highest GDP** (excluding the tiny principalities of Monaco and Lichtenstein) at $110,424 (£65,384).

Most murders per capita
While Brazil has the most murders in an absolute sense (see above), per capita the record is held by Honduras. The Central American country has 82.1 murders per 100,000 people, according to research by *The Economist*.

Most prisoners per capita
According to the International Centre for Prison Studies, in 2011 the USA had a record prison population of 2,239,751, and a rate of 716 prisoners for every 100,000 residents – the most prisoners per capita. By comparison, the microstate of San Marino had just two prisoners – or six prisoners per 100,000.

Most fatal snake bites per country

India reports a greater number of fatalities from snake bites than any country, recording 81,000 "envenomings" annually. Of these, 11,000 eventually prove to be fatal, according to conservative estimates published in *The Global Burden of Snakebite* (2008).

Largest global toxic threat
According to a report from 2010 by the Blacksmith Institute (USA), 10 million people are at risk from lead poisoning. The next most toxic global pollutants, in order, are: mercury, chromium, arsenic, pesticides and radionuclides. These can cause mental and physical disabilities, cancers and even death.

> ## GLOBAL PEACE INDEX: THE LEAST PEACEFUL COUNTRIES

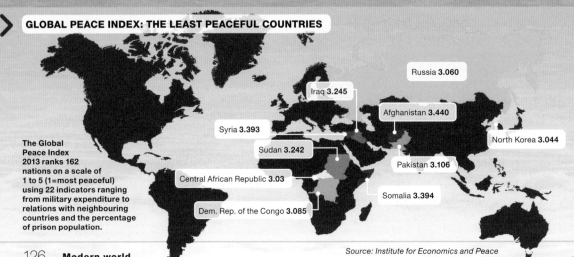

The Global Peace Index 2013 ranks 162 nations on a scale of 1 to 5 (1=most peaceful) using 22 indicators ranging from military expenditure to relations with neighbouring countries and the percentage of prison population.

Russia **3.060**
Iraq **3.245**
Afghanistan **3.440**
Syria **3.393**
North Korea **3.044**
Sudan **3.242**
Pakistan **3.106**
Central African Republic **3.03**
Somalia **3.394**
Dem. Rep. of the Congo **3.085**

Country comparisons

Highest death rate: Ukraine, with 16.2 deaths per 1,000 population projected for 2010–15.

Highest cancer death rate: Hungary, with 316 deaths per 100,000 population in 2009.

Highest heart disease death rate: Ukraine, with 1,070.5 deaths per 100,000 population in 2011.

Highest obesity rate: the island state of Nauru in the South Pacific, with 71.1% of people in 2008.

Source: Institute for Economics and Peace

Most polluted major city

A 2011 report by the WHO measured air pollution by the mass of particles smaller than 10 microns in diameter per m³ of air (known as PM_{10}). Ahwaz in Iran was the main offender, with a PM_{10} of 372 micrograms per m³.

Worst air pollution

In 2011, the World Health Organization (WHO) reported that the air in Mongolia had an annual average of 279 micrograms of PM_{10} per m³ (see Glossary). Many of the country's factories burn coal and many people live in *gers*: yurt-like felt-lined tents with central stoves. See above for the **most polluted major city**.

On a lighter note, the WHO report also stated that Whitehorse in Yukon, Canada, has an annual average of only 3 micrograms of PM_{10}, making it the **least polluted city**.

Worst land pollution

In Nov 1994, thousands of tonnes of crude oil flowed across the pristine Arctic tundra of the Komi Republic near Usinsk, Russia. Estimates of the amount of oil lost vary from 14,000 to 200,000 tonnes, and the total contaminated area measured 21.1 million m² (227.11 million sq ft), almost the same area occupied by El Salvador. The cost of the accident was estimated at more than 311 billion roubles ($11 bn; £7.5 bn).

Unhappiest country

According to a survey of 156 nations conducted in 2013 by the UN Sustainable Development Solutions Network, the citizens of the West African nation of Togo are the unhappiest, with a score of 2.936 out of 10. The survey looked at factors such as quality and quantity of life, mental health and personal liberty. At the other end of the scale was Denmark with a score of 7.693 – making it the **happiest country**.

Most tornadoes by area

The Netherlands has one twister for every 1,991 km² (769 sq mi) of land. The USA has one per 8,187 km² (3,161 sq mi).

Most deaths from natural disasters

In 2013, the Centre for Research on the Epidemiology of Disasters, Belgium, provided a report of fatalities from disasters such as earthquakes, floods and hurricanes during 2012. The most deaths – 2,385 – occurred in the Philippines, with China in second place with 802. In Dec 2012, almost 2,000 people in the Philippines were killed by Typhoon Bopha alone.

Most robberies per capita

In 2013, *The Economist* reported that Belgium has 1,714 robberies for every 100,000 people in a population of 10.8 million. The figures include an audacious heist on 18 Feb 2013 when cars with police markings were used to steal £33 m ($50 m) of diamonds from a plane at Brussels Airport – without a shot being fired.

Most dangerous resort for shark attacks

New Smyrna Beach in Florida, USA, has recorded 238 attacks and the beach has become known as the shark attack capital of the world, although most of the bites have been nibbles from hungry juveniles. Pictured here are surfers with a blacktip shark not far behind them – a photo snapped in 2008 by Kem McNair, who had finished surfing for the day.

FACT

Experts believe New Smyrna's reputation as a shark diner is simply down to the large numbers of people in the water who venture in despite frequent shark sightings.

 State of danger

From our first edition: "Taking figures for the decade (1940–1950) that part of the world with the highest annual average murder rate is the state of Georgia, USA, with 167.3 per million." By 2012 the figure had dropped to 59 per million, according to the FBI. The record holder per capita is now Honduras (see main text).

Hard news: journalists in danger

The **most dangerous country for journalists** is Iraq, with 153 killed since 1992. A total of 1,014 journalists have been killed worldwide since 1992, according to the Committee to Protect Journalists (CPJ). The problem is compounded by impunity – when governments deliberately don't investigate murders because they don't want to have abuses of power and human rights violations reported. The second most dangerous country is the Philippines, with 73 journalists killed since 1992.

Glossary

PM_{10}: Used to assess the extent of air pollution, this refers to "particulate matter" smaller than 10 micrometres wide. (The full stop at the end of this sentence is about 1,000 micrometres wide.) At this size, particulate matter such as dust, salts and the products of industrial processes are sufficiently small to penetrate into the deepest part of the lungs and cause a range of health problems such as asthma and lung cancer.

Travel & tourism

Mexico City is sinking by 10 cm per year – **10 times faster** than Venice

Most northerly ski resort

The Tromsø Alpinsenter ski resort is located in Kroken, Norway, more than 300 km (186 mi) inside the Arctic Circle. The resort has two drag lifts, a 500-m (1,640-ft) children's tow and four slopes with varying levels of difficulty. The longest run extends for some 2 km (1.2 mi).

Highest tourist receipts
In 2011, global receipts (earnings) from tourism topped $1 tr (£0.6 tr) for the first time in history, according to the United Nations World Tourism Organization (UNWTO). In 2012, however, total exports from international tourism rose yet again, to reach a record level of $1.3 tr (£0.8 tr).

Greatest spending on tourism (country)
The Chinese spent $102 bn (£63 bn) on tourism in 2012 – an increase of 37% on the country's 2011 spending and an eightfold increase from the $13 bn (£8.7 bn) spent in 2000. Germany's tourists spent the next largest amount internationally – $83.8 bn (£51.8 bn) – with the USA third, spending $83.5 bn (£51.6 bn).

Highest earnings from tourism
According to the UNWTO, tourism in the USA was worth $126.2 bn (£78 bn) in 2012 and single-handedly accounted for 8.5% of international tourism takings. Spain was second, with $56 bn (£34 bn), and France third, with $54 bn (£33 bn).

Most international tourist arrivals in one year
In 2012, according to a UNWTO report, the number of international tourist arrivals was 1.035 billion.

The same source reports that the **most popular country for tourism** is France, with 83 million international arrivals. The country accounts for just over 8% of the global

Fastest-growing tourist region

Tourist arrivals in Asia and the Pacific rose 7% in 2012, the equivalent of 15 million more international tourist visitors than in 2011. Among Asian subregions, south-east Asia posted the highest growth, with 9% more arrivals than the previous year, and Thailand saw a growth of 16% in absolute terms over 2011. This was the second year in a row that this region posted a record increase, according to the UNWTO.

tourism market. Its nearest rivals are the USA (with 67 million visitors) and China (with 57.7 million).

Europe remains the **most-visited tourism region**, with 534.2 million arrivals in 2012 according to the UNWTO. Asia and the Pacific are its nearest rivals, with 233.6 million arrivals. In third place are the Americas, with 163.1 million.

Most continents visited in one calendar day
Gunnar Garfors (NOR) and Adrian Butterworth (UK) visited five continents in one calendar day, taking scheduled transport between the east side of Istanbul in Turkey (Asia), Casablanca in

 For truly epic journeys, see p.156

Largest apartment ship

Launched in 2002, MS *The World* incorporates 165 residential units comprising 106 apartments, 19 studio apartments and 40 studios. While it continuously circumnavigates the world, its residents are able to conduct their professional lives while living and relaxing on board. The average stay lasts for around three to four months of the year and average occupancy is 150 residents (with an average age of 65).

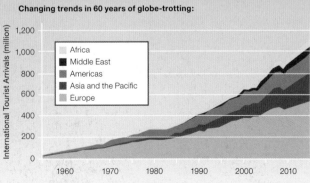

THE WORLD

WANDERERS OF THE WORLD: INTERNATIONAL TOURISM

Changing trends in 60 years of globe-trotting:

International Tourist Arrivals (million)

- Africa
- Middle East
- Americas
- Asia and the Pacific
- Europe

1,200 / 1,000 / 800 / 600 / 400 / 200 / 0

1960 1970 1980 1990 2000 2010

Source: UNWTO Tourism Highlights 2013 Edition

Transportation mode
- Air 52%
- Road 40%
- Rail 2%
- Water 6%

Purpose of visit
- Leisure 52%
- Health; religion; friends/family; other 27%
- Business 14%
- Not specified 7%

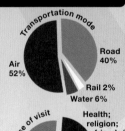 **Plus ça change...**
China has overtaken the USA in terms of tourist spending, and over the years London and Paris have vied for the honour of being the most-visited city. But for years now, one country has consistently proved to be the most popular for tourists: France. Back in 1999, it welcomed 73 million visitors. As of 2012, 83 million of us chose France for its rich cultural heritage, beautiful countryside, beaches, ski resorts, culinary delights, historic castles and cathedrals... and, of course, to see the "city of light", Paris.

FACT
Only an estimated 1,000th of 1% of the world's population has visited Antarctica.

Towering achievement
Every seven years, the Eiffel Tower receives a fresh coat of paint. In all, some 60 tonnes of paint are required to cover its 250,000-m^2 surface area.

Largest marina

In terms of inhabitants, Marina del Rey in Los Angeles County, California, USA, is the largest marina, with a population of 8,866 according to a 2010 census. It is home to 6,500 boats. The Dubai Marina, however – a 3-km-long (2-mi) canal city in Dubai, UAE, inaugurated in 2003 – will accommodate approximately 120,000 people. It has a provisional completion date of 2015.

Most international visits by a US president

Two US presidents have each visited 74 unique nations in office. The first was Bill Clinton, whose trips began on 3–4 Apr 1993 in Vancouver, Canada, where he had a summit meeting with President Yeltsin (RUS) and a meeting with Canadian Prime Minister Brian Mulroney. His final trip was to the UK on 12–14 Dec 2000, and included meetings with Prime Minister Tony Blair and Queen Elizabeth II. In all, Clinton made 133 trips.

George W Bush, the 43rd president, visited 74 unique nations during 140 trips in his two terms. The first, on 16 Feb 2001, was to San Cristóbal in Mexico, where he met with President Fox. The final visit was to Kabul in Afghanistan, from 14 to 15 Dec 2008, to meet President Karzai and visit US military personnel.

Most popular city for tourism

According to the MasterCard Global Destination Cities index, the city that attracted the greatest number of tourists in 2012 was London, UK, with some 16.9 million international visitors. The same report noted that tourists to London spent $21.1 bn (£13 bn), a 10.3% increase on 2011. No doubt the city's role as host of the 2012 Olympics played a part in this achievement.

Morocco (Africa), Paris in France (Europe), Punta Cana in the Dominican Republic (North America) and Caracas in Venezuela (South America) on 18 May 2012. The entire trip took 28 hr 25 min, but the changing time zones ensured that Garfors and documentary film-maker Butterworth cleared customs in each country on the same day.

Most national capitals visited in 24 hours by scheduled transport

Sarah Warwick and Lucy Warwick (both UK) visited London, Paris, Brussels, Prague, Vienna and Bratislava from 24 to 25 Sep 2013.

Largest national park

The Northeast Greenland National Park covers 972,000 km² (375,290 sq mi), from Liverpool Land in the south to the northernmost island, Oodaaq, off Peary Land. Established in 1974 and enlarged in 1988, much of the park is covered by ice and is home to a variety of protected flora and fauna, including polar bears, musk ox and birds of prey.

The **oldest national park** is Yellowstone National Park, USA. It was given its status in 1872 by US president Ulysses S Grant, who declared that it would always be "dedicated and set apart as a public park or pleasuring ground for the benefit and enjoyment of the people". It covers 8,980 km² (3,470 sq mi), mostly in the state of Wyoming.

Most-visited art gallery

The Louvre Museum in Paris, France, attracted 9,720,260 visitors in 2012. Housed in the Palais du Louvre on the Right Bank of the Seine, the museum first opened in 1793. In 1989, a glass pyramid designed by architect I M Pei was controversially added to its main courtyard (below).

According to *The Economist*, the Tate Modern in London, UK, remains the **most-visited modern art gallery**. In 2012, it drew 5,300,000 art lovers.

Water resistance: Venice in peril

The historic Italian city of Venice, a UNESCO World Heritage Site, is increasingly threatened with subsidence and serious flooding of its lagoon and canals. In 2002, a scheme was inaugurated to control water surges from the Adriatic Sea into the lagoon. Named the Moses Project, it envisages building 78 giant steel gates across three inlets to the lagoon, and sinking 300-tonne hinged gates (see bottom left) – each around 27 m wide – into huge concrete bases dug into the seabed. This represents the **largest project to save a tourist resort**.

The final frontier

First space tourist: Businessman Dennis Tito (USA), trip to *International Space Station*, 28 Apr to 6 May 2001

First space tourist (female): Anousheh Ansari (IRN), trip to *ISS*, 18 to 29 Sep 2006

Most trips into space by a tourist: Charles Simonyi (USA, b. HUN) embarked on first trip to *ISS* on 7 Apr 2007; made second trip, aged 60, on 26 Mar 2009

Shipping

In a year, the average container ship will cover the distance of a trip to the **Moon and halfway back**

Greatest lifting capacity for a ship

The MV *Fairplayer* and MV *Javelin*, operated by Jumbo Shipping of Rotterdam (NLD), are J-class mega-ships. Equipped with two Huisman mast cranes, each is capable of carrying a load of 900 tonnes (2 million lb), giving a maximum lifting capacity of 1,800 tonnes (4 million lb).

Busiest shipping lane

The Dover Strait marks the narrowest part of the English Channel between the UK and continental Europe. Through its shipping lane pass 500–600 ships a day.

First container ship

Shipborne containers were employed – usually on short-sea routes – from the early 20th century. Modern containerization started in the 1950s, one of the first vessels being the former tanker *Ideal X*, modified by Sea-Land Service (USA) in 1955. Standard container sizes were adopted in the 1960s alongside the introduction of purpose-

built ships. A unit of cargo capacity can be measured by TEU – Twenty-foot Equivalent Unit – based on the volume of one standard, 6.1-m-long (20-ft) container.

Largest container shipping line

Maersk (DNK) runs more than 600 vessels that make a total of 3.4 million

Busiest ocean trade route

A total of 7.52 million cargo containers were transported from North America to Asia in 2012, and 14.42 million containers shipped in the opposite direction. In all, the route saw 21.94 million units.

container moves annually. The company reported that they call at 35,000 ports annually and, in 2012, their work included shipping 8.4 billion bananas.

Largest ship ever

The oil tanker *Mont* (formerly *Jahre Viking*, *Happy Giant* and *Seawise Giant*) had a deadweight tonnage of 564,763 tonnes (622,544 tons). She was 458.45 m (1,504 ft) long, 68.8 m (226 ft) wide and had a draught of 24.61 m (80 ft 9 in). In 2010, she became the **largest ship to be scrapped**.

Fastest ship-building

The World War II ship-building programme at Kaiser's yard in Portland, Oregon, USA, built 10,000-tonne (22-million-lb)

Longest container ship

The Maersk (DNK) Triple E-class ships are each 400 m (1,312 ft) long and 20 have been ordered. The lead, *Maersk Mc-Kinney Møller*, was launched in Geoje, South Korea, on 24 Feb 2013. Each of the ships will contain as much steel as eight Eiffel Towers and, placed in Times Square, New York City, USA, would tower above the billboards and most of the buildings. Each ship has enough space to accommodate 36,000 cars or 863 million tins of baked beans.

LARGEST SHIPS

For comparison:
Eiffel Tower, 324 m tall

Largest privately owned yacht:
Azzam, owned by Sheikh Khalifa bin Zayed Al Nahyan (UAE), 180 m (cost: approx. £390 m)

Largest passenger liner: Royal Caribbean International Oasis class, 362 m, DWT (deadweight tonnage) 15,000 tonnes

Largest oil tanker: Daewoo Shipbuilding & Marine Engineering T1 class, 379 m, DWT 441,585 tonnes

Longest container ship: Maersk Triple E class, 400 m, DWT 196,000 tonnes

Largest ship ever: *Mont*, 458.45 m, DWT 564,763 tonnes

i Modelling big ships

For the ship enthusiast who needs a Maersk in their life, LEGO® have created a model version of the Triple E-class ship (see **longest container ship**). It comes in 1,519 pieces and measures 21 cm in height, 65 cm in length and is 9 cm wide.

👁 Deadweight tonnage (DWT)

Largest oil tanker – current: *Hellespont Alhambra*, Daewoo Shipbuilding & Marine Engineering (KOR), 11 Jun 2001, 441,585 tonnes

Largest bulk carrier ship: *Vale Beijing* (Dec 2011) and *Vale Qingdao* (Jun 2012), STX Offshore & Shipbuilding (KOR), 404,389 tonnes

Largest dry bulk carrier ship: *Berge Stahl*, Bergesen (NOR), 1986, 364,767 tonnes

Largest pipe-laying ship: *Solitaire*, Allseas Group (NDL), 1998, 127,435 tonnes

Busiest port for cargo volume

The Port of Shanghai turned over 736 million tonnes (724.3 million tons) of cargo in 2012, handling more than 32 million containers. It has a total quay length of around 20 km (12.43 mi), with 125 berths for container ships.

FACT

In 1992, 29,000 plastic yellow ducks and other toys were released into the wild when they were spilled from a container ship in the Pacific.

Most powerful nuclear-powered cargo ship

The Russian *Sevmorput* is not only the most powerful but is now the only nuclear-powered cargo ship left of the four that were originally produced. Nuclear power has not been widely adopted in shipping, and *Sevmorput* itself was to be scrapped until it was announced in Dec 2013 that it is to be restored by 2016.

ships in as little as 4 days 15 hr 30 min. In 1942, the SS *Robert E Peary* had her keel laid on 8 Nov, launched on 12 Nov and was operational on 15 Nov. Prefabrication speeded up production.

Largest ship builder

Hyundai Heavy Industries (KOR) is said to account for 15% of total world ship production. According to a report from a South Korean news agency in Feb 2014, a fall in ship prices meant that the giant's profits were down 86% in 2013, at 146.3 bn South Korean Won (£88 m; $136 m). In Jan 2014, it began work on a container ship with a capacity of 19,000 TEU.

Largest offshore mast crane

Onboard the *Seven Borealis* is a crane, built by Huisman (NLD), that lifts payloads of up to 5,000 tonnes (11 million lb). The *Seven Borealis* crane extends a record 150 m (492 ft) above deck level, although other cranes lift heavier weights. The structure revolves on a bearing that is 11 m (36 ft) in diameter. The ship began work in 2012.

Largest open-deck transport ship

The semi-submersible *Dockwise Vanguard* is 275 m (902 ft) long and has a flat deck measuring 70 x 275 m (230 x 902 ft). It can carry oversized cargo weighing 110,000 tonnes (242 million lb). The carrier, operated by Dockwise (NLD), submerges its deck to a depth of 16 m (52 ft) to allow it to load cargoes such as oil and gas platforms by floating underneath them.

SHIPWRECKS

Deepest

The *Rio Grande* was a German World War II blockade runner, evading enemies to deliver cargo. In Jan 1944, she was sunk by American ships and was discovered in 1996 by Blue Water Recoveries (UK) at a depth of 5,762 m (18,904 ft).

Another World War II casualty was UK merchant ship SS *Gairsoppa*, from which was retrieved the **deepest salvage of cargo from a shipwreck**. She was sunk by a German U-boat submarine and lay at a depth of 4,700 m (15,420 ft). In 2011, the ship was discovered by Odyssey Marine Exploration (USA), who had retrieved 47.9 tonnes (105,821 lb) of silver by Jul 2013.

Largest

The 321,186-tonne (708-million-lb) deadweight crude-oil carrier *Energy Determination* broke in two in the Strait of Hormuz, Persian Gulf, on 12 Dec 1979. The ship was not carrying any cargo at the time but had a hull value of $58 m (£26 m).

Oldest

A single-mast sailing ship, discovered in 1912, was wrecked off Uluburun, near Kaş in southern Turkey, in the 14th century BC.

Longest big ship canal

The Suez Canal has allowed ships to navigate from the Red Sea to the Mediterranean Sea, without sailing around Africa, since opening on 17 Nov 1869. Ten years in the making, it is 162.2 km (100.8 mi) in length and varies in width between 300 m (984 ft) and 365 m (1,198 ft).

Spinning around: a propeller with a twist

FACT

Emma Maersk can transport approximately 528 million bananas in one voyage – one each for every person in Europe or North America.

The *Emma Maersk* was launched in 2006 and featured the world's **largest propeller**. Made by Mecklenburger Metallguss GmbH (DEU), the single-piece, 130-tonne propeller has six blades and measures 9.6 m in diameter. Because of its size, the metal alloy from which it's made required two weeks to cool after casting. The blades are turned by a 14-cylinder Wärtsilä-Sulzer RTA96C two-stroke engine, the world's **largest diesel engine**. In Feb 2013, however, as the ship entered the Suez Canal, an engine-room flood put it out of service for some months.

Glossary

Deadweight tonnage: The total weight that a ship can carry, including crew, passengers, supplies, etc.

Gross tonnage: The total enclosed space within a ship (i.e., not a weight measurement).

Displacement tonnage: The weight of the water that a ship displaces when floating with full fuel tanks and stores. It is the actual weight of the ship, as a floating body displaces its own weight in water.

World of chance

In 2013, **$9.4 bn** was gambled by the 39.7 million people who visited Las Vegas

Most money lost by a nation to gambling per capita

According to international gambling organization H2 Gambling Capital, during 2010 the average Australian aged 17 or over lost £775. Around 70% of Australians are believed to participate in some form of gambling.

Greatest winning streak
In Dec 1992, Greek-American Archie Karas arrived in Las Vegas, USA, with $50 (£27) in his pocket. By early 1995, he had turned this sum into $40 m (£25 m) by playing pool, poker and dice. It's the largest winning streak in history, and even has its own name in gambling lore: "The Run". Karas's love of dice and (later) baccarat were his downfall: by mid-1995, he had lost all of the money.

First bookmaker
The first person to turn a profit as a bookmaker is thought to have been Harry Ogden (UK), who operated on Newmarket Heath, Suffolk, UK, during the mid-1790s. Prior to this, people who wished to bet on horse racing would simply make bets against one another. Ogden was the first to look at the entire field and offer different odds on every horse, calculating its chance of winning so that he would make a profit.

First offshore bookmaker
Victor Chandler International, now trading as BetVictor, decided to move its entire operation offshore in 1997 to evade the UK gambling tax, a move that was completed in 1999. The company relocated to Gibraltar – where the betting tax is zero. Many other bookmakers now also have a presence on the "Rock".

Largest horse-racing win
Scottish race horse owner Harry Findlay scooped £1.85 m ($3 m) over the British May Bank Holiday weekend in 2007. Findlay had placed bets of £140,000 ($276,000) with online pool betting firm RaceO. He ended up with 16 winners, comprising two eight-horse accumulators (a multiple, high-risk bet that only pays out if every horse wins).

Most successful horse-racing gambler
William Benter (USA) makes some $10 m (£5 m) per year betting on horses at the two

Largest win in a televised poker game

Tom Dwan (USA) picked up £0.6 m ($1.1 m) from one hand of televised poker against fellow American Phil Ivey during Full Tilt Poker's Million Dollar Cash Game, filmed in London, UK, in Sep 2009. Both players had drawn a "straight" (five cards of any suit ranked in order), but Dwan's 3-4-5-6-7 beat Ivey's Ace-2-3-4-5.

Largest lottery win donated to charity

In Jul 2010, Canadians Allen and Violet Large won CAN$11.2 m ($10.8 m; £7.1 m) on the Lotto 6/49 draw. They gave away some 98% – CAN$10.9 m ($10.5 m; £6.9 m) – to local groups, including the Red Cross and hospitals where Violet had cancer treatment.

Largest claw machine

"Santa Claw" is a claw machine measuring 5.1 x 2.4 x 3.6 m (17 x 8 x 12 ft) that was operated via the internet on thesantaclaw.com website between 3 Jan and May 2011. Around 100,000 players tried their luck during this period, and more than 4,000 prizes were grabbed; winners received their prizes by post.

TOP 10 BIGGEST GAMBLING LOSSES PER ADULT (PER ANNUM)

$1,000

In absolute terms, populations of larger countries such as the USA and China naturally lose more money to gambling than smaller countries. (Macau in China is the **largest gambling city by revenue** – more than $38 bn was generated by its casinos and other gaming services in 2012.) But measured in proportion to their overall population, gambling's biggest losers tend to be the smaller nations:

Source: H2 Gambling Capital, 2011; all figures quoted in US$

Australia: $1,199

Singapore: $1,093

$500

Hong Kong: $468
Italy: $481
Finland: $514
Canada: $528
Ireland: $547

Spain: $389
Greece: $391
Norway: $416

$0

FACT

The chances of winning the jackpot in a 6/49 lottery (i.e., selecting six numbers correctly out of a choice of 49) are 1 in 13,983,816.

AZ Glossary

Jackpot: maximum prize; the name originates from a type of poker in which the stakes built up until a player could open with a pair of jacks or better.

Bingo & Slots FRIENDZY

First Facebook game to offer cash prizes

On 7 Aug 2012, the British online gaming company Gamesys launched the first Facebook game to offer real cash prizes. Titled *Bingo Friendzy*, it featured 90 mini-games. Only Facebook users over the age of 18 are legally allowed to play the game.

tracks in Hong Kong, China. Benter trained as a physicist and used his scientific skills to build a computer model that takes into account more than 100 statistics – quantifying horses, jockeys, trainers, tracks and race conditions – to calculate each runner's exact chance of winning.

Longest craps roll

On 23 May 2009, at the Borgata Hotel Casino in Atlantic City, New Jersey, USA, craps player Patricia Demauro (USA) threw a pair of dice 154 times before a 7 ended her winning streak. It took her 4 hr 18 min, beating odds of 1,560 billion to 1.

Largest win in a poker competition

Antonio Esfandiari (USA, b. Iran) won $18,346,673 (£11,701,800) at the World Series of Poker tournament (WSOP2012) in Las Vegas, Nevada, USA, on 3 Jul 2012.

Largest online poker tournament

PokerStars (UK) organized an online poker tournament with 225,000 participants on 16 Jun 2013. Each player paid 60p ($1), with a £15,000 ($25,000) top prize.

Largest slot-machine tournament

A total of 3,001 players attended a slot-machine event organized by Bally Technologies (USA) at Mohegan Sun in Uncasville, Connecticut, USA, on 27 Apr 2013.

Most lottery prizes given in a year

Pronósticos para la Asistencia Pública (MEX) awarded 97,909,447 lottery prizes during 2008, distributed across eight different games.

Most members of a family to win a national lottery

In Sep 2012, teenager Tord Oksnes became the

Greatest national lottery jackpot

By 30 Mar 2012, the American Mega Millions lottery jackpot reached an annuity value of $656 m (£412 m), or $474 m (£298 m) in cash. The three unidentified winners (all USA) split the cash sum between them.

third member of his family to hit the jackpot in the Norwegian National Lottery when he won 12.2 m kroner (£1.3 m; $2.1 m). Three years previously, Tord's sister Hege Jeanette claimed 8.2 m kroner (£880,000; $1.27 m). Three years before that, Tord and Hege's father Leif scooped a win of 8.4 m kroner (£900,000; $1.5 m).

Largest Tote betting win

Sixty-one-year-old Steve Whiteley (UK) won an incredible £1,445,671.71 ($2,356,444.89) on a £2 ($3.25) Tote Jackpot accumulator bet in which he successfully predicted the winner of all six races from the meeting at Exeter, UK, on 8 Mar 2011. Afterwards, he was quoted as saying: "I'm a heating engineer – well, I was."

Lottery winners: what do they spend it on?

Source: Camelot Group

As of Mar 2012, the **largest national lottery** (see Lottery legends, right) had created 3,000 millionaires, each winning an average of £2.8 m. So how did they choose to spend their windfalls?

Property: £3.3 bn

Investments: £2.1 bn

Future needs (inc. provisions for children): £1.6 bn

Dream holidays: £21 m

Cars: £463 m

Lottery legends

Highest prize pot for a lottery: *El Gordo* ("The Fat One") in Spain is an annual lottery that, in 2013, had a total prize pool of 2.6 bn euros (£2 bn).

Largest lottery win: $314.9 m (£197.5), by Andrew "Jack" Whittaker Jr (USA) for a Powerball jackpot on 24 Dec 2002.

Largest national lottery: The UK National Lottery had total ticket sales of £95 bn as of 31 Mar 2013.

Fakes, frauds & forgeries

In 1496, the young **Michelangelo** faked an "ancient" statue of Cupid

Most expensive fake diaries

In 1983, *Stern* magazine paid some 9 million German marks (£3.3 m; $5 m) for 62 diaries allegedly written by Adolf Hitler, Germany's leader during World War II. US expert Kenneth W Rendell later proved that they were forged. The forger, Konrad Kujau (DEU), was jailed for 3 years 6 months, as was Gerd Heidemann, (DEU, above) the man who "uncovered" them.

Most lucrative art fraud by a woman

On 16 Sep 2013, Glafira Rosales (MEX) pleaded guilty in New York City, USA, to nine counts of fraud. She had taken part in a scheme to sell more than 60 fakes of abstract and Impressionist art, allegedly by 73-year-old American-Chinese artist Pei-Shen Qian, for more than $80 m (£50 m). The forgeries included copies of works by Mark Rothko and Jackson Pollock.

Most prolific forger of Shakespearean work

In 1794–95, manuscripts appeared in London, UK, supposedly written by William Shakespeare (1564–1616), among them a love poem to his wife, a letter

Largest collection of fake masterpieces

French artist Christophe Petyt owns just over 2,500 fake paintings of some of the world's most famous artworks. His company, L'Art du Faux, employs a selection of highly talented artists to copy masterpieces, which are then officially registered as a reproduction and sold.

from Queen Elizabeth I, revisions to his work, and two new plays. They were, in fact, forgeries by William Henry Ireland (UK). One of the new dramas, *Vortigern and Rowena*, was performed in 1796.

Most lucrative wine fraud

On 16 Oct 2013, two Italian wine merchants suspected of faking at least 400 bottles of the exclusive Romanée-Conti burgundy wine were arrested. The fraudsters may have made some £1.7 m ($2.75 m) from the scheme.

Most prolific art forger

At his trial in 1979, Thomas Keating (UK, 1917–84) put his output of fake pictures at more than 2,000 works, representing 121 different artists across a 25-year period.

Highest career earnings for a forger

Han van Meegeren (NLD, 1889–1947) is often cited as the most successful and influential art forger of all time. Estimates of his earnings vary, but by 1943 he had made the equivalent today of £15.6–18.8 m ($25–30 m), and also had property investments in the region of £300 m ($500 m). He focused on forgeries of work by the artists Johannes Vermeer and Pieter de Hooch.

Most successful defence equipment faker

On 2 May 2013, James McCormick (UK) received a 10-year sentence for selling devices that he claimed could detect explosives and drugs, but which were actually modified novelty golf-ball finders. He sold them for around £27,000 ($40,000) each, making an estimated £50 m ($77 m) overall.

Largest ATM fraud

In May 2013, it was reported that cyber criminals had stolen $45 m (£29 m) by hacking into a database of pre-paid credit cards in a scheme dubbed "PIN cashing" or "carding". Seven US citizens were arrested and accused of removing withdrawal limits, creating access codes and using associates to spread the data online to leaders of "cashing crews", who drained cash machines.

CONFOUNDING THE COUNTERFEITERS

The Swiss have the most secure banknotes (see right). Security features include:

Bank of Guinness World Records
Ten Dollars

$10 / $10

01 777 700 555

1 777 700 55

- Colour-shifting ink: changes colour when viewed from different angles
- Holographic strip
- Watermark, visible when held up to the light
- Hidden numbers, visible when held up to the light
- Very fine lines – difficult to replicate
- Raised printing
- Security thread, embedded in the note
- Microprint text – difficult to replicate
- Made from multi-layer polymer plastic; changes colour when tilted

Splashing the plastic

In 2006, we declared Swiss franc notes to be the **most secure banknote**. The 1,000-franc note incorporated 14 security features including micro lettering, fluorescent ink and braille. Several nations – including Australia, Canada and Brunei – have now abandoned paper notes in favour of plastic film. They are also four times more durable than paper banknotes: on average, the US dollar bill lasts only for around 18 months before it wears out.

FACT

In all, 830 million UK banknotes – worth £11.4 bn – had to be destroyed in 2013 owing to their poor condition.

Finance agents

The US Secret Service, a law-enforcement agency, was originally created at the end of the American Civil War (1861–65) to tackle counterfeit currency.

Largest bitcoin fraud

Bitcoin – a virtual monetary system based on digital tokens – was conceived in 2008, and by Nov 2013 its value had soared to £600 ($1,000) per bitcoin. The currency has already suffered from fraud losses, the worst being that of the Bitcoin Savings and Trust. By the time it was shut down in 2012, the savings scheme had reportedly lost the equivalent of £3.4 m ($5.6 m).

Largest fine for pharmaceutical fraud

In Jul 2012, British company GlaxoSmithKline received a £1.9-bn ($3-bn) penalty after admitting to history's biggest healthcare fraud. From 1997 to 2004, the company was alleged to have bribed doctors to prescribe drugs linked with safety concerns and promoted drugs that were not approved for their intended purpose.

Greatest goldsmith fraud

In 1896, the Louvre Museum in Paris, France, exhibited a large gold helmet weighing more than 800 g (1 lb 12 oz). The "Tiara of Saitaphernes" allegedly dated from either the late 3rd or 2nd century BC. The Louvre bought the object for 200,000 gold French francs, but it was later shown to be a fake that had been crafted by Russian goldsmith Israel Rouchomovsky.

Largest fine for mortgage fraud

On 19 Nov 2013, the largest US bank – JPMorgan Chase – concluded a settlement with officials from the US Justice Department. This included a fine that amounted to $13 bn (£8 bn) – the largest civil settlement with any one company resulting from the sale and misrepresentation of residential mortgage-backed securities (RMBS).

Largest fake army

Before allied forces invaded Europe, via Normandy in France, on "D-Day" (6 Jun 1944), a ruse was invented. Operation Bodyguard gave the illusion of two field armies, one set to menace Pas-de-Calais, comprising 1 million men. As a result, many German troops stayed in Pas-de-Calais instead of Normandy – preserving many allied lives on the day of the invasion.

For genuine works of art, view p.170

Largest fraud by a rogue trader

On 24 Jan 2008, French bank Société Générale declared that it had uncovered 4.9 bn euros (£3.6 bn; $7.16 bn) of losses following rogue trading by a member of its staff. Bank trader Jérôme Kerviel (FRA) was taken into police custody and was said to have admitted hiding his activities from his superiors. He was sentenced to five years in prison, with two years suspended. In 2010, however, he published a memoir entitled *Downward Spiral: Memoirs of a Trader*, in which he claims that his employers were aware of his trading activity.

Longest time under an assumed identity

In 1914, newspaper editor Anton Ekström (SWE) had a breakdown after the death of his wife and the loss of his wealth.

He became a hermit in the countryside under the name Magnusson. In 1955, after 41 years, he was exposed and reunited with his bewildered children.

Highest annual cost of cybercrime

Stolen identities, raided bank accounts and hacked emails are all forms of cybercrime. The 2013 Norton Report puts the annual cost of consumer cybercrime at £68 bn ($113 bn), or £180 ($298) per victim, of which there are more than 1 million every day or one every 3 sec.

Worrying signs: the rogue interpreter

Nelson Mandela's memorial service took place on 10 Dec 2013 in the 95,000-capacity FNB Stadium in Soweto, South Africa. It was attended by leaders and dignitaries from more than 100 countries and some 60,000 South Africans. As US President Barack Obama and South African President Jacob Zuma spoke, the official interpreter for the deaf stood beside them and made signs. These were later described by experts as childish hand gestures relating neither to the signs associated with the country's 11 official languages, nor to any of the related facial gestures. According to one international expert, the man – identified as Thamsanqa Jantjie – had also falsely interpreted at a military event in 2012.

Financial finagling

Longest prison sentence for fraud: 141,078 years, for Chamoy Thipyaso (THA) and seven associates in 1989, for swindling some 16,000 Thai citizens out of their life savings.

Greatest banknote forgery: the Third Reich's Operation Bernhard, during World War II, produced approximately 9 million counterfeit British notes valued at around £130 m ($520 m).

Money & economics

1,616 tonnes of gold was recycled in 2012, generating **£15 bn**

Largest gender gap

According to the World Economic Forum's 2013 Global Gender Gap Index, Yemen has the largest gender gap of any country. The measurement is made by scoring four indicators: economic participation and opportunity, educational attainment, health and survival, and political empowerment. Yemen scored 0.5128 (with 1 as the highest possible score). The country with the **smallest gender gap** was Iceland, scoring 0.8731. The USA scored 0.7392 and the UK 0.7440.

Fastest rising brand
Facebook's brand value increased by 43% to take it to No.52 in the Interbrand list of 2013, the only social media brand to claim a place on the Top 100 Best Global Brands. Its global user base increased by 26% to an incredible 1.19 billion MAU (monthly active users) and its mobile user base went up by 51% to 751 million in the year to Sep 2013.

Largest advertising agency
In Jul 2013, Publicis (FRA) and Omnicom (USA) announced that they would merge to create the Publicis Omnicom Group, which would have had $23 bn (£14 bn) in revenue had it been in existence during 2012. As it stands, WPP reported record revenues of $16.8 bn (£10.4 bn) in the same period.

FACT
Big givers: the Bill and Melinda Gates Foundation has given away $28 bn since its instigation in 1997.

Highest annual earnings by a CEO

John H Hammergren (USA), chief executive of pharmaceutical firm McKesson, received $131.19 m (£81.1 m) in 2012. Of this, "just" $1.66 m (£1 m) was earned salary; $4.65 m (£2.9 m) was a bonus, $112.12 m (£69.3 m) came as stock options, and the remaining $12.76 m (£7.9 m) was categorized as "other".

Greatest economic freedom
With a score of 89.3 (out of 100), Hong Kong, China, enjoys the greatest economic freedom according to the Heritage Foundation's Index of Freedom. Economic freedom is a measurement of the right of workers to control their own labour, consumption, investments and property.

Highest economic growth
Sierra Leone ended a decade of often barbaric civil war in 2002, and growth has been relatively speedy given how poor its citizens are in absolute terms. The country saw a 15.2% increase in GDP (Gross Domestic Product) in 2011–12. However, citizens also have the lowest **average life expectancy**, at 45 years.

In 2011, South Sudan gained independence from Sudan after another long civil war. The fledgling country went on to experience the **lowest economic growth**, with an enormous drop of 55.8% in 2011–12. Next door, Sudan recorded the second lowest growth with -10.1%.

Most innovative economy
As of Jul 2013, Switzerland had a score of 66.59 in the annual Global

Most unequal society

According to World Bank data from 2009 (the most recent figures available), South Africa is the economy in which disparities of income between richest and poorest are at their worst. The country with the **most equal distribution of income** is Slovakia.

Richest media tycoon

Former mayor of New York City Michael Bloomberg (USA) is the richest media mogul. His Bloomberg LP empire, which includes the Bloomberg financial news firm, is worth $27 bn (£17.7 bn), according to Forbes' list of billionaires from Mar 2013.

> **ECONOMY SIZES: LARGEST GDP**

Source: worldbank.org

USA $16.24 tr
China $8.22 tr
Japan $5.95 tr
Germany $3.42 tr
France $2.61 tr
UK $2.47 tr
Brazil $2.25 tr
Russia $2.01 tr
Italy $2.01 tr
India $1.84 tr

FACT
The GDP of the USA is $16.24 tr (£10 tr). But how long would it take you to count this out in $1 bills? Fast (human) money counters can count 200 notes in a minute; at 12,000 per hr, that's more than 154,000 years – non-stop – to count all 16.24 trillion bills!

Prosperous people

Richest person (ever): John D Rockefeller (USA, 1839–1937), $189 bn (£114 bn), if adjusted to 2013 figures.

Richest person (current): Bill Gates (USA), $75.9 bn (£45.5 bn), Feb 2014.

Richest investor: Warren Buffett (USA), $58.6 bn (£35.1 bn), Feb 2014.

Richest woman: Christy Walton (USA), $36.9 bn (£22.1 bn), Feb 2014.

Most valuable brand

According to the 2013 Interbrand Top 100 Best Global Brands rankings, Apple is worth $98.31 bn (£59.61 bn) – a 28% rise over the previous year. The record ends 13 years of domination by Coca-Cola, which dropped to third behind Google. There are 72 million Mac computers in use, and 9 million iPhone 5s and 5c models were sold in launch weekend alone. In 2013, the App Store reached the 50-billion download mark after just five years.

Innovation Index, published by Cornell University, the business school INSEAD and the World Intellectual Property Organization. Measurements are taken in such areas as institutions, infrastructure, research, the sophistication of the market and in business, creativity and technology.

Highest budget for...
• **Defence:** According to *The Economist*, Iraq spent 11.3% of its GDP on defence in 2012.
• **Health:** World Bank figures from 2011 put Liberia top of health spending with 19.5% of its GDP.
• **Education:** In 2012, Lesotho put 13% of its GDP towards education, according to figures from *The Economist*.

Highest budgetary expenditure
The USA spent $3.53 tr (£2.3 tr) in 2012, a figure that excludes social benefits of approximately $2.3 tr (£1.5 tr). The USA accounts for more than 15% of worldwide budgetary expenditure and also brings in the **highest revenue**, with an estimated $2.44 tr (£1.6 tr) in 2012. This excludes social contributions revenue of some $1 tr (£652 bn).

Highest cost of living
According to a Dec 2012 survey by the Economist Intelligence Unit, Japan is the most expensive nation to live in for expatriate executives and their families. Prices for products of international comparable quality in stores in New York City, USA, are used as a base, with the USA scoring 100. Japan is the priciest, with a score of 152, followed by Australia (137). The country with the **lowest cost of living** is Pakistan, with a rating of 44.

Largest municipal bankruptcy

On 18 Jul 2013, Detroit in Michigan, USA, filed for the largest bankruptcy in modern times, with debts estimated at $18–20 bn (£11–12 bn). Up to 40% of street lights are broken in the city that is home to over 150,000 deserted buildings. Among them is the former Packard car factory (pictured), a 325,160-m² (3.5-million-sq-ft) property that is the **largest abandoned factory**. Closed since 1956, Packard once produced 75% of the world's cars in Detroit – known as "Motor City".

Worst modern recession

The ongoing downturn in Greece has been more severe than in any other country in the developed world since World War II. In 2013, the economy shrank by 23–25%, compared with 20% in 2012. The jobless rate increased from 25% to 27% and youth unemployment leapt from 50% to 60%.

⚡ Costly quaffs
As an indicator of how our spending habits have changed since 1955, the **most expensive bottle of wine** then was a 1949 Feinste Trockenbeerenauslese priced at £8; adjusting for inflation means that this would cost £178 today. But the most expensive wines commercially available currently sell for c. £32,000 – that's 180 times more than the adjusted figure!

Starship enterprise: high transactions
Russian cosmonaut Pavel Vinogradov was in the *International Space Station* orbiting at an altitude of 419 km (260 mi) above Earth when he made the **highest-altitude financial transaction**, a land tax payment of 616 roubles (£11.31; $18.51) on 22 Apr 2013. The money was transferred to the Federal Tax Service of Russia and represents the first time that anyone has paid their tax bill – or indeed any kind of bill – from space!

⚡ Gross world product
Totalling the gross domestic product (GDP) of every country gives you the "gross world product" – in other words, the value of all goods and services in the world. Sixty years ago, this figure stood at $5.43 tr (or $1,966 per person); in 2014, this is an estimated $72.21 tr (or $10,316 per person). This means our economy today is more than 13 times bigger than it was back in 1955.

:Internet

By 2015, **44%** of the world will have internet access at home

FACT
Google's Trekker helped collect images for the **southernmost Street View** (right). Trekker is a backpack with a battery-powered 19-kg camera on a mast. Its 15 lenses are differently angled and their images later stitched into a 360° panorama.

Most viewed online video advertisement

"Dove Real Beauty Sketches" was watched 134,265,061 times – in 25 languages in more than 110 countries – as of 1 May 2014, by which date it had been shared 4,517,422 times. The video was posted on 14 Apr 2013 and data was collected by Unruly for their Viral Video Chart.

Southernmost location on Google Street View

On 17 Jul 2012, Google released images on its ground-level perspective Street View service showing the South Pole. Other areas of Antarctica available on Street View include penguin colonies, Ernest Shackleton's hut and Robert Falcon Scott's supply hut. Users can guide their cursors inside the buildings and take a virtual tour of these icons of exploration.

First Google hoax
On 1 Apr 2000, Google perpetrated the "MentalPlex" hoax to mark April Fool's Day. It invited users of its search engine to stare at an animated gif on its homepage and think of what they wanted to find on the net. Later japes included 2007's Google TiSP (Toilet Internet Service Provider).

First webcam
In 1991, computer scientists at Cambridge University, UK, set up a camera and a computer to monitor the status of their coffee pot without having to leave their room. The system was upgraded in Nov 1993 when it was linked to the net, and live images of the famous coffee pot were broadcast until the feed was turned off in 2000.

Highest communications bandwidth between Earth and the Moon
A two-way laser lunar net link was established with download speeds of 622 megabits per sec between a NASA spacecraft orbiting the Moon – allowing a gigabyte to be transferred in 5 min. NASA and the Massachusetts Institute of Technology (USA) ran tests in Oct 2013, including an HD video sent between the Moon and Earth in 7 sec.

Most Facebook "likes" on an item

On 30 Nov 2013, *Fast & Furious* star Paul Walker (USA, left and below) died in a car crash in California, USA. Friend Vin Diesel, aka Mark Vincent (USA, right and below), posted the photo shown below right on Facebook, where it had 6,817,898 "likes" as of 7 May 2014. The previous record-holding item was a 2012 photo on Barack Obama's Facebook page showing his embrace with wife Michelle after being elected US president for a second term. As of 7 May 2014, it had 4,433,487 "likes".

Most mentions of a brand name on Twitter in 24 hours

A chocolate-coated biscuit stick called Pocky was mentioned 3,710,044 times on Twitter on 11 Nov 2013. That works out at slightly over 4,294 mentions per sec for the Ezaki Glico Co, Ltd (JPN) snack. Everything from emojis (Japanese smileys) to straight retweets were counted in the attempt.

WHAT HAPPENS IN AN INTERNET MINUTE

email
204 million emails sent

flickr
20 million photo views

Google
2 million searches

facebook
1.8 million "likes"

skype
1.4 million connection minutes

twitter
278,000 tweets

YouTube
3 days of video uploaded

tumblr.
20,000 new photos

iTunes
15,000 tracks downloaded

Pinterest
11,000 active users

Source: Intel and qmee.com, 2013

Email spamming

Anyone who has ever used email has received spam – unsolicited messages. Billions of the nuisances are sent daily but, before the phenomenon had a name, Gary Thuerk (USA) sent the **oldest spam**, on 3 May 1978. His memo was quite innocent – a message to 397 email accounts on the ARPAnet of the US Department of Defense, with an invitation to attend a product demonstration.

FACT
Tim Berners-Lee had the idea for the **first hypertext browser** – what became the World Wide Web – in Mar 1989. Marking its 25th anniversary, in 2014 Berners-Lee called for a bill of rights to keep the Web free and open. "Our rights are being infringed... on every side and the danger is that we get used to it... the key thing is getting people to fight for the Web."

First Instagram from space

"Back on *ISS*, life is good" wrote Steve Swanson (USA) from the *International Space Station* on 7 Apr 2014, posing in a T-shirt from cult TV sci-fi show *Firefly* (USA, 2002).

The **most "liked" image on Instagram** (inset) shows actor Will Smith (USA) and Justin Bieber (CAN), posted in Aug 2013. "Me and uncle Will," noted the pop star, who posted the image. It has been "liked" more than 1.5 million times.

currency that exists only online – belonged to Ross Ulbricht (USA), who is accused of running the Silk Road, an online marketplace for drugs.

Northernmost underwater communications cable

Longyearbyen in Norway, at a latitude of 78.22°N, is the landing point of the Svalbard Undersea Cable System, which provides a fibre-optic internet connection with the Norwegian mainland. The two-cable system is 2,714 km (1,686 mi) long and provides fast access to data from Svalbard's SvalSat. This is one of only two ground

Most retweeted message on Twitter

The selfie above, organized by 2014 Oscars host Ellen DeGeneres (USA), exceeded 1 million retweets within about an hour of being tweeted on Oscars night, 3 Mar 2014. Smiling alongside stars such as Bradley Cooper, Jennifer Lawrence, Brad Pitt, Kevin Spacey and Meryl Streep, DeGeneres tweeted, "If only Bradley's arm was longer. Best photo ever. #oscars." As of 5 May 2014, the message had been retweeted 3,428,897 times.

stations optimally located to download data from all 14 polar-orbiting satellites.

In Apr 2014 he documented his split from wife and fellow vlogger Alli.

Largest internet census by a botnet

A botnet – from robot network – consists of many computers linked together to run services. In 2012, an anonymous hacker hijacked 420,000 devices that had only default passwords and used them to conduct an illegal mapping of the internet, particularly insecure devices. His control program was called the Carna Botnet.

Largest seizure of virtual currency

On 25 Oct 2013, the US Federal Bureau of Investigation (FBI) revealed that it had seized 144,000 bitcoins worth around $28.5 m (£17.2 m). The FBI allege that the tranche of bitcoins – a

Fastest time to reach 1 million followers on Twitter

On 11 Apr 2014, Twitter was a-flutter to learn that Robert Downey Jr (USA) had joined the site with a "Talk to me, Twitter" (@robertdowneyjr). Within a day, the star had attracted 1,017,322 fans, but he still lags behind the **most followers on Twitter for an actor**. Ashton Kutcher (USA; @aplusk) had 16,022,147 followers as of 6 May 2014.

For more top tech turn to pp.206–207

Most consecutive daily personal video blogs on YouTube

As of 6 May 2014, Charles Trippy (USA) had posted 1,831 vlogs, without missing a day, on his YouTube channel Internet Killed Television.

Most expensive property sold at online auction

A plot of land in the same area of Dubai as the Burj Khalifa sold for 94,176,000 United Arab Emirates dirham (£16,565,558; $25,634,707) on 19 Feb 2013 through Emirates Auction (UAE).

Most subscribers on YouTube

As of 6 May 2014, "PewDiePie", aka Felix Arvid Ulf Kjellberg (SWE), had 26,540,250 YouTube subscribers for his comedic videogaming highlights.

FACT

Robert Downey Jr also operates a Facebook account which had been "liked" by 16,373,295 fans as of 7 May 2014.

Turn it off and on again: rebooting the net

Seven experts (including Moussa Guebre, BFA, above left) form the **first international group capable of rebooting the World Wide Web**, or at least certain aspects of it, in the event of a major catastrophe such as a cyber attack. They are the back-up for a security system called DNSSEC that adds a digital signature to website names, helping in the battle to stop hackers redirecting surfers to fake sites. Should a disaster take out DNSSEC, five of the seven global keyholders would be summoned to a secure US location to save the day. Each of the team has a swipe card that provides one-fifth of the reboot key.

Glossary

DNS: stands for Domain Name System. It manages navigation of the internet by resolving proper names used by websites into the strings of numbers understood by computers.

DNSSEC: stands for Domain Name System Security Extensions, a set of standards to ensure that our browsers are not being sent to fake sites with malicious code.

○ ○ ○

Crowdsourcing

A bank robber used crowdsourcing to hire a team of identically dressed workmen, aiding his escape

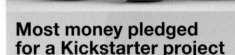

in the Jun 2006 edition of *Wired* under the title "The Rise of Crowdsourcing".

Largest platform for crowdfunding

From Kickstarter's launch on 28 Apr 2009 until 4 Mar 2014, 5.7 million people pledged a total of $1,001,567,335 (£598,870,000). This support has aided 57,171 projects to meet their funding goals.

First crowdsourced military vehicle design

The XC2V FLYPMode, made by Local Motors and the US Defense Advanced Research Projects Agency (DARPA), used design ideas from

Most money pledged for a Kickstarter comic project

Graphic designer Rich Burlew (USA) couldn't afford to reprint *The Order of the Stick* himself, so turned to his fans. Almost 15,000 people had pledged $1,254,120 (£790,570) by the time the project closed on 21 Feb 2012.

First use of the term "crowdsourcing"

In 2005, US journalist Jeff Howe coined the term "crowdsourcing" while pitching an article about how the internet was being used to outsource work to the general public, or "crowd". The article appeared

Most money pledged for a Kickstarter project

The Pebble (USA) is a customizable watch with internet connectivity, message and email alerts, and access to sports and fitness apps. The watch received pledges of $10,266,845 (£6,468,610) by 19 May 2012, surpassing its goal 10-fold.

more than 150 people. Built to replace the Humvee, the prototype was presented to President Obama in 2011.

Highest chart placing by a crowdfunded album

Theatre is Evil, an album by Amanda Palmer and The Grand Theft Orchestra (USA, see above right), achieved a top 10 placing on the *Billboard* 200 on its release in Sep 2012 – the highest position achieved by a crowdfunded music release.

First crowdsourced car design

The Rally Fighter, an off-road racer produced by Local Motors (USA), represents the culmination of 35,000 designs by 2,900 people from more than 100 countries. The car made its debut at the Specialty Equipment Market Association Show in Las Vegas, Nevada, USA, on 3 Nov 2009.

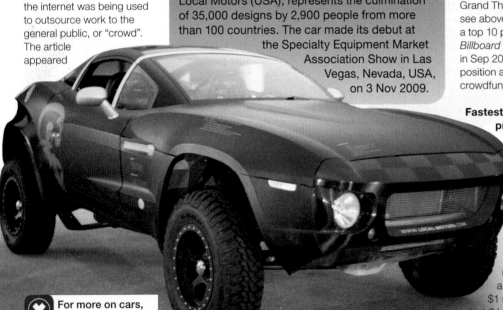

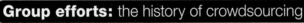

Fastest Kickstarter project to reach $1 m

On 27 Oct 2013, "Reaper Miniatures Bones II" (USA) – a project created to fund an expansion of the miniatures range – sped to a pledge total of $1 m (£618,000) in just 2 hr 41 min 51 sec.

Most money pledged on Kickstarter for photography

On 1 Jul 2013, US-based Planetary Resources raised more than $1.5 m (£989,000) for "A Space Telescope for Everyone". The project aims to launch a publicly accessible telescope that could take photos of space or allow people to have their photo displayed above Earth.

⊗ For more on cars, turn to p.186

Group efforts: the history of crowdsourcing

Crowdsourcing is nothing new. In the UK, the Oxford English Dictionary (left) received six million suggestions from the public when it first solicited entries in the 1850s, while Nelson's Column (below left, erected 1843) was paid for in part from public subscriptions (crowdfunding). In 1567, England's Queen Elizabeth I effectively crowdfunded the enlarging of the Navy by initiating the first national lottery. Competitions can also be considered a form of crowdsourcing: the Longitude Prize in the 1700s, for example, sought to find a solution to determining a ship's longitude at sea – a problem finally solved in 1756 by John Harrison (right).

i What is Kickstarter?

Kickstarter was founded by Perry Chen, Yancey Strickler and Charles Adler (all USA) in New York, USA, and launched on 28 Apr 2009. The concept allows investors to pledge money towards creative projects in return for rewards and experiences. However, the funds are only handed over if the project's entire funding goal is met. ○○○

Most crowdfunded music project

Amanda Palmer (USA) initiated a Kickstarter appeal to fund her album with the aim of raising $100,000. By the time the appeal closed on 1 Jun 2012, she had received pledges of $1,192,793 (£771,211), making hers the most successful crowdfunded music project of any kind.

MOST MONEY PLEDGED FOR A KICKSTARTER...

Art project
The Marina Abramović Institute, a performance and education centre in New York City, USA, aimed to raise $600,000.

The goal was surpassed on 25 Aug 2013, with pledges of $661,452 (£424,750).

Dance project
STREB Extreme Action (USA) beat their $45,000 goal on 25 Nov 2013 with pledges of $45,512

(£28,043). *FORCES* is described as a theatrical show centred on "action".

Fashion project
Jake Bronstein (USA) is so sure of his lifetime-lasting hoodie that he provides a 10-year free mending service. He passed his funding goal on 21 Apr 2013 with pledges of $1,053,830 (£690,000).

Food project
Scott Heimendinger's (USA) "Sansaire Circulator" uses *sous vide* – a method of cooking using exact temperature control – in a product designed for the home cook. Final pledges reached $823,003 (£527,000) on 6 Sep 2013.

Publishing project
Planet Money's (USA) project leads the consumer on an innovative journey through a T-shirt's creation. Each T-shirt has a barcode linking to a web page featuring photos of the people who made it, from cotton growers to factory workers. Pledges of $590,807 (£385,076) were received by 14 May 2013.

Theatre project
Tim O'Connor (USA) raised $175,395 (£108,041) by 24 Sep 2012 to upgrade Catlow Theater in Barrington, Illinois, USA, with modern audio and visual equipment.

Most crowdfunded stage project

The story of serial killer Patrick Bateman may seem an unlikely source for a musical, but *American Psycho* opened in London, UK, in Dec 2013 with ex-*Doctor Who* star Matt Smith as the lead. Producer Jesse Singer of Act 4 Entertainment (USA) had raised pledges of $154,929 (£97,000) in May 2013 to help fund the production.

Most crowdfunded videogame console

The Kickstarter appeal to back the OUYA (USA) raised $8,596,474 (£5,500,090) by 9 Aug 2012. The £99 eighth-generation console is an Android-based device that connects to a standard modern TV set and allows users to play free-to-try games.

Most crowdfunded project (overall)

Efforts to fund *Star Citizen*, a space-based trading and combat adventure videogame, resulted in the largest single amount ever raised via crowdsourcing. As of 4 Mar 2014, publisher Cloud Imperium Games (USA) had raised $39,680,576 (£23,726,300) via its own website appeal alone. Chris Roberts designed the game, scheduled for release in 2015.

KICKSTARTER CATEGORIES WITH THE MOST SUCCESSFUL PROJECTS

Category	Total	Funded	Unfunded
Music	$94.20 m	15,011	12,203
Film & Video	$163.95 m	13,096	19,594
Art	$30.24 m	5,613	6,101
Publishing	$40.42 m	5,125	10,756
Theatre	$19.69 m	3,556	1,974
Games	$189.97 m	2,948	5,435
Design	$125.13 m	2,537	4,040
Food	$30.69 m	2,089	3,121
Comics	$22.96 m	1,762	1,814

Source: kickstarter.com, 4 Mar 2014

Kickstarter's most funded...

- **Art book:** *Masters of Anatomy* (CAN), $532,614 (£330,662), 20 Nov 2013
- **Children's book:** *Hello Ruby*, Linda Liukas (USA), $380,747 (£228,545), 22 Feb 2014
- **Fiction:** *The Warden and the Wolf King*, Andrew Peterson (USA), $118,188 (£73,631), 31 Oct 2013
- **Poetry:** *A Bruise on Light* by Shane Koyczan (CAN), $91,154 (£54,656), 26 Feb 2014

Great journeys

Each continent has a **Pole of Inaccessibility** – its farthest point from an ocean

First 360° panorama filmed on the summit of Mount Everest

The first fully spherical 360° video from the summit of Mount Everest was recorded in May 2013. The footage was captured with 360Heros' 360° video gear for a documentary by Everest Media Productions about Nepalese climber Apa Sherpa, who also acted as a consultant for the shoot. The veteran sherpa summitted the mountain 21 times between 1990 and 2011, the **most conquests of Mount Everest**.

Slotting into place
The 3D-printed H3PRO6 holder was invented by Michael Kintner (USA), CEO of 360Heros. On Everest, six GoPro cameras were slotted into the holder and software was later used to create the final footage.

"Little Planet" mode
As well as being available as a fully interactive 3D video, the panorama can also be viewed in "little planet" or "miniplanet" mode, which creates a spherical or "stereographic" projection.

FACT
In Nepal the name of Everest is *Sagarmatha* ("forehead of the sky"), and in Tibet it is *Chomolungma* ("mother goddess of the world").

North Pole

The ocean at the North Pole is more than **4,000 m deep**

First traverse of the North Pole by motorized vehicle

The Russian Marine Live-Ice Automobile Expedition MLAE 2013 (Sergey Isayev, Nikolay Kozlov, Afanasy Makovnev, Vladimir Obikhod, Alexey Shkrabkin and Andrey Vankov, led by Vasily Elagin) left Golomyanny Island, Russia, on 1 Mar 2013. Driving two 6 x 6 low-pressure-tyre ATVs, the team arrived at the North Pole on 6 Apr, then continued to the Canadian coast, which they reached on 30 Apr. The 60-day journey covered approximately 4,000 km (2,480 mi) in all.

Most polar expeditions completed by an individual
Richard Weber (CAN) has successfully completed eight polar expeditions. He reached the geographic North Pole from the coast six times between 2 May 1986 and 14 Apr 2010, and the geographic South Pole twice from the coast on 7 Jan 2009 and 29 Dec 2011.

First solo expedition to the North Pole
At 4:45 a.m. GMT on 1 May 1978, Japanese explorer and mountaineer Naomi Uemura became the first person to reach the North Pole in a solo expedition across the Arctic sea-ice. He had travelled 770 km (478 mi), setting out on 7 Mar 1978 from Ellesmere Island in

Canada. The expedition was dog-supported and Uemura had access to re-supplies.

First person to ski to both poles (unassisted, unsupported)
Marek Kamiński (POL/USA) reached the North Pole from Cape Columbia on 23 May 1995, and the South Pole from Berkner Island on 27 Dec 1995. He completed both trips under his own power and without any external assistance.

FASTEST...

Surface journey to the North Pole
On 21 Mar 2005, Tom Avery and George Wells (both UK), Matty McNair and Hugh Dale-Harris (both CAN), Andrew Gerber (ZAF) and 16 husky dogs left Cape Columbia on Ellesmere Island in Canada. They reached the North Pole 36 days 22 hr 11 min later, on 26 Apr 2005. Their journey was an attempt to recreate as closely as possible the disputed 1909 expedition of US explorer Robert Peary.

Three Poles Challenge

The **first person to complete the Three Poles Challenge** was Erling Kagge (NOR), who reached the North on 8 May 1990, the South on 7 Jan 1993, and Everest on 8 May 1994. The latest challenger was Johan Ernst Nilson (SWE, pictured), who topped Everest in May 2007. He began the polar stages by being dropped at the North Pole on 22 Jun 2011 and walking to land, and completed a South Pole trek on 19 Jan 2012. Having left from 90°N, Nilson achieved the **first Three Poles Challenge – North Pole to land.**

Youngest female to ski to the North Pole (unsupported, unassisted)

Amelia Darley (née Russell, UK, b. 29 Aug 1982) was 27 years 239 days old when she reached the geographic North Pole on 25 Apr 2010. Her journey of 780 km (484 mi) began at Cape Discovery, McClintock Inlet, on Ward Hunt Island, Canada. Amelia travelled in a two-person expedition accompanied by her boyfriend, Dan Darley (UK).

Ski journey to the North Pole by a women's team
Catharine Hartley and Fiona Thornewill (both UK) skied to the North Pole (with support in the form of re-supplies en route) in 55 days between 11 Mar and 5 May 2001. They began their expedition from Ward Hunt Island in Nunavut, Canada.

Trek to the North Pole
David J P Pierce Jones (UK), Richard Weber and Tessum Weber (both CAN) and Howard Fairbanks (ZAF) took 41 days 18 hr 52 min to trek to the North Pole, from 3 Mar to 14 Apr 2010. The team set out from 82°58'02"N and 77°23'3"W and were picked up after reaching the North Pole, at 90°N.

Solo trek to the North Pole (unsupported, unassisted)
Børge Ousland (NOR) skied his way to the North Pole from Cape Ar
Arkticheskiy on the archipelago of Severnaya Zemlya in the Russian Federation. He undertook the trip without external assistance in 52 days, from 2 Mar to 23 Apr 1994. This also makes him the **first person to make a solo journey to the North Pole from land (unsupported, unassisted).**

The **fastest trek to the North Pole by a woman (unsupported)** was achieved by Cecilie Skog (NOR). She left Ward Hunt Island with Rolf Bae and Per Henry Borch (both NOR) on 6 Mar 2006, reaching the Pole 48 days 22 hr later.

Marathon on each continent and the North Pole (male)
From 26 Feb to 9 Apr 2013, Ziyad Tariq Rahim (PAK) ran a marathon on each continent and one at the North Pole, taking 41 days 20 hr 38 min 58 sec in all.

The "Three Poles"
Adventurers consider Earth to have three poles: the North and South poles and Mount Everest. The latter is regarded as a "pole" in this context, owing to its relative inaccessibility.

Magnetic North Pole: Unlike the geographic North Pole, this is not a fixed point; it moves by some 60 km each year, driven by fluctuations in the Earth's magnetic field. This is the "north" to which magnetic compasses align themselves.

Canada

Greenland

Svalbard archipelago

Norway

Geographic North Pole: Also known as "True North", this is located at 90°N. All the lines of longitude on Earth converge at this point.

"Our carbon paddles were lightweight, but durable. The sharp blade helped us to cut through thin ice layers and make a channel."

"This small outdoor weather station allowed us to measure wind speed, temperature, air pressure and humidity. It was also of some help to us in predicting the weather."

"A very simple and ordinary GPS. It's lightweight and consumes less energy than those with colour maps. In the Arctic Ocean, there is no need for GPS maps: there is nothing to be mapped."

"Ski goggles protect the eyes and part of the face in harsh weather conditions. The yellow and red lenses also enhance contrast and give a better definition in overcast and white-out conditions."

"A waterproof 'spray skirt' covers the cockpit and prevents water from getting in when we paddle in high winds and heavy waves."

"To protect our hands from the wind and cold, weatherproof mittens are a must."

"Waterproof Gore-Tex dry suits made paddling through the freezing cold Arctic waters both comfortable and safe."

"For some reason, we managed to break all our plastic spoons. So we had to improvise and combine new ones from the leftovers."

"This type of camping stove is simple and sturdy – exactly what you need in the Arctic Ocean. It is such a crucial part of our gear that we had a spare."

"A sledge, rather than this kayak, would have been more appropriate to pull across the sea-ice of the Arctic Ocean. But we needed it to cross the large open areas of water at the later stages of the expedition in order to get on land and continue along the fjords."

THREE POLES CHALLENGE

First woman to complete the Three Poles Challenge

Sweden's Tina Sjögren reached the North Pole on 29 May 2002 with her husband Thomas. She had summitted Everest on 26 May 1999 and reached the South Pole on 1 Feb 2002. The couple's two polar journeys also mark the **fastest time to reach both poles unsupported**.

First person to complete the Three Poles Challenge without the use of oxygen on Everest

As of Mar 2014, the only person to complete the Three Poles Challenge unsupported and without the use of supplementary oxygen is Antoine de Choudens (FRA), who accomplished this breathtaking feat from 25 Apr 1996 to 10 Jan 1999.

Fastest time to complete the Three Poles Challenge

The shortest time taken to reach the three extreme points on Earth is 1 year 217 days by Adrian Hayes (UK). He summitted Everest on 25 May 2006, reached the North Pole on 25 Apr 2007 (from Ward Hunt Island, Canada), and claimed the South Pole, journeying from the Hercules Inlet in western Antarctica, on 28 Dec 2007.

The **fastest time to complete the Three Poles challenge by a woman** is 1 year 336 days, and was accomplished by Cecilie Skog (NOR). She summitted Mount Everest on 23 May 2004, reached the South Pole on 27 Dec 2005, and got to the North Pole on 24 Apr 2006.

Fastest journey from the North Pole to land (unsupported, unassisted)

In 1895, Fridtjof Nansen and Hjalmar Johansen (both NOR) almost became the first people to reach the North Pole, but were forced to retreat at 86°14'N. In 2012, Audun Tholfsen (NOR) and Timo Palo (EST), pictured right, set out on what would have been Nansen and Johansen's return route. The duo left the North Pole on 23 Apr 2012. Using skis and kayaks, but no external support or re-supplies, they negotiated 1,150 km (715 mi) of drifting ice and curious polar bears to reach Phippsøya island, in Norway's Svalbard archipelago, 55 days later. They arrived at Longyearbyen, Svalbard, on 3 Jul, having covered 1,620 km (1,060 mi) in all.

South Pole

Approximately **90% of the ice on Earth** is located in Antarctica

Fastest trek to the South Pole by a team (unsupported)

Norwegians Mads Agerup (main picture, above), Christian Eide (photographer, reflected), Morten Andvig and Rune Midtgaard skied from the Messner Start on the Filchner Ice Shelf to the geographic South Pole in 24 days 8 hr 57 min between 2 Dec and 26 Dec 2008.

First expedition to reach the South Pole

The South Pole was conquered on 14 Dec 1911 by a Norwegian party of five men led by Captain Roald Amundsen, after a 53-day march with dog sledges from the Bay of Whales, then part of Antarctica's Ross Ice Shelf.

A total of 19 expeditions in Antarctica were undertaken in 2011, the **most expeditions to the South Pole in a single year**. Most of the expeditions were launched with the aim of marking the centenary of Captain Robert Scott (UK) and Roald Amundsen's race to the South Pole. Around 500 people were involved in the various attempts,

either as participants or working as support staff.

The **first person to walk to both poles** was Robert Swan OBE (UK). He led the three-man "In the Footsteps of Scott" expedition, which reached the South Pole on 11 Jan 1986, and three years later headed the eight-man "Icewalk" expedition, which arrived at the North Pole on 14 May 1989.

First solo expedition to the South Pole

Erling Kagge (NOR) became the first person to reach the South Pole after a solo and unsupported surface trek on 7 Jan 1993. His 1,400-km (870-mi) journey from Berkner Island took 50 days.

The **first woman to complete a journey to the South Pole solo (unsupported)** was Liv Arnesen (NOR), who trekked solo from the Hercules Inlet on 4 Nov 1994, arriving at the pole 50 days later on 24 Dec.

Fastest journey to the South Pole overland

Two-man team Jason De Carteret and Kieron Bradley (both UK) set off from Patriot Hills in western Antarctica on 18 Dec 2011 in their Thomson Reuters polar vehicle. They arrived at their destination 1 day 15 hr 54 min later. Having

Youngest person to trek to the South Pole

Lewis Clarke (UK, b. 18 Nov 1997) was 16 years 61 days old when he reached the geographic South Pole on 18 Jan 2014. He had skied 1,123.61 km (698.18 mi) from Hercules Inlet on the Ronne Ice Shelf with guide Carl Alvey (aged 30). The duo were unsupported but were assisted with three re-supplies by air.

Farthest distance skied by a team (unsupported)

James Castrission and Justin Jones (both AUS, above left and right) skied 2,270 km (1,410 mi) from the Hercules Inlet to the South Pole and back, finishing on 27 Jan 2012 after an 89-day trek. They crossed the finish line with Aleksander Gamme (NOR, centre), who had completed the trip solo (see opposite).

covered 1,114 km (692 mi) at an average speed of 27.9 km/h (17.34 mph), they also recorded the **fastest average speed to the South Pole overland**.

Fastest walk to the South Pole (unsupported, unassisted)

Ray Zahab, Kevin Vallely and Richard Weber (all CAN) reached the South Pole from the Hercules Inlet, on the south-western edge of the Ronne Ice Shelf, on 7 Jan 2009 after 33 days 23 hr 30 min.

Farthest distance skied solo (unsupported)

Aleksander Gamme (NOR) skied solo for 2,270 km (1,410 mi) across Antarctica, completing his epic journey on 25 Jan 2012 (local time). He set off from the Hercules Inlet and travelled to the South Pole, then returned to

First person to cycle to the South Pole (supported, assisted)

British cyclist Maria Leijerstam departed from the Russian Novo air-force base on Antarctica on 16 Dec 2013 on her recumbent tricycle. She reached the South Pole 10 days 14 hr 56 min later, despite suffering from a knee injury.

Records for the **first** and **fastest person to reach the South Pole by bicycle** – that is, a two-wheel cycle – are currently in research. Two expeditions were attempted during the winter of 2013/14 but evidence has yet to be collated.

Ronne-Filchner Ice Shelf: second-largest ice shelf in Antarctica, covering 30,000 km².

Hercules Inlet: located on the south-west edge of the Ronne Ice Shelf, this ice-packed inlet is frequently chosen as a starting point for Antarctic treks.

Ross Ice Shelf: Earth's most southerly navigable point. It is some 472,000 km² in size.

South Pole: located at 90°S. Ice is about 2,800 m thick here. As with the North Pole, there is also a magnetic South Pole, which fluctuates with Earth's magnetic field. It is presently in the Southern Ocean, some 2,825 km from the geographic South Pole.

"Antarctica is right beneath the ozone hole, so there is little or no natural protection from the Sun's harmful UV rays. Without these ski goggles for eye protection, I would quickly have gone snow-blind."

"These mittens have both a fleece inner glove and down outer glove for extra warmth and are completely windproof."

"In the extreme cold, my face had to be covered at all times. This face mask has a clever system that allows me to breathe freely without losing too much heat."

"This jacket is lightweight but it is a very effective wind barrier and so keeps me warm when I am skiing. It has deep, well-placed pockets so I had easy access to the equipment I needed while skiing."

"These meals were made especially for me with added carbohydrate and fat for energy. Once cooked, the meals are dehydrated to make them light to carry. To eat them, I simply had to pour hot water into the bag and wait a few minutes."

"The sledges were made of strengthened plastic that was lightweight and resilient. I dragged two sledges, one behind the other, together containing all my equipment."

"These boots are hand-made in Norway, based on a traditional design. Inside the canvas and leather outer boot is an inner liner made of pressed wool surrounded by a fleece sock."

FACT

Antarctica is larger than the entire continent of Europe (and bigger than the USA), and is nearly twice the size of Australia.

1 km (0.6 mi) from his start. There, he waited two days to cross the finish line with two other skiers – James Castrission and Justin Jones (both AUS) – who had travelled a similar route.

On 27 Jan 2012, the three men returned to their starting point at the Hercules Inlet. They had travelled without food drops, snowmobiles, kites or other means of assistance, thereby setting the record for the **first ski trip to the South Pole and back (unassisted)**.

Most expeditions to the South Pole

Hannah McKeand (UK) made six expeditions to the South Pole from 4 Nov 2004 to 9 Jan 2013. By skiing to the pole in 39 days 9 hr 33 min from 19 Nov to 28 Dec 2006, she also made the **fastest solo journey to the South Pole by a woman (unsupported, unassisted)**.

First solo Antarctic traverse by a woman

In Nov 2011, Felicity Aston (UK) skied solo from the Ross Ice Shelf to the South Pole, then carried on across Antarctica to the Hercules Inlet on the Ronne Ice Shelf, arriving 59 days later on 23 Jan 2012. Aston made the 1,744-km (1,084-mile) journey – with re-supplies – on Nordic cross-country skis, dragging 85 kg (187 lb) of provisions on two sledges in temperatures as low as -40°C (-40°F).

Youngest person to traverse Antarctica (supported and wind-assisted)

Teodor Johansen (NOR, b. 14 Aug 1991) traversed Antarctica at the age of 20 years 151 days. Johansen started out on his journey from the Axel Heiberg Glacier on 26 Nov 2011, reaching the South Pole on 18 Dec 2011 and completing the trip at the Hercules Inlet on 12 Jan 2012. In all, Johansen covered 1,665 km (1,034 mi).

First circumnavigation via both poles (surface)

Sir Ranulph Fiennes (UK) – named in 1984 by GWR's Founding Editor Norris McWhirter as the greatest living explorer – travelled south with Charles Burton (UK) from Greenwich in London, UK, on 2 Sep 1979. They reached the South Pole on 15 Dec 1980, the North on 10 Apr 1982, and returned to Greenwich on 29 Aug 1982 after a 56,000-km (35,000-mi) journey.

"The highlight of my day was crawling into the tent when I had finished skiing, taking off my ski boots and slipping my feet into my treasured down booties. Warm and comfortable, I often slept in them too!"

"This shovel was a vital piece of kit. At the end of each day, the tent has to be dug into the snow for protection against high winds. And in the morning, all the snow that has accumulated overnight has to be dug away."

"One of the major hazards in Antarctica are crevasses that are hidden from the surface by a thin layer of snow. Skiing, especially long ones, spread out the skier's weight and reduce the likelihood of falling through the snow into an unseen crevasse."

Mount Everest

It took **16 attempts** before the highest peak was finally conquered

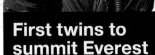

First astronaut to summit Everest

On 20 May 2009, former NASA astronaut Scott Parazynski (USA) successfully topped Everest, becoming the first person to travel in space and climb Earth's highest mountain. According to NASA, Parazynski participated in five space flights and spent more than 1,380 hr in space. Once at the top of Everest, he left a small Moon rock that he had collected during one of his seven space walks.

Most ascents of Everest (female)
Lakpa Sherpa (NPL) reached the 8,848-m-high (29,029-ft) summit of Everest for the sixth time on 11 May 2006. She made the climb accompanied by her husband, Gheorghe "George" Dijmarescu (ROM/USA), who was completing his eighth ascent of Everest. For the **most conquests of Everest** overall, see p.142.

Most ascents of Everest in one day
On 19 May 2012, a total of 243 climbers summitted Everest – the most on a single day. The **most ascents of Everest in one year** came in 2013, with 658 ascents, up from 623 in 2007.

Tragically, an avalanche near Everest's base camp on 18 Apr 2014 killed 16 Nepalese climbers, the **most deaths on Everest in one day**.

Longest stay on the summit of Everest
Babu Chhiri Sherpa (NPL) completed a stay of 21 hr at the summit of Everest, without the use of bottled oxygen, in May 1999.

Oldest man to climb Everest
Yuichiro Miura (JPN, b. 12 Oct 1932) reached the top of Everest on 23 May 2013, at the age of 80 years 223 days. This is the third time that he has held this record: he previously climbed to the highest point on Earth as the world's oldest summiteer in 2003 and again during 2008. The achievement also makes Miura the **oldest man to climb any mountain over 8,000 m**.

Tamae Watanabe (JPN, b. 21 Nov 1938) climbed Everest for the second time on 19 May 2012, aged 73 years 180 days, making her the **oldest woman to climb Everest**.

Fastest time to ski down Everest
Slovenian ski instructor Davo Karničar skied from the summit of Everest to Base Camp (located at an altitude of 5,350 m, or 17,550 ft) in just 5 hr on 7 Oct 2000. By contrast, it took him a whole month to get to the mountain top, as he was obliged to stop at several camps to acclimatize to the extreme altitude.

First woman to climb Everest twice in a season

Chhurim Dolma Sherpa of Nepal conquered Everest twice in the same climbing season. She reached the peak from the Nepalese side for the first time on 12 May 2011, and again seven days later as leader of the same expedition.

First twins to summit Everest

On 23 May 2010, Damián and Willie Benegas (b. ARG, now USA) became the first twins to climb Everest. They set out from the South Col – a pass located between Everest and Lhotse (the world's fourth-highest mountain, at 8,516 m, or 27,940 ft) – situated on Nepalese territory.

Youngest woman to climb Everest (south side)

Ngim Chhamji Sherpa (NPL, b. 14 Nov 1995) reached the summit from the Nepali side on 19 May 2012, aged 16 years 187 days. She and her father, Dendi Sherpa (NPL), are the **first father and daughter to climb Everest together**. The **youngest woman to climb from the north side** (Tibet) was 15-year-old Mingkipa Sherpa (NPL, b. 1987) on 22 May 2003.

Fastest ascent of Everest (south side)
Pemba Dorje Sherpa (NPL) climbed from Base Camp to the peak of Everest in a time of 8 hr 10 min on 21 May 2004.

FIRST...

Ascent of Everest
At 11:30 a.m. on 29 May 1953, Edmund Percival Hillary (NZ) and Tenzing Norgay (IND/Tibet) became the first people to conquer Everest. The successful expedition was led by Colonel (later Honorary Brigadier) Henry Cecil John Hunt. Hillary was knighted by Queen Elizabeth II and Norgay awarded the George Medal.

Junko Tabei (JPN) achieved the **first ascent of Everest by a woman**, reaching the summit on 16 May 1975.

Ascent of Everest without oxygen
Reinhold Messner (ITA) and Peter Habeler (AUT) made the first successful ascent of Everest without supplemental oxygen, on 8 May 1978. This feat is regarded by some purist mountaineers as the first "true" ascent of Everest, because overcoming the effects of altitude (i.e., the low oxygen content of the air) is the greatest challenge facing high-altitude climbers.

Highest-altitude cricket match

The Everest Test 2009 (UK) was played 5,164 m (16,942 ft) above sea level at the Gorak Shep plateau near Everest on 21 Apr 2009. This epic feat saw two 15-man squads, three qualified cricket umpires, four medics, two members of the press and 10 spectators scale the heights to the plateau. Team Hillary defeated Team Tenzing.

First female twins to summit Everest

Tashi and Nungshi Malik (both IND) are the first twin sisters to have climbed Everest, doing so on 19 May 2013. They reached the peak alongside Samina Baig, the first Pakistani woman to complete the climb. All three successful climbers raised the flags of both countries in a symbolic gesture of peace.

On 20 Aug 1980, Messner also became the **first person to ascend Everest solo**. It took him three days to make the climb from his base camp at 6,500 m (21,325 ft) – again without the benefit of supplementary oxygen.

Blind person to climb Everest

Erik Weihenmayer (USA) was born with retinoschisis, an eye condition that left him blind by the age of 13. Despite this, on 25 May 2001, he topped Everest, the first – and so far only – blind person to have done so.

Erik's other notable feats include his 2008 completion of the Seven Summits – the highest mountain on each of the seven continents (see p.150) – making him the **first blind person to climb the Seven Summits including Carstensz**.

Married couple to climb Everest

On 7 Oct 1990, Andrej and Marija Štremfelj (both SVN) became the first married couple to conquer Everest, climbing via the South Col.

On the same day, Jean-Noël and Bertrand "Zébulon" Roche (both FRA) became the **first father and son team to summit Everest**.

First person to climb Everest from both sides in one season

David Liaño González (MEX) reached the peak of Everest from Nepal on the south side on 11 May 2013 and returned to the peak on 19 May 2013, climbing from Tibet on the north side. This is the first time that any climber has scaled the mountain from both sides in one climbing season.

"Oxygen levels at the summit of Everest are approximately one-third of those available at sea level. This mask mixes pure oxygen from a tank with ambient air."

"I use this ice axe for self-arrest in case I have a fall and for additional support while climbing."

"For nourishment at high altitudes, I rehydrate freeze-dried food by adding water to it from melting ice."

"These goggles protect my eyes from hurricane-speed winds and the Sun reflected on the snow, which can cause blindness. The LED headlamp illuminates my way when I'm climbing at night."

"The outermost layer of this suit is filled with goose down, which is still one of the best materials for insulation while climbing."

"This is an ascender: a safety device that allows climbers to clip into ropes and anchors already set up on the route. It's attached to the mountaineering harness by a length of climbing cord."

"Fingers are one of the first body parts to get injured because of extreme cold. These mittens are filled with goose down to protect my hands against frostbite."

"The backpack is expandable, to accommodate big loads – such as those carried to the lower camps – and small loads – such as those carried on summit day."

"This solar panel provides clean energy to power electronics such as radios, satellite phones and cameras on the mountain."

"The double-layer boots protect the toes against frostbite and are comfortable enough to be worn for hours and hours. The crampons are easily attached to the boots, and allow climbers to ascend steep ice sections where boots alone would slip."

FASTEST TIME TO CLIMB HEIGHT OF EVEREST BY...

Machine (such as a Versaclimber stepping machine). Requires climbing the equivalent of 8,848 m (29,029 ft)

Individual	2 hr 53 min 47 sec	Richard Pemberton (AUS)
Male (team)	1 hr 56 min 8 sec	Richard Saville, Edward Kerry, Steve Wilson, Chris Grimshaw, Charlie Boyes, Dan Levy, Dave Rome and Kevin Williams (all UK)
Female (team)	2 hr 45 min 53 sec	Bridget Funnell, Victoria Brown, Natasha Jones, Sarah Ruscombe-King, Sandra Heard, Margaret Reeve, Sandra Cann and Nicola Hammond (all UK)

Indoor climbing wall

Individual	13 hr 25 min	Tom Lancaster (UK)
Team	4 hr 24 min 33 sec	The Climbing Society at Texas A&M University-Commerce (USA)

Mountaineering

The Seven Summits' combined height is the equivalent of **113 Eiffel Towers**

First ascent of Nanga Parbat via the Mazeno Ridge

In 1953, Hermann Buhl (AUT) became the **first person to climb Nanga Parbat** – the ninth-highest mountain, situated in the Himalayas at 8,125 m (26,656 ft). It was not until 15 Jul 2012 that it was ascended via the technically difficult Mazeno Ridge or west-southwest route – one of the most demanding challenges in alpinism – by Sandy Allan and Rick Allen (both UK).

FIRST...

Person to climb the Seven Summits

The highest mountains on each of the continents are known as the "Seven Summits" (see table). Two lists have been compiled: the "Bass list", which includes Mount Kosciuszko in New South Wales, Australia, and the more difficult "Messner list", which recognizes Oceania's highest point as Puncak Jaya in Indonesia. Patrick Morrow (CAN) completed the Messner list on 5 Aug 1986 with a summit of Puncak Jaya.

Woman to climb the Seven Summits

On 28 Jun 1992, Junko Tabei (JPN) topped Puncak Jaya, completing Messner's list. Tabei also recorded the **first ascent of Everest by a woman**, when she climbed it on 16 May 1975.

It took Vanessa O'Brien (USA) 295 days to climb both Messner's and Bass's list – the **fastest Seven Summits ascent (female)**. Vanessa began with Everest on 19 May 2012 and finished on Kilimanjaro on 10 Mar 2013.

Person to climb all 8,000-m mountains

Reinhold Messner (ITA) began his quest to climb each of the 14 mountains higher than 8,000 m (26,246 ft) in Jun 1970. He completed the feat with a summit of Lhotse, on the Nepal-Tibet border, on 16 Oct 1986. The feat is so difficult that as of 25 Apr 2014 – nearly 30 years later – only 32 people had successfully tackled all 14 mountains.

Woman to climb all 8,000-m mountains

On 17 May 2010, Edurne Pasaban Lizarribar (ESP) completed her climb of the 14 mountains over 8,000 m (undisputed) by summitting Shisha Pangma in Tibet. A month earlier, Oh Eun-Sun (KOR) had claimed this title, but doubt was cast on one of her summits and her record remains disputed.

The **first woman to summit all 8,000ers without bottled oxygen** was Gerlinde Kaltenbrunner (AUT) on 23 Aug 2011.

Person to complete the Explorers' Grand Slam

The Explorers' Grand Slam comprises climbing the Seven Summits, the 14 mountains over 8,000 m and trekking to the North and South poles on foot. Park Young-Seok (KOR) began by climbing Everest on 16 May 1993 and completed the feat when

First ascent of Puncak Jaya

The 4,884-m-high (16,024-ft) peak of Puncak Jaya, aka Carstensz Pyramid, in Indonesia was first topped by Heinrich Harrer (AUT), Philip Temple, Russell Kippax (both NZ) and Albertus Huizenga (NLD). The team reached the summit on 13 Feb 1962. It is considered the most difficult of the Seven Summits to climb.

he reached the North Pole on 30 Apr 2005. Sadly, Park died in Oct 2011 on Annapurna, renowned as the world's **deadliest mountain**.

Ascent of K2

On 31 Jul 1954, Italians Achille Compagnoni and Lino Lacedelli completed the first ascent of K2, which at 8,611 m (28,251 ft) is the world's second-highest mountain. K2 is situated in the Karakoram range, on the border between Pakistan and China.

Wanda Rutkiewicz (POL) became the **first woman to climb K2** on 23 Jun 1986.

Russia's Andrew Mariev and Vadim Popovich completed the **first ascent of K2's west face**, on 21 Aug 2007, after a gruelling 10-week climb. The pair –

Fastest time to climb the Seven Summits (both lists)

Vernon Tejas (USA) climbed the combined Kosciuszko and Carstensz lists of summits, beginning with Vinson Massif on 18 Jan 2010 and ending with McKinley, aka Denali, on 31 May 2010. This musically minded climber has also played guitar on top of each of the summits and at the North and South poles.

led by Viktor Kozlov (RUS) – conquered this notoriously vicious face and reached the peak without the use of supplementary oxygen.

Ascent of Kangchenjunga

The third-highest mountain (8,586 m; 28,169 ft) was first climbed on 25 May 1955 by George Band and Joe Brown (both UK).

First to summit Annapurna via the south face (female)

Wanda Rutkiewicz (POL) reached the peak of Annapurna (8,091 m; 26,545 ft) from the south face in the Himalayas, Nepal, on 22 Oct 1991. Rutkiewicz was also the **first woman to ascend K2**, doing so on 23 Jun 1986.

THE SEVEN SUMMITS

As with many mountaineering distinctions, the definition of the "Seven Summits" is disputed. Some climbers include Kosciuszko in Australia over Carstensz. Others place Elbrus within the borders of Asia, and thus regard Mount Blanc as Europe's highest mountain.

Continent	Mountain	Location	Height	First climbed
Africa	Kilimanjaro	Tanzania	5,895 m	6 Oct 1889
Antarctica	Vinson Massif	Antarctica	4,892 m	18 Dec 1966
Asia	Everest	Nepal/China	8,848 m	29 May 1953
Australasia	Puncak Jaya, aka Carstensz	Indonesia	4,884 m	13 Feb 1962
Europe	Elbrus	Russia	5,642 m	27 Jul 1874
North America	McKinley, aka Denali	USA	6,194 m	7 Jun 1913
South America	Aconcagua	Argentina	6,962 m	14 Jan 1897

Source: www.8000ers.com

FACT

Kim Chang-Ho made a sea-to-summit ascent of Everest, starting from sea level at the Bay of Bengal.

"Helmet: to protect the head from falling rocks and chunks of ice."

"Glasses: to protect the eyes from the Sun's UV radiation and wind."

"Gloves: to protect against the cold."

Fastest time to climb all 8,000ers

Kim Chang-Ho (KOR) climbed the 14 mountains over 8,000 m (26,246 ft) in a time of 7 years 310 days, starting with his summit of Nanga Parbat on 14 Jul 2005 and ending with Everest on 20 May 2013. Significantly, he completed all climbs without supplemental oxygen.

"Ice axe: to climb on icy terrain."

"Rope: for protection in case of a fall and to rappel [abseil]."

The **first female to climb Kangchenjunga** was Ginette Harrison (UK), who summitted via the north-west face on 18 May 1998.

OLDEST...

Person to climb the Seven Summits (Messner list)
Male: Takao Arayama (JPN, b. 4 Oct 1935) completed his final Seven Summits climb on Kilimanjaro in Tanzania on 18 Feb 2010, at the age of 74 years 138 days.
Female: Carol Masheter (USA, b. 10 Oct 1946) completed her last Seven Summits climb of the Messner list with an ascent of Carstensz Pyramid on 12 Jul 2012, at the age of 65 years 276 days. Masheter also climbed Kosciuszko on 17 Mar 2012, thus becoming the **oldest female to climb the Bass list**.

Person to climb the Seven Summits (Bass list)
Ramón Blanco (ESP, b. 30 Apr 1933) completed the last mountain on the Bass list on 29 Dec 2003, aged 70 years 244 days old.

Person to climb an 8,000er without bottled oxygen
Only five people older than 65 have summitted an 8,000er without the use of bottled oxygen. The oldest was Boris Korshunov (RUS, b. 31 Aug 1935), who climbed Cho Oyu on 2 Oct 2007 aged 72 years 32 days. However,

as some alpinists dispute Korshunov's claim, the undisputed record goes to Carlos Soria (ESP, b. 5 Feb 1939), who summitted Manaslu on 1 Oct 2010, aged 71 years 238 days.

First person to climb the Triple Seven Summits

Building on the idea of the Seven Summits, the Triple Seven Summits refers to climbing the three highest mountains on each continent. Christian Stangl (AUT) was the first to achieve the feat when he finished with Europe's third-highest mountain, Shkhara, on 23 Aug 2013.

While achieving this hat-trick, Stangl also became the **first person to climb the Seven Second Summits** and the **Seven Third Summits**, having conquered the second-highest mountain on each continent by 15 Jan 2013.

"Harness: provides the link between your body and the rope."

"Carabiners and quickdraws: for safety and to provide quick connection to the rope while climbing."

"Trousers and jacket: waterproofed and with insulation."

Continent	Second Summits	Third Summits
Africa	Batian (5,199 m)	Mawenzi (5,148 m)
Antarctica	Tyree (4,852 m)	Shinn (4,660 m)
Asia	K2 (8,611 m)	Kangchenjunga (8,586 m)
Australasia	Sumantri (4,870 m)	Puncak Mandala (4,758 m)
Europe	Dykh-tau (5,205 m)	Shkhara (5,193 m)
North America	Logan (5,959 m)	Orizaba (5,636 m)
South America	Ojos del Salado (6,893 m)	Pissis (6,795 m)

"Crampons: steel frame with spikes, essential to get a grip on icy ground."

"Boots: waterproofed and with good insulation."

"Trousers and jacket: waterproofed and with insulation."

Crossing the seas

Youngest person to row across any ocean (non-solo)

Eoin Hartwright (UK, b. 17 Jan 1997) was 16 years 340 days old when he left La Gomera in the Canary Islands, Spain, to row the Atlantic Ocean east to west. The team, also consisting of Simon Hartwright (Eoin's uncle), Matthew Collier and Tom Alden, reached Antigua in the *Trilogy Extra* on 4 Feb 2013, in just under 44 days.

Fastest single-handed transatlantic sailing

Francis Joyon (FRA) sailed from New York City, USA, to Cornwall, UK, in 5 days 2 hr 56 min. He arrived on 16 Jun 2013 after a trip of 2,880 nautical mi (5,333 km; 3,314 mi). Joyon still holds the **fastest global solo circumnavigation sailing** record, set back in 2008 at 57 days 13 hr 34 min. He sailed 21,600 nautical mi (38,900 km; 24,170 mi).

Fastest row across the Indian Ocean, east to west

Maxime Chaya (LBN), Livar Nysted (DNK) and Stuart Kershaw (UK) rowed from Geraldton, Australia, to Mauritius on board *tRIO*.

First person to row across two different oceans in a year

Livar Nysted (DNK) rowed the Atlantic east to west in a team of eight from Gran Canaria to Barbados from 17 Jan to 22 Feb 2013. After a few months' rest, on 9 Jun, he rowed a second ocean, crossing the Indian Ocean east to west in a team of three from Australia to Mauritius (see left), arriving on 5 Aug 2013. He spent a total of 93 days 4 hr at sea during the two voyages.

Fastest single-handed sail from Cádiz to San Salvador

Following a similar route to that of Christopher Columbus – leading to its name "The Discovery Route" – Armel Le Cléac'h (FRA) sailed from Cádiz in Spain to San Salvador in The Bahamas in 6 days 23 hr 42 min. Le Cléac'h sailed in his 31.4-m (103-ft) trimaran *Banque Populaire 7* and completed the 3,884-nautical-mi (7,193.17-km; 4,469.62-mi) route on 23–30 Jan 2014 at an average speed of 23.16 knots (42.89 km/h; 26.65 mph).

On 26–27 Jan, during the voyage, veteran sailor Le Cléac'h also achieved the **greatest distance sailed in 24 hours single-handedly**, covering 682.85 nautical mi (1,264.64 km; 785.81 mi).

Longest unsupported open ocean journey by jet ski

Frederico Rezende (PRT) jet-skied 963 km (598.4 mi) in the Atlantic Ocean between the Portuguese cities of Lisbon and Funchal on 11–13 Sep 2013. The voyage took him 48 hr 55 min, during which time he was the sole pilot and had no sleep.

Their trip – which took 57 days 15 hr 49 min, from 9 Jun to 5 Aug 2013 – also represents the **first team of three to row an ocean**.

First person to row mid-Pacific west to east solo

Sarah Outen (UK) rowed on board *Happy Socks* from Chōshi in Japan to Adak in Alaska, USA, taking 149 days 13 hr between 27 Apr and 23 Sep 2013.

Prior to this, at the age of 23 years 310 days, Outen (b. 26 May 1985) had become the **youngest female to row the Indian Ocean solo**. She made her epic east-to-west crossing between 1 Apr and 3 Aug 2009.

Longest distance rowed solo non-stop in the Atlantic (female)

Janice Jakait (DEU) rowed 5,705 km (3,545 mi) as the crow flies, east to west from Portugal to Barbados, from 23 Nov 2011 to 21 Feb 2012. This also makes her the **first woman to row across the Atlantic east to west from mainland Europe to the West Indies solo**, a feat unmatched as of Apr 2014.

Youngest tandem row across an ocean

UK rowers Jamie Sparks (b. 11 Jan 1992) and Luke Birch (b. 4 Jul 1992) set off on 4 Dec 2013 in the *Maple Leaf* from La Gomera, Spain, on the Talisker Whisky Atlantic Challenge. Aged, respectively, 21 years 327 days and 21 years 153 days on departure, they reached English Harbour in Antigua 54 days 5 hr 56 min later, on 27 Jan 2014, having covered 4,722.6 km (2,934.48 mi).

Youngest person to row solo across an ocean

On 14 Mar 2010, Katie Spotz (USA, b. 18 Apr 1987) completed her 70-day row across the Atlantic, east to west from Senegal to Guyana. When she set off on 3 Jan 2010, she was aged 22 years 260 days.

Tommy Tippetts (UK, b. 26 Mar 1989) was 22 years 301 days old at the start of his trip east to west across the Atlantic, making him the **youngest male to row solo across an ocean**. His trip took place from 21 Jan to 12 Apr 2012.

Fastest monohull solo circumnavigation (40-ft class)

Guo Chuan (CHN, above left) sailed the world in 137 days 20 hr 1 min, finishing on 4 Apr 2013. In 2005–06, he was the first Chinese sailor to take part in the Clipper Round the World Yacht Race, founded by Sir Robin Knox-Johnston (UK, above right, with GWR's Frank Chambers). Sir Robin became the **first person to sail solo around the world (non-stop)** on 22 Apr 1969, as the only finisher of the Golden Globe Race.

"A tracking beacon charts the boat's progress every step of the way and relays data to team members on dry land."

"The sun hat provides neck protection, which is vital in temperatures exceeding 40°C on the mid-Atlantic route."

First crossing of the Tasman Sea by kayak

James Castrission and Justin Jones (both AUS) travelled from Australia to New Zealand across the Tasman Sea in *Lot 41*. They left Foster in Victoria on 13 Nov 2007 and rowed 3,318 km (2,061.7 mi) over 62 days, reaching New Plymouth in New Zealand on 13 Jan 2008.

"An off-shore life jacket with spray hood, whistle and reflective tape; this is designed to keep a rower's head above water in case of becoming unconscious."

"White flares are set off to avoid collision and red flares are to ask for help."

"A safety harness keeps the rower attached to the rowing boat at all times."

TASMAN SEA

First solo row

From 6 Feb to 10 Apr 1977, Colin Quincey (NZ) rowed solo in the *Tasman Trespasser* across the Tasman Sea – a stretch of water approximately 2,000 km (1,200 mi) wide and known locally as "The Ditch". Quincey rowed from Hokianga in New Zealand to Marcus Beach in Queensland, Australia, taking 63 days 7 hr.

The **first person to row across the Tasman Sea west to east** (from the mainland) is Shaun Quincey (NZ) – Colin's son. He rowed in *Tasman Trespasser 2* from New South Wales in Australia to Ninety Mile Beach in New Zealand. The trip took him 53 days, between 20 Jan and 14 Mar 2010.

First team to row east to west

Steven Gates, Andrew Johnson, Kerry Tozer and Sally Macready (all AUS) rowed from Hokianga in New Zealand to Sydney Harbour, Australia, between 29 Nov and 30 Dec 2007.

The **first team to row west to east** was Nigel Cherrie, Martin Berka, James Blake and Andrew McCowan (all NZ), from Sydney to the Bay of Islands, between 26 Nov 2011 and 16 Jan 2012.

"The satellite phone is for safety first and foremost but it's good to hear news from back at home and tell loved ones how the rowers are getting on."

"Fenders are only used in port and not taken on the trip. They prevent damage to the boat when moored."

"Desalinated water is heated in the Jetboil cooker to rehydrate the freeze-dried food rations – and is good for making the odd cup of tea too!"

"Specifically designed for ocean rowing, the oars provide the only means of propelling the boat."

Most ocean rows by one person

Simon Chalk (UK, b. 12 Sep 1972) has made a total of eight ocean rows. He rowed east to west across the Atlantic Ocean in teams of two (1997), five (2007/08), six (2013), eight (2012 and 2014) and 14 (2011). He rowed the Indian Ocean east to west, solo, in 2003 – making him the **youngest male rower to cross the Indian Ocean** – and in a team of eight in 2009.

"The throwing line is used as a first rescue attempt in the event of man overboard."

Endurance

We can survive for about two months without food, but only around five days **without water**

Fastest speed in a human-powered vehicle (single rider)

Sebastiaan Bowier (NLD) notched up a speed of 133.78 km/h (83.13 mph) in his streamlined recumbent bicycle *VeloX3* at the World Human Powered Speed Challenge near Battle Mountain in Nevada, USA, on 14 Sep 2013. Sebastiaan is pictured left, with team-mate Wil Baselmans.

Fastest speed in a human-powered vehicle (multiple riders)
On 14 Sep 2013, Tom Amick and Phil Plath (both USA) reached 117.61 km/h (73.08 mph) in their streamlined recumbent bicycle *Glowworm* on a flat road surface at the World Human Powered Speed Challenge near Battle Mountain in Nevada, USA.

Fastest circumnavigation by bicycle (female)
In just 152 days 1 hr, Juliana Buhring (DEU) cycled a total distance of 29,069 km (18,063 mi). The journey started and finished at Piazza Plebiscito in Naples, Italy, and lasted from 23 Jul until 22 Dec 2012.

Fastest human-powered propeller submarine
In Jun 2007, the two-person, propeller-driven submarine *OMER 5* reached 8.035 knots (14.9 km/h; 9.2 mph) at the 9th International Submarine Races held at the David Taylor Model Basin in Bethesda, Maryland, USA. It was piloted by Sebastien Brisebois and Joel Brunet (both CAN) of the École de Technologie Supérieure at the University of Quebec, Canada.

Most countries visited by bicycle in seven days
Between 29 Apr and 5 May 2013, Glen Burmeister (UK) cycled through 11 countries, from Břeclav in the Czech Republic to Shkodër in Albania. Burmeister passed through Austria, Slovakia, Hungary, Slovenia, Croatia, Romania, Serbia, Bosnia and Herzegovina and Montenegro.

Longest time flying in a human-powered vehicle
Kanellos Kanellopoulos (GRC) kept his *Daedalus 88* aircraft aloft for 3 hr 54 min 59 sec on 23 Apr 1988, while pedalling the 115.11 km (71.93 mi) between Heraklion, Crete, and the Greek island of Santorini. Unfortunately, a gust of wind broke off the plane's tail and it crashed just before reaching shore.

Farthest distance to swim under ice with breath held

Wearing fins and a diving suit, Stig Åvall Severinsen (DNK) swam 152 m (500 ft) under ice, with his breath held, at Qorlortoq Lake on Ammassalik Island, Greenland, on 16 Apr 2013. He returned the next day to make the **farthest swim under ice with breath held (no fins, no diving suit)**: 76 m (250 ft).

LONGEST JOURNEY...

By bicycle (individual)
The greatest mileage amassed in a cycle tour was more than 646,960 km (402,000 mi), by the itinerant lecturer Walter Stolle (CZE) from 24 Jan 1959 to 12 Dec 1976. He

Longest walk on flower petals

Between 2 and 27 Jan 2013, a group of 1,128 Buddhist monks walked 448.4 km (278.6 mi) between temples, across eight provinces in Thailand, stepping on marigold petals. The walk was part of the Second Dhammachai Dhutanga pilgrimage to welcome in the year 2013.

Farthest distance barefoot (24 hours)

Peter Wayne Botha (NZ, b. ZAF) ran 211.51 km (131.43 mi) barefoot on 5–6 Oct 2013, in the 16th annual Sri Chinmoy 24-hour race in Auckland, New Zealand. En route, he clocked the **fastest 100 km barefoot**, in 8 hr 49 min 42 sec.

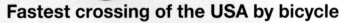

Fastest crossing of the USA by bicycle

During the Race Across America in 2013, Christoph Strasser (AUT) cycled across the USA in 7 days 22 hr 11 min, completing the trip on 19 Jun. In doing so, the indefatigable cyclist also became the first person to cross the USA coast to coast in under 8 days.

Fastest time to climb El Capitan (female)

Mayan Smith-Gobat (NZ, above) and Libby Sauter (USA) successfully climbed the "Nose" route of El Capitan in Yosemite National Park in California, USA, on 29 Sep 2013. The duo took 5 hr 39 min to complete the ascent, beating the previous record by almost two hours.

visited 159 countries, starting out from Romford in Essex, UK.

On crutches
From 21 Mar to 27 Jul 2011, Guy Amalfitano (FRA) journeyed 4,004 km (2,488 mi) through France on crutches. His journey took him from Salies-de-Béarn to the Centre Hospitalier in Orthez.

On roller skis
Between 11 May and 5 Jul 2012, César Baena (VEN) travelled 2,246.21 km (1,395.73 mi) on roller skis from Stockholm in Sweden to Oslo in Norway.

On inline skates
Khoo Swee Chiow (SGP) covered a distance of 6,088 km (3,782 mi) on inline skates. Khoo departed

from Hanoi in Vietnam on 20 Oct 2007 and arrived in Singapore on 21 Jan 2008.

Swimming in open water
Martin Strel (SVN) swam 5,268 km (3,273 mi) down the length of the Amazon River in Peru and Brazil from 1 Feb to 8 Apr 2007.

Walking backwards
To date, the greatest exponent of reverse pedestrianism is Plennie L Wingo (USA). From 15 Apr 1931 to 24 Oct 1932, he walked 12,875 km (8,000 mi) from Santa Monica in California, USA, to Istanbul in Turkey at a rate of 24.89 km (15.47 mi) per day.

Fastest speed in a human-powered vehicle (female)

On 15 Sep 2010, Barbara Buatois (FRA) reached a speed of 121.81 km/h (75.69 mph) pedalling her streamlined recumbent bicycle *Varna Tempest*. She achieved the feat on a flat road surface at the World Human Powered Speed Challenge near Battle Mountain in Nevada, USA.

"I used these beat-up binoculars for 20–30 years. They were small but clear for finding a way over difficult mountains or ravines. Also, to see in wars, where the shooting and bombing was."

"I wore these sunglasses out in two years across Africa. The dust on dirt roads from passing trucks rose up in huge clouds. I also wore contact lenses. These were almost priceless."

"My greatest treasure and necessity. When faced with dangers, death and struggles I pull it out and hold it in my hand."

Longest ongoing pilgrimage

As of 24 Apr 2013, the greatest distance claimed for an "around the world" pilgrimage is 64,752 km (40,235 mi) by Arthur Blessitt (USA), who has been walking on a mission since 25 Dec 1969. He has visited all seven continents, including Antarctica, having traversed 321 nations, island groups and territories carrying a 3.7-m-tall (12-ft) wooden cross and preaching from the Bible throughout.

"I've used this hipster for 20 years. It carries my small Bible and sometimes my passport. Sometimes I have food snacks in it, too. It's like a small backpack. I still use it."

"A true pleasure, these utensils fit inside a plastic holder with a salt and pepper shaker. So even with dirty hands on the road and awful food at least I have something clean to eat with."

"My army knife is one thing that always goes with me. It fits right on my belt with its bottle- and can-opener, sewing kit, paper, writing pen, magnifying glass, saw, wrench, scissors, screwdriver and stone for sharpening."

"My water canteen, last used in the Darién Gap in Panama/Colombia in 1978. I've never gotten sick from the water sources I used on the roads of the world. Jesus did it. It is very emotional to see this…"

"Keep the passport dry, out of sight and away from sticky fingers – some border police of remote areas would hold the passport for a bribe. Interestingly, it's the smallest countries that have a full-page stamp!"

"In 1969, there were only working boots – it was years before specialist walking shoes became developed. I learned the hard way to get walking shoes that were larger than my typical shoe size: I would have to cut holes on the side for my toes. I tighten my shoe laces in the morning and loosen them as my feet expand."

"The wheel for my cross, this one used on my trip across southern Africa in 1985–86 and China in 1987. The cross wood wears away as it drags on the rocks and pavement, and I'd have to replace the cross every few weeks without the wheel."

Epic journeys

We walk the equivalent of about **four times** around Earth in a lifetime

Youngest person to circumnavigate by aircraft

Between 2 May and 29 Jun 2013, Jack Wiegand (USA, b. 22 Jun 1992) flew around the world in a Mooney M20R Ovation aircraft, covering approximately 38,600 km (24,000 mi) in all and making 22 stops en route. Jack was 21 years 7 days old when he touched down in Fresno, California, USA, at the conclusion of his trip.

applicable in 1989 and 1991 embracing more than an equator's length of driving (24,901 road miles; 40,075 km), is held by Saloo Choudhury and his wife Neena Choudhury (both India). The journey took 69 days 19 hours 5 minutes from 9 September to 17 November 1989. The couple drove a 1989 Hindustan "Contessa Classic" starting and finishing in Delhi, India.

Longest journey...
• **Barefoot:** Michael Essing (DEU) walked 1,488.09 km (924.65 mi) on his bare feet between the German towns of Flensburg and Efringen-Kirchen from 30 May to 5 Sep 2013.

Longest journey by 50-cc scooter

Theodore Rezvoy and Evgeniy Stoyanov (both UKR) rode 14,434 km (8,968 mi) from Odessa in Ukraine to Ulan-Ude in Russia on two 50-cc Honda Zoomer scooters between 11 Jul and 11 Sep 2013. In doing so, they surpassed the previous record, set in 2010, by approximately 2,000 km (1,240 mi).

BY AIR

Fastest circumnavigation by microlight
Colin Bodill (UK) circled the globe in his Mainair Blade 912 Flexwing microlight aircraft in 99 days from 31 May to 6 Sep 2000, starting and landing at Brooklands airfield in Weybridge, Surrey, UK. Accompanying him was Jennifer Murray (UK), who made the **fastest circumnavigation by helicopter (female)** on the trip, flying in a Robinson R44. The pair covered some 35,000 km (21,750 mi).

Longest journey...
• **By ultralight aircraft:** Roberto Bisa and Antonio Forato (both ITA) of ASD Riding the Skies flew an ultralight aircraft 20,126 km (12,505 mi) from Cassola in Italy to Southport in Queensland, Australia, from 8 to 31 Oct 2013.

• **Kite surfing in 24 hours:** On 26 Feb 2012, Rimas Kinka (LTU) covered 645.6 km (401.2 mi) off the coast of Islamorada in Florida, USA.

• **Kite surfing (female):** No woman has kite-surfed for longer than Germany's

Longest journey by solar-powered car

A team from SolarCar Projekt Hochschule Bochum (DEU) carried out a 29,753-km (18,487-mi) trip by electric vehicle, leaving Adelaide in Australia on 26 Oct 2011 and arriving in Mount Barker, Australia, on 15 Dec 2012. They spent a total of 168 days driving. Eight days were devoted to recharging the vehicle; the remaining days were spent exhibiting the SolarCar at various locations, events and universities and being transported between continents.

• **By car:** As of 3 Apr 2013, Emil and Liliana Schmid (both CHE) had covered 677,281 km (420,842 mi) in a Toyota Land Cruiser. Their trip began on 16 Oct 1984.

• **By non-solar electric vehicle:** Duane Leffel (USA) drove 5,688.68 km (3,534.77 mi) from Charleston in South Carolina to Laguna Hills in California, USA, from 4 Jul to 24 Aug 2013.

• **By motorcycle in one country:** Buck Perley (USA) and Amy Mathieson (UK) rode 33,357.15 km (20,727.13 mi) across China from 19 Jul to 11 Dec 2013.

• **By motorized bicycle:** From 14 Jul to 4 Sep 2012, Danny Halmo (CAN) rode

Anke Brandt, who covered 135.16 nautical mi (250.32 km; 155.54 mi), between Amwaj Marina and Al Dar Island, Bahrain, on 1 Mar 2014.

BY LAND

Fastest circumnavigation by car
The record for the first and fastest man and woman to have circumnavigated the Earth by car covering six continents under the rules

LONGEST JOURNEY BY...			
Vehicle	Distance	Record holders	Dates
Bus	87,367 km	Hughie Thompson, John Weston and Richard Steel (all UK)	6 Nov 1988–3 Dec 1989
Fire engine	50,957 km	Stephen Moore (UK)	18 Jul 2010–10 Apr 2011
Hovercraft	8,000 km	British Trans-African Hovercraft Expedition, led by David Smithers (UK)	15 Oct 1969–3 Jan 1970
Motorcycle	735,000 km	Emilio Scotto (ARG)	17 Jan 1985–2 Apr 1995
Quadbike	56,239 km	Valerio De Simoni, Kristopher "Ted" Davant and James Kenyon (all AUS)	10 Aug 2010–22 Oct 2011
Skateboard	12,159 km	Rob Thomson (NZ)	24 Jun 2007–28 Sep 2008
Tandem	38,143 km	Phil and Louise Shambrook (UK)	17 Dec 1994–1 Oct 1997
Tractor	21,199 km	Vasilii Hazkevich (RUS)	25 Apr–6 Aug 2005
Wheelchair	40,075 km	Rick Hansen (CAN)	21 Mar 1985–22 May 1987

6,721 km (4,176 mi) within Canada, from English Bay in Vancouver, British Columbia, to Halifax Harbour, Nova Scotia.

• **By rickshaw:** Tim Moss (UK) rode a rickshaw 1,377.96 km (856.22 mi) from Aviemore to West Molesey, UK, between 26 Apr and 19 May 2010.

BY WATER

First person to swim from Cuba to Florida without a shark cage
Diana Nyad (USA, b. 22 Aug 1949) swam from Havana, Cuba, to Key West, Florida, USA, in 52 hr 54 min 18.6 sec on 31 Aug–2 Sep 2013, aged 64 years 11 days.

Longest journey...
• **Swimming non-stop in open water (male):** Martin Strel (SVN) swam 504.5 km (313.1 mi) down the Danube, from Melk in Austria to Paks in Hungary, in 84 hr 10 min on 3–6 July 2001. He was escorted by four kayakers, a safety escort boat and six road vehicles.

• **Rowed in 24 hours by a team (men):** On 14–15 Jun 2013, Dutch rowers Ansgar John Brenninkmeijer, Gert Jan Keizer, Oscar Dinkelaar, Jacques Klok, Jeroen van Renesse and Hans-Jan Rijbering covered 295.2 km (183.4 mi) up- and downstream on the Amstel river in the Netherlands.

Longest journey by electric motorcycle

As part of the Meneghina Express event – a project to investigate global food nutrition and sustainability – Nicola Colombo and Valerio Fumagalli (both ITA) covered 12,379 km (7,691 mi) on electric motorcycles. The duo rode from Shanghai, China, to Milan, Italy, between 10 Jun and 23 Jul 2013.

First row of the navigable length of the Amazon

Embarking from Nauta in Peru on 13 Sep 2013, Anton Wright (UK, below left) and Dr Mark de Rond (NLD, below right) rowed down the Amazon river to Macapá in Brazil, arriving on 14 Oct 2013. Altogether, they covered more than 3,200 km (2,000 mi) in their Woodvale Pairs-class ocean rowing boat, made out of plywood and reinforced with glass fibre and resins.

"Tropical storms can whip up quickly in the Amazon basin. These JL splash jackets provided ideal protection from the torrential rain."

"Wearing a sun hat is a must when rowing the Amazon to prevent sunstroke and provide protection from the blistering Sun."

"One of our most important pieces of equipment by far was this GPS device. It would indicate where we were on the river, how much progress we'd made and what we could expect ahead."

"A life vest is a non-optional accessory, and for good reason: tropical storms and strong currents have claimed the lives of plenty of strong swimmers in the past."

"Oars made of reinforced carbon fibre are ideal for their durability and strength. They are also surprisingly lightweight."

Arts & media

Highest-grossing action-movie heroine

The phenomenal success of the first two *Hunger Games* movies (USA, 2012 and 2013) means that the character of Katniss Everdeen – portrayed by Jennifer Lawrence (USA) – is the cinema's most successful action heroine at the box office, with both movies grossing a total of $1.55 bn (£928 m) internationally. *The Hunger Games: Catching Fire* was the **highest-grossing post-apocalypse movie**, taking $424,668,047 (£255,278,000) in the USA and $864,565,663 (£519,711,000) worldwide.

Contents

○ ○

FACT
According to Forbes'
2013 list of the most
powerful celebrities,
Jennifer Lawrence was
the second-highest-
scoring actress. Only
Angelina Jolie (USA)
ranked higher.

60 years on screen

The film industry has seen a huge increase in technological sophistication over the past six decades, but how has this affected our appetite for movies? Are we going to the cinema more than ever? Are we releasing as many films? And are new releases just as successful if you account for inflation?

All figures in US$

In the past 60 years on screen, everything has changed, and yet nothing has changed. In 1955, the highest-grossing film of all time was *Gone with the Wind* (USA, 1939). Adjusting for current inflation, it seems likely it will still be the highest-grossing film of all time at the end of 2015.

American cinemas made today's equivalent $10.68 billion in 1954, and $10.90 billion in 2012. Does this mean that movies are as popular as they've ever been? Well, it's estimated that US cinemas sold approximately 2.5 billion tickets in 1955, compared with 1.3 billion in 2012.

While most people visit the cinema less regularly than they did in 1955, the rise of blockbusters – with their ever-spiralling budgets and technical breakthroughs – means that the public is prepared to pay more when they do.

The rise of affordable video technology has also helped the total number of films made around the world each year to spiral, creating grass-roots industries such as Nigeria's Nollywood, which now produces over 1,000 films each year, beating the USA into third place on the list of the most prolific film-making countries.

Blockbusters pre-1955

Below is a list of the highest-grossing movies since 1955. Only two films in the all-time top 10 list of **most successful movies** pre-date 1955: *Gone with the Wind* (1939) and *Snow White and the Seven Dwarfs* (1937). When adjusted to today's ticket prices, the former remains at the No.1 slot, with a gross of $3.44 bn.

NUMBER OF FEATURE FILMS RELEASED PER YEAR (WORLDWIDE)

There has been a steady increase in the number of movies released annually, from 1,904 in 1955 to 10,048 in 2013. The affordability of high-end film-making technology has led to a rapid rise in the past 10 years.

Cleopatra (USA, 1963)
Most expensive movie produced (adjusted): $306.86 m in today's money

Peak of 3,248 releases in 1968; not surpassed until 1990

12,000 / 10,000 / 8,000 / 6,000 / 4,000 / 2,000 / 0

AVERAGE PRICE OF A US CINEMA TICKET

Prices have crept up over the last six decades, as you would expect, but when adjusted for inflation (the lighter colour) there is plenty of variation over the years, peaking in 1971. Of course, this is just the cost of the seat, not the parking, the popcorn, the drinks, the 3D glasses…

Average ticket price peaks in 1971 at $9.35 (in today's money)

Doctor Zhivago (USA, 1965)
First movie to win five Golden Globe awards: Best Film, Director, Actor, Screenplay and Score; five Globes is also a record, shared with four other movies

$10 / $9 / $8 / $7 / $6 / $5 / $4 / $3 / $2 / $1 / $0

US CINEMA ADMISSIONS

It's been a bumpy ride when it comes to theatre admissions. As ticket prices grew, so the number of visits to the cinema dropped drastically, reaching a low at the start of the 1970s. The advent of the blockbuster and multiplexes has seen this trend reverse, but not back to the glory days of the 1940s and 50s.

Jaws (USA, 1975)
First blockbuster movie: the first movie to earn $100 m at the box office

Record low of 709 million admissions in 1971

The Golden Age of Hollywood peaked at 4.7 billion admissions in 1947; by 1964, with the rise of TV, the figure had dropped below 1 billion

3,000,000,000 / 2,500,000,000 / 2,000,000,000 / 1,500,000,000 / 1,000,000,000 / 500,000,000 / 0

TOTAL US BOX-OFFICE GROSS

The money earned by the theatres has fluctuated annually between a high of c. $12 bn and a low of $6 bn.

2001: A Space Odyssey (USA/UK, 1968)
Largest film budget for special effects: Stanley Kubrick's mind-altering sci-fi classic spends more than 60% of its budget on special effects

Adjusted peak of $11.98 bn in 1956; remains unbeaten until 2002

$12,000,000,000 / $10,000,000,000 / $8,000,000,000 / $6,000,000,000 / $4,000,000,000 / $2,000,000,000

1955 / 1960 / 1965 / 1970

TOP 10 FILMS OF THE PAST 60 YEARS...

1956

The Ten Commandments
Chart position: 6
Ticket sales: 262.0 m
Adjusted gross: $2.187 bn
Biblical epic starring Charlton Heston as Moses, tasked with freeing the Hebrew slaves

1961

101 Dalmatians
Chart position: 10
Ticket sales: 199.8 m
Adjusted: $1.003 bn
A litter of dalmatian dogs must be rescued before they become the fashion victims of Cruella de Vil

1965

Doctor Zhivago
Chart position: 7
Ticket sales: 248.2 m
Adjusted: $2.073 bn
A doctor/poet experiences illicit love and hardship during the Bolshevik Revolution

1965

The Sound of Music
Chart position: 4
Ticket sales: 283.3 m
Adjusted: $2.366 bn
The hills are alive with the sound of children and their nanny fleeing Nazi-occupied Austria

1973

The Exorcist
Chart position: 9
Ticket sales: 214.9 m
Adjusted: $1.794 bn
The Church is called in after a demonic entity takes possession of a young girl

Ranking based on number of tickets sold, seat prices and box-office gross

Most prolific movie industry

India continues to be the source of more movies than any other country: 1,255 releases in 2011, compared with 819 in the USA. In May 2013 – during Bollywood's 100th anniversary year – Vijay Krishna Acharya (IND) released *Dhoom 3*, the **highest-grossing Bollywood movie**, which raked in $88 m internationally.

GUINNESS WORLD RECORDS

FACT

More Americans went to the movies in 2011 than attended sporting events or theme parks combined. But in the same year, India recorded twice as many theatre visits as the USA.

E.T.: The Extra-Terrestrial (USA, 1982)
Most weekends at No.1: enjoys 16 (non-consecutive) weekends as the highest-ranking movie; seen by an estimated 161 million people in the USA alone

The Rescuers Down Under (USA, 1990)
First fully digital feature film: made using a digital ink system developed by Disney and Pixar (both USA)

Peak of 3,482 releases in 1990; not surpassed until 1999

Releases exceed 4,000 for first time; 1,041 of them originate in India

Avatar (USA, 2009)
First movie to gross $2 bn: surpasses $2 bn globally by the weekend of 29–31 Jan 2010

FACT

The average spend in a US cinema in 2013 was $20 per person – of which only $8.12 was for the seat.

True Lies (USA, 1994)
First film to have a $100-m budget: James Cameron ups the ante on the spectacle of film-making; it ends up making back $378 m

FACT

The Japanese pay the most for their cinema tickets, as of 2013 – the equivalent of $22 per seat.

The Twilight Saga: Eclipse (USA, 2010)
Widest movie release: opens in 4,468 cinemas in the USA on 30 Jun

Tron (USA, 1982)
First major motion picture to use CGI: producers desperate to keep cinema audiences growing discover the benefits of computer-generated imagery

Attendances peak at 1.6 billion in 2002, with *The Lord of the Rings*, *Harry Potter*, *Men in Black* and *Star Wars* all enjoying chart-topping sequels

Titanic (USA, 1997)
Most consecutive weekends at No.1: 15 weekends as the highest-ranking movie

The Avengers (USA, 2012)
Fastest time to gross $100 m at the domestic box office: two days (4–5 May)

Star Wars helps annual grosses to peak at $9.5 bn in 1978 – a figure not surpassed for another 20 years

Super Mario Bros. (USA, 1993)
First live-action film based on a videogame: movie producers, looking for inspiration from popular licences, turn to videogaming for the first time

US box-office takings peak in 2003, with combined adjusted earnings of $12.06 tr

The 12 biggest movies of 2009's Christmas weekend (25–27 Dec) earn a combined $259.9 m in three days at the domestic (US) box office – the **biggest weekend at the cinema**

Star Wars (USA, 1977)
Highest-grossing sci-fi series: George Lucas's blockbuster and its sequels (and prequels) go on to gross an adjusted $2.65 bn

Titanic (see above) becomes the **first movie to gross $1 bn**

Harry Potter and the Deathly Hallows Part 2 (UK/USA, 2011)
Highest-grossing film – single day: earns $91 m on 15 Jul in the USA alone

1980 | 1985 | 1990 | 1995 | 2000 | 2005 | 2010 | 2015

1975

Jaws
Chart position: 8
Ticket sales: 242.8 m
Adjusted: $2.027 bn
A man-eating great white shark terrorizes a US tourist hotspot at the height of the summer season

1977

Star Wars
Chart position: 2
Ticket sales: 338.4 m
Adjusted: $2.825 bn
Swashbuckling adventure set a long time ago in a galaxy far, far away…

1982

E.T.: The Extra-Terrestrial
Chart position: 5
Ticket sales: 276.7 m
Adjusted: $2.310 bn
An alien visitor to Earth is left stranded and befriends a young boy, who helps him "phone home"

1997

Titanic
Chart position: 3
Ticket sales: 301.3 m
Adjusted: $2.516 bn
James Cameron's epic tale of the sinking of the "unsinkable" ocean liner

2009

Avatar
Chart position: 1
Ticket sales: 238.6 m
Adjusted: $3.02 bn
Cameron again, this time setting the sci-fi action on the distant planet Pandora

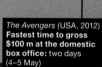

Movies

Cinema visits in Senegal cost the **equivalent of 38p**

Highest box office film gross for an animation

Frozen (USA, 2013) surpassed *Toy Story 3* (USA, 2010) as the most successful animated movie at the global box office, earning $1.112 bn (£664.7 m) – and counting – as of 14 Apr 2014. The Disney musical, inspired by Hans Christian Andersen's fairy tale *The Snow Queen*, broke the record while still on general release.

Most expensive year in Hollywood

The 50 biggest blockbusters released by major Hollywood studios in 2010 cost a combined total of $5.2 bn (£3.37 bn) – the highest in US cinematic history.

In 2013, the USA experienced the **highest box-office summer gross**, with cinemas taking a total of $4.76 bn (£2.96 bn) between 1 May and 31 Aug.

Most extensive digital object

For the final battle sequence in *Ender's Game* (USA, 2013), US effects studio Digital Domain created 333,443 individual spaceships, all of which appeared simultaneously in shots comprising more than 27 billion polygons.

Largest total cinema attendance (current)

There were some 3.17 billion trips made to cinemas in India in 2011. The **largest annual cinema attendance** in a given year occurred in 1929, when 4.49 billion admissions were made to US movie theatres.

Largest international movie market

North America represents the largest market for films, with box-office receipts in USA and Canada totalling $10.8 bn (£6.6 bn) in 2012.

Largest annual movie output

According to UNESCO, India is the most prolific movie-making nation. The Bollywood industry produces up to 1,000 feature films a year, and in 2011 1,255 movies were made, in 24 languages,

Longest continuously running movie franchise

Despite several significant gaps in production, the scheduled release of *Godzilla* (USA/JPN) on 16 May 2014 means that Japan's Toho studios have owned and promoted the *Godzilla* (Gojira) franchise for nearly 60 years. The original film by Ishirō Honda (JPN) was released in Nov 1954.

compared with 819 movies produced in the USA.

Most movies made in one language

The most recent UNESCO cinematic survey found that in 2011, 1,302 movies were made exclusively in English

FACT

Max Brooks, author of *World War Z*, is the son of comedy director Mel Brooks, whose movies include horror spoofs *Young Frankenstein* (USA, 1974) and *Dracula: Dead and Loving It* (USA, 1995).

Highest box-office gross for a zombie movie

The 2013 blockbuster *World War Z* (UK/USA) took a worldwide box-office gross of more than $540 m (£337 m) by the time it closed in cinemas on 10 Oct 2013. The film is based on a book of the same name by Max Brooks and stars Brad Pitt. In Jun 2013 it was announced that there would be a *World War Z* sequel.

BUDGET vs BOX OFFICE: BIGGEST RETURNS ON INVESTMENT

Charted here are the top 10 most profitable movies, as identified by the-numbers.com as of 14 May 2014. Profit is estimated from global box-office figures and domestic video/DVD sales. At the top is *Paranormal Activity* (USA, 2009), which cost $450,000 (£225,300) to make but netted $89.7 m (£44.9 m).

Legend: Budget / Gross / Return

Profit (estimated)	Return on investment (%)
Paranormal Activity (2009)	19,850%
The Devil Inside (2012)	3,644%
Peter Pan (1953)	3,443%
Grease (1978)	3,056%
Paranormal Activity 2 (2010)	2,474%
Insidious (2011)	2,079%
Jaws (1975)	1,730%
Reservoir Dogs (1992)	1,632%
The King's Speech (2010)	1,154%
Beauty and the Beast (1991)	1,148%

Source: www.the-numbers.com/Nash Information Services; budget and profit scales are not proportional

Just the ticket

In our 1955 book, we reported that the Brits were the most prolific cinema-goers: "The people of the United Kingdom go to the cinema more often than any other country in the world. Each week on average half the total population visit a cinema, of which there are a total of 4,595." Fast forward to the present day and Iceland has the **largest annual cinema attendance per capita**, with an average of 5.24 trips per person per year according to a 2011 survey by UNESCO. (For **largest total attendance**, see above.)

French came second with 293 movies and Spanish was third with 263. Although India makes the most movies, a range of languages were featured including Hindi, Tamil and Telugu.

Most times an actor has played themselves

Legendary *lucha libre* wrestler El Santo (MEX) starred as himself in 50 action-adventure movies made over 24 years, beginning with *Santo contra el cerebro del mal* in 1958 and concluding with *Santo en la furia de los karatekas* in 1982.

Most expensive movie

Pirates of the Caribbean: At World's End (USA) had a production budget of $300 m (£146 m) in 2007. Even if movie budgets are adjusted for inflation to 2014 prices, *At World's End* remains the most expensive production of all time. Its $339-m (£204-m) budget narrowly beats *Cleopatra* (1963, USA), starring Elizabeth Taylor and Richard Burton (both UK), which cost $44 m (£16 m) in 1963 – the equivalent of $337 m (£202 m) today.

Most expensive movie series

The eight *Harry Potter* films (USA/UK, 2001–09) had a combined production budget of $1.15 bn (£718 m). However, it is *James Bond* that takes the record of **most expensive movie series adjusted for inflation**, with costs of around $2.07 bn (£1.29 bn) across 23 films and 50 years.

HIGHEST GROSSING...

- **Movie:** *Avatar* (USA, 2009), $2.78 bn (£1.77 bn)
- **Bollywood movie:** *Dhoom: 3* (IND, 2013), $88 m (£53 m)
- **James Bond movie:** *Skyfall* (UK/USA, 2012), $1.10 bn (£742 m)
- **Post-apocalypse movie:** *The Hunger Games: Catching Fire* (USA, 2013), $864 m (£519 m)

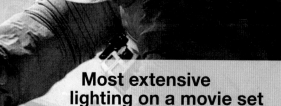

Most swearing in one film

In the film *The Wolf of Wall Street* (USA, 2013), there are at least 687 expletives – an average of 3.81 swear words per minute. The movie, which is directed by Martin Scorsese and stars Leonardo DiCaprio (both USA), is based on a memoir by Wall Street trader Jordan Belfort. The film was nominated for five Oscars.

Most extensive lighting on a movie set

"Zero-gravity" footage for the movie *Gravity* (USA, 2013) was filmed within a custom-built light box containing 1.8 million high-powered LEDs. The LEDs were individually controlled by the film's effects team to help recreate the natural light and shade of outer-space photography. The light box took the form of a hollow cube, within which the actors were suspended.

⊗ For more movies turn over the page

Crowdfunded: Veronica Mars

Veronica Mars (right) is the **most crowdfunded movie**, having received $5,702,153 (£3,708,480) via the Kickstarter crowdfunding site as of 13 Apr 2013. The appeal, which began in response to the cancellation of the *Veronica Mars* TV show, funded the movie, which premiered on 14 Mar 2014, a year and a day after the appeal launch.

The **first crowdfunded Oscar winner**, *Inocente* (left), won the Best Documentary (short feature) award on 24 Feb 2013. The film, about a homeless Californian girl's efforts to become an artist, was directed by Sean Fine and Andrea Nix.

FACT
Pledges totalling $52,527 (£33,502) were raised on Kickstarter to help fund *Inocente* (2012).

👁 Stand-out studios

Most billion-dollar movies by a studio: Buena Vista International (USA), seven (*Pirates of the Caribbean: Dead Man's Chest, Alice in Wonderland, Toy Story 3, Pirates of the Caribbean: On Stranger Tides, The Avengers, Iron Man 3* and *Frozen*)

Highest average gross for a studio: Pixar (USA) has earned an average of $252.6 m (£151 m) across 14 movies ○ ○ ○

Movie makers

Johnny Depp once worked for a **telemarketing** firm, selling pens

Bollywood big-hitters

Topping the *Forbes* list as the **highest-earning Bollywood actor** is Shah Rukh Khan (IND), with estimated earnings in 2013 of 220.5 crore (2.2 bn rupees; £22.08 m; $37.06 m). Khan is pictured here in the 2012 romantic drama *Jab Tak Hai Jaan* (*As Long as I Live*) with Katrina Kaif (HKG/UK), the **highest-earning Bollywood actress**, with earnings of 63.75 crore (637 m rupees; £6.38 m; $10.7 m) during the same period.

Highest box-office film gross for a director
The 27 theatrically released films thus far directed by Steven Spielberg (USA) – from *The Sugarland Express* (USA, 1974) to *Lincoln* (USA, 2012) – have grossed a total of $9.01 bn (£5.66 bn) worldwide.

Most billion-dollar movies at the box office for a director
Three directors have each made two films that have grossed at least $1 bn at the box office. They are: Canada's James Cameron, for *Titanic* (USA, 1997) and *Avatar* (USA/UK, 2009); New Zealand's Sir Peter Jackson, for *The Lord of the Rings: The Return*

of the King (USA/NZL, 2003) and *The Hobbit: An Unexpected Journey* (USA/NL, 2012); and the UK's Christopher Nolan, for *The Dark Knight* (USA/UK, 2008) and *The Dark Knight Rises* (USA/UK, 2012).

Most overpaid actor
According to business magazine *Forbes*, Adam Sandler (USA) returned an average of $3.40 (£2.23) for every $1 (61p) he was paid, based on the last three films he starred in to 1 Jun 2013. For the same period, *Forbes* ranked Katherine Heigl (USA) as the **most overpaid actress**, with an average return of $3.50 (£2.30) for every $1 earned. (See also: "Payback with interest", below.)

Highest box-office gross for a female director

With a total worldwide box-office gross of $1,152,567,728 (£716,897,126) for her six films as director, including *What Women Want* (USA, 2000) and *It's Complicated* (USA, 2009), US film-maker Nancy Meyers remains the highest-grossing female film director of all time.

Most powerful actor

Best known for his role as Wolverine, Hugh Jackman (AUS) topped Forbes' 2013 list of most powerful actors and is 11th overall in the list of most powerful celebrities. The list measures fame in terms of factors such as earnings, media exposure and internet presence.

Oldest actress in a leading role
Lillian Gish (USA, b. 14 Oct 1893) was 93 years old when she starred in *The Whales of August* (USA), released on 16 Oct 1987.
  The **oldest actress to debut in a leading role** is Harue Akagi (JPN, b. 14 Mar 1924), who was 88 years 175 days old when she starred in *Pekorosu no Haha ni Ai ni Iku* (JPN), released on 9 Nov 2013.

HIGHEST...

Annual earnings for a producer
Steven Spielberg (USA) earned $100 m (£65 m) from Jun 2012 to Jun 2013 according to Forbes' Celebrity 100 list. The total gross of Spielberg-produced movies stands at more than $6.4 bn (£3.9 bn).

Highest average box-office gross for a leading role

Harry Potter star Emma Watson (UK) has an average box-office gross of $775,303,380 (£482,238,702). Her *Harry Potter* co-star Daniel Radcliffe (UK) took top billing in one more non-*Harry Potter* film than Watson, which has reduced his per-film lead role average slightly to $712,856,021 (£443,396,445).

HOLLYWOOD ROYALTY: THE MOST INDIVIDUAL OSCAR WINS

Most Oscars won in a lifetime: Walt Disney (USA), 26

Most Oscars won in a lifetime (female): Edith Head (USA), eight

Most Best Director Oscars won: John Ford (USA), four

Most Best Actress Oscars won: Katharine Hepburn (USA), four

Most Best Actor Oscars won: Daniel Day-Lewis (UK), three

Walt and Oscar

In 1955, *The Guinness Book of Records* noted that "Walt Disney has won more 'Oscars' – awards of the United States Academy of Motion Picture Arts and Sciences instituted 1929 – than any other person." Back to the present day... and Disney (USA) still holds the record for **most Oscars awarded in a lifetime**: a career total of 26. His final Academy Award – Best Short Subject (Cartoon) for *Winnie the Pooh and the Blustery Day* (1968) – was awarded posthumously.

Payback with interest

Best investment return for an actress: according to Forbes, as of Dec 2010 Emma Stone (USA) returned an average of $80.70 for every $1 she was paid. Other actors with a super-competitive rate of return include Mila Kunis (USA), at $68.70 for every $1 paid, and Jennifer Lawrence (USA), at $68.60. The **best investment return for an actor** was that of The Rock aka Dwayne Johnson (USA), with $31.10 in returns for every $1 paid.

Most billion-dollar movies at the box office for an actor

Johnny Depp achieved three billion-dollar box-office smashes with *Pirates of the Caribbean* movies *On Stranger Tides* and *Dead Man's Chest*, and *Alice in Wonderland*. Hugo Weaving (AUS, top inset) matches him with *The Hobbit: An Unexpected Journey*, *Transformers: Dark of the Moon* and *The Lord of the Rings: The Return of the King*. Gary Oldman (UK, bottom inset) scores for *Harry Potter and the Deathly Hallows: Part 2*, *The Dark Knight* and *The Dark Knight Rises*.

Box-office gross for an actor

Samuel L Jackson (USA) has a career worldwide gross of $12,126,213,694 (£7,542,504,918) from the 94 films in which he has appeared. These include supporting roles in box-office record-breakers *The Avengers* and *Iron Man 2* (USA, 2010).

Average box-office gross for a director (male)

Lee Unkrich (USA) has an average US gross of $332.9 m (£207 m) as a director, with a worldwide overall gross of $2.97 bn (£1.84 bn) as of 8 Nov 2013. His highest-grossing film is *Toy Story 3* (USA, 2010).

Average earnings for a film composer

John Williams (USA) has written scores for 76 films, each grossing an average of $289.6 m (£179.9 m) at the box office. They include

Highest annual earnings for an actor

According to Forbes, two actors share the record for the highest earnings over a 12-month period. Robert Downey Jr (USA, main picture) earned around $75 m (£46.6 m) from Jun 2012 to Jun 2013, benefiting from the success of *The Avengers* and *Iron Man 3*. Tom Cruise (USA, below right) earned a similar figure from May 2011 to May 2012, during which *Mission: Impossible: Ghost Protocol* (USA/UAE/CZE, 2011) grossed some $700 m (£430 m).

Most bankable Hollywood figure

Steven Spielberg (USA) contributed the equivalent of $26,344,040 (£15,831,000) annually to the movie industry as of Feb 2014, according to the-numbers.com. His annual earnings (see **highest earnings for a producer**, p.164) also make him the **highest-earning director**.

the six *Star Wars* films and several of the *Harry Potter* movies. The **highest career box-office film gross for a composer** is $22.48 bn (£13.98 bn) by Hans Zimmer (DEU), nearly $4 bn (£2.4 bn) more than John Williams, his nearest rival. His credits include *The Dark Knight Rises* and three *Pirates of the Caribbean* movies.

 Cruising to success

In the past eight years, Tom Cruise, seen here as Jack Reacher, has been the highest-earning film actor three times. His big-screen debut came back in 1981.

Super-cameo-Man: Stan Lee

With films based on his creations breaking box-office records around the world, it's perhaps unsurprising that Marvel Comics mastermind Stan Lee (USA), aged 91 years 68 days as of 5 March 2014, would want to play his part in the action. The 19 films in which he has made cameo appearances since his cinematic debut in *Mallrats* (USA, 1995) – including *X-Men 3: The Last Stand* (USA, 2006; above left), *Spider-Man 3* (USA, 2007; centre left) and *Fantastic Four* (USA, 2005; bottom left) – have grossed $10,077,831,163 at the global box office, making Stan Lee the **highest-grossing actor from cameo appearances**.

 And finally...

- **Most appearances in $100-m-grossing movies:** Bruce Willis (USA), with 25 such movies as of 21 Jan 2014.
- **Most powerful actress:** Angelina Jolie (USA), ranked 41 in Forbes' 2012–13 Celebrity 100 list.
- **Most screenwriters credited:** 51, for *50 Kisses*, (UK, 2014) produced by the London Screenwriters' Festival (UK). ○ ○ ○

Pop music

There are more than **26 million songs** in the iTunes catalogue

Most travelled musician in one year

According to research carried out by the live music events website Songkick, electro-house musician, DJ and producer Steve Aoki (USA) clocked up 389,221 km (241,850 mi) performing a total of 168 shows in 41 countries in 2012.

Most Facebook "likes" for a musician

As of 25 Apr 2014, Shakira (COL) had the most "likes" with 90,938,442. Not far behind was Rihanna (BRB) with 87,042,153, and at No.3 was Eminem (USA) with 86,136,651.

Over on Twitter, the **musician with the most followers** is Katy Perry (USA) with 52,463,838. Next up are Justin Bieber (CAN) with 51,140,907 and Lady Gaga (USA) with 41,297,293.

Highest-earning dead celebrity

American singer Michael Jackson earned $160 m (£99 m) from Oct 2012 to Oct 2013. If Forbes included the dead, he would top the 2013 highest-earning celebs.

Most consecutive years with a UK No.1 single

Three acts in the 62-year history of the UK's Official Singles Chart have achieved No.1 singles in seven consecutive years: Elvis Presley (USA) in 1957–63, The Beatles (UK) in 1963–69, and in 2007–13 Rihanna, whose latest chart-topper, "The Monster", debuted at No.1 on 9 Nov 2013.

First act to play a concert on every continent

Metallica (USA) became the first music act to play on all seven continents when they entertained 120 scientists and competition winners at Antarctica's Carlini Station on 8 Dec 2013. The show was dubbed "Freeze 'Em All".

First act to debut at No.1 in USA with first three albums

One Direction (UK) completed a hat-trick of No.1 debuts on the *Billboard* 200 albums chart when *Midnight Memories* entered in pole position with first-week sales of 546,000 on 14 Dec 2013. It followed the chart-topping success of *Up All Night* and *Take Me Home* in 2012.

Longest officially released song

"Zwei Jahre" ("Two Years"), performed by German band Phrasenmäher, lasts 1 hr 30 min 10 sec. It was released via iTunes, Amazon and Spotify on 10 Jan 2014.

Fastest-selling iTunes album

On 13 Dec 2013, Beyoncé (USA) unexpectedly released self-titled studio album *BEYONCÉ* – with 14 new tracks and 17 videos – exclusively on iTunes. In its first three days of availability as a download, it sold 828,773 copies worldwide.

Longest-running album series

There have been 87 albums in the *NOW That's What I Call Music!* series (Virgin/EMI). The first was released in 1983 and the most recent on 7 Apr 2014.

- **First:** *NOW That's What I Call Music!*, 28 Nov 1983
- **Editions:** 87
- **Songs:** 3,440
- **Units sold:** more than 100 million
- **Most appearances:** Robbie Williams (33)
- **Most appearances on one album:** Calvin Harris (3)

BIGGEST MUSIC FESTIVALS BY ATTENDANCE

***Source:** mtviggy.com*

- **Exit** (SRB) 200,000 in 2013
- **Paléo** (CHE) 230,000 in 2013
- **Ultra** (USA) 330,000 in 2013
- **Sziget** (HUN) 385,000 in 2011
- **Przystanek** (POL) 550,000 in 2012
- **Coachella** (USA) 675,000 in 2013
- **Rock in Rio** (BRA) 700,000 in 2011
- **Summerfest** (USA) 849,000 in 2013
- **Mawazine** (MAR) 2.5 million in 2013
- **Donauinselfest** (AUT) 3.2 million in 2013

Still a "White Christmas"

The **best-selling single** (or "gramophone record" as it was then known) in 1955 was "White Christmas" (1942), written by Irving Berlin. Including Bing Crosby's famous version, it had sold 18 million copies. Today, the record is held by... "White Christmas", the festive favourite having sold an estimated 50 million copies (this figure can be doubled if you include sales of albums on which it has appeared).

Silver stars

Oldest US Hot 100 entrant: Fred Stobaugh (USA), 96 years 23 days ("Oh Sweet Lorraine", No.42, 14 Sep 2013).

Oldest UK albums chart-topper: Dame Vera Lynn (UK), 92 years 183 days (*The Very Best of Vera Lynn – We'll Meet Again*, 19 Sep 2009).

Oldest UK singles chart-topper: Robert "Bobby" Elliott (UK, Hollies drummer), 71 years 21 days ("He Ain't Heavy, He's My Brother" by The Justice Collective, 29 Dec 2012).

Most words in a hit single

"Rap God" by Eminem (USA) packs 1,560 words into a fast and furious 6 min 4 sec – that's a tongue-twisting average of 4.28 words every second! In one 15-second segment alone, "Slim Shady" spits out 97 words (6.46 words per sec) at supersonic speed.

Longest time between UK No.1 albums

On 22 Jun 2013, British rock band Black Sabbath returned to the top of the UK albums chart with their 19th studio set, *13*, some 42 years 255 days after first topping the chart with their second album, *Paranoid*, on 10 Oct 1970.

Most cover versions of a single charted before the original

Seven cover versions of "I Love It", by Swedish duo Icona Pop and singer-songwriter Charli XCX, aka Charlotte Aitchison (UK), made the Top 200 of the UK's Official Singles Chart before the original debuted at No.1 on 6 Jul 2013.

Largest TV audience for a Super Bowl half-time performance

The half-time show by Bruno Mars and the Red Hot Chili Peppers (both USA) at Super Bowl XLVIII attracted 115.3 million US viewers, according to data supplied by Nielsen. The 2014 Super Bowl was contested by the Denver Broncos and the Seattle Seahawks at MetLife Stadium in East Rutherford, New Jersey, USA, on 2 Feb. The game itself was watched by an average of 111.5 million – the **largest TV audience for a Super Bowl**.

Best-selling album ever

Thriller by Michael Jackson (USA), released in Nov 1982, has sold more than 65 million copies worldwide. *Thriller* and the Eagles' (USA) *Their Greatest Hits (1971–1975)* have been certified 29x platinum by the Recording Industry Association of America (RIAA) and are joint holders of the **best-selling album in the USA**.

According to the Official Charts Company, the **best-selling album in the UK** is Queen's *Greatest Hits* (1981). In 2014, it became the first album to sell 6 million copies in the UK.

GWR'S POP MUSIC POWER INDEX

	Name	Power rating
1	Lady Gaga (USA)	100
2	Justin Bieber (CAN)	75.5
3	Taylor Swift (USA)	66.8
4	Katy Perry (USA)	66.2
5	Rihanna (BRB)	64.2
6	Shakira (COL)	62.9
7	One Direction (UK/IRL)	56.2
8	Madonna (USA)	49.0
9	Britney Spears (USA)	47.0
10	Miley Cyrus (USA)	46.3

Index accounts for earnings, social media presence, video views and search hits, as of 6 Mar 2014; benchmarked to Lady Gaga = 100.

Best-selling female artist

Madonna has sold more than 300 million albums in her career. Her earnings of $125 m (£82 m) for Jun 2012–Jun 2013 were also the **highest annual earnings ever for a female pop star**, dwarfing those of record holder Celine Dion for 1998 – $56 m ($80 m, or £49 m, today).

Most searched-for pop star

According to Google, Miley Cyrus (USA) was the most searched-for pop star in 2013. No.5 on the overall list, her internet popularity peaked after she "twerked" with Robin Thicke at the 2013 MTV Video Music Awards.

Most weeks on US singles chart (one single)

"Radioactive", by the US rock band Imagine Dragons, spent a total of 86 non-consecutive weeks on the US Hot 100 singles chart between 18 Aug 2012 and 3 May 2014. It reached a peak chart position of No.3.

Most weekly radio impressions

Robin Thicke's (USA/CAN) controversial single "Blurred Lines" had 228.9 million audience impressions on *Billboard*'s Radio Songs chart on 24 Aug 2013. Impressions are calculated according to the number of times a song is played and the radio station's audience size.

Calvin climbs: superstar DJs

The **highest-paid DJ in one year** is Calvin Harris (UK), with earnings of £30 m ($46 m) in the 12 months to Jun 2013, according to Forbes, including up to $300,000 (£200,000) for one night's work in Las Vegas, USA. Electronic dance music has become very popular in the USA in the last decade and is worth $4 bn (£2.4 bn) a year. Harris proved his worth on 16 May 2013 when he was named Songwriter of the Year at the 58th Ivor Novello Awards. Harris has collaborated with artists such as Rihanna, Dizzee Rascal, Kylie Minogue and Ellie Goulding.

FACT

The UK's Glastonbury festival began in 1970, attracting 1,500 fans. Fast forward to 2013: all 135,000 tickets were sold in just 1 hr 40 min.

Pop videos

After Robin Thicke performed "Give it 2 U" at 2013's MTV MVAs, the single's sales **leapt by 251%**

1958: First music videos
The Big Bopper, aka Jiles Perry Richardson (USA), booms "Hello, baby!" in his "Chantilly Lace" video of 1958, miming into a prop phone. He was the first to use the term "music video", only weeks before he died in the plane crash that also claimed Buddy Holly. The Bopper filmed clips for three songs on the same day.

1981: First music video shown on MTV
On 1 Aug 1981, MTV used "Video Killed the Radio Star" by The Buggles (UK duo Geoff Downes and Trevor Horn) as its opening track. On 27 Feb 2000, the same video was the millionth to be broadcast by the channel.

1982: First music video banned by MTV
Tame by today's standards, Queen's "Body Language" was full of sweaty, writhing, Lycra-clad bodies in a dimly lit steam room. While the band was fully clothed, the flesh and alleged "homoerotic undertones" worried MTV.

1982: First Grammy for Video of the Year
Elephant Parts (Pacific Arts, 1981) was an hour-long mix of five songs with comedy by former Monkee Michael Nesmith (USA) that won at the 1982 Grammys. Short- and long-form video awards were separated in 1984.

1986–99: Most wins at the MTV Music Video Awards
Madonna (USA) has won a total of 20 MTV Music Video Awards (MVAs): Video Vanguard Award (1986); one for "Papa Don't Preach" (1987); three for "Express Yourself" (1989); one for "Like a Prayer" (1989); three for "Vogue" (1990); one for *The Immaculate Collection* (1991); two for "Rain" (1993); one for "Take a Bow" (1995); five for "Ray of Light" (1998); one for "Frozen" (1998); and one for "Beautiful Stranger" (1999).

1987: Most MTV MVAs for a single video
In 1987, Peter Gabriel's (UK) "Sledgehammer" (1986) won nine awards,

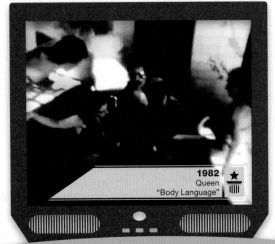

1982
Queen
"Body Language"

1982
Michael Nesmith
Elephant Parts

1990
Madonna
"Vogue"

1958
The Big Bopper
"Chantilly Lace"

1981
The Buggles
"Video Killed the Radio Star"

1987
Peter Gabriel
"Sledgehammer"

TOP OF THE POPS: MOST VIEWED AND TOP TRENDING MUSIC VIDEOS OF 2013

#	Most viewed music videos of 2013	Top trending music videos of 2013
1	PSY – "Gentleman M/V" **598 million**	Ylvis – "The Fox (What Does The Fox Say?)" **265 million**
2	Miley Cyrus – "Wrecking Ball" **393 million**	Kenneth Håkonsen – "Harlem Shake (Original Army Edition)" **95 million**
3	Miley Cyrus – "We Can't Stop" **304 million**	SteveKardynal – "Wrecking Ball (Chatroulette Version)" **67 million**
4	Katy Perry – "Roar (Official)" **251 million**	thelonelyisland – "YOLO (feat. Adam Levine & Kendrick Lamar)" **53 million**
5	P!nk – "Just Give Me A Reason ft. Nate Ruess" **236 million**	ERB – "Mozart vs Skrillex: Epic Rap Battles of History Season 2" **41 million**

Listed here are the top five most viewed music videos of 2013 alongside the year's top five trending music videos. Both sets of figures represent the total viewing figures for each video as of Dec 2013.

Video firsts
First video featuring unauthorized use of an act's music: "Up All Night" (2011), Blink-182, compiled from clips taken from fan-made videos

First video in Simlish: "Smile" (2007), Lily Allen in *The Sims 2: Seasons* (2007)

First video to receive one billion views on YouTube: "Gangnam Style", PSY, Dec 2012

including Best Special Effects and Video of the Year. Lady Gaga, aka Stefani Germanotta (USA), is second with seven awards for "Bad Romance" (2009).

1991: Largest TV audience for a music video premiere
An estimated 500 million people in 27 countries watched "Black or White" by Michael Jackson (USA) on 14 Nov 1991. The 11-min clip was filmed by "Thriller" director and movie-maker John Landis.

2010
Lady Gaga and Beyoncé
"Telephone"

2004: First official fan-made music video
Placebo (BEL/SWE/UK) were so impressed by fan Grégoire Pinard's (ZAF) claymation clip for "English Summer Rain" that they adopted it as the official promo video for the song.

2010: Most product placement in a video
Lady Gaga has approximately a dozen brands on show in "Telephone" (featuring Beyoncé), including Virgin Mobile, Beats Electronics, Polaroid, Chanel sunglasses,

Wonder bread, Kraft salad dressing and Diet Coke cans imaginatively utilized as her hair rollers.

2013: First video in space
On 12 May 2013, Commander Chris Hadfield (CAN) posted a video of himself singing David Bowie's "Space Oddity" on board the *International Space Station*. Read an interview with Chris on p.17.

2013: Longest video
Pharrell Williams (USA) released the "world's first 24-hour music video". *Happy* features fans dancing to the four-min track of the same name, which is looped 360 times. Pharrell appears in the video on the hour every hour.

2013: Longest wait for an official video
An interactive video for Bob Dylan's (USA) "Like a Rolling Stone" appeared on his website on 19 Nov 2013, more than 48 years after the song was a hit. Viewers could flick through different "channels" to watch artists lip-sync the song.

2004
Placebo
"English Summer Rain"

2013
Chris Hadfield
"Space Oddity"

1991
Michael Jackson
"Black or White"

2013
Pharrell Williams
"Happy"

2013
Bob Dylan
"Like a Rolling Stone"

Take your partners: biggest dances

Record attempts can be inspired by music videos. Pictured right is the **largest "Thriller" dance**, in which 13,597 "zombies" pulled Michael Jackson moves in Mexico City, Mexico, on 29 Aug 2009. "Harlem Shake" by Baauer inspired the **highest Harlem Shake** (below left), danced at an altitude of 19,000 m on a British Airways plane on 10 Mar 2013. "Cha Cha Slide" (DJ Casper, 2000) prompted 3,231 dancers to achieve the **largest Cha Cha Slide** (above left) at the Pleasure Beach in Blackpool, UK, on 8 Oct 2011.

ℹ **Distinctive Dylan**
Described by one website as "a Dylan cable network with 16 channels of mindless entertainment", the star-studded interactive video (see above) features a host of celebrities and musicians including vintage footage of Dylan himself performing "Like a Rolling Stone". According to the video's creator, Interlude, no viewer will see the same video twice.

Works of art

On 21 Aug 1911, the **Mona Lisa** was stolen from Paris's Louvre

Most expensive sculpture (living artist)

On 12 Nov 2013, the 3.6-m-tall (12-ft) stainless steel sculpture *Balloon Dog (Orange)* by Jeff Koons (USA) sold for $58.4 m (£36.8 m) at Christie's in New York City, USA.

Most frequently stolen painting

The Ghent Altarpiece – also known as *The Adoration of the Mystic Lamb* – is a large, early-15th-century Flemish panel painting by Hubert and Jan van Eyck. It has been stolen seven times since it was first unveiled. Police are still searching for one missing panel.

Most expensive sculpture

A 1.8-m-tall (6-ft) bronze sculpture entitled *L'Homme qui marche I (The Walking Man I)* (1960), created by Alberto Giacometti (CHE), sold to an anonymous bidder at Sotheby's in London, UK, for £65 m ($104 m) on 3 Feb 2010.

Actual Size

Oldest sculpture

In Sep 2008, excavations at Hohle Fels Cave in south-west Germany uncovered a 35,000–40,000-year-old female figurine carved from a mammoth's tusk.

Most expensive painting

The Card Players, painted by Paul Cézanne (FRA), was sold to the royal family of Qatar for $250 m (£158.3 m) in 2011. The painting, created in the early 1890s, is one of five in a series by the renowned post-Impressionist.

Oldest painting

Discovered in the 1870s, paintings of animals and handprints from a cave called El Castillo in Puente Viesgo in the province of Cantabria, Spain, have now been proved to be at least 40,800 years old.

Most expensive painting sold at auction

On 12 Nov 2013, *Three Studies of Lucian Freud* (1969), a triptych by Francis Bacon (UK), was sold to an unnamed client for $142.4 m (£89.6 m) at Christie's in New York City, USA.

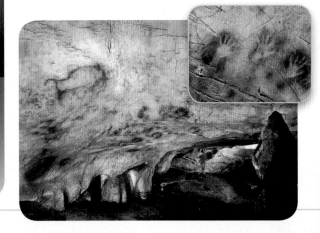

Largest horse-head sculptures

In Nov 2013, two 30-m-tall (100-ft) equine sculptures were unveiled in Falkirk, UK. *The Kelpies* were designed by artist Andy Scott (UK) as a tribute to the local tradition of working horses.

Largest Rubik's Cube mosaic

Created by Josh Chalom (USA), the largest mosaic made out of Rubik's Cubes measured 68.78 m (225 ft 7 in) long by 4.03 m (13 ft 2 in) high and was unveiled at One Central Macau, China, on 7 Dec 2012. The mosaic depicted famous views in Macau and comprised 85,626 cubes.

Anamorphic art: seeing is believing

Anamorphic art is a 2D artwork that looks 3D when seen from one point of view. The **largest anamorphic pavement art** (above) covers 1,570 m² (16,899 sq ft) and was created to promote tourism in Wilhelmshaven, Germany, on 4 Aug 2012. Above left is the **largest anamorphic print**: a 4,227.5-m² (45,504-sq-ft) image commissioned by Renault Trucks (FRA) and realized by François Abélanet (FRA) in Lyon, France, on 6 Jul 2013.

Smallest hand-made sculpture

Golden Journey is a gold sculpture measuring just 0.1603 mm (0.006 in) long. It was hand-crafted by artist Willard Wigan (UK) and sits in a hollowed-out section of a single hair. The measurement was verified in Birmingham, UK, on 19 Jun 2013.

Longest wood sculpture

Designed by Zheng Chunhui (CHN), the lengthiest wooden carving measures 12.28 m (40 ft 3 in) and was unveiled in Putian, Fujian, China, on 14 Nov 2013. It took the record holder and his 20 co-workers four years to complete the highly intricate work from camphor wood.

Publishing

Harry Potter creator J K Rowling **does not have a middle name**

BEST-SELLING...

Fiction book
Owing to a lack of audited figures, it is impossible to state which single work of fiction has the highest sales. However, Charles Dickens' (UK) *A Tale of Two Cities* (1859) is believed to have sold in excess of 200 million copies.

Children's book series
J K Rowling's (UK) seven-part *Harry Potter* saga began in 1997 and ended in 2007, with *Harry Potter and the Deathly Hallows*. By 2008, the series had sold a combined total of *c.* 400 million copies.

The **best-selling children's trilogy** is Suzanne Collins' (USA) *Hunger Games*; during 2012 alone, the three books – *Hunger Games* (2008), *Catching Fire* (2009) and *Mockingjay* (2010) – sold a total of 27.7 million copies across both printed and digital formats.

Non-fiction book
Even without exact sales numbers, there is little doubt that the Bible is the world's best-selling and most widely distributed book. A survey by the Bible Society concluded that around 2.5 billion copies were printed between 1815 and 1975, but more recent estimates put the number at more than 5 billion.

Regularly updated book
The *Xinhua Zidian* (New China Character Dictionary) is the world's most popular reference work. Originally published in 1953, the dictionary has been revised 11 times, had over 200 print runs and sold well in excess of 400 million copies.

Highest *New York Times* ranking for a "mash-up"

A "mash-up" is a work of fiction that combines pre-existing text (often a literary classic with expired copyright) and new text written by a contemporary author.
Pride and Prejudice and Zombies – a hybrid of Jane Austen's 19th-century period romance and Seth Grahame-Smith's (left) alternative-universe zombie horror – reached No.3 on the *New York Times* best-seller list in 2009.

FIRST...

Encyclopedia
Speusippus compiled the earliest known encyclopedia in Athens, Greece, in *c.* 370 BC. As of 2014, it would have been compiled 2,384 years ago.

Detective novel
According to the British Library, *The Notting Hill Mystery* (1863) by Charles Felix (UK) was the first detective novel. Starting with a murder, the plot reveals the twists and turns leading up to the crime, establishing many features of the now-ubiquitous detective genre.

Digital library
Currently offering around 133,000 free eBooks, Project Gutenberg was established in 1971 with the aim of

> **FACT**
> Bob's collection weighs an estimated 7.6 tonnes – about the same as 118 adult men!

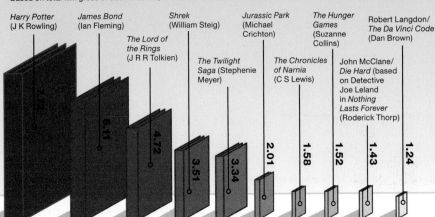

Largest comic-book collection

Bob Bretall (USA) has amassed a collection of 94,268 comic books. The tally was made at his home in Mission Viejo, California, USA, on 1 May 2014 and includes unique comic books only. Bretall began collecting comics at the age of eight years old, when he purchased *The Amazing Spider-Man* #88.

HIGHEST-GROSSING LITERARY CREATIONS AT THE MOVIES

Based on total film gross of each creation, measured in billions of dollars

Harry Potter (J K Rowling)	7.72
James Bond (Ian Fleming)	6.11
The Lord of the Rings (J R R Tolkien)	4.72
Shrek (William Steig)	3.51
Jurassic Park (Michael Crichton)	3.34
The Twilight Saga (Stephenie Meyer)	2.01
The Chronicles of Narnia (C S Lewis)	1.58
The Hunger Games (Suzanne Collins)	1.52
John McClane/Die Hard (based on Detective Joe Leland in *Nothing Lasts Forever* (Roderick Thorp))	1.43
Robert Langdon/The Da Vinci Code (Dan Brown)	1.24

Lucrative literature
Highest annual earnings for an author (2012–13): $95 m (£62 m), E L James (UK), *Fifty Shades...* trilogy
Highest annual earnings for a children's author (2012–13): $55 m (£36 m), Suzanne Collins (USA), *Hunger Games* trilogy
Largest advance for a non-fiction book: $15 m (£7.8 m), US President Bill Clinton for his memoir, *My Life*

> **FACT**
> Self-published author John Locke (USA) has sold more than 2 million Kindle-formatted eBooks on Amazon using the Kindle Direct Publishing service. He passed the 1-million milestone in Jun 2011, and to date has published 21 novels plus one non-fiction book, entitled – appropriately enough – *How I Sold 1 Million eBooks in 5 Months*.

FACT
Only 250 copies of the 22-page book were printed between Apr and Dec 2012.

Smallest printed book

The illustrated reference book *Flowers of the Four Seasons* measures 0.74 x 0.75 mm (0.02 x 0.02 in) and was printed by Toppan Printing Co. Printing Museum in Bunkyo, Tokyo, Japan.

making 10,000 of the most consulted books available to the public at little or no cost.

Graphic novel
The term "graphic novel" first appeared in 1976 on the dust jacket of *Bloodstar* by Richard Corben and Robert E Howard (both USA).

Author to earn $1 bn
In 2004, J K Rowling (UK) – one of only five self-made female billionaires – became the first author to earn $1 bn

(£519 m). Her *Harry Potter* books have been published in at least 55 languages.

Author to sell one million eBooks
By 6 Jul 2010, James Patterson (USA), creator of *Alex Cross* and *Women's Murder Club*, had exceeded sales of one million eBooks.

MOST...

Prolific computer-assisted author
With a little help from computers, a team of programmers and a clever software algorithm that he designed, Philip M Parker (USA) has "written" in excess of 200,000 books. His algorithm gathers information freely available in the public domain and compiles it into book form. Digital files are produced in around 13 min and printed on demand. Given the specialist nature of the content, cover prices are

Youngest Booker Prize winner
Eleanor Catton (NZ, b. 24 Sep 1985) was aged 28 years 22 days when she won the Booker Prize on 15 Oct 2013 for her novel *The Luminaries*.

often high – for example, £795 ($1,300) in the case of *The 2007–2012 World Outlook for Floor Lamps*.

Booker Prize wins
Awarded since 1969, the Booker Prize has been won twice by four authors as of 2013: J G Farrell (UK), J M Coetzee (ZAF), Peter Carey (AUS) and Hilary Mantel (UK).

Pseudonyms
A total of 325 pen names were listed for humorist Konstantin

Arsenievich Mikhailov (RUS) in the 1960 *Dictionary of Pseudonyms*. Most were abbreviations of his real name.

Translated author
According to the Index Translationum – UNESCO's book translation inventory – Agatha Christie (UK) has had an astonishing 6,598 translations of her novels, short stories and plays.

Blank pages in a published book
Sheridan Simove's (UK) book *What Every Man Thinks About Apart from Sex...* (2011) contains 196 blank pages.

Largest book
A photography book measuring 5.01 x 8.08 m (16 ft 5 in x 26 ft 6 in) was created by Samsung Electronics in Berlin, Germany, on 7 Sep 2013. The 16-page book consists of 28,000 photos sent via Facebook to Samsung. It was unveiled in the Museum für Kommunikation Berlin.

Diamond seller: the record-breaking record book

The 100-millionth copy of *Guinness World Records* was sold in 2004, although the book by then had already earned its own entry in the records archive. In the edition published in 1975 (right), our founding editors Norris and Ross McWhirter announced that, in Nov 1974, the *Guinness Book of Records* "first sold in October 1955 and [with] total sales in 14 languages now running at 60,000 a week, surpassed the 23,916,000 of *The Common Sense Book of Baby and Child Care* by Dr Benjamin Spock". We continue to be the **biggest-selling annual book**.

 Nobel Prize in Literature

The Nobel Prize in Literature has been awarded to 110 authors since 1901. According to Alfred Nobel's will, the winner should have produced "...the most outstanding work in an ideal direction..." Doris Lessing (UK, 1919–2013) was the **oldest recipient of the Literature Prize**, winning it in 2007 aged 87 years 355 days.

 And finally...

• **Fastest-selling non-fiction book (UK):** *My Autobiography*, by retired soccer manager Sir Alex Ferguson (UK), published on 24 Oct 2013 – first week sales of 115,547 copies.

• **Fastest-selling videogame guide (UK):** *Grand Theft Auto V Signature Series Strategy Guide*, published on 17 Sep 2013 – first week sales of 21,530 copies.

Bermuda has more TV sets per capita than any other country (1,024 per 1,000)

First 3D television
We often think of 3D TV as a modern invention, but stereoscopic 3D television was first demonstrated by Scottish inventor John Logie Baird at his company's premises at 133 Long Acre in London, UK, on 10 Aug 1928. Baird pioneered a variety of 3D TV systems using electro-mechanical and cathode-ray tube techniques, including simultaneous left- and right-eye images for true stereoscope viewing. It took until 12 Apr 2008, however, for the **first commercially available 3D TV set** to go on sale, made by Hyundai in Japan.

Most pirated TV programme

Game of Thrones retains the No.1 spot of Torrent Freak's top 10 list of most pirated TV shows, with some 5,900,000 downloads per episode in 2013. One reason is HBO's refusal to license the series to Netflix; HBO and Warner Bros executives also stated, controversially, that "receiving the title of 'most-pirated' was better than an Emmy", creating a "much-needed cultural buzz".

Highest-rated TV series (current)

As of the 2013–14 season, the first series of Canal+'s *The Returned* (aka *Les Revenants*, FRA) had a rating of 92 out of 100 on Metacritic. Based on the French 2004 film *Les Revenants*, the creepy story revolves around a French village where the dead start to return from the grave.

Most powerful person in television
According to Forbes, Oprah Winfrey (USA) tops the list of most powerful celebrities. The list assesses fame by taking into account income, exposure in print and on TV, internet presence, public opinion and marketability. Her estimated earnings from Jun 2012 to Jun 2013 were $77 m (£50 m), the **highest annual earnings for a TV personality (female)**.

Ashton Kutcher (USA), who joined sitcom *Two and a Half Men* (CBS, 2003–present) in 2011, has earned an estimated $24 m (£15.7 m) from Jun 2012 to Jun 2013, the **highest annual earnings for a TV actor (current)**.

Highest annual earnings for a TV chef
Gordon Ramsay (UK) earned $38 m (£25 m)

between Jun 2012 and Jun 2013, according to Forbes. He is known for TV shows such as *Hell's Kitchen* and *The F Word*.

Highest box-office gross for a TV simulcast
The *Doctor Who: The Day of the Doctor* simulcast on 23 Nov 2013 (see below) grossed $10.2 m (£6.2 m) at the global cinema box office. In the USA alone, 320,000 tickets were sold, earning $4.7 m (£2.89 m) at more than 650 sites. That made it the second biggest attraction of the day after *The Hunger Games: Catching Fire* (USA, 2013), but the per-screen average for *Doctor Who* was higher at $13,607 (£8,384), compared with $12,300 (£7,578).

Longest career as a TV news anchor (same programme)
Guillermo José Torres (USA) worked on WAPA-TV's *Noticentro* in Guaynabo, Puerto Rico, for 43 years 303 days, until 5 Aug 2013. He was awarded his GWR certificate as a surprise during his final telecast.

Largest TV drama simulcast

At 7:50 p.m. (GMT) on 23 Nov 2013, the 50th-anniversary episode of *Doctor Who* (BBC, UK) was broadcast in 98 countries across six continents. Themed around a Time War between Timelords and Daleks, the episode featured three Doctors, played by Matt Smith, David Tennant and John Hurt (main picture, right). The inset picture shows (left to right) Executive Producer Steven Moffat, Matt Smith and Jenna-Louise Coleman, who plays the Doctor's companion, Clara.

FACT
The first US president to appear on television was Franklin D Roosevelt, on 30 Apr 1939.

 TV gets a cool reception

There were no television broadcasts in Iceland during July until 1983. And Icelanders had to wait until 1987 before state television broadcast on Thursdays.

A dose of reality: *Got Talent*

The **most successful reality TV format** is *Got Talent* (Fremantle Media/Syco), sold to 58 countries – including India, below left – since debuting as *Britain's Got Talent* in the UK in Jun 2007. Simon Cowell (UK, right) and Howard Stern (USA, top left) – judges on the UK and US editions respectively – enjoy the **highest annual earnings by a TV celebrity**. Each earned $95 m (£62.4 m) for the year ending Jun 2013. In Forbes' annual list of the most powerful celebrities, however, Cowell (No.17) outranks Stern (No.45), factoring in areas such as marketability and social media ranking.

Most Primetime Emmy Awards for a TV series

Saturday Night Live (NBC, USA, 1975–present) won four trophies at the 2013 Primetime Emmy Awards, bringing its overall haul to 40 awards. The late-night comedy sketch show, which was created by Lorne Michaels and developed by Dick Ebersol, is in its 39th season as of 2014.

As of the 2013 ceremony, *Saturday Night Live* has also received the **most Primetime Emmy Award nominations** (171).

Highest-rated reality-competition series

As of Feb 2014, *Project Runway: Season 2* (Lifetime/Bravo, USA, 2005–06) boasts a Metacritic rating of 86. The 14-week show, fronted by model Heidi Klum, saw designers compete to have their work selected for the catwalk in New York Fashion Week.

Most Emmy Awards won by an individual

Producer Sheila Nevins (USA), President of Documentary and Family Programming for HBO and Cinemax, has won 25 Primetime Emmy Awards. Most recently, she took home two statuettes in 2013: Outstanding Documentary or Non-fiction Special for *Manhunt* (2013) and Exceptional Merit in Documentary Filmmaking for *Mea Maxima Culpa: Silence in the House of God* (2012).

Camera operator Hector Ramirez (USA) has been nominated for an Emmy Award

Highest annual earnings for a TV actress (current)

Modern Family star Sofía Vergara (COL) celebrates her second year as the best-paid actress on TV, with earnings estimated at $30 m (£19.7 m) by Forbes. This makes her the **highest paid actor in absolute terms** – earning more than her male counterpart, Ashton Kutcher (see left).

71 times in his 40-year career, the **most Emmy Award nominations received by an individual**. His first nod came in 1978 for *CBS: On the Air*. As of the 2013 ceremony, he had won 17 awards.

The **most nominations for a game show producer** is 37 for Harry Friedman (USA), Executive Producer of *Wheel of Fortune* and *Jeopardy!*

Most BAFTA Children's Awards won by a TV series

The BBC's educational sketch series *Horrible Histories* (UK) is the first programme to win four successive BAFTAs at the Children's Awards (2010–13). Commissioned by CBBC and produced by Richard Bradley of Lion TV, it is based on Terry Deary's award-winning books.

LONGEST-RUNNING TV SERIES BY CATEGORY

Category		Duration
Documentary series: *Meet the Press* (NBC, USA), 6 Nov 1947–present		66 years 119 days
Sports programme: *Hockey Night in Canada* (CBC, CAN), 11 Oct 1952–present		61 years 145 days
Children's magazine programme: *Blue Peter* (BBC, UK), 16 Oct 1958–present		55 years 140 days
Cookery show: *Hasta La Cocina* (Canal 4, MEX), 1 Dec 1960–present		53 years 94 days
Soap opera: *Coronation Street* (ITV, UK), 9 Dec 1960–present		53 years 86 days
Quiz show: *It's Academic* (NBC4, USA), 7 Oct 1961–present		52 years 149 days
Variety show: *Sábado Gigante* (Univision Television Network, CHL/USA), 8 Aug 1962–present		51 years 209 days
Educational show: *Teleclub* (Canal 13, CRI), 8 Feb 1963–present		51 years 25 days
Animated series: *Sazae-san* (Fuji Television Network, JPN), 5 Oct 1969–present		44 years 151 days
Medical drama: *Casualty* (BBC, UK), 6 Sep 1986–present		27 years 180 days

1945 1950 1955 1960 1965 1970 1975 1980 1985 1990 1995 2000 2005 2010

Statistics correct as of 5 Mar 2014

 "D'oh!"

Longest running sitcom (episodes): *The Simpsons* (FOX, USA), 546 episodes, 17 Dec 1989–30 Mar 2014

Most guest stars in a TV series: *The Simpsons*, 671 guest stars, 17 Dec 1989–30 Mar 2014

Most Emmy Awards won by an animated TV series: *The Simpsons*, 29 awards, 1990–2013

○ ○ ○

 Small-screen millionaires

In 1954, US comedian Jackie Gleason signed the most lucrative TV contract up to that date: $65,000 per episode for CBS's *The Honeymooners*, a half-hour, once-weekly TV show. Even though this is worth a cool $555,000 in today's money, it still doesn't beat Ashton Kutcher (USA), currently the **highest-paid TV actor per episode**, who picks up $750,000 for each instalment of *Two and a Half Men*.

Videogamers

According to the ESA, **58% of Americans** play videogames

Longest marathon on a dance videogame

Carrie Swidecki (USA) danced herself into the record books with a body-pumping 49-hr 3-min 22-sec session on *Just Dance 4* (Ubisoft, 2012) at Otto's Video Games & More! in Bakersfield, California, USA, between 15 and 17 Jun 2013.

Longest NHL videogame marathon

Hockey-mad Canadians James Evans (left) and Bruce Ashton (right) racked up a thumb-numbing 24-hr 2-min game of *NHL 10* (EA, 2009) in Orillia, Ontario, Canada, from 30 to 31 Jul 2011. Bruce's Winnipeg Jets fantasy team won the 45-game series against James and his Detroit Red Wings by a score of 32–13.

Youngest pro gamer

Born on 6 May 1998, "Lil Poison", aka Victor De Leon III (USA), picked up a Dreamcast Controller aged just two to play *NBA 2K* (Sega). In 2005, aged seven, he signed an exclusive deal with the organizers of Major League Gaming.

Largest competitive *Pokémon* gaming family

Pokémon's family-friendly charm is amply affirmed by the five-strong Arnold family from Frankfort, Illinois, USA, who take part in official *Pokémon* videogame world championships. Pictured from left to right are Ryan, mum Linda, Ryan's twin David, dad Glenn and youngest child Grace.

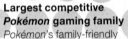

Most international *Street Fighter* competition wins

Ryan Hart (UK) won more than 450 *Street Fighter* events from 1998 to 2011. On 27 Mar 2010, he also set the record for the **longest winning streak on *Street Fighter IV*** with 169 unbeaten matches at GAME in Hull, UK. Hart is pictured here with "Kayane", aka Marie-Laure Norindr (FRA) – the **first woman to win a pro-*Street Fighter* event**.

Arts & media

Highest score at Level 1-1 of "Poached Eggs" on *Angry Birds* for Chrome

Stephen Kish (UK) notched up 37,510 points at this level on *Angry Birds* for Chrome (Rovio, 2011) in East Sussex, UK, on 23 Aug 2011.

On the same day, he also ran up the **highest score on World's Biggest PAC-Man** (Soap Creative, 2011), with 5,555,552 points.

Fastest completion of *Batman: Arkham City*

On 27 May 2012, Sean "DarthKnight" Grayson (USA) flew through *Batman: Arkham City* in just 2 hr 3 min 19 sec. The game settings were single-segment (played without stopping) and "normal" difficulty (including Catwoman DLC story-driven episodes).

FACT
The Joker is voiced in the game by Mark Hamill, who played Luke Skywalker in the original *Star Wars* trilogy.

Fastest completion of *Super Mario Kart* Circuit 1

Speedy Sami Çetin (UK) took the chequered flag for the fastest completion of the iconic Circuit 1 on the first game in the series, *Super Mario Kart* (Nintendo, 1992). Sami holds the record on both the PAL and NTSC versions of the game, with times of 58.34 sec and 56.45 sec respectively.

FACT
Sami's niece Leyla Hasso (UK) is also an *SMK* star, having held 30 time-trial records.

Largest joypad

Officially verified in Aug 2011 as the largest console gamepad, this fully functional NES pad measures 3.66 x 1.59 x 0.51 m (12 ft x 5 ft 3 in x 1 ft 8 in). Its main creator is engineering student Ben Allen (right), who was helped by Stephen van't Hof and Michel Verhulst, all students at Delft University of Technology in the Netherlands at the time.

Highest score on *Guitar Hero III* (female)

On 30 Sep 2010, at her home in San Francisco, California, USA, Annie Leung achieved a record score of 789,349 – the highest by a female gamer – playing the DragonForce track "Through the Fire and Flames" on *Guitar Hero III: Legends of Rock* (Neversoft, 2007).

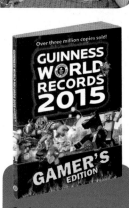

Guinness World Records Gamer's Edition

All these gamers were photographed for our record book dedicated to videogaming. Look out for *Gamer's Edition 2015* – packed with new gaming achievements and coming soon!

There are **766 cars** for every 1,000 people in Liechtenstein

World's Largest

FACT
Frederick's titanic trolley has a capacity of 27,332,836 cm³, making it 227 times bigger than a typical 120,000-cm³ shopping cart.

Largest motorized shopping trolley

Powered by a 7,439-cc engine, this mammoth cart measures 8.23 m (27 ft) long, 4.57 m (15 ft) tall and 2.43 m (8 ft) wide and incorporates 3,265 kg (7,200 lb) of stainless steel. Built by Frederick Reifsteck (USA), it was displayed in South Wales, New York, USA, on 20 Apr 2012.

It's not the **largest shopping trolley** overall, though. That honour goes to a 9.6-m-long (31-ft 5-in), 13.6-m-tall (44-ft 7-in), 8.23-m-wide (27-ft) behemoth created by Migros Ticaret A.Ş. (TUR) in Istanbul, Turkey, and unveiled on 14 Jun 2012.

Telecoms revolution

The entirety of the data on the internet **weighs about the same as a strawberry**

In just one lifetime, we've undergone an unprecedented transformation in how we communicate with each other. Here we chart the development in technology that has underpinned this telecoms revolution over the past 60 years.

When Guinness World Records launched in 1955, it wasn't even possible to make a transatlantic telephone call: today, we can send all of the data in this book down a phone line between our London and New York offices in seconds. We are living through a truly epoch-defining digital revolution.

The timeline below highlights the major record-breaking milestones that have dictated style, fashion and communication trends over the past 60 years and reveals the extent of this spectacular change. The technology we have today can transmit audio and video at a blistering pace that would have been inconceivable to our colleagues in the 1950s. Just imagine what we've got to look forward to in the next 60 years!

1979 First true laptop is the GRiD Compass, designed by William Moggridge (UK) for GRiD Systems (USA); boasts 512 K of RAM

1972 First all-in-one desktop computer is the HP 9830, launched by Hewlett-Packard

1981 Oldest archived Usenet post, written by Mark Horton (USA), describes how the bulletin-board forerunner should be run; unlike forums, Usenet content is sent between servers as news feeds

1962 First active direct relay communications satellite is *Telstar 1*, launched on 10 Jul; transmits intercontinental TV, phone and telegram signals

1955/56 First transatlantic telephone call becomes possible after TAT-1 cable is laid between Gallanach Bay in Scotland, UK, and Clarenville, Canada, in 1955; public phone service starts on 25 Sep 1956

1963 First touch-tone telephone used at Bell Labs (USA) on 18 Nov, replacing "pulse" dialling

1973 First cellular phone invented by Motorola's Martin Cooper (USA), who first uses it to call his rival at Bell Labs, Joel Engel

1981 First IBM Personal Computer (model 5150) launches, operating with Microsoft's MS-DOS; becomes the first "true" home PC

1955 — *1965* — *1975* — *1985*

1974 First Voice over Internet Protocol (VoIP) carried out in Aug 1974 using Network Voice Protocol (NVP) over the ARPANET; enables multiple computers to "talk" to each other over a single wire connection

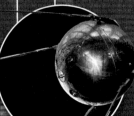

1957 First artificial satellite, *Sputnik 1*, put in orbit from Kazakhstan on 4 Oct; transmits signals for three weeks to Soviet scientists and radio enthusiasts

1964 First fax machine or Long Distance Xerography (LDX) is launched by Xerox

1982 First digital emoticons entered by Scott Fahlman (USA) on a bulletin board to signify emotion and avoid misunderstandings in emails: :-) and :-(

1984 First successful PC using a graphical user interface (GUI) is the Apple Macintosh; Microsoft's DOS interface is text-only

1969 First remote computer connection made from the University of California, USA, to Stanford Research Institute

1976 First public fibre-optic cable network installed in Hastings, UK, by Rediffusion (UK), leading to faster and farther telecommunications

1958 First monolithic integrated circuit (microchip) patented by Jack Kilby (USA, pictured). He and Robert Noyce (USA) etch transistors and connections on to silicon, key to modern telecoms

1988 First ISDN (Integrated Services Digital Network) standard defined by the International Telecommunication Union to allow digital transmission over copper telephone wires

FACT
It was Ray Tomlinson, sender of the **first email** (see right), who decided to use the @ symbol to separate the recipient's name and location.

1971 First email sent is the rather unimaginative "QWERTYUIOP" by Ray Tomlinson (USA), who programs a system to exchange messages between computers in the same office (above) linked through the US Department of Defense's ARPANET

1977 *Voyager 1* launches; in 2014, it is still sending back data, from 19 billion km away – the **longest communications distance**

1987 First MMORPG (multiplayer online videogame) with graphics, *Air Warrior*, is released by Kesmai on the GEnie (USA) service

Timeline not to scale

1990 **First hypertext browser** launched by Tim Berners-Lee (UK, above) and released on the internet as the World Wide Web in 1991

2006 **First tweet** sent by Twitter founder Jack Dorsey (USA, above) at 9:50 p.m. PST on 21 Mar 2006: "just setting up my twittr"

2007 **First land-based mobile phone call from the summit of Mount Everest** is made, at 8,848 m, by Rod Baber (UK) on a Motorola MOTO Z8 satellite phone

2012 First neutrino message

On 13 Mar 2012, it was announced that scientists working at Fermilab in Batavia, Illinois, USA, had used a beam of neutrinos to send a message to a detector for the very first time. The word "neutrino" was sent across 1 km – 240 m of which was solid rock – at a data rate of 0.1 bits per sec. Subatomic neutrinos pass through matter easily, as they rarely interact with it, but require massive equipment to be detected so are unlikely to replace email any time soon!

1991 **First email sent from space** by Shannon Lucid (inset) and James C Adamson (both USA) on an Apple Macintosh Portable on the Space Shuttle

1993 **First internet radio show**, "Geek of the Week", produced by Internet Talk Radio (USA)

2007 **Best-selling smartphone** is the original Apple iPhone; in its first month on sale, it shifts 2.31 million units

2011 **Highest-capacity communications satellite**, with a throughput of 134 gigabits per sec, is *ViaSat-1* in geostationary orbit above North America

2014 Facebook buys the instant messaging service WhatsApp for $19 bn (£11 bn) – **the largest acquisition of a venture-backed company**

2012 **Fastest internet connection** reaches 200 Gbit per sec at The Gathering IT event in Norway, meaning users can download a BluRay movie in 2 sec

2008 **First online legal summons** served by lawyers Mark MacCormack and Jason Oliver (both AUS) on Facebook

1996 **First public GPS network** introduced, though already used by the US government since the 1980s

2000 **Longest submarine fibre-optic cable**, the Sea-Me-We 3. It is 39,000 km long and connects users in Europe, Australia and Japan

2002 Scientists at Essex University, UK, transmit data at a rate of 1.02 terabits per sec (equivalent to 15.9 million phone calls), becoming the **first fibre transmission system to exceed 1 terabit per sec**

2009 **First video phone watch** is LG's GD910 Watch Phone, with colour screen, voice recognition and video-call capability

2009 **First 3D broadcast on the internet** is a 20-min set by rock band Keane (UK) from Abbey Road Studios in London, UK

2012 **Largest email service provider** becomes Google's Gmail, with 425 million users, surpassing previous record holders Yahoo! Mail and Microsoft Hotmail

2012 **First Google+ Hangout in space** conducted with Akihiko Hoshide (JPN) of the Japan Aerospace Exploration Agency (JAXA) on board the *International Space Station*

2005 Facebook – originally known as thefacebook – launches worldwide to become the **largest social network**, with 1.19 billion monthly active users by late 2013

2010 **Fastest-selling consumer electronics device** is the iPad (pictured with Apple's Steve Jobs), 3 million of which are sold in the first 80 days of its launch; the iPad 2, launched in Mar 2011, sells at a rate of 311,666 per day

Do not print the internet...

In May 2013, the TechHive website calculated that if you wanted to print out the entirety of the internet, you would need 4.73 billion sheets of paper – creating a stack 492 km high. If you factored in just one year of emails, the stack of paper would grow to nearly 5.5 million km tall!

Roller-coasters

There are **3,360 roller-coasters** in the world: 3,186 steel and 174 wood

FACT
When looping the loop, acceleration is stronger than gravity at the top, keeping you in your seat.

Largest roller-coaster loop

Full Throttle at Six Flags Magic Mountain in Valencia, California, USA, has the largest loop, at 38.75 m (127 ft 1 in). Its name doesn't lie: riders accelerate into the record-breaking loop at a fearsome 110 km/h (70 mph) and are turned upside down twice in less than a minute.

Most roller-coasters in one country
The nation with the greatest number of coasters of any kind is China, which has 824. Next up is the USA with 653 and then Japan with 212.

Most roller-coasters in one theme park
As of 20 Jan 2014, Six Flags Magic Mountain in Valencia, California, USA, has 18 operating roller-coasters. The theme park opened on 29 May 1971.

Most roller-coasters ridden in 24 hours
The greatest number of different roller-coasters

ridden in one 24-hour period is 74. On 9 Aug 2001, Philip A Guarno, Adam Spivak, John R Kirkwood and Aaron Monroe Rye (all USA) rode cars in 10 parks in four US states, using helicopters to travel between them.

Most naked people on a theme park ride
On 8 Aug 2010, 102 coaster fans bared all on the *Green Scream* roller-coaster at Adventure Island in Southend-on-Sea, UK.

Most costumed riders on a theme park ride
Dorney Park & Wildwater Kingdom in Allentown, Pennsylvania, USA, saw 330 costumed riders – all dressed as zombies – enjoy the *Steel Force* roller-coaster on 18 Aug 2011.

Longest marathon on a roller-coaster
Richard Rodriguez (USA) rode the *Pepsi Max Big One* and *Big Dipper* roller-coasters at the Pleasure

Most track inversions on a roller-coaster

The Smiler at Alton Towers Resort in Staffordshire, UK, inverts its riders 14 times. The (possibly misleadingly named) ride also includes optical illusions, blinding lights and near misses as it reaches speeds of 85 km/h (52.82 mph) through drops of up to 30 m (98 ft).

Highest thrill ride
The aptly named *Sky Drop* sits at the top of the 485-m (1,591-ft) mast of the Canton Tower in Guangzhou, Guangdong, China. Visitors are dropped 31 m (101 ft 8 in) back to the top deck at 16 m/s (48 ft/s).

Steepest steel roller-coaster

The *Takabisha* ride at Fujikyu (aka Fuji-Q) Highland amusement park, Fujiyoshida City, Japan, stands 43 m (141 ft) at its highest. Its steepest drop – at an angle of 121° down a 3.4-m (11-ft 2-in) stretch – takes a mere 0.38 sec.

> ## THE FORCE IS WITH YOU: WHAT A ROLLER-COASTER DOES TO YOUR BODY

In 2013, the *Washington Post* provided a fascinating step-by-step guide to what happens to your body during a roller-coaster ride.

1: A linear G-force (G for gravity) launch of 0–120 mph in under 5 sec pushes riders back, and fear and adrenaline kick in.

2: The drop makes riders feel extra-heavy – positive G-force, anything up to 5G, briefly.

3: Upside-down riders stay in their seats through centripetal force exerted over the course of the loop. Riders may feel queasy, though, as gravity isn't keeping their lunch where it should be.

4: Just the right amount of negative G-force makes your insides float momentarily (too much would make your eyeballs explode).

5: Bumpy corners make you feel the lateral G-force that – when uncontrolled, such as in car crashes – can result in whiplash injuries.

Largest pleasure beach

Stretching 45 km along the Atlantic Ocean is Virginia Beach in Virginia, USA, which offers 147 hotels and 2,323 campsites. Back in 1955, the record was held by Coney Island in New York, USA. "As well as its five-mile beach it features more than 350 business and amusement places... An estimated 50 million visit Coney Island and each spends about $1.25 (8s 11d [45p])."

Source: "Roller coasters: feeling loopy", washingtonpost.com, 1 Jul 2013

Biggest drop on a wooden roller-coaster

El Toro at Six Flags Great Adventure near Jackson, New Jersey, USA, is 57.3 m (188 ft) tall and features a drop of 54 m (176 ft). As if that weren't enough, this heart-stopping plunge is tilted at an angle of 76° and is taken at 110 km/h (70 mph).

built at Lakemont Park in Altoona, Pennsylvania, USA, in 1902. It closed, seemingly for good, in 1985, but funds were raised for its restoration and it reopened in 1999.

Most expensive roller-coaster
Expedition Everest at Walt Disney World Resort in Florida, USA, opened in 2006 at a cost of $100 m (£51 m). The concept is a train journey through the Himalayas via Forbidden Mountain, wherein lies a huge Yeti: a 6.7-m-tall (22-ft) audio-animatronic beast covered in 93 m² (1,000 sq ft) of fur.

Steepest wooden roller-coaster

Outlaw Run at Silver Dollar City in Branson, Missouri, USA, has a drop at an angle of 81°. The coaster – which can achieve a reported speed of 109 km/h (68 mph) – has been open since 15 Mar 2013 and is estimated to have cost more than $10 m (£6.6 m) to build.

Beach in Blackpool, UK, for 405 hr 40 min from 27 Jul to 13 Aug 2007.

Fastest accelerating roller-coaster
Dodonpa, the 52-m-tall (170-ft 7-in) steel roller-coaster at Fuji-Q Highland in Fujiyoshida, Yamanashi Prefecture, Japan, accelerates its eight riders from 0 to 172.03 km/h (106.9 mph) in 1.8 sec.

Fastest roller-coaster

After going from 0–100 km/h (62 mph) in 2 sec, the steel *Formula Rossa* at Ferrari World Abu Dhabi, in the UAE, can accelerate to 240 km/h (149 mph) and move 52 m (170 ft) upwards – higher than the Statue of Liberty – in just 4.9 sec.

Oldest roller-coaster operating continuously
The Scenic Railway, a traditional wooden coaster at Luna Park in St Kilda, Victoria, Australia, opened on 13 Dec 1912 and has been running ever since.

Oldest roller-coaster fully restored
Leap-the-Dips, another old wooden ride, was

Biggest roller-coaster drop

Kingda Ka at Six Flags Great Adventure near Jackson, New Jersey, USA, includes a drop of 127.4 m (418 ft) and sees riders reach 206 km/h (128 mph) just seconds after launch. *Kingda Ka* is no ordinary ride – at 139 m (456 ft), it's the world's **tallest roller-coaster**.

LONGEST...

Roller-coaster
Don't hold your breath on *Steel Dragon 2000* at Nagashima Spa Land in Kuwana, Mie, Japan – it's 2.48 km (1.54 mi) long.

Flying roller-coaster
Six Flags Magic Mountain in Valencia, California, USA, has the longest flying coaster, *Tatsu*, measuring 1.09 km (0.68 mi), as well as the **longest stand-up coaster**, *The Riddler's Revenge*, which is 1.33 km (0.82 mi) long.

Floorless roller-coaster
The Dominator at Kings Dominion in Doswell, Virginia, USA, continues for 1.28 km (0.79 mi).

Wooden roller-coaster
The 2.28-km (1.40-mi) *Beast*, at Kings Island in Ohio, USA, lasts for 3 min 40 sec.

Track records: coasters identified

In addition to the typical "sit down" coaster (which you ride above the track in a seated position), look out for:
Flying: riders are strapped parallel to the track, as if flying (top left: *Tatsu*, Six Flags, Valencia, California, USA)
Fourth dimension: riders sit either side of the track, allowing seats to rotate (bottom left: *Eejanaika*, Fuji-Q, Yamanashi, Japan)
Floorless: riders are seated above the track but with their legs dangling (top right: *Griffon*, Busch Gardens, Williamsburg, Virginia, USA)
Inverted: seats are suspended under the track (bottom right: *Wicked Twister*, Cedar Point, Ohio, USA)

ℹ The deadly coaster

In 2010, Julijonas Urbonas, a student at the Royal College of Art in London, UK, drafted plans for the *Euthanasia Coaster*: a thrill ride designed to kill its passengers. This controversial coaster – thankfully just a concept – kills by subjecting riders to seven 10-*g* inversions and cutting the oxygen supply to the brain. It is, says Urbonas, "engineered to humanely – with elegance and euphoria – take the life of a human being".

Bridges & tunnels

The bridge that inspired Winnie the Pooh's **Pooh sticks** cost £30,000 to renovate

Largest ferris wheel bridge

The Tianjin Eye on the Yongle Bridge is 120 m (394 ft) high. Opened on 5 Apr 2009 in Tianjin, China, the wheel bisects the bridge and road itself. The bridge has two layers: the upper for six lanes of traffic and the lower for pedestrians and the entrance to the Eye.

Most bridges in a city

Hamburg in Germany has between 2,300 and 2,500 bridges – more than Venice, Amsterdam and London combined. The oldest is Zollenbrücke (1663). A more accurate figure is hard to find, partly because bridges are added and destroyed all the time and partly because sources disagree on how big a river, stream or channel has to be to qualify for needing a bridge.

First Leonardo da Vinci bridge to be built

Italy's master artist and inventor Leonardo da Vinci designed the Golden Horn bridge in 1502 to cross the Bosphorus in Istanbul, Turkey. It would have been the longest bridge in the world but Ottoman Empire ruler Sultan Bayezid II believed the bridge wouldn't work and it was not until 2001 that the design was realized. It was finally built as a footbridge, measuring 100 m (328 ft) long and 8 m (26 ft 3 in) wide, over the E18 motorway in Ås, Norway. It was created by artist Vebjørn Sand (NOR) with Norway's National Roads Authority.

Highest sky bridge

A double-decker bridge connects the Petronas Twin Towers in Kuala Lumpur, Malaysia, at the 41st and 42nd floors. (The buildings are distinct, rather than one structure as with other contenders.) The bridge is 170 m (558 ft) above the ground, 58 m (190 ft) long and weighs 750 tonnes (1.65 million lb).

Largest spiral bridge access

Traffic approaches the Nanpu Bridge over the Huangpu river in Shanghai, China, via a sweeping swirl of an elevated road section that minimizes the steepness of the gradient. The final section is 180 m (590 ft) in diameter, 7.5 km (4.66 mi) long, and cars complete two full rotations on the way up. The road, opened in 1991, was designed by the Shanghai Municipal Engineering Design Institute and Tongji Architectural Design and Research Institute.

Longest canal bridge

The Mittellandkanal and Elbe-Havel canals in Germany are joined by the Magdeburg Water Bridge over the Elbe river. The bridge is 918 m (3,012 ft) long and was opened on 10 Oct 2003. The 43-m-wide (142-ft) structure contains 24,000 tonnes (52.9 million lb) of steel and carries ships of up to 1,350 tonnes (2.9 million lb).

Largest double helix bridge

Taking inspiration from the structure of DNA, the Helix Bridge in Singapore was designed by Cox Architecture and Architects 61. If the steel that created its complex tubular truss was to be stretched out, it would measure 2.25 km (1.4 mi) – but the bridge still uses five times less steel than its regular box girder equivalent.

Longest bridge over water (continuous)

The Lake Pontchartrain Causeway joins Mandeville and Metairie in Louisiana, USA. It is 38.42 km (23.87 mi) long and was completed in 1969. It runs alongside a slightly shorter bridge that was opened in 1956 – each has two lanes for traffic.

FACT

The Causeway withstood the effects of Hurricane Katrina in 2005 when nearby bridges were destroyed.

Longest tunnel

The 1955 *Guinness Book of Records* suggested that the **longest road tunnel** was the 4.6-km-long Birkenhead (aka Queensway or Mersey) Tunnel joining Liverpool and Birkenhead in Merseyside, UK. It was later determined that, between 1948 and 1964, the record was, in fact, held by the Vielha Tunnel in Catalonia, Spain, at 5.23 km. (The Birkenhead Tunnel, however, was the **longest underwater tunnel** as of 1955.)

RECORD-BREAKING BRIDGES AND TUNNELS

Longest bridge: 164.80 km
Danyang–Kunshan Grand Bridge, Beijing–Shanghai High-Speed Railway, China

Longest road bridge: 54 km
Bang Na Expressway, Bang Na–Bang Pakong Highway, Thailand

Longest bridge over water (aggregate): 42.50 km
Qingdao Haiwan road bridge, Jiaozhou Bay, Shandong, China

Longest *Minecraft* tunnel: 10.001 km
Eric McCowan's (USA) tunnel created in the *Minecraft* videogame covered 10,001 blocks, equating to 10.001 km

Longest rail tunnel: 57.00 km
Gotthard Rail Tunnel, Switzerland

Longest road tunnel: 24.50 km
Lærdal Tunnel, Aurland–Lærdal, Norway

Longest multi-coloured light tunnel

The Bund Sightseeing Tunnel connects East Nanjing Road and Pudong in Shanghai, China: a distance of 646 m (2,121 ft). Tourists ride on driverless trains through the tunnel, illuminated with different coloured lights and accompanied by sound effects.

against a South Vietnamese government backed by the USA in the 1960s. At their peak, the claustrophobic, snake-and-spider-infested tunnels stretched for 250 km (150 mi), an extent of which has been preserved to be explored by tourists.

First tunnel under a navigable waterway

The Thames Tunnel was 365 m (1,300 ft) long and completed in 1843 by engineer Sir Marc Brunel (FRA) to connect Rotherhithe and Wapping in London, UK. On the opening day, 50,000 people paid a penny each to wander through the attraction and within 10 weeks one million had visited it, although it was never used for traffic. It is today part of the London rail network. The tunnel used the **first tunnelling shield**, also developed by Brunel, to act as a temporary support structure. The basic idea is still used to allow workers

First tilting bridge

The Millennium or "Winking" Bridge was opened on 28 Jun 2001 over the River Tyne in Newcastle upon Tyne, UK. The bridge rotates rather than lifts up, turning on pivots on both sides of the river. It gets its nickname from the way it mimics a (very slow) blink of an eye when opening to allow boats to pass underneath.

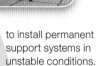

to install permanent support systems in unstable conditions.

Most expensive rail tunnel

The rail link underneath the English Channel between the UK and France was opened in 1994 at a total cost of around £12 bn ($20 bn), including train stock. The link consists of two 50-km (31-mi) rail tunnels, each 7.6 m (25 ft) in diameter, and one 4.8-m-diameter (16-ft) service tunnel that runs between them.

First curling bridge

Rather than opening up rigidly, the Rolling Bridge curls up its eight segments like a scorpion's tail to let boats pass. Thomas Heatherwick (UK) designed the pedestrian bridge and it was built in 2004 in London's Paddington Basin, UK.

Longest self-anchored suspension span bridge

While a suspension bridge is anchored in the ground, a self-anchored bridge is secured to the road deck ends. This latter form was chosen to replace the eastern span of the San Francisco–Oakland Bay Bridge, USA, which centres on Yerba Buena Island. The span is 624 m (2,047 ft) long, supported from a 160-m-high (525-ft) tower.

Largest system of military infiltration tunnels

The tunnels of Cu Chi in Ho Chi Minh City, Vietnam, became a key part of the Viet Cong insurgency fight

Longest bridge-supported airport runway

A runway extension to accommodate larger aircraft at Madeira Airport was built partially over the sea. A bridge supporting this part is 1,020 m (3,346 ft) long and 180 m (591 ft) wide, and sits on 180 pillars. It cost a total of 520 m euros (£432.75 m; $707.76 m) and was opened in Dec 2011.

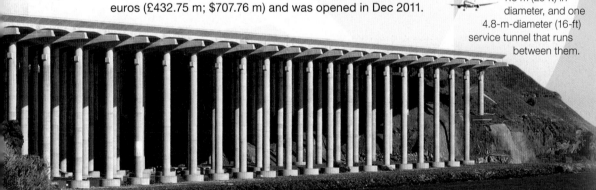

Changing channels: bridge tunnels

The **longest bridge tunnel** is the Chesapeake Bay Bridge Tunnel, which was opened to traffic on 15 Apr 1964, extending 28.40 km from the Eastern Shore region of the Virginia Peninsula to Virginia Beach, Virginia, USA. Bridges on each side give way to a tunnel, allowing ships access from the Atlantic along the Thimble Shoals and Chesapeake shipping channels. The longest bridge section is Trestle C at 7.34 km and the longest tunnel is the Thimble Shoal Channel Tunnel at 1.75 km.

FACT

The Channel Tunnel between England and France was first proposed in 1802, by French engineer Albert Mathieu-Favier. It was finally completed in 1994.

Tunnel vision

- **Deepest road tunnel:** Eiksund road tunnel, Norway, 287 m below sea level
- **Most expensive road tunnel:** Central Artery/Tunnel Project, Boston, USA, $14.6 bn (£7.3 bn)
- **Longest sewage tunnel:** Chicago TARP (Tunnels and Reservoir Plan), currently 176 km (extending to 211 km when completed in 2029)

Cars

Every year, commuters in the USA spend an average of **38 hr stuck in traffic**

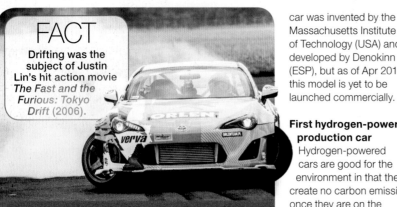

FACT

Drifting was the subject of Justin Lin's hit action movie *The Fast and the Furious: Tokyo Drift* (2006).

Fastest vehicle drift

Regular drivers might react with panic when taking a turn so fast that their back wheels swing out and their car slides into an uncontrolled drift. For others, it's a skill and a sport. Jakub Przygoński (POL) drifted at a speed of 217.97 km/h (135.44 mph) at Biała Podlaska Airport near Warsaw, Poland, on 3 Sep 2013.

Largest producer of vehicles

Toyota (JPN) ended General Motors' 77-year winning streak as the biggest maker of cars in 2008, and the two companies have traded places twice since. In 2013, Toyota sold 9.98 million vehicles across all its divisions, again ahead of General Motors (9.71 million) and just short of 10 million units – a figure as yet never reached by a manufacturer in a single year.

Best-selling two-seater sports car

The Mazda MX-5 (known as the Miata in North America) has held the record for best-selling two-seater since 1999. By the first half of 2014, it had sold over 940,000 units.

First folding car

An electric car with a chassis that folds itself up, the Hiriko Fold shrinks from a length of 2.63 m (8 ft 7 in) to 2.07 m (6 ft 9 in). Three Hirikos can park in the same space as one four-door saloon. The two-seater car was invented by the Massachusetts Institute of Technology (USA) and developed by Denokinn (ESP), but as of Apr 2014 this model is yet to be launched commercially.

First hydrogen-powered production car

Hydrogen-powered cars are good for the environment in that they create no carbon emissions once they are on the move. The Honda FCX, introduced in 2002, was the first hydrogen-powered production car. Although only a handful are currently on the road, manufacturers such as Toyota and Honda

Cheapest consumer car

The 1922 Briggs & Stratton Flyer, known as the "Red Bug" for its paint job and small size, was built by Briggs & Stratton of Wisconsin, USA, and listed at $125–150 (£28–34; today, $1,600–1,920; £1,160–1,390). Following close behind is the Nano car, made by Tata Motors of India and launched in 2009 at a cost of 100,000 rupees (£1,350; $1,900).

Most expensive car commercially available

Prices for cars in Bugatti's six-part "Legends" series range from 2.09 m euros (£1.76 m) for the "Meo Costantini" to 2.35 m euros (£1.91 m) for the "Ettore Bugatti", the final edition to be unveiled. The Legends series – based on the Veyron 16.4 Grand Sport Vitesse – is limited to just three cars per edition. Prices exclude tax and transportation.

are planning to have more affordable versions available by 2016.

Highest vehicle mileage

On 18 Sep 2013, Irvin Gordon (USA) clocked up his three-millionth mile (4.28 million km) in the 1966 Volvo P1800S that he had driven continuously for 48 years. By 1 May 2014, the retired science teacher had driven 3,039,122 mi (4.89 million km). Irv now has a brand-new XC60R AWD, and plans to "give my 1800 a bit of a break".

FACT

The 2.18-m euro (£1.77-m) "Rembrandt", right, is named after founder Ettore Bugatti's younger brother.

TOP 10 LARGEST PARADES OF...

1.	VWs (Beetle) 2,728
2.	Porsches 2,325
3.	Minis 1,450
4.	Ferraris 964
5.	Jaguars (E-Type, 1961 model) 767
6.	Mazdas (MX-5) 683
7.	Renaults 678
8.	Fords (Mustang) 620
9.	Volvos 570
10.	Hondas (Beat) 569

KEY:

x1 = 400 cars

Oldest "horseless carriage"

The Grenville Steam Carriage was a three-wheeled vehicle built in 1875. More than 45 years after featuring in our first edition as the oldest "horseless carriage" still in working order, it completed the 87-km London to Brighton Veteran Car Run of 2000 in less than 9 hr. In 2009, it was moved from Bristol to the Beaulieu National Motor Museum – and, as of Apr 2014, is still in working order. Robert Neville Grenville of Somerset, UK, designed the self-propelled vehicle, which holds four passengers and boasts a top speed of 24 km/h.

FACT

In 2010, there were an estimated 6.75 vehicles in operation for every human on Earth (see right). According to predictions made by the International Monetary Fund, by 2050 the number of cars on the road will have risen to 3 billion worldwide. CO_2 emissions from cars could contribute 8.1% to the overall figure of emissions.

Most expensive car at auction

A 1963 Ferrari 250 GTO racer was sold to a private buyer in Oct 2013 for $52 m (£32 m). The competition car was formerly owned by US collector and racer Paul Pappalardo. Only 39 of the GTO cars were made, with an original retail price of around $18,000 (£4,623; today's equivalent would be $135,000; £83,500).

Longest fuel range (standard tank)
Marko Tomac and Ivan Cvetković (both HRV) drove a Volkswagen Passat 1.6 TDI BlueMotion for 2,545.8 km (1,581.88 mi) on one tank of fuel between 27 and 30 Jun 2011 in Croatia.

Longest journey by car in a single country
Durga Charan Mishra and Jotshna Mishra (both IND) toured continuously throughout India between 23 Feb and 1 Apr 2014, clocking up 18,458 km (11,469 mi). They started and finished their epic 38-day road trip in Puri in the state of Odisha, averaging 485.7 km (301.7 mi) per day.

Most expensive veteran car
Only cars built before 1905 are classed as "veteran" – qualifying for entry in the UK's annual London to Brighton Veteran Car Run. A Rolls-Royce built in 1904 was sold for £3.52 m ($7.24 m) in the UK on 3 Dec 2007. It has the serial number 20154 and is the oldest existing Rolls-Royce.

Tightest parallel parking of two cars
On 9 Jan 2014 in the city of Jiangyin, China, Tian Linwen and Xia Hongjun (both CHN) drove into a parking space that was just 42 cm (16.5 in) longer than their two cars combined. This is the length of an A3 sheet of paper.

Fastest automated parking facility
At Volkswagen's Autostadt in Wolfsburg, Germany, cars fresh from the production line are retrieved and delivered by an automated system that travels at up to 2 m/sec (3 ft 3 in/sec). The entire parking process from the entrance of the Autostadt to the farthest parking box takes 1 min 44 sec.

Largest automated parking facility
The car park at Emirates Financial Towers in Dubai, UAE, stores up to 1,191 cars in an area of 27,606.14 m² (297,150 sq ft).

Largest production car engine (ever)

Three cars had engines of 13.5-litre-capacity (823.8-cu-in) – the Pierce-Arrow 6-66 Raceabout (1912–18, above), the Peerless 6-60 of 1912–14 and a 1918 Fageol (all USA). But big is not always better. Their power output was 49 kW (65.7 hp), roughly the same as a typical modern family car with a capacity of 1.3–2 litres (79.3–122 cu in).

Largest production car engine (current)

Chrysler's (USA) 2014 SRT Viper has an 8.39-litre (512-cu-in) V10 engine. Even Bugatti's mighty Veyron has only an 8-litre (488-cu-in) engine. The Viper can produce 477 kW (640 hp) of power, 814 Nm (600 lb/ft) of torque and accelerates from 0 to 96.5 km/h (60 mph) in 3.3 sec.

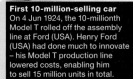

First 10-million-selling car
On 4 Jun 1924, the 10-millionth Model T rolled off the assembly line at Ford (USA). Henry Ford (USA) had done much to innovate – his Model T production line lowered costs, enabling him to sell 15 million units in total.

First 20-million-selling car
On 15 May 1981, Volkswagen's iconic Beetle – originally designed in 1938 for the Nazis as a cheap option for the German masses – hit the 20-million milestone. By the time that production ceased in 2003, around 22 million Beetles had been made.

First 30-million-selling car
In 2005, the Toyota Corolla sold its 30-millionth car, and in 2013, as reported by the manufacturer, was the **first car to sell 40 million units**, making the Corolla overall the **best-selling car**.

Driving seat: big producers

China was the **largest producer of cars** in 2013, making 18,085,213 of a total of 65,386,596 automobiles (excluding commercial vehicles). This contributes to 2013 being the **biggest year on record for car sales**, according to data from the International Organization of Motor Vehicle Manufacturers. Japan was in second place, with 8,189,323 sales, and Germany came in third with 5,439,904. According to industry experts WardsAuto, the number of vehicles on the road (including commercial traffic) hit 1 billion in 2010, rising from 250 million in 1970.

Most people crammed in...

an original Fiat 500: 14 students from ESSCA business school in Paris, France, on 2 Apr 2011.

a classic model Mini Cooper: 25 people organized by Virgin Mobile in Johannesburg, South Africa, on 2 Oct 2013.

a new model Mini: 28 people organized by Dani Maynard and the David Lloyd Divas (UK) in London, UK, on 15 Nov 2012.

a Smart car: 20 people organized by Glendale College Cheerleading Team (USA) in Los Angeles, USA, on 28 Sep 2011.

Urban transport

Japan is home to **45 of the 51 busiest train stations** in the world; almost half are in Tokyo alone

Longest driverless metro network

The two lines of the driverless Dubai Metro have a combined length of 74.69 km (46.41 mi). They were constructed by the Roads & Transport Authority in Dubai, UAE, and officially inaugurated on 9 Sep 2011.

At 52.1 km (32.3 mi) in length, the Dubai Metro Red Line is the **longest driverless metro line**. The second line, Green Line, is 22.5 km (13.9 mi) long.

The **longest metro system by total length** is the Seoul Metropolitan Subway in South Korea, with 940 km (580 mi) of routes across 17 lines as of 2013.

Largest underground train depot (metro)

Singapore's Kim Chuan Depot, which opened in 2009, measures 800 m (2,624 ft) long, 160 m (524 ft) wide and 23 m (75 ft) high, and has a volume of 2.9 million m^3 (1,057 million cu ft).

The depot took five years and 295 million Singapore dollars (£131 m; $209 m) to construct. It houses equipment and stabling

First congestion scheme

In 1975, Singapore implemented the Area Licensing Scheme (ALS). Owners of vehicles entering the Central Business District or the "Restricted Zone" had to buy a special paper licence. In 1998, the system was upgraded to the Electronic Road Pricing (ERP) programme.

Busiest underground network (current)

The Tokyo Metro served a ridership of 3.102 billion passengers in 2012. The city's underground system stretches 310 km (190 mi) altogether and caters to a metropolitan area of 35 million residents. It incorporates 13 lines and 290 stations in total.

The Moscow Metro is the **busiest underground network ever**, with 3.3 billion passenger journeys in a year at its peak, although by 1998 the figure had declined to 2.55 billion. The system has been serving the Russian capital since 1935, and incorporates 3,135 carriages covering 159 stations and 212 km (132 mi) of track.

Most cycle rickshaws in one city

There are some 500,000 cycle rickshaws in Dhaka, Bangladesh (above). In this city of 15 million people, they account for nearly 40% of all trips.

As of 2012, an estimated 120,000–160,000 autorickshaws were active in Mumbai, India (inset), the **most autorickshaws in one city**. They are used by up to 85% of residents.

Longest buses

Currently trialling in Germany is the AutoTram Extra Grand (pictured), a bi-articulated (three-section) bus 30.7 m (100 ft 9 in) long that is designed to carry 256 passengers. In China, meanwhile, the Youngman JNP6250G bus is being piloted, a 25-m-long (82-ft) vehicle that will transport 300 passengers.

Neither will beat the **longest buses ever**, though: the 32.2-m-long (105-ft 7-in) articulated DAF Super CityTrain buses in the Democratic Republic of the Congo.

MOST EXPENSIVE PUBLIC TRANSPORT SYSTEMS

Ticket to ride: the 10 most expensive cities, by cost of a single metro, bus or tram ticket

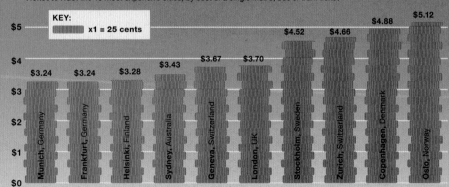

KEY: x1 = 25 cents

Munich, Germany	$3.24
Frankfurt, Germany	$3.24
Helsinki, Finland	$3.28
Sydney, Australia	$3.43
Geneva, Switzerland	$3.67
London, UK	$3.70
Stockholm, Sweden	$4.52
Zurich, Switzerland	$4.66
Copenhagen, Denmark	$4.88
Oslo, Norway	$5.12

Source: therichest.com. Figures correct as of 2012

Tram-packed

The **largest urban tram network ever** was in Argentina's capital Buenos Aires. Inaugurated in 1897, by the 1960s it had 857 km of tramways, including some underground. The lines were finally discontinued to save money and make way for buses. Today's **most extensive tram system** is more than three times smaller. Located in Melbourne, Victoria, Australia, it runs to "just" 250 km, with 487 trams, 1,763 tram stops and 30 routes.

FACT

In Japan, some metro cars are set aside for women, to provide greater personal safety.

ℹ Test drive

All of London's black-cab drivers have to pass "The Knowledge", to test their familiarity with 320 routes, across 25,000 streets, in the capital. The training can take four years to complete.

Largest ships by capacity

Although other ships can potentially carry more passengers, the vessels with the largest "standard" passenger loads are the Staten Island Ferry sister ships *Andrew J Barberi* and *Samuel I Newhouse* in New York City, USA, each of which can carry 6,000 passengers. They are 95 m (310 ft) long and 21 m (69 ft 10 in) wide, with a service speed of 16 knots (30 km/h; 19 mph).

and provides maintenance facilities for up to 70 three-car driverless trains.

Most expensive public transit commute

According to the UBS Price and Earnings Report 2012, which assessed 72 cities in 58 countries, Oslo in Norway has the most expensive transit ticket fare (based on a 10-stop bus, tram or subway trip): £3.21 ($5.12).

The same report also noted that Zurich in Switzerland offers the **most expensive taxi ride**, at £18.17 ($28.93). This calculation is based on a taxi journey over a distance of 5 km (3 mi), taken during the day within the city limits.

Farthest distance by a battery-powered tram (one charge) in 24 hours

Stadler Pankow GmbH (DEU)

ran the battery-powered Variobahn tram 18.98 km (11.79 mi) on a single charge at Velten/Hennigsdorf rail-test track near Berlin, Germany, on 25 May 2011.

The **most southerly tramway terminus** is at Brighton East in Melbourne, Victoria, Australia, on route

Largest bicycle-share programme

The Hangzhou Public Bicycle programme in Hangzhou, China, is the largest bicycle-sharing system. In 2013, its fleet included 69,750 bicycles, with 2,965 stations spread across the city. Users can easily access the system as stations are placed less than 1 km (0.6 mi) apart.

Longest intracity tram route

The 501 Queen route in Toronto, Canada, is 24.5 km (15.2 mi) long, and averages 52,000 passengers daily, 24 hr a day, seven days a week. It runs from Long Branch in the west to Neville Park in the east.

number 64 at the junction of Hawthorn Road and Nepean Highway.

The **longest tram route** is the Kusttram service that runs along the Belgian coast from Knokke in the north to Adinkerke in the south – a distance of 68 km (42 mi).

Largest bus rapid transit (BRT) system

The TransJakarta bus rapid transit system in Jakarta, Indonesia, boasts some 194 km (120 mi) of dedicated busways. It carries more than 300,000 passengers daily on 12 "corridors".

Oldest railway tunnel

British engineer Benjamin Outram (UK) built a 27-m-long (88-ft) railway tunnel at Fritchley near Crich in Derbyshire, UK, in 1793. It remained in use until 1933. Both ends were sealed in the 1960s.

As of Jan 2014, the **oldest railway workshop in continuous operation** is the Boston Lodge Works of the Ffestiniog Railway near Minffordd, UK. Wagon maintenance began there in 1838 with a blacksmith's shop, from which the current complex has grown.

Liverpool Road station in Manchester, UK, is the **oldest railway station**. It opened on 15 Sep 1830 and closed on 30 Sep 1975.

Largest rail freight yard

Bailey Yard in North Platte, Nebraska, USA, is 12.8 km (8 mi) long and covers an area of 11.5 km² (4.4 sq mi). It is operated by the Union Pacific Railroad.

Metro mania: station masters

For some, going underground provides a direct route to breaking records. Chris Solarz and Matthew Ferrisi (both USA, top left) achieved the **fastest time to travel to all New York City Subway stations** (22 hr 52 min 36 sec) from 22 to 23 Jan 2010. Tim Littlechild and Chantel Shafie (both UK; Chantel seen bottom left) recorded the **fastest time to travel to all Hong Kong metro stations** (8 hr 18 min 8 sec) on 30 Dec 2013. Geoff Marshall and Anthony Smith (both UK, right) set the **fastest time to travel to all London Underground stations** (16 hr 20 min 27 sec) on 16 Aug 2013.

Premier service

First regular passenger railway service: the Oystermouth Railway, later the Swansea and Mumbles Railway, in Swansea, UK, began on 25 Mar 1807.

First motorized taxicab service: operated by the Daimler Motorized Cab Company in Stuttgart, Germany, in 1897. The taxi was able to travel 70 km a day. The fleet was increased to seven vehicles just two years later.

Alternative transport

As of 2013, around 95.4% of the USA's energy needs are still met by **fossil fuels**

Highest cable car above ground

The Peak 2 Peak Gondola in Whistler, British Columbia, Canada, rises to 436 m (1,430 ft). The three-cable gondola lift runs for around 4.4 km (2.7 mi) and connects the peaks of the Whistler and Blackcomb mountains. The vertiginous ride also incorporates the **longest unsupported span between two cable-car towers** – a length of 3,024 m (9,921 ft).

operation today, it is now used as a 13.2-km-long (8.2-mi) tourist ride.

Longest non-stop aerial tram

Wings of Tatev, constructed in collaboration with the National Competitiveness Foundation of Armenia, is a non-stop cable-car tramway measuring 5,752 m (18,871 ft) long. It links the Tatev monastery and Halidzor, Armenia.

Highest ascent by a non-stop cable car

The Bà Nà Hills single-track cable car in Da Nang, Vietnam, opened on 29 Mar

Steepest railway gradient

The Katoomba Scenic Railway in the Blue Mountains, New South Wales, Australia, has a 52°-angle slope. The 310-m-long (1,017-ft) funicular was built in 1878, originally for mining purposes, but was converted into a tourist ride in 1945.

2013, takes 15 min to rise 1,368 m (4,488 ft) between its start and end stations.

Longest funicular

The Sierre to Crans-Montana funicular is 4.192 km (2.604 mi) long. It connects passengers to the ski resort of Crans-Montana from the Swiss city of Sierre and was built in 1911 as two separate funiculars. The two lines were merged and rebuilt as one system in 1997. The funicular travels at speeds of 8 m/sec (26 ft/sec) and completes the journey in 12 min.

Longest cable car beneath sea level

A 1,328-m-long (4,359-ft), 12-cabin cable car connects Elisha's Spring with the Mount of Temptation in Jericho, Palestine. The lower station is 219.86 m (721 ft 3 in) below sea level; the upper station is 50.29 m (164 ft 11 in) below sea level.

Longest cable car ever

A cable car of approximately 96 km (60 mi) in length was first opened in 1943 to transport ore from Kristenberg to Boliden in Sweden. Constructed in lieu of a road, owing to the shortage of rubber and gasoline during World War II, the system was only decommissioned for ore transport as late as 1987. Still in

Longest monorail

The most extensive monorail system is 74.4 km (46.2 mi) long and forms part of the Chongqing Rail Transit. The most recent stretch of line was completed in Dec 2012.

The **longest monorail line** is line 3 of the Chongqing Rail Transit system. It is 55 km (34 mi) in length.

First maglev train to enter public service

A 600-m (1,970-ft) maglev line operated between

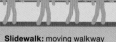

Busiest public-transit cable car

Line K of the Metrocable system in Medellín, Colombia, is the busiest cable-car line built for public transportation, with a ridership of 6,330,713 passengers in 2012. The 2-km (1.2-mi) line, opened in 2004, was designed to connect the impoverished hillside communities to the city's metro network.

For cutting-edge science, see p.202

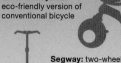

ECO TRANSPORT: THE FUTURE OF TRAVEL

The latest developments in public transport may mark the beginning of the end for fossil fuels:

Backpack helicopter: motor and rotor from helicopter strapped to the back

Zeppelin: fuel-efficient and does not require a runway

SkyTran: automated cabins, running on non-stop aerial "guideways"

Electric bicycles: eco-friendly version of conventional bicycle

Driverless pods: automated four-seater that runs on a guideway

Slidewalk: moving walkway for public pavements; allows for faster movement and helps reduce pedestrian congestion

Segway: two-wheeled, electric-powered, scooter-like vehicle

Maglev train: faster, quieter and less CO_2-hungry than conventional trains

Rise of the zeppelins

The **largest airships** were the 245-m-long, 213.9-tonne German *Hindenburg* (LZ 129) and *Graf Zeppelin II* (LZ 130). Although their heyday had passed by 1940, our 1955 edition included the **longest non-rigid airship**, the US Navy anti-submarine airship ZP2N, with a capacity of 27,400 m³ (970,000 cu ft) of helium. Interest in these eco-friendly giants revived with such designs as Germany's Zeppelin Luftschifftechnik and Worldwide Aeros (USA).

FACT

The first flight of a zeppelin took place on 2 Jul 1900 over Lake Constance in Germany.

Aerial survey

All cable-car records on this spread refer to aerial carriages that are propelled by a steel cable. The term "cable car" is also sometimes used to refer to land-based street cars.

Source: EU Infrastructure

Longest suspended monorail

Measuring 15.2 km (9.45 mi), the Chiba Urban Monorail near Tokyo, Japan, is the longest suspended monorail train system. The first 3.2-km (1.98-mi) stretch opened on 20 Mar 1979, although the line has been expanded three times since then. The monorail has 18 stations, and an average of 120 trains run on the system per day.

Birmingham International Airport and the nearby Birmingham International Interchange in West Midlands, UK, from 1984 to 1995. It was taken out of service due to the high cost of replacing worn parts and succeeded by a conventional cable-drawn shuttle system.

Fastest maglev train
A MLX01 maglev train operated by the Central Japan Railway Company and Railway Technical Research Institute attained a speed of 581 km/h (361 mph) on the Yamanashi Maglev Test Line in Yamanashi Prefecture, Japan, on 2 Dec 2003.

The **fastest maglev train in public service** links China's Shanghai International Airport and the city's financial district and reaches a speed of 431 km/h (267 mph) on each 30-km (18-mi) trip. Built by Germany's

Transrapid International, the train had its official maiden run on 31 Dec 2002.

Highest-capacity funicular
The Funicular de Montjuïc in Barcelona, Spain, can transport 16,000 people per hr (8,000 people each way). It can hold 400 people

at a time and travels at a top speed of 10 m/sec (32 ft/sec) or 36 km/h (22 mph).

First public electric railway
The earliest public electric railway opened on 12 May 1881 in Lichterfelde near Berlin, Germany. It was 2.5 km (1.5 mi) long, ran on 100-V current and carried 26 passengers at 48 km/h (30 mph).

The Volk's Electric Railway, which runs along the seafront at Brighton, UK, between the pier and the marina, is the **oldest electric railway in operation**. Designed

by Magnus Volk (UK), the railway first opened for business on 4 Aug 1883.

Largest fleet of electric taxis
Shenzhen in China is home to a fleet of 800 "e6" model electric taxis built

Shortest funicular

The Fisherman's Walk Cliff Railway in Bournemouth, UK, is 39 m (128 ft) long. Built in 1935 by borough engineer F P Dolamore, the system travels on a 1.77-m-gauge (5-ft 10-in) railway track with a 45° incline. It has transported more than 4 million passengers.

by Chinese automobile manufacturer BYD. Each taxi can travel 300 km (185 mi) on one charge. The fleet's total mileage is estimated to have now exceeded 100 million km (62 million mi).

First "duck" tour

"Ducks" are amphibious vehicles widely used in sightseeing tours. The first ever duck tour company was established in 1946 by Mel Flath and Bob Unger (both USA) in Wisconsin Dells, Wisconsin, USA. The original company has changed ownership since then, and today operates under the name Original Wisconsin Ducks. Flath's family also owns another duck tour company, bearing the name Dells Army Ducks.

Who's driving this? Driverless cars

For several years now, Google has been trialling driverless cars (below), controlled by on-board computers that also keep track of the cars' locations. A qualified driver would still be required to sit at the wheel – but only to take over in emergencies. To date, Google's autonomous automobiles have racked up more than 300,000 km on the road without any major incidents, and the company claims that they could be safer than human drivers. Above left: children peer inside a self-driving car at Google's HQ in California, USA. Below left: a street as interpreted by a driverless car.

Glossary

Funicular: a cable railway, enabling travel on gradients too steep for conventional trains. The word is derived from the Latin *funiculus*, meaning "rope" or "cord".

Maglev: an abbreviation of "magnetic levitation". Maglev vehicles are propelled by magnets – supported by a magnetic field that runs around the train tracks – rather than wheels.

○ ○ ○

Wacky wheels

Wheels were already being used for transport **5,500 years ago**, but not like this!

FACT

Matt smashed his own record for this feat – a mere 73.61 km/h – which he had set during the previous month.

Fastest motorized shopping trolley

Bringing a whole new meaning to the words "fast food", Matt McKeown (UK) reached 113.2 km/h (70.4 mph) in a shopping trolley at Elvington Airfield in North Yorkshire, UK, on 18 Aug 2013.

Fastest toilet

The *Bog Standard* consists of a motorcycle and sidecar hidden under a bathroom set comprising a Victorian-style throne toilet, bathtub, sink and laundry bin. Created by Edd China (UK), this mobile restroom can reach a speed of 68 km/h (42.25 mph).

A past master in mobile furniture, Edd has also made the **fastest garden shed** (94 km/h; 58 mph), **bed** (111 km/h; 69 mph) and **office** (140 km/h; 87 mph)!

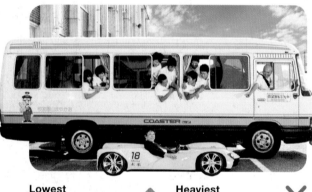

Lowest roadworthy car

The *Mirai* car measures just 45.2 cm (1 ft 5 in) from the ground to its highest part. Students and teachers of the Automobile Engineering Course of Okayama Sanyo High School in Asakuchi, Japan, unveiled it on 15 Nov 2010. "Mirai" means "future" in Japanese.

Heaviest rideable tricycle

Wouter van den Bosch (NLD) has constructed a tricycle that's truly off the scale, weighing in at a colossal 750 kg (1,650 lb). Wouter took his heavyweight creation for a ride in Arnhem, Netherlands, in May 2010.

Smallest caravan

The QTvan is just 2.39 m (7 ft 10 in) long, 1.53 m (5 ft) high and 79 cm (2 ft 7 in) wide. It was manufactured by the Environmental Transport Association (UK) and measured in Aylesbury, UK, on 5 Jun 2013. Below, designer Yannick Read (UK) shows off his compact creation.

Smallest roadworthy car

The ideal complement for the smallest caravan, this diminutive car measures 63.5 cm (2 ft 1 in) high, 65.4 cm (2 ft 1.75 in) wide and 1.26 m (4 ft 1.75 in) long. It was made by Austin Coulson (USA) and measured in Carrollton, Texas, USA, on 7 Sep 2012.

Largest monster truck

Bigfoot 5 is 4.7 m (15 ft 6 in) tall with 3-m-high (10-ft) tyres and weighs in at more than 17 tonnes (38,000 lb). It is one of a fleet of 17 Bigfoot trucks created by Bob Chandler (USA) and was built in 1986. Permanently parked in St Louis, Missouri, USA, *Bigfoot 5* makes occasional exhibition appearances at local shows.

Tallest limousine car

Gary and Shirley Duval (both AUS) have made a lofty limo that measures 3.33 m (10 ft 11 in) tall. The record-breaking car has an eight-wheel independent suspension system and sits on eight monster truck tyres. It has eight-wheel steering, two engines and took a little over 4,000 hours (166 days) to complete.

FACT

The Hornster was built to highlight the dangers cyclists face on busy roads. It's louder than a clap of thunder!

Loudest bicycle horn

Not content simply with creating the **smallest caravan** (left), the Environmental Transport Association has developed a bicycle horn capable of emitting a honk measuring 136.2 dB(A) (decibels) from a distance of 2.5 m (8 ft 2 in). *The Hornster* uses a modified freight train horn powered by a scuba-diving tank and was demonstrated by Yannick Read on 13 Feb 2013 in Weybridge, Surrey, UK.

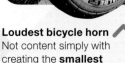

Longest golf cart

From bumper to bumper, the longest golf cart stretches an impressive 9.62 m (31 ft 6 in) and was created by Mike's Golf Carts (USA). The cart was measured in Perry, Georgia, USA, on 30 May 2013.

 For wild wheel skills, flip to p.114

Military hardware

On average, there are **88.8 firearms per 100 people** in the USA

First 3D-printed pistol

In 2013, Solid Concepts, based in Austin, Texas, USA, produced a 3D-printed gun using laser-sintering – a process that creates objects from powders, in this case metal powders. The gun is a replica of the 1911 Browning pistol and has fired 50 rounds successfully. The purpose of the project was to demonstrate that 3D metal printing provides strong, reliable and accurate products.

ON LAND

First javelin
A study published by the journal *PLOS ONE* on 13 Nov 2013 dated the use of projectile weapons akin to javelins to more than 279,000 years ago. An examination of fossils indicated that pointed stone artefacts were used on throwing weapons. The stone-tipped weapons were found at Gademotta in Ethiopia, suggesting that eastern Africa was a source of more modern culture and biology than previously thought. The weapons ultimately allowed humans to leave Africa and out-compete Neanderthals.

First hand grenades
Grenades appeared in the Eastern Roman (Byzantine) Empire in *c.* AD 741, when soldiers realized that Greek fire – a buoyant incendiary weapon – could also be thrown at the enemy in stone, ceramic or glass containers. The use of grenades spread, with evidence found in a Chinese military writing from 1044, *Wujing Zongyao* (*Compilation of Military Classics*).

IN THE AIR

First air-to-air refuelling by hose
On 27 Jun 1923, at Rockwell Field in San Diego, California, USA, a successful refuelling of one aircraft from another

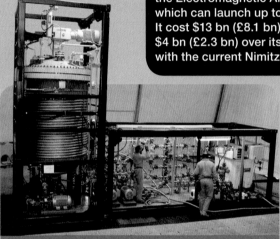

Newest deployable chemical weapon destroyer

The US Defense Threat Reduction Agency commissioned a mobile unit that can destroy chemical weapons, following Syria's agreement to surrender them. The Field Deployable Hydrolysis System works by splitting chemical weapon molecules into small fragments that can then be disposed of like normal hazardous waste.

Most expensive supercarrier

The USS *Gerald R Ford*, a 332-m-long (1,092-ft) carrier, is scheduled for service in 2016. It has capacity for 75 fighter and strike aircraft, and comes equipped with a new type of catapult – the Electromagnetic Aircraft Launch System – which can launch up to 220 air strikes a day. It cost $13 bn (£8.1 bn) to build, but will save $4 bn (£2.3 bn) over its lifetime compared with the current Nimitz-class carriers.

took place. An Airco DH.4B passed 284 litres (75 gal) of gasoline through a hose to a craft of the same type.

First manned missile
In 1944, during World War II, German V1 missiles were found to lack accuracy. This led the German Research Institute for Sailplane Flight to design a manned missile. The Fieseler Fi 103R-4 Reichenberg could be guided to its target by a pilot, who would bail out. The plan was abandoned, as getting out of a 650-km/h (400-mph) speeding missile was impossible without death or serious injury.

MILITARY MIGHT: GLOBAL FIRE POWER 2014

#	Country	Manpower	Land vehicles	Aircraft	Seacraft
1.	USA	145,212,012	39,162	13,683	473
2.	Russia	69,117,271	57,503	3,082	352
3.	China	749,610,775	23,664	2,788	520
4.	India	615,201,057	15,681	1,785	184
5.	UK	29,164,233	6,935	908	66
6.	France	28,802,096	8,672	1,203	120
7.	Germany	36,417,842	5,124	710	82
8.	Turkey	41,637,773	15,948	989	115
9.	South Korea	25,609,290	13,158	1,393	166
10.	Japan	53,608,446	4,611	1,595	131

KEY:
x1 = 30,000,000 manpower
x1 = 5,000 land vehicles
x1 = 1,000 aircraft
x1 = 100 seacraft

Source: globalfirepower.com

Submarine spotlight

Largest non-nuclear submarine: 121-m-long World War II I-400 Japanese submarines of the Sen-Toku class (1946)

Longest-range stealth mini-submarine: Torpedo SEAL, 2013, capable of transporting two divers and equipment at 4 knots (7.4 km/h) over a range of 10 nautical mi (18.5 km)

Newest class of submarine: Iran's Fateh class, 2013, a diesel-electric submarine

FACT

The total known land area occupied by US nuclear weapons bases and facilities is 40,544 km².

Glossary

SEALs: SEa, Air and Land – the US Navy's main operations force

UAS/UAV: Unmanned Aerial System/Vehicle

Most expensive military aircraft programme

By 2012, the Lockheed Martin F-35 Lightning Joint Strike Fighter had costs of $336 bn (£207 bn) – a 52.8% increase from 2001 – with some reports putting it as high as $392 bn (£242 bn), for the USA. This 50-year, multinational programme has an estimated sustainment cost for the USA of $0.85–1.5 tr (£530–927 bn) over its lifetime.

Most expensive UAV
A US General Accountability Office Report in Mar 2013 gave the Northrop Grumman Global Hawk a unit cost of $222 m (£146 m), making it the most expensive UAV yet.

IN THE SEA

First sea mine
A reference to sea mines can be found in *Huolongjing,* a Chinese military manual from the early Ming Dynasty (1368–1644). It describes the "Submarine Dragon King" – a wrought-iron mine weighted by stones with an explosive contained in an ox bladder, ignited via a joss stick enclosed in a goat's intestine.

First successful combat submarine
On 17 Feb 1864, during the American Civil War, the *H L Hunley* became the first combat submarine to sink an enemy warship when it sunk the USS *Housatonic* off Charleston in South Carolina. The 12-m-long (40-ft) *H L Hunley* – which sank minutes after engagement – was recovered in 2000 and, after restoration work, displayed in Jan 2013.

First self-propelled torpedo
In 1866, Robert Whitehead (UK) developed a new weapon in the shape of a self-propelled underwater torpedo, which was fired via compressed air. Whitehead's weapon could hit a target as far away as 640 m (2,100 ft) with an 8-kg (18-lb) charge of explosive, at a speed of 7 knots (13 km/h; 8 mph).

The **first ship sunk by a self-propelled torpedo** was *Intibah* in Jan 1878. Whitehead torpedoes launched from Russian torpedo boats sank the Turkish ship during the 1877–78 Russo-Turkish War.

First drone launch from a submerged combat submarine

On 5 Dec 2013, the XFC (eXperimental Fuel Cell) unmanned aerial system was launched from a submerged submarine. It can undertake video reconnaissance and intelligence missions, and relay its output to its command centre.

First pilotless aircraft to cross the Pacific Ocean

On 23 Apr 2001, the Northrop Grumman RQ-4A began its flight at the Edwards Air Force Base in California, USA. The unmanned aerial vehicle (UAV) flew for 22 hr non-stop across the Pacific Ocean before landing at the Royal Australian Air Force Base in Edinburgh, Adelaide, Australia.

Largest anti-mine naval exercise

On 13 May 2013, a fleet of 34 ships, 100 divers and 18 unmanned submarines began an anti-mine exercise in the Persian Gulf. The aim was to show how the strategically important Strait of Hormuz – a critical route for the world's oil supplies – could be kept open in the event that a hostile nation would seek to block it.

Longest-serving bomber

The Boeing B-52 jet bomber, which entered service with the US Air Force in 1954, is the longest-serving currently operational bomber aircraft. With 60 years of service already, it is scheduled to remain in use until 2044 and will receive a further $24.6 m (£14.9 m) of upgrades to increase its ability to carry smart weapons.

Mouse droppings: aerial assault

The snake population on the island of Guam in the Pacific grew to some 2–3 million following their arrival in freight from Australia and Papua New Guinea. The snakes threatened native fauna and cost the Guam Power Authority up to $4 m (£2.4 m) annually in repairs. The solution? The **largest aerial assault by paramice**. On 1 Dec 2013, 2,000 dead mice tied to miniature parachutes (left) were air-dropped on to Guam by US authorities. Each mouse contained 80 mg of the over-the-counter painkiller paracetamol: a fatal dose for snakes.

And finally...

• **Most common fighter aircraft (current):** US F-16 Fighting Falcon, made by US General Dynamics and Lockheed Martin: 2,281 combat aircraft (15% of global total)

• **Largest air force by number of fighter aircraft (current):** USA: 2,271 active fighters/interceptors, according to globalfirepower.com (see full table, left) ○ ○ ○

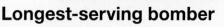

Architecture

"Skyscraper" originally referred to a triangular sail at the top of a ship's mast

Largest planetarium

The planetarium of Nagoya City Science Museum in Japan has a hemispherical dome with an internal diameter of 35 m (114 ft 10 in). The almost perfectly spherical section that houses the planetarium measures 39.2 m (129 ft) tall and is suspended 11.4 m (37 ft) above the ground.

Largest architectural practice (employees)
According to the "2013 World Architecture 100" survey by the UK's *Building Design* magazine, the largest firm of architects in terms of the number of employees is Gensler, with a 1,468-strong workforce on its books. Gensler's headquarters are in San Francisco, USA, but it also has 43 offices in 14 countries worldwide.

Logically enough, according to the "Top 300 Architecture Firms" list compiled by US magazine *Architectural Record*, the **largest firm of architects by revenue** is also Gensler, with earnings of $807 m (£499 m) in 2012.

Largest glass greenhouse

The Flower Dome greenhouse at Gardens by the Bay in Singapore covers 1.28 ha (3.16 acres) under its glass roof. Designed by architects Wilkinson Eyre, the column-free gridshell and arch shape allow for maximum sunlight and climate control. Along with the smaller Cloud Forest conservatory, it was completed in Jun 2012.

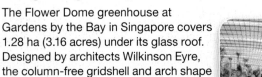

OLDEST...

Continuously inhabited city
Archaeologists have discovered settlements in Jericho, part of the Palestinian territories, that date back to 9000 BC. The city, located near the Jordan River in the West Bank, is today home to approximately 20,000 people. Its population in 8000 BC is thought to have numbered 2,000 to 3,000.

Minaret
The Great Mosque of Kairouan in Tunisia houses a minaret that was largely built in the 9th century and completed by AD 836. It is 31.5 m (103 ft 4 in) high and rests on a square base measuring 10.7 x 10.7 m (35 ft 1 in x 35 ft 1 in).

Surviving skatepark
The Albany Skate Track in Albany, Western Australia, was completed in Mar 1976. It consists of a 140-m-long (459-ft) concrete "snake run" with steeply banked sides, varying from 6 m to 8 m (19 ft 8 in–26 ft 2 in) wide. The facility cost AUS$15,000 (£9,700; $18,600).

LARGEST...

Airport passenger terminal roof
The roof of the Hajj terminal at King Abdulaziz International Airport near Jeddah, Saudi Arabia, covers 260,129 m^2 (2.8 million sq ft). Designed by Skidmore, Owings

Tallest art nouveau church

La Sagrada Família in Barcelona, Spain, was begun in 1882 under architect Francisco de Paula del Villar y Lozano and taken over in 1883 by Antoni Gaudí (both ESP). It is not expected to be completed until at least 2026. Currently 107 m (351 ft) high, the tallest of the 18 towers will reach 170 m (560 ft) when finished.

Tallest building

Developed by Emaar Properties, the 828-m-tall (2,716-ft) Burj Khalifa opened in Dubai, UAE, on 4 Jan 2010. Almost 26,000 hand-cut glass panels were used in the exterior cladding of the building, which has residential, office and hotel use.

Z Glossary

Biome: in the wild, a significant local or worldwide community defined by its climatic conditions and its prevailing plant life. Examples include desert and grassland. The biomes at the Eden Project are climatically controlled environments in which plants and crops from specific ecosystems are cultivated.

Dome grown: Eden Project

The Eden Project, near St Austell in Cornwall, UK, is the **largest greenhouse**. It comprises two giant transparent domes ("biomes"), the larger of which – the humid tropics, or rainforest biome – is 55 m tall, covers 25,390 m^2 and has a volume of 415,730 m^3. The smaller warm temperate, or Mediterranean, biome has 6,540 m^2 of floor space and a volume of 85,620 m^3. Both are made of steel frames carrying hexagons and pentagons of flourine-based plastic. The site also features an unroofed outdoor biome.

& Merrill, the Teflon-coated roof modules are supported by 45-m-high (147-ft) pylons.

Basket-shaped building
Completed in 1997, the seven-storey headquarters of the Longaberger basket company in Ohio, USA,

Largest building shaped like a musical instrument

The Piano House in Huainan, China, is around 16 m (52 ft) tall. It was designed by students of Hefei University of Technology in 2007. Visitors enter through a "violin", then proceed via an escalator that takes them into the main, piano-shaped section of the building.

resembles a giant basket and has 16,722 m² (180,000 sq ft) of floor space. With a maximum length of 63.4 m (208 ft) and a width of 43.3 m (142 ft), it is 160 times larger than Longaberger's "Medium Market Basket".

Opera house
Designed by architect Wallace K Harrison, the Metropolitan Opera House at the Lincoln Center in New York City, USA, can accommodate an audience of 3,975 – based on 3,800 seats and 175 standing-room places. It cost $45.7 m (£15.9 m) and was opened on 16 Sep 1966.

Television building
The China Central Television building in Beijing is 234 m (768 ft) tall, contains 54 floors and cost 850 million euros (£702 million) to construct. It was designed by architects Office for Metropolitan Architecture (NDL) with engineers Arup (UK), and

officially completed on 16 May 2012. The total floor space measures 473,000 m² (5,091,300 sq ft) – equivalent to 85 American football fields – and includes areas for news and programme production, TV broadcasting and parking. Beijing residents have nicknamed the building the "giant shorts" owing to its unique shape.

Tallest summit cross
Built in 1926–28 to honour the dead of World War I, Heroes' Cross (aka the Caraiman Cross) is 39.5 m (129 ft 7 in) tall with its concrete base. It sits 2,291 m (7,516 ft) up Mount Caraiman in Romania's Bucegi Mountains.

Vertical garden
Keppel Land Limited completed a 2,125.56-m² (22,879.33-sq-ft) green wall in Singapore's Ocean Financial Centre on 13 Sep 2013. It took three years to create the garden, which features 25 species of plants.

Tallest twisted tower

The Cayan Tower in Dubai, UAE, stands 307.3 m (1,008 ft) tall and features a 90° twist. Each floor has a 1.2° rotation, which creates a helix shape. It was developed by Cayan Real Estate Investment & Development and opened on 10 Jun 2013.

The **first twisted skyscraper** was the HSB Turning Torso in Malmö, Sweden (2005).

Highest building jack-up

The Main Yuzhen Palace Gate, East Palace Gate and West Palace Gate of the Ancient Building Complex in Hubei Province, China, were lifted 15 m (50 ft) – from an elevation of 160 m (524 ft) to 175 m (574 ft) – between 15 Aug 2012 and 16 Jan 2013 to avoid the risk of flooding from a water-diversion project.

ℹ️ **Kingdom Tower**

So far, work has only begun on its foundations, but when completed – possibly by 2019, and at a cost of around £726 m – the Kingdom Tower will become the first building ever to break the 1-km barrier. Its sloping exterior and triangle-shaped footprint are designed to help reduce the impact of wind on the super-tall building.

TALLEST BUILDINGS AROUND THE WORLD

- **Under construction:** Kingdom Tower, Jeddah, Saudi Arabia: **1,000 m**
- **Building:** Burj Khalifa, Dubai, UAE: **828 m**
- **Tower:** Tokyo Skytree, Japan: **634 m**
- **In North America:** One World Trade Center, New York, USA: **541.3 m**
- **Office:** Taipei 101, Chinese Taipei, China: **508 m**
- **Residence:** Princess Tower, Dubai, UAE: **413 m**
- **Hotel:** JW Marriott Marquis Hotel Dubai Towers 1 and 2, Dubai, UAE: **355 m**
- **In Oceania:** Q1, Queensland, Australia: **322.5 m**
- **In Europe:** Eurasia, Moscow, Russia: **308.9 m**
- **Twisted building:** Cayan Tower, Dubai, UAE: **307.3 m**
- **In South America:** Torre Costanera, Santiago, Chile: **300 m**
- **In Africa:** Carlton Centre, Johannesburg, South Africa: **222.5 m**

⚡ **Scraping the sky**

In 1955, the **tallest building** was the Empire State Building in New York City, USA, measuring "1,472 feet [488.6 m] high to the top of the television tower". A succession of buildings have held that coveted title since, the latest being the Burj Khalifa, which is nearly twice as tall as that 1955 record holder. The Sky City skyscraper in Changsha, China, was to top out at 10 m taller but, by 2013, work stalled on the challenging prefabricated design.

Castles

Oldest castle
The earliest recorded castle is located in the old city of Sana'a, Yemen. Known as Gomdan or Gumdan Castle, it dates from before AD 200 and is believed to have originally comprised 20 storeys.

Largest inhabited castle
The royal residence of Windsor Castle at Windsor, Berkshire, UK, is originally of 12th-century construction and takes the form of a waisted parallelogram measuring 576 x 164 m (1,890 x 540 ft). The entire site covers 53,000 m² (570,000 sq ft) – larger than seven soccer pitches – in the centre of which stands the iconic 65.5-m-tall (214-ft) Round Tower topped off with gothic-style battlements.

Largest non-palatial residence
St Emmeram Castle (or Abbey) in Regensburg, Germany, has 517 rooms and a floor area of 21,460 m² (231,000 sq ft). Originally a Benedictine monastery (founded in AD 739), it was acquired in 1812 by the Thurn und Taxis family, who built up a fortune from their exclusive control of the mail service in Bavaria over the course of 200 years. Princess Gloria von Thurn und Taxis still uses the castle as her primary residence.

Longest castle siege
The cathedral fort of Ishiyama Hongan-ji, in what is today Osaka, Japan, first came under attack from the renowned warrior Oda Nobunaga in Aug 1570, but the defending Ikkō-ikki warrior monks under Abbot Kōsa held out for a decade until Aug 1580, when the complex was finally burned to the ground. Osaka Castle was constructed on the site and continues to be a popular tourist destination.

Largest brick castle
Poland's Malbork Castle was built largely in the 13th and 14th centuries by Teutonic Order crusader knights. It encompasses a 21-ha (52-acre) site and is built almost entirely from locally made bricks of a distinctive red hue. Its grandiose Knights' Hall refectory could house up to 400 visiting knights and guests.

Northernmost castle
At a latitude of 64.2295°, Kajaani Castle in Finland is the most northerly castle. One of the smallest stone castles in Europe, it was built on a river island between 1604 and 1619 and first used as a prison. Today, it is a roofless ruin.

Largest cave castle
More than 35 m (115 ft) in height, Predjama Castle near Postojna, Slovenia, is built in the entrance to a cave system (inset). Set halfway up a 123-m-high (403-ft) cliff face, the castle dates back to at least the 13th century, and was rebuilt in a Renaissance style in 1570.

FACT
Predjama's most famous resident was a "robber baron" named Erazem. The castle's defensive advantages enabled him to withstand a siege by Austrian Habsburg troops for a whole year before a servant betrayed him.

Longest castle
Constructed mainly between c. 1255 and 1490, the Burg zu Burghausen measures 1,051 m (3,448 ft) long and is built on a ridge that runs above the town of Burghausen in Germany. It was once a residence of the dukes of Bavaria and is composed of a main inner courtyard – where the family lived – and five large outer courtyards, all of which would have been protected by portcullises, moats and drawbridges.

 Glossary

Castle: specifically, a defensively constructed residence for rulers, often with state-of-the-art military hardware. Sometimes a generic term for fortified structures.

Citadel: a fort or fortress used to defend a town or city.

Fort: a heavily defended military outpost but not always designed as a residence for royalty or aristocracy.

Palace: the non-fortified residence of a leader.

ANATOMY OF A CASTLE

- Drawbridge
- Lower bailey
- Round mural tower
- Middle bailey
- Forebuilding
- Upper bailey
- Siege engine tower
- Arsenal tower
- Watchtower
- Gateway to middle bailey
- Keep
- Gateway to upper bailey
- Moat
- Mill tower
- Curtain wall
- Rocky cliff

FACT
In all, 40 monarchs have lived in Windsor Castle, from Henry I to the present British queen, Elizabeth II.

 Narrow advantage

The term "loophole" originally referred to the narrow slit in a castle wall through which arrows could be fired.

Largest ancient castle

Prague Castle in the Czech Republic was constructed in the 9th century. It is an oblong irregular polygon with an axis of 570 m (1,870 ft) and an average transverse diameter of 128 m (420 ft), resulting in a total surface area of 7.28 ha (18 acres).

Oldest museum

The Royal Armouries museum in the Tower of London (UK) – the city's most famous castle – is the oldest museum. It first opened its doors to the public in 1660, although it was possible to view the collection by appointment for up to eight years prior to this date.

Tallest theme-park castle

The Cinderella Castle at Disney's Magic Kingdom in Florida, USA, is 57.3 m (189 ft) high. Partly based on picturesque real-life castles such as those at Neuschwanstein (Germany), Segovia (Spain) and Moszna (Poland), the "forced-perspective" design of the steel, concrete and fibre-glass structure makes it seem even taller than it is. It opened in 1971.

Largest inflatable (bouncy) castle

Designed by Dana Caspersen and William Forsythe (both USA) and produced in three weeks by Southern Inflatables, UK, the largest inflatable castle stands 12 m (39 ft) tall and is 19 m² (62 sq ft) at the base. Made from 2,725 m² (29,330 sq ft) of white-PVC-coated polyester, it takes 6 hr to fully construct and 15 min to fill with 385 m³ (13,500 cu ft) of air. Between 24 Mar and 11 May 1997, it served as an architectural

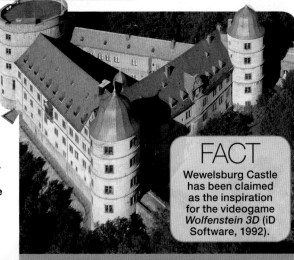

> **FACT**
> Wewelsburg Castle has been claimed as the inspiration for the videogame *Wolfenstein 3D* (iD Software, 1992).

Largest triangular castle

Wewelsburg Castle in Büren, Germany, was constructed between 1603 and 1609. The Renaissance-style structure has a total perimeter of 240 m (787 ft). Originally used by the Prince-Bishopric of Paderborn, it later became notorious as one of the centres for the Nazi SS under Heinrich Himmler.

Tallest self-built castle

The 48.75-m-tall (160-ft) stone-and-steel Bishop Castle in Colorado, USA, has been a work in progress by American welder Jim Bishop since Jun 1969. It features stained-glass windows, three towers, a grand ballroom and a sculpture of a fire-breathing dragon!

installation in Camden, London, UK. Since then, it has been used at a range of events worldwide.

A more modest inflatable, measuring 3.6 x 4.5 m (12 x 15 ft) at the base, was used for the **longest marathon on a bouncy castle by a team**. Eight bouncers from the logistics company Wincanton and the Tesco supermarket in Rugby,

Warwickshire, UK, clocked a time of 37 hr 14 sec on 30–31 Aug 2013.

Largest can sculpture

A 5.5-m-tall (18-ft) reproduction of Yoshida Castle in Toyohashi, Japan, was built from 104,840 aluminium drinks cans by Junior Chamber International in Toyohashi Park, Aichi, Japan, on 21 Sep 2013.

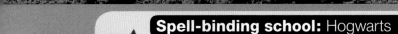

Spell-binding school: Hogwarts

One of the most instantly recognizable castles is Hogwarts School of Witchcraft and Wizardry from J K Rowling's *Harry Potter* series. The **largest model of Hogwarts castle** was made by the art department of Warner Bros (UK) in 2011. The 1:24-scale model (pictured right, with model supervisor José Granell) is 15.25 m wide and can be visited at the Warner Bros studio tour in London.
The **largest model of Hogwarts made from LEGO®** was created by Alice Finch (USA, left) in 2012; 4 m long, it used around 400,000 bricks.

Armoured division

Largest suit of armour made for an animal: adult Asian elephant suit, weighing 118 kg, in Royal Armouries museum, Leeds, UK

Most expensive suit of armour sold at auction: suit of armour made for Henri II in 1545 by Giovanni Negroli, sold for £1,925,000 on 5 May 1983, from Hever Castle collection, Kent, UK

Tallest suit of armour: 2.05 m high, dated to *c.* 1535, in the White Tower at HM Tower of London, UK

Sports architecture

A UK home valued at £70 m in 2005 boasted a squash court, bowling alley and five pools

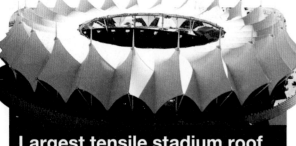

Largest tensile stadium roof

Tensile structures are held in place using tension, anchored by cables rather than bent or compressed with poles. The King Fahd International Stadium in Riyadh, Saudi Arabia, covers 47,000 m² (505,900 sq ft) and was completed in 1987 from a design by Ian Fraser Associates. Its 24 masts support a 246-m-wide (807-ft) roof shaped like Bedouin tents. The roof protects more than 67,000 spectators from the desert climate.

of Rome's temples. First begun in the 6th century BC, the Circus Maximus reached its largest form under Trajan in AD 103. It remains most famous for the chariot races that were recreated in *Ben-Hur* (USA, 1959), as well as for athletics and gladiator combat. The last race in the Circus Maximus was recorded in AD 550.

Largest marble stadium
The Panathenaic Stadium is unique in being constructed almost entirely out of white marble. It was first built in the 6th century BC in Athens, Greece, rebuilt in marble in

Largest soccer stadium

The Rungnado May Day Stadium is on an island in the middle of the Taedong River in Pyongyang, North Korea. It was inaugurated on 1 May 1989 and is also used for the Arirang Festival (inset, the 2013 event) that celebrates the country's late leaders. It has a current capacity of 150,000.

Largest ancient stadium
The Circus Maximus in Rome, Italy, could accommodate 255,000 spectators in a triple-banked structure measuring some 610 m (2,000 ft) long and 200 m (650 ft) wide. Writer Pliny the Younger said it rivalled the beauty

329 BC by Lycurgus, and has been enlarged and renovated many times since. It hosted the first modern Olympic Games in 1896.

Highest-capacity Olympic stadium
Stadium Australia was constructed to hold approximately 110,000 people for the Sydney Olympics of 2000, but more than 114,000 spectators crammed into the stadium for the closing ceremony. Also known as the ANZ Stadium, the venue is still used, although with a reduced capacity of 83,500. Four other Olympic cities have had stadia with

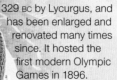

Largest floating sports platform

The Float at Marina Bay, Singapore, was completed in 2007 and has 19,960 m² (214,847 sq ft) of usable space plus a grandstand for 27,000 fans on the shore. The platform is secured by six pylons and can support the weight of 9,000 people.

Largest solar-powered stadium

The National Stadium in Kaohsiung, Chinese Taipei, is topped with 8,844 solar panels covering 14,155 m² (152,362 sq ft). They can generate 1.14 million kWh of electricity every year: 80% of the venue's needs. If it were powered by traditional power stations, 660 tonnes (1.45 million lb) of carbon dioxide would be released annually. Designed by Toyo Ito (JPN), the stadium's shape is said to be based on that of a curled dragon.

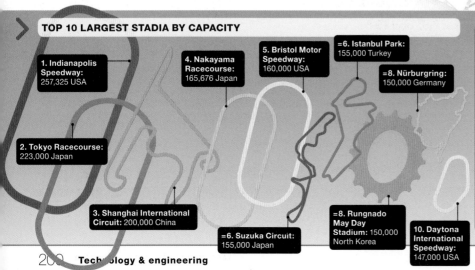

TOP 10 LARGEST STADIA BY CAPACITY

1. Indianapolis Speedway: 257,325 USA

2. Tokyo Racecourse: 223,000 Japan

3. Shanghai International Circuit: 200,000 China

4. Nakayama Racecourse: 165,676 Japan

5. Bristol Motor Speedway: 160,000 USA

=6. Istanbul Park: 155,000 Turkey

=6. Suzuka Circuit: 155,000 Japan

=6. Nürburgring: 150,000 Germany

=8. Rungnado May Day Stadium: 150,000 North Korea

10. Daytona International Speedway: 147,000 USA

ℹ️ Supersized stadia

Building for top sports comes at a cost. Portugal spent 536.5 m euros (£380 m) to host soccer's Euro 2004, with seven new stadia in a country about the size of Indiana, USA. For the 2002 soccer World Cup, Japan spent ¥526 bn (£2.7 bn) on new venues and renovations. For the Olympics, Greece's 2004 Games cost 9.4 bn euros (£6.6 bn) and China spent ¥293 bn (£29.6 bn) in 2008.

Source: World Stadiums

⚡ Largest stadium

The **largest stadium** in 1955 was the Strahov Stadium in Prague, Czechoslovakia. Completed in 1934, it could house 240,000 fans, typically watching more than 40,000 gymnasts. Today, the Strahov's grand gymnastic displays are a distant memory and the record holder is the Indianapolis Motor Speedway in Indiana, USA, with 257,325 seated. The future for Prague's striking monolith of the Communist era remains uncertain.

Largest floating golf green

To play the 14th hole of the Coeur d'Alene golf course in Idaho, USA, you have to take a boat trip. Measuring some 1,390 m² (15,000 sq ft), the green is on a computer-controlled island that can be moved between 75 m (246 ft) and 175 m (574 ft) from the shore. Golfers reach the island by an electrically powered water taxi in a course that was completed in 1991.

capacities of more than 100,000: Los Angeles, USA (101,574 in 1932); Berlin, Germany (110,000 in 1936); Melbourne, Australia (100,000 in 1956); and Moscow, Soviet Union (103,000 in 1980).

Largest sumo stadium

The Ryōgoku Kokugikan in Tokyo, Japan, has a capacity of 11,908. Spectators in the *suna-aburi-seki* ringside seats are so close to the action in the *dohyō* central ring that they are often sprayed with sand during bouts. The venue opened in Jan 1985 and holds three of the country's six official sumo tournaments.

18 curves. Riders can reach speeds as high as 135 km/h (83.9 mph).

Tallest ski-flying hill

Ski-flying is a more extreme version of ski-jumping. The ski-jump facility at Vikersundbakken in Vikersund, Norway, is partly man-made and partly modified natural hill. It reaches a dizzying height of 225 m (738 ft) – almost two-and-a-half times the height of the Statue of Liberty. Begun in 1935, Vikersundbakken had been modified into its current form by 2011. On 11 Feb of that year, Johan Remen Evensen (NOR) set the **longest competitive ski jump** on the hill, with a distance of 246.5 m (809 ft).

Newest real tennis court

The court may be new, but the game is old. Real tennis is a precursor of modern

Longest bobsled track

The 2014 Winter Olympics track at the Sliding Center Sanki in Sochi, Russia, is the most fiendish yet. It has a competition length of 1.5 km (0.93 mi) and drops 131.9 m (432 ft 8 in) at an average grade of 9.3% over its

First retractable grass pitch

The GelreDome in Arnhem, Netherlands, opened on 25 Mar 1998. Home to soccer club Vitesse Arnhem, its playing surface sits in a concrete tray that takes 5 hr to slide outside the stadium (inset) to prepare for concerts.

The **largest retractable roof** covers the Toronto Blue Jays' Rogers Center (formerly SkyDome) in Toronto, Canada. It spans 209 m (685 ft) and covers 3.2 ha (8 acres).

Longest motor-racing circuit

The longest purpose-designed circuit in use is Nürburgring in Nürburg, Germany. Built in 1927, the "Nordschleife" ("north loop") measures 20.81 km (12.93 mi) and the "Südschleife" ("south loop"), which was rebuilt in 1984, is 5.148 km (3.199 mi) long. When combined for the annual 24-hr endurance event, the track is 25.958 km (16.129 mi) long, with more than 180 corners.

tennis, played on a hard court surrounded by four walls. Fewer than 50 courts exist today; their numbers were swelled in 2012 by the Racquet Club of Chicago, Illinois, USA.

The **oldest surviving real tennis court** is at Falkland Palace in Fife,

UK. It was constructed for James V of Scotland between Apr 1539 and late 1541 and is home to the Falkland Palace Royal Tennis Club, which was founded in 1975.

Sky-high sports: top courts

You'd need serious danger money to be a ballboy on the **highest tennis court**, 211 m above the ground. The court was temporarily installed on the helipad of the Burj Al Arab hotel in Dubai, UAE, on 22 Feb 2005 as Roger Federer (CHE) and Andre Agassi (USA) played a friendly game to promote the ATP's Dubai Duty Free Men's Open. "Do you think I can knock this guy off his boat?" joked Agassi as they paused to peer over the side of the sheer drop to the shallows far below. If you were ever on the beach in Dubai and wondered where that tennis ball came from – it was from former world No.1 Andre Agassi!

Motorsports venues

First motor-racing circuit: Brooklands in Weybridge, UK, opened 17 Jun 1907

Longest Formula One circuit (all time): Pescara Circuit (used for F1 racing 1959–61), at 25.7 km

Shortest Formula One circuit (all time): Circuit de Monaco, Monte Carlo (used for F1 racing since 1929), 3 km (1929–79)

Cutting-edge science

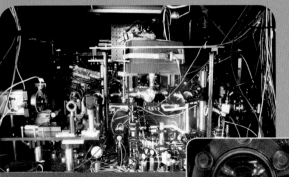

Most accurate clock

Researchers at the Joint Institute for Laboratory Astrophysics (JILA) – a project initiated by the University of Colorado and the US National Institute of Standards and Technology – have used the element strontium to create an atomic clock that will neither gain nor lose a second in 4.5 billion years. The research was announced on 22 Jan 2014. Because the SI definition of the second is based on the caesium atom, caesium clocks were previously regarded as the most accurate.

First country to mine gas hydrates

Gas hydrates, aka "flammable ice", are a solid resembling water ice. They contain methane gas trapped in a crystalline structure and occur beneath sediments on the ocean floor. In Mar 2013, Japan announced that it had successfully extracted methane gas from hydrate deposits in the Nankai Trough, 50 km (30 mi) offshore from Japan. Scientists estimate that there could be enough hydrate deposits in the Nankai Trough to meet Japan's energy needs for a decade.

First photon interaction

In Sep 2013, researchers from Harvard University and the Massachusetts Institute of Technology (both USA) completed an experiment that compared the interaction of protons to the behaviour of lightsabers, the fictional weapons used in *Star Wars*. Researchers observed an attractive force between two photons – the basic particles that form light – which interacted to form a joined, two-photon molecule. This indicated that photons could be manipulated to create a solid "blade" of light, like a lightsaber.

Highest man-made RPM

Scientists at the University of St Andrews in the UK created a tiny sphere of calcium just 4 micrometres (0.004 mm; 0.00015 in) across, around 10 times narrower than a human hair. They suspended the sphere using laser light inside a vacuum and made it spin by altering the polarity of the light. On 28 Aug 2013, the team published the results of their research, which observed the calcium sphere reaching 600 million revolutions per min (RPM) before disintegrating.

Thinnest man-made material

In Oct 2004, British and Russian scientists announced the discovery of the nanofabric graphene. With a thickness of just one single atom

Most accurate electron mass measurement

On 19 Feb 2014, the Max Planck Institute for Nuclear Physics (DEU) announced the mass of an electron measured at 0.000548579909067 of an atomic mass unit. It was measured by binding a single electron to a bare carbon nucleus in a Penning trap (above) and manipulating it with electric and magnetic fields. The result is *c.* 13 times more accurate than previous efforts.

Fastest computer

The supercomputer "Tianhe-2", developed by China's National University of Defense Technology, performs at 33.86 petaFLOPS on the Linpack benchmark (see below). The list of the most powerful supercomputers was announced on 17 Jun during the opening session of the 2013 International Supercomputing Conference.

COMPUTING EFFICIENCY

Computations per kilowatt-hour

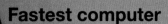

1e+16	
1e+15	Apple Macintosh
1e+14	SiCortex SC5832
1e+13	
1e+12	Dell Dimension 2400
1e+11	
1e+10	Compaq Deskpro 386/20e
1e+9	SDS 920
1e+8	Altair 8800
1e+7	
1e+6	UNIVAC III
1e+5	
1e+4	Commodore 64
1e+3	
1e+2	
1e+1	UNIVAC II
1e+0	

1955 1960 1965 1970 1975 1980 1985 1990 1995 2000 2005 2010 2015

⚡ Enormous instruments

In 1955, the **largest scientific instrument** was the Radio Telescope of the Manchester University Experimental Station in Cheshire, UK. "The filigree skeletal bowl and 180-ft [54-m] high supports weigh 1,500 tons [1,524 tonnes]." Today, the record is held by the Large Electron-Positron storage ring collider at CERN in Geneva, Switzerland, which was built to examine the smallest and most fundamental particles of matter. This huge device is a circular tube with an overall circumference of 27 km.

FACT

A supercomputer's performance is measured in FLOPS – FLoating-point Operations Per Second. A floating-point operation is the calculation of a mathematical equation, so a petaFLOP, as used to measure the fastest supercomputer (above), means 1,000,000,000,000,000 calculations per sec.

First proof of the Higgs boson

On 14 Mar 2013, it was confirmed that an experiment performed at the Large Hadron Collider (above) at CERN in Geneva, Switzerland, had revealed the existence of the Higgs boson. The confirmation of this elementary particle – known as the "God particle" – is the most important discovery in physics for decades. It strengthens the idea of the Standard Model: a unified theory about the nature of the universe that connects fundamental particles and the forces acting between them.

Thinnest transistor

A transistor is a small device that opens or closes an electrical circuit, or amplifies a signal. On 19 Feb 2012, scientists from the Centre for Quantum Computation & Communication Technology (AUS) unveiled a transistor less than 1 nanometre (0.000001 mm) high. The active element in this transistor is a single phosphorus (P) atom positioned within a silicon (Si) crystal. All elements of the device are fabricated on a single atomic plane, so the entire transistor is only one atomic layer in height. It is termed a "single atom transistor".

First earthquake detected from orbit

On 17 Mar 2009, the European Space Agency launched *GOCE*, a satellite that can map Earth's gravitational field from an orbit of 254.9 km (158.3 mi). On 11 Mar 2011, as it passed through the weak sound waves of Earth's thermosphere, the spacecraft detected the devastating earthquake that struck Japan.

of carbon, graphene can exist as a single sheet of a theoretically infinite size.

In Jan 2012, researchers from the University of California in Riverside (USA) showed that when just 10% graphene was added to other materials, a 23-fold increase in thermal conductivity was seen – the **highest increase in thermal conductivity**

by a material. These composite materials have potential for use as thermal interface materials; for example, they are used in electronic devices to avoid overheating, by absorbing the heat generated.

Highest projectile velocity

Scientists at the Naval Research Laboratory in Washington, DC, USA, have used the Nike krypton fluoride laser to propel a sphere less than 300 micrometres (12-thousandths of an inch) in size to velocities in excess of 1,000 km/s (621 mi/s). This figure is some 300 km/s (186 mi/s) faster than previous attempts.

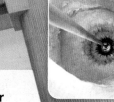

Largest neutrino detector

IceCube is a US-led international telescope designed to detect neutrinos – subatomic particles with almost no mass. Located at the Amundsen-Scott South Pole Station in Antarctica, it consists of 5,160 detectors in 86 vertical cables buried 1,450–2,450 m (4,750–8,050 ft) below sea level, where the ice is optically clear.

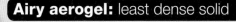

Airy aerogel: least dense solid

Professor Gao Chao and his team from the Department of Polymer Science and Engineering at Zhejiang University in China have produced graphene aerogel with a density of just 0.16 mg/cm³. The team freeze-dried solutions of carbon nanotubes and large sheets of graphene oxide, then chemically removed oxygen to leave a conductive, elastic, solid foam. Aerogel is lighter than air itself and has numerous applications, from mopping up oil spills to capturing dust from comet tails. The breakthrough was announced in *Nature* magazine on 27 Feb 2013.

Glossary

Caesium: an alkali metal element ($_{55}$Cs) that provides the basis of the SI unit of measurement for the second; one second equals 9,192,631,770 oscillations of a caesium atom with an atomic weight of 133 atomic units ($^{133}_{55}$Cs).

Carbon nanotube: an allotrope of carbon ($_8$C) in which the molecules are in the shape of a cylinder 50,000 times smaller than a human hair.

Robots & AI

In the Middle East, **robot jockeys** are replacing children in camel racing

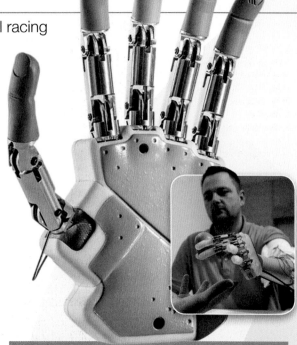

First robot trumpeter

A bipedal robot made by Toyota (JPN) in 2004 mastered the embouchure (complex coordination of mouth, lips and tongue) to play the trumpet. Fellow robots were constructed to play tuba and drums.

First public reference to robots

The word "robot" was introduced into English by Karel Čapek (CZE) in his 1921 play *R.U.R.* (*Rossum's Universal Robots*). The story features "artificial people" who have been designed to enjoy hard work. The word, suggested by the playwright's brother Josef, derives from the Czech word "*robota*", meaning slave labour.

First computer to play in the Draughts World Championship

Chinook, a computer program designed to play draughts, was developed at the University of Alberta, Canada, in 1989. In 1990, it won the right to compete in the Draughts World Championship by being rated second in the US nationals behind Marion Tinsley (USA), one of the greatest draughts players of all time. Chinook won the World Championship in 1994, following Tinsley's retirement due to ill health.

Most dexterous robot band

Z-Machines is a band created by engineers at the University of Tokyo, Japan, in 2013. As well as keyboardist Cosmo, the group consists of guitarist Mach (who boasts 78 "fingers") and drummer Ashura (who can play with 22 drumsticks). The group released their debut album,

composed by the UK electronic music artist Squarepusher, in Apr 2013.

Longest journey by an unmanned autonomous surface vehicle

On 14 Feb 2013, "Benjamin Franklin" the Wave Glider® – developed by Liquid Robotics (USA) – finished a 14,703-km (7,939-nautical mile) journey across the Pacific Ocean from San Francisco in California, USA, to Lady Musgrave Island in Queensland, Australia. It is one of four Wave Gliders; they convert wave energy into thrust and use solar energy to generate electricity for sensors, communications and navigation.

Largest planetary rover

The *Curiosity* rover landed on Mars on 6 Aug 2012 as part of NASA's Mars Science Laboratory mission. It is 3 m (9 ft) long and weighs 900 kg (1,900 lb), including 80 kg (176 lb) of scientific instruments. As of Mar 2014, the rover had travelled

First bionic hand with real-time sensory feedback

Dennis Aabo Sørensen (DNK) was the test subject for a prosthetic hand that was wired into his nerves. According to a report issued on 5 Feb 2014 by École Polytechnique Fédérale de Lausanne in Switzerland, he was able to tell how hard he was grasping and to distinguish between objects, including their shape and softness.

First self-organizing robot construction swarm

TERMES robots are shoe-sized and their design, by Harvard University, USA, was inspired by termites. As reported on 14 Feb 2014, TERMES robots are able to use blocks to construct towers, pyramids and other structures. They require no centralized command, operating as a swarm to complete the task collectively.

almost 5 km (3 mi). *Curiosity* uses an arm and "hand" to collect samples; having analyzed them, it sends the resulting data back to Earth. Scientists believe that its current location may have once been a river bed.

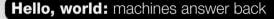

Glossary

Artificial narrow intelligence: typically focused on a narrow task, such as playing chess or fulfilling requests, as Apple's Siri does in iOS.

Artificial general intelligence: theory of human-like intelligence, including the ability to display reason, strategy, planning and make complex judgements.

Hello, world: machines answer back

In 2011, IBM's *Watson* (right) responded in real time to questions to record the **highest score by a computer on the TV game show *Jeopardy!*** (USA, 1964–present). Its $77,147 (£49,914) total beat the show's two human contestants. IBM also built *Deep Blue*, the **first computer to beat a world chess champion under regular time controls**, defeating Garry Kasparov (RUS) on 11 May 1997 (below right). Mike Dobson and David Gilday (both UK) built *CUBESTORMER 3* (left), which achieved the **fastest time to solve a Rubik's Cube by a robot**, taking just 3.253 sec on 15 Mar 2014.

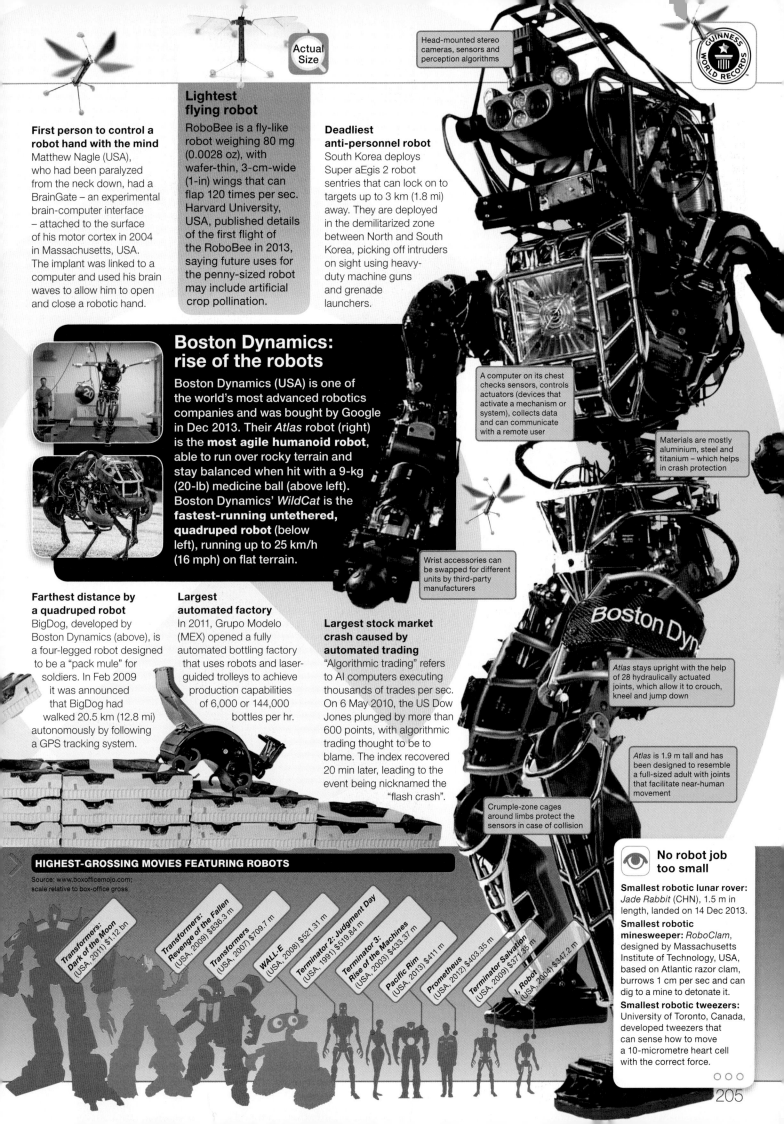

First person to control a robot hand with the mind
Matthew Nagle (USA), who had been paralyzed from the neck down, had a BrainGate – an experimental brain-computer interface – attached to the surface of his motor cortex in 2004 in Massachusetts, USA. The implant was linked to a computer and used his brain waves to allow him to open and close a robotic hand.

Lightest flying robot
RoboBee is a fly-like robot weighing 80 mg (0.0028 oz), with wafer-thin, 3-cm-wide (1-in) wings that can flap 120 times per sec. Harvard University, USA, published details of the first flight of the RoboBee in 2013, saying future uses for the penny-sized robot may include artificial crop pollination.

Deadliest anti-personnel robot
South Korea deploys Super aEgis 2 robot sentries that can lock on to targets up to 3 km (1.8 mi) away. They are deployed in the demilitarized zone between North and South Korea, picking off intruders on sight using heavy-duty machine guns and grenade launchers.

Actual Size

Head-mounted stereo cameras, sensors and perception algorithms

A computer on its chest checks sensors, controls actuators (devices that activate a mechanism or system), collects data and can communicate with a remote user

Materials are mostly aluminium, steel and titanium – which helps in crash protection

Wrist accessories can be swapped for different units by third-party manufacturers

Boston Dynamics: rise of the robots
Boston Dynamics (USA) is one of the world's most advanced robotics companies and was bought by Google in Dec 2013. Their *Atlas* robot (right) is the **most agile humanoid robot**, able to run over rocky terrain and stay balanced when hit with a 9-kg (20-lb) medicine ball (above left). Boston Dynamics' *WildCat* is the **fastest-running untethered, quadruped robot** (below left), running up to 25 km/h (16 mph) on flat terrain.

Farthest distance by a quadruped robot
BigDog, developed by Boston Dynamics (above), is a four-legged robot designed to be a "pack mule" for soldiers. In Feb 2009 it was announced that BigDog had walked 20.5 km (12.8 mi) autonomously by following a GPS tracking system.

Largest automated factory
In 2011, Grupo Modelo (MEX) opened a fully automated bottling factory that uses robots and laser-guided trolleys to achieve production capabilities of 6,000 or 144,000 bottles per hr.

Largest stock market crash caused by automated trading
"Algorithmic trading" refers to AI computers executing thousands of trades per sec. On 6 May 2010, the US Dow Jones plunged by more than 600 points, with algorithmic trading thought to be to blame. The index recovered 20 min later, leading to the event being nicknamed the "flash crash".

Atlas stays upright with the help of 28 hydraulically actuated joints, which allow it to crouch, kneel and jump down

Atlas is 1.9 m tall and has been designed to resemble a full-sized adult with joints that facilitate near-human movement

Crumple-zone cages around limbs protect the sensors in case of collision

HIGHEST-GROSSING MOVIES FEATURING ROBOTS
Source: www.boxofficemojo.com; scale relative to box-office gross

Transformers: Dark of the Moon (USA, 2011) $1.12 bn

Transformers: Revenge of the Fallen (USA, 2009) $836.3 m

Transformers (USA, 2007) $709.7 m

WALL·E (USA, 2008) $521.31 m

Terminator 2: Judgment Day (USA, 1991) $519.84 m

Terminator 3: Rise of the Machines (USA, 2003) $433.37 m

Pacific Rim (USA, 2013) $411 m

Prometheus (USA, 2012) $403.35 m

Terminator Salvation (USA, 2009) $371.35 m

I, Robot (USA, 2004) $347.2 m

No robot job too small
Smallest robotic lunar rover: *Jade Rabbit* (CHN), 1.5 m in length, landed on 14 Dec 2013.

Smallest robotic minesweeper: *RoboClam*, designed by Massachusetts Institute of Technology, USA, based on Atlantic razor clam, burrows 1 cm per sec and can dig to a mine to detonate it.

Smallest robotic tweezers: University of Toronto, Canada, developed tweezers that can sense how to move a 10-micrometre heart cell with the correct force.

Boston Dyn

Top tech

"**Gadget**": may originate from French – *gâchette* (lock tumbler) or *gagée* (tool)

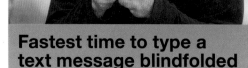

Fastest-selling portable gaming system

Apple reported opening-weekend sales of the iPhone 5c and 5s in Sep 2013 of 9 million units, breaking its own record of 5 million for the iPhone 5 in 2012 and becoming the fastest-selling device capable of playing videogames. Apple's sales were boosted by releasing two models rather than one, and for the first time debuting in China on the same day as the USA.

Highest power drawn from a fruit battery
Da Vinci Media (DEU), an educational TV channel, generated 1.21 watts by connecting 1,500 lemons together in Budapest, Hungary, on 27 Apr 2013.

Largest animated mobile phone mosaic
At the inaugural China Smart Device Games – held at the National Olympic Sports Centre in Beijing on 13 Jul 2013 – China Unicom, Sohu IT and HTC created an animated mobile phone mosaic using 400 smartphones. The devices were linked via China Unicom's WCDMA HSPA+ network; each screen showed a different video that, in combination with the others, formed a video advert.

Fastest time to type a text message blindfolded

Mark Encarnación (USA) used a smartphone to type a specified text message in 25.9 sec in Redmond, Washington, USA, on 24 Apr 2013. Without a blindfold, the **fastest time to type a text message on a smartphone** is 18.44 sec, achieved by Gaurav Sharma (USA), who was also in Redmond, on 16 Jan 2014.

Most consumer electronics recycled in 24 hours
Sims Recycling Solutions (USA) recycled electronics weighing a total of 57,308 kg (126,344 lb) at seven locations in the USA and Canada on 20 Apr 2013. The event, staged as part of Earth Day 2013, saw the company collecting unwanted electronics from locations in California, Hawaii, Illinois, Nevada, New Jersey and Ontario.

First bluetooth gloves commercially available
In Oct 2012, Italian company hi-Fun released a range of knitted and leather gloves with built-in bluetooth communication for mobile phones. Users can make mobile calls by speaking into the glove's little finger and listening via the thumb.

Largest loop-the-loop by a remote-controlled vehicle

On 15 Jun 2013, Jason Bradbury – host of *The Gadget Show* (Channel 5, UK) and pictured left with co-host Rachel Riley – guided a remote-controlled car in a 3.18-m-wide (10-ft 5-in) loop-the-loop. Other records from the show include the **heaviest machines moved using a brain-control interface** (in which cranes weighing 56.2 tonnes (123,899 lb) were used to move a car with an electromagnet in 2011, bottom left) and the **largest architectural projection-mapped game** (a game of *PAC-Man* covering 2,218.65 m² (23,881 sq ft) played in London, UK, in 2013, below right).

❌ For cutting-edge science, turn to p.202

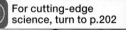

TOP 10 MOST FREQUENTLY USED SMARTPHONE APPS

Google Maps 54%	Facebook 44%	YouTube 35%	Google+ 30%	WeChat 27%

Facebook Messenger 22%	Skype 22%	Twitter 22%	WhatsApp 17%	Instagram 11%

⚡ Phone alone
When we first published in 1955, the country with the most telephones was deemed to be the USA, with approximately 50 million. We calculated that this provided 31 phones per 100 population, adding that Canada made the most calls, with an annual average of 459. By 2011, according to the International Telecommunication Union (ITU), the world had gone mobile, with 6 billion subscriptions (these were for sim cards rather than phones).

FACT
The Oxford Dictionary recognized "selfie" as 2013's word of the year, defining this as "a photograph that one has taken of oneself, typically one taken with a smartphone or webcam, and uploaded to a social media website". It beat competition from "twerk", "binge-watch", "whackadoodle" and "showrooming".

Source: GlobalWebIndex survey, Aug 2013

First 3D-printed titanium alloy bicycle frame

Empire Cycles (UK) designed a bike frame that was constructed by UK manufacturing firm Renishaw from titanium. The 3D laser melting process ensured that there was less waste, and made it easier to create a more organic form. The MX-6 Evo prototype frame of 2014 weighs 1.4 kg (3 lb), making it 33% lighter than conventional frames.

3D PRINTING

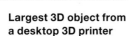

Fastest ultra-high-resolution 3D printer
Researchers have developed a printer that can make models the size of a grain of sand. The super-fast nano printer at the Vienna University of Technology in Austria uses a liquid resin, which is hardened by a laser beam. The applications for the printer's nano models in the future include biomedical technology and nanotechnology.

Largest 3D object from a desktop 3D printer
Skylar Tibbits, Marcelo Coelho (both USA), Natan Linder and Yoav Reches (both ISL) used a desktop 3D printer to create "folded" items within a print chamber measuring 12.4 x 12.4 x 16.5 cm (4.9 x 4.9 x 6.5 in). The 2013 project linked each part of the larger structure in a chain and the team created a chandelier approximately five times larger in volume than the printer's chamber.

Most 3D printers operating simultaneously
Students of Dr Jesse French (USA) in 2013 were required to make a 3D printer as part of their engineering course at LeTourneau University in Longview, Texas, USA. A total of 102 undergraduates assembled with their printers on 4 Apr 2014 and printed a special coin designed for the event.

Most money pledged for a Kickstarter 3D-printer project

As of 1 May 2014, the Micro printer by M3D had attracted pledges of $3.15 m (£1.98 m) – towards an initial goal of $50,000 (£31,300) – on the crowdsourcing website kickstarter.com. As 3D printing is becoming increasingly popular, it is used to create everything from plastic ornaments to whole houses, and the price of printers has been coming down. The Micro is aimed at the consumer market, with a cube-shaped printer chamber measuring 18.5 cm (7.3 in) on each side. It costs $299 (£187).

Most used smartphone app

A global study of smartphone owners aged 16–64 (below left) asked them to complete an online questionnaire that found 54% use Google Maps. The GlobalWebIndex data was published in Aug 2013, showing users opened the app at least once in the previous month. In second place (44%) was the Facebook mobile app.

First 3D-printed complete lower-jaw implant

In Jun 2011, an 83-year-old woman underwent surgery at the Orbis medical centre in the Netherlands, during which she was implanted with a lower jaw "printed" from titanium powder fused together using a laser. It was created by LayerWise in collaboration with scientists at Hasselt University (both BEL).

First selfie
In Oct 1839, Robert Cornelius (USA) took a self-portrait using the daguerreotype technique: a photographic process employing a polished silver plate that is afterwards exposed to mercury vapour. He sat for the shot – which typically would need 3–15 min to expose – in the back yard of his family's store in Philadelphia.

First selfie in space
On 18 Jul 1966, *Gemini 10* launched with astronauts John Young and Michael Collins (both USA). A day later, while in orbit, Collins took this picture of himself sitting in the capsule.

First selfie in open space
On 13 Nov 1966, Edwin "Buzz" Aldrin, Jr (USA) started the second of three space walks during the *Gemini 12* mission. During the 2-hr 6-min tethered walk in open space, he took photos of the visible star fields and of himself.

Need for 3D: real printing

The **first 3D-printed football cleat shoes** (left) were tailored by Nike in 2013 for NFL American footballers. Nike's Vapor Laser Talon boots have soles made by "selective laser sintering", in which lasers fuse small particles of plastic. The **first 3D-printed record** (above right) was made in 2013 by researcher Amanda Ghassaei (USA), who wrote code to transform audio files into 3D files. And Blizzident (ESP) produced the **first 3D-printed toothbrush** (right) in 2013, in which 400 bristles are mounted in a plastic mould made from scans of your mouth; you brush using a chewing motion.

Remote-control model vehicles

Fastest speed by a jet-powered aircraft: 706.97 km/h on 14 Sep 2013, by a turbine-powered 1.3-m-long plane built by Niels Herbrich (DEU).

Fastest speed by a battery-powered car: 276.74 km/h on 19 Dec 2012, by the R/C Bullet, designed, built and driven by Nic Case (USA).

Longest ramp jump by a remote-control car: 36.9 m by a Carson Specter 6S, controlled by Thomas Strobel (DEU) on 30 Jul 2011.

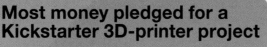

On average, a tennis game lasts for two-and-a-half hours – of which the ball is in action for just **20 min**

Most "powerful" sports star (female)

The highest-ranked female athlete in Forbes' "most powerful" list is tennis player Serena Williams (USA). The list measures fame by taking into account celebrity earnings, exposure in print and on television, the strength of a star's internet presence, public opinion and marketability.

Serena also became the **first female athlete to win $50 million [£31.9 million] in prize money** when she won the US Open at Flushing Meadows in New York, USA, on 8 Sep 2013. And on 27 Oct 2013, aged 32 years 31 days, she became the **oldest female tennis player to be ranked world No.1**.

What's more, she has enjoyed the **longest span of Grand Slam titles in the open era**, male or female. Her win over Victoria Azarenka at the US Open on 8 Sep 2013 came 13 years 362 days after her maiden Slam against Martina Hingis, in the same tournament, on 11 Sep 1999.

Contents

FACT
Serena's sister Venus shares a world record with Brenda Schultz-McCarthy (NLD) for the **fastest tennis serve (female)** – an incredible 207.6 km/h.

American football

The 2013 Super Bowl was watched on TV by **164.1 million people**

Longest NFL touchdown run by a quarterback

Terrelle Pryor of the Oakland Raiders ran for 93 yards before scoring a touchdown. The record run was set during an NFL (National Football League) game against the Pittsburgh Steelers on 27 Oct 2013.

Kansas City Chiefs and Minnesota Vikings. Andersen also scored records for the **most points** (2,544), **most successful field goals** (565) and **most attempted field goals** (709) in an NFL career.

Most consecutive games played

Jeff Feagles appeared in 352 consecutive games between 1988 and 2009 while playing for the New England Patriots, Philadelphia Eagles, Arizona Cardinals, Seattle Seahawks and New York Giants.

Most tackles in an NFL game

Luke Kuechly of the Carolina Panthers made 24 tackles in a game against the New Orleans Saints on 22 Dec 2013, tying the single-game NFL record set by David Harris of the New York Jets, playing against the Washington Redskins, on 4 Nov 2007.

NFL

Most seasons played

George Blanda played for four different teams across 26 NFL seasons. He first played in 1949 and ended his career with the Oakland Raiders in 1967–75.

Most seasons played for the same team

Jason Hanson spent 21 seasons (1992 to 2012) with the Detroit Lions.

Most games played

Between 1982 and 2007, place-kicker Morten Andersen (DNK) played in 382 games with the New Orleans Saints, Atlanta Falcons, New York Giants,

Most points by a player in a season

San Diego Chargers' LaDainian Tomlinson scored 186 points in 2006. In the same year, the running back secured the **most touchdowns in a season**, with 31.

Most points by a team in a season

Colorado's Denver Broncos scored 606 points during the 2013 season.

Most points in a game

Ernie Nevers scored 40 points for the Chicago (now Arizona) Cardinals on 28 Nov 1929. Also in 1929, Nevers racked up the **most touchdowns in an NFL game** (six), a feat matched by William "Dub" Jones in 1951 and Gale Sayers in 1965.

Most consecutive games scoring a touchdown

Two footballers managed at least one touchdown in 18 consecutive games: Lenny Moore from 1963 to 1965 and LaDainian Tomlinson in 2004–05.

Most field goals in a season

David Akers kicked 44 field goals in the 2011 season for the San Francisco 49ers. In the same year, he recorded the **most field goals attempted in a season** (52).

Most NFL career yards gained by interception return

Baltimore Ravens, Houston Texans and New York Jets star Ed Reed accumulated 1,590 interception return yards from 2002 to 2013. He also recorded the **longest interception return for a touchdown**, with 107 yards while playing for the Ravens against the Philadelphia Eagles on 23 Nov 2008. He broke his own record of 106 yards, set against the Cleveland Browns on 7 Nov 2004.

Most NFL career interception returns for touchdown

Rod Woodson scored 12 touchdowns after intercepting a pass during an NFL career played with the Pittsburgh Steelers, Baltimore Ravens and Oakland Raiders from 1987 to 2003.

Most yards rushing in a game

On 4 Nov 2007, Minnesota Vikings running back Adrian Peterson gained 296 yards rushing in a game. The 2007 season saw Peterson named NFL Offensive Rookie of the Year.

Most pass completions in a play-off game

Drew Brees completed 40 passes for the New Orleans Saints in a play-off game against the San Francisco 49ers on 14 Jan 2012.

SUPER BOWL GAME RECORDS

Most yards gained passing	407	St Louis Rams (2000)
Most yards gained rushing	280	Washington Redskins (1988)
Most yards gained by interceptions	172	Tampa Bay Buccaneers (2003)
Most rushing attempts	57	Pittsburgh Steelers (1975)
Most points	55	San Francisco 49ers (1990)
Largest margin of victory	45	San Francisco 49ers vs Denver Broncos, 55–10 (1990)
Most passes completed	34	Denver Broncos (2014)
Most first downs	31	San Francisco 49ers (1985)
Most penalties	12	Dallas Cowboys (1978)
		Carolina Panthers (2004)
Most punts	11	New York Giants (2001)
Most kick-off returns	9	Denver Broncos (1990)
		Oakland Raiders (2003)
Most turnovers	9	Buffalo Bills (1993)
Most fumbles	8	Buffalo Bills (1993)
Most touchdowns	8	San Francisco 49ers (1990)
Most punt returns	6	Washington Redskins (1983)
		Green Bay Packers (1997)
Most interceptions	5	Tampa Bay Buccaneers (2003)
Most field goals	4	Green Bay Packers (1968)
		San Francisco 49ers (1982)

Correct as of 3 Feb 2014

Most career return touchdowns

Devin Hester and Deion Sanders have achieved 19 return touchdowns each.

Most career receiving yards by a tight end

Tony Gonzalez gained 15,127 receiving yards for the Kansas City Chiefs and the Atlanta Falcons from 1997 to 2013.

SUPER BOWL

Most games played

Mike Lodish has played in six Super Bowl games: four for the Buffalo Bills in 1991–94 and two for the Denver Broncos in 1998–99.

Most points in a game

Four players have scored 18 points in a Super

Bowl game: Roger Craig in 1985, Jerry Rice twice, in 1990 and 1995, Ricky Watters in 1995 and Terrell Davis in 1998.

Most career touchdowns

Jerry Rice racked up eight touchdowns in Super Bowl games, as well as the **most career NFL touchdowns** (208) in 1985–2004.

Most career field goals

Adam Vinatieri scored seven field goals in Super Bowl games in 2001–06.

Most yards rushing in a game

During Super Bowl XXII (1988), the Washington Redskins' Timmy Smith gained 204 yards rushing.

Longest NFL field goal

Denver Broncos' Matt Prater set the NFL field goal record by kicking a 64-yard goal in a game against the Tennessee Titans on 8 Dec 2013. The previous mark of 63 yards was set by New Orleans Saints' Tom Dempsey in 1970 and had later been tied three times.

CFL

Most touchdown passes in a career

Anthony Calvillo has thrown 455 touchdown passes in his CFL (Canadian Football League) career. He played for the Las Vegas Posse and Canada's Hamilton Tiger-Cats and Montreal Alouettes from 1994 to 2013.

Highest pass completion percentage in a season

Ricky Ray completed 77.23% of his passes (234 of 303) for the Toronto Argonauts (CAN) in 2013.

Most career pass completions

From 1994 to 2013, Anthony Calvillo set many CFL records, including 5,892 pass completions and the **most pass attempts in a career** (9,437).

Most yards rushing in a Grey Cup game

The 101st CFL Grey Cup on 24 Nov 2013 saw Kory Sheets run for 197 yards while leading the Saskatchewan Roughriders (CAN).

First player to record 200 receiving yards in consecutive NFL games

Josh Gordon of the Cleveland Browns recorded 237 receiving yards on 24 Nov 2013 and then 267 receiving yards on 1 Dec 2013. It marked the first time in NFL history that a player had logged consecutive 200-yard receiving games.

 For soccer, see pp.236–39

Pig in a blanket

American footballs were originally made from natural materials, most commonly a pig's bladder wrapped in leather.

All players and teams USA unless otherwise stated.

If he could sustain his peak speed, it would take Usain Bolt **44 days** to sprint around the globe

Most IAAF Athlete of the Year trophies won

Male: Usain Bolt (JAM) has won the International Association of Athletics Federations' (IAAF) Athlete of the Year trophy five times, in 2008–09 and 2011–13.
Female: The women's record belongs to Yelena Isinbayeva (RUS) with three wins, in 2004–05 and 2008.

DIAMOND LEAGUE

Youngest meeting winner
Male: Conseslus Kipruto (KEN, b. 8 Dec 1994) won the 3,000-m steeplechase Diamond League title in 2012 aged 17 years 225 days old.
Female: Francine Niyonsaba (BDI, b. 5 May 1993) is the youngest female winner, taking the 800-m crown on 7 Sep 2012, at the age of 19 years 126 days.

Oldest meeting winner
Male: Discus-thrower Virgilijus Alekna (LTU, b. 13 Feb 1972) was 39 years 175 days old when he won the London meet in 2011.
Female: Brigitte Foster-Hylton (JAM, b. 7 Nov 1974) took the 100-m hurdles title in Doha, Qatar, aged 37 years 187 days in 2012.

Most titles won
A man and a woman have each won four Diamond Race titles. Renaud Lavillenie (FRA, above)

i League of their own

The Diamond League was established in 2010, replacing the Golden League as the premier annual athletics competition.

OLYMPICS

Most northerly Summer Games
The XV Olympiad (1952) in Helsinki, Finland, was located at 60.1° latitude and 24.6° longitude. By contrast, the 1956 Summer Games in Melbourne, Australia, were the **most southerly**, at a latitude of 37.5° and a longitude of 144.6°.
The **highest altitude Summer Games** were the XIX Games in Mexico

Highest indoors pole vault (male)

Renaud Lavillenie (FRA) achieved 6.16 m (20 ft 2.5 in) in the indoors pole vault at Pole Vault Stars in Donetsk, Ukraine, on 15 Feb 2014. The previous record of 6.15 m (20 ft 2.12 in), set by pole vault legend Sergey Bubka, had stood for almost 21 years.

City, Mexico, 2,250 m (7,380 ft) above sea level, on 12–27 Oct 1968.

Most athletics golds
Male: Paavo Nurmi (FIN) won nine athletics golds in 1920–28. Carl Lewis (USA) matched his feat between 1984 and 1996.
Female: Six women have four golds to their name, the most recent being

won the pole vault from 2010 to 2013 and Milcah Chemos Cheywa (KEN) won four 3,000-m steeplechase events between 2010 and 2013.

Sprinting hat-trick

Shelly-Ann Fraser-Pryce (JAM) became the **first woman to win three sprint golds at one World Championships** when she won the 100 m, 200 m and 4 x 100 m relay at the 2013 IAAF event on 12–18 Aug. Maurice Greene (USA) was the **first athlete** to achieve the feat, doing so at the 1999 World Championships in the same three events.

OUTDOOR TRACK EVENTS (MALE)

Event	Time	Name (Nationality)	Date
100 m	9.58	Usain Bolt (JAM)	16 Aug 2009
200 m	19.19	Usain Bolt (JAM)	20 Aug 2009
400 m	43.18	Michael Johnson (USA)	26 Aug 1999
800 m	1:40.91	David Lekuta Rudisha (KEN)	9 Aug 2012
1,000 m	2:11.96	Noah Ngeny (KEN)	5 Sep 1999
1,500 m	3:26.00	Hicham El Guerrouj (MAR)	14 Jul 1998
1 mile	3:43.13	Hicham El Guerrouj (MAR)	7 Jul 1999
2,000 m	4:44.79	Hicham El Guerrouj (MAR)	7 Sep 1999
3,000 m	7:20.67	Daniel Komen (KEN)	1 Sep 1996
5,000 m	12:37.35	Kenenisa Bekele (ETH)	31 May 2004
10,000 m	26:17.53	Kenenisa Bekele (ETH)	26 Aug 2005
20,000 m	56:26.00	Haile Gebrselassie (ETH)	27 Jun 2007
25,000 m	1:12:25.4	Moses Cheruiyot Mosop (KEN)	3 Jun 2011
30,000 m	1:26:47.4	Moses Cheruiyot Mosop (KEN)	3 Jun 2011
3,000 m steeple-chase	7:53.63	Saif Saaeed Shaheen (QAT)	3 Sep 2004
110 m hurdles	12.80	Aries Merritt (USA)	7 Sep 2012
400 m hurdles	46.78	Kevin Young (USA)	6 Aug 1992
4 x 100 m relay	36.84	Jamaica	11 Aug 2012
4 x 200 m relay	1:18.68	Santa Monica Track Club (USA)	17 Apr 1994
4 x 400 m relay	2:54.29	USA	22 Aug 1993
4 x 800 m relay	7:02.43	Kenya	25 Aug 2006
4 x 1,500 m relay	14:36.23	Kenya	4 Sep 2009

OUTDOOR FIELD EVENTS (MALE)

Event	Metres	Name (Nationality)	Date
High jump	2.45	Javier Sotomayor (CUB)	27 Jul 1993
Pole vault	6.14	Sergey Bubka (UKR)	31 Jul 1994
Long jump	8.95	Mike Powell (USA)	30 Aug 1991
Triple jump	18.29	Jonathan Edwards (UK)	7 Aug 1995
Shot put	23.12	Randy Barnes (USA)	20 May 1990
Discus	74.08	Jürgen Schult (GDR)	6 Jun 1986
Hammer	86.74	Yuriy Sedykh (USSR)	30 Aug 1986
Javelin	98.48	Jan Železný (CZE)	25 May 1996

Event	Points	Name (Nationality)	Date
Decathlon	9,039	Ashton Eaton (USA)	23 Jun 2012

Statistics correct as of 12 Mar 2014

OUTDOOR TRACK EVENTS (FEMALE)

Event	Time	Name (Nationality)	Date
100 m	10.49	Florence Griffith-Joyner (USA)	16 Jul 1988
200 m	21.34	Florence Griffith-Joyner (USA)	29 Sep 1988
400 m	47.60	Marita Koch (GDR)	6 Oct 1985
800 m	1:53.28	Jarmila Kratochvílová (TCH)	26 Jul 1983
1,000 m	2:28.98	Svetlana Masterkova (RUS)	23 Aug 1996
1,500 m	3:50.46	Yunxia Qu (CHN)	11 Sep 1993
1 mile	4:12.56	Svetlana Masterkova (RUS)	14 Aug 1996
2,000 m	5:25.36	Sonia O'Sullivan (IRL)	8 Jul 1994
3,000 m	8:06.11	Junxia Wang (CHN)	13 Sep 1993
5,000 m	14:11.15	Tirunesh Dibaba (ETH)	6 Jun 2008
10,000 m	29:31.78	Junxia Wang (CHN)	8 Sep 1993
20,000 m	1:05:26.6	Tegla Loroupe (KEN)	3 Sep 2000
25,000 m	1:27:05.9	Tegla Loroupe (KEN)	21 Sep 2002
30,000 m	1:45:50.0	Tegla Loroupe (KEN)	6 Jun 2003
3,000 m steeplechase	8:58.81	Gulnara Samitova-Galkina (RUS)	17 Aug 2008
100 m hurdles	12.21	Yordanka Donkova (BGR)	20 Aug 1988
400 m hurdles	52.34	Yuliya Pechenkina (RUS)	8 Aug 2003
4 x 100 m relay	40.82	USA	10 Aug 2012
4 x 200 m relay	1:27.46	USA "Blue"	29 Apr 2000
4 x 400 m relay	3:15.17	USSR	1 Oct 1988
4 x 800 m relay	7:50.17	USSR	5 Aug 1984
4 x 1,500 m relay	17:09.75	Australia	25 Jun 2000

OUTDOOR FIELD EVENTS (FEMALE)

Event	Metres	Name (Nationality)	Date
High jump	2.09	Stefka Kostadinova (BGR)	30 Aug 1987
Pole vault	5.06	Yelena Isinbayeva (RUS)	28 Aug 2009
Long jump	7.52	Galina Chistyakova (USSR)	11 Jun 1988
Triple jump	15.50	Inessa Kravets (UKR)	10 Aug 1995
Shot put	22.63	Natalya Lisovskaya (USSR)	7 Jun 1987
Discus	76.80	Gabriele Reinsch (GDR)	9 Jul 1988
Hammer	79.42	Betty Heidler (DEU)	21 May 2011
Javelin	72.28	Barbora Špotáková (CZE)	13 Sep 2008

Event	Points	Name (Nationality)	Date
Heptathlon	7,291	Jackie Joyner-Kersee (USA)	24 Sep 1988
Decathlon	8,358	Austra Skujytė (LTU)	15 Apr 2005

Statistics correct as of 12 Mar 2014

Sanya Richards-Ross (USA) and Allyson Felix, who added to their tallies in 2012.

PARALYMPICS

Most athletics medals
Male: Heinz Frei (CHE) competed in 14 Paralympic competitions between 1984 and 2012 – both Winter and Summer games. He won 34 medals in total, 22 of which were in athletics events.

Youngest World Championship relay medallist
Female: Dina Asher-Smith (UK, b. 4 Dec 1995) won 4 x 100-m bronze aged 17 years 247 days in 2013.
Male: Darrel Brown (TTO, b. 11 Oct 1984) was 16 years 305 days old when he won 4 x 100-m silver in 2001.

Female: Chantal Petitclerc (CAN) won 21 Paralympic athletics medals between 1992 and 2008 in track distances between 100 m and 1,500 m.
Chantal also holds the record for the **most Paralympic athletics gold medals** (14), a record she shares with male athlete Franz Nietlispach (CHE).

IAAF WORLD CHAMPIONSHIPS

Most appearances
Male: Spanish 50-km walker Jesús Ángel García competed in 11 IAAF World Championships between 1993 and 2013.
Female: Susana Feitór (POR) also appeared 11 times, contesting three different events

between 1991 and 2011: the 10,000-m walk, 10-km walk and 20-km walk.

Most gold medals
Four athletes – three men and one woman – have won eight gold medals at the World Championships. Carl Lewis (USA) was the first in 1983–91, a feat matched by Michael Johnson (USA, 1991–99), Allyson Felix (USA, 2005–11) and Usain Bolt (2009–13).

Most 200-m wins
Female: Allyson Felix won three consecutive 200-m golds, in 2005–09.
Male: Usain Bolt matched her record in 2009–13.

Most consecutive 4 x 400-m relay wins LaShawn Merritt (USA) won gold in four World Championships in a row in 2007–13.

Most points in Diamond League athletics meetings

Female: The most points scored in a Diamond League career is 94, by Valerie Adams (NZ, above) in the shot put in 2010–13. An athlete scores points by finishing in the top three at a meeting.
Male: Renaud Lavillenie (see left) has scored the most points for a man. By the end of the 2013 Diamond League season he had 86 points.

Most medals won at the IAAF World Championships

Male: The most medals accumulated by a man at the World Championships is 10, by Carl Lewis (below), who won eight gold, one silver and one bronze between 1983 and 1993. His feat was equalled by Usain Bolt (left), who won eight gold and two silver medals between 2007 and 2013.
Female: Merlene Ottey (JAM) won 14 medals – three gold, four silver and seven bronze – from 1983 to 1997.

Ball sports

A brutal Mayan ball game played 3,000 years ago may have used **severed human heads**

Highest team score in a Netball World series final

New Zealand scored the most points in a final of netball's top competition, aka Netball Fast5, when they beat Australia on 10 Nov 2013. The Ferns won by 29, with a final score of 56–27.

Largest attendance for a netball match
The Allphones Arena in Sydney, Australia, recorded an official attendance of 14,339 for the Australia vs New Zealand international game on 13 Nov 2004. Australia won 54–49.

Highest total score in a women's World Handball Championship final
On 14 Dec 2003, France and Hungary met in the World Championship final in Croatia. France won by 32 points to 29 for an aggregate score of 61.

Most World Polo Championships won
Argentina have won the World Championships four times since its inauguration in 1987 – taking the crown in 1987, 1992, 1998 and 2011.

FIELD HOCKEY

Most World Cups
Female: The Dutch women's team won the field hockey World Cup six times between 1974 and 2006.
Male: Pakistan hold the record for the most men's World Cup wins with four between 1971 and 1994.

Most international goals scored
Defender Sohail Abbas (PAK) scored 348 goals between 1 Mar 1998 and 5 Aug 2012.

Most wins of the men's African Cup for Nations
The field hockey African Cup for Nations is a qualifier for the World Cup and in some years the Olympic Games. The greatest number of wins is seven, by South Africa between 1993 and 2013.

Largest margin of victory in an Olympic match
Male: The third men's field hockey match at the 1932 Olympics in Los Angeles, California, USA, saw India beat the home team 24–1.
Female: South Africa beat the USA 7–0 at London 2012 on 6 Aug.

GAA

Most All-Ireland Hurling championships won
The GAA (Gaelic Athletic Association) sport of hurling is a fast-moving Irish stick-and-ball sport (not unlike a free-form version of hockey). Kilkenny won its top competition – contested by inter-county teams – 34 times between 1904 and 2012.

Most All-Ireland Senior Camogie championships
Camogie is hurling, but played by women. Dublin have the greatest number of All-Ireland titles with 26.

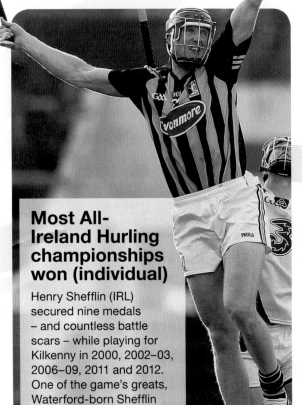

Most All-Ireland Hurling championships won (individual)

Henry Shefflin (IRL) secured nine medals – and countless battle scars – while playing for Kilkenny in 2000, 2002–03, 2006–09, 2011 and 2012. One of the game's greats, Waterford-born Shefflin (nicknamed "King Henry") is a centre-forward and works as a bank official when not winning trophies.

Most All-Ireland Gaelic Football championships
Gaelic football is roughly a cross between rugby and soccer. Kerry have won 36 championships – more than any other side.

KORFBALL

Highest score in a mixed World Championship final
Korfball is a mixed-gender sport similar to netball and basketball. The final on 5 Nov 2011 saw the Netherlands score 32 points against Belgium in Shaoxing, China.

Most Europa Cup titles
Dutch team PKC won the Europa Cup seven times, in 1985, 1990, 1999–2000, 2002, 2006 and 2014.
The Dutch national team have the **most World Games titles** (8) having won

Largest winning margin in a men's World Handball Championship final

The biggest score difference in an International Handball Federation men's World Championship final is 16 goals. It was achieved by Spain, who beat Denmark 35–19 in the 2013 final at the Palau Sant Jordi stadium in Barcelona, Spain, on 27 Jan. Pictured is pivot Julen Aguinagalde (ESP, left) vying with Denmark's left-back Mikkel Hansen.

FACT
A type of handball was played by the ancient Greeks in Homer's *Odyssey*, using a ball made of purple wool.

Most women's Volleyball World Grand Champions Cups

Brazil became the first women's team to win the FIVB World Grand Champions Cup twice when they triumphed in Tokyo, Japan, on 17 Nov 2013. The first five editions were won by different countries; Brazil had previously won it in 2005.

every korfball tournament at the World Games between 1985 and 2013.

LACROSSE

Most men's World Championship titles
Between 1967 and 2010, the men's USA team won nine World Lacrosse Championship titles. The USA also hold the record

Most points scored in a lacrosse season

The highest points tally accumulated in a single Major League Lacrosse season is 72, by Paul Rabil (USA) while playing for the Boston Cannons in the 2012 season.

for **most women's Lacrosse World Cup titles**, with seven golds between 1982 and 2013.

Fastest shot
Mike Sawyer (USA) recorded 183 km/h (114 mph) in Charlotte, North Carolina, USA, on 13 Jul 2013.

VOLLEYBALL

Most men's FIVB Volleyball World League titles
The Fédération Internationale de Volleyball World League is an annual event in which teams compete in pools before the best sides progress to the final round. The most men's World League wins is nine, by Brazil in 1993, 2001, 2003–07 and 2009–10.

Most FIVB Volleyball World League participants (men)
In 2013, 18 countries from four continents took part in the FIVB Volleyball World League. Russia were the eventual winners, seeing off Brazil 3–0 in the final.

Most appearances by a pair in men's FIVB beach volleyball events
Norwegian duo Vegard Høidalen and Jørre Kjemperud recorded

135 appearances in FIVB beach volleyball events between 1987 and 2010.

FACT

In 1363, hockey was banned in England by King Edward III, along with soccer and other "idle games".

Most goals by an individual in the Euro Hockey League

The top scorer in the Euro Hockey League (field hockey's top competition) is Jeroen Hertzberger (NLD). The striker notched up 32 goals for HC Rotterdam between 27 Oct 2007 and 25 Oct 2013.

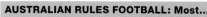

AUSTRALIAN RULES FOOTBALL: Most...		
Career games	426	Michael Tuck (1972–91)
Consecutive games	244	Jim Stynes (1987–98)
Career goals	1,360	Tony Lockett (1983–2002)
Goals in a season	150	Bob Pratt (1934)
		Peter Hudson (1971)
Goals in a game	18	Fred Fanning (1947)
CANADIAN FOOTBALL: Most...		
Career games	408	Lui Passaglia (1976–2000)
Consecutive games	353	Bob Cameron (1980–2000)
Career touchdowns	147	Milt Stegall (1992–2008)
Touchdowns (season)	23	Milt Stegall (2002)
Touchdowns (game)	6	Eddie James (1932)
		Bob McNamara (1956)

Most tournament titles in women's beach volleyball

Kerri Walsh Jennings (USA) has the most tournament wins with 113. This total comprises 67 domestic and 46 international wins from May 2001 to 28 Oct 2013. Walsh Jennings has won 113 (60%) of the 189 tournaments she has entered, most of which were alongside Misty May-Treanor (USA), whose record she broke on 28 Oct 2013.

Baseball

Most home runs in a career by a designated hitter

David Ortiz (DOM) has hit 381 career home runs – a Major League Baseball (MLB) record for a designated hitter – from an overall total of 431 home runs, playing for the Minnesota Twins and the Boston Red Sox since 1997. His 47 home runs for the Red Sox in 2006 represent the **most home runs by a designated hitter in a season**. His overall home run total was 54.

Most grand-slam home runs in a MLB career

A grand-slam home run is a homer hit with batters on all the bases. Since 1994, Alex Rodriguez has hit 24 of them for the Seattle Mariners, Texas Rangers and New York Yankees.

MOST GAMES...

Finished in a career
Playing for the New York Yankees between 1995 and 2013, Mariano Rivera (PAN) was the last pitcher for his team in 952 games. With the Yankees, he also recorded the **most games pitched with one team**: 1,115.

Won consecutively by a pitcher
Masahiro Tanaka (JPN) won 30 successive games pitching for Japan's Tohoku Rakuten Golden Eagles from 26 Aug 2012 to 27 Oct 2013. Tanaka also recorded the **most consecutive baseball games won by a pitcher during regular-season play** (28), again for the Tohoku Rakuten Golden Eagles, from 26 Aug 2012 to 8 Oct 2013. For the same team, Tanaka set the **most consecutive baseball games won by a pitcher in a season** (24), from 2 Apr to 8 Oct 2013.

Won consecutively by a pitcher in the MLB
Roger Clemens (USA) won 20 consecutive games for the Toronto Blue Jays and New York Yankees from 3 Jun 1998 to 1 Jun 1999.

Most strikeouts by a pitching staff in a season

Detroit Tigers pitchers struck out 1,428 batters during the 2013 season. Their achievement surpasses the previous record of 1,404, by the Chicago Cubs' pitching staff in 2003.

MOST HOME RUNS...

By a catcher
Mike Piazza (USA) hit 396 home runs (with an overall total of 427) while playing for the Los Angeles Dodgers, Florida Marlins, New York Mets, San Diego Padres and Oakland Athletics from 1992 to 2007.

By a switch hitter
Playing for the New York Yankees from 1951 to 1968, Mickey Mantle (USA) hit 536 home runs.

Most combined wins and saves
Andy Pettitte (USA) and Mariano Rivera (PAN) combined for a win and a save 72 times while pitching for the New York Yankees from 1996 to 2013.

Oldest player to hit a walk-off home run
A walk-off home run is a game-ending homer on the final pitch of the game that results in a victory for the home team. At 42 years 202 days old, Jason Giambi (USA, b. 8 Jan 1971) is the oldest player in MLB history to perform such a feat. Giambi accomplished the record with a pinch-hit homer in the ninth innings to defeat the Chicago White Sox on 29 Jul 2013.

Most doubles hit in a season
Earl Webb (USA) hit 67 doubles playing for the Boston Red Sox

in 1931. The **most triples hit in a season by an individual player** is 36, by "Chief" Wilson (USA) for the Pittsburgh Pirates in 1912.

Youngest player to hit 30 home runs and steal 30 bases in a season

At the age of 21 years 53 days, Mike Trout (USA, b. 7 Aug 1991, left) became the youngest MLB player ever to hit 30 or more home runs and steal 30 or more bases within just one season. He accomplished this feat while playing for the Los Angeles Angels of Anaheim in 2013. Before Trout, the youngest person to do this had been 22-year-old Alex Rodriguez, while playing for the Seattle Mariners in 1998.

Most consecutive baseball crowd sell-outs

The longest home sell-out streak in major pro sports history (i.e., Major League Baseball, the National Basketball Association, the National Football League and the National Hockey League) lasted 820 games. The Boston Red Sox set it with every home game at Fenway Park in Boston, USA, from 15 May 2003 to 10 Apr 2013.

By a second baseman
Jeff Kent (USA) scored 351 home runs as a second baseman (with an overall total of 377) with the Toronto Blue Jays, New York Mets, Cleveland Indians, San Francisco Giants, Houston Astros and LA Dodgers from 1992 to 2008.

The **most home runs in one season hit by a third baseman** stands at 52 (with an overall total that season of 54), scored by Alex Rodriguez (USA) for the New York Yankees in 2007.

First father-and-son home runs in sequential at bats

Ken Griffey and his son Ken, Jr (USA) hit back-to-back home runs for the Seattle Mariners on 14 Sep 1990. They also became the **first father-son duo to play on the same team at the same time**, on 31 Aug 1990.

MOST STRIKEOUTS...

By a batter in a post-season
Alfonso Soriano (DOM) struck out 26 times in 17 games while playing for the New York Yankees in the 2003 post-season.

By a pitching staff in a post-season series
Detroit Tigers pitchers struck out 73 Boston Red Sox batters over the course of the six-game American League Championship Series in 2013.

By a batter in a season
The MLB record for most strikeouts by a batter in a season is 223, by Mark Reynolds (USA) for the Arizona Diamondbacks in 2009. In doing so, he surpassed his own mark of 204, established in 2008.

By a pitcher in a career
Nolan Ryan (USA) recorded 5,714 strikeouts while playing for the New York Mets, California Angels, Houston Astros and Texas Rangers from 1966 to 1993.

By a team in a season
Houston Astros (USA) batters struck out 1,535 times during the 2013 season, surpassing the previous mark of 1,529 by the Arizona Diamondbacks in 2010.

By batters in a post-season (team)
Boston Red Sox (USA) batters struck out 165 times in 16 play-off games during the 2013 post-season.

Across all teams in a season
Major league batters struck out 36,710 times in the 2013 regular season.

First siblings to hit home runs in successive at bats

On 23 Apr 2013, B J Upton and his brother Justin (USA, above) struck back-to-back home runs for the Atlanta Braves against the Colorado Rockies, becoming only the second pair of siblings to do so. The first were Lloyd and Paul Waner (USA) of the Pittsburgh Pirates, who hit successive homers on 15 Sep 1938. The Uptons' feat marked the 27th time in MLB history that brothers had homered in the same game.

Most saves in a career

The MLB record for most career saves is 652, achieved by Mariano "Sandman" Rivera (PAN) playing for 19 seasons with the New York Yankees from 1995 – when he made his MLB debut – to his retirement in 2013. New York mayor Michael Bloomberg declared 22 Sep 2013 "Mariano Rivera Day" in his honour.

The last 42 in history
Rivera was the last baseball player to wear a number 42 shirt in baseball history. The shirt was retired across the major leagues on 15 Apr 1997, in memory of baseball legend Jackie Robinson of MLB's Brooklyn Dodgers.

MAJOR LEAGUE BASEBALL (MLB) WORLD SERIES RECORDS

Team		
Most titles (first awarded in 1903)	27	New York Yankees
Most consecutive titles	5	New York Yankees, 1949–53
Largest cumulative attendance	420,784	Six games between Los Angeles Dodgers and Chicago White Sox, 1–8 Oct 1959; Dodgers won 4–2
Individual		
Most home runs, one series	5	Chase Utley (USA) of Philadelphia Phillies, 2009 World Series against New York Yankees
		"Reggie" Jackson (USA) of New York Yankees, 1977 World Series against Los Angeles Dodgers
Most games pitched	24	Mariano Rivera (PAN) of New York Yankees, 1996, 1998–2001, 2003, 2009
Most MVP (Most Valuable Player) awards	2	Sanford "Sandy" Koufax (USA), 1963, 1965
		Robert "Bob" Gibson (USA), 1964, 1967
		"Reggie" Jackson (USA), 1973, 1977

Statistics correct as of the end of the 2013 season

Basketball

The late "Chick" Hearn is credited with coining the phrase **"slam dunk"**

Most games in an NBA career

Robert Parish played 1,611 NBA (National Basketball Association) regular-season games from 1976 to 1997. His 21-season career saw him play for the Golden State Warriors (1976–80), Boston Celtics (1980–94), Charlotte Hornets (1994–96) and Chicago Bulls (1996–97).

rebounds aged just 27 years 130 days old. He took the record while playing for the Los Angeles Lakers in a game against the Houston Rockets on 17 Apr 2013.

Oldest player to record 20 rebounds in a game

On 2 Mar 2007, at the age of 40 years 251 days, Dikembe Mutombo (COD, b. 25 Jun 1966) of the Houston Rockets became the oldest player in NBA history to get more than 20 rebounds in a game, with 22.

Most free throws attempted in a game

Dwight Howard equalled his own record of 39 while playing for the Los Angeles Lakers on 12 Mar 2013.

Most free throws in a WNBA career

As of 12 Feb 2014, Tamika Catchings had made 1,709 free throws in Women's National Basketball Association (WNBA) games. Catchings – who has played for the Indiana Fever since 2002 – also holds the record for **most steals in a WNBA career,** with 930.

NBA

Most career minutes

During Kareem Abdul-Jabbar's 20-year NBA pro-career, he spent 57,446 min on court for the Milwaukee Bucks and the Los Angeles Lakers (1969–89) – that's almost 40 days!

First players to win an NBA and Olympic title in one year

In 1992, Michael Jordan and Scottie Pippen won the NBA finals playing with the Chicago Bulls, then won an Olympic basketball gold as part of the USA team.

Most consecutive games played

A C Green played in 1,192 consecutive games for the Los Angeles Lakers, Phoenix Suns, Dallas Mavericks and Miami Heat from 19 Nov 1986 to 18 Apr 2001.

Youngest player to reach 9,000 rebounds

Dwight Howard (b. 8 Dec 1985) had recorded 9,000

FACT

The NBA three-point line is 7.23 m from the middle of the basket, while the WNBA line is 6.75 m from the top of the key.

Most three-pointers attempted by a team in an NBA season

The New York Knicks attempted 2,371 three-point field goals during the 2012/13 season, 891 of which were successful – the **most three-pointers scored in a season**. The Knicks also hold the record for the **longest post-season losing streak**, with 13 consecutive playoff games lost from 2001 to 2012.

Most consecutive games scoring a three-pointer

Kyle Korver's run of scoring a three-pointer per game hit 127, ending on 5 Mar 2014. It began on 4 Nov 2012, and beat Dana Barros' 89-game record on 6 Dec 2013.

Most three-pointers in a game

Kobe Bryant (Los Angeles Lakers) and Donyell Marshall (Toronto Raptors) each scored 12 three-pointers, on 7 Jan 2003 and 13 Mar 2005 respectively.

Most wins of Defensive Player of the Year

Two players have been named NBA Defensive Player of the Year four times, as of the end of the 2014 season. Dikembe Mutombo (COD) won for the Denver Nuggets, Atlanta Hawks and Philadelphia 76ers between 1994 and 2001, and Ben Wallace (above left) was awarded the title for the Detroit Pistons between 2001 and 2006.

Most three-pointers in a season

Stephen Curry accumulated 272 three-point field goals while playing for the Golden State Warriors during the 2012–13 season, surpassing the 269 recorded by Ray Allen in 2005–06.

As of 16 Apr 2014, Allen still holds the record for the **most three-point field goals in a career**, with 2,973 sunk since 1996. Allen joined Miami Heat in 2012.

Most three-pointers in an NBA Finals

Danny Green scored 27 three-point field goals in the 2013 NBA Finals. Green was playing for the San Antonio Spurs against Miami Heat in the Finals, which lasted seven games. He beat Ray Allen's 22 with the Boston Celtics in 2008.

NBA & WNBA – CAREER RECORDS

Individual	NBA		WNBA	
Most points	Kareem Abdul-Jabbar (1969–89)	38,387	Tina Thompson (1997–present)	7,488
Most rebounds	Wilt Chamberlain (1959–73)	23,924	Lisa Leslie (1997–2009)	3,307
Most field goals made	Kareem Abdul-Jabbar (1969–89)	15,837	Tina Thompson (1997–present)	2,630
Most assists	John Stockton (1984–2003)	15,806	Ticha Penicheiro (PRT, 1998–2012)	2,599
Most free throws made	Karl Malone (1985–2004)	9,787	Tamika Catchings (2002–present)	1,709
Most blocks	Hakeem Olajuwon (NGA, 1984–2002)	3,830	Margo Dydek (POL, 1998–2008)	877
Most steals	John Stockton (1984–2003)	3,265	Tamika Catchings (2002–present)	930
Team	**NBA**		**WNBA**	
Most Championship titles	Boston Celtics (1957, 1959–66, 1968–69, 1974, 1976, 1981, 1984, 1986 and 2008)	17	Houston Comets (1997–2000)	4
Most Finals appearances	Los Angeles Lakers (1949–50, 1952–54, 1959, 1962–63, 1965–66, 1968–70, 1972–73, 1980, 1982–85, 1987–89, 1991, 2000–02, 2004 and 2008–10)	31	Houston Comets (1997–2000)	4
			Detroit Shock (2003 and 2006–08)	
			New York Liberty (1997, 1999, 2000 and 2002)	

Correct as of 12 Feb 2014

The **most three-pointers in a game by a team** is 23, a record shared by the Orlando Magic (13 Jan 2009) and the Houston Rockets (5 Feb 2013).

Most three-pointers in a quarter
Joe Johnson scored eight three-pointers for the Brooklyn Nets on 16 Dec 2013, equalling Michael Redd's 2002 record.

WNBA

Most games in a career
As of 20 Dec 2013, Tina Thompson had played in 496 Women's National Basketball Association (WNBA) games. Her career began in 1997 with the Houston Comets; she has since played with the Los Angeles Sparks and is currently with Seattle Storm.

Thompson has also clocked up the **most minutes played in a WNBA career**, with 16,088 – the equivalent of more than 11 days on court.

Most free throws attempted in a game
Two women have attempted 24 free throws in a game: Cynthia Cooper did so on 3 Jul 1998, and Tina Charles followed suit on 29 Jun 2013.

Longest basketball shot
On 11 Nov 2013, Corey "Thunder" Law of the Harlem Globetrotters threw a basketball 33.45 m (109 ft 9 in) into the net. His record-breaking basket occurred at the US Airways Center in Phoenix, Arizona, USA, in celebration of GWR Day 2013. Three fellow Globetrotters gave it their best shot, but fell short of Law's length.

Highest rebounds per game average
Tina Charles – playing for the Connecticut Sun since 2010 – also holds the record for rebounds per game: an unrivalled average of 10.8.

Most three-pointers in a career
Katie Smith had scored 906 three-pointers as of 12 Feb 2014, since her career began in 1999. Smith has played for five teams: Minnesota Lynx, Detroit Shock, Washington Mystics, Seattle Storm and New York Liberty.

On 8 Sep 2013, Riquna Williams scored the **most three-pointers in a game**, with eight for the Tulsa Shock. Williams equalled the mark set twice by Diana Taurasi for Phoenix Mercury, on 10 Aug 2006 and 25 May 2010.

Largest half-time lead
Connecticut Sun led New York Liberty by a massive 34 points (61–27) at half-time on 15 Jun 2012. The Suns went on to win the match with a comfortable 97–55 victory. Their half-time lead also bested Seattle Storm's 33-point margin against Tulsa Shock on 7 Aug 2010.

Most points scored in an NBA career
Kareem Abdul-Jabbar scored 38,387 points (at an average of 24.6 points per game) in his regular-season career from 1969 to 1989. He also scored 5,762 points in playoff games, which ranks second to 5,987 by Michael Jordan from 1984 to 1998.

Fewest turnovers in an NBA game
The Oklahoma City Thunder committed just two turnovers against the Los Angeles Lakers on 5 Mar 2013, equalling the mark set by the Milwaukee Bucks in 2006 and Cleveland Cavaliers in 2009.

The **fewest turnovers in an NBA Finals game** is four, by the Detroit Pistons on 16 Jun 2005 and San Antonio Spurs on 6 Jun 2013.

All players and teams USA unless otherwise stated.

Combat sports

Size matters: there are **no weight divisions** in pro sumo wrestling

Most siblings to win world boxing titles

As of 1 Aug 2013, brothers Kōki, Daiki and Tomoki Kameda (JPN) had each won a world boxing title. Tomoki won the WBO bantamweight title, Kōki secured the WBA bantamweight crown and Daiki started the brothers' success by winning the WBA flyweight title.

WRESTLING

Most freestyle wrestling world titles (male)

Two men have won seven freestyle wrestling world titles: Aleksandr Medved (BLR) in the over-100-kg class between 1962 and 1971, and Valentin Jordanov (BGR) in the 55-kg class between 1983 and 1995.

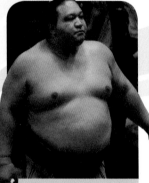

Most career matches won by a sumo wrestler

Kaiō Hiroyuki (JPN) won 1,047 (of 1,731) bouts between Mar 1988 and Jul 2011. Remarkably, Kaiō initially doubted if he was good enough to make it as a sumo wrestler.

Most freestyle wrestling world titles

Between 2002 and 2013, Saori Yoshida (JPN) won a record 11 championships in the 55-kg wrestling class. This achievement – unmatched by any man or woman in Japan or anywhere else – saw Yoshida receive a Japanese People's Honour Award in Nov 2013.

Heaviest living athlete

Sumo wrestler Emmanuel "Manny" Yarborough of Rahway, New Jersey, USA, stands 203 cm (6 ft 8 in) tall and weighs 319.3 kg (704 lb).

Most arm wrestling matches in 24 hours

On 12 Feb 2012, world champion Ion Oncescu (ROM) contested 1,024 arm wrestles in Bucharest, Romania. He won every match.

FENCING

Most individual world fencing titles

Male: Christian d'Oriola (FRA) won six foil titles in World Championships and Olympics between 1947 and 1956. Russian Stanislav Pozdnyakov matched this feat with six sabre wins from 1996 to 2007.

BOXING

Most world title fights

Julio César Chávez (MEX) won 31 of his 37 fights contested between 1984 and 2000 in the super featherweight, lightweight and light welterweight divisions.

Most flash KOs in a pro career

Mike Tyson (USA) managed nine under-60-sec knockouts during his career.

Shortest world title fight

Just 17 sec was all it took for Daniel Jiménez (PRI) to knock out Harold Geier. Jiménez was defending his WBO super bantamweight title at Wiener Neustadt in Austria on 3 Sep 1994.

Highest-selling pay-per-view boxing match

The junior middleweight fight between Saúl "El Canelo" Álvarez (MEX, left) and Floyd Mayweather Jr (USA, right) on 14 Sep 2013 grossed $150 m (£91 m) from 2.2 million TV viewers. In addition, the venue in Las Vegas, Nevada, USA, sold out and a further $20 m (£12 m) was taken in gate receipts.

Most siblings to win gold at a taekwondo championships

The López family (USA) won three gold medals at the World Taekwondo Championships in Madrid, Spain, in Apr 2005. Steven won the welterweight title, younger brother Mark the featherweight crown, and sister Diana took featherweight gold. Their coach was dad Jean.

Female: Valentina Vezzali (ITA) won nine individual foil titles: three Olympic golds and six at the World Fencing Championships. She won the titles in 1999–2011.

Most golds at the World Championships (country)

In 2013, Italy became the first nation to win more than 100 golds at the Fencing World Championships. As of the end of 2013, their tally stood at 101 gold, 97 silver and 114 bronze medals.

MARTIAL ARTS

Most World Taekwondo Championships wins
Male: Steven López (USA) won five Championships: lightweight in 2001 and four welterweights in 2003–09.
Female: Jung Myung-suk's (KOR) three heavyweight wins came in 1993–97, a feat equalled by Brigitte Yagüe (ESP), who won finweight in 2003 and flyweight in 2007 and 2009.

Most single-leg martial arts kicks in one minute
Raul Meza (USA) performed 335 single-leg kicks at Meza's Karate America in Sioux Falls, South Dakota, USA, on 17 Nov 2011.

Most gold medals won at the World Combat Games

Russia's tally from 2010 in Beijing, China, and 2013 in St Petersburg, Russia, is 65. The latter featured 97 nations and 135 events. Shown here is Nikita Selyanskiy in the 71-kg full-contact kickboxing category.

Most men's team kumite World Karate Championships wins

The first World Karate Championships were held in 1970. Since then the French men's team have won the kumite title seven times, in 1972, 1994, 1996, 1998, 2000, 2004 and 2012.

UFC

Most fights won by decision
Georges St-Pierre (CAN) won 12 Ultimate Fighting Championship (UFC) fights by decision from 16 Apr 2005 to 16 Nov 2013. St-Pierre also holds the record for the **most UFC wins** – 19 – from 31 Jan 2004 to 16 Nov 2013.

Most fights won by KO
Anderson "The Spider" Silva (BRA) secured 20 knockout wins between 2000 and 2012. Silva also has the **most consecutive UFC wins** – 17 – in 2006–12.

BOXING WINS – OLDEST AND YOUNGEST

Record	Age	Boxer	Title (date)
Oldest...			
World champion (male)	48 years 53 days	Bernard Hopkins (USA, b. 15 Jan 1965)	IBF light heavyweight (9 Mar 2013)
World champion (female)	46 years 61 days	Alicia Ashley (USA/JAM, b. 23 Aug 1967)	WBC super bantamweight (23 Oct 2013)
Youngest...			
World champion (male)	17 years 176 days	Wilfred Benítez (USA, b. 12 Sep 1958)	WBA light welterweight (6 Mar 1976)
World champion (female)	18 years 342 days	Ju Hee Kim (KOR, b. 13 Jan 1986)	IFBA light flyweight (19 Dec 2004)

Correct as of 23 Jan 2014

  For more strength, turn to p.104

For more strength, turn to p.104

Most World Judo Championships wins

Male: Teddy Riner (FRA) has won six titles – five at heavyweight (over-100 kg) in 2007, 2009–11 and 2013, and one with the French men's team in 2011.
Female: Ryoko Tani (JPN) won seven titles in the under-48-kg category in 1993–2007.

Shortest average contest time

The shortest average UFC contest time is 2 min 20 sec, achieved by Drew McFedries (USA) in 17 fights from 8 Sep 2001 to 25 Jan 2013.

Tallest UFC fighter

Stefan "Skyscraper" Struve (NLD), who competes as a heavyweight in the UFC, measures 211 cm (6 ft 11 in); he also reportedly has a phenomenal 2.13-m (7-ft) reach.

Longest total fight time in a UFC career

The longest overall time spent in the octagon (the eight-sided enclosure where Ultimate Fighting Championship bouts take place) is 5 hr 28 min 21 sec, achieved by Georges St-Pierre (CAN) between 25 Jan 2002 and 16 Nov 2013. Pictured is St-Pierre (left) – fighting Jake Shields – on his way to successfully defending the welterweight title on 30 Apr 2011.

FACT

The only rules for the freestyle combat sport of pankration (recorded in the Olympic Games of 648 BC) were no biting and no eye-gouging.

Cricket

With c. 3 billion fans, cricket is the world's **second most popular sport**

Longest cricket ban
In Sep 2013, Indian bowler Shanthakumaran Sreesanth was handed a lifetime ban from cricket. He was found guilty of spot-fixing in the Indian Premier League match between Rajasthan Royals and Kings XI Punjab on 9 May 2013.

Fastest delivery of a cricket ball
Shoaib Akhtar (PAK) bowled a ball at a speed of 161.3 km/h (100.23 mph) on 22 Feb 2003, during a World Cup match against England in Cape Town, South Africa.

Most wickets in a T20 International career (female)
Spin bowler Anisa Mohammed (TTO) is the leading wicket-taker in women's Twenty20 Internationals. As of 9 Mar 2014, she had claimed 74 wickets in 59 matches playing for the West Indies, at an average of 13.68 runs conceded per wicket.

Most Champions League Twenty20 wins
The annual Champions League Twenty20 (T20) is contested by leading domestic teams from seven countries. Mumbai Indians (IND) are the only team to have won the title twice. Their first win came on 9 Oct 2011, and most recently they claimed a 33-run win against Rajasthan Royals (IND) in Delhi, India, on 6 Oct 2013.

Highest single-day Test match attendance
A crowd of 91,092 people packed out the Melbourne Cricket Ground in Australia on day one of the fourth Ashes Test between Australia and England on 26 Dec 2013.

Most wins of a domestic first-class cricket competition
New South Wales won Australia's Sheffield Shield 45 times between 1895–96 and 2007–08.

WICKETS

Most wickets without conceding a run in a women's ODI
Two women have taken three wickets without conceding a run in an ODI (One-Day International). Olivia Magno (AUS) snapped up three tail-end wickets in 1.4 overs on 14 Dec 1997, a feat matched by England's Arran Brindle in two maiden overs in Mumbai, India, on 5 Feb 2013.

RUNS

Highest Test match 10th-wicket partnership
Australians Ashton Agar (98) and Phillip Hughes (81 not out), batting at 11 and 6 respectively, made 163 runs in 31.1 overs in the 2013 Ashes at Trent Bridge in the UK on 11 Jul.

Most runs in a T20 match
Chris Gayle (JAM) finished on 175 not out – the highest score by a player in any professional T20 innings – for Royal Challengers Bangalore in the Indian Premier League on 23 Apr 2013. Gayle hit 100 runs in 30 balls – the **fastest T20 century** – and 13 fours and 17 sixes, the **most T20 runs scored in boundaries** (154).

Fastest international century
Corey Anderson (NZ) hit a century from just 36 balls in an ODI against the West Indies on 1 Jan 2014. Anderson struck 14 sixes and six fours in an unbeaten 131 from 47 balls.

FACT
Cricketers batting in positions 8 to 11 are known as the lower order or "tail".

Most runs by a No.11 batsman in a Test match innings
Test match debutant Ashton Agar (AUS) rewrote the record books when he scored 98 runs in the opening Test of the 2013 Ashes series against England at Trent Bridge in Nottingham, UK, on 11 Jul. Agar's astonishing 101-ball knock featured 12 fours and two sixes and rescued Australia from a perilous 117 for 9.

Most runs scored by a player in a T20 International
The highest individual score in a Twenty20 International is 156 runs, by Australian Aaron Finch against England at the Ageas Bowl in Southampton, UK, on 29 Aug 2013. Opening batsman Finch hit 14 sixes in his 63-ball innings to guide Australia to a formidable 248 for 6.

Most catches by a wicket-keeper in a Test series
Australia gloveman Brad Haddin broke a 30-year-old Test record when he claimed 29 catches in the 2013 Ashes series between hosts England and Australia – despite his team losing the five-match series 3–0. Haddin pouched the record on 25 Aug 2013 – day five of the fifth Test – from another Australian wicket-keeper, Rod Marsh, who took 28 catches in five Test matches in 1982–83.

RUNS, WICKETS AND CATCHES

Test matches (men)

Most runs	15,921	Sachin Tendulkar (IND), 1989–2013
Most wickets	800	Muttiah Muralitharan (LKA), 1992–2010
Most catches	210	Rahul Dravid (IND), 1996–2012

Test matches (women)

Most runs	1,935	Janette Brittin (ENG), 1979–98
Most wickets	77	Mary Duggan (ENG), 1949–63
Most catches	25	Carole Hodges (ENG), 1984–92

One-Day Internationals (men)

Most runs	18,426	Sachin Tendulkar (IND), 1989–2012
Most wickets	534	Muttiah Muralitharan (LKA), 1993–2011
Most catches	201	Mahela Jayawardene (LKA), 1998–2013

One-Day Internationals (women)

Most runs	5,432	Charlotte Edwards (ENG), 1997–2014
Most wickets	180	Cathryn Fitzpatrick (AUS), 1993–2007
Most catches	50	Jhulan Goswami (IND), 2002–14

Source: www.espncricinfo.com, as of 4 Feb 2014 (catches excluding wicket-keepers)

Highest match aggregate in a T20 International

England made 209 for 6 in reply to Australia's 248 for 6 at the Ageas Bowl in Hampshire, UK, on 29 Aug 2013, for a match aggregate of 457 runs.

SIXES

Highest aggregate in a Test match series

In the five-match 2013–14 Ashes series between

Most sixes by a player in a first-class innings

Jamaican cricketer Chris Gayle cleared the boundary 17 times on his way to a Twenty20 record of 175 not out. His set of sixes came in the record-breaking Indian Premier League match on 23 Apr 2013 (see left).

Australia and England, 65 sixes were recorded. Australia, who won the series 5–0, contributed 40 maximums – the **most sixes by one team in a Test match series**. Chief contributions came from Aussies Brad Haddin (nine) and George Bailey (eight), with six each from Shane Watson (AUS), Ian Bell and Stuart Broad (both ENG).

Bailey hit three of his sixes in one over during the third Test in Perth on 16 Dec 2013, when he equalled the 28-run record for the **most runs scored off an over in a Test match**. West Indies batsman Brian Lara had achieved the feat on 14 Dec 2003.

Most in an ODI

Rohit Sharma (IND) hit 16 sixes in Bangalore, India, on 2 Nov 2013. Opening batsman Sharma made 209 – the second highest score in ODI history – off 158 balls.

Most in a Test match innings

Wasim Akram (PAK) scored 12 sixes in an innings of 257 not out against Zimbabwe in Sheikhupura, Pakistan, on 19–20 Oct 1996.

Most in an IPL career

At the conclusion of the 2013 Indian Premier League tournament on 26 May 2013, Chris Gayle (JAM) had scored a total of 180 maximums in his five-season career (2009–13).

First multi-format series in international cricket

A Test match, three Twenty20 Internationals and three One-Day Internationals determined the winner of the multi-format women's Ashes series between England and Australia in Aug 2013. Captained by Charlotte Edwards, hosts England clinched the series by 12 points to 4 and regained the Ashes crown that they had lost on Australian soil in 2011.

For sports architecture, see pp.200–01

THE CENTURION OF CRICKET

Sachin Tendulkar's career totals (1989–2013)

Most centuries in internationals	100
Most centuries in Test matches	51
Most centuries in One-Day Internationals	49
Most international centuries scored in a partnership (career) – with Sourav Ganguly (IND)	38

Source: www.espncricinfo.com

Most Test matches played

Batsman Sachin Tendulkar (IND) – known by his fans as the "God of Cricket" – retired on 16 Nov 2013 after a 24-year career, but not before playing a record 200th Test, against the West Indies at Mumbai's Wankhede Stadium. Tendulkar has 20 Guinness World Records titles to his credit, the highlights of which are listed in the tables above.

Origin of the "Ashes"

The Sporting Times mourned the death of English cricket in 1882, when England lost to Australia on home soil for the first time. The mock obituary of English cricket read: "The body will be cremated and the ashes taken to Australia."

Most by a team in a T20 International

The Netherlands struck 19 sixes in a World T20 group match against Ireland at Sylhet Stadium, Bangladesh, on 21 Mar 2014, reaching their target of 190 with 37 balls to spare to progress to the Super 10 stage of the tournament.

Cycling

175, during the 2012 Vuelta a España (Tour of Spain) from 18 Aug to 9 Sep 2012.

Fastest 4-km pursuit (women)
The Great Britain team consisting of Katie Archibald, Elinor Barker, Danielle King and Joanna Rowsell completed the 4-km team pursuit in 4 min 16.552 sec to win gold at the Union Cycliste Internationale (UCI) Track Cycling World Cup in Aguascalientes, Mexico, on 5 Dec 2013.

OLYMPICS

Most cycling medals
The greatest number of Olympic cycling medals won by an individual is seven, by Bradley Wiggins and Chris Hoy (both UK). Wiggins won four gold, one silver

Most Olympic cycling medals won (female)

Leontien Zijlaard-van Moorsel (NLD) won six Olympic cycling medals including four golds. Her medals were won at Sydney 2000 and Athens 2004.

Oldest Olympic road cycling gold medallist

When Kristin Armstrong (USA, b. 11 Aug 1973) successfully defended her time trial title at the 2012 Games in London, UK, on 1 Aug, she became the oldest road cycling winner. Aged 38 years 356 days, Kristin rode the 29-km (18-mi) course in 37 min 34.82 sec.

Greatest distance cycled in 12 hours
Marko Baloh (SVN) cycled 475.26 km (295.31 mi) solo and unpaced in 12 hr at the Montichiari Velodrome in Brescia, Italy, on 8 Oct 2010. He completed 1,901 full laps of the 250-m (820-ft) course in the allotted time.

Baloh continued his solo, unpaced cycling for another 12 hr and went on to achieve the **greatest distance cycled in 24 hours** with 903.76 km (561.57 mi), or 3,615 full laps.

Largest cycling race
The 2004 Cape Argus Pick n Pay Cycle Tour held in Cape Town, South Africa, on 14 Mar 2004 began with 42,614 entrants, 31,219 of whom finished the race.

Most riders to finish a Grand Tour
The greatest number of cyclists to complete an edition of a Grand Tour is

Oldest person to win a cycling Grand Tour

Chris Horner (USA, b. 23 Oct 1971) won the 2013 Vuelta a España aged 41 years 327 days in Madrid, Spain, on 15 Sep 2013. He also became the **oldest winner of a stage in a Grand Tour** when he took stage 10 of the race aged 41 years 314 days in Alto de Hazallanas, Spain, on 2 Sep 2013.

and two bronze medals in 2000–12. Hoy's seven came from six golds and one silver, also between 2000 and 2012.

Chris Hoy's six golds give him the record for the **most Olympic track cycling gold medals**. He picked up gold in the 1-km time trial at Athens 2004, the individual sprint, team sprint and Keirin at Beijing 2008, and the team sprint and Keirin at London 2012.

Most cycling gold medals won at one Olympic Games
On 5 Aug 1904, at the Olympic Games in St Louis, USA, Marcus Hurley (USA) won four gold medals, in the quarter mile, third mile, half mile and 1 mile events.

Most medals won at both Summer and Winter Olympics (female)
Canadian athlete Clara Hughes won a total of six medals across both Summer and Winter Games. She won two bronze medals in cycling events at the 1996 Summer Games in Atlanta, USA, before switching to speed skating. In this new discipline, Hughes won a bronze medal at the 2002 Winter Olympics in Salt Lake City, USA, a gold and silver medal at the 2006 Games in Turin, Italy, and another bronze medal at the 2010 Winter Olympics in Vancouver, Canada.

FACT
Prior to Horner's victory, the oldest Grand Tour winner was Firmin Lambot (BEL), who won the Tour de France in 1922, aged 36.

First to win the Tour de France and Olympic gold in the same year
Bradley Wiggins capped a memorable summer for British cycling when he eased to victory in the men's time

Most podium finishes in the Tour de France

Raymond Poulidor (FRA) finished in the top three of the Tour de France eight times. He came second on three occasions (1964, 1965 and 1974) and third five times (1962, 1966, 1969, 1972 and 1976).

i On tour

The cycling Grand Tours are: the Tour de France, the Giro d'Italia and the Vuelta a España, which date from 1903, 1909 and 1935 respectively.

TRACK CYCLING – ABSOLUTE

Men	Start	Time/Distance	Name & Nationality	Place	Date
200 m	flying	9.347	François Pervis (FRA)	Aguascalientes, Mexico	6 Dec 2013
500 m	flying	24.758	Chris Hoy (UK)	La Paz, Bolivia	13 May 2007
1 km	standing	56.303	François Pervis (FRA)	Aguascalientes, Mexico	7 Dec 2013
4 km	standing	4:10.534	Jack Bobridge (AUS)	Sydney, Australia	2 Feb 2011
Team 4 km	standing	3:51.659	Great Britain (Steven Burke, Ed Clancy, Peter Kennaugh and Geraint Thomas)	London, UK	3 Aug 2012
1 hour	standing	49.7 km	Ondřej Sosenka (CZE)	Moscow, Russia	19 Jul 2005
Women	**Start**	**Time/Distance**	**Name & Nationality**	**Place**	**Date**
200 m	flying	10.384	Kristina Vogel (DEU)	Aguascalientes, Mexico	7 Dec 2013
500 m	flying	29.481	Olga Streltsova (RUS)	Moscow, Russia	29 May 2011
3 km	standing	3:22.269	Sarah Hammer (USA)	Aguascalientes, Mexico	11 May 2010
1 hour	standing	46.065 km	Leontien Zijlaard-van Moorsel (NLD)	Mexico City, Mexico	1 Oct 2003

Statistics correct as of 7 Dec 2013

Most UCI Mountain Bike Marathon World Championships

Christoph Sauser (CHE) has won the UCI Mountain Bike Marathon World Championships a total of three times, in 2007, 2011 and 2013.

Most World Championships in cyclo-cross (female)

Marianne Vos (NLD) has won six cyclo-cross World Championships, in 2006 and consecutively in 2009–13. The championships began in 2000. She also won Olympic gold in different cycling events at the Beijing and London games.

trial in 50 min 39 sec at the London Olympics on 1 Aug 2012 – just 10 days after becoming the first Brit to win the Tour de France.

TOUR DE FRANCE

Longest
In 1926, the Tour de France totalled 5,745 km (3,569 mi) and was won by Lucien Buysse (BEL).

Most wins
Four riders have won the Tour five times: Jacques Anquetil (FRA) in 1957 and 1961–64; Eddy Merckx (BEL) in 1969–72

Most UCI Trials World Championships won
Male: Benito Ros Charral (ESP) won nine elite men's UCI Trials World Championships, in 2003–05 and 2007–12.
Female: Karin Moor (CHE) won the women's title nine times between 2001 and 2011.

❌ A bit too slow? Try Motorsports, p.232

and 1974; Bernard Hinault (FRA) in 1978–79, 1981–82 and 1985; and Miguel Indurain (ESP) in 1991–95. With 34 victories, Merckx also enjoyed the **most Tour de France stage wins**, between 1969 and 1978.

Closest
In the 1989 Tour de France, after 3,267 km (2,030 mi) ridden over a period of 23 days (1–23 July), Greg LeMond (USA) finished the race in 87 hr 38 min 35 sec, beating Laurent Fignon (FRA) by only 8 sec.

Largest attendance at a sporting event
The most spectators at any sporting event is an estimated 12 million people over a three-week period for the 2012 Tour de France. The Tour took place in Belgium, Switzerland and France from 30 June to 22 July. The organizers estimate that 80% of spectators were French and that 70% were men.

BMX

Most World Championships won
Male: The most UCI BMX World Championships won by an individual is three, by Kyle Bennett (USA) in 2002–03 and 2007.
Female: Two women have won three titles: Gabriela Diaz (ARG) in

2001–02 and 2004, and Shanaze Reade (UK) in 2007–08 and 2010.

Most Olympic medals
BMX was first incorporated into the Olympics in 2008. Since then, only one rider has won two medals. Māris Štrombergs (LVA) won the individual men's event in 2008 and 2012.

First person to win the cycling Triple Crown

The inaugural winner of cycling's Triple Crown was Eddy Merckx (BEL), who won the Tour de France, Giro d'Italia and UCI Road World Cycling Championships in 1974. The only other person to achieve this feat was Stephen Roche (IRL) in 1987.

Golf

The word **"caddy"** comes from the French *cadet*, meaning junior or student

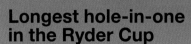

First winner of the FedEx Cup and Race to Dubai in one year

Henrik Stenson (SWE) won the US Professional Golfers' Association (PGA) Tour's FedEx Cup (inset) on 22 Sep 2013 and the PGA European Tour's Race to Dubai (main picture) on 17 Nov 2013. The scale of his achievement is indicated by the fact that no player has even won both tours in *different* years before.

was part of the 18 Tour titles that Nelson won in the same year. He turned professional in 1932 and retired from full-time golf in the 1946 season, by which time he had amassed a career total of 52 PGA titles.

Most PGA Player of the Year awards

The greatest number of PGA Player of the Year awards won by an individual golfer is 11, by Tiger Woods (USA) in 1997, 1999–2003, 2005–07, 2009 and 2013. Inaugurated in 1948, this award is based on a points system, including variables such as wins, top 10 finishes, performances in major

Longest hole-in-one in the Ryder Cup

Paul Casey (UK, above) holed a 194-m (213-yd) drive at the 14th hole (par 3) at the K Club in Straffan, County Kildare, Ireland, on 23 Sep 2006. Incredibly, the feat was repeated by Scott Verplank (USA) the next day at the same hole on the final day of the tournament. The Ryder Cup is contested every two years between the USA and Europe.

Longest golf hole
The seventh hole (par 7) of the Satsuki gold course in Sano, Japan, measures 881 m (964 yd) long.

Longest hole-in-one in a PGA Tour event
On 25 Jan 2001, Andrew Magee (USA) shot a 303-m (332-yd) hole-in-one on the 17th hole (par 4) in the first round of the Phoenix Open at TPC of Scottsdale in Arizona, USA.

The **longest hole-in-one in the US Masters** is 194 m (213 yd), by Jeff Sluman (USA) at the par-3 fourth hole at Augusta National Golf Club in Georgia, USA, on 9 Apr 1992.

Most consecutive PGA Tour titles won
Byron Nelson (USA) won 11 PGA Tour titles in a row in 1945. The run, commonly referred to as "The Streak",

tournaments and scoring average. Woods has almost twice as many awards as his nearest rival, Tom Watson (USA), who won the award on six occasions.

LOWEST ROUNDS

Lowest single-round score (18 holes) in the US Masters
Two players have each recorded a single-round score of 63 at the US Masters, which is played at the Augusta National Golf Club. They are Nick Price (ZWE) in 1986 and Greg Norman (AUS) in 1996.

Lowest score at the British Open
Eight players have played a round of 63 at the British Open golf championships:

FACT
The 2014 Humana Challenge had a total prize purse of $5.7 m (£3.4 m), with $1.026 m (£0.62 m) going to Patrick Reed for winning the event.

MOST WINS AND LOWEST SCORES (72 HOLES)

British Open		
Most wins	6	Harry Vardon (UK)
Lowest total score	267	Greg Norman (AUS), 1993
US Open		
Most wins	4	Willie Anderson (USA)
		Bobby Jones Jr (USA)
		Ben Hogan (USA)
		Jack Nicklaus (USA)
Lowest total score	268	Rory McIlroy (UK), 2011
US PGA		
Most wins	5	Walter Hagen (USA)
		Jack Nicklaus (USA)
Lowest total score	265	David Toms (USA), 2001
US Masters		
Most wins	6	Jack Nicklaus (USA)
Lowest total score	270	Tiger Woods (USA), 2007

Statistics correct as of 24 Feb 2014

Lowest score below par after 54 holes in a PGA Tour event

Patrick Reed (USA) scored 27 under par after 54 holes during the 2014 Humana Challenge on the PGA West course in La Quinta, California, USA, on 16–18 Jan. Reed received a congratulatory call afterwards from former US President Bill Clinton. The tournament is held in partnership with the Clinton Foundation.

Most appearances by a pair in the Ryder Cup

The most frequent pairing in Ryder Cup history is that of Spaniards Severiano "Seve" Ballesteros (above right) and José María Olazábal (above left), who played together 15 times for Europe in foursomes and four-ball from 1987 to 1993. The duo ended with an overall record of 11 wins, two draws and two losses.

Mark Hayes (USA) at Turnberry, South Ayrshire, in 1977; Isao Aoki (JPN) at Muirfield, East Lothian, in 1980; Greg Norman (AUS) at Turnberry in 1986; Paul Broadhurst (UK) at St Andrews, Fife, in 1990; Jodie Mudd (USA) at Royal Birkdale, Southport, in 1991; Nick Faldo (UK) and Payne Stewart (USA), both at Royal St George's, Sandwich, in 1993; and Rory McIlroy (UK) at St Andrews in 2010.

Highest annual earnings from golf

Released in 2013, Forbes' Celebrity 100 list ranks Tiger Woods (USA) as both the highest-earning golfer and the **highest-earning athlete**. His earnings for 2012–13 came to an estimated $78 m (£51 m).

Lowest score under par in a pro golf tournament (single round)

Richard Wallis (UK) shot 59 at the PGA Southern Open Championship OOM Pro-Am on the par-73 course at The Drift Golf Club, East Horsley, Surrey, UK, on 2 Jun 2013. This represents a score of 14 under par.

Lowest below-age score

Two golfers have had a score of 17 below their ages. James D Morton (USA) hit a 72 at Valleybrook Golf and Country Club, Hixson, Tennessee, USA, on 21 Apr 2001, aged 89 years, and Keith Plowman (NZ) hit 72 at Maungakiekie Golf Club, Auckland, New Zealand, also aged 89, on 20 Nov 2007.

YOUNGEST AND OLDEST

Youngest golfer to make the cut at the US Masters

Aged 14 years 171 days, Guan Tianlang (CHN, b. 25 Oct 1998) made the cut with 4 over par after 18 holes at the 77th US Masters on 13 Apr 2013. The tournament was staged at Augusta National Golf Club in Georgia, USA.

Guan had already become the **youngest golfer to play at the US Masters** when he teed off at the

same tournament two days beforehand, aged 14 years 169 days. His final score was 300 (73, 75, 77, 75).

Youngest golfer to score their age

Tsugio Uemoto (JPN, b. 3 Jul 1928) scored 68 at the Higashi Hiroshima Country Club, Hiroshima, Japan, on 22 Oct 1996.

The **oldest player to score their age** is C Arthur Thompson (CAN, 1869–1975), who scored 103 on the 5,682-m (6,215-yd) Uplands Golf Club course in Victoria, British Columbia, Canada, in 1973.

Youngest Ryder Cup captain

Arnold Palmer (USA) was 34 years 31 days old when he captained the US Ryder Cup team at East Lake Golf Club in Atlanta, Georgia, USA, in 1963.

The **oldest Ryder Cup captain** is Tom Watson (USA, b. 4 Sep 1949), who was selected on 13 Dec 2012, at the age of 63 years 100 days, to lead the US team. The 2014 Ryder Cup at Gleneagles in Scotland,

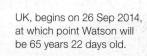

Most LPGA Player of the Year awards

Sweden's Annika Sörenstam has won a total of eight Ladies Professional Golfers' Association (LPGA) Player of the Year awards. Her victories came in 1995, 1997–98 and 2001–05.

UK, begins on 26 Sep 2014, at which point Watson will be 65 years 22 days old.

Youngest golfer to play in the Ryder Cup

Sergio García (ESP, b. 9 Jan 1980) competed for Europe in the Ryder Cup in 1999, aged 19 years 229 days.

The **oldest golfer to play in the Ryder Cup** is Raymond Floyd (USA b. 4 Sep 1942), who competed in the 1993 tournament aged 51 years 20 days. Floyd retired from professional golf in Apr 2010, but Tom Watson recruited him as a vice-captain for his 2014 Ryder Cup team.

Oldest golfer to score a hole-in one

Switzerland's Otto Bucher (b. 12 May 1885) hit a hole-in-one on the 119-m (130-yd) 12th hole at La Manga in Spain on 13 Jan 1985, at the age of 99 years 244 days.

Oldest golf club president

Jack Miles (UK, b. 10 Mar 1913), who is the president of Wimbledon Common Golf Club, celebrated his 101st birthday in 2014. Jack has been an active playing member of the club since 1947.

Most consecutive golf majors won in a single year (female)

Mildred Ella "Babe" Didrikson Zaharias (USA, main picture) won three successive majors in 1950, a feat matched by Inbee Park (KOR, inset) in 2013. Their three wins also represent the **most majors won in a year (female)**, a record shared with Mary "Mickey" Wright (USA, 1961) and Pat Bradley (USA, 1986).

Solheim Cup

The female equivalent of the Ryder Cup is the Solheim Cup, held every two years since 1990. The USA has won eight times to Europe's five.

Ice hockey

Pucks used to be made from **frozen cow dung**

FACT

Jágr started playing ice hockey at the age of three.

Most game-winning goals in an NHL career

As of 30 Dec 2013, the Czech Republic's Jaromír Jágr had scored 122 game-winning goals in his National Hockey League (NHL) career. He has also scored the **most regular-season NHL career goals in overtime**, with 18 for the Pittsburgh Penguins, Washington Capitals, New York Rangers, Philadelphia Flyers and New Jersey Devils from 1990 to 2013.

Longest undefeated run by an NHL team

From 14 Oct 1979 to 6 Jan 1980, the USA's Philadelphia Flyers had an unbeaten run of 35 games, with 25 wins and 10 ties. (For the **longest NHL winning streak**, see the table below right.)

Most career games in professional ice hockey

Canadian right-winger Gordon "Gordie" Howe (b. 31 Mar 1928) featured in 2,421 professional games over 26 seasons from 1946 to 1980, including NHL and WHA (World Hockey Association) games. When Howe retired in 1980, he was 52 years old, an age that made him the **oldest player in NHL history**.

Oldest goal-scorer in Olympic ice hockey

At the age of 43 years 234 days, Teemu Selänne (FIN, b. 3 Jul 1970) scored twice in the Olympic bronze medal match against the USA in Sochi, Russia, on 22 Feb 2014. Selänne's goals helped Finland to a 5–0 victory over the Americans and also made him the **oldest medallist in Olympic ice hockey**.

Most wins in an NHL season

The Detroit Red Wings (USA) won 62 times in the 1995/96 NHL season.

Most assists in an NHL season

Wayne Gretzky (CAN) made 163 assists playing for the Edmonton Oilers during the 1985/86 NHL season.

Gretzky also recorded the **most assists in an NHL career**, with 1,963 for the Edmonton Oilers, Los Angeles Kings, St Louis Blues and New York Rangers from 1979 to 1999.

Most penalty minutes in an NHL game

Playing for the Los Angeles Kings in a game against the Philadelphia Flyers on 11 Mar 1979, Canadian Randy Holt racked up 67 penalty minutes.

The player with the **most penalty minutes in NHL history**, however, is Dave "Tiger" Williams (CAN), with 3,966 in 17 seasons between 1974 and 1988, playing for the Toronto Maple Leafs, Vancouver Canucks, Detroit Red Wings, Los Angeles Kings and Hartford Whalers.

Fastest coach to reach 200 NHL wins

Pittsburgh Penguins' 3–1 win over the Ottawa Senators on 22 Apr 2013 gave Dan Bylsma (USA) his 200th win from 316 games coached.

Fastest NHL hat-trick

On 23 Mar 1952, Canadian right-winger Bill Mosienko scored a hat-trick in 21 sec for the Chicago Blackhawks vs the New York Rangers at Madison Square Garden, New York City, USA. The Blackhawks went on to triumph 7–6.

Most consecutive NHL games played

Doug Jarvis (CAN) played 964 games for the Montreal Canadiens, Washington Capitals and Hartford Whalers from Oct 1975 to Oct 1987.

Most consecutive games played by an NHL defenceman

Jay Bouwmeester (CAN) had featured in 635 consecutive NHL regular-season games as of the end of the 2012/13 season. Chris Chelios (USA) played the **most career regular-season games by an NHL defenceman**, with 1,651 for various teams from 1983 to 2010.

Most shoot-out wins by an NHL goaltender

Henrik Lundqvist (SWE) achieved 44 shoot-out wins while playing for the New York Rangers – more than any other NHL goalie.

Most tickets sold for an NHL match

A total of 105,491 tickets were sold for the 2014 Bridgestone NHL Winter Classic game between the Detroit Red Wings (USA) and the Toronto Maple Leafs (CAN). The match was held at the University of Michigan Football Stadium in Ann Arbor, Michigan, USA, on 1 Jan 2014.

 Stay cool: visit the Poles, from p. 144

Highest save percentage by a goaltender in an NHL season

Craig Anderson (USA) recorded a .941 save percentage while playing for the Ottawa Senators during the 2012/13 season, surpassing the previous mark of .940 set by Brian Elliott (CAN) of the St Louis Blues in 2011–12.

1956, 1963–71, 1973–75, 1978–79, 1981–83, 1986 and 1989–90) and four wins as Russia (in 1993, 2008–09 and 2012).

Most women's ice hockey World Championships

The women's IIHF World Championships was first held in 1990 and has been staged annually since then apart from Olympic years and in 2003, during the SARS outbreak. The Canadian team have won 10 titles in total: in 1990, 1992, 1994, 1997, 1999–2001, 2004, 2007 and 2012. The USA has won five times, most recently in 2013.

Most NHL career points

Wayne Gretzky (CAN) scored a remarkable 2,857 points for the Edmonton Oilers, Los Angeles Kings, St Louis Blues and New York Rangers between 1979 and 1999. This total comprises 894 goals and 1,963 assists in 1,487 games. In addition to these regular-season goals and 122 Stanley Cup goals, Gretzky scored 56 goals in the World Hockey Association (WHA) in 1978–79.

Most overtime goals in an NHL season

The NHL record for overtime goals in a season is five, by Steven Stamkos (CAN) in the 2011/12 season for Tampa Bay Lightning.

Most shoot-out goals in an NHL career

Zach Parise (USA) has scored 34 shoot-out goals in the service of the New Jersey Devils and Minnesota Wild since 2005.

Most goals by a rookie in an NHL season

In the 1992/93 NHL season, Finland's Teemu Selänne racked up 76 goals for the Winnipeg Jets.

Most goals on an NHL debut

On 9 Oct 2010, Derek Stepan (USA) became only the fourth player to score a hat-trick on his NHL debut, playing for the New York Rangers in a 6–3 victory over the Buffalo Sabres. The others are: Alex Smart (CAN) on 14 Jan 1943, Réal Cloutier (CAN) on 10 Oct 1979 and Fabian Brunnström (SWE) on 15 Oct 2008.

Most men's ice hockey World Championships

The men's IIHF (International Ice Hockey Federation) World Championships were first held in 1920. The Soviet Union/Russia have won more times than any other nation, with 22 victories as the Soviet Union (in 1954,

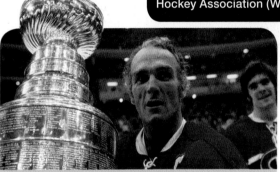

Most individual wins of the Stanley Cup

Henri Richard (CAN) won the Stanley Cup 11 times with the Montreal Canadiens from 1956 to 1975. The shorter sibling of legendary right-winger Maurice "The Rocket" Richard, Henri was nicknamed "The Pocket Rocket".

Youngest captain of a Stanley Cup-winning team

At 21 years 309 days, Sidney Crosby (CAN, b. 7 Aug 1987) became the youngest captain of any team to win the Stanley Cup when the Pittsburgh Penguins beat the Detroit Red Wings in the 2009 finals.

Fewest goals conceded in a Stanley Cup finals series

The fewest goals conceded by a goaltender in a Stanley Cup finals series is eight, by Tim Thomas (USA) for the Boston Bruins vs the Vancouver Canucks in 2011.

NATIONAL HOCKEY LEAGUE		
Most Stanley Cup Final appearances	34	Montreal Canadiens (CAN), 1916–93
Most Stanley Cup wins	24	Montreal Canadiens (CAN), 1916–93
Most games played in a career	1,767	Gordie Howe (CAN), for the Detroit Red Wings and Hartford Whalers, 1946–80
Longest winning streak	17	Pittsburgh Penguins (USA), from 9 Mar to 10 Apr 1993
Most goals scored	894	Wayne Gretzky (CAN), for the Edmonton Oilers, Los Angeles Kings, St Louis Blues and New York Rangers
Most goals in a game by a player	7	Joe Malone (CAN), for the Quebec Bulldogs vs Toronto St Patricks on 31 Jan 1920
Most goals in a game by a team	16	Montreal Canadiens, in a 16–3 victory over the Quebec Bulldogs (both CAN) on 3 Mar 1920
Most goals in a season by a player	92	Wayne Gretzky (CAN), for the Edmonton Oilers in 1981–82
Most goals in a season by a team	446	Edmonton Oilers (CAN), 1983–84
Most saves by a goaltender	27,312	Martin Brodeur (CAN), for the New Jersey Devils, 1993–present

All statistics correct as of 29 Jan 2014

Marathons

London Marathon runners have raised some **£663 m** for charity

Deepest marathon
The Crystal Mine Underground Marathon is run in an old salt mine located 500 m (1,640 ft) below sea level. It has taken place in Sondershausen, Thuringia, Germany, annually since 2002.

Coldest marathon
In 2001, the Siberian Ice Marathon in Omsk, Russia, registered a temperature of -39°C (-38°F), making it the coldest regular marathon.
Some 94°C (169°F) warmer, the **hottest marathon** is the Badwater Ultramarathon held between Death Valley and Mount Whitney in California, USA, which registers temperatures of 55°C (131°F).

Fastest marathon (female)
Paula Radcliffe (UK) finished the London Marathon on 13 Apr 2003 in 2 hr 15 min 25 sec, making her the fastest female marathon runner of all time. She also ran the **fastest Chicago Marathon (female)**, on 13 Oct 2002, finishing in 2 hr 17 min 18 sec.

Fastest aggregate World Marathon Majors time
The "World Marathon Majors" comprise the Olympic and World Championship marathons as well as those held in Berlin, Boston, Chicago, London and New York City. Kjell-Erik Ståhl (SWE) completed the seven Majors in an aggregate time of 15 hr 36 min 47 sec. His record-breaking sequence began at the Moscow 1980 Olympic Games and ended in Berlin in 1991.

Most northerly marathon
The North Pole Marathon held at the geographic North Pole has been run annually since 2002. In 2007, Thomas Maguire (IRL) ran the **fastest men's North Pole marathon** in 3 hr 36 min 10 sec. A year later, Cathrine Due (DNK) recorded the **fastest women's** in 5 hr 37 min 14 sec.
The **most southerly marathon** is the Antarctic Ice Marathon, held on the Antarctic mainland at a latitude of 80° south.

Fastest marathon
The Berlin Marathon in Germany was the setting for the fastest marathon ever. It took Wilson Kipsang (KEN) just 2 hr 3 min 23 sec to complete the course on 29 Sep 2013. Kipsang has also won the Frankfurt Marathon twice (2010–11) and the London Marathon twice (2012 and 2014).

Fastest Olympic marathon
Female: On 5 Aug 2012, Tiki Gelana (ETH) clocked 2 hr 23 min 7 sec to take gold in the women's marathon at the London 2012 Games. However, the Olympic record isn't her personal best: she ran the Rotterdam Marathon in the Netherlands in 2 hr 18 min 58 sec on 15 Apr 2012.
Male: Samuel Wanjiru (KEN) won the marathon in Beijing in 2 hr 6 min 32 sec on 24 Aug 2008.

Most World Marathon Majors races won
Female: Grete Waitz (NOR) won 12 Majors: nine in New York, two in London and one World Championship between 1978 and 1987.
Male: Bill Rodgers (USA) won eight Majors: four in Boston and four in New York from 1975 to 1980.

Most ITU World Triathlon Series medals
Female: Michellie Jones (AUS) won two gold, two silver and four bronze medals at the International Triathlon Union World Championships. She won her eight medals in 1991–2003.
Male: Simon Lessing (UK) collected seven World Championship medals: four

2014 VIRGIN MONEY LONDON MARATHON: NEW WORLD RECORDS

While marathon running is a serious business for elite athletes, such as those featured above, for others it is a great excuse to have some fun and raise money for charity – and where better to have it than at the world's premier marathon event: the London Marathon! Pictured below are some of the colourful characters who took part this year, listed in order of their running times.

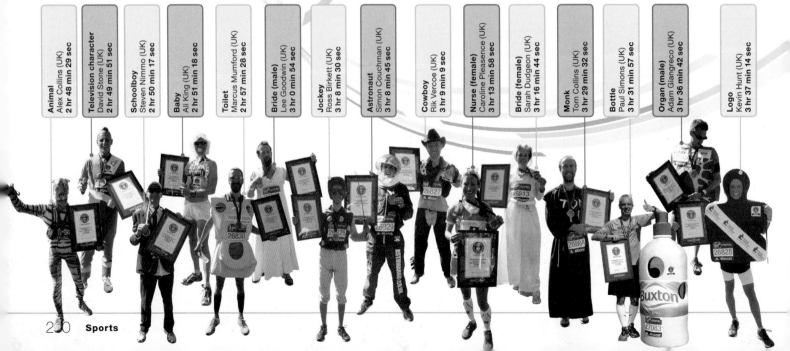

Animal Alex Collins (UK) 2 hr 48 min 29 sec

Television character David Stone (UK) 2 hr 49 min 51 sec

Schoolboy Steven Nimmo (UK) 2 hr 50 min 17 sec

Baby Ali King (UK) 2 hr 51 min 18 sec

Toilet Marcus Mumford (UK) 2 hr 57 min 28 sec

Bride (male) Lee Goodwin (UK) 3 hr 0 min 54 sec

Jockey Ross Birkett (UK) 3 hr 8 min 30 sec

Astronaut Simon Couchman (UK) 3 hr 8 min 45 sec

Cowboy Rik Vercoe (UK) 3 hr 9 min 9 sec

Nurse (female) Caroline Pleasence (UK) 3 hr 13 min 58 sec

Bride (female) Sarah Dudgeon (UK) 3 hr 16 min 44 sec

Monk Tom Collins (UK) 3 hr 29 min 32 sec

Bottle Paul Simons (UK) 3 hr 31 min 57 sec

Organ (male) Adam Giangreco (UK) 3 hr 36 min 42 sec

Logo Kevin Hunt (UK) 3 hr 37 min 14 sec

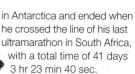

BIGGEST MARATHONS

Marathon	Most finishers	Fastest (male)	Fastest (female)
Berlin, Germany	36,544 29 Sep 2013	Wilson Kipsang (KEN), 2:03:23, 29 Sep 2013	Mizuki Noguchi (JPN), 2:19:12, 25 Sep 2005
Boston, Massachusetts, USA	35,868 15 Apr 1996	Geoffrey Mutai (KEN), 2:03:02, 18 Apr 2011	Rita Jeptoo (KEN), 2:18:57, 21 Apr 2014
Chicago, Illinois, USA	39,122 13 Oct 2013	Dennis Kimetto (KEN), 2:03:45, 13 Oct 2013	Paula Radcliffe (UK), 2:17:18, 13 Oct 2002
London, UK	36,672 22 Apr 2012	Wilson Kipsang (KEN), 2:04:29, 13 Apr 2014	Paula Radcliffe (UK), 2:15:25, 13 Apr 2003
New York City, New York, USA	50,062 3 Nov 2013	Geoffrey Mutai (KEN), 2:05:06, 6 Nov 2011	Margaret Okayo (KEN), 2:22:31, 2 Nov 2003
Osaka, Japan	27,674 27 Oct 2013	Ser-Od Bat-Ochir (MNG), 2:11:52, 25 Nov 2012	Lidia Şimon (ROM), 2:32:48, 30 Oct 2011
Paris, France	38,690 7 Apr 2013	Kenenisa Bekele (ETH), 2:05:04, 6 Apr 2014	Feyse Tadese (ETH), 2:21:06, 7 Apr 2013
Tokyo, Japan	35,308 24 Feb 2013	Dickson Chumba (KEN), 2:05:42, 23 Feb 2014	Tirfi Tsegaye (ETH), 2:22:23, 23 Feb 2014

Statistics correct as of 30 Apr 2014. The IAAF rules the Boston course ineligible to set world records

gold, two silver and one bronze from 1992 to 1999. The record was equalled by Javier Gómez (ESP), with three golds, three silvers and one bronze in 2007–13.

Fastest time to complete the Hawaiian Ironman
Male: The Ironman World Championship, aka the "Hawaiian Ironman", was first held on 18 Feb 1978 in Kailua-Kona, Hawaii, USA. It was described as "Swim 2.4 miles! Bike 112 miles! Run 26.2 miles! Brag for the rest of your life!" Craig Alexander (AUS) holds the course record of 8 hr 3 min 56 sec, which he set on 8 Oct 2011 with a 3.8-km swim in 51 min 56 sec, a 180-km cycle in 4 hr 24 min 5 sec and a marathon run in 2 hr 44 min 2 sec.

First winner of the wheelchair marathon Grand Slam

Tatyana McFadden (USA) completed the wheelchair marathon "Grand Slam" in 2013. The feat comprises wins of the wheelchair marathons in Boston, London, Chicago and New York in a single year. Tatyana also recorded the **fastest women's wheelchair London Marathon** in a time of 1 hr 46 min 2 sec on 21 Apr 2013.

Female: On 12 Oct 2013, Australia's Mirinda Carfrae recorded the fastest women's time, in 8 hr 52 min 14 sec. Her nearest rival was more than 5 min behind.

The **oldest person to complete the Hawaiian Ironman** is Lew Hollander (USA, b. 6 Jun 1930), who was aged 82 years 129 days when he crossed the finish line on 13 Oct 2012.

Fastest time to run an ultramarathon on each continent
Ziyad Tariq Rahim (PAK) ran seven 50-km (36.6-mi) ultramarathons – one on each continent from 26 Jan to 8 Mar 2014. The timing for this record began when Ziyad started his first ultramarathon

in Antarctica and ended when he crossed the line of his last ultramarathon in South Africa, with a total time of 41 days 3 hr 23 min 40 sec.

Andrei Rosu (ROM) set the **fastest time to run a marathon and an ultramarathon on each continent** in 1 year 217 days. He started with the Australian Outback Marathon on 31 Jul 2010 and ended with the Supermaratona Cidade do Rio Grande ultramarathon in Brazil on 4 Mar 2012.

Fastest time to complete 10 marathons in 10 days
Male: Adam Holland (UK) ran the 2010 Brathay 10 in 10 challenge in Cumbria, UK, from 7–16 May. His total time was 30 hr 20 min 54 sec.
Female: Sally Ford (UK) ran the same challenge two years later on 11–20 May, taking 36 hr 38 min 53 sec.

Fastest marathon barefoot
Male: Abebe Bikila (ETH) ran the 1960 Olympic marathon in his bare feet. He set a time of 2 hr 15 min 16.2 sec in Rome, Italy, on 10 Sep 1960.
Female: It took just 2 hr 29 min 45 sec for barefooted Kenyan Tegla Loroupe to run the Olympic marathon in Sydney, Australia, on 24 Sep 2000.

Virgin money LONDON MARATHON 2014

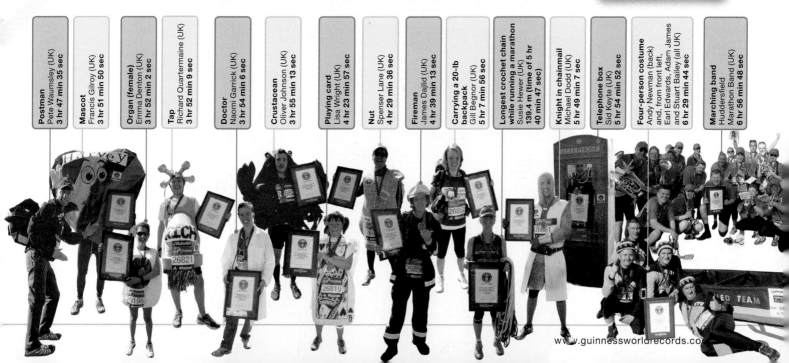

Postman Pete Waumsley (UK) 3 hr 47 min 35 sec

Mascot Francis Gilroy (UK) 3 hr 51 min 50 sec

Organ (female) Emma Denton (UK) 3 hr 52 min 2 sec

Tap Richard Quartermaine (UK) 3 hr 52 min 9 sec

Doctor Naomi Garrick (UK) 3 hr 54 min 6 sec

Crustacean Oliver Johnson (UK) 3 hr 55 min 13 sec

Playing card Lisa Wright (UK) 4 hr 23 min 57 sec

Nut Spenser Lane (UK) 4 hr 29 min 36 sec

Fireman James Dajlid (UK) 4 hr 39 min 13 sec

Carrying a 20-lb backpack Gill Begnor (UK) 5 hr 7 min 56 sec

Longest crochet chain while running a marathon Susie Hewer (UK) 139.4 m (time of 5 hr 40 min 47 sec)

Knight in chainmail Michael Dodd (UK) 5 hr 49 min 7 sec

Telephone box Sid Keyte (UK) 5 hr 54 min 52 sec

Four-person costume Andy Newman (back) and, from front left, Earl Edwards, Adam James and Stuart Bailey (all UK) 6 hr 29 min 44 sec

Marching band Huddersfield Marathon Band (UK) 6 hr 56 min 48 sec

Motorsports

There are approximately **80,000 components** in every Formula One car

Most finishers in the Baja 1000 off-road race

The 1,000-km (620-mi) Baja 1000 is staged on Mexico's Baja California peninsula. The off-road race allows motorcycles, cars and trucks to compete together. Unmarked challenges include harsh desert conditions, wandering animals and traps made by spectators for their own amusement. The most drivers to complete the race is 237, out of the 424 starters in 2007.

on to win the 2013 MotoGP World Championship at Circuit Ricardo Tormo in Spain, becoming the **youngest MotoGP world champion**, at 20 years 266 days, on 10 Nov 2013.

Fastest Isle of Man TT Superbike race

Michael Dunlop (UK) set a time of 1 hr 45 min 29.98 sec on his 1000-cc TT Legends Honda in a six-lap Isle of Man TT Superbike race in Douglas, Isle of Man, UK, on 2 Jun 2013.

Most wins of the Motocross des Nations

Staged on off-road circuits, the Motocross des Nations,

Most consecutive NASCAR Sprint Cup Series wins

Jimmie Johnson (USA) won five successive National Association for Stock Car Auto Racing (NASCAR) Sprint Cup Series championships between 2006 and 2010. His streak ended when Tony Stewart (USA) won in 2011, but Johnson regained the title in the 2013 series. This brings his total to six series titles overall in 2006–13.

BIKES

Most MotoGP championships won

MotoGP is one of the three classes in the Road Racing World Championship Grand Prix, motorcycling's premier road-racing competition since it replaced the 500-cc class in 2002. The greatest number of victories in the MotoGP championships is six and was achieved by Valentino Rossi (ITA) in 2002–05 and 2008–09.

The **most wins of the MotoGP championships by a constructor** is seven,

achieved by Honda (JPN) in 2002–04, 2006 and 2011–13.

Youngest rider to achieve a MotoGP pole position

On 20 Apr 2013, Marc Márquez (ESP, b. 17 Feb 1993) took pole position at the 2013 Motorcycle Grand Prix of the Americas at the Circuit of the Americas in Austin, Texas, USA, aged 20 years 62 days.

The next day, Márquez won the race, becoming the **youngest MotoGP race winner**, at the age of 20 years 63 days. He went

also known as the "Olympics of Motocross", has been contested annually since 1947. The team with the most wins is the USA, with 22 between 1981 and 2011.

CARS

Most F1 victories by a constructor

The greatest number of Formula One (F1) Grand Prix wins by one manufacturer is 221, by Italian constructor Ferrari between 1951 and 2013. The team's first victory came at the 1951 British Grand Prix held at Silverstone, Northamptonshire, UK, which was won by Argentinian driver José Froilán González. Ferrari has also recorded the **most consecutive F1 Grand**

Most leaders in an Indianapolis 500 race

There were 14 different leaders of the 2013 edition of the Indianapolis 500 race at Indianapolis Motor Speedway in Indiana, USA, on 26 May 2013. In order, they were: Carpenter, Kanaan, Andretti, Hunter-Reay, Power, Jakes, Viso, Muñoz, Allmendinger, Tagliani, Bell, Hinchcliffe, Castroneves and Dixon. The race was won by Tony Kanaan.

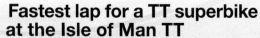

Fastest lap for a TT superbike at the Isle of Man TT

In a TT Superbike-class race in Douglas, Isle of Man, UK, on 2 Jun 2013, John McGuinness (UK) completed a lap on a Honda CBR1000RR in just 17 min 11.57 sec. McGuinness set the record with his sixth and final lap of the Mountain Course, during which he maintained an average speed of 211.90 km/h (131.67 mph).

MOST WINS OF THE ...		
Competition	Wins	Champion
International Isle of Man TT (Tourist Trophy) Race	26	Joey Dunlop (UK) in 1977, 1980, 1983–88, 1992–98 and 2000
Motocross des Nations	22	USA in 1981–93, 1996, 2000 and 2005–11
Formula One World Constructors' Championship	16	Ferrari (ITA) in 1961, 1964, 1975–77, 1979, 1982–83, 1999–2004 and 2007–08
Road Racing World Championship Grand Prix	15	Giacomo Agostini (ITA) 500-cc in 1966–72 and 1975; and 350-cc in 1968–74
Motocross World Championship	10	Stefan Everts (DEU) 125-cc in 1991; 250-cc in 1995–97; 500-cc in 2001–02; MXGP in 2003; and MX1 in 2004–06
World Rally Championship	9	Sébastien Loeb (FRA) in 2004–12
Formula One World Drivers' Championship	7	Michael Schumacher (DEU) in 1994–95 and 2000–04
NASCAR Sprint Cup Series Drivers' Championship	7	Richard Petty (USA) in 1964, 1967, 1971–72, 1974–75 and 1979
		Dale Earnhardt, Sr (USA) in 1980, 1986–87, 1990–91 and 1993–94
Karting World Championship	6	Mike Wilson (UK) in 1981–83, 1985 and 1988–89
MotoGP Championship	6	Valentino Rossi (ITA) in 2002–05 and 2008–09
Dakar Rally	5	Stéphane Peterhansel and Jean-Paul Cottret (both FRA) in 2004–05, 2007 and 2012–13
Superbike World Championship	4	Carl Fogarty (UK) in 1994–95 and 1998–99

Statistics correct as of 25 Mar 2014

Most consecutive Formula One Grand Prix wins

Sebastian Vettel (DEU) won nine Formula One Grands Prix driving for Red Bull in the 2013 season from 25 Aug to 24 Nov 2013. Vettel also became the **youngest F1 world champion** when he won the 2010 Abu Dhabi Grand Prix, aged 23 years 134 days, on 14 Nov 2010.

to win at least one Grand Prix in the eight successive seasons up to and including his victory at the Grand Prix in Sepang, Malaysia, on 30 Mar 2014.

Most wins in a NASCAR Sprint Cup Series season
In the 1967 season, Richard Petty (USA) recorded 27 wins in the NASCAR Sprint Cup Series. In the same year, he set the mark for the **most consecutive NASCAR race wins**, with 10 victories from 12 Aug to 1 Oct 1967.

First F1 driver to finish every debut season Grand Prix

Max Chilton (UK) completed all 19 races during his debut season in 2013, driving for Marussia. True, he didn't secure a single point, but he became the first rookie in the 64-year history of the F1 championship to finish every race.

Prix points finishes by a constructor. The team enjoyed 71 successive points finishes between the German Grand Prix staged on 25 Jul 2010 and the Chinese Grand Prix on 20 Apr 2014. Since 2010, a driver must finish in the top 10 to earn points for both themselves and their constructor.

Most points by a driver in an F1 career
The greatest number of points in an F1 career is 1,647, by Fernando Alonso (ESP) between 9 Mar 2003 and 20 Apr 2014.

Most F1 Grand Prix wins by a driver in a season
Michael Schumacher (DEU) won 13 Grands Prix in the 2004 season. His feat was equalled by Sebastian Vettel (DEU) in 2013.

Most consecutive seasons to win an F1 Grand Prix from debut
British driver Lewis Hamilton made his F1 Grand Prix debut in 2007 and his first win was in Canada that year. He went on

Most NASCAR race victories in a career

Richard Petty (USA) enjoyed 200 wins during his NASCAR career from 1958 to 1992. He also had the **most NASCAR pole positions** (126) and **most NASCAR race wins from pole position** (61).

Most WRC points in a season by a driver

Sébastien Ogier (FRA) scored 290 points driving for Volkswagen during the 2013 World Rally Championship (WRC) season. Ogier ended Sébastien Loeb's record run of nine consecutive championships by winning the 2013 season, and in the process scored 14 more points than Loeb amassed in 2010.

Rugby

Scotland beat England in the first international rugby match

Most international appearances in rugby union

Brian O'Driscoll (IRL, above with daughter Sadie) made 141 international appearances from 12 Jun 1999 to 15 Mar 2014, playing for Ireland 133 times and eight times for the British and Irish Lions (2001, 2005, 2009 and 2013 tours). He scored 47 international tries and won 81 matches, ending with the 22–20 victory over France that secured the 2014 Six Nations trophy.

Bernard Norman (all AUS), playing for Annandale in the New South Wales Rugby League (the predecessor of the NRL) in the 1910 season. More than 100 years later, the feat was equalled by Sam, Luke, Tom and George Burgess (all UK), who played for South Sydney Rabbitohs against Wests Tigers at the Allianz Stadium in Sydney, Australia, on 30 Aug 2013.

Longest drop-kick
Joseph "Joe" Lydon (UK) scored a 56-m (183-ft) drop-kick for Wigan against Warrington in a Challenge Cup semi-final held at Maine Road in Manchester, UK, on 25 Mar 1989.

Most points scored in a Super League career

Kevin Sinfield (UK) scored 3,498 points for Leeds Rhinos from 13 Sep 1998 to 14 Mar 2014. In 2012, the loose forward won the coveted *Rugby League World* Golden Boot Award, given to the player judged to be the best in the world.

LEAGUE

Fastest try
Tim Spears (UK) scored for Featherstone Rovers just 7.75 sec into a game against Wakefield Trinity Wildcats at Post Office Road in Featherstone, West Yorkshire, UK, on 12 Jan 2014. This (just) beat the previous record of 7.9 sec set by Rochdale Hornets' Danny Samuel (UK) in 2010.

Largest attendance at a World Cup final
A crowd of 74,468 fans watched the Rugby League World Cup final between Australia and New Zealand at Old Trafford in Manchester, UK, on 30 Nov 2013 (see right).

Most siblings to play in the same NRL team
Four brothers have played for the same National Rugby League (NRL) team twice in history. The first set of brothers to achieve this was Ray, Roy, Rex and

Highest margin of victory in a World Cup final

Australia's 32-point win over New Zealand in the 2013 Rugby League World Cup final on 30 Nov 2013 represents the greatest victory margin ever recorded in this competition, which has been held since 1954.

Most points in an international career
Between 5 May 2006 and 30 Nov 2013, Australia's Johnathan Thurston scored 318 points in international rugby league matches. He finally surpassed Mick Cronin's long-standing record of 309 points when he kicked seven goals for 14 points in the 2013 World Cup final against New Zealand.

Oldest player with an international cap in union and league
Tom Calnan (b. 22 Oct 1976) is the oldest person to have won a "double cap" in international rugby, by playing in both codes. Calnan was aged 36 years 50 days when he made his debut for the UAE rugby union side against Hong Kong in Dubai, UAE, on 11 Dec 2012. He had previously represented the UAE rugby league side in a match against Pakistan on 30 Mar 2012.

Youngest international player
Gavin Gordon (b. 28 Feb 1978) played for Ireland vs Moldova on 16 Oct 1995 at Spotland in Rochdale, UK, aged 17 years 229 days. He scored a hat-trick of tries in this debut game, which Ireland won 48–26.

MOST INTERNATIONAL...

Rugby union		
Caps	141	Brian O'Driscoll (IRL, 1999–2014)
Points	1,442	Dan Carter (NZ, 2003–13)
Tries	69	Daisuke Ohata (JPN, 1996–2006)
Rugby league		
Caps	59	Darren Lockyer (AUS, 1998–2011)
Points	318	Johnathan Thurston (AUS, 2006–13)
Tries	41	Mick Sullivan (GB, 1954–63)
Statistics correct as of 15 Mar 2014		

GUINNESS WORLD RECORDS

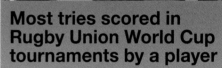

FACT

Farrell's debut, aged just 17, for Saracens against the Llanelli Scarlets in 2008 made him the youngest player in English professional rugby at that time.

Most penalties scored in the Heineken Cup by a player

Owen Farrell (UK) kicked 10 penalties for Saracens vs Racing Métro 92 in the Heineken Cup match held at Stade de la Beaujoire in Nantes, France, on 12 Jan 2013.

Bloemfontein in South Africa. During this match, the All Blacks scored 21 tries.

Youngest World Cup player
On 30 Sep 2007, Thretton Palamo (b. 22 Sep 1988) played for the USA vs South Africa, aged 19 years 8 days, at Stade de la Mosson in Montpellier, France.

Most tries scored in Rugby Union World Cup tournaments by a player

Jonah Lomu (NZ) scored 15 tries in the 1995 and 1999 Rugby Union World Cups. His top tally in a single match was four tries, in a 45–29 win against England on 18 Jun 1995. Above, Lomu is shown playing in the 1999 World Cup, in what proved to be a commanding 101–3 win over Italy.

UNION

Fastest try
Just 7.24 sec into a game on 23 Nov 2013, Tyson Lewis (UK) scored a try for Doncaster Knights vs Old Albanians at Woollam Playing Fields in St Albans, UK.

Fastest sending-off in an English Premiership match
London Scottish player Mike Watson (UK) was sent off after 42 sec against Bath at the Recreation Ground in Bath, UK, on 15 May 1999.

Most consecutive international wins
Cyprus had 21 successive victories from 29 Nov 2008 to 30 Nov 2013.

Most consecutive World Cup defeats
Namibia suffered 15 Rugby Union World Cup losses in a row between 1 Oct 1999 and 26 Sep 2011.

Highest aggregate score in a World Cup match
New Zealand beat Japan 145–17 on 4 Jun 1995 at

First person to play Australian rules, rugby league and rugby union
Karmichael Hunt (AUS) began his career in the NRL with Brisbane Broncos in 2004, switching to rugby union with Biarritz in 2009/10. In 2011, he played in the AFL for the Gold Coast Suns.

Most successive matches to score a try in the English Premiership
Mark Cueto (UK) scored tries in eight consecutive games for Sale Sharks from 9 Apr to 25 Sep 2005.

Most Heineken Cup points scored by a player
Ronan O'Gara (IRL) scored 1,365 points in Heineken Cup matches for Munster from 7 Sep 1997 to 27 Apr 2013.

The **most Heineken Cup tries scored by a player** is 35, by Vincent Clerc (FRA) for Stade Toulousain from 13 Oct 2002 to 13 Jan 2013.

Most tries in a Super Rugby career
Doug Howlett (NZ) scored 59 tries for the Auckland Blues from 1999 to 2007.

Oldest international player
Mark Spencer (b. 21 May 1954) was 57 years 340 days old when he played for Qatar in the Asian 5 Nations competition against Uzbekistan in Dubai, UAE, on 25 Apr 2012. Mark was born in the USA but took up Qatari residency, allowing him to represent the national side.

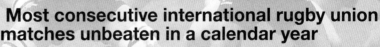

Most consecutive international rugby union matches unbeaten in a calendar year

New Zealand's All Blacks remained unbeaten for 14 international matches during 2013, from 8 Jun to 24 Nov. Not only was the team undefeated, but it also won all of the 14 matches played. In 2003, England won more games (16) but were not unbeaten, having lost one match.

Club soccer

More than **265 million people** play soccer worldwide

FACT
The Copa Libertadores and Champions League are the most prestigious continental competitions in South America and Europe respectively.

First player to score a hat-trick in the Copa Libertadores and the Champions League

On 11 Dec 2013, Barcelona's Neymar (BRA) scored a hat-trick in a Champions League game at the Nou Camp in Spain. Having previously achieved the feat in the Copa Libertadores on 7 Mar 2012 for Brazilian side Santos, he became the first player to score hat-tricks in both contests.

Most valuable soccer club
According to Forbes, as of 17 Apr 2013 Real Madrid was valued at $3.3 bn (£2.15 bn). The Spanish side, who won a 32nd La Liga title in 2011/12, ended Manchester United's run at the top of the rich list.

Most red cards in a game
In an Argentine Primera D match between Club Atlético Claypole and Victoriano Arenas on 27 Feb 2011, 36 players (both sides and all substitutes) were sent off by Damián Rubino (ARG).

First player to hold four major continental trophies simultaneously
When Chelsea won the Europa League on 15 May 2013, Fernando Torres and Juan Mata (both ESP) held four of soccer's most prestigious titles:

by 4.7 billion people across 212 territories. The total was boosted by its broadcast on terrestrial TV in China.

Most goals in a single national top-division season by an individual
Archibald Stark (UK) scored 67 times for Bethlehem Steel in the American Soccer League between 15 Sep 1924 and 18 May 1925.

Most consecutive top-division league titles
Skonto FC, from capital city Riga, won the Latvian Higher League 14 consecutive times from 1991 to 2004.

Most hat-tricks in La Liga
Telmo Zarra (ESP) scored 22 hat-tricks for Athletic Bilbao from 1940 to 1953. Alfredo Di Stéfano (ARG/ESP) matched the feat playing for Real Madrid and Espanyol from 1953 to 1966.

Most MLS championships
Two teams have won the USA's Major League Soccer Cup four times: Washington's DC United (1996–97, 1999 and 2004) and LA Galaxy from California (2002, 2005 and 2011–12).

the World Cup, European Championship, Champions League and Europa League.

DOMESTIC

Most viewed domestic soccer league (global)
In 2010/11, the English Premier League was viewed

Most consecutive losses
A home defeat by Rothwell Corinthians saw Woodford United FC (UK) record

Longest unbeaten streak in the Bundesliga

Bayern Munich were unbeaten in the Bundesliga – the top division in German soccer – for 53 games from 3 Nov 2012 to 29 Mar 2014. The run finally ended on 5 Apr 2014 against Augsburg, who beat them 1–0. The previous record of 36 games unbeaten had been set by Hamburg in 1983.

62 consecutive losses. The United Counties League match finished 6–2 at Byfield Road stadium in Woodford Halse, UK, on 26 Oct 2013.

Youngest man to play in all four English Football League divisions
Jack Hobbs (UK, b. 18 Aug 1988) made his debut for League One side Leicester City on 9 Aug 2008 aged 19 years 357 days. Hobbs had previously played for Lincoln City in League Two, Liverpool in the Premier League and Scunthorpe in the Championship.

Most appearances in the English top division
Goalkeeper Peter Shilton (UK) recorded 848 appearances for Leicester City, Stoke City, Nottingham Forest, Southampton and Derby County from 3 May 1966 to 11 May 1991.

Most appearances for the same club

Rogério Ceni (BRA) appeared in 1,081 competitive matches for São Paulo Futebol Clube between 7 Jul 1993 and 27 Nov 2013. Keeper Ceni regularly takes free kicks and penalties, securing him the record for **most goals by a goalkeeper** (113) as of 13 Nov 2013.

Most expensive player
The transfer fee for winger Gareth Bale (UK) from Tottenham Hotspur (UK) to Real Madrid (ESP) on 1 Sep 2013 was a reported £85.3 m ($132 m), eclipsing the £80 m ($132 m) Real Madrid paid for Cristiano Ronaldo on 1 Jul 2009.

MOST WINS OF A MAJOR CONTINENTAL TROPHY

Team	Country	Trophy	Wins
Real Madrid	Spain	European Cup/Champions League	9
Al Ahly	Egypt	African/CAF Champions League	8
AC Milan	Italy	European Cup/Champions League	7
Independiente	Argentina	Copa Libertadores	7
Boca Juniors	Argentina	Copa Libertadores	6
Cruz Azul	Mexico	CONCACAF Champions' Cup/League	6
América	Mexico	CONCACAF Champions' Cup/League	5
Auckland City	New Zealand	OFC Champions League	5
Bayern Munich	Germany	European Cup/Champions League	5
Liverpool	England	European Cup/Champions League	5
Peñarol	Uruguay	Copa Libertadores	5
Zamalek	Egypt	African/CAF Champions League	5

Statistics correct as of 25 Apr 2014

Most consecutive weeks leading La Liga

Barcelona spent 59 weeks at the top of La Liga, the Spanish top division, from 19 Aug 2012 to 27 Jan 2014. Barcelona also hold the record for the **most consecutive La Liga victories**. They racked up 16 wins in a row between 16 Oct 2010 and 5 Feb 2011, outscoring their opponents by 60 goals to 6 during the streak.

EUROPEAN

Oldest player to make a Champions League debut
Mark Schwarzer (AUS, b. 6 Oct 1972) took to the pitch aged 41 years 66 days in his Champions League debut for Chelsea against Steaua Bucharest at Stamford Bridge in London, UK, on 11 Dec 2013.

Tottenham keeper Brad Friedel (USA, b. 18 May 1971) was 42 years 305 days old when he played against Benfica on 20 Mar 2014, making him the **oldest player in the UEFA Europa League**.

FACT

Ronaldo is a record-breaker off the pitch too. He has the **most Twitter followers for an athlete**, with 25,229,560 as of 1 Apr 2014.

Most appearances in the Champions League
Ryan Giggs (UK) has racked up 151 appearances for Manchester United in the UEFA Champions League. His debut came in Sep 1993, and more than 20 years later, on 1 Apr 2014, he played in a quarter-final match against Bayern Munich.

Most Europa League appearances
Ola Toivonen (SWE) appeared in 36 UEFA Europa League games for PSV Eindhoven between 30 Jul 2009 and 12 Dec 2013.

Most Champions League wins by an individual
Spanish midfielder Xavi won 83 matches playing for Barcelona from 16 Sep 1998 to 12 Mar 2014.

Most consecutive Champions League matches with a goal
Real Madrid scored in 35 consecutive Champions League games from 3 May 2011 to 2 Apr 2014.

Highest total score in a European Cup match
A first-round European Cup match between Feyenoord (NLD) and KR Reykjavík (ISL) saw a total of 14 goals scored. The match, which took place on 17 Sep 1969, saw a Dutch 12–2 victory.

The **most goals in a single Champions**

Longest goal scored

On 2 Nov 2013, when Stoke City's goalie Asmir Begović (BIH) cleared the ball 13 sec into a Premier League game, something very unusual happened. The ball, caught by the wind, flew over the head of the Southampton keeper, scoring Begović a goal from 91.9 m (301 ft 6 in) away. Only Ledley King has scored faster in the Premier League, his goal coming after just 10 sec.

League match is 11, and was achieved when Monaco (FRA) beat Deportivo La Coruña (ESP) 8–3 at home on 5 Nov 2003.

Most Champions League goals in a calendar year

Cristiano Ronaldo (POR) found the back of the net 15 times for Real Madrid between 13 Feb and 10 Dec 2013, beating the record of 13 goals set by his Barcelona rival Lionel Messi in 2012.

International soccer

The average soccer player runs 11 km in a 90-min match

SPAIN 10 - 0 TAHITI
TORRES 5' 33' 57' 78'
DAVID SILVA 31' 89'
VILLA 39' 49' 64'
MATA 66'

Highest margin of victory in a FIFA tournament (men)

A Confederations Cup match on 20 Jun 2013 saw Spain put 10 goals past Tahiti at the Estádio do Maracanã in Rio de Janeiro, Brazil. Tahiti – a team of amateur players – had been surprise qualifiers following their victory in the 2012 Oceania Football Confederation Nations Cup.

Most international caps

Kristine Lilly (USA) won 352 caps during her international career – more than any other man or woman. Her first cap came in 1987 and her last was on 5 Nov 2010.

The record for the **most international caps by a man** belongs to Ahmed Hassan (EGY), who won 184 caps between 29 Dec 1995 and 22 May 2012.

Most international wins by a player

Goalkeeper Iker Casillas racked up 112 wins playing in 153 games for Spain between 3 Jun 2000 and 5 Mar 2014.

Longest unbeaten run in competitive internationals

Spain went unbeaten for 29 games between 21 Jun 2010 and 27 Jun 2013. Their winning streak came to an end at the hands of Brazil in the 2013 Confederations Cup final. If friendly matches were included, Spain and Brazil would share the record.

Youngest player to reach 100 caps

South Korea's Cha Bum-Kun (b. 22 May 1953) was aged 24 years 139 days playing his 100th game on 9 Oct 1977 against Kuwait.

Oldest international player

On 31 Mar 2004, MacDonald Taylor Sr (VIR, b. 27 Aug 1957) played for the US Virgin Islands at the age of 46 years 217 days.

Most teams in UEFA European Championship qualifying

Following Gibraltar's addition to the Union of European Football Associations (UEFA) in 2013, a record 53 teams will attempt to qualify for the 2016 European Championship.

Most consecutive losses

On 4 Sep 2004, San Marino began a losing streak of 57 matches in a row. Their most recent match, on 15 Oct 2013, saw an 8–0 hammering by Ukraine. Prior to Gibraltar joining UEFA, San Marino was the smallest side competing in European soccer, with a population of just 30,000.

Most international goals

No soccer player – male or female – has scored more international goals than American striker Abby Wambach (left). As of 12 Mar 2014, she had 167 goals to her name, scored since 9 Sep 2001. Wambach surpassed her old team-mate Mia Hamm's record of 158 goals to take the record in Jun 2013 with four goals against South Korea in Harrison, New Jersey, USA.

Most hat-tricks in the Confederations Cup

Fernando Torres (ESP) is the only player to have scored two hat-tricks in the FIFA (Fédération Internationale de Football Association) Confederations Cup. Torres scored them on 14 Jun 2009 and 20 Jun 2013.

FIFA WORLD CUP

Most tournaments won

The Brazilian men's team have won five World Cups, taking the crown in 1958–62, 1970, 1994 and 2002.

The **most Women's World Cup wins** is two, first achieved by the USA in 1991 and 1999 and then matched by Germany in 2003–07.

Most international goals (men)

Ali Daei earned 149 caps for Iran in his career. He scored in more than half of the matches – 109 goals in total – between 25 Jun 1993 and 1 Mar 2006. In second place is Hungarian Ferenc Puskás, who scored 84 goals in 85 matches.

Oldest coach to win the European Championship

Luis Aragonés (ESP, 1938–2014) was aged 69 years 337 days when he coached Spain to a UEFA European Championship title. The win came at the Ernst-Happel Stadium in Vienna, Austria, on 29 Jun 2008.

Highest goal average at a World Cup finals

The 1954 World Cup in Switzerland saw an average of 5.38 goals scored per match. The **lowest goal average at a World Cup finals** was 2.21 per game in 1990.

Most goals scored

Men: Brazilian striker Ronaldo, aka Ronaldo Luís Nazário de Lima, scored 15 goals across three World Cup tournaments in 1998–2006.

MOST CONFEDERATION CHAMPIONSHIP WINS

Men's competition	No.	Country
Asian Football Confederation (AFC): Asian Cup	4	Japan
Confederation of African Football (CAF): African Cup of Nations	7	Egypt
Confederation of North, Central American and Caribbean Association Football (CONCACAF): Gold Cup	6	Mexico
Union of European Football Associations (UEFA): European Championship	3	Spain
		Germany
Confederación Sudamericana de Fútbol/Confederação Sul-Americana de Futebol (CONMEBOL): Copa América	15	Uruguay
Oceania Football Confederation (OFC): Nations Cup	4	New Zealand
		Australia

Women's competition	No.	Country
AFC: Asian Cup	8	China
CAF: African Women's Championship	8	Nigeria
CONCACAF: Gold Cup	4	USA
UEFA: European Championship	8	Germany
CONMEBOL: Sudamericano Femenino	5	Brazil
OFC: Oceania Cup	4	New Zealand

Statistics correct as of 11 Mar 2014

Women: Birgit Prinz (DEU) scored 14 goals at four World Cups between 1995 and 2007. Marta (BRA) matched the feat over three World Cups in 2003–11.

Highest margin of victory

Women: The very first match at the Women's World Cup on 10 Sep 2007 saw Germany put 11 goals past the Argentinian defence. Germany went on to lift the trophy, beating Brazil 2–0.
Men: On 17 Jun 1954, five Hungarians scored in a 9–0 thrashing of South Korea. Subsequently, Yugoslavia defeated Zaire 9–0 in 1974 and Hungary beat El Salvador 10–1 in 1982.

Most players sent off in one finals match

Nicknamed "The Battle of Nuremberg", a match between the Netherlands and Portugal at the 2006 World Cup had four players seeing red, two from each side, in Nuremberg, Germany, on 25 Jun.

Most teams represented at the FIFA World Cup

FIFA rules prohibit players from switching nationalities at senior level; however, Dejan Stanković has represented three Balkan countries as political borders have shifted. He played in three World Cups, representing Yugoslavia in 1998 (above), Serbia and Montenegro in 2006 (above inset) and Serbia in 2010 (right).

Most qualifiers played

Between 4 Mar 1934 and 20 Nov 2013, the Mexican men's team participated in 141 World Cup qualifying matches. Mexico won 92 of the games – the **most World Cup qualifiers won**.

West Germany recorded the **most consecutive World Cup qualifiers won**, with 16 in a row between 10 May 1969 and 30 Apr 1985.

Most wins of the FIFA World Cup by a player

The only soccer player to have won the FIFA World Cup three times is Pelé (BRA), who won the 1958, 1962 and 1970 titles with Brazil.

From 7 Sep 1956 to 1 Oct 1977, Pelé scored 1,279 goals in 1,363 games — the **most career goals**.

Most wins of the Confederations Cup

The Brazilians have won the FIFA Confederations Cup four times, in 1997 and 2005–13. They also have the **most consecutive Confederations Cup match wins**, with 12 from 25 Jun 2005 to 30 Jun 2013.

 Cup competitors

The Confederations Cup is contested every four years by the winners of the six FIFA confederation championships (see table above), the FIFA World Cup holder and the host nation.

Tennis & racket sports

Wimbledon is the only tennis Grand Slam tournament still played on grass

FACT

Graf won 22 Grand Slam singles titles, starting and ending with the French Open in 1987 and 1999.

First tennis player to win a "Career Super Slam"

A "Career Super Slam" involves winning all four Grand Slams, the Davis Cup (male)/Fed Cup (female), the ATP World Tour Finals (male)/ WTA Tour Championships (female) and an Olympic gold medal. In 1988, Steffi Graf (DEU) became the first tennis player to achieve this. Her husband, Andre Agassi (USA), became the **first male tennis player to win a "Career Super Slam"**, doing so in 1999.

Female: Four Chinese women have won the singles title twice: Li Lingwei, Han Aiping, Ye Zhaoying and, most recently, Xie Xingfang in 2005 and 2006.

Longest rally in competition

On 18 Mar 2010, during the third set of a Swiss Open match in Basel, 154 strokes were played by Petya Nedelcheva (BGR) and Anastasia Russkikh (RUS) vs Shizuka Matsuo and Mami Naito (both JPN).

SQUASH

Most European Team Championships won
England hold both the **male** and **female** records for this competition with 38 and 35 wins respectively.

Most World Open wins
Male: Jansher Khan (PAK) won a record eight

FACT

Jahangir Khan and Jansher Khan were fierce rivals. However, they are not related.

Longest unbeaten squash run

Male: The longest unbeaten run in men's squash is 555 games, by Jahangir Khan (PAK) from Nov 1981 to Nov 1986.
Female: Heather McKay (AUS) was unbeaten in 1962–81, and lost just two matches in her career.

World Open titles: in 1987, 1989–90 and 1992–96.
Female: The women's title has been won seven times by Nicol David (MYS), in 2005–06 and 2008–12.

Most World Series Finals
Male: Jansher Khan has had the most wins of the World Series Finals, with four titles between 1993 and 1998.

Female: The women's World Series Finals have been held twice. Nicol David won both times, in 2012 and 2013.

Longest singles marathon
Guy Fotherby and Darren Withey (both UK) endured 31 hr 35 min 34 sec playing squash singles at Racquets Fitness Centre in Thame, Oxfordshire, UK, on 13–14 Jan 2012. Darren won 422 of 465 games.

BADMINTON

Most Sudirman Cup wins
The Sudirman Cup – held every two years since 1989 – is the mixed-team world championship. China accumulated nine wins between 1995 and 2013. The 2013 final also saw China record the **most consecutive Sudirman Cup wins**: five triumphs in a row (2005–13).

Most Thomas Cup wins
Also known as the World Men's Team Championships, the Thomas Cup was won 13 times by Indonesia between 1958 and 2002.

Most singles BWF World Championships titles
Male: When China's Dan Lin won the singles title at the Badminton World Federation (BWF) World Championships on 11 Aug 2013, he did so for the fifth time.

TENNIS

Most prize money for a Grand Slam
Total prize money for the US Open rose to $34.3 m (£21.8 m) for the 2013 tournament. The singles champions, Rafael Nadal and Serena Williams, each collected $2.6 m (£1.7 m).

Most retirements in one day at a Grand Slam
On 26 Jun 2013, at the Wimbledon Championships in London, UK, seven players retired mid-match or withdrew before making it on to court. Dubbed "Wipeout Wednesday", the day saw injuries to one shoulder, one arm, one hamstring and four knees.

Most "powerful" athlete

Swiss sensation Roger Federer is the top sports star on Forbes' list of the world's most powerful celebrities, ranking No.8 overall. Federer holds a wealth of men's tennis records including **most Grand Slam singles titles (17)**, **most Grand Slam matches won (265)** and **most weeks ranked world No.1 (302)**. Forbes' list measures fame by considering earnings, TV and print exposure, strength of internet presence, public opinion and marketability.

108 mph

FACT

Federer earned an estimated £46 m ($71 m) from Jun 2012 to Jun 2013, according to Forbes.

First duo to win each Grand Slam together

Serena Williams (USA) and Rafael Nadal (ESP) are the only duo to win each tennis Grand Slam singles tournament together, both claiming titles at the 2009 Australian Open, Wimbledon in 2010 and Roland Garros in 2013. They completed their set at the US Open on 8–9 Sep 2013.

Most singles titles won at one Grand Slam

Female: No one, male or female, has won more open era (since 1968) singles titles at one Grand Slam than Martina Navratilova (USA). Between 1978 and 1990, she won Wimbledon nine times.

Male: Rafael Nadal won an eighth French Open title when he defeated David Ferrer in straight sets on 9 Jun 2013.

MOST TENNIS GRAND SLAM SINGLES WINS		
Australian Open		
Female	11	Margaret Court (AUS, 1960–1973)
Male	6	Roy Emerson (AUS, 1961–67)
French Open (Roland Garros)		
Male	8	Rafael Nadal (ESP, 2005–13)
Female	7	Chris Evert (USA, 1974–86)
Wimbledon		
Female	9	Martina Navratilova (USA, 1978–90)
Male	7	W C Renshaw (UK, 1881–89)
		Pete Sampras (USA, 1993–2000)
		Roger Federer (CHE, 2003–12)
US Open		
Female	8	Molla Mallory (NOR, 1915–26)
Male	7	Richard Sears (USA, 1881–87)
		William Larned (USA, 1901–11)
		Bill Tilden (USA, 1920–29)

TABLE TENNIS

Most World Table Tennis Championships singles
Female: Angelica Rozeanu (ROM) won six consecutive singles titles in 1950–55.
Male: The men's singles crown was won five times by Viktor Barna (HUN), in 1930 and 1932–35.

Most ITTF World Tour Grand Finals singles titles

Female: Zhang Yining (CHN) claimed four International Table Tennis Federation (ITTF) World Tours, taking the singles crown in 2000, 2002 and 2005–06.
Male: Two Chinese men have won three ITTF singles titles: Wang Liqin (1998, 2000 and 2004) and Ma Long (2008–09 and 2011).

Most Olympic golds

Male: Ma Lin (CHN) has won three table tennis golds, winning doubles in 2004, and singles and team in 2008.
Female: Three Chinese women have won four Olympic golds: Yaping Deng at the 1992 and 1996 Games; Nan Wang in 2000, 2004 and 2008; and Yining Zhang in 2004 and 2008.

Youngest Olympic table tennis gold medallist

On 21 Aug 2004, Chen Qi (CHN, b. 15 Apr 1984) – one of the few top-ranked Chinese left-handers – won the men's doubles aged 20 years 128 days with his partner Ma Lin (CHN).

Most consecutive wins of the ITTF World Tour Grand Finals

Female: Liu Shiwen (CHN, left) won consecutively from 2011–13.
Male: Two Chinese men have won two consecutive ITTF Grand finals: Ma Long (2008–09) and Xu Xin (2012–13).

Most IRF World Championships won (male)

Americans Rocky Carson (above) and Jack Huczek have each won the International Racquetball Federation (IRF) World Championships three consecutive times: Huczek in 2002–06, and Carson in 2008–12.

Fastest serve

On 9 May 2012, Samuel Groth (AUS) served an ace at 263 km/h (163.4 mph).

Most Grand Slams before first title win (female)

Marion Bartoli (FRA) won her first Grand Slam title at her 47th attempt, defeating Germany's Sabine Lisicki in the Wimbledon final on 6 Jul 2013. Her Grand Slam debut was at the 2001 French Open.

Water sports

Michael Phelps eats a mammoth **12,000 calories a day** during training

First open-water swimmer to win a World Championships gold in every discipline (male)

Thomas Lurz (DEU) was the first man to win a FINA World Championships gold in every open-water event, winning the 5, 10 and 25-km races between 2005 and 2013. The **first female** to achieve the same feat was Viola Valli (ITA), between 2001 and 2003.

Most nations in a FINA World Championships

The 15th FINA (Fédération Internationale de Natation) World Championships included participants from 181 nations. It was held in Barcelona, Spain, in 2013.

DIVING

Most consecutive FINA World Championships titles

Guo Jingjing (CHN) won five 3-m diving titles in both individual and synchronized events from 2001 to 2009.

Youngest Summer Olympic medallist in an individual event

Nils Skoglund (SWE, 1906–80) was just 14 years 11 days old when he won silver in the plain high-diving event at the 1920 Olympics.

Most Olympic medals

Male: Dmitri Sautin (RUS) won eight Olympic medals, including two golds, in 1992–2008.
Female: Two Chinese divers have six Olympic medals: Guo Jingjing (2000–08) and Wu Minxia (2004–12).

SWIMMING

Most individual Olympic medals (male)

Michael Phelps (USA) has won more individual medals than any other man across any discipline. He swam his way to 13 medals in individual events at Athens 2004, Beijing 2008 and London 2012. Only one athlete has won more individual medals than him: gymnast Larisa Latynina (USSR/UKR), who won 14.

Phelps also holds Olympic men's records for **most individual event golds** (11), **most golds** (18) and **most swimming medals** (22), as well as seven speed records (see table below).

Most Olympic golds at one Games (female)

Kristin Otto (GDR) won a sensational six swimming gold medals at the 1988 Olympic Games in Seoul.

Most consecutive golds in synchronized swimming at the FINA World Championships

From 23 Jul 2009 to 27 Jul 2013, Russia won 17 synchronized swimming golds at the FINA World Championships, with their latest clean sweep of seven golds in Barcelona, Spain. Russia hope to add to their medal run on home soil at the 2015 Championships in Kazan.

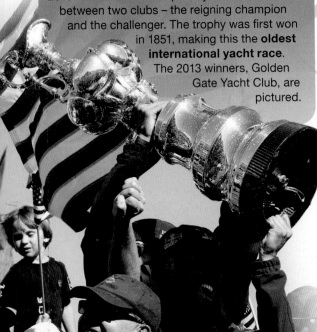

Most America's Cup wins

US teams have won 30 of the 35 America's Cup sailing competitions held between 1851 and 2013. The America's Cup is a yacht race held between two clubs – the reigning champion and the challenger. The trophy was first won in 1851, making this the **oldest international yacht race**. The 2013 winners, Golden Gate Yacht Club, are pictured.

MEN'S SWIMMING – FASTEST...

Event	Time	Name (Nationality)	Time	Name (Nationality)
Freestyle	**Short course**		**Long course**	
50 m	20.30	Roland Schoeman (ZAF)	20.91	Cesar Filho Cielo (BRA)
100 m	44.94	Amaury Leveaux (FRA)	46.91	Cesar Filho Cielo (BRA)
200 m	1:39.37	Paul Biedermann (DEU)	1:42.00	Paul Biedermann (DEU)
400 m	3:32.25	Yannick Agnel (FRA)	3:40.07	Paul Biedermann (DEU)
800 m	7:23.42	Grant Hackett (AUS)	7:32.12	Zhang Lin (CHN)
1,500 m	14:10.10	Grant Hackett (AUS)	14:31.02	Sun Yang (CHN)
4 x 100 m	3:03.30	USA	3:08.24	USA
4 x 200 m	6:49.04	Russia	6:58.55	USA
Butterfly	**Short course**		**Long course**	
50 m	21.80	Steffen Deibler (DEU)	22.43	Rafael Muñoz (ESP)
100 m	48.48	Evgeny Korotyshkin (RUS)	49.82	Michael Phelps (USA)
200 m	*1:48.56	Chad le Clos (ZAF)	1:51.51	Michael Phelps (USA)
Backstroke	**Short course**		**Long course**	
50 m	22.61	Peter Marshall (USA)	24.04	Liam Tancock (UK)
100 m	48.94	Nicholas Thoman (USA)	51.94	Aaron Peirsol (USA)
200 m	1:46.11	Arkady Vyatchanin (RUS)	1:51.92	Aaron Peirsol (USA)
Breaststroke	**Short course**		**Long course**	
50 m	25.25	Cameron van der Burgh (ZAF)	26.67	Cameron van der Burgh (ZAF)
100 m	55.61	Cameron van der Burgh (ZAF)	58.46	Cameron van der Burgh (ZAF)
200 m	2:00.67	Dániel Gyurta (HUN)	2:07.01	Akihiro Yamaguchi (JPN)
Medley	**Short course**		**Long course**	
200 m	1:49.63	Ryan Lochte (USA)	1:54.00	Ryan Lochte (USA)
400 m	3:55.50	Ryan Lochte (USA)	4:03.84	Michael Phelps (USA)
4 x 100 m	3:19.16	Russia	3:27.28	USA

*As of 19 Mar 2014 (*pending FINA approval)*

Event	Time	Name (Nationality)	Time	Name (Nationality)
Freestyle	Short course		Long course	
50 m	23.24	Ranomi Kromowidjojo (NLD)	23.73	Britta Steffen (DEU)
100 m	51.01	Lisbeth Trickett (AUS)	52.07	Britta Steffen (DEU)
200 m	1:51.17	Federica Pellegrini (ITA)	1:52.98	Federica Pellegrini (ITA)
400 m	3:54.52	Mireia Belmonte (ESP)	3:59.15	Federica Pellegrini (ITA)
800 m	7:59.34	Mireia Belmonte (ESP)	8:13.86	Katie Ledecky (USA)
1,500 m	*15:26.95	Mireia Belmonte (ESP)	15:36.53	Katie Ledecky (USA)
4 x 100 m	3:28.22	Netherlands	3:31.72	Netherlands
4 x 200 m	7:35.94	China	7:42.08	China
Butterfly	Short course		Long course	
50 m	24.38	Therese Alshammar (SWE)	25.07	Therese Alshammar (SWE)
100 m	55.05	Diane Bui Duyet (FRA)	55.98	Dana Vollmer (USA)
200 m	2:00.78	Liu Zige (CHN)	2:01.81	Liu Zige (CHN)
Backstroke	Short course		Long course	
50 m	25.70	Sanja Jovanović (CRO)	27.06	Zhao Jing (CHN)
100 m	55.23	Shiho Sakai (JPN)	58.12	Gemma Spofforth (UK)
200 m	2:00.03	"Missy" Franklin (USA)	2:04.06	"Missy" Franklin (USA)
Breaststroke	Short course		Long course	
50 m	*28.71	Yulia Efimova (RUS)	29.48	Rúta Meilutyté (LTU)
100 m	*1:02.36	Rúta Meilutyté (LTU)	1:04.35	Rúta Meilutyté (LTU)
200 m	2:14.57	Rebecca Soni (USA)	2:19.11	Rikke Moeller-Pederson (DNK)
Medley	Short course		Long course	
200 m	2:03.20	Katinka Hosszú (HUN)	2:06.15	Ariana Kukors (USA)
400 m	4:20.85	Katinka Hosszú (HUN)	4:28.43	Ye Shiwen (CHN)
4 x 100 m	3:45.56	USA	3:52.05	USA

As of 19 Mar 2014 (*pending FINA approval)

Fastest short-course 100-m medley (female)

Hungarian swimmer Katinka Hosszú completed the 100-m short-course medley in 57.45 sec. She set the record at the FINA Swimming World Cup in Berlin, Germany, on 11 Aug 2013. Hosszú also holds two other short-course speed records (see table left).

Fastest short-course 800-m freestyle (female)

On 10 Aug 2013, Mireia Belmonte (ESP) finished the 800-m short-course freestyle in a time of 7 min 59.34 sec – the first woman to break the 8-min barrier – in Berlin, Germany. Belmonte was awarded the title of Best Spanish Athlete of 2013, alongside tennis star Rafael Nadal.

 Surf's up

Garrett McNamara (USA) caught a wave measuring 23.77 m off the coast of Praia do Norte in Portugal on 1 Nov 2011, the **largest unlimited wave surfed**.

WATER POLO

Most Olympic golds
Hungary won gold on nine occasions, including consecutive wins in 2000, 2004 and 2008. Eleven men have recorded three Olympic water polo golds. Women's water polo was introduced into the Olympics in 2000, but no country has won gold more than once.

Most Water Polo World League wins
Male: The Serbian national team have collected seven FINA Water Polo

World League titles (two as Serbia and Montenegro), between 2005 and 2013. The competition was inaugurated in 2002.
Female: The women's competition was added in 2004 and has seen the USA score seven titles in 2004, 2006–07 and 2009–12.

SURFING

Most ASP World Tour event wins
The surfer with the most ASP (Association of Surfing Professionals) World Tour event wins is Kelly Slater (USA), with 54 titles between 1992 and 2014.

Slater also boarded his way to the **most ASP World Championship Tour titles** – won by the surfer with the most points at the end of the year. Slater's 11 wins between 1992 and 2011 put him seven ahead of the man in second place: Mark Richards (AUS).

Layne Beachley (AUS) has the **most women's ASP**

World Championship Tour titles, winning six consecutively from 1998 to 2003 and a seventh in 2006.

CANOEING

Most Olympic appearances (female)
Josefa Idem (ITA, b. FRG) has participated in eight Olympic Games in the canoe sprint – the most for any female athlete. Idem competed for West Germany in 1984 to 1988 and Italy from 1992 to 2012. During her Olympic career, she won five medals, including gold in the K-1 500-m event at Sydney 2000.

Most individual canoe-slalom Olympic medals
Michal Martikán (SVK) won five Olympic canoe-slalom medals. He picked up two gold, two silver and a bronze between 1996 and 2012.

Most canoe-slalom Olympic golds
Tony Estanguet (FRA) claimed his third Olympic gold medal in canoe-slalom on 31 Jul 2012.

Youngest ASP World Tour champion (female)

Carissa Moore (USA, b. 27 Aug 1992) became the youngest female ASP World Tour champion when she won the 2011 Tour aged 18 years 322 days on 15 Jul 2011. Hawaiian-born Carissa won the title on her second attempt, having finished third in 2010. She broke the 27-year-old record held by Frieda Zamba (USA), who won the 1984 title as a teenager, aged 19 years 164 days.

Winter sports

Downhill skiers can attain speeds of up to **250 km/h**

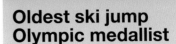

Highest score in free dance figure skating

US gold medallists Meryl Davis and Charlie White achieved a score of 116.63 at the XXII Winter Olympics in Sochi, Russia, on 17 Feb 2014. Their high score was set in the free dance section of the ice dancing event, which they performed to Rimsky-Korsakov's "Scheherazade".

First shared gold medal in alpine skiing

The women's downhill skiing event at the 2014 Games saw Tina Maze (SVN) and Dominique Gisin (CHE) record the exact same time, 41.57 sec, on 12 Feb.

FASTEST...

Ski-bob
On 19 Apr 2006, during the Pro Mondial speed skiing event at Les Arcs, Rhône-Alpes, France, Romuald Bonvin (CHE) attained a speed of 204.43 km/h (127.03 mph) on a ski-bob.

Oldest ski jump Olympic medallist

Noriaki Kasai (JPN, b. 6 Jun 1972) won bronze in the men's ski jump team event aged 41 years 256 days in Sochi, Russia, on 17 Feb 2014. He is also the **oldest ski jump World Cup winner**, taking gold in the ski flying event aged 41 years 219 days in Tauplitz, Austria, on 11 Jan 2014.

MOST...

Skiing Nations' Cup wins
The skiing Nations' Cup is based on the combined men's and women's results at the Alpine Ski World Cup. It was won 35 times by Austria between 1969 and 2014.

FACT
Snowboarding was first included in the Winter Olympics in 1998.

Youngest Olympic snowboard medallist

Ayumu Hirano (JPN, b. 29 Nov 1998) was just 15 years 74 days old when he won silver in the snowboard halfpipe in Sochi, Russia, on 11 Feb 2014. The record for the **youngest Olympic freestyle skiing medallist (female)** was also set in Sochi, by Justine Dufour-Lapointe (CAN, b. 25 Mar 1994), who won gold in the moguls event aged 19 years 321 days on 8 Feb 2014.

WINTER OLYMPICS

Most expensive Olympics (Winter or Summer)
The 2014 Winter Olympics in Sochi, Russia, were widely reported to have cost $50 bn (£30 bn) to stage, including all sports-related and infrastructure costs.

The Sochi Games also set the record for the **most participating countries at a Winter Olympics**: 87 National Olympic Committees entered athletes. Of these, the **largest Winter Olympics team** was the USA, with 230 athletes.

Most medals won by a country
By the close of the 2014 Sochi Games, Norway's all-time haul of Winter Olympics medals had grown to 329: 118 gold (the **most Winter Olympics gold medals won by a country**), 111 silver and 100 bronze.

Most gold medals won by an individual
Male: Two Norwegian Olympians have each won eight golds: Ole Einar Bjørndalen (see opposite page) in the biathlon in 1998–2014, and cross-country skier Bjørn Dæhlie in 1992–98.
Female: Three Olympians share this record with six gold medals apiece: speed skater Lydia Skoblikova (USSR) in 1960–64, and cross-country skiers Lyubov Yegorova (EUN/RUS) in 1992–94 and Marit Bjørgen (NOR) in 2010–14.

First women's Olympic curling team to win every first-round game
The round-robin format was introduced to curling at the 1998 Winter Olympics in Nagano, Japan. Canada is the only women's team to have won every first-round game, with nine wins in Sochi from 10 to 18 Feb 2014.

Speed skating 500 m
Male: Jeremy Wotherspoon (CAN) skated 500 m in 34.03 sec in Salt Lake City, Utah, USA, on 9 Nov 2007.
Female: Lee Sang-Hwa (KOR) took 36.36 sec to skate 500 m, also in Salt Lake City, on 16 Nov 2013.

Speed skating 1,000 m
Male: On 7 Mar 2009, multiple record holder Shani Davis (USA) skated 1,000 m in 1 min 6.42 sec in Salt Lake City, Utah, USA.

Female: Brittany Bowe (USA) skated 1,000 m in 1 min 12.58 sec, also in Salt Lake City, on 17 Nov 2013.

Bobsleigh skeleton
Male: Alexander Tretyakov (RUS) and Sandro Stielicke (DEU) both reached 146.4 km/h (90.96 mph) during the Winter Olympics in British Columbia, Canada, on 19 Feb 2010.
Female: Marion Trott (DEU) recorded a speed of 144.5 km/h (89.78 mph), also during the 2010 Winter Olympics competition at Whistler, on 19 Feb.

Most appearances at the Winter Olympics

Two athletes have competed in seven consecutive Winter Olympics: ski-jumper Noriaki Kasai (JPN) and luger Albert Demchenko (RUS, above) appeared in every Winter Games from Albertville 1992 to Sochi 2014.

Most consecutive individual Olympic medals

Armin Zöggeler (ITA) won six consecutive individual Olympic medals from 1994 to 2014: two gold, one silver and three bronze, all in the men's singles luge. The previous record was also held by a luger, Georg Hackl (DEU), who won five consecutive individual medals from 1988 to 2002.

PARALYMPIC WINTER GAMES

Most...	Total	Athlete	Dates
Medals (female)	27	Ragnhild Myklebust (NOR)	1988–2002
Medals (male)	22	Gerd Schönfelder (DEU)	1992–2010
Gold medals (female)	22	Ragnhild Myklebust (NOR)	1988–2002
Gold medals (male)	16	Gerd Schönfelder (DEU)	1992–2010
Most medals in...	**Total**	**Athlete**	
Alpine skiing (male)	22	Gerd Schönfelder (DEU)	1992–2010
Alpine skiing (female)	19	Reinhild Möller (DEU)	1980–98, 2006
Cross-country skiing (male)	17	Frank Höfle (DEU)	1988–2006
Cross-country skiing (female)	16	Ragnhild Myklebust (NOR)	1988–2002
Ice sledge speed racing (male)	12	Knut Lundstrøm (NOR)	1988, 1994–98
Ice sledge speed racing (female)	11	Brit Mjaasund Øjen (NOR)	1980–84, 1994
		Sylva Olsen (NOR)	1980–88
Biathlon (male)	7	Vitaliy Lukyanenko (UKR)	2002–14
Biathlon (female)	7	Olena Iurkovska (UKR)	2002–14

Most Paralympic cross-country skiing gold medals

Male: Frank Höfle (DEU), Terje Loevaas (NOR) and Brian McKeever (CAN, above) have each won 10 golds in Paralympic cross-country skiing. McKeever added three golds to his tally in 2014.
Female: Norway's Ragnhild Myklebust won 16 Paralympic gold medals in cross-country skiing between 1988 and 2002.

Most Winter Olympics medals

Male: Ole Einar Bjørndalen (NOR) won 13 Olympic biathlon medals between 1998 and 2014.
Female: Three women have won 10 cross-country skiing medals: Raisa Smetanina (USSR/EUN), Stefania Belmondo (ITA) and Marit Bjørgen (NOR).

WSOC medals
Relay: Finland has won 38 World Ski Orienteering Championships (WSOC) medals across the three relay categories (men, women and mixed).

Individual (male): Eduard Khrennikov (RUS) has won 11 WSOC medals, including seven golds.
Individual (female): Fellow Russian Tatiana Vlasova has taken 10 individual medals.

Bobsleigh Skeleton World Cup race wins (male)
Martins Dukurs (LVA) won 31 bobsleigh Skeleton World Cup races between 8 Feb 2008 and 25 Jan 2014.

YOUNGEST...

Curling rink (team) to win an Olympic medal (female)
The Great Britain side of Eve Muirhead, Anna Sloan, Vicki Adams, Claire Hamilton and Lauren Gray had an average age of 23 years

Most points in a single end of an Olympic curling match

An "end" in curling is complete when both teams have delivered all eight rocks. The most points scored by a team in a single end of an Olympic match is seven, by Great Britain against the USA in Sochi, Russia, on 11 Feb 2014. Great Britain won the game 12–3, needing only six of the 10 possible ends to do so.

255 days when they won bronze in Sochi, Russia, on 20 Feb 2014.

World Women's Curling Championship winning skip
Scottish skip Eve Muirhead (UK, b. 22 Apr 1990) led her team to victory aged 22 years 336 days in Riga, Latvia, on 24 Mar 2013.

OLDEST...

Individual Winter Olympics medallist
Luge silver-medallist Albert Demchenko (RUS, b. 27 Nov 1971) was 42 years 74 days old when he won in Sochi, Russia, on 9 Feb 2014. The **oldest individual Winter Olympics gold medallist** is Ole Einar Bjørndalen (NOR, b. 27 Jan 1974), who was 40 years 12 days old when he won the 10-km biathlon sprint on 8 Feb 2014.

Skiing World Cup slalom race winner (male)
Mario Matt (AUT, b. 9 Apr 1979) finished first aged 34 years 250 days in Val d'Isère, France, on 15 Dec 2013.

Most Olympic short track speed skating golds (male)

Viktor Ahn (KOR/RUS, b. Ahn Hyun-Soo) won three short track speed skating gold medals for South Korea at the 2006 Olympics in Turin, Italy, and a further three golds for Russia at the 2014 Games in Sochi. Ahn represented South Korea at the 2006 Games, but in 2011 he became a Russian citizen and so represented Russia at the Sochi Olympics.

Sports round-up

In 1927, the first world snooker champion received **prize money of £6.50**

Most wins of the individual long-distance World Orienteering Championships

The World Orienteering Championships long-distance event has been contested annually since 1966. Simone Niggli-Luder (CHE) has taken the crown eight times, more than any other person – man or woman. Her wins came in 2001, 2003, 2005–06, 2009–10 and 2012–13.

Most competitive 147 breaks in snooker
Ronnie O'Sullivan (UK) has racked up 12 maximum breaks in competitive snooker matches. He achieved his 147s from 24 Apr 1997 to 2 Mar 2014.

O'Sullivan has also made the **most century breaks at the World Snooker Championship** (144), from 15 Apr 1995 to 5 May 2014.

First female snooker player to qualify for the final stages of a ranking event
Reanne Evans (UK) – 10-time ladies' world champion – qualified for the televised stages of China's Wuxi Classic with a 5–4 victory over male snooker player Thepchaiya Un-Nooh (THA) in a qualifying match at the South West Snooker Academy in Gloucester, UK, on 28 May 2013.

Most century breaks in a season
Neil Robertson (AUS) made 103 century breaks in 22 tournaments in the 2013–14 season that ran from 7 Jun 2013 to 5 May 2014. As of 3 May 2014, Robertson had made 361 century breaks as a professional. He is the fifth best all-time century-maker, on a list that is headed by Stephen Hendry (UK) with 775.

Longest snooker ban
On 25 Sep 2013, an independent tribunal found professional snooker player Stephen Lee (UK) guilty of fixing seven matches in 2008 and 2009. Lee was banned from playing in any match sanctioned by the World Professional Billiards and Snooker Association for 12 years.

Most Professional Bowlers Association tour event appearances
Between 1976 and 2013, Tom Baker (USA) competed in 840 Professional Bowlers Association (PBA) ten-pin bowling tour events.

Carmen Salvino (USA, b. 23 Nov 1933) is the **oldest ten-pin tour bowler**. He played in the 2014 PBA Tournament of Champions aged 80 years 58 days at Thunderbowl Lanes in Michigan, USA, on 20 Jan.

Walter Ray Williams, Jr (USA) has the **most PBA ten-pin bowling titles**. His tally stands at 47 titles; the latest was won at the USBC Masters on 14 Feb 2010.

Most players to score a televised nine-dart finish in one day
The fewest throws needed to score 501 points in a game of darts is nine, aka the nine-dart finish. Two players achieved this feat during the televised 2014 PDC World Darts Championship in London, UK: Terry Jenkins (UK) and Kyle Anderson (AUS), in different matches, on 14 Dec 2013.

First woman to win the Mongol Derby
When Lara Prior-Palmer (UK, b. 24 Jun 1994) won the Mongol Derby on 10 Aug 2013, she became the first woman to do so. The competition takes place over a gruelling 1,000-km (621-mi) course and is the **longest multi-horse race**. Lara's 2013 title also made her the youngest **Mongol Derby winner**, at the age of 19 years 47 days.

Most Grade 1 victories by a horse
Hurricane Fly (IRL) won 19 Grade 1 races – the premium class of horse racing – from 30 Nov 2008 to 26 Jan 2014.

Most 180s in a World Darts Championship

At the 2014 Professional Darts Corporation (PDC) World Championship, held at Alexandra Palace in London, UK, from 13 Dec 2013 to 1 Jan 2014, a total of 603 maximums (180s) were recorded, beating the 588 achieved in the 2012 competition. The title was eventually won by Michael van Gerwen (NLD, pictured), who hit 16 of the maximums.

Youngest X Games medallist
Alana Smith (USA, b. 20 Oct 2000) was 12 years 210 days old when she won a silver medal in the Women's Skateboard Park competition at the X Games in Barcelona, Spain, on 18 May 2013.

Tom Schaar (USA, b. 14 Sep 1999) is the **youngest X Games gold medallist**. He was 12 years 229 days old when he won the Mini Mega category on 30 Apr 2012.

Most Archery World Cup recurve wins

Female: Yun Ok-Hee (KOR) has won the women's recurve competition twice at the Archery World Cup. Ok-Hee's wins came in 2010 and 2013. The World Cup was instituted in 2006 and comprises four separate events in different locations before a final competition.
Male: Brady Ellison (USA) has also scored two recurve World Cup wins, in 2010–11.

Most USASF Cheerleading Worlds international titles

Cheer Athletics of Kentucky, USA, had won 15 international All Star Federation Cheerleading Worlds titles as of the end of 2013. Their wins include both all-girl and co-ed, levels 5 and 6.

- **200-m road (female):** Jersy Puello (COL) skated 200 m on the road in 17.677 sec on 27 Aug 2013 in Ostend, Belgium.
- **1,000-m track (male):** Bart Swings (BEL) skated 1,000 m on a track in 1 min 20.923 sec on 25 Aug 2013 in Ostend, Belgium.
- **1,000-m track (female):** Barbara Fischer (DEU) set a track time of 1 min 27.06 sec in Inzell, Germany, on 27 Aug 1988.

Youngest World Artistic Gymnastics Championships floor gold medallist (male)

Kenzo Shirai (JPN, b. 24 Aug 1996) won the floor event at the World Artistic Gymnastics Championships aged 17 years 43 days in Antwerp, Belgium, on 6 Oct 2013. Shirai also became the **first person to perform a quadruple twist in a major final** (pictured above).

Most jump racing wins

Tony "AP" McCoy (UK) rode 4,106 jump-racing winners in his career between 26 Mar 1992 and 26 Apr 2014. McCoy also has the **most jump racing wins in a season** (289 in 2001/02) and the **most jump racing Champion Jockey titles** (19, awarded from 1996 to 2014).

Fastest speed skating

- **200-m road (male):** On 9 Dec 2012, in San Benedetto del Tronto, Italy, Ioseba Fernandez (ESP) finished the 200-m individual time trial in 15.879 sec.

- **10,000-m track (male):** On 23 Aug 2013, inline skating world champion Fabio Francolini (ITA) covered 10,000 m on a track in Ostend, Belgium, in just 14 min 23.54 sec.

- **10,000-m track (female):** Yang Hochen (TWN) recorded a time of 15 min 26.970 sec in a 10,000-m track skate in Ostend, Belgium, on 24 Aug 2013.

Most appearances in the World Equestrian Games

Anky van Grunsven (NLD) appeared in the Fédération Equestre Internationale (FEI) World Equestrian Games six times between 1990 and 2010. She is the only rider to have appeared in every edition of the tournament since its inception in 1990.

Longest raft race

The Great River Amazon Raft Race has been staged annually since 1999 between the Peruvian locations of Pescadores Island and the Club de Caza y Pesca in Bella Vista. The race, which covers some 180 km (112 mi), was created by Mike Collis (UK). It challenges four-person teams to build a log raft and paddle the course in three stages over three days.

FACT

The All-Around title is awarded to the leading money winner in a single season in two or more events.

Most Rodeo World Championships

Between 2002 and 2013, Trevor Brazile (USA) won 19 titles at the Professional Rodeo Cowboys Association World Championships. His titles were won across four events: All-Around, Tie-Down Roping (individual and team) and Steer Wrestling. Brazile also has the **most All-Around Rodeo World Championships titles**, with 11 wins in 12 years.

PARALYMPIC (IPC) POWERLIFTING

Category	Weight	Name	Year
Male			
<49 kg	181 kg	Yakubu Adesokan (NGR)	2014
<59 kg	190 kg	Ali Jawad (UK, b. LBN)	2014
<80 kg	236 kg	Xiao Fei Gu (CHN)	2014
<97 kg	240 kg	Mohamed Eldib (EGY)	2013
107+ kg	285 kg	Siamand Rahman (IRN)	2014
Female			
<41 kg	103 kg	Nazmiye Muslu (TUR)	2014
<50 kg	122 kg	Olesya Lafina (RUS)	2014
<61 kg	135.5 kg	Fatma Omar (EGY)	2014
<73 kg	150 kg	Souhad Ghazouani (FRA)	2013
86+ kg	151 kg	Precious Orji (NGR)	2014

Statistics correct as of 21 Apr 2014

Index

Index

Acknowledgements

Guinness World Records would like to thank the following for their help in compiling this edtion:

Across the Pond (Rob, Aaron, Julie, Karen, Katie and all their colleagues); API Laminates Ltd (Simon Thompson); Asatsu-DK Inc. (Motonori Iwasaki, Shinsuke Sakuma); Charlotte Atkins; Eric Atkins; Freya Atkins; Simon Atkins; BAFTA; Alexander Balandin; Elle Bartlett; BBC; Oliver Beatson; Sarah Bebbington; Andrew Benson (Carnegie Institution for Science); BFI; Anisa Bhatti; Alexander Boatfield; Joseph Boatfield; Luke Boatfield; Bodyflight Bedford (Bryony Doughty, Ged Parker); Sam Borden; Chiara Bragato; Patrick Bragato; Veronica Bridges (Featherstone Rovers RLFC); Broadcast; Colin Burgess (Stoke City FC); Nicola Campbell (Camelot Group); Canton Classic Car Museum, Ohio, USA; Carousel Candies, California, USA; CCTV (Guo Tong, Wang Wei and all their colleagues); Frank Chambers; Richard M Christensen (Professor Research Emeritus, Stanford University); The Chunichi Shimbun (Tetsuya Okamura, Tadao Sawada); Adam Cloke; Collaboration Inc. Japan (Mr Suzuki, Miho, Kyoto and all their colleagues); Connexion Cars (Rob and Tracey); Ken Cook (Caboose Hobbies, Denver, Colorado, USA); Anne Cowne (Information Officer, Information Centre, Lloyd's Register); Pietro D'Angelo; Panos Datskos; Anastassia Davidzenka; Martyn Davis; Denmaur Independent Papers Limited (Julian Townsend); Frank Dimroth; Gemma Doherty; Emmys (Academy of Television Arts & Sciences); Europroduzione (Renato, Gabriela, Carlo, Paola and all their colleagues); Toby and Amelia Ewen; Eyeworks/Warner Bros. Germany (Michael, Martin, Käthe and all their colleagues); Benjamin Fall; Rebecca Fall; Daniel Fernandez; Jonathan de Ferranti; FJT Logistics Limited (Ray Harper, Gavin Hennessy); Forbes; Martin Fuechsle; Gemological Institute of America (Kristin Mahan, Shane McClure, Stephen Morisseau, Gwen Travis); Damien Gildea; Andrew Goodwin; Brandon Greenwood; Jordan Greenwood; Ryan Greenwood; Victoria Grimsell; GWRJ internship students (Jiani Xie, Natsumi Kawakami, Chisaki Iijima, Maho Miyamoto, Yumina Murata); Carmen Alfonzo de Hannah; Alexia Hannah Alfonzo; Amy Hannah Alfonzo; Rod Hansen (Museum of Idaho, Idaho Falls, Idaho, USA); Ellie Hayward; Dr Haze (Circus of Horrors); Bob Headland; Matilda and Max Heaton; High Noon (Brad, Jim, Dana and all their colleagues); The Himalayan Database; Hololens Technology Co., Ltd; Stephen J Holroyd (US Soccer Archives); Claire Holzman (Houghton Mifflin Harcourt); Marsha K Hoover; Dora Howard; Tilly Howard; Colin Hughes; Cynthia Hunt; Sarah Icken (Camelot Group); Integrated Colour Editions Europe (Roger Hawkins, Susie Hawkins, Clare Merryfield); Richard Johnston, Barbara Jones (Information Centre Manager, Lloyd's Register); Stephanie Jones (Great British Racing); Raymond S Jordan, Drogheda, Ireland; Justin Kazmark (Kickstarter); Harry Kikstra; Laleham Camping Club, UK; Orla Langton; Thea Langton; Sophie Lawrenson (Royal Collection Trust); Frederick Horace Lazell; Sydney Leleux; Lion Television (Simon, Jeremy, Tom and all their colleagues); Lloyd's Insurance (Oonagh Bates, Jonathan Thomas); London Pet Show; London Wonderground; Rüdiger Lorenz; Luci Producciones (Maria, Shaun, Stefano); Ciara Mackey; Sarah & Martin Mackey; Theresa Mackey; Christian de Marliave; Missy Matilda; Dave McAleer; Chelsea McGuffin; Clare Merryfield; Metacritic; Jeremy Michell, Historic Photographs and Ships Plans Manager, Royal Museums Greenwich; Miditech (Niret, Nivedith, Nikhil and all their colleagues); John Jackson Miller; Tamsin Mitchell; Harriet Molloy; Sophie, Joshua and Florence Molloy; Colin Monteath; Dan Morrison; Steven Munatones (Open Water Source); Museum of the Weird, Austin, Texas, USA; Anikó Németh-Móra (International Weightlifting Federation); James Ng; Jim Nicholls; David Oberlink; Caitlin Penny; Periscoop (Peri, Elsy and all their colleagues); Karen Perkins (World Alternative Games); Tom Pierce; Sophie Procter (British Airways); Robert Pullar; Miriam Randall; John Reed (World Speed Sailing Records Council); Kevin Rochfort (FISB); Dan Roddick (World Flying Disc Association); Roller Coaster Database; Kate Rushworth (YouTube); Nick Ryan (Xpogo); Nick Ryuan (Xpogo); Eric Sakowski; Paolo Scarabaggio; Rob Schweitzer (Historic Hudson Valley); Nellie Scott (Brick Artist); Michael Serra (São Paulo Futebol Clube); Bill Sharp (Billabong XXL Big Wave Awards); Ang Tsering Sherpa; Dawa Sherpa; Patrice Simon; Athena Simpson; Chris Skone-Roberts; Katy Smith (John Wiley & Sons, Inc.); Spectratek Technologies, Inc (Terry Conway, Mike Foster); Glenn Speer; Bill Spindler; St Mary's University, UK; Ray Stevenson; Stephen Sutton; Charlie, Holly and Daisy Taylor; Terry and Jan Todd (H J Lutcher Stark Center for Physical Culture and Sports, University of Texas, USA); Matthew Tole; Anaelle Torres; Cliff Towne (Professional Disc Golf Association); truTV (Michael, Chris, Stephen, Angel, Marissa and all their colleagues); Sheryl Twigg, Press & PR Manager, Royal Museums Greenwich; UPM Plattling, Germany; Kripa Varanasi; Variety; Virgin (Charmaine Clarke, Philippa Russ); Craig Walter; Lara and Sevgi White; Oli White; Robert White; Paul Winston (Zippos Circus); Robert Wood; Daniel Woods; Madeleine Wuschech; Hayley Wylie-Deacon; Rueben George Wylie-Deacon; Tobias Hugh Wylie-Deacon; Zodiak Clips (Sandra, David, Dom, Cath and all their colleagues); Zodiak Kids (Karen, Gary and all their colleagues); Zodiak Rights (Andreas, Tim, Barney and all their colleagues)

Picture credits

1: Kevin Scott Ramos/GWR **2**: Getty Images **3**: Hilary Morgan/Alamy, Erik C Pendzich/Rex, V&A Images/Alamy, Getty Images, Lloyds of London/AP/PA, Lloyds of London/AP/PA, Lionel Cironneau/AP/PA **5**: Paul Michael Hughes/GWR **7**: Kevin Scott Ramos/GWR Paul Michael Hughes/GWR **8** (UK): Steven Peskett **9** (UK): Andy Chubb, Christian Black **10** (UK): Richard Bradbury/GWR, Richard Bradbury/GWR, Crown Copyright **11** (UK): Alex Walker, Marc O'Sullivan, Paul Michael Hughes/GWR, Pete Jones **8** (US): Rick Kern/Bravo, James Ellerker/GWR, Zef Nikolla **9** (US): SYCO **10** (US): Peter Kramer/NBC, Virginia Sherwood/NBC, Peter Kramer/NBC, Ross Halfin, Dan MacMedan/Chevrolet **11** (US): Greg Lemaster, Heidi Gutman/ABC, Rich Pedroncelli/AP/PA, Kevin Scott Ramos/GWR **9** (CAN): Kevin Scott Ramos/GWR **10** (CAN): Mark Blinch/Reuters, Sergey Ilnitsky/Alamy **11** (CAN): Dylan Martinez/Reuters, Ints Kalnins/Reuters **8** (AUS): Joe Murphy **9** (AUS): Mark Metcalfe/Getty Images, M Cranna, David Gray/Reuters **10** (AUS): Brian Lee, Daniel Chew, Glen Yearbury **11** (AUS): Ross Kummer, Jeremy Guzman, Richard Birch **12**: Getty Images, Photoshot, Clive Limpkin/Rex, Fox TV, Getty Images, Paul Michael Hughes/GWR **13**: ITV/Rex, John Wright/GWR **14**: NASA, NASA/Science Photo Library, NASA **15**: NASA **16**: NASA, Getty Images, Alamy **17**: NASA, Reuters, ESA, Mike Blake/Reuters **18**: NASA **19**: ESO, NASA, Alamy **20**: NASA, NASA/Alamy, German Aerospace Center **21**: NASA, Mark A Garlick/Science Photo Library, Joongi Kim, Robert Matton/Alamy **22**: NASA, ESA, Denysov Dmytro/iStock, Science Photo Library **23**: MPIA, Gavin Collins, NASA, Sci-Fi Photo Journal **24**: NASA, Getty Images **25**: Eberly College of Science, Zeit News, Alamy **26**: NRAO/AUI, redOrbit.com **27**: Large Binocular Telescope Observatory, NRAO/AUI, Alamy, Stefan Schwarzburg/ H.E.S.S. Collaboration, Pablo Bonet/IAC, Javier Larrea/Alamy, Alamy **28**: Thomas Senf/Mammut **30**: Getty Images, NASA, NOAA, Kara Lavender, Argo Information Centre, University of California, Tomas Munita/Evevine, Getty Images, Holger Leue/Corbis **31**: University of Texas, NASA, ESA, Curtin University of Technology, NOAA, Alamy, Ralph White/Corbis, Bill Waugh/Reuters, Dean Conger/Corbis, Getty Images **32**: Australian Science, AP/PA, Reuters, NASA/Reuters, NASA, Roger Coulam/Alamy **33**: AP/PA, Alamy, Reuters, NASA, Addi Bischoff, Stefan Ralew/sr-meteorites.de, NASA **34**: NASA **35**: NASA **36**: Getty Images, Maps for Free, Alamy, Royal Geographical Society **37**: Susanna Wikman, Galen Rowell/Corbis, Dianne Blell/Getty Images, British Antarctic Survey **38**: Bay of Bengal Large Marine Ecosystem Project, Andrew McLachlan/Superstock, Massimo Brega/Science Photo Library, Massimo Brega/Science Photo Library **39**: W Robert Moore/National Geographic, Doug Perrine/Corbis, Colorado State University, Anderson Aerial Photography, Alamy, Gary Bell/Oceanwide Images **40**: Dave Bunnell/Under Earth Images, David Kilpatrick/Alamy, Robbie Shone/Alamy **41**: Carsten Peter/Getty Images, Getty Images, Alamy, Stephen L Alvarez/National Geographic **42**: Martin Strmiska/Alamy **44**: Alamy, Getty Images, Nurlan Kalchinov/Alamy, Bio-Ken Snake Farm, Dirk Ercken/Alamy, Image Quest Marine, Image Quest Marine, Jodi Rowley, Tilo Nadler, Richard Porter/Ardea, Alamy, Nicole Dutra **45**: Daniel Heuclin/Nature PL, AP/PA, Bruce Rasner/Nature PL, Sebastian Kennerknecht/FLPA, Alamy, Miguel Rangel Jr, Peter Kappeler, Public Library of Science, Knud Andreas Jønsson, Mahree-Dee White, Samuel Nienow **46**: Alamy, Steve Bloom/Alamy, Alamy, Human Dynamo Workshop **47**: Martin Strmiska/Alamy, Alamy, Justin Hofman/Alamy **48**: Anup Shah/Getty Images, Thomas Marent/Corbis, H Lansdown/Alamy, Corbis **49**: Masahiro Iijima/Ardea, FLPA, Denis Palanque/FLPA, Getty Images, Alamy, Dave Watts/Alamy **50**: Corbis, Photoshot, Frans Lanting/Corbis, Eric Nathan/Photoshot **51**: Alamy, Donald M Jones/FLPA, Corbis, Barry Mansell/Nature PL **52**: Alamy, Kevin Elsby/Alamy, Alamy, M Watson/Ardea, Getty Images **53**: Jim Zipp/Ardea, Photoshot, Cyril Laubscher/Getty Images, Alamy, Steven David Miller/Nature PL, Chris Howarth/Alamy **54**: Milos Manojlovic/iStock, Andrew Murray/Nature PL, Alamy, Danté Fenolio **55**: Alamy, Stan Osolinski/Getty Images, Chris Mattison/Alamy, A & J Visage/Alamy **56**: Zeb Hogan/WWF, Chris Radburn/PA, Catalina Island Marine Institute **57**: Doug Perrine/Nature PL, Jesse Cancelmo/Alamy, Steve Bloom Images/Alamy, David Jenkins/Caters News **58**: Corbis, Getty Images, Reuters **59**: www.aphotomarine.com, Chris Skone-Roberts/GWR, Koen G H Breedveld/Spring Rivers Ecological Sciences, Corbis, Alamy, creepyanimals.com **60**: Morley Read/Alamy, Dale Ward, Alamy, Caters, California Academy of Sciences **61**: Csiro Ecosystem Sciences, Maximilian Weinzierl/Alamy, Getty Images, Louise Murray/Alamy, Natural History Museum, London **62**: Barry Durrant/Getty Images, SWNS, Alamy, Jeff Rotman/Getty Images, Andrey Nekrasov/Alamy, Andrey Nekrasov/Alamy **63**: snailworld.eu, Seren/Bangor University, MMurphy/NPWS **64**: David Crump/Rex, Kevin Scott Ramos/GWR **65**: James Ellerker/GWR, Ryan Schude/GWR, Ryan Schude/GWR, Sophie Davidson/GWR, Getty Images, Corbis, Elaine Thompson/AP/PA **66**: James Ellerker/GWR, Ryan Schude/GWR, James Ellerker/GWR, Kevin Scott Ramos/GWR, Howard Burditt/Reuters **67**: Ranald Mackechnie/GWR, David Moir/Reuters, Kevin Scott Ramos/GWR **68**: Silvia Vignolini/PNAS, Paul Street/Alamy, Vinayaraj, Jerry Lampen/Reuters **69**: Frans Lanting/Corbis, Redfern Natural History, Getty Images, Alamy **70**: Paul Michael Hughes/GWR **72**: Ron Siddle/AP/PA, Corbis, Buddhika Weerasinghe/Getty Images, John Wright/GWR, Corbis, Irish Independent, Birmingham Mail, Getty Images **73**: John Wright/GWR, Paul Michael Hughes/GWR, The Burns Archive, Getty Images, Alamy **74**: Roslan Rahman/Getty Images, PA, Sam Green **75**: Naturex, Getty Images **76**: Gary Wainwright, Devon Steigerwald, Reuters, Simon Pizzey/The Citizen, Tyler Hicks/Eyevine, Alamy, Reuters **78**: Drew Gardner/GWR, James Ellerker/GWR, Lorenz Schadeberg/Rex **79**: Kimberly Cook/GWR, James Ellerker/GWR, Paul Michael Hughes/GWR, John Wright/GWR, **80**: Rex, Tomas Bravo/GWR **81**: Hank Walker/Getty Images, Sean Sexton/Getty Images, Corbis, Paul Michael Hughes/GWR **83**: D L Anderson, Lakruwan Wanniarachchi/Getty Images **84**: Corbis **85**: Alamy, Getty Images, Wellcome Images, Rex Features, John A Secoges/AP/PA **86**: Ranald Mackechnie/GWR **88**: Sam Christmas/GWR, Richard Howard/Getty Images, Tengku Bahar/Getty Images **90**: Philip Robertson/GWR, Shinsuke Kamioka/GWR, Richard Bradbury/GWR **91**: Frank Espich/The Indianapolis Star, Richard Bradbury/GWR, Alamy, Mike Sonnenberg/iStock, Alamy **92**: Kevin Scott Ramos, Pete Jenkins/Alamy **93**: Ranald Mackechnie/GWR, Dan Kitwood/Getty Images, Peter Byrne/PA, Steve Parsons/PA, Steve Parsons/PA, David Cripps/Royal Collection **94**: Ranald Mackechnie/GWR **95**: Fredrik Naumann/Felix Features **96**: Richard Bradbury/GWR, Ryan Schude/GWR, Ranald Mackechnie/GWR **97**: Ranald Mackechnie/GWR, Kate Melton, Paul Michael Hughes/GWR **98**: Ryan Schude/GWR **99**: Ryan Schude/GWR **100**: Dan Rowlands/Caters, Ryan Schude/GWR **101**: David Parry/PA, David Parry/PA, Reuters **102**: Ryan Schude/GWR, John Wright/GWR, Rob Loud/Getty Images **103**: Ranald Mackechnie/GWR, Drew Gardner/GWR **104**: Ryan Schude/GWR, Paul Michael Hughes/GWR **105**: Paul Michael Hughes/GWR, Ranald Mackechnie/GWR, Keith Heneghan/Phocus **106**: Richard Keith Wolff/Getty Images, Ryan Schude/GWR **107**: Ryan Schude/GWR, Matt Crossick/GWR, John Wright/GWR, Ranald Mackechnie/GWR **108**: Ranald Mackechnie/GWR, Paul Michael Hughes/GWR **109**: Richard Birch, Paul Michael Hughes/GWR, Ranald Mackechnie/GWR, Nathan King/Alamy, Tomasz Rossa, Alexander Nemonov/Getty Images **110**: Aly Song/Reuters **111**: WSSA **112**: Paul Michael Hughes/GWR **113**: Andrew Schwartz/Corbis, Marcel Wichert, Jeff Holmes, The Strong, Alamy **114**: Rick Belden, Capture the Moment Photography **115**: Christiane Kappes, Mirja Geh/Red Bull, Michael G Nightengale **116**: Philip Robertson/GWR, Rentsendorj Bazarsukh/Reuters, Anne Caroline/GWR **117**: Theo Cohen, Ilya S Savenok/Getty Images, Daniel Berehulak/Getty Images, Sanjay Kanojia/Getty Images **118**: Ruud van der Lubben/PA, Ryan Schude/GWR, Paul Michael Hughes/GWR **119**: Paul Michael Hughes/GWR, Mark Radford **120**: Ryan Schude/GWR **122**: Getty Images, Tim Rooke/Rex, National Archives, Shel Hershorn/Getty Images, Alamy, Corbis **123**: Alamy, Corbis, Alamy, Nati Harnik/AP/PA, Gus Ruelas/Reuters, Keith Dannemiller/Alamy **124**: Ahmad Masood/Reuters, Thomas Mukoya/Reuters, Ho New/Reuters, Soe Zeya Tun/Reuters **125**: Getty Images, Reuters, Reuters, Ho New/Reuters, Reuters, Athar Hussain/Reuters **126**: Christophe Simon/Getty Images, Evaristo Sa/Getty Images, Krishnendu Halder/Reuters, Ezequiel Abiu Lopez/AP/

PA, Kem McNair/Getty Images **127:** Global Times, Onur Coban/ Getty Images, Wim Scheire/Getty Images, Mahmoud Raouf Mahmoud/Reuters **128:** Ragnhild Gustad, Chaiwat Subprasom/ Reuters **129:** United States Geological Survey, Alamy, Oleksandr Rupeta/Alamy, Pascal Ducept/Alamy, Giorgio Marcoaldi/ CVN, Reuters, Manuel Silvestri/ Reuters **130:** Kristijan Vuckovic, National Center for Ecological Analysis and Synthesis, Jahre-Wallern, Michael Kooren/ Reuters **131:** Aly Song/Reuters, Marine Traffic, Reuters **132:** Cameron Laird/Rex, Pablo Blazquez Dominguez/Getty Images **133:** Mark Bialek/Alamy, Phil Mingo/Pinnacle **134:** Thomas Grimm/AP/PA, Michael Urban/ Getty Images, Paul Cooper/Rex, Alamy, Alamy **135:** Alamy, RMN-Grand Palais/Musée du Louvre/Hervé Lewandowski, Roger Viollet/Getty Images, Alamy **136:** Tina Hager/Getty Images, Chao-Yang Chan/Alamy, George Nikitin/AP/PA, Craig Barritt/Getty Images **137:** Toru Hanai/Reuters, Alamy, Rebecca Cook/Reuters, Yorgos Karahalis/Reuters, NASA **138:** Dove, Google Maps, Universal Pictures/Alamy, Facebook, Alamy **139:** Instagram, Instagram, AP, Lucy Nicholson/ Reuters, Andrew Kelly/Reuters, Laurence Mathieu/The Guardian **140:** Mike Goldwater/Alamy, Alamy **141:** Alastair Muir/Rex **142:** Everest Media Productions **144:** Afanassi Makovnev, Getty Images **145:** Jarek Jõepera/GWR **147:** Getty Images, Paul Michael Hughes/GWR **148:** Will Wintercross **149:** James Ellerker/ GWR **150:** British Nanga Parbat 2012 Expedition, Philip Temple, Paul A Souders/Corbis, Frieder Blickle/Camera Press **151:** Paul Michael Hughes/GWR **152:** Felipe Souza, Ben Duffy **153:** Daniel Deme/Rex, Torsten Blackwood/Getty Images, Paul Michael Hughes/GWR **154:** Bas de Meijer, Lars Stenholt Kirkegaard, Lupi_Spuma, Shutterstock **155:** John Dickey, Claudia Marcelloni, James Ellerker/GWR, James Ellerker/ GWR **157:** Paul Michael Hughes/ GWR **158:** Lionsgate/Alamy **160:** MGM/Alamy, Walt Disney Productions, Twentieth Century Fox, MGM/Alamy, Universal, MGM/Alamy, Paramount, Walt Disney Productions/Rex, MGM, Twentieth Century Fox, Warner Bros. **161:** Universal/Alamy, Yash Raj Films, Walt Disney Pictures, Twentieth Century Fox/Alamy, Twentieth Century Fox, Summit Entertainment, Walt Disney Productions, Twentieth Century Fox, Marvel, Lucasfilm, Hollywood Pictures, Warner Bros., MGM/ Alamy, Lucasfilm, Universal, Twentieth Century Fox, Twentieth Century Fox **162:** Lionsgate, Warner Bros., Paramount Pictures **163:** Paramount Pictures, Warner Bros., Salty Features, Warner Bros. **164:** Yashraj Films, Twentieth Century Fox, Alamy, Cross Creek Pictures, Alamy **165:** Alamy, Mario Anzuoni/ Reuters, Alamy, Walt Disney Pictures, Karen Ballard/Paramount Pictures, Fred Prouser/Reuters **166:** Getty Images, Brian Snyder/ Reuters **167:** Lucy Nicholson/ Reuters, Steven Klein, Terry Richardson, Isaac Brekken/Getty Images **168:** YouTube **169:** Girlguiding North West, Matt Crossick/GWR **170:** Don Emmert/ Getty Images, Alamy, PA, Marijan

Murat/PA, Alamy, Rodrigo de Balbin Behrmann **171:** WENN, WENN, Russell Cheyne/Reuters, Alain Perus/L'Oeil du Diaph **172:** Ryan Schude/GWR, Alamy **173:** Olivia Harris/Reuters, Benjamin Pritzkuleit **174:** Rex Features, Haut et Court, Virginia Sherwood/Getty Images, Yogen Shah/Getty Images, Samir Hussein/Getty Images **175:** A & E Networks, Bob D'Amico/Getty Images, BBC **176:** Ryan Schude/ GWR, Kevin Scott Ramos/GWR, Paul Michael Hughes/GWR, Ryan Schude/GWR, Richard Bradbury/ GWR **177:** Ranald Mackechnie/ GWR, Richard Bradbury/GWR, Ryan Schude/GWR **178:** Kevin Scott Ramos/GWR **180:** Alcatel-Lucent, Topfoto, HP Museum, Eric Risberg/AP/PA, Getty Images, AP/ PA, NASA, Getty Images, Gene J Puskar/AP/PA, Science Photo Library **181:** Elise Amendola/AP/ PA, Getty Images, Rebecca Cook/ Reuters, Fabrizio Bensch/Reuters, Reidar Hahn, Getty Images, Kimberly White/Reuters, Denis Closon/Rex **182:** Mathew Imaging, Ho New/Reuters, Justin Garvanovic/Coaster Club **183:** Iain Masterton/Alamy, Stan Honda/ Getty Images, Craig T Mathew/ Mathew Imaging, Kazuhiro Nogi/ Getty Images **184:** Corbis, J S Callahan/Alamy, Alamy **185:** Rex Features, Alamy, Getty Images, Ray Roberts/Rex **186:** Damian Kramski, Max Earey/ Newspress **187:** Alamy, Canton Classic Car Museum, Chrysler Group LLC, Alamy, Alamy, Kim Kyung Hoon/Reuters, Tobias Schwarz/Reuters, Reuters **188:** Maciej Dakowicz/Alamy, iStock **189:** Peter Brogden/Alamy, Robert Nickelsberg/Alamy, PA **190:** Andy Clark/Reuters, Alison Thompson/Alamy, Colombia Travel, Alamy **191:** Shadow Fox, Mark L Simpson/Electric Lemonade Photography, Wisconsin Duck Tours, Marcio Jose Sanchez/AP/PA, Rex **192:** Paul Michael Hughes/GWR, Paul Michael Hughes/GWR, Shinsuke Kamioka/GWR, Paul Michael Hughes/GWR, Ranald Mackechnie/GWR, James Ellerker/ GWR **193:** Paul Michael Hughes/ GWR, Richard Bradbury/GWR, Drew Gardner/GWR, Kevin Scott Ramos/GWR **194:** Solid Concepts, US Navy, Reuters, USAF **195:** US Navy, Alamy, USDA **196:** Sean Pavone/Alamy, Gustau Nacarino/ Reuters, Rory Daniel, Rex Features, Alamy, Alamy, Alamy **197:** Jianan Yu/Reuters, Rex Features, iStock **198:** iStock, Postojna Cave, Jim Zuckerman/ Alamy **199:** Jorge Royan, Glenn Asakawa/Getty Images, Alice Finch, Alamy **200:** Khaled Al-Sayyed/Getty Images, Dominique Debaralle/Corbis, Ed Jones/Getty Images, Chi Po-lin, Pichi Chuang/Reuters, Christian Haugen **201:** Joel Riner, Hans Blossey/Corbis, Cor Mulder/EPA, Reuters, David Cannon/Getty Images, David Cannon/Getty Images, Getty Images **202:** Baxley/JILA, Baxley/JILA, Long Hongtao/Rex, Long Hongtao/Rex, Sven Sturm/MPI for Nuclear Physics **203:** ESA, Felipe Pedreros/IceCube/NSF, Jim Haugen/IceCube/NSF, Alamy **204:** Alamy, Iberpress, Harvard School of Engineering and Applied Sciences, Seth Wenig/AP/PA, Peter Morgan/Reuters **205:** Kevin Ma and Pakpong Chirarattananon/ Harvard Microrobotics Lab, Boston Dynamics **206:** Kumar Sriskandan/Alamy **207:** Alamy,

NASA, NASA **208:** Stephane Mahe/Reuters **210:** Ezra Shaw/ Getty Images, Jeremy Brevard/ Reuters, Lucy Nicholson/Reuters, Reuters **211:** Alamy, Jack Dempsey/AP/PA, John Leyba/ Getty Images **212:** John Thys/ Getty Images, Dylan Martinez/ Reuters, Pascal Lauener/Reuters **213:** Ian Walton/Getty Images, Alamy, Alamy **214:** Hannah Johnston/Getty Images, Lorraine O'Sullivan/Inpho, Lluis Gene/Getty Images, Toshifumi Kitamura/Getty Images **215:** Alamy, Marco Garcia/ Getty Images **216:** Ray Stubblebine/Reuters, Alamy, Mike Cassese/Reuters **217:** Martin Thomas/Alamy, Keith Charles/ Getty Images, Getty Images, Mike Blake/Reuters **218:** Dick Raphael/ Getty Images, Ron Hoskins/Getty Images, Joe Skipper/Reuters, Reuters, Mike Segar/Reuters **219:** Layne Murdoch Jr/Getty Images, Getty Images **220:** Getty Images, Alamy, Al Bello/Getty Images, Kristian Dowling/Getty Images **221:** David Finch/Getty Images, Nathan Denette/PA **222:** Christopher Lee/Getty Images, Philip Brown/Reuters, Philip Brown/Reuters, David Gray/ Reuters **223:** Aijaz Rahi/AP/PA, Alamy, Philip Brown/Reuters **224:** Stefano Rellandini/Reuters, Reuters **225:** Javier Lizon/Alamy, Getty Images, John Sommers/ Corbis, PA, Corbis, Leo Mason/ Corbis **226:** Caren Firouz/Reuters, Tami Chappell/Reuters, Daren Staples/Reuters, Alamy, Alamy **227:** Phil Sheldon/Getty Images, Andy Lyons/Getty Images, Jim Young/Reuters, Harry Warnecke/ Getty Images, Denis Balibouse/ Reuters **228:** Reuters, Antti Aimo-Koivisto/PA, B Bennett/ Getty Images, Reuters, Alamy, Reuters **229:** Dick Raphael/Getty Images **230:** Reuters, Tobias Schwarz/Reuters, Chris Helgren/ Reuters **231:** Reuters, Reuters, Alamy, Reuters, Alamy **232:** Cody Duncan/Alamy, Alamy, Tannen Maury/Alamy, Mervyn McClelland/ Presseye **233:** Adrees Latif/ Reuters, Lars Baron/Getty Images, Dozier Mobley/Getty Images, Lehtikuva/Reuters **234:** Cathal McNaughton/Reuters, Alamy, Alamy **235:** Jean Sebastien Evrard/Getty Images, Alamy, Reuters, Eddie Keogh/Reuters **236:** Josep Lago/Getty Images, Michaela Rehle/Reuters, Paul Hanna/Reuters, Alamy **237:** Alamy, Paul Burrows/Action Images, Alex Morton/Action Images, Susana Vera/Reuters **238:** Reuters, Christophe Simon/ Getty Images, Wolfgang Rattay/ Reuters, Getty Images, Juan Medina/Reuters **239:** Alamy, Clive Brunskill/Getty Images, Goran Tomasevic/Reuters, Alamy, Jorge Silva/Reuters **240:** Adam Stoltman/ Corbis, Bob Thomas/Getty Images, Mike Hewitt/Getty Images **241:** Darren Carroll/Getty Images, Stan Honda/Getty Images, Charles Platiau/Reuters **242:** Albert Gea/ Reuters, Matthias Oesterle/Alamy, Alamy **243:** Alamy, Alamy, Alex Laurel/Red Bull **244:** Lucy Nicholson/Reuters, Michael Dalder/ Reuters, Alamy, Fabrizio Bensch/ Reuters, Alamy **245:** Alamy, Sergei Karpukhin/Reuters, Alamy, Alexander Demianchuk/Reuters **246:** Lehtikuva Lehtikuva/Reuters, Bryce Kanights/ESPN Images, Alamy, Franck Fife/Getty Images, Getty Images, Alamy, Dan Abraham, Isaac Brekken/AP/PA **254:** Derek Wade Alamy **255:** Birmingham Mail, Kevin Scott Ramos/GWR

Country codes

ABW	Aruba	GIB	Gibraltar	PAK	Pakistan
AFG	Afghanistan	GIN	Guinea	PAN	Panama
AGO	Angola	GLP	Guadeloupe	PCN	Pitcairn Islands
AIA	Anguilla	GMB	Gambia	PER	Peru
ALB	Albania	GNB	Guinea-Bissau	PHL	Philippines
AND	Andorra	GNQ	Equatorial Guinea	PLW	Palau
ANT	Netherlands Antilles	GRC	Greece	PNG	Papua New Guinea
ARG	Argentina	GRD	Grenada	POL	Poland
ARM	Armenia	GRL	Greenland	PRI	Puerto Rico
ASM	American Samoa	GTM	Guatemala	PRK	Korea, DPRO
ATA	Antarctica	GUF	French Guiana	PRT	Portugal
ATF	French Southern Territories	GUM	Guam	PRY	Paraguay
		GUY	Guyana	PYF	French Polynesia
ATG	Antigua and Barbuda	HKG	Hong Kong	QAT	Qatar
		HMD	Heard and McDonald Islands	REU	Réunion
AUS	Australia			ROM	Romania
AUT	Austria	HND	Honduras	RUS	Russian Federation
AZE	Azerbaijan	HRV	Croatia (Hrvatska)		
BDI	Burundi			RWA	Rwanda
BEL	Belgium	HTI	Haiti	SAU	Saudi Arabia
BEN	Benin	HUN	Hungary	SDN	Sudan
BFA	Burkina Faso	IDN	Indonesia	SEN	Senegal
BGD	Bangladesh	IND	India	SGP	Singapore
BGR	Bulgaria	IOT	British Indian Ocean Territory	SGS	South Georgia and South SS
BHR	Bahrain	IRL	Ireland	SHN	Saint Helena
BHS	The Bahamas	IRN	Iran	SJM	Svalbard and Jan Mayen Islands
BIH	Bosnia and Herzegovina	IRQ	Iraq		
		ISL	Iceland		
BLR	Belarus	ISR	Israel	SLB	Solomon Islands
BLZ	Belize	ITA	Italy		
BMU	Bermuda	JAM	Jamaica	SLE	Sierra Leone
BOL	Bolivia	JOR	Jordan	SLV	El Salvador
BRA	Brazil	JPN	Japan	SMR	San Marino
BRB	Barbados	KAZ	Kazakhstan	SOM	Somalia
BRN	Brunei Darussalam	KEN	Kenya	SPM	Saint Pierre and Miquelon
		KGZ	Kyrgyzstan		
BTN	Bhutan	KHM	Cambodia	SRB	Serbia
BVT	Bouvet Island	KIR	Kiribati	SSD	South Sudan
BWA	Botswana	KNA	Saint Kitts and Nevis	STP	São Tomé and Príncipe
CAF	Central African Republic			SUR	Suriname
		KOR	Korea, Republic of	SVK	Slovakia
CAN	Canada			SVN	Slovenia
CCK	Cocos (Keeling) Islands	KWT	Kuwait	SWE	Sweden
		LAO	Laos	SWZ	Swaziland
CHE	Switzerland	LBN	Lebanon	SYC	Seychelles
CHL	Chile	LBR	Liberia	SYR	Syrian Arab Republic
CHN	China	LBY	Libyan Arab Jamahiriya		
CIV	Côte d'Ivoire			TCA	Turks and Caicos Islands
CMR	Cameroon	LCA	Saint Lucia		
COD	Congo, DR of	LIE	Liechtenstein	TCD	Chad
COG	Congo	LKA	Sri Lanka	TGO	Togo
COK	Cook Islands	LSO	Lesotho	THA	Thailand
COL	Colombia	LTU	Lithuania	TJK	Tajikistan
COM	Comoros	LUX	Luxembourg	TKL	Tokelau
CPV	Cape Verde	LVA	Latvia	TKM	Turkmenistan
CRI	Costa Rica	MAC	Macau	TMP	East Timor
CUB	Cuba	MAR	Morocco	TON	Tonga
CXR	Christmas Island	MCO	Monaco	TPE	Chinese Taipei
		MDA	Moldova	TTO	Trinidad and Tobago
CYM	Cayman Islands	MDG	Madagascar		
		MDV	Maldives	TUN	Tunisia
CYP	Cyprus	MEX	Mexico	TUR	Turkey
CZE	Czech Republic	MHL	Marshall Islands	TUV	Tuvalu
				TZA	Tanzania
DEU	Germany	MKD	Macedonia	UAE	United Arab Emirates
DJI	Djibouti	MLI	Mali		
DMA	Dominica	MLT	Malta	UGA	Uganda
DNK	Denmark	MMR	Myanmar (Burma)	UK	United Kingdom
DOM	Dominican Republic				
		MNE	Montenegro	UKR	Ukraine
DZA	Algeria	MNG	Mongolia	UMI	US Minor Islands
ECU	Ecuador	MNP	Northern Mariana Islands		
EGY	Egypt			URY	Uruguay
ERI	Eritrea	MOZ	Mozambique	USA	United States of America
ESH	Western Sahara	MRT	Mauritania		
		MSR	Montserrat	UZB	Uzbekistan
ESP	Spain	MTQ	Martinique	VAT	Holy See (Vatican City)
EST	Estonia	MUS	Mauritius		
ETH	Ethiopia	MWI	Malawi	VCT	Saint Vincent and the Grenadines
FIN	Finland	MYS	Malaysia		
FJI	Fiji	MYT	Mayotte		
FLK	Falkland Islands (Malvinas)	NAM	Namibia	VEN	Venezuela
		NCL	New Caledonia	VGB	Virgin Islands (British)
FRA	France	NER	Niger		
FRG	West Germany	NFK	Norfolk Island	VIR	Virgin Islands (US)
FRO	Faroe Islands	NGA	Nigeria		
FSM	Micronesia, Federated States of	NIC	Nicaragua	VNM	Vietnam
		NIU	Niue	VUT	Vanuatu
		NLD	Netherlands	WLF	Wallis and Futuna Islands
FXX	France, Metropolitan	NOR	Norway		
		NPL	Nepal	WSM	Samoa
GAB	Gabon	NRU	Nauru	YEM	Yemen
GEO	Georgia	NZ	New Zealand	ZAF	South Africa
GHA	Ghana	OMN	Oman	ZMB	Zambia
				ZWE	Zimbabwe

Stop press

Largest Garfield collection

Cathy Kothe (USA) has 6,190 unique Garfield items, as listed by her official cataloguer – husband Robert – and verified in Huntington Station, New York, USA, on 10 Apr 2014. The collection includes three slot machines and an inflatable measuring 7.6 m (25 ft) tall – higher than the couple's house!

Most haikus about one town

As of 29 Apr 2014, a total of 1,663 haikus had been written about Luton in Bedfordshire, UK, by the local *Clod Magazine*. The Luton Haiku team – Andrew Kingston, Tim Kingston, Andrew Whiting and Stephen Whiting – began posting haikus online each weekday from 23 Jan 2007.

Most pubs visited

As of 29 Jan 2014, Bruce Masters (UK) had visited 46,495 pubs and drinking establishments, sampling local brews where available. He began his tour in 1960, and visited 936 pubs in 2013 alone. The most popular UK pub name so far, says Bruce, is the Red Lion.

Longest group drum roll

To celebrate the 350th anniversary of the Royal Marines (founded in 1664), the Corps of Drums of Her Majesty's Royal Marines Band Service (UK) achieved a group drum roll lasting 64 hr 27 min 59 sec. Beginning on 30 Apr 2014, 40 members of the Corps took it in turns to drum on the same snare drum at the Tower of London, London, UK, finishing on 3 May 2014.

Largest game of "What's the time, Mr Wolf?"

The playground favourite was played by 494 staff of Royal London (UK) at the EICC in Edinburgh, UK, on 6 Feb 2014.

Largest charity walk

Iglesia Ni Cristo (PHL) organized a walk with 175,509 people, starting at the Quirino Grandstand in Manila, Philippines, on 15 Feb 2014. Money was raised for victims of 2013's Typhoon Haiyan.

Most southerly navigation

On 27 Jan 2014, the *Arctic P*, skippered by Russell Pugh and owned by the Packer family (both AUS), reached the Bay of Whales in the Ross Ice Shelf of Antarctica. An instrument on the bow recorded 78°43.042'S 163°42.069'W, the most southerly point. The latitude of the shelf is dynamic due to the ice calving – when ice melts and breaks off the shelf.

Telmex triple certification

Telmex (MEX) achieved a GWR treble at Aldea Digital in Mexico City, Mexico, from 11 to 27 Apr 2014. CEO Héctor Slim (centre) receives the certificate for **largest digital inclusion event** (258,896 people), plus those for **most people trained in IT in one month** (177,517, at the same event) and for **most scans of an Augmented Reality app in eight hours** (49,273, on 26 Apr).

Most consecutive rolls by an aircraft

Kingsley Just (AUS) rolled his Pitts Special biplane 987 times at Lethbridge Airpark in Victoria, Australia, on 1 Mar 2014. Kingsley rolled his aircraft continuously for just under an hour without any break.

Largest observation wheel

The Las Vegas High Roller is 167.5 m (549 ft 8 in) tall. Opened on 31 Mar 2014 in Las Vegas, Nevada, USA, it has 28 cabins, each holding 40 people. A full revolution of the wheel takes 30 min.

Rumeysa Gelgi

The new record holder tells us: "I'm adapting everything to my height. It has good and bad sides but, anyway, I feel lucky myself."

Oldest boxing world champion

Bernard Hopkins (USA, b. 15 Jan 1965) broke his own record when, aged 49 years 94 days, he outpointed Beibut Shumenov (KAZ) for the WBA (super) light heavyweight, IBA light heavyweight and IBF light heavyweight titles on 19 Apr 2014.

Largest greetings card

A Mother's Day card measuring 10.19 m (33 ft 5 in) tall and 7.09 m (23 ft 3 in) wide was unveiled by Nestlé Middle East FZE (UAE) at Dubai Mall, United Arab Emirates, on 21 Mar 2014.

Tallest teenager (female)

Measuring 213.6 cm (7 ft 0.09 in) at full standing height, Rumeysa Gelgi (TUR, b. 1 Jan 1997) is the tallest female under the age of 18. Rumeysa, pictured left with niece Zeynep Ravza Yakut, was diagnosed with Weaver syndrome, a rare genetic disorder that causes rapid growth. She was measured by Dr Ömer Hakan Yavaşoğlu (inset) in Karabük, Turkey, on 19 Mar 2014.

Most bungee jumps in 24 hours

Fitness coach Colin Phillips (UK) recorded 151 bungee jumps from a 100-m-tall (328-ft) crane in aid of charity Breast Cancer Arabia. His attempt was set with Gravity Zone at Dubai Autodrome in the United Arab Emirates on 21 Mar 2014. He dislocated a finger and afterwards admitted to feeling "a bit beaten up, to be honest".

Most siblings to celebrate diamond wedding anniversaries

Edward Thomas and Ellen Jane Howell (UK) had five children, all of whom had celebrated 60 years of marriage as of 4 Mar 2014:
• Gwendoline Jean Howell and Douglas Derek Bennett: 61 years
• John Edward Howell and Sylvia Beryl (née Winter): 61 years
• Doris Winifred Howell and Donald Street: 66 years
• Stanley Frederick Howell and Margaret Elizabeth (née Sharpe): 65 years
• William George Howell and Hazel Pauline (née Freeman): 60 years.

Largest aquarium

The whale shark tank at Chimelong Ocean Kingdom in Hengqin, Guangdong, China, has a dome with a diameter of 12 m (39 ft 4 in). The attraction was opened on 28 Jan 2014 and set five world records, including one for the **largest underwater viewing dome** (shown above). It uses 48.75 million litres (10.72 million UK gal; 12.87 million US gal) of salt and fresh water.

Most valuable life-insurance policy

The identity of the Silicon Valley billionaire who holds an insurance policy worth $201 m (£120.44 m) remains anonymous, but with more than 100 billionaires resident in the famous strip of California, USA, there is no shortage of candidates. The policy was brokered by Dovi Frances (ISR) of the advisory firm SG, LLC (USA), and certified by a public notary in Santa Barbara, California, USA, on 28 Feb 2014. This beats the long-standing record for a $100-m (£51.8-m) policy sold by Peter Rosengard (UK) for US media mogul David Geffen back in 1990.

Most weight lifted by dumbbell rows in one minute with one arm

Strongman Robert Natoli (USA) set five records in an hour at the Pacific Health Club in Liverpool, New York, USA, on 22 Mar 2014 to raise money for the Patterson family, whose three children had been badly injured in a car crash that claimed the life of their mother. He lifted 1,975.85 kg (4,356 lb) with dumbbell rows and recorded the **most pull-ups in one minute with a 40-lb pack** (23); the **most step-ups in one minute with** an 80-lb pack (41); the **most step-ups in one minute with a 100-lb pack** (38); and the **most knuckle push-ups in one minute** (58).

In a separate charity event in Oswego, New York, USA, on 4 Apr 2013, Natoli achieved two further records: the **most step-ups in one minute with a 40-lb pack** (52) and the **most step-ups in one minute with a 60-lb pack** (47).

Most people people making heart-shaped hand gestures

Stephen Sutton (UK, 1994–2014) and 553 friends gathered to make a heart symbol with their hands on 4 May 2014 in Staffordshire, UK. Stephen, diagnosed with terminal cancer, made headlines in 2014 with his fund-raising efforts, and stated that one of his dreams was to secure a Guinness World Records title.

Longest time ranked as chess world No.1 (female)

As confirmed by the International Chess Federation, Judit Polgár (HUN) has been the world No.1 female player since 1 Feb 1989 and retains the spot as of 17 Apr 2014.

Fastest lawnmower

The *Mean Mower* can cut grass while moving at a speed of 187.61 km/h (116.57 mph) and was constructed and raced by Honda and Team Dynamics (both UK) at Applus+ IDIADA's test track in Tarragona, Spain, on 8 Mar 2014. *Top Gear* journalist Piers Ward drove the mower.

Tallest teenager

Broc Brown (USA, b. 15 Apr 1997) measured 217.17 cm (7 ft 1.5 in) tall when verified in Apr 2014. A student at Vandercook Lake High School in Jackson, Michigan, USA, Broc was diagnosed with Sotos syndrome and his condition has resulted in frequent hospital stays.

WANT MORE?

GET YOUR FREE EBOOK
Go behind the scenes at GWR to see how records are judged and test your record-breaking knowledge with our quiz of the year!
DOWNLOAD NOW AT
GUINNESSWORLDRECORDS.COM/BONUS

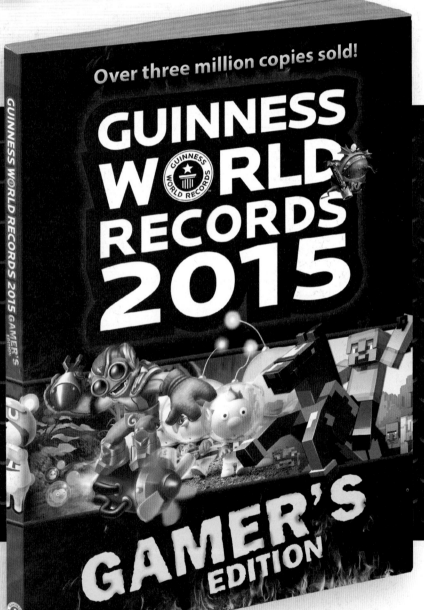

Over three million copies sold!

GUINNESS WORLD RECORDS 2015

GAMER'S EDITION

ARE YOU A VIDEOGAMER?

The GWR *GAMER'S EDITION* is the world's **best-selling videogaming annual** and a must-have for every keen gamer.

Be sure to check in regularly for special offers available exclusively on
GUINNESSWORLDRECORDS.COM/ GAMERS

The ultimate guide to videogame superlatives!

ACCESS EXCLUSIVE VIDEOS AND RECORD-BREAKING NEWS

Keep up to date with your favourite superlative achievements from around the world at:

GUINNESSWORLDRECORDS.COM

Facebook.com/
GuinnessWorldRecords

Twitter.com/
GWR

Youtube.com/
GuinnessWorldRecords

Plus.Google.com/
+guinnessworldrecords

Instagram.com/
guinnessworldrecords

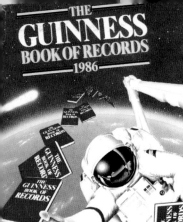

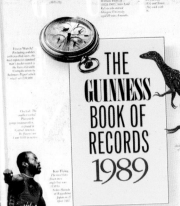